MW00390127

Hawai'i Place Names

*Kailua Beach, Kailua, Oʻahu. North end of Kailua's
famous 2.5 mile-long beach.*

HAWAI'I PLACE NAMES
Shores, Beaches, and Surf Sites

JOHN R. K. CLARK

UNIVERSITY OF HAWAI'I PRESS
Honolulu

07   06   05   04   03   02   6   5   4   3   2   1

Library of Congress Cataloging-in-Publication Data

Clark, John R. K., 1946–
    Hawai'i place names : shores, beaches, and surf sites / John R. K. Clark.
        p. cm.
    Includes bibliographical references.
    ISBN 0–8248–2451–2 (alk. paper)
    1. Names, Geographical—Hawaii. 2. Hawaii—Gazetteers.
3. Hawaiian language—Etymology—Names—Dictionaries. 4. Hawaii—
History, Local. I. Title.

DU622 .C546   2002
919.69'001'4—dc21   2001037027

Designed by Santos B. Barbasa

All photos © 2001 Mike Waggoner. All rights reserved.

Printed by Versa Press, Inc.

For my parents,
who started me on my journey
with a love of the ocean
and a Hawaiian sense of place.

Aloha ʻia no ka huakaʻi
mai ka hikina i Kumukahi
i ka welona i Lehua,
Hoʻi mai ka manaʻo i na
moʻolelo o na pana o ke kai.

Beloved is the journey
from the sunrise at Kumukahi
to the sunset at Lehua,
Our thoughts return
to the stories of the famous
places of the sea.

CONTENTS

PREFACE

In 1966 the University of Hawai'i Press published the first edition of *Place Names of Hawai'i*. Written by Mary Kawena Pukui and Samuel H. Elbert, it contained 1,125 entries, all of which were place names in the Hawaiian language. In 1974 the press published the second edition by Pukui, Elbert, and Esther T. Mo'okini. It contained some four thousand entries, and this time it included place names in English and other languages. This edition, in the words of the authors, provided "a glossary of important place names in the State, including names of valleys, streams, mountains, land sections, surfing areas, towns, villages, and Honolulu streets and buildings." During the years that have followed its publication, the second edition of *Place Names of Hawai'i* has become a standard reference in the literature of Hawai'i.

In May 1972, I began gathering information for a book that I had decided to write about O'ahu's beaches. My idea was to identify every beach on the island and describe its physical characteristics, including its dangers, its use as a recreational resource, and its value as a historic and cultural site. As a result, the University of Hawai'i Press published *The Beaches of O'ahu* in 1977, *The Beaches of Maui County* in 1980, *Beaches of the Big Island* in 1985, *Beaches of Kaua'i and Ni'ihau* in 1990, and *Hawai'i's Best Beaches* in 1999. My original idea for a book on O'ahu's beaches evolved into the beaches of Hawai'i series that inventories and describes every beach in the Hawaiian Islands. During the course of writing these books, I interviewed hundreds of informants to gather information, many of whom were native Hawaiians. I soon realized that many of the place names I was collecting were not in standard references such as *Place Names of Hawai'i* and that much of the anecdotal information I was being given to describe the shores and beaches was not recorded. In an effort to preserve some of this information, I put as much as I thought appropriate into the beaches of Hawai'i books, but a significant amount still remained only in my notebooks and in my memory. I have always thought that the glossary approach in *Place Names of Hawai'i* is a good format for presenting and consolidating large amounts of diverse information, so in 1998 I asked the University of Hawai'i Press if they would be interested in a shores and beaches supplement to *Place Names of Hawai'i*. In it I proposed to include all of the information that I have gathered from researching the beaches of Hawai'i series and from spending a lifetime swimming and surfing on Hawai'i's beaches. They agreed, and the result is this volume, *Hawai'i Place Names: Shores, Beaches, and Surf Sites.*

During the last century, more new place names were added to Hawai'i's collective body of place names than at any other time in the postcontact period—the period beginning in 1778, the year of Captain Cook's arrival. The twentieth century was a time of phenomenal growth in population and infrastructure in the Hawaiian Islands. Streets, subdivisions, homes, hotels, condominiums, office buildings, boat ramps, harbors, military bases, pineapple canneries, sugar mills, and myriad other structures built across the Islands made lasting marks on the land and gave us thousands of place names. Street names on the island of O'ahu alone now number over seven thousand. All of these land-based names have been recorded in telephone books, maps, magazines, newspapers, construction plans, land sale contracts, and other similar documents. In addition, the use of computers and the development of the Internet have revolutionized record keeping and made records and names accessible to everyone.

At the same time that Hawai'i experienced its explosive growth of population and infrastructure on land, an equally explosive growth took place in the ocean. The Hawaiian Islands offer almost every type of ocean recreation activity in the world, so new residents and visitors followed the Hawaiians into the ocean. Hawai'i saw the rise of swimming and the rebirth of surfing in the early 1900s, the development of outrigger canoe racing in the 1930s, the introduction of scuba diving and the rise of bodysurfing during the 1950s, the international explosion of surfing in the 1960s with the introduction of mass-produced foam surfboards, the rise of the spin-off sports of bodyboarding and windsurfing in the 1970s, and the introduction of extreme, or tow-in, surfing and kite surfing in the 1990s. These activities and many more spawned an ocean recreation industry that is a significant source of revenue in the state and that has contributed thousands of new place names.

The place names on our shores and beaches, however, have been largely unrecorded, historians having judged them colorful but ephemeral. It is true that many names of ocean recreation sites are short-lived, especially those introduced by commercial tour operators who may be in business only a short time. They introduce names that they believe will have commercial advertising value—names that will attract customers—and often only their company uses these names. During the past twenty-five years, for example, "turtle" names have proliferated, the assumption being that visitors want to swim with turtles when they snorkel and scuba dive. Yet in spite of the constant inundation of ephemeral and esoteric names, many place names on our shores and beaches have survived the test of time. They have passed from one generation to the next and from one user group to another. These are names that I have attempted to record.

The 2,500 entries in this book are names that are associated with the ocean. They are the names of *shores*, the lands at the edge of the ocean; the names of *beaches*, the dynamic sites on the shores that are composed of loosely consolidated material such as sand, cinder, or pebbles; and of the names of *sites* on or near the shores and beaches where people practice recreational and subsistence activities such as beachcombing, bodyboarding, bodysurfing, boating, fishing (pole, spear, surround net, and throw net), gathering (seaweed, sea cucumbers, sea anemone, shellfish, salt, and sea urchins), kayaking, paddling, sailing, scuba diving, skimming, snorkeling, surfing, swimming, waterskiing, and windsurfing. The entries are also the names of significant features or landmarks on or near the shores such as fishponds, monuments, navigational lights, and shrines, in addition to significant sites offshore such as buoys, channels, reefs, rocks, and small islands. Entries that include two or more sites with the same name are listed alphabetically by island, and if the sites with the same name are on the same island, they are listed alphabetically by district.

Surfing sites, with over six hundred entries, comprise the largest single group of shore and beach place names. Surfers and other wave riders, including bodyboarders, bodysurfers, and windsurfers, are always looking for new, uncrowded sites, so many of the English entries reflect the sport and its culture as new sites are named. Surfers, like fishermen, name sites for the landmarks they use to triangulate their spots, typically a house or some other feature on the beach. Brown's, Horner's, Fujioka's, Kamisugi's, Paty's, and Ruddle's are sites that are or were off someone's home. Iron Bridge, Lighthouse, Pillboxes, Pinetrees, and Shipwrecks are sites named after features onshore. Other site names suggest the dangers of the sport, such as Gas Chambers, Impossibles, Insanities, Razors, and Suicides; describe wave characteristics, such as Infinities, Pipeline, Pounders, and Wrap Arounds; identify geographical features, such as Black Rock, Blue Hole, and Rocky Point; and show humor, such as Dog Bowls, No Can Tell, and Pray for Sex. During the 1980s, younger surfers began modifying many of the existing place names by shortening and pluralizing them. The trend continued through the 1990s, so many names today are abbreviated versions of former names, and almost all of them end with an *s*. Ala Moana Bowl is Bowls, China Wall is Chinas, and Sandy Beach is Sandys.

One of the challenges in collecting Hawaiian place names is that thousands of them are found in legends and other accounts in Hawaiian language newspapers, old books, land court documents, and so on, but many of them are not connected to an exact site. All of the names in this book are connected to exact sites, and while some of these names may not be familiar to everyone, they are names that are in use by at least one generation or user group, with one exception. Today many of our shores and beaches have English names, especially our surfing and diving sites. In the interest of preserving Hawaiian place names, if I knew the Hawaiian name for a site, I included it whether it is in use or not, and I cross-referenced it with all of the variant names.

In general, secondary or lesser-used sites often have more than one name, while primary or more frequented sites usually have one popular name that is known to everyone. Guidebooks and literature for tourists identify popular places, event promoters use them as venues for competitive events, and government agencies turn them into parks. Primary place names are reinforced to all of us on signs, in books, on T-shirts, and by the media. Secondary site names do not get the publicity that primary sites do, so they often have more than one name. The number of names they have depends on how many different groups use the sites and how much interaction there is between the groups. If there is no interaction between the user groups, each of them may have a different name for the site and each group will think that theirs is the correct name. Naming a site or knowing its name is important for most of us. It gives us a sense of ownership. If we use a place, know its name, and understand the story behind its name, then we are part of the place. We feel like we belong there.

One of the important rules about place names in the Hawaiian language is that you never know the true meaning of a name unless you know the *mo'olelo*, or story, that goes with it. Anyone can take a Hawaiian place name, separate it into its component parts, and make an attempt at a literal translation, but unless you know the original story, tradition, or legend behind the name, all you really have is an educated guess. Without the *mo'olelo*, we do not know if a place name is a proper name, a geographical feature, a shortened form of the original name, or even a misspelling of the original name. Hawaiian translations in the text that are not from references such as *Place Names of Hawai'i*, the *Hawaiian Dictionary* (Pukui and Elbert, University of Hawai'i Press, 1986), or other valid sources are prefaced by the word *perhaps* to indicate that they are educated guesses made by contemporary Hawaiian linguists. Entries without translations are those that are too obscure for even an educated guess. Other entries without translations are surnames. Translations of these names should be left to the families who have these names.

As I have gathered information over the years, I have always kept the *moʻolelo* rule in mind, and I have tried to learn the stories behind every place name—whether of Hawaiian, English, or other origin. Collecting *moʻolelo*, ancient and modern, is an exciting pursuit. Place names are a reflection of culture and history, a reflection of us. They are a reflection of the who, what, when, where, and why at the time they were given, and like the culture they are dynamic and subject to change no matter how established or traditional they are. During the last century, the influence of English on our shores and beaches was considerable and many Hawaiian place names were replaced, especially as the number of native Hawaiian speakers—individuals raised in Hawaiian-speaking families—has significantly decreased. English is the common denominator of culture in Hawaiʻi today, and as the language of our daily activities, it is the dominant language of our new place names and modern *moʻolelo.*

In addition to reflecting culture, place names recognize value. In general, we name the places that we want to go back to. These are the places that have value for us, that meet our individual needs. On our shores and beaches, our needs today are primarily for recreational activities and secondarily for subsistence activities, but whether they identify primary or secondary sites, place names identify localities that are significant resources. Although many of these sites are in the ocean, they are still just as important as golf courses, soccer fields, or gardens on land, and they should be recognized for their value as resource sites.

The entries span a period of approximately a hundred years— the twentieth century. I began interviewing people in 1972, and the oldest of my informants was born in 1887. The last hundred years have been a time of major transition for the Hawaiian Islands, and this shows clearly in the information provided by the informants. Most of the informants I interviewed over the years are identified in the acknowledgments, which follow. They kindly answered my questions and contributed invaluable information to the entries in the book. I assume complete responsibility, however, for any errors or oversights and invite the reader to contact me by mail or email through the University of Hawaiʻi Press with any additions, changes, corrections, or comments. I will address them along with my own revisions in the next edition of *Hawaiʻi Place Names: Shores, Beaches, and Surf Sites.*

ACKNOWLEDGMENTS

The real history of a place can only be found in the stories of its people.

—Ron Youngblood, *Maui News*

From 1972 to 2001, I interviewed over nine hundred people as I gathered information about Hawai'i's shores, beaches, and surf sites. All of them graciously shared the stories of their places with me and made this book possible. Everyone whose name I was able to record is listed below, a small token of my appreciation.

Ackerman, Brant
Ackerman, Doug
Ah Sam, Ronnie
Aikala, Charles
Aikau, Clyde
Aikau, Solomon
Aila, William
Aiu, Francis
Aiu, Stella
Akana, Ernie
Akana, John
Akau, Bill, Jr.
Akeo, Harold
Akina, Alex
Akina, Charlie
Akiyama, Gerald
Ako, Emma
Akuna, Abraham
Alapai, Aaron
Alford, John
Aluli, Irmgard
Anderson, Eve
Anderson, Reid
Andrade, Carlos
Andrews, Joseph
Angel, Jose
Angel, Mozelle
Apo, Henrietta

Arine, Torako
Armitage, Betty
Asano, Ken
Ashdown, Inez
Auhoy, Fanny
Auwae, Henry
Avant, Wiley
Avishham, Dottie
Awai, Jimmy

Bacon, Ann
Bacon, Nat
Bacon, Pat
Bail, Linda
Bailey, Charlie
Bailey, Ken
Baird, Peter
Baker, Adam
Baker, Bernie
Balazs, George
Barnes, Bob
Barnes, Edean
Barnes, Preston
Barnett-Sallee, Betty Ann
Barrère, Dorothy
Barrett, Henry
Bartram, Paul

Bass, Bill
Beamer, Mahi
Beans Beans
Bechert, Doug
Beck, Alex
Beck, Elizabeth
Beck, Nick
Beck, William
Beckley, James Kahea
Berkemeyer, Dave
Bethel, Steven
Bieber, Don
Bieber, Glenda
Birnie, Ian
Bishop, Danny
Black, A. Duane
Blaich, Beryl
Blaich, Gary
Blakemore, Paul
Blanchard, Emily Kainanui
Blanchard, Henry
Bland, Ben
Blankenfeld, Bruce
Blomfield, Barry
Blomfield, Kolohe
Blomfield, Tinker
Bollin, Suzanne

Bond, Robin
Boshard, Henry
Bouret, Pierre
Bowman, Craig
Bowman, Elizabeth
Bowman, Lani
Bowman, Pierre
Bowman, Winifred
Boyd, Mae
Boynton, David
Bradbury, Ronald
Brady, Jean
Bredin, Jack
Bregman, Ron
Brennan, Joe
Brennecke, Marvin
Brenner, Alexander
Brown, Aileen
Brown, Chris
Brown, Kelii
Brown, Kent
Brown, Nancie
Brown, Timothy
Brown, Woody
Brown, Zadock
Bruce, Robert
Brundage, Barbara
Bryan, Edwin H., Jr.
Buck, Mark
Bumatay, Edward
Burley, Blake
Busby, Charles
Butchart, David
Butchart, Gail

Cachola, Fred
Cambra, John
Campbell, James
  Kimo
Cano, Terry
Carper, John
Carr, Dougie
Carroll, Bob
Carter, Lloyd
Cater, John
Cates, Bobby
Cauldwell, Jean
Cauldwell, Keith
Cauldwell, Paul
Chang, Brian

Chang, Deborah
Chang, Eddie
Chang, Elden
Char, Wayne
Ching, Patty
Ching, Val, Jr.
Chong Kee, Kenneth
Choquette, Lisa
Choy, Agnes
Christenson, Floyd
Christian, George
Chu, Barlow
Chun, Shorty
Chung, Yan Hoon
Clarey, Jean
Clark, Agnes
Clark, Bruce
Clark, Dave
Clark, Harriet
Clemens, Michael
Clissold, Grant
Cluney, Johanna
Coakley, Jeff
Coakley, Lani
Cockett, Ruth
Cole, Peter
Coleman, Mark
Collins, Lei
Colotario, Reginald
Conrad, Agnes
Cook, Chris
Cook, Frank
Cooke, George
  "Peppy"
Cooke, Pat
Corell, Allen
Cornuelle, Richard
  "Ditto"
Cowan, David
Cowan, Richard
Cowden, Charlie
Cox, David
Crusat, Jay-nyn
Cunha, Irma
Cunningham, Mark
Curtis, Betsy
Curtis, Eric

Dairo, Agnes
Damron, Roy

Davidson, Dougie
Davidson, Jamie
Davis, Alan
Davis, Edgar
Davis, Sue
Dawson, Puna
Delos Santos, Andre
Derby, Steven
Desha, Adolph
  "Swede"
Desha, Edean
Diffenderfer, Mike
Dinson, Pearl
Dodge, Robert, Jr.
Domingo, Hattie
Donohugh, Don
Doty, Bud
Downing, George
Dowsett, Carol
Dowsett, Wade
Doyle, David
Duarte, Mary
Dudoit, John
Dudoit, Loretta
Dudoit, Moana
Dudoit, Valentine
Dunbar, Kippy
Duncan, Francine
Dunford, Kellen
Dungate, Peter
Dunn, James
Durkin, Pat
Dye, Tessa
Dykes, Del

Eberle, Jackie
Elliott, Rex
Ellis, Elizabeth
Emmons, Brian
Emory, Kenneth
English, Joseph
Enoka, Bill
Enos, Ruby
Erdman, Pardee
Estrellas, Edna
Ettinger, Tom
Evensen, Sonja

Fairbanks, Keoni
Fairfull, Tom

Falau, Raul
Farden, Lucy
Farm, George
Farr, Beverly
Farr, Meredith
Fernandez, Albert
Fiene-Severns,
    Pauline
Fink, John
Fleming, Bill
Fleming, David
Fleming, James
Flores, Destry
Forrest, Skipper
Fortner, Heather
Foster, Jeanette
Foti, John
Fragale, Mark
Frazier, Paul
Frazier, Tom
Frederick, John
Frias, Kathy
Froiseth, Teene
Froiseth, Wally
Fujikawa, Goro
Fujio, Guy
Fukunaga, Tadashi
Fullard-Leo, Ellen
Funai, Brian
Furukawa, Mike
Furutani, Elton

Gaffney, Rick
Garcia, Donna
Gardner, Chris
Gaudet, Pete
Gaudet, Philip
Gayner, Vicki
Gerard, Paul
Getzner, Sid
Gilman, J. Atherton
Gleason, Karen
Gleason, Michael
Goldstein, Virginia
Gomez, Henry
Gordon, Mike
Gorst, Bill
Goto, Ralph
Gough, Michael
Gouveia, Dennis

Grace, Jean
Graham, Roy
Green, Wayne
Greenwell, Alan
Greenwell, Jean
Greenwell, John
Greenwell, Marc
Greenwell, Norman
Greenwood, Bruce
Griffey, John
Griffin, Don
Grout, Dave
Gulick, Bill
Guerrero, Hugh
Gutmanis, June

Haley, Fred, Jr.
Hamasaki, Kent
Hanson, Patricia
Hapai, Alice
Hapai, Kaniu
Harada, Ivan
Harris, Roger
Hartman, Jackson
    "Chip"
Harvey-Hall, Barbie
Helms, David
Hemmings, Fred
Hendricks, Pete
Herrman, Kurt
Hillen, Thurston
Hind, Robert, Jr.
Ho, Anthony
Ho, Bernadette
Ho, Harry
Ho, Kaipo
Hoddick, Howard
Hodgins, Aka
Hodgins, Bill
Hoepfl, Scott
Hoeppner, Carroll
Hoeppner, Mark
Hoffman, James
Holmes, Steve
Holmes, Tommy
Holt, Henrietta
Holt, James
Hong, Alan
Hookala, Annie
Hookala, Daniel

Hooper, Doug
Hoopii, Floyd
Hoopii, Sonny
Hope, Dale
Hosaka, Don
Hosaka, Yaichiro
Hoshijo, Kona
Hoshiko, Arthur
Howard, Howie
Howard, Jeanette
Howe, Jim
Hubbard, Louis
Huddy, Bill
Huntley, Lou

Iaea, Bulla
Ikeda, Greg
Inenaga, Gerald
Inouye, Reid
Isaacs, Illinois
Isayama, Todd
Ishikawa, Wade
Ivey, Garner

Jackman, Yvette
Jackson, Hartman
Jardin, Manuel
Jahrling, Frank
Jensen, Robert
Jewett, Mike
Joao, Larry
Johns, Kevin
Johnson, Alice
Johnson, Bill
Johnson, Chuck
Johnson, Norman
Johnson, Pilali
Johnson, Rachael
Johnson, Stephen
Johnston, Paul

Kaaiea, John
Kaanehe, Anna May
Kaawaloa, Minnie
Kaden, Bob
Kaeo, Aloha
Kaeo, Pauline
Kahana, January
Kahele, Gilbert
Kahele, Mona

Kahoohanohano, Whitey
Kaido, Rodney
Kaimikaua, Pualani
Kainard, Chris
Kaipo, Ivar "Little Joe"
Kalama, Charles
Kalama, Clyde
Kaleikini, Jacob, Jr.
Kalepa, Archie
Kalepa, Dallas
Kalili, John
Kalima, Haywood
Kalua, James
Kalua, Mary
Kaluahine, Gordon, Sr.
Kam, Kent
Kamaka, David
Kamakeeaina, Herbert, Sr.
Kamano, Mike
Kamisugi, Art
Kamoku, Elvin
Kamoku, Harold
Kanahele, Pualani
Kanuha, Dwayne
Kanuha, Red
Kaokai, Wally
Kaona, John
Kaona, Lucy
Kaopuiki, Lydia
Kaopuiki, Sol
Kaowili, Steven
Kapuni, Lani
Kapuniai, Daniel
Kau, Peter
Kauahikaua, Hazel
Kauwe, Kauluokala
Kauwe, Kula
Kauhane, Francis
Kauhane, Rawlins "Sonny"
Kaupiko, Eugene
Kaupiko, Willy
Kawamoto, Ann
Ke, Alapai
Keawe, Kala
Keakealani, Leinaala

Kekipi, Greg
Kekona, Martha
Keliiliki, Leroy
Kelly, John
Kelly, Marion
Kenn, Charles
Kenolio, Helen
Keoho, George
Kerr, Larry
Keaulana, Brian
Keaulana, Momi
Keaulana, Richard "Buffalo"
Kikuchi, Bill
Kimak, Rick
Kin In, Bucky
Kini, Sid
Kino, Keoni
Kliks, Michael
Knudsen, Herbie
Kohn, Steve
Kon, Eugene
Ku, George
Kuala, Joe
Kuloloio, Leslie
Kupele, David
Kuramoto, Charles

Lake, Russell
Lambert, Jay
Lambert, Steve
Lane, Ben
Lani, Helen
Lauer, Jack
Lee, Bruce
Lee, Michael
Lee, Rachel
Lee, Sam
Lee, Stephen
Lee Loy, Marion
Lee Loy, Pili
Lee Loy, Samuel
Lelepali, Rose
Leong, Arthur
Leong, Gwen Moana
Leser, Curtin
Lett, Turner
Levy, Winona
Liebke, Paul
Lightfoot, Blakey

Lightfoot, Bobby
Lind, John
Lindsey, Annabel
Lipp, Jane
Littlejohn, Robbie
Logan, Ha'aheo
Logan, Kaha'i
Loomis, Paula
Lopes, Eddie
L'Orange, Hans
Louie, Kinney
Lovell, Abraham
Lovell, Wayne
Lua, Makahiwa
Lucas, Clorinda
Lucas, Jimmy
Lucas, Lorre
Lui-Kwan, Tim
Lum, Alice Makaiwa
Lum, Curt
Lum, Gary
Lum King, Henry
Lung, Glenn
Lutkenhouse, Dan
Luuwai, John
Lyman, Arthur
Lyman, Barbara
Lyman, Danny
Lyman, Kimo

MacDonald, Virginia
Machado, Colette
Machida, Michael
MacPherson, Aileen
MacPherson, George
MacPherson, Michael
Magelssen, Mark
Mahaulu, Bertram
Mahoe, Louis
Mahoe, Solomon
Mahoney, Dennis
Maio, Henry
Maki, Clarence "Mac"
Maki, David
Maliikapu, Moses
Malo, Elroy Makia
Mamuad, Kaimi
Manantan, Robert
Manley, Mark

Manner, Marshall
Manner, Mildred
Markrich, Mike
Marsteller, Ann
Martin, J. Noel
Martinez, Daniel
Marvin, Richard
Matney, Greg
Matsuura, Harold
Matthew, Craig
Matthews, B'Gay
Matthews, Mo
Maynard, Sherwood
McCloskey, Rick
McClure, Keith
McConkey, J. R.
    "Mac"
McCrary, Chuck
McGrath, Ed
McGregor, Calvin
McGregor, Daniel
McShane, Marsue
Medeiros, Johnny
Meeker, Heidi
Meheula, Barbara
    "Bobbie"
Meheula, Harold
Meheula, Kalehua
Meheula, William
Mesker, Roy
Meyers, Ted
Michaelson, Geoff
Midgett, Richard
Mikasobe, Lucy
Milikan, Alex
Miller, Bolo
Miller, Kala'i
Mills, Barbara
    "Bobbee"
Mills, Joe
Minvielle, A. E.
    "Toots", Jr.
Mitchell, Donald
    Kilolani
Mitsumura, Chris
Miyao, Glen
Moberly, Ralph
Moir, John, Jr.
Moncrief, Bob
Moncrief, Rob

Moncrief, Scott
Moniz, John
Moody, Max
Moon, Sarah
Moore, Bill
Morris, Russell
Moore, Claude
Morelock, Jeff
Morgan, James
Morinaka, Stanford
Morris, Russ
Moses, Don
Mossman, Joe
Motteler, Lee S.
Mundon, Michael
Munro, Hector
Mur, Teddi
Murata, Clarence
Murphy, Nancy
Myers, Amy
Myers, Charles
Myers, Dick

Nakahara, Sidney
Nakama, Keo
Nakoa, Rachael
Naone, Howard
Napoka, Nathan
Nary, Ben
Naughton, John
Neill, Alika
Neill, Caroline
Neves, Dodie
Nihipali, Ben
Nihipali, Ida
Nihipali, Larry
Niino, Roy
Nishida, Jean
Nishihira, Jerry
Nishikawa, Earl
Nonaka, Mel
Norton, Ann Marie
Nottage, David
Nozawa, Jerome

O'Brian, Danny
O'Brian, Tom
Ogata, Roy
O'Halloran, Terry
Okawa, Dwight

Okita, Richard
Olds, Haunani
Olds, Kenny
Oliveira, Ella
Olsen, Marie
Olsen, Willy
Onuma, Masa
Oshiro, Kiyoshi
Orcutt, Annie
Orr, Annette
Orr, John
Owen, Vance

Paakonia, Herman
Paauhau, Lillian
Padeken, George
Padeken, Michael
Palumbo, Charles
Panui, William
Pascua, Norberto
Paty, Bill
Paty, Randy
Pavao, Muriel
Pavcek, Joe
Pedro, David
Pegeder, Dionne
Pekelo, Noah
Pelekai, Henry
Penhallow, Richard
Pereira, Luika
Perry, Richard "Black"
Perry, Thomas
Pestana, Edmund
Petro, Joaquin
Phillips, Pat
Piianaia, Ilima
Piianaia, Norman
Pili, Meli
Pili, Titai
Pfluger, Mary
Pfluger, Nancy
Pfund, Rose
Poepoe, Mac
Power, Lowrey
Preece, Henry
Profilet, Leo
Pua, Susan
Puleloa, Bill
Punikaia, Bernard
Pupule, Bernice

Rapoza, Tim
Ramos, David
Rarick, Randy
Rath, Jackie
Rath, Robert
Raymond, Stanley
Rego, Anson
Reid, Jimmy
Renner, Janet
Requilman, Sarah
Rhodes, Larry
Rice, Arthur
Richards, Atherton
Rietow, Alan
Robello, Billy
Roberson, John
Roblin, Tommy
Rocheleau, Bob
Rodrigues, Colin
Rodrigues, Hamilton
Rodrigues, John, Jr.
Rosa, Joe
Ross, May Cunha
Rothstein, Jerry
Rowland, Robert E.
Russell, Steve
Rust, Kenny
Ryan, Annie
Ryan, Tim

Sablas, Lori
Sadowski, John
Sadowski, Lui
Sallee, Harriett
Sallee, Ralph
Samala, Bruno
Samura, Gary
Sanburn, Curt
Santos, Herbert
Santos, Violet
Sasaki, Clyde
Sasaki, Larry
Sato, Glenn
Sawyer, Richard
Scelsa, Bud
Schatteuer, George
Schimmelfenning,
   Chad
Schladermundt, Eric
Schmitt, Robert

Schoenstein, Sybil
Scholtz, Stanley
Schmidt, Robert
Schultz, Florence
Seddon, Tony
Shepard, Barbara
Sherman, Cheryl
Shigeoka, Chester
Shigeoka, Francis
Shigeta, Albert
Shimizu, Paul
Shimoda, Jerry
Shindo, Gary
Shipley, Jack
Silva, Allan
Silva, Dane
Silva, Kenneth
Silva, Robert
Simeona, Ed
Simeona, Jackie
Simmons, Maili
Sizemore, Chuck
Smith, Andy
Smith, George
Smith, Kale
Smith, Sanford
Smith, Steve
Smythe, Francis
Solomon, Alfred
Solomon, Tommy
Soria, Harry B., Jr.
Souza, Kamakani
Souza, Palani
Souza, Wayne
Sox, David
Springer, Pilipo
Springer, Thelma
Sproat, Bill
Sproat, Clyde
Sproat, Dale
Sproat, David
Stapleton, Frankie
Stephenson, William
Stevens, Tom
Stone, Tom
Stubenberg, Arthur
Suganuma, Larry,
   Sr.
Summers, Catherine
Summers, Mary

Sutherland, Audrey
Sutherland, Gavin
Sutherland, James
Sutherland, Jock
Sutter, Fred
Sutton, Sue
Svetin, Kimberly
   Mikami
Swanson, Karen
Swapp, Wylie
Swezey, Joe
Sylva, Rene
Sylva, Richard

Takahashi, Char
Takahashi, Mike
Takamoto, Robert
Takata, Christine
Takata, Howard
Takayama, Donald
Tamura, George
Tanabe, George
Tanemoto, Takume
Tannehill, Jimmy
Tanoura, Grant
Tavares, William
Taylor, Leighton
Taylor, Vernon
Teller, Suzanne
Teraoka, Wesley
Terukina, Kerry
Tester, Keith
Thomas, Robert
Thompson, Sara
Thronas, Henry
Thurston, Robert
Tiepel, Joe
Tojio, Clyde
Tom, Kevin
Tom, Richard
Tomita, Roy
Toms, Helen
Tongg, Michael
Tracy, L.R. Skip
Trent, Theodore
Tsark, Warren
Tsuji, Nelson
Tsuneishi, Lani
Tsutsumi, Mrs.
   Yasukei

Uchimura, Donald
Uchimura, Teruo
Uno, Kathy
Upchurch, Bill
Ursal, Bob

Valentine, Val
Valier, Kathy
Van Gieson, George
Vasconcellos, Graley
Velzy, Dale
Ventura, Mel
Victor, Angeline
Vierra, Dahlia
Villa, Gordon
Vincent, Emily
Vogt, Bill
Vogt, William

Waddoups, Mickey
Wagenman, Eric
Wagner, Peter

Wagner, Ron
Walker, Don
Walker, Donna
Walker, Ronald
Wallace, Jeff
Walsh, Francis
Ward, Megan
Warrington, Nakoolani
Watanabe, Farley
Waterhouse, John
Watson, Katheryn Kekapa
Wayman, David
Wayman, Debbie
Webb, Adrian
Weir, Randy
White, Mary
Whitney, Joe
Wietecha, Barney
Wilcox, Carol
Wilcox, John

Willars, Jon
Williams, Steve
Wilmington, Ann
Wilson, C.B.
Wilson, Elmer
Winsley, George
Winstedt, Charles
Wirtz, Cable
Wong, Danny
Woods, Andrea
Woolaway, Christine

Yamada, Tom
Yent, Martha
Yonover, Robert
Young, Aaron
Young, Betty
Young, Kalani
Young, Stephen
Youngblood, Ron

Ziemke, Debbie

Finally, I would like to thank my family and friends for their support during the compilation of this book and the years of research that contributed to it.

Ambrose, Greg
Bartram, Paul
Blair, Janyce
Bowen, John
Bushnell, Betty
Campbell, Alan "Soupy"
Chip, Reuben
Clark, George
Clark, Jason
Clark, Koji
Clark, Lei
Clark, Sachi
Davis, Carter
Desha, Piilani
Hakes, Dennis
Hamilton, William
Higdon, Alexis
Ikeda, Masako
Kiang, Stuart
Lane, John C.
Leatherman, Stephen

Leonardi, Attilio
Logan, Dwayna
Logan, Kalele
Longstaff, Kathy
Longstaff, Richard
Mace, Ross
Makua, Kainoa
Makua, Nelson
Mann, J. Cline
Mookini, Ester "Kiki"
Moriarty, Dan
Moriarty, Donald
Moriarty, Hannah
Moriarty, Linda
Moriarty, Mary
Mowat, Bill
Mowat, Bridget
Mowat, Gayla
Mowat, Harry James
Mowat, Karl
Ortiz, Diane "Ting"
Pedro, Rodney

Perez, Rosalynn
Picadura, Daryl
Pierceall, Mike
Rath, Robbie
Silva, Carol
Smith, Riley
Soria, Harry
Stanley, Alice
Stanley, Larry
Tannehill, Bo
Tsukazaki, Ben
Ushio, Julie
Ushio, Sai
Ushio, Sam
Waggoner, Mike
Werjefelt, Christian
Wessel, Irene
Wessel, Macy
Yee, Brady
Young, Pat Leilani

Hawai'i Place Names

GLOSSARY

AA Buoy. Fish aggregating device, Port Allen, Kaua'i. Buoy anchored at approximately 960 fathoms. Landmarks: Kokole Point, Hanapēpē Buoy Light, and Makahū'ena Point Light.

'A'alaloloa. Sea cliffs, Pāpalaua, Maui. The cliffs are named in the September 5, 1863, edition of the Hawaiian language newspaper *Ka Nūpepa Kū'oko'a*. In telling the legend of 'Ele'io, writer W. N. Pualewa gives a series of Maui shore place names, including the name of the cliffs, while describing how 'Ele'io ran from the ghost 'A'ahuali'i: "Thus they ran until they passed Wailuku, Kama'alaea, the cliff of 'Aalaloloa, and down the incline of Papalaau [*sic*]. He ['Ele'io] exerted himself and ran past Ukumehame, on to and past Olowalu, on to and past Awalua, on to and past Kulanaokala'i, on to and past Launiupoko, and on to Wainanukole. There 'A'ahuali'i almost caught up with him." Also known as Lahaina Pali. Name of a wind.

'A'awa. Fishing site, Mākena, Maui. At Nahuna Point, the north point of Mākena Bay. *Lit.*, wrasse fish.

'A'awa Iki. Island (.35 acres, 40 feet high), Kahakuloa, Maui. *Lit.*, small wrasse fish.

'A'awa Nui. Island (.9 acres, 40 feet high), Kahakuloa, Maui. *Lit.*, large wrasse fish.

A-Bay. Surf site, 'Anaeho'omalu, Hawai'i. A-Bay is an abbreviation of 'Anaeho'omalu Bay. The surf site is on the reef off 'Anaeho'omalu Point at the north end of the bay.

A Buoy. Fish aggregating device, South Point, Hawai'i. Buoy anchored at approximately 900 fathoms. Landmarks: South Point, Pālima Point.

Acid Drop. Surf site, Po'ipū, Kaua'i. Steep wave that breaks on a shallow reef. Named in 1968 by a surfer from Po'ipū who was into the psychedelic lifestyle of the day. The name is a play on the word *drop*. In surfing, the drop is the travel distance from the takeoff to the bottom of the wave, and at the time this name was given, "dropping acid," or taking lysergic acid dieth-

3

ylamide (LSD), an illegal hallucinatory drug, was a popular psychedelic phrase. So an acid drop would be an extremely steep drop. Surfers in the 1960s believed that the drop here was comparable to that at Sunset on O'ahu.

 mo'olelo

I was living in L.A. after I was discharged from the navy, and I heard about a job for an air traffic controller at Barking Sands. I applied, got the job, and moved to Kaua'i in May 1968. I lived in Kekaha and decided to take up surfing. I started at the small breaks right in front of Kekaha and actually learned to surf pretty quickly. As I got better, I started surfing other places and started meeting other surfers. Two guys that I became good friends with, Gaylord and Mike, lived at Po'ipū in a house near Spouting Horn, so I started surfing the breaks out there with them. We could see **Acid Drop** from their house, but no one ever surfed it. One day we decided to try it and ended up surfing it almost every day for about two weeks on the usual small waves. Then a south swell hit and it got big. When it's over 6 feet, the peak is steep and really throws out, and it can get pretty scary on the takeoffs because it's so shallow. When you take off, the drop is vertical and you can see the bottom. When it gets bigger, it gets really mean. Mike was from the mainland, and he was into the psychedelic lifestyle of the sixties, so one day after we rode it big, he said, "You know that drop—it's like taking acid. We should call it 'Acid Drop'." After awhile the name spread, and the rest of the guys on Kaua'i started calling it Acid Drop. That was the summer of '68.

 Steven Bethel, October 25, 2000

Admiral Clarey. Bridge, Pearl Harbor, O'ahu. The 4,700-foot-long bridge that joins Ford Island in Pearl Harbor with Makalapa on the shore of O'ahu. It was dedicated on April 15, 1998, and named for Admiral Bernard "Chick" Clarey (1912–1996), a former commander-in-chief, U.S. Pacific Fleet. Clarey was one of the U.S. Navy's most highly decorated officers, with three Navy Crosses, five Distinguished Service Medals, the Silver Star, the Legion of Merit, and the Bronze Star Medal with Combat "V." He was also an active community leader in Honolulu. Also known as Ford Island Bridge.

A. D.'s. Surf site, Hawai'i Kai, O'ahu. A. D. are the initials of Alan Davis, the owner of Wāwāmalu Ranch from 1932 to 1946. Davis' home on Kalama Stream was near the surf site. Also known as Alan Davis, Left Point.

Ahalanui. Beach park (6 acres), Pohoiki, Hawai'i. Site of Hot Pond, a brackish pool warmed by a thermal spring. The park is in the land division of Ahalanui. See Hot Pond.

Ahelu. Beach, Waiheʻe, Maui. Section of beach near the mouth of Waiheʻe Stream.

ʻAhihi Bay. Dive site, snorkeling site, Mākena, Maui. Part of the ʻAhihi-Kinaʻu Natural Area Reserve.

ʻAhihi-Kinaʻu. Natural area reserve, Mākena, Maui. Established in 1973 by the State Board of Land and Natural Resources, the reserve includes (1) the lava flows forming Cape Kinaʻu and their developing dryland vegetation, (2) an inshore marine ecosystem, and (3) the mixohaline ponds. Consumptive activities are prohibited on the lands and in the waters of the reserve.

Āhole. Island (.15 acres, 40 feet high), Kīpahulu, Maui. Adult Hawaiian flagtail fish *(Kuhlia sandvicensis).*

Āholehole Flats. Fishing site, Kamākaʻipō, Molokaʻi. Section of Kamākaʻipō Beach that was a thrownet site for *āholehole,* the juvenile Hawaiian flagtail fish *(Kuhlia sandvicensis).*

Āhole Hōlua. Historic site, Kapuʻa, Hawaiʻi. Best-preserved sled ramp *(hōlua)* in Hawaiʻi, on the shore of Puʻu Hinahina Bay. The narrow, ski jump-shaped structure is approximately 105 feet long with a 25-foot runway and an 85-foot ramp, both constructed of rocks. Hawaiians covered the surface of the ramp with pili grass and *kukui* nut oil and then rode down it toward the ocean on narrow sleds with hardwood runners. *Lit., āhole* sled ramp.

ʻĀhua. Reef, Hickam Air Force Base, Oʻahu. West of Hickam Harbor and off Fort Kamehameha housing. Remnant of the large reef that was dredged during the 1940s during the construction of the seaplane runways in Keʻehi Lagoon and at ʻĀhua Point, filled in the 1970s to accommodate the Reef Runway, and dredged in the 1970s to construct the Hickam Harbor Channel. The remnant of the reef lies between Hickam Harbor Channel and Pearl Harbor Channel. Near shore the reef is a shallow tidal flat that is a popular fishing and reef-walking site. *Lit.,* heap.

Ahuʻena. *Heiau,* Kailua, Hawaiʻi. Shrine fronting Kamakahonu Beach that was part of King Kamehameha I's royal residence until his death in 1819. *Lit.,* red-hot heap.

Ahukini. Dive site, landing, state recreation pier (.9 acres), Līhuʻe, Kauaʻi. On the south point of Hanamaʻulu Bay. This site was known as Ahukini Landing when it was a landing for interisland steamers. During the early 1920s, Ahukini Terminal Company constructed a 300-foot pier and breakwater and dredged a turning basin. The pier was the first on Kauaʻi that could accommodate large vessels and was used extensively until the end of World War II. After the war, shipping operations were relocated to Nāwiliwili Harbor, which had been improved to accommodate vessels too large to enter Ahukini. The facilities at Ahukini were abandoned by 1950. The pier was dismantled, and in 1978 the state converted the landing into a park. The dive site is off the park and is used for beginning divers. *Lit.*, altar [for] many [blessings] or many altars.

Ahu o Laka. Island (3.1 acres, awash at high tide), Kahalu'u, O'ahu. When the island— actually a sandbar—is emergent at low tide, it is a popular picnic and recreation site for boaters in Kāne'ohe Bay. Also known as the Sandbar. *Lit.*, altar of [the deity] Laka.

Ahupū. Bay, beach, northwest shore, Kaho'olawe. Large sheltered bay that falls within the coastal boundaries of the 'ili, or land division, of Ahupū. A detrital sand beach lines its shore. *Lit.*, heap together.

Ahupū Iki. Bay, beach, northwest shore, Kaho'olawe. Sheltered bay that falls within the coastal boundaries of the *'ili*, or land division, of Ahupū. A detrital sand beach lines its shore. *Lit.*, small Ahupū (heap together).

'Aiea Bay. State recreation area (20 acres), 'Aiea, O'ahu. Park on the shore of East Loch, Pearl Harbor, dedicated on October 13, 1998. No in-water activities are permitted in Pearl Harbor from the park. *Lit.*, the *Nothocestrum* tree.

Aikau. Memorial, Waimea, O'ahu. Plaque at Waimea Bay for Eddie Aikau (1946–1978). Aikau was a veteran big-wave surfer and lifeguard at Waimea. On March 17, 1978, he was a crewmember on the Hawaiian sailing canoe *Hokule'a* when it swamped at sea in the Moloka'i Channel. Taking a surfboard that he had onboard the canoe, he attempted to paddle to Lāna'i for help, but he disappeared at sea and was never seen again. Aikau is also memorialized in the famous saying, "Eddie would go," meaning that no matter how big a wave was, he would catch it, or in surfing terminology, he would "go."

'Aimakapā. Fishpond (35 acres), Honokōhau, Hawai'i. Inland of Honokōhau Beach and part of the Kaloko-Honokōhau National Historical Park. As the largest freshwater pond on the Kona Coast, it is an important habitat for native and migratory waterbirds.

'Āina Haina. Surf site, 'Āina Haina, O'ahu. In 1924, Robert Hind purchased 2,090 acres in Wailupe Valley and used the land to operate the Hind-Clarke Dairy. The first subdivision in the valley was developed in 1947 and named 'Āina Haina in honor of Robert Hind. *'Āina* means "land" and *Haina* is the Hawaiianization of Hind. The entire valley has been known as 'Āina Haina since then. The surf site is off 'Āina Haina Shopping Center. Also known as 'Āina's. *Lit.*, Hind's land.

'Āinamalu. Beach, Diamond Head, O'ahu. Section of Ka'alawai Beach. 'Āinamalu was the name of the former George Brown estate in the center of Ka'alawai Beach at the foot of Diamond Head. When the estate was subdivided, the subdivision was named 'Āinamalu. *Lit.*, shady land.

'Āina Moana. County beach park (43 acres), Honolulu, O'ahu. 'Āina Moana is a man-made peninsula at the east end and part of Ala Moana Beach Park. Completed in 1964, it was originally named Magic Island by its developers, who intended it to be the site of a resort complex. The complex was never built, and the peninsula became a state park. In 1972, the Division of State Parks decided to give it this name because the peninsula was created from dredged coral fill. In spite of the new name assigned by park planners, it is still commonly called Magic Island. *Lit.*, land [from the] sea.

'Āina's. Surf site, 'Āina Haina, O'ahu. Same as 'Āina Haina.

'Ai'ōpio. Fishpond, Honokōhau, Hawai'i. Small, circular pond at the south end of Honokōhau Beach and part of the Kaloko-Honokōhau National Historical Park. *Lit.*, food [of the] youngsters.

Airplane Wreck. Dive site, Keāhole, Hawai'i. South of Unualoha Point at approximately 115 feet. Little remains of the wreck, so it is dived infrequently.

Airport. Beach, dive site, Kā'anapali, Maui. Off the former Kā'anapali Airport. Also known as Kahekili Beach Park, North Beach.

Airports. Surf site, Pacific Missile Range Facility, Kaua'i. Off the runway, or "airport," at PMRF. Also known as Kinikini.

'Akahi Kaimu. Pond, swimming site, 'Anaeho'omalu, Hawai'i. On the rocky shore, approximately one-quarter mile south of Kapalaoa Beach. L-shaped, spring-fed anchialine pond with good water clarity. The swimming site is the pond. Also known as Lone Palm.

Akeo Point. Hawai'i Kai, O'ahu. Small, partially submerged limestone shelf at the base of the Koko Head sea cliffs west of Hanauma Bay. In 1990, veteran kayak paddler Harold Akeo inadvertently went aground here during a training run and had to walk on the shelf with his kayak in hand before resuming paddling. His paddling companions believed that the incident should be immortalized and named the shelf "Akeo Point."

 mo'olelo

For the past sixteen years, a group of Hawai'i Kai and Waimānalo kayakers has paddled each Tuesday, Thursday, and Sunday. The most common training run is from Hawai'i Kai to Hanauma Bay, Lāna'i Lookout, or Blowhole, depending upon conditions. This is some of the roughest water on the island, and the area from

A

Portlock Point to Hanauma Bay is referred to as "The Wall," as in, for example, "Are we paddling up The Wall today?" The group calls itself the Up The Wall Gang. It's a great training run because if you can paddle there, the rest of the racing areas are easy by comparison. In 1990, on a flat calm day, Harold Akeo ran aground on a semisubmerged limestone shelf on the west side of Hanauma Bay, just past the partially detached rock that marks the west side of the bay. Everyone, including Harold, had his head down as we raced toward home. If you aren't careful, the swell bends slightly shoreward in this area, and it is easy to get sucked toward the ledge. We noticed Harold standing on the ledge, holding his kayak under his arm. Because it was calm, he managed to get off the ledge and back on his kayak with the only damage being that to his pride. Naturally, our group started calling the spot **"Akeo Point."** This is one of the natural gathering places on the paddling runs from Makapu'u to Hawai'i Kai, and word of the new name spread quickly. At Harold's forty-first birthday party—his *yakudoshi* party—we presented him with a fake plaque from National Geographic commending him on his discovery of a new point, and also a framed nautical chart of the area with "Akeo Point" superimposed on it. The point is now known by almost all one-man and kayak racers as Akeo Point.

 Bob Rocheleau, January 3, 2000

Aki's. Beach, surf site, Mākaha, O'ahu. Cove with a small calcareous sand beach between 'Upena and Moua Streets. Walter Aki, father of former state Senator James Aki, bought the property adjacent to the beach in 1948 when the subdivision was first opened. The Aki family home has been there since then. The surf site is a shorebreak on the beach. Also known as Kiddies Beach, Laukinui.

Ako. Channel, point, Kū'au, Maui. During the early 1900s, an elderly man named Ako lived on Kū'au Point. Fishermen named the point and a narrow channel through the rocks on the point after him. Also known as Kū'au to windsurfers.

Akua House. Bay, Mokulē'ia, O'ahu. Alternate name for Kawaihapai Bay. *Akua* is Hawaiian for "god." The Akua House is the O-Jizosan Shrine on the shore that was built by Japanese fishermen in 1913 to protect shorecasters along the entire Mokulē'ia shore. The name is used primarily by commercial fishermen who net and spearfish offshore.

Aku Bowls. Surf site, Kuli'ou'ou, O'ahu. When the surf site Tunas was named in the early 1970s, Stanley Ogino, one of the regular Kuli'ou'ou surfers, started calling it "Aku's" for fun. *Aku* is the

Hawaiian word for tuna. The bowl is the curved or bowl-shaped section at the start of the wave. Also known as Aku's, Tunas, Tuna Bowls.

Aku's. Surf site, Kuli'ou'ou, O'ahu. Same as Aku Bowls. Also known as Tunas, Tuna Bowls.

'Alaeloa. Beach, Nāpili, Maui. Small pocket of calcareous sand. *Lit.,* distant mudhen, or long fern.

Alahao Airport Park. Beach park, windsurf site, Kahului, Maui. Wide calcareous sand beach on the north side of Kanahā Beach Park. The undeveloped backshore is under the control of the State Department of Transportation, Airports Division. Alahao Road is the major road to the site. *Alahao* means "railroad tracks," and the road was a former right-of-way for the railroad. Also known as Kooks Beach. *Lit.,* iron road, or railroad tracks.

Ala Kahakai. National historic trail, Hawai'i. The 175-mile coastal trail that runs from the eastern boundary of the Hawai'i Volcanoes National Park through the districts of Ka'ū, Kona, and Kohala to 'Upolu Point. The name was first suggested by planners from the Division of State Parks in a 1973 report called "Nā Ala Hele" (literally, the trails). The report recommended a Nā Ala Hele Statewide Trail System and proposed a demonstration trail from Keāhole Point to Kawaihae that would be known as the Ala Kahakai. The Ala Kahakai National Historic Trail connects the demonstration trail with other coastal trail remnants and includes many county, state, and federal lands. It was established on November 13, 2000, when President William Clinton signed into law the Ala Kahakai National Trail Act as Public Law 106–509. Section 3 of this law describes the location of the trail and provides that no land may be acquired by the Secretary of the Interior without the consent of the landowner. It also provides that the Secretary shall encourage communities and landowners along the trail to participate in the planning, development, and maintenance of the trail, and consult with affected federal, state, and local agencies, native Hawaiian groups, and landowners in the administration of the trail. The National Park Service is the trail manager. *Lit.,* trail [by the] sea, or beach trail.

Alāla. Fishing shrine, point, Kailua, Oahu. Point at the south end of Kailua Beach that separates Kailua and Lanikai. The point takes its name from the fishing shrine, a natural stone formation on the ridge above. Wailea, a companion fishing shrine, is located at the south end of Lanikai. *Lit.,* awakening.

Ala Moana. 1. Beach. The 4,000-foot-long and 150-foot-wide calcareous sand beach that fronts Ala Moana Regional Park. 2. Channel, Honolulu, O'ahu. The 1,000-meter swimming channel that parallels the beach in Ala Moana Regional Park.

It was formerly a boat channel that was dredged through Ala Moana Reef to connect the Ala Wai Boat Harbor and Kewalo Basin, but it was closed at its west end in 1955. 3. Reef, Honolulu, Oʻahu. An approximately half-mile-long reef between Magic Island and Kewalo Channel. 4. Regional park (120 acres), Honolulu, Oʻahu. Land for the park was set aside in 1931. Facilities were completed and dedicated in 1934. Originally known as Moana Park, its name was changed to Ala Moana in 1947. Ala Moana Regional Park is one of the most popular and heavily used beach parks in urban Honolulu. 5. Surf site, Honolulu, Oʻahu. Off Ala Wai Boat Harbor. Named after Ala Moana Boulevard, the road in Waikīkī that leads to the site. Also known as Ala Moana Bowls, Bowls. *Lit.*, deep sea path.

Ala Moana Bowls. Surf site, Honolulu, Oʻahu. This site was first called Ala Moana in the 1950s after Ala Moana Boulevard, the road in Waikīkī that leads to it, and "Bowls" was added later. The bowl is the curved or bowl-shaped section at the west end of the wave. Also known as Ala Moana, Bowls.

Alan Davis. 1. Beach, Hawaiʻi Kai, Oʻahu. Calcareous sand beach and rocky shore named for Alan Sanford Davis, former head trustee of Campbell Estate, who lived here from 1932 to 1946. Davis leased 3,000 acres from Bishop Estate as a cattle ranch that he called Wāwāmalu Ranch. Shorecasters and thrownet fishermen began calling the shore here "Alan Davis" in the 1930s. Also known as Ka Iwi Coast, Ka Iwi Shoreline, Queen's Beach, Wāwāmalu. 2. Fishing site, Hawaiʻi Kai, Oʻahu. Sea cliffs between Makapuʻu Light and the Balancing Rock. *Ulua* fishermen extended the name Alan Davis to include this side of Makapuʻu Head. 3. Surf site, Hawaiʻi Kai, Oʻahu. Off the calcareous sand beach. Also know as A. D.'s, Left Point.

 moʻolelo

Sam Damon had the lease for the ranch before I did. He and I were friends and we'd go out there on weekends and round up the cattle, which were wild. When his lease was up, I took a 30-year lease on the property from Bishop Estate, beginning in 1932, and made my home there. The property included all the land from the gap near Kamiloiki to Makapuʻu Point. We knew the entire area as Wāwāmalu and that's what I named the ranch. It means "shady valley," but there never were any wooded areas to go with the name. Fishing was very good, especially for *moi* and *āholehole,* and we often had fish for dinner.

We were home on April 1, 1946, when the tidal wave struck. The first wave came in between six and seven in the morning. I had just finished shaving when I heard water lapping against the sisal fence outside the house. We'd had previous wave warnings, so I knew immediately what it was. I quickly gathered everyone up, my wife and my two daughters, Linda and Nancy, and we drove up the valley to higher ground. I returned to the house between the third and fourth waves to make sure everyone else was out and to try and get our dogs and personal belongings. The inside of the house was turned upside down. As I was walking through the mess, another wave struck. I was so startled, I grabbed a painting off the wall and ran. The water around the house was knee-deep, but I managed to get back to the road. I still have that painting—a picture of a large wave.

Alan Davis, October 10, 1972

The next wave destroyed the house and came farther up the valley. My dad was afraid that another one might come all the way up the valley and spill through the gap into Makapuʻu Beach, so as the water receded, we drove up the road to the lighthouse. The men on duty did not realize what was happening. From the lighthouse we watched the water recede all the way out to the island next to Rabbit Island. When the water returned, the noise was tremendous, and it still sticks in my memory. Wāwāmalu was the most fantastic childhood imaginable, but after the tidal wave we never went back.

 Nancy Davis Pfluger, October 8, 1972

ʻAlau. Island (4.5 acres, 40 feet high), Haneoʻo, Maui. Off Koki Beach Park. Part of the Hawaiʻi State Seabird Sanctuary. *Lit.,* many rocks, or dividing, branching.

Ala Wai. 1. Canal, Honolulu, Oʻahu. Inland waterway 9,700 feet long (approximately 1.8 miles) and 250 feet wide that was dredged by Hawaiian Dredging Company from 1921 to 1928. It begins behind the Waikīkī-Kapahulu Library and ends at the Ala Moana Boulevard Bridge where its waters flow into the Ala Wai Small Boat Harbor. It is the most heavily used inland waterway in the state for ocean recreation activities, especially outrigger canoe paddling. 2. Channel. The boat channel that connects the Ala Wai Boat Harbor to the open ocean. 3. Small Boat Harbor, Honolulu, Oʻahu. Originally dredged in the late 1920s with the Ala Wai Canal. Facilities include 699 berths, 85 moorings, a ramp, 22 dry storage spaces, and a vessel washdown area. The harbor is also home to the Hawaiʻi Yacht Club and the Waikīkī Yacht Club. 4. Yacht Harbor. The Ala Wai Small Boat Harbor is often called the Ala Wai Yacht Harbor because of the presence of the Hawaiʻi Yacht Club and the Waikīkī Yacht Club within the harbor. *Lit.,* freshwater path.

ʻAleʻale. Point, sea stack, south shore, Kahoʻolawe. Steep sea stack connected to the point by a thin land bridge and the home of the last known *kanaloa* plants *(Kanaloa kahoolawensis)* on Kaho'olawe. *Lit.,* ripple.

'Alekoko. Fishpond, Nāwiliwili, Kaua'i. Same as Menehune Fishpond. *Lit.,* bloody ripples or rainbow-hued ripples.

Ali'i. 1. Fishpond, Kaunakakai, Moloka'i. 2. Beach, Hale'iwa, O'ahu. Same as Hale'iwa Ali'i Beach Park. *Lit.,* chief.

'Aliomanu. Beach, reef, Kaua'i. Narrow calcareous sand beach fronted by a long, wide, shallow reef. The reef is one of the island's famous seaweed harvesting sites for *limu kohu,* or *Asparagopsis taxiformis.* This prized edible seaweed is found elsewhere in Hawai'i, but local consumers believe the best *limu kohu* comes from Kaua'i and specifically from the reefs at 'Aliomanu, Ka'aka'aniu, and Pīla'a. Commercial harvesting on these reefs has for generations been the domain of a small group of Hawaiian families from Anahola and Moloa'a, the communities closest to the reefs. *Limu kohu* grows at the edge of the reef where there is a constant flow of water from breaking waves. After it is harvested and cleaned, it is soaked overnight in fresh water to reduce its iodine flavor, drained, and lightly salted. If it is to be sent to market, it is rolled into tight balls. Hawaiians differentiate between *limu kohu līpehe,* a milder flavored light red variety, and *limu kohu koko,* a stronger flavored dark red variety. *Lit.,* scar made by birds.

Allertons. Surf site, Lāwai Kai, Kaua'i. Lāwai Kai, or "seaward Lāwai," was purchased in 1937 by Robert Allerton, a millionaire from Chicago. Allerton, with his adopted son, John Gregg Allerton, turned the property into a tropical garden known as the Allerton Estate. Before his death in 1964, Robert Allerton designated a portion of the estate to be the Pacific Tropical Botanical Garden. The groundbreaking ceremony was held on January 1, 1970. When John Gregg Allerton died in 1986, the remainder of the Allerton Estate became a part of the garden. The Lāwai Kai shore is a calcareous sand beach fronted by a shallow sandbar. The surf site is a shorebreak on the sandbar. Also known as Lāwai.

Alligator. Rock, Kawailoa, O'ahu. Massive limestone rock on the beach, the seaward point of which is shaped like the head and snout of an alligator. The beach here is called Ka'alaea.

Alligators. Surf site, Hale'iwa, O'ahu. Off Alligator Rock. Also known as Baby Sunset, Little Sunset.

Aloha 'Āina. 1. Beach, southwest shore, Kaho'olawe. An otherwise unnamed calcareous sand beach near Maka'alae. In 1976, a group called the Protect Kaho'olawe 'Ohana dedicated itself to stopping the U.S. Navy's bombing of Kaho'olawe and to preserving the cultural, historical, and environmental integrity of the island. The group's efforts evolved into a statewide movement that was finally rewarded on May 8, 1994, when the island was returned to state ownership. In 1982, several of the group's members secretly paddled to Kahoʻolawe to occupy the island in protest of the RIMPAC exercises. They eluded the military search parties, but wanted to make sure the navy knew that they were there. On the side of a sand dune in this small unnamed bay, with large driftwood letters they spelled out "Aloha ʻĀina," the group's motto. The beach has since been known by this name. 2. Park, Pearl Harbor, Oʻahu. On the shore near the Pearl Harbor Officers' Club. *Lit.*, love [of the] land.

Aloha Tower. Harbor landmark, Honolulu, Oʻahu. The ten-story tower at Pier 10 that at 184 feet 2 inches was the tallest building in Honolulu when it was built in 1926. A 40-foot flagstaff tops the tower. After Diamond Head, it is the most widely recognized landmark on the shore of Honolulu, where it serves as the control tower for shipping traffic in Honolulu Harbor.

Alternatives. Surf site, Olowalu, Maui. On the east side of Olowalu between Ukumehame State Wayside Park and Olowalu. One of the many "alternative" surf sites along this stretch of Honoapiʻilani Highway.

Aluea. Island (.14 acres, 40 feet high), Keʻanae, Maui.

Alula. Beach, Honokōhau, Hawaiʻi. Small calcareous sand and lava fragment beach at the entrance to Honokōhau Small Boat Harbor. Also known as Manta Ray Beach.

Amelia Earhart. Monument, Diamond Head, Oʻahu. In the center lookout of Kuilei Cliffs Beach Park. Kate Kelly, Honolulu's leading sculptor of the 1930s and wife of artist John Kelly, made the memorial plaque to honor aviator Amelia Earhart (1898–1937). In July 1937, Earhart was lost in the South Pacific during an attempt to fly around the world in her Lockheed Electra.

Americas. Surf site, Ala Moana, Oʻahu. Off Ala Moana Beach Park and inshore of Big Lefts. Primarily a bodyboarding site on the reform waves on the inside reef.

Ammonias. Surf site, Nāwiliwili, Kauaʻi. On a shallow reef off the seawall in Nāwiliwili Park. Named for the ammonia smell from commercial ammonia tanks in the harbor industrial area.

Ammo Reef. Dive site, Waiʻanae, Oʻahu. Bullets and other ammunition from a former target range onshore are found on the ocean floor here. Southwest of Waiʻanae Small Boat Harbor at approximately 40 feet. Also known as Aquarium Reef.

Amphitheater. Dive site, Hawaiʻi Kai, Oʻahu. Large amphitheater-shaped rock formation at 15 to 50 feet off Kawaihoa Point.

ʻAnaehoʻomalu. Bay, beach, beach park, surf site, windsurf site, ʻAnaehoʻomalu, Hawaiʻi. Calcareous sand and lava fragment beach approximately 900 feet long at the head of a wide bay.

Two fishponds, Ku'uali'i and Kahapapa, and a large coconut grove are in the backshore. A small beach park with public parking is at the south end of the beach. The surf site is on the reef at the north end of the beach. Windsurfers launch and land primarily at the south end of the beach fronting the beach park. *Lit.*, restricted mullet, or protected mullet.

'Anaeho'omalu Point. Dive site, 'Anaeho'omalu, Hawai'i. Off the north point of 'Anaeho'omalu Bay.

Anahola. Beach park (1.5 acres), landing, surf site, Anahola, Kaua'i. Long, wide calcareous sand beach fronted by a shallow sandbar. Surf sites are located in the shorebreak on the sandbar. Unreals is the name of the surf site next to the ruins of the former interisland steamer landing. The beach park at the north end of the beach is Hawaiian Homes' land that has been leased from the state since 1955.

Anakaluahine. Cave, Kalaupapa, Moloka'i. One of a series of sea caves on the north side of the peninsula. Also known as Keanaokaluahine, Old Lady's Cave. *Lit.*, cave [of] the old lady.

Ananoio. Cave, Kalaupapa, Moloka'i. One of a series of sea caves on the north side of the peninsula. Also known as Bird Cave, Keananoio. *Lit.*, noddy tern cave. Noddy terns nest here.

Anchorage. Boat ramp, Hawai'i Kai, O'ahu. Private boat ramp in Hawai'i Kai Marina for residents of the Anchorage.

Anglerfish Reef. Dive site, Hawai'i Kai, O'ahu. Semicircular, undercut ledge at 25 to 45 feet deep, straight out from Hawai'i Kai Channel; remnants of a boat wreck are nearby. Jackie James, the owner of Aloha Dive Shop in Hawai'i Kai Marina since 1970, found a small anglerfish, or frogfish, here in the late 1970s. It was always in the same place during her dives and became like a personal pet. James never saw the fish again after Hurricane 'Iwa struck the islands in 1982. Also known as Anglers Reef.

'Anini. 1. Beach park, channel, ramp, reef, snorkeling site, windsurf site, 'Anini, Kaua'i. Narrow calcareous sand beach inshore of 'Anini Reef, one of the longest and widest fringing reefs in Hawai'i at 2 miles long and 1,600 feet wide at its widest point. The beach park is midway along the beach. 'Anini Channel, a wide sand-bottomed channel, cuts through the reef to the west of the beach park. The windsurf site, especially good for beginners, is west of the boat ramp. The snorkeling site is west of the channel. The ramp facility in the beach park is for smaller, shallow-draft boats. *Lit.*, dwarfish, stunted.

Antennas. Surf site, Kamalino, Ni'ihau. The antennas are the radio towers of a former Ni'ihau loran station at Waiu, a communication facility that was built in 1944, during World War II, and decommissioned in 1951. The residents of Ni'ihau knew the station as Waiu and composed a song in its honor called "Po'e Koa o Ni'ihau," or the "Soldiers of Ni'ihau." Also known as Kamalino.

Ant Man's. Surf site, 'Anaeho'omalu, Hawai'i. Big-wave, second-reef site that breaks off 'Anaeho'omalu Point and is usually ridden only when A-Bay, or 'Anaeho'omalu Bay, to the north is closed out.

Apo. Pond, Miloli'i, Hawai'i. Large natural pond south of Miloli'i Beach Park that is used as an anchorage for shallow-draft boats. Named for the Apo family living onshore.

Āpua. 1. Point, surf site, Hawai'i Volcanoes National Park, Hawai'i. Coastal campsite on a low, flat, rocky point that marks the coastal boundary between the districts of Puna and Ka'ū. The surf site is on the west side of the point. Also known as Trains. 2. Coastal plain, Kualoa, O'ahu. The land that comprises Kualoa Regional Park. *Lit.*, fish basket or fish trap.

 *mo'olelo*

I was born in 1915 on Gandle Lane in Honolulu, but we moved to Hilo in April 1924 when my dad got a job there. He was the court reporter, the only one in town. We lived there until 1930 when we moved back to Honolulu, and I transferred from Hilo High to McKinley. During those five years on the Big Island my dad organized about eight goat drives in Kīlauea National Park. The Board of Agriculture was trying to protect the park and the grazing lands, and they encouraged the drives and paid half the cost. Whoever did the drive, though, had to dispose of the goats, and our drives netted from seven hundred to four thousand goats per drive.

We had relatives in Kalapana, the Lane family, and I spent several summers with them. From the Lanes we knew some of the other Kalapana families such as the Pea's, Hauanio's, Kaipo's, and Kamelamela's. My dad would hire about thirty of them as cowboys and pay them five dollars a day, plus their meals. They had to bring their own horses. They rode *mauka* and stayed overnight at 'Āinahou Ranch before starting the drive.

The first day the cowboys would fan out from the Chain of Craters to Hilina Pali and slowly herd the goats toward **'Āpua Point** on the ocean. 'Āpua was the first night's stop. The cowboys kept about one-quarter mile behind the goats so they wouldn't get spooked and bolt. A fence was laid flat across the point and when the goats were driven over it, the cowboys raised it, penning the goats. The point was surrounded by water. The Pea family was from 'Āpua, and told my dad that the 1868 tidal wave had wiped out their village, so they had moved to Kalapana. They still knew the area well, and everyone got water from the brackish water well for their former village. It was within 150 feet of the point and could only be reached by climbing down into a deep crack.

On one drive I got lost in the Ka'ū Desert. A violent sandstorm swept over us and I lost sight of the other riders. My horse stepped in a hole, reared up to free his foot, and I slid off. I hit the ground really hard, but jumped up right away to grab him. Luckily, he was only walking. My dad had told me many times if I was ever lost to just give the horse its head. I did and he walked us back toward 'Āpua Point.

The second stop was Ka'ena where there was another pen, and by then the goats were tired and easy to handle. They were almost like a domesticated herd. At the last stop in Punalu'u, the goats were penned, slaughtered, and skinned immediately. The hides were salted and placed in the shade to cure, and the carcasses were thrown in the ocean for the sharks. After the hides were cured, they were bundled, trucked to Hilo, and shipped to the mainland.

George V. Clark, August 31, 1980

During the evenings on the goat drives, the cowboys would sit around talking and joking, and sometimes tell riddles. This is one that I remember:

> *O keia kanaka nui*
> *Nui kona leo*
> *Lohe na po'e apau*
> *Ma ka laho.*

In English it means:

> This is a big man
> He has a loud voice
> All of the people hear him
> From his balls.

The answer is a church bell.

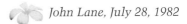 *John Lane, July 28, 1982*

'Āpuakehau. 1. Shore, Mākena, Maui. Near Keawala'i Church on Mākena Bay. 2. Stream, Waikīkī, O'ahu. Prior to the completion of the Ala Wai Canal in 1928, 'Āpuakehau was the major stream that drained the wetlands inland of Waikīkī Beach into the ocean. It crossed the beach between the Royal Hawaiian and the Outrigger Waikīkī Hotels. *Lit.*, basket [of] dew. Probably the name of a rain.

Aquarium. 1. Dive site, Kealakekua, Hawai'i. Shallow reef at 15 feet with a dropoff to 115 feet off the Captain Cook Monument. Also known as Ka'awaloa Cove. The name attests to the wide variety of fish found here. 2. Dive site, Kohanaiki,

Hawaiʻi. One of the Pine Trees dive sites. 3. Dive site, Nāwili-wili, Kauaʻi. Shallow reef with lava ledges and small valleys south of Nāwiliwili Harbor. Remnants of a wreck are also found here. 4. Dive site, Makena, Maui. Cove on the shore of ʻĀhihi-Kinaʻu Natural Area Reserve. 5. Aquarium, Waikīkī, Oʻahu. Same as Waikīkī Aquarium.

Aquarium Reef. Dive site, Waiʻanae, Oʻahu. Southwest of Waiʻanae Small Boat Harbor at approximately 40 feet. The name attests to the wide variety of fish found here. Also known as Ammo Reef.

Arch. 1. Geographical feature, north shore, Kahoʻolawe. Weathered hole through a rocky point near Makaʻalae. 2. Dive site, north coast, Niʻihau. Series of arches, caves, and chimneys that are an underwater extension of the protruding rocks and small islands at Kamakalepo Point.

Arches. 1. Dive site, Makalawena, Hawaiʻi. Underwater arches, caves, tunnels. First used as a commercial dive site in the early 1970s by the former Kona Dive Lodge at Mahaiʻula. 2. Dive site, Diamond Head, Oʻahu. Off Kaʻalāwai Beach fronting the former Lester McCoy home; it has three large arches on its seaward side. Surfers call this site Brown's.

Arizona Memorial. National park, Pearl Harbor, Oʻahu. Same as USS *Arizona* Memorial.

Arma Hut. Surf site, Sunset Beach, Oʻahu. During the early 1960s, Dr. Willis Butler bought a beachfront home at Rocky Point. His son Bruce was an avid surfer and began riding the waves in front of their home, a large green quonset hut. As a joke, one of Bruce's friends said that Bruce resembled an Armadoon, a cross between an armadillo and a baboon, so the quonset hut was soon known as Arma Hut. Arma Hut was home to many transient surfers and by the mid-1960s was also the name of the surf site off the house on the north side of Rocky Point. During the 1970s, Rocky Point replaced Arma Hut as the name of the surf site. Some surfers still use the name Arma Hut for a secondary surf site between Rocky Point and Monster Mush. This site is also known as Stone Zone.

Armchair Reef. Dive site, southeast coast, Lānaʻi. Near Kamaiki Point at approximately 40 feet.

Army. 1. Beach, Waiʻanae, Oʻahu. Same as the Waiʻanae Kai Military Reservation. 2. Museum, Waikīkī, Oʻahu. Same as U.S. Army Museum.

Army Beach. Surf site, Mokulēʻia, Oʻahu. The army had a recreation facility in Haleʻiwa until the lease expired in 1970 and they moved to Mokulēʻia. The Mokulēʻia Army Beach Recreation Center included 14 acres and one-half mile of beach near the west end of Dillingham Airfield until it closed in May 1989. Today only the concrete slab of the former beach volleyball court is left. The surf site is off the concrete slab.

Atlantis Reef. Waikīkī, Oʻahu. Artificial reef built by Atlantis Submarines at the east end of Waikīkī approximately one mile offshore in 100 feet of water. The reef was started in 1989 as an attraction for Atlantis' submarine tours and includes a 111-foot-long line fishing vessel, a 174-foot navy yard oiler, the remains of two aircraft, and other fish aggregation devices.

Atlantis Wreck. Dive site, Waikīkī, Oʻahu. A 174-foot navy yard oiler that is part of the Atlantis Reef. Also known as Waikīkī Wreck, Y.O., Y.O. 257.

ʻAukai. Beach Park (.2 acres), Hauʻula, Oʻahu. Across the street from Hauʻula Fire Station. Alfred ʻAukai ʻAluli was the owner of the property when it was condemned for a public park.

Auntie Kaleiʻs. Island, Kawela, Oʻahu. Same as Kaleiʻs Island.

Au Street. Surf site, Mokulēʻia, Oʻahu. Off ʻĀweoweo Beach Park. The beach park is on Au Street. Also known as ʻĀweoweo, Pyramids. *Lit.*, swordfish street.

Avalanche. 1. Surf site, tow-in surf site, Haleʻiwa, Oʻahu. Second-reef, big-wave surf site. A small group of local surfers from Haleʻiwa named this site in 1954 while watching it from shore on a big day. Its huge, powerful waves, spilling massive amounts of whitewater, reminded them of an avalanche. Veteran big wave surfers Henry Preece, Buzzy Trent, and Fred Van Dyke were the first to surf it in 1955. 2. Surf site, Waimānalo, Oʻahu. At the east end of the reef off Makai Research Pier. Named by surfers from Waimānalo during the late 1950s after the surf site of the same name on the North Shore. Also known as Makai Pier, Submarines.

 *moʻolelo*

I was born in Nānākuli on April 13, 1929, and I started surfing about 1947 on the old redwood boards. George Downing made me my first good redwood board, and Wally Froiseth made me my second, a redwood laminated with balsa. One of the places in Nānākuli where I learned to surf was Keaulanaʻs, which was named for Buffalo Keaulanaʻs uncle. He had a house there on the point. As I got better, I started surfing big waves at Mākaha and Māʻili Point, which is what we used to call Green Lanterns. In 1953, I moved to the North Shore, and for three years from 1954 to 1957, I lived in a shack on the beach where the surf center is now at Aliʻi Beach. One day after work about eight or ten of us were drinking at my place—Bobby Chun, Buffalo, who was a lifeguard at the old Army Beach, David Pahoa, and some other *guys. We were just talking and watching these huge waves breaking on the second reef to the west of us. Somebody commented that when the waves broke, they looked like an avalanche, and from then on that was its name. I surfed it in 1955 with Fred Van Dyke and Buzzy Trent. It was really big, and each of us only caught one wave. As far as I know, that was the first time anyone surfed it.*

 Henry Preece, October 12, 2000

'Awahua. Beach, Kalaupapa, Moloka'i. One of five beaches on the Kalaupapa Peninsula. Long, wide detrital sand beach at the foot of the Kalaupapa Trail on the west side of the peninsula. Also known as Black Sands Beach, Ke One Ne'e o 'Awahua, and Puahi. *Lit.*, bitterness.

Awake'e. Dive site, Awake'e, Hawai'i. South of Pu'u Kuili at approximately 45 feet. *Lit.*, bent harbor or bent channel.

Awalua. 1. Bay, beach, landing, north shore, Lāna'i. Narrow calcareous sand beach at the head of a small bay on Shipwreck Beach. Used as a boat landing during the late 1800s. Site of one of the two remaining shipwrecks on Shipwreck Beach, a shipyard oil tanker that went aground under mysterious circumstances in the early 1950s. 2. Beach, Olowalu, Maui. Narrow calcareous sand beach along the highway west of Olowalu. *Lit.*, double harbor.

'Āweoweo. Beach park (1.4 acres), surf site, Mokulē'ia, O'ahu. The park was named for the street that leads to it from Waialua Beach Road. The surf site is off the beach park and is also known as Au Street, Pyramids. *Lit.*, bigeye or scad fish (Priacanthidae family). The streets in this subdivision are named for Hawaiian fish.

Āwili. 1. Bay, fishing site, Keaukaha, Hawai'i. 2. Beach, fishing site, point, Manukā, Hawai'i. Black sand beach on the south side of 'Āwili Point at the base of a small littoral cone. Near the end of Road to the Sea. The point is one of the Big Island's famous *ulua* fishing sites. *Lit.*, swirl.

Baboon Point. Sea cliff, Hawai'i Kai, O'ahu. The outline of the sea cliff at Pai'olu'olu Point on the west side of Hanauma Bay resembles the face of a baboon from the lookout above the beach, especially the pointed nose. It is also known as Baboon Face and Baboon Nose.

Baby. 1. Beach, Po'ipū, Kaua'i. Section of beach at Po'ipū Beach Park that is protected from the open ocean by a seawall. The seawall is semicircular and forms a "pool" that is a popular swimming site for little children. Also known as Children's Pool. 2. Park, Pā'ia, Maui. Small or "baby" beach park on Pā'ia Bay. Also known as Pā'ia Park.

Baby Canoes. Surf site, Waikīkī, O'ahu. Secondary or "baby" surf site with smaller waves inshore of Canoes surf site.

Baby Castles. Surf site, Waikīkī, O'ahu. Secondary or "baby" surf site with smaller waves inshore of Castles. Also known as No Name, No Place.

Baby Cunha's. Surf site, Waikīkī, O'ahu. Secondary or "baby" surf site with smaller waves inshore of Cunha's. Also known as Ins-and-Outs.

Baby Hale'iwas. Surf site, Ala Moana, O'ahu. Waves here resemble those at Hale'iwa on the North Shore of O'ahu, although they are a smaller or "baby" version. Like Hale'iwa, the lineup here is a long right that ends on a shallow reef.

Babyland. Surf site, Mā'ili, O'ahu. Opposite Mā'ili Pink Market. Popular swimming and surf site for neighborhood children and families with babies.

Baby Makapu'u. Bay, surf site, Makapu'u, O'ahu. Small bay at the north end of Kaupō Beach Park. Baby Makapu'u was originally the name of the surf site at the east end of the park now called Suicides. After the name Suicides was introduced in the 1980s, Baby Makapu'u migrated to the north end of the park where it was applied to the bay and a popular novice surf site in the bay. The bay is also used as a site to scatter ashes following memorial services on the beach. Also known as The Bay, Cockroach Bay, Kumu Cove.

Baby Moke. Island, Kailua, O'ahu. Smaller or "baby" of the two Mokulua Islands, Moku Nui and Moku Iki, off Wailea Point in Lanikai. "Moke" is a slang abbreviation of Mokulua. Also known as Moku Iki.

Baby Queens. Surf site, Waikīkī, O'ahu. Secondary or "baby" surf site with smaller waves inshore of Queens.

Baby Royals. Surf site, Waikīkī, O'ahu. Secondary or "baby" surf site with small waves on the shallow sandbar fronting the Royal Hawaiian Hotel. Named for its location fronting the hotel. Also known as Cornucopia.

Baby Sunset. Surf site, Hale'iwa, O'ahu. Waves here are a smaller or "baby" version of those at Sunset. Also known as Alligators.

Back. Channel, Hanalei, Kaua'i. Small sand-bottomed channel into Hanalei Bay through the reef off Pu'u Poa Beach. This is a secondary or "back" channel in deference to the nearby primary channel into the bay at the Hanalei River mouth.

Backdoor. 1. Channel, Hanauma Bay, O'ahu. Channel through the east end of the reef. The name refers to the channel's location at the end of the reef that leads into the outer bay. It is the backdoor or lesser-used channel, as opposed to the primary or more frequently used channel into the bay, the Cable Channel at the west end of the reef. 2. Surf site, Sunset Beach, O'ahu. Same as Backdoor Pipeline. 3. Surf site, Ka'alawai, O'ahu. The inside, or reform, of the left at Brown's, a surf site ridden primarily to the right. Also known as In Betweens.

Backdoor Chun's. Surf site, Kawailoa, O'ahu. Left at Chun's Reef. Most surf sites are surfed best in one direction, either to the left of the takeoff spot or to the right. When a surfer rides the opposite way of the usual direction of the wave, he or she is said to be riding through the "backdoor." Riding left at Chun's Reef is riding through the backdoor. Also known as Piddleys.

Backdoor Pipeline. Surf site, Sunset Beach, O'ahu. Most surf sites are surfed best in one direction, either to the left of the takeoff spot or to the right. If a site is best surfed to the left, it is called a left. If a site is best surfed to the right, it is called a right. When a surfer rides the opposite way of the normal direction of the wave, he or she is said to be riding through the "backdoor." Probably the most famous backdoor is the right at Pipeline, a surf site that is a world-famous left. Also known as Backdoor.

Backsides. Surf site, Kailua, O'ahu. On the backside or seaward side of Flat Island off Kailua Beach Park.

Back Wall. Dive site, Molokini Island, Maui. On the backside of the island.

Backyards. 1. Surf site, Kawailoa, Oʻahu. Off the backyards of the first beachfront homes on Pāpaʻiloa Road. Small wave break that disappears when Himalayas is breaking. 2. Surf site, windsurf site, Sunset Beach, Oʻahu. Off the backyards of the beachfront homes on the north side of Sunset Point.

Bakers. Beach, Hilo, Hawaiʻi. On the shore of Hilo Bay between Reeds Bay and Pier 3. Like the beach in Reeds Bay, Bakers Beach is man-made. The coral rubble and calcareous sand that comprise the beach are spoil materials from the dredging operations that enlarged the Hilo Harbor basin. They were deposited on the shore here between 1925 and 1930. The newly created beach fronted the home of prominent Hilo businessman Adam Baker, whose three-story house with its beautiful lawns, rock gardens, and large fruit and shade trees was a famous landmark. Baker was the son of John Timoteo Baker, the last appointed governor of the Big Island under the Hawaiian monarchy.

Balancing Rock. Rock formation, Hawaiʻi Kai, Oʻahu. At the west end of Makapuʻu Head above the small breakwater built by Henry J. Kaiser. When viewed from Kalanianaʻole Highway near the entrance to the Hawaiʻi Kai Golf Course, part of the rock formation appears to be a pedestal, or "balancing," rock. Also known as Pele's Chair, Rebel Rock.

Baldwin. Beach park (17 acres), surf site, Kahului, Maui. Named after Harry A. Baldwin (1871–1946), son of Henry P. Baldwin, cofounder of Alexander and Baldwin, Inc. (A&B). The park was originally developed as a company recreation facility by Hawaiian Commercial and Sugar Company, a division of A&B, but eventually became a public beach park when the county leased the land from A&B. The shorebreak here is one of Maui's most popular bodysurfing and bodyboarding sites.

Bamboo Ridge. Point, Hawaiʻi Kai, Oʻahu. Small, flat lava point or ridge on the west side of the Hālona Blowhole. This is one of the most popular fishing sites on Oʻahu's south shore, and bamboo poles of *ulua* fishermen have lined the edge of the point since the 1920s.

Banyans. Surf site, Kona, Hawaiʻi. Off a large banyan tree on the grounds of the Kona Bali Kai Hotel on Aliʻi Drive.

Banyan Tree. Park, Lahaina, Maui. On Front Street, behind Lahaina Small Boat Harbor. The banyan tree in the center of the park, the largest banyan in Hawaiʻi, is ¼ mile in circumference and 60 feet high. It is a *Ficus benghalensis* from India and was planted on April 24, 1873 by William Owen Smith, the Sheriff of Lahaina, to commemorate the fiftieth anniversary of the American Protestant Mission in Lahaina.

Banyan Tree Reef. Dive site, Mākena, Maui. North of Nahuna Point. A large banyan tree stands on the low sea cliff inshore of the site.

Banzai. Beach, Sunset Beach, Oʻahu. Calcareous sand beach between Ke Waena and Ke Nui Roads. The origin of this name for the section of beach between Banzai Rock and Rocky Point is unknown, but surfing movie producer and artist John Severson recalled that the name was in use when he arrived in 1957. During the 1960s the name was applied to a lava rock formation at the southwest end of the beach, the Banzai Rock, and attached to the surf site in the center of the beach, the Banzai Pipeline. *Banzai* is a Japanese word meaning "Ten Thousand Years" and is commonly used as a toast at festive occasions to wish someone a long life. In the past it has also been used as a war cry. During World War II, a banzai charge was a death-defying attack by Japanese soldiers against their enemies. This latter definition of *banzai* is the one applicable to the beach and its dangerous waves.

Banzai Pipeline. Surf site, Sunset Beach, Oʻahu. Same as Pipeline.

Banzai Rock. Beach support park (2.3 acres), Sunset Beach, Oʻahu. Named for the Banzai Rock, a natural lava rock formation at the edge of the calcareous sand beach fronting the park. Also known as Rockpile.

Barbed Wires. Surf site, Mokulēʻia, Oʻahu. Off Mokulēʻia Polo Field. The polo field is a former Dillingham Ranch pasture that was surrounded by barbed wire.

Barbers. Point, ʻEwa, Oʻahu. During a trading voyage to China, Captain Henry Barber arrived in Hawaiʻi in October 1795 in his ship, the *Arthur*. He stopped at Waikīkī for provisions and then sailed for Kauaʻi. Soon after passing the entrance to Pearl Harbor, the *Arthur* wrecked on a reef in high surf and was completely destroyed. Six of the crew drowned, but Barber and the other fifteen members of his crew made it ashore in their small boats. The point where the wreck occurred was known thereafter as Barbers Point. Also known as Kalaeloa.

Barbers Point. 1. Beach park (7.4 acres), ʻEwa, Oʻahu. Narrow calcareous sand beach bordered by a rocky shelf. Named after the point. 2. Harbor, Kalaeloa, Oʻahu. One of two deep-draft harbors on Oʻahu. Originally dredged in 1961 as a barge harbor, it is also known as Kalaeloa Barbers Point Harbor. 3. Light, ʻEwa, Oʻahu. Established in 1888 at Puhilele, Kalaeloa. The 72-foot concrete light tower was built in 1933, and the light was automated in 1964. 4. Naval air station. In 1940 the U.S. Navy purchased the site of the naval air station from the Campbell

Estate and established the 'Ewa Marine Corps Air Station. On April 15, 1942, the station was commissioned as Barbers Point Naval Air Station. On July 1, 1999, the 3,700-acre station was closed in a series of nationwide base closings. The navy retained 1,173 acres for a housing complex, a medical center, and a golf course. The remaining acreage was dispersed among other federal, state, and county agencies. White Plains and Nimitz Beaches were opened to the public and became part of a 333-acre regional park that is managed by the county. The station was renamed the Kalaeloa Community Development District.

B

Barge Harbor. Dive site, south coast, Lāna'i. Shallow reef on the north side of Kaumalapa'u Harbor that extends several hundred feet out from shore and drops to 110 feet.

Barking Sands. 1. Beach, Polihale, Kaua'i. Section of Polihale Beach at Nohili Point. 2. Beach, Kaluakahua, Ni'ihau. 3. Beach, 'Ōhikilolo, O'ahu. "Barking sands," or "singing sands" as they are called in other parts of the world, are acoustical sands that emit noises when they are disturbed. Early English speakers in Hawai'i likened the noises from the sands to the woofing or barking of a dog and called them "barking sands." The Hawaiians called these sites *keonekani,* or "the sounding sands." The Kaua'i site is often referred to as Keonekani o Nohili in chants and songs. The three sites identified in Hawai'i are places where there are extensive dunes.

Bascule. Bridge, Honolulu, O'ahu. Bridge that connects Sand Island to O'ahu. A bascule bridge is one that is counterweighted so that it can be raised and lowered easily. The Sand Island bascule bridge is no longer raised and lowered due to the heavy traffic on Sand Island Road. Also known as the Drawbridge, Slattery Bridge.

Bathtub. Beach, Lā'ie, O'ahu. Opposite the Polynesian Cultural Center where the ocean has severely eroded the shore, exposing a limestone shelf. The "bathtub" is the pond between the shelf and the beach.

Battery Randolph. Museum, Waikīkī, O'ahu. On the shore of Ft. DeRussy and the site of the U.S. Army Museum. Battery Randolph is a former gun emplacement that was completed in 1911 as a key installation in the coastal artillery defense of Honolulu and Pearl Harbor. It was equipped with two 14-inch cannons that could shoot 14 miles out to sea. The guns were mounted on a disappearing carriage so that the recoil would cause them to drop behind the concrete wall after firing. Fire was directed from Diamond Head, but the guns were not used often as their blasts caused buildings in Honolulu to shake. In 1946 Battery Randolph's guns were dismantled, and in 1969 it was scheduled for demolition. The building, however, had been designed to withstand direct artillery hits and demolition proved to be a problem. A new use for the building was found, and the U.S. Army Museum opened in it on December 7, 1976.

Battleship _Missouri_. Memorial, Pearl Harbor. Memorial operated by the National Park Service that commemorates the battleship USS _Missouri,_ the "Mighty Mo." On September 2, 1945, General Douglas MacArthur accepted the Japanese surrender that ended World War II on the deck of the _Missouri._ On May 4, 1998, Secretary of the Navy John H. Dalton signed the donation contract officially transferring the historic battleship to the USS _Missouri_ Memorial Association (MMA) of Hawai'i. The ship was docked at Ford Island, Pearl Harbor, on June 22 after a 2,300-mile voyage across the Pacific from Bremerton, Washington, that began May 23. The _Missouri_ is moored to a pier on "Battleship Row," near the _Arizona_ Memorial. It was opened as a memorial and museum on January 29, 1999.

Battleship Rock. Dive site, Mākena, Maui. Near Pu'u 'Ola'i. Rock formation at 110 feet that resembles a ship. The rock is a seaward extension of Hawaiian Reef.

Bay, The. 1. Surf site, Waimānalo, O'ahu. This site in Kaupō Beach Park was first surfed regularly by Waimānalo residents in the late 1950s. They named it The Bay because the surf site is in a small bay. Also known as Baby Makapu'u, Cockroach Bay, Kumu Cove. 2. Surf sites, all islands. Many surf sites in bays, such as Waimea Bay, O'ahu, Hanalei Bay, Kaua'i, and Honolua Bay, Maui, are called The Bay.

Bayfront. Park, surf site, Hilo, Hawai'i. Bayfront is an abbreviation of Hilo Bayfront Park. The surf site is off the highway bridge over the Wailuku River at the north end of the park and is also known as Iron Bridge.

Bayviews. Surf site, Kahuku, O'ahu. Adjacent to the Turtle Bay Hilton Hotel on the north side of the point. The Bayview Lounge in the hotel overlooks the surf site. Also known as Hotels, Keyholes.

BB Buoy. Fish aggregating device, Moloa'a, Kaua'i. Buoy at approximately 395 fathoms. Landmarks: Kīlauea Point Light, Kāhala Point Light.

B Buoy. Fish aggregating device, Miloli'i, Hawai'i. Buoy anchored at approximately 850 fathoms. Landmarks: Miloli'i Light, 'Au'au Point, Kānewa'a Point.

Beach House. 1. Arch, beach, dive site, snorkeling site, surf site, Po'ipū, Kaua'i. Small pocket beach of calcareous sand on the west side of the Beach House Restaurant. The snorkeling and surf sites are on the reef off the beach. The arch and the dive site are beyond the reef. Also known as Longhouse Beach. 2. Surf site, Kualoa, Oʻahu. Off the beach houses north of the old sugar mill.

Beach Parks. 1. Surf site, ʻEwa Beach, Oʻahu. Off ʻEwa Beach Park. 2. Surf site, windsurf site, Mokulēʻia, Oʻahu. Off Mokulēʻia Beach Park. Also known as Park Rights.

Beach 69. Beach, Wailea, Hawaiʻi. Calcareous sand beach fronting a small community of beachfront homes. The beach is accessed from a section of Puakō Road that parallels the shore between Hāpuna Beach and the Puakō community. The utility poles along the road are numbered in ascending order heading toward Puakō, and the pole marking the secondary road to Wailea Beach is number 69, the origin of the name. Also known as Wailea State Park.

Beachtree. Surf site, Kūkiʻo, Hawaiʻi. Off the Beachtree Bar & Grill on the shore of the Four Seasons Resort Hualālaʻi. The restaurant is on the beach and adjacent to a large beach heliotrope tree.

Beanʻs. Beach, Honokokau, Hawaiʻi. Several small pockets of calcareous sand and coral rubble in the lava shore north of Old Kona Airport State Recreation Area. Captain Beans Beans (his personal choice for his legal name) was a tour boat operator who leased the Queen Liliʻuokalani Trustʻs campsite at Papawai for snorkeling and picnic tours in the 1960s and early 1970s. During that period the beach was named Beanʻs Beach. Although Beans sold his snorkeling business and concentrated on glass bottom boat tours and dinner cruises until his death in April 1983, the beach is still known by his name. Also known as Papawai, Pāwai.

Beaverʻs. Surf site, Niu, Oʻahu. On the west side of Niu Channel. Named after Steve "The Beaver" Saunders, one of the regular Niu surfers here in the late 1950s.

Beckʻs Cove. Bay, east shore, Kahoʻolawe. In 1905, a survey crew on the USS *Patterson* mapped Kahoʻolawe. They were unfamiliar with the islandʻs traditional names, so apparently named some of the major physical features after themselves. One of the members of the survey crew was H. L. Beck. The Hawaiian name is Kanapou Bay.

Bellows Field. Beach park (54.2 acres), Waimānalo, Oʻahu. In 1917, the Waimānalo Military Reservation was established on 1,500 acres of sand dunes and sugarcane fields. In 1933, it was renamed Bellows Field for Second Lieutenant F. B. Bellows, who had been killed in an airplane accident. The beach park with its calcareous sand beach is at the south end of the base, between Waimānalo and Inoaʻole Streams.

Berm. Island, water-skiing site, Keʻehi, Oʻahu. Long, narrow island off Keʻehi Small Boat Harbor and adjacent to the mooring area. The section of the lagoon on the seaward side of the Berm is the major water-skiing site in Honolulu. Also known as Slipper Island.

Bermuda Triangle. Reef, Kanahā, Maui. Off the middle of Kanahā Beach Park. Windsurfers named the site because it is an area they try to avoid like boaters try to avoid the famous Bermuda Triangle in the Atlantic. Currents over the reef are strong and waves cross it from many different angles.

Big. 1. Beach, Mākena, Maui. Calcareous sand beach 3,300 feet long at Mākena State Park. The names Big Beach and Little Beach for the two beaches in Mākena State Park were popularized from 1968 to 1972 by a transient hippie community that lived at Puʻu Ōlaʻi at the north end of the park. Also known as Long Sands, Mākena Beach, Oneloa. 2. Beach, Kahuku, Oʻahu. Calcareous sand beach on the east side of Kahuku Point. Also known as Hanakaʻilio, Marconi. 3. Rock, Kaluakoʻi, Molokaʻi. Same as Puʻu o Kaiaka.

Big Eel Reef. Dive site, Niu, Oʻahu. Long ledge at 35 to 50 feet deep. In addition to reef fish and turtles, several types of moray eels are commonly found here.

Big Gulch. Beach, backshore, Hakioawa, Kahoʻolawe. Name used by fishermen and hunters for the large gulch that runs down to the shore. The Hawaiian name is Hakioawa.

Big Lefts. Surf site, Ala Moana, Oʻahu. Left at Baby Haleʻiwas that breaks only on a big swell.

Big Moke. Island, Kailua, Oʻahu. Larger of the two Mokulua Islands, Moku Nui and Moku Iki, off Wailea Point in Lanikai. *Moke* is a slang abbreviation of Mokulua. Also known as Moku Nui.

Big Mouth Cave. Dive site, Mākaha, Oʻahu. Large cave below a ledge west of Lahilahi Point. The mouth of the cave is about 80 feet wide and bottoms at 80 feet. Also known as Ulua Cave.

Big Reef. Dive site, reef, ʻAnaehoʻomalu, Hawaiʻi. Large reef off the beach homes at Kapalaoa at the south end of ʻAnaehoʻomalu Bay.

Big Reef Lefts. Surf site, ʻAnaehoʻomalu, Hawaiʻi. Left on Big Reef, the large reef off the beach homes at Kapalaoa at the south end of ʻAnaehoʻomalu Bay. Big Reef Lefts is a big-wave, second-reef site that breaks seaward of Big Reef Rights.

Big Reef Rights. Surf site, ʻAnaehoʻomalu, Hawaiʻi. Right on Big Reef, the large reef off the beach homes at Kapalaoa at the south end of ʻAnaehoʻomalu Bay.

Big Rights. 1. Surf site, Kaluakoʻi, Molokaʻi. Off the resort dining room. 2. Surf site, Makaweli, Kauaʻi. South of Pākala

Point. 3. Surf site, Ala Moana, O'ahu. Right to the west of Concessions that breaks only on a big swell. Named in the early 1960s.

Big Sandy. Bay, snorkeling site, Kohala, Hawai'i. Large sand patch in Waiaka'īlio Bay that gives it its popular name, Big Sandy Bay. A reef adjacent to the sand provides snorkeling opportunities. Also known as Waiaka'īlio.

Bird. 1. Cave, Kalaupapa, Moloka'i. Sea cave on the north side of the peninsula. Noddy terns nest here. Also known as Ananoio. 2. Island, Ke'anae, Maui. One of two islands near Pauwalu Point. It is the only place on Maui where '*iwa,* or frigate birds, land. Also known as Mokumana. 3. Island, Kailua, O'ahu. Solitary island at the north end of Kailua Bay that is part of the Hawai'i State Seabird Sanctuary. Parts of the island are covered with white guano deposited by roosting seabirds. The guano is visible from a distance and is the origin of the island's name. Also known as Black Rock, Mokolea Island.

Bird Island. Surf site, Kailua, O'ahu. The surf site is adjacent to the island. Also known as Black Rock.

Bird Rock. Dive site, Kailua, O'ahu. Mokolea Island in Kailua Bay is used as a roosting site by seabirds. The dive site is adjacent to the island. Also known as Bird Island, Black Rock, Mōkōlea Island.

Black Hole. Dive site, Keāhole, Hawai'i. South of Keāhole Point at approximately 60 feet. A vertical lava tube in the reef looks like a "black hole" from above.

Blackouts. Surf site, Kailua, O'ahu. Big-wave, second-reef site in Kailua Bay to the east of Kapoho Point. Kailua surfers from the Kaimalino neighborhood began surfing here in the late 1950s. They noted that when they paddled to this deep-water site between Castle Point and Castles, the ocean bottom disappeared from view, or "blacked out."

Black Point. 1. Fishing site, North Kohala, Hawai'i. South of Keawanui Bay. 2. Fishing site, Kahuku, Hawai'i. Between Kāki'o and Pu'u Kaimu'uala. 3. Blowhole, fishing site, Diamond Head, O'ahu. Black Point, or Kupikipiki'o, is the southernmost point on O'ahu. The blowhole is in the low sea cliffs on the west side of Black Point. The fishing site is on the same sea cliffs adjoining the blowhole. 4. Pool, Diamond Head, O'ahu. Private, saltwater swimming pool in the sea cliffs on the east side of Black Point that is for the use of Black Point Road residents only. The pool is one of two that were built by the military as part of the Fort Ruger support facilities prior to the development of Black Point as a residential community. The second pool is in the backyard of a private home on Kaiko'o Place. 5. Surf site, Kāhala, O'ahu. On the eastern side of Black Point. Also known as Blacks, Duke's. The "black" in all the Black Point names refers to the black lava that comprises the points.

Black Pot. Beach park, Hanalei, Kaua'i. Beach park on Hanalei Bay's 2-mile calcareous sand beach that is located between the Hanalei Landing, a 300-foot pier, and the Hanalei River. The property that is now the beach park has always been an informal gathering place for the Hanalei community. Prior to its development as a county park in 1973, a group of Hanalei residents kept a large black communal cooking pot here, which for many years was a focal point of social activity.

Black Rock. 1. Dive site, surf site, southwest shore, Kaho'olawe. On Ku'ia Shoal off Kealaikahiki Point. Black Rock, or Pōhaku Ku'ike'e, was a small black island that was deliberately destroyed by the U.S. Navy during the Rim of the Pacific (RIMPAC) exercise in 1982. RIMPAC is an international maritime exercise held in Hawaiian waters that tests the tactical proficiency of military warships and aircraft from many Pacific nations, such as Australia, Canada, Chile, Republic of Korea, United Kingdom, and the United States. Black Rock was apparently determined to be a hazard to navigation for the dozens of warships that were traversing the waters around Kaho'olawe. Although the rock is gone, the dive and surf sites remain and are still known as Black Rock. 2. Dive site, snorkeling site, Kā'anapali, Maui. Pu'u Keka'a, a cinder cone in the center of Kā'anapali Beach, is commonly known as Black Rock. The dive and snorkeling sites are on its seaward side and are also known as Sheraton. 3. Surf site, Ka'ena, O'ahu. Off a large black rock on the north side of Ka'ena Point State Park. 4. Island, surf site, Kailua, O'ahu. Except for the white guano deposits, the island looks black from a distance. Also known as Mōkōlea Island. 5. Island, Makapu'u, O'ahu. Except for a red cinder cone, the island is composed of black lava. Also known as Kāohikaipu. 6. Island, surf site, Mokulē'ia, O'ahu. The island looks black. The surf site is adjacent to the island. Also known as Devil's Rock, Rock, Stone Island. 7. Point, surf site, Nānākuli, O'ahu. Point at the east end of Pōhakunui Avenue. The rocks on the point are black. The surf site is at the point. 8. Point, surf site, Mākaha, O'ahu. The point is also known as Mauna Lahilahi. The rocks on the point are black. The surf site is on the west side of the point. 9. Point, surf site, Wai'anae, O'ahu. The point is also known as Kāne'ilio Point. The rocks on the point are black. The surf site is on the east side of the point.

Black Rock Arches. Dive site, Nānākuli, O'ahu. Several large arches at 20 to 45 feet off Black Rock in Nānākuli.

Blacks. Surf site, Kāhala, Oʻahu. On the east side of Black Point. Blacks is an abbreviation of Black Point. Also known as Duke's.

Black Sand. 1. Beach, Kehena, Hawaiʻi. Narrow black sand beach at the base of low sea cliffs. The beach was formed in 1955 when a lava flow from Kīlauea reached the ocean and generated large amounts of black cinder sand. Also known as Black Sand Beach. 2. Beach, Punaluʻu, Hawaiʻi. Black sand and pebble beach backed by low dunes between the boat ramp and Punaluʻu Beach Park. 3. Bay, fishing site, Kaupakalua, Maui. Well-known fishing site for surround-netting *akule,* or bigeyed scad. *Akule* congregate here over a large pocket of black sand on the bottom of the bay. Also known as Keone, Uaoa Bay.

Black Sand Mānele. Beach, Mānele, Lānaʻi. Prior to the construction of Mānele Bay Small Boat Harbor, a detrital or "black" sand beach lined the head of the bay. It was called Black Sand Mānele Beach to differentiate it from White Sand Mānele Beach, the calcareous sand beach in Hulopoʻe Bay to the west.

Black Sands. Beach, Kalaupapa, Molokaʻi. One of five beaches on the Kalaupapa Peninsula. Long, wide detrital sand beach at the foot of the Kalaupapa Trail on the west side of the peninsula. Also known as ʻAwahua Beach, Ke One Neʻe o ʻAwahua, Puahi.

Blaisdell. Park (25.9 acres), Pearl City, Oʻahu. On the shore of Pearl Harbor at the foot of Kaʻahumanu Street. Named after Neil Blaisdell, mayor of the City and County of Honolulu from 1955 to 1968.

Blockhouse. 1. Gathering site, Hāmākua Poko, Maui. Also known as Mauna Kohala. 2. Surf site, Kawailoa, Oʻahu. Also known as Police Beach. 3. Surf site, Mokulēʻia, Oʻahu. At the west end of the reef fronting Camp Erdman. All of the Blockhouse sites are named for a concrete blockhouse, also known as a pillbox, from World War II that is located inshore of the site.

Blonde. Reef, Hilo, Hawaiʻi. Fringing reef in Hilo Bay upon which the Hilo Breakwater is built. Named for the British frigate HMS *Blonde.* In 1825, Lord George Anson Bryon, cousin of the poet, arrived in Hilo aboard the *Blonde* to return the bodies of King Kamehameha II (Liholiho) and his wife Kamamalu. The Hawaiian king and queen had died of measles within six days of each other while on a visit to London. The *Blonde* stopped briefly at Hilo Bay and then proceeded on to Maui and Oʻahu. In June 1825, Kaʻahumanu, regent of the kingdom, returned to Hilo aboard the *Blonde* with Bryon. She declared that the reef that protects the bay would be known as Blonde Reef in honor of the ship that had returned the bodies of the royal couple to their homeland.

Blonde Reef. Surf site, Hilo, Hawai'i. Infrequent big-wave site off the north end of the Hilo Breakwater. The breakwater was constructed on Blonde Reef.

Blowhole. 1. Blowhole, Hawai'i Kai, O'ahu. Same as the Hālona Blowhole. 2. Dive site, Hawai'i Kai, O'ahu. Off Hālona Blowhole. 3. Surf site, Mākaha, O'ahu. Named for a blowhole at Mākaha Point that is now filled in with rocks. During big, "point surf" days, the takeoff in line with the blowhole was called thus. 4. Surf site, Waikīkī, O'ahu. Between Canoes and First Break. During a big south swell, sand from the ocean bottom boils to the surface here with a blowhole-type action.

Bluebirds. Surf site, Waikīkī, O'ahu. During the 1930s, *bluebird* was a surfing term for a very large wave, one that came out of deep blue water. The surf site Bluebirds is a peak in line with Castles, but to the west where it breaks primarily on a westerly south swell. Also known as Papanui.

Blue Hole. 1. Surf site, Hā'ena, Kaua'i. Deep pocket of sand on the seaward side of the reef. 2. Surf site, Niu, O'ahu. Deep pocket of sand on the shoreward side of the reef. At both the Hā'ena and Niu sites, the calcareous sand at the bottom of the holes gives them a distinct turquoise or "blue" color compared to the darker sea around them.

Blue Moons. Surf site, Hawai'i Kai, O'ahu. Second-reef, big-wave site off Portlock Road between Seconds and Pillars. A blue moon is a second full moon in a calendar month, a rare occurrence. This surf site breaks only during the biggest south swells, or "once in a blue moon."

Blue Pool. Waterfall plunge pool, Ula'ino, Maui. On a boulder beach near Hāna at the base of a waterfall. Also known as Blue Pond.

Boat, The. Surf site, Mokulē'ia, O'ahu. During the construction of the boat *Day Star* on the beach here, the surf site was called The Boat or Ironboat before the boat was named. Same as Day Star.

Boat House. Beach, Kalaupapa, Moloka'i. Center section of Papaloa Beach where an outrigger canoe shed or "boat house" once stood in the backshore.

Boatwreck Reef. Dive site, Kainaliu, Hawai'i. One of the Red Hill dive sites.

Bobo's. Surf site, Hā'ena, Kaua'i. In the early 1970s, Carlos Andrade and Stanford Morinaka were surfing at Cannons. It was crowded, so Andrade suggested that they paddle west and check out a site near the mouth of Limahuli Stream. The reef was shallow, but it turned out to be a good spot, so Andrade named it for Morinaka whose nickname then was "Bobo." Also known as Pu'u Kahuaiki.

BO Buoy. Fish aggregating device, Kalaeloa, Oʻahu. Buoy anchored at approximately 850 fathoms. Landmarks: Pōkaʻī Bay Light, Honolulu Harbor Buoy Light, Barbers Point Light.

Boilers. 1. Surf site, Kaluakoʻi, Molokaʻi. Off the Kaluakoʻi Resort restaurant. 2. Surf site, Lāʻie, Oʻahu. Inshore of Pulemoku Island. Both sites are named for the water that "boils" up to the surface through rock formations on the ocean bottom when waves pass over them.

Boils. Surf site, Waimea, Oʻahu. Site in the Waimea lineup where water "boils" up to the surface from a rock formation on the ocean bottom when waves pass over it. Veteran Waimea surfers use Boils to determine if "true" or classic big-wave Waimea is breaking. If they take off outside Boils, then the waves are 20 feet or higher, and they are riding "true" Waimea.

Bomb Bay. Beach, Poʻolau, Molokaʻi. During World War II, the pastures inland of Poʻolau Bay were used by the military for bombing practice. A member of the Cooke family, the founders of Molokaʻi Ranch, found a large unexploded bomb here and gave the bay its popular name. Also known as Poʻolau Beach.

Bomboras. 1. Surf site, Pākala, Kauaʻi. Big-wave, second-reef site that breaks outside the normal lineup at Pākala. 2. Surf site, Ala Moana, Oʻahu. Off Magic Island. Also known as Islands, Magic Island. The names at both sites are from *bombora,* an Australian term for an isolated, second-reef surf site that breaks only during periods of high surf.

Bones. Surf site, Wailupe, Oʻahu. Off the center of Wailupe Peninsula. Waves here end on a shallow reef that was named the Boneyard in the late 1950s but has since been shortened to Bones.

Bongs. Surf site, Waialeʻe, Oʻahu. Between Waialeʻe Beach Park and Kawela Bay. In the 1970s, waterpipes, or "bongs," were popular drug paraphernalia for smoking marijuana. The first surfers to ride here often smoked a bong before going out, so they named the site after their paraphernalia of choice.

Bonk's. Beach, Waikīkī, Oʻahu. Small pocket of calcareous sand adjoining the outermost parking lot in the Ala Wai Small Boat Harbor. Surfers commonly use the beach to access the surf sites from Kaisers to Ala Moana Bowls.

Boulders. Surf site, Mōkapu, Oʻahu. Near the intersection of the runway and North Beach at Marine Corps Air Station Kāneʻohe Bay. A cluster of loose boulders on the ocean bottom marks the site.

Bowfin. Memorial, Pearl Harbor, Oʻahu. Same as USS *Bowfin* Submarine Museum and Park.

Bowl. 1. Surf site, Hanalei, Kauaʻi. The final section at Hanalei. Named for the curved or bowl-shaped section at the west end of the wave. 2. Surf site, Mākaha, Oʻahu. Named for the curved or bowl-shaped section at the east end of the wave during big winter point surf.

Bowling Alleys. Surf site, Anahola, Kaua'i. At the north end of Anahola Beach. Series of reform breaks offshore on a second reef.

Bowls. 1. Surf site, Kaimū, Hawai'i. East of Kaimū. Named for its curved or bowl-shaped section in the wave. 2. Surf site, Lanikai, O'ahu. Same as Dog Bowls. 3. Surf site, Waikīkī, O'ahu. Named for the curved or bowl-shaped section at the west end of the wave at the edge of the Ala Wai Channel. Same as Ala Moana, Ala Moana Bowls.

Box, The. Surf site, Mokulē'ia, O'ahu. Off Owen's Retreat, a beach vacation rental complex adjacent to the west end of Mokulē'ia Beach Park. The name was introduced by Australian surfers who compared the waves here to The Box in Australia, a surf site south of Perth famous for its steep, dangerous waves that break on an extremely shallow reef. Also known as Middles, Straight Outs.

Breakwalls. Surf site, Lahaina, Maui. On the east side of the channel and off the breakwater, or "breakwall," that protects Lahaina Small Boat Harbor. The site is a left that breaks into the channel. Also known as Harbor Lefts.

Breakwater. Fishing site, Kukuihaele, Hawai'i. Small peninsula at the base of the sea cliffs between Kukuihaele Light and Waipi'o Valley. The name is linked to the construction of the 2-mile long breakwater in Hilo Bay, which was started in 1908 and completed in 1929. Boulders from the peninsula were loaded on barges and towed to Hilo Bay, where they were used in the construction of the second phase of the breakwater.

Brennecke's. Beach, bodyboarding site, bodysurf site, Po'ipū, Kaua'i. Small pocket of calcareous sand fronted by a shallow sandbar at the east end of Po'ipū Beach Park. Named for Dr. Marvin Brennecke, who came to Kaua'i in 1931 and worked as a plantation doctor until he retired in 1972. Brennecke bought a lot at the beach in 1934 and built a beach house on it in 1936. On November 23, 1982, his beach house was destroyed by Hurricane 'Iwa, and he never rebuilt. The county eventually acquired the lot to expand Po'ipū Beach Park. The bodyboarding and bodysurf site is a shorebreak on the sandbar. A 1972 state regulation prohibits surfboards here.

 mo'olelo

My last name is German, and I'm originally from Jackson, Missouri. I graduated from Washington University Medical School in St. Louis, and I came to Kaua'i in 1931 as the assistant plantation doctor at Līhu'e Plantation to Dr. J. M. Kuhns. In 1933 I took

Dr. A. H. Waterhouse's place for McBryde, Kōloa, and Līhu'e Terminals, and then in 1942 I became the plantation doctor for Waimea Plantation, Kekaha Plantation, Gay and Robinson, and Olokele Sugar until I retired in 1972.

In 1934 I bought a lot at Po'ipū from the late mayor of Kaua'i, Anthony Vindinha, and in 1936 I built a beach house on it. In 1941 I renovated the beach house and made an addition to it. It was finished on the morning of December 7. I remember the contractor was cleaning up when we heard the news about Pearl Harbor. The house stood unchanged until Hurricane 'Iwa in 1982.

After 'Iwa, I tried to sell the property to the county and state to expand Po'ipū Beach Park, but they wouldn't buy it, so I deeded it to my alma mater, Washington University Medical School. The bodysurfing site was at the sand beach below the seawall fronting my home.

 Marvin Brennecke, December 7, 1988

Brennecke's Drop. Dive site, Po'ipū, Kaua'i. Lava shelf off Brennecke's Beach with a drop from 60 to 95 feet that creates a long ledge with overhangs and holes.

Broken Road. Landing, Kahuku, Hawai'i. In April 1955, the county completed a concrete boat landing on the west side of Ka Lae, or South Point. It was intended to assist fishermen who moor their boats at the point where they use hoists to haul fish and equipment up and down the sea cliffs. In less than a year the landing and its access road collapsed under the onslaught of seasonal high surf and were never rebuilt. Area residents call the ruins Broken Road.

Brown's. Surf site, Ka'alawai, O'ahu. Off the former estate of George Brown, now a subdivision called 'Āinamalu. 'Āinamalu was the name of Brown's home. This site was first surfed and named in the late 1920s by John Kelly and Fran Heath who lived nearby at Black Point.

Brown's Bay. Surf site, Kawailoa, O'ahu. Same as John Brown's.

Buzz's. Surf site, Mā'alaea, Maui. Off Buzz's Wharf, a restaurant on the shore at the west end of Mā'alaea Small Boat Harbor. Also known as Buzz's Wharf.

Buzz's Wharf. Surf site, Mā'alaea, Maui. Same as Buzz's.

Cabins. Surf site, Kalaeloa, Oʻahu. Off the officers' cabins at the west end of White Plains Beach.

Cable Channel. Dive site, Hanauma Bay, Oʻahu. Channel cut through the reef to house a submarine communications cable for Hawaiian Telephone.

California Reef. Dive site, ʻĀina Haina, Oʻahu. Introductory dive site at 40 feet, with some ledges that have a wide diversity of marine life; like California, the ledges have a wide diversity of everything.

Calvary by the Sea Lutheran Church. Memorial, ʻĀina Haina, Oʻahu. Two stone monuments established in 1979 in the beachfront garden of the church. The monuments have rows of individually inscribed metal plates that are "in loving memory of those who have been buried at sea." One of these plates is for Kala Kukea (1943–1996), who lived in ʻĀina Haina and whose ashes were scattered offshore. In a state renowned for its exceptional watermen, Kukea, a rescue captain in the Honolulu Fire Department, was one of the best. He excelled in surfing, diving, kayaking, and outrigger canoe paddling and was a highly respected coach for the Hui Nalu Canoe Club.

Campbell. National wildlife refuge, Kahuku, Oʻahu. The U.S. Fish and Wildlife Service leases two wetland parcels from the James Campbell Estate: the Kiʻi Unit (126 acres) and the Punamanō Unit (38 acres). The Kiʻi Unit is man-made, consisting of several wastewater settling basins built by Kahuku Sugar Company before it closed in 1971. Punamanō is a natural spring-fed marsh. Both sites attract migratory and native waterbirds that frequent the shore of Kahuku Point, including Hawaiian ducks, Hawaiian moorhens, Hawaiian coots, Hawaiian stilts, black-crowned night herons, and over two dozen species of migratory seabirds and waterfowl. Also known as James C. Campbell National Wildlife Refuge.

C

Campbells. Surf site, Campbell Industrial Park, Oʻahu. Off the public right-of-way on Kaomi Loop in Campbell Industrial Park.

Camp Erdman. Recreation site, Mokulēʻia, Oʻahu. Named in 1932 for Harold Randolph Erdman (1905–1931), who was killed in a fall from a horse during a polo game. The land for the camp had been leased in 1926 from Walter Dillingham, but upon Erdman's death the Dillingham family donated the land to the YMCA. Erdman was Dillingham's nephew, the son of his sister, Marion Dillingham Erdman.

Camp Hālena. Recreation site, Hālena, Molokaʻi. George P. Cooke, the first president of Molokaʻi Ranch, was an enthusiastic scouting supporter and sponsored the construction of Camp Hālena, a cluster of small cabins and related buildings on Hālena Beach.

Camp Homelani. Recreation site, surf site, Mokulēʻia, Oʻahu. Salvation Army camp on Crozier Drive. Camp Homelani was originally a half-acre site on the beach when it was acquired in 1948 by Major Adolf Kranz, the Salvation Army officer who had been Hawaiʻi's division commander during World War II. The Salvation Army is a Christian organization and Kranz named it Homelani, or "heavenly home," to reflect their religious beliefs. It now includes a 1-acre site on the beach and 8 acres on the opposite side of Crozier Drive. The surf site is off the camp and is also known as Homelani.

Camp Kokokahi. Recreation site, Kāneʻohe, Oʻahu. A YWCA camp and hostel at the southeast end of Kāneʻohe Bay. The camp was founded in 1935 by Reverend Theodore Richards, who also named it Kokokahi, "one blood." Kokokahi is a name he devised to signify that all races have similar blood and are, therefore, equal.

Camp Mokulēʻia. Recreation site, surf site, Mokulēʻia, Oʻahu. In August 1947, the Episcopal Diocese, under the leadership of Bishop Harry S. Kennedy, purchased Camp Mokulēʻia's 2.5 acres from the estate of James D. McInerny for $40,000. The original buildings on the site, built in the 1920s, were part of McInerny's beachfront home. The camp was dedicated on September 14, 1947. In 1978, the camp's property was expanded when an additional 27 acres of land between its west boundary and Mokulēʻia Beach park were leased from Mokulēʻia Ranch. The surf site is offshore and is also known as Camps, Razors.

Camp Naue. Recreation site, Hāʻena, Kauaʻi. YMCA camp on Kauaʻi's north shore established in 1926. Naue is a coastal area that was famous for its *hala,* or pandanus, grove. The epithet *nā hala o Naue,* or "the pandanus of Naue," appears in chants and songs about Kauaʻi.

Camp One. 1. Dive site, Wahiawa, Kaua'i. Off Weli Point near Wahiawa Bay. A former McBryde Sugar Company plantation camp was here on the shore. Also known as Weli Point. 2. Windsurf site, Pā'ia, Maui. A former Hawaiian Commercial and Sugar (HC&S) plantation camp, Camp One, was on the now undeveloped shore between the end of the runway and the stables.

Camps. 1. Surf site, Mokulē'ia, O'ahu. Also known as Camp Homelani. 2. Surf site, Mokulē'ia, O'ahu. Also known as Camp Mokulē'ia, Razors.

Cannons. Surf site, Hā'ena, Kaua'i. The first surfers here in the 1950s discovered that on a big, no-wind day the booming of the breaking waves is like the sound of a cannon firing and even seems to echo off the mountains. They also discovered the waves are so hollow that completing a good ride is like being shot out of a cannon, so they named it Cannons for both of these cannon-related features. Also known as Cannons Reef, Hauwa.

 mo'olelo

The first few times I rode it, I called it Wichman's since the break was just to the west of Juliette Wichman's Hā'ena home with a great view of the lineup. Then one day we paddled out, and it looked 4 to 6 feet. It was perfect—a glassy day, just a slight off-shore breeze coming out of Limahuli, and a west swell coming up. But when we got out there, the waves were much bigger than they looked from the road above and kept getting bigger. It was well overhead, but it was so perfect. The tubes [were] so big and awesome, and the water was really clear and blue. What got me that day was how loud the sound of the waves was when the tube exploded and spit out foam and whitewater. It even seemed to echo off the mountains behind Juliette's house, sounding like a cannon going off. And then making those first few tubes was like getting shot out a cannon. So after that, it became **Cannons.**

Nick Beck, January 6, 1999

Cannons Reef. Dive site, surf site, Hā'ena, Kaua'i. Reef at the Cannons surf site. The outer edge of the reef is a long ledge with lava tubes where turtles and white tip sharks are common. The surf site is also known as Cannons.

Canoe. Beach, Hanaka'o'o, Maui. Outrigger canoe clubs practice, hold regattas, and store their canoes here. Also known as Hanaka'o'o Beach.

Canoes. Surf site, Waikīkī, O'ahu. One of Waikīkī's most famous surf sites. Outrigger canoes surf the waves here daily, the only place in the world where this occurs. The site was named for this activity. Also known as Canoes Surf.

Canoes Surf. Surf site, Waikīkī, Oʻahu. Same as Canoes.

Can Opener. Rock, Hawaiʻi Kai, Oʻahu. Sharp rock on the west edge of the reef at Half Point in Sandy Beach Park that has caused many injuries, especially cuts and lacerations, which gave it this name.

Canyons. Dive site, Mākaha, Oʻahu. Same as Mākaha Canyons.

Canyons Reef. Dive site, Waikīkī, Oʻahu. Spur and groove reef southeast of the Ala Wai Small Boat Harbor at approximately 35 feet. Also known as Turtle Canyon, Turtle Canyons.

Capehart. Beach. Also known as Iroquois Beach. Named after Capehart Housing, the Navy housing at Keahi Point.

Cape Kaʻea. Light, Palaoa, Lānaʻi. Established in 1934 at Palaoa Point, but called the Cape Kaʻea Light.

Cape Kinaʻu. Point, Honuaʻula, Maui. In approximately 1790, lava from the southwest rift zone of Haleakalā reached the ocean north of La Pérouse Bay and formed Cape Kinaʻu. This was apparently the last volcanic eruption on Maui.

Cape Kumukahi. Light, Kumukahi, Hawaiʻi. Established as an automatic light in 1929 at the easternmost point in the Hawaiian Islands. The 115-foot steel skeleton tower was built in 1934 approximately 156 feet above sea level. In 1960 it was nearly overrun by lava flowing into the ocean from an eruption nearby in Kapoho. Lava came within several feet of the tower, then divided into two streams, passing on either side of it.

Captain Cook. Monument, Kaʻawaloa, Hawaiʻi. Monument erected at Kaʻawaloa on the north side Kealakekua Bay at the site where Captain James Cook was killed. The monument is a 27-foot white obelisk surrounded by twelve metal posts linked by chains. The plaque on the obelisk reads: "In memory of the great circumnavigator Captain James Cook, R.N., who discovered these islands on the 18th day of January AD 1778 and fell near this spot on the 14th day of February AD 1779. This monument was erected in November AD 1874 by some of his fellow countrymen." A second plaque at the jetty fronting the monument reads: "The Commonwealth of Australia in memory of Captain James Cook, R.N., the discoverer of both Australia and these islands erected this jetty." A third plaque at the site reads: "In commemoration of the 200th anniversary of the arrival in the Pacific Ocean of Captain James Cook, R.N., on his voyage of discovery 1768–1771 in the bark *Endeavor.* Presented by Swedish American Line on the occasion of a visit by M.S. *Kungsholm* to Kealakekua Bay, April 1st, 1969."

Carrier Dove. Wreck, Kaupōa, Molokaʻi. The *Carrier Dove* was a four-masted schooner carrying copra from Tonga that went aground on a reef near Kaupōa in November 1921. Some of the wreckage is still visible on the ocean bottom.

Carter. 1. Beach, point, Nāwiliwili, Kaua'i. Boulder beach and the south point of Nāwiliwili Harbor. 2. Estate, Honua'ula, Maui. A 17-acre estate and home of former territorial governor George R. Carter at La Pérouse Bay.

Castle. 1. Beach, Mālaekahana, O'ahu. North section of Mālaekahana Beach fronting Mālaekahana State Recreation Area, Kahuku Section. Young surfers in the 1960s from Kawela Bay and Kahuku thought that some of the large beachfront homes here were more like castles than homes. 2. Point, Kailua, O'ahu. Named after Harold Kainalu Long Castle who owned the land at the point and who, in 1925, developed the Kalama Tract, the first housing tract in Kailua. Prior to its development as a residential community, the point was used by the Honolulu Skeet Club as a firing range from 1938 to 1977. Also known as Kapoho Point. 3. Rock, Mokulē'ia, O'ahu. Small rock island off the Mokulē'ia Polo Field that has been compared to an underwater castle. Also known as Black Rock, Devil's Rock, Rock, Stone Island.

Castle's. 1. Dive site, Ke'e, Kaua'i. Underwater pinnacle that resembles a castle on the ocean floor. 2. Surf site, windsurf site, Kailua, O'ahu. At the north end of Kailua Bay adjacent to Kapoho Point. Harold K. L. Castle formerly owned the land at the point and his descendants have a beach home inshore in Kainalu Park. 3. Surf site, Mālaekahana, O'ahu. Off Castle Beach. 4. Surf site, Waikīkī, O'ahu. Samuel Northrup Castle arrived in Hawai'i with the eighth company of missionaries in 1837. He left the mission in 1851 and, with Amos Cooke, founded Castle and Cooke Company. The Castle family's three-story beachfront home, Kainalu, was a prominent landmark in Waikīkī and the landmark for the takeoff at Castles. It was razed in 1958 for the construction of the Elks Club. Castles is the south shore's most famous big-wave surf site. A second-reef site, it does not break unless wave heights are 10 feet or greater. In 1930, Duke Kahanamoku caught a now-legendary wave here and rode it standing all the way to Waikīkī Beach. Also known as Kalehuawehe.

 mo'olelo

Castle's was named for the Castle home on the beach. To us, Castle's was Castle's—there was only one. The other names people use for it, like Bluebirds and Steamer Lane, were not actually Castle's. Bluebirds is to the west of Castles, outside of Techniques, and it forms only on a special swell, a more westerly swell. That's the spot that the Duke named Papanui. When Duke

C

made his famous ride from Castle's to Canoes, he was riding a 16-foot-long skegless redwood board. To make that ride, the angle of his slide would have been important, especially to get from Castle's past Cunha's. That in-between section is Techniques, and it's a difficult section to get through. You had to have good technique to make it, especially on the old boards. "Steamer Lane" was a term that was used to describe Waikīkī when it was breaking at its biggest, as in, "We have a Steamer Lane swell today." It happened when the lineup put you so far offshore that you were in the shipping lanes used by the former interisland steamers. But it wasn't one specific site.

In the years that followed Duke's ride, there was talk among other surfers if he really did it or not—if anyone could actually make a wave from Castle's to Canoes. This bothered me, and I wanted to prove to myself that the Duke could have done it. In the early 1950s, I was out at Castle's on a big day, but using a smaller board, a 10-foot balsa/redwood with a skeg. I made the ride three times from Castle's to Canoes. In fact, I ended up past Canoes, inside of Populars, and there's no doubt in my mind that I could have made the Halekūlani Hotel. But out of respect for the Duke's ride, I never went ashore. The Duke was something special, and I tried to be respectful of his image and what he did. I proved to myself that it could be done, and that if the Duke said he did it, he did it. The smaller board took a lot of maneuvering, compared to Duke's 16-foot board, which had a lot of glide, and the paddle back out between waves took at least 45 minutes. During the rides I remember thinking, "All right, I'm still going!" and at the end of each ride, I was always amazed that I had ridden so far.

Castle's on a big day is a massive wave. The current is strong, and it's so hard to line up that lots of waves come through un-ridden. You drift quickly and really have to watch your markers. The big sets usually clean everyone out. To make that ride to Canoes takes a special wave, the more from the south the better, and it is probably one of the longest rides in the world on one wave. The ride takes you from one end of the bay to the other. From Castle's it's the same wave, one long swell, and you go through section after section. Each section has a peak, and you have to turn down into the peak and then accelerate forward. All of the riding is done outside of the regular spots like Publics and Cunha's.

June 1995 is the last time I surfed at Castle's, and the swell then lasted three days. I had a pair of binoculars, and from the beach I counted over five hundred people in the water from Castle's to Populars. This is what makes Waikīkī so unique—so many sites in one bay, in one place. When we get a gigantic *swell, the wave train breaks outside and regenerates itself inside in many different spots. These are the waves that produce lots of good memories that live in your mind forever.*

 George Downing, October 13, 2000

Cat Bowls. Surf site, Waimānalo, Oʻahu. On the Waimānalo side of the Mokulua Islands. The name is a play on words for the surf site Dog Bowls, which is between the two islands.

Cathedrals. Dive site, Mānele, Lānaʻi. Two dive sites with similar underwater features that are known collectively as Cathedrals, and individually as First Cathedral and Second Cathedral. Several pinnacles rise from 60 feet to just below the surface. Spacious caverns in the pinnacles have a cathedral-like appearance when shafts of sunlight crisscross the interiors through skylights in the exterior walls. This dive site was discovered and named in the late 1950s by the first commercial black coral divers from Maui, Jack Ackerman and Larry Windley. The first commercial dive tours were conducted here in the late 1960s by Roy Damron and Don Bieber, who were leading scuba tours as Undersea Adventures Unlimited on Maui, Lānaʻi, and Molokaʻi.

 moʻolelo

I honestly cannot take credit for the discovery of the **Cathedral,** but perhaps my learning of its existence may be of some interest to you. To begin my story, I spent twenty-four years in the motion picture industry in Hollywood. Part of my time was spent doing stunt work that included scuba diving during the latter 1950s, and this led to a dive trip to do underwater filming in Tahiti. We planned to be there three weeks, but went native and stayed three months. This changed my entire life plan, and in 1962 I ended up on Maui when Lahaina looked very much like Papeete.

The only "dive shop" was an old store taken over by the Lahaina black coral divers. The shop was started by two of them from Oʻahu who went to Maui to shoot an underwater commercial. They fell in love with the place, soon discovered black coral, and found that tourists would buy black coral jewelry. They were Jack Ackerman and Larry Windley. By the time I met them, Larry had had his spinal hit from too much deep diving and was confined to a wheelchair. Since he could no longer dive, he had become very active with the Lahaina Restoration Foundation. At the time, they were restoring the old Baldwin Home. He and I became immediate close friends and spent several days discussing diving and Maui history. It was he who told me about the

Cathedral and how to find it. Cathedral II was unknown at that time. He also told me about Molokini.

Later in the sixties, when I moved from Hollywood to Honolulu, I met Don Bieber, who was converting a surplus navy liberty launch into the dive boat *Scuba Belle*. When we began taking dive groups to Maui, our best dives were Cathedral and Molokini. I knew where they were thanks to that wonderful guy, Larry Windley, who, due his incapacitating problems, sailed off into the sunset, never to be seen again.

 Roy Damron, February 28, 2000

Cattle Chute. Dive site, Mānele, Lāna'i. Off the ruins of a cattle chute on the shore of Mānele Bay that was constructed in 1921 by the Lāna'i Ranch Company to load cattle on interisland steamers.

Cattle Guard. Surf site, Ka'ena, O'ahu. Off a former cattle guard in the road in Ka'ena Point State Park.

Cave, The. Surf site, Honolua, Maui. One of three sections of the surf site at Honolua Bay. The Cave is the innermost section on the shallow reef fronting the large sea cave at the base of the sea cliffs.

C Buoy. Fish aggregating device, Hōnaunau, Hawai'i. Buoy anchored at approximately 969 fathoms. Landmarks: Kealakekua Bay Light, Loa Point, Miloli'i.

CC Buoy. Fish aggregating device, Ka'ena Point, Lāna'i. Buoy anchored at approximately 410 fathoms. Landmarks: Ka'ena Point, Palaoa Point Light.

Cement City. Beach, Mokulē'ia, O'ahu. Section of Mokulē'ia Beach that fronts a cluster of concrete or "cement" low-rise condominiums on Au Street. As the only low-rises in Mokulē'ia, a community of single-family residences, the buildings are a prominent landmark.

Cemeteries. Surf site, Nukoli'i, Kaua'i. Off Nukoli'i Beach Park. Carlos Andrade named this site in the mid-1960s as a play on words for not making a ride through the tube of a hollow wave. When surfers wipe out in the tube, they often say they were "buried," which is the connection between the surf site and the term *cemetery*.

Chains. Dive site, surf site, Kailua, O'ahu. Seaward of Flat Island. The spur and groove rock formations on the ocean bottom resembled chains to skin divers here in the 1960s.

Chambers. 1. Surf site, Hawai'i Kai, O'ahu. Peak in the shorebreak at Sandy Beach at the west end of the beach. 2. Surf site, Sunset Beach, O'ahu. On the west side of Rocky Point. The names at both sites are an abbreviation of Gas Chambers.

Changes. Surf site, Mokulē'ia, O'ahu. Off Crozier Loop. Surf conditions here, including the lineup and the takeoff spot, change abruptly and often with the swell direction, the wave size, the wind, and the tide.

Chang's. Beach, Mākena, Maui. South section of Po'olenalena Beach. Longtime Mākena residents, the Chang family farmed the land behind the beach for many years. Several members of the family are buried in a small graveyard at Pamolepo on the point bordering the south end of the beach. After the military put in the road past the beach during World War II, fishermen began calling the area Chang's Beach. Also known as Paipu, Po'olenalena Beach.

Channel Marker. Dive site, Hawai'i Kai, O'ahu. Reef at 15 to 20 feet near the outermost channel marker of the Hawai'i Kai Channel. Introductory site with the wreck of a barge that was used by Henry J. Kaiser when he was dredging the channel and Hawai'i Kai Marina in the 1970s.

Channels. 1. Surf site, Kailua, O'ahu. In the channel between the Mokulua Islands. 2. Surf site, Hawai'i Kai, O'ahu. On the west side of Hawai'i Kai Channel near the outermost channel markers. This site is often "surfed" by jet ski riders. Also known as Shark Pit. 3. Surf site, Nānākuli, O'ahu. At the mouth of Ulehawa Channel, the concrete drainage canal for Ulehawa Stream. Also known as Ulehawa. 4. Surf site, Waikīkī, O'ahu. Big-wave, second-reef site between Suicides and Graveyards that breaks outside of the channel through the reef off Mākālei Beach Park.

Charlie's Reef. Surf site, Mākaha, O'ahu. Off the west end of 'Upena Street. Named for Charlie Borges, a former area resident who lived opposite the public right-of-way and surfed here regularly.

Charlie Young. Beach, bridge, Kīhei, Maui. Charles Clinton Young (1905–1974) came to Hawai'i in 1932 as a military reporter to cover the Massie Case and decided to make his home in the Islands. He and his wife Betty purchased a beachfront parcel on Kama'ole Beach north of Kama'ole I Beach Park in 1940 and built their home there in 1950. Young became a well-known public figure as a reporter for the *Maui News* and the *Honolulu Star-Bulletin* and for his involvement in many social, civic, and business activities. The section of Kama'ole Beach below his home is known as Young's Beach or Charlie Young Beach. A bridge at Cove Park at the intersection of 'Ili'ili and Kīhei Roads is also named after him.

Chicken Creek. Surf site, 'Ewa Beach, O'ahu. Off One'ula Beach Park. During the 1960s, a large chicken farm was here near the drainage ditch, or the "creek," at the entrance

45

to the park. Many residents of ʻEwa Beach bought eggs from the farm.

Chicken Wing. Surf site, Hanalei, Kauaʻi. Near the end of Waipa Reef. The left on this wave hooks back into the bay like a chicken wing as it follows a bend in the reef.

Children's Pool. Swimming site, Poʻipū, Kauaʻi. Section of beach at Poʻipū Beach Park that is protected from the open ocean by a seawall. The seawall is semicircular and forms a "pool." Also known as Baby Beach.

Chimney. Dive site, Kainaliu, Hawaiʻi. Sand canyon with lava walls and a lava tube, or "chimney," which begins at 40 feet, ends at 10 feet, and is open on both ends.

Chinaman's Hat. Island, Kualoa, Oʻahu. Off Kualoa Regional Park. The outline of the island resembles a wide-brimmed, Chinese-style hat. Also known as Mokoliʻi Island and Pake Pāpale Island.

Chinas. Surf site, Hawaiʻi Kai, Oʻahu. Same as China Walls.

China Walls. 1. Surf site, Hawaiʻi Kai, Oʻahu. Long left with many sections at Kawaihoa, or Portlock Point, that begins with a steep takeoff next to a large submerged rock. Named in 1948 by Richard Okita, a surfer from Kuliʻouʻou, who with a small group of friends was the first to surf here. Okita had learned about the Great Wall of China in school and adapted the name to describe the length of the waves on a big day. Also known as China's, Portlock Point. 2. Dive site, Hawaiʻi Kai, Oʻahu. Ledge at 15 to 70 feet. A continuation of this site from 80 to 130 feet is known as Deep China Walls.

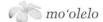 *moʻolelo*

My family moved from Damon Tract to Kuliʻouʻou in 1944, and I started surfing the Portlock area in 1948. I think we were probably the first ones to surf out at the point. Our first boards were big redwood planks that were so heavy, it took two of us to carry them. Sometimes we would just put the boards in the water at Kuliʻouʻou and paddle all the way out. Richard Okita was the one who came up with the name **China Wall** for that quarter-mile-long wave at the point. With those heavy boards, we did a lot of pearl diving, but when it was big, China Wall was an awesome wave.

Alexander Brenner, November 15, 2000

My family moved to Kuliʻouʻou in 1939 when I was six years old. The valley wasn't developed then, so all the neighborhood kids would go down to Kuliʻouʻou Park to hang out and play basketball. No one surfed any of the spots outside the park like they do now, and the reef at Turtles was where we dived for fish. Several of the families in the valley fished for *ulua* at the point out-

side Portlock, and in those days when the adults went some-
place, the kids would go, too. So when they went fishing, we
went with them. Portlock Road only went half way to the point,
so you had to walk the rest of the way. Nobody else went out
there except the fishermen. Their favorite casting spots were on
the cliffs and on the big rock that's called Finger Rock today. It's a
dangerous area and several fishermen died when they were
washed off the cliffs by high surf. A monument was erected for
one of them, a man from Kuli'ou'ou. It was a wooden pole with
his name on it. But when we went with them and we saw the
waves, we realized that you could surf them.

We started surfing there in 1948, after the war. Our gang was
Alexander Brenner, Clifford Murakami, Donald Ishii and his
brother Roger, and me. As far as I know, we were the first to surf
there. First, we rode our *paipo* boards on the left over the shallow
reef next to Finger Rock. That reef had more *wana* [spiny sea
urchins] than any other reef I ever saw, but that's where we
started. When the surf got bigger, we would bodysurf and *paipo*
the left that hugs the cliffs straight out from Finger Rock. When
the surf was really big, we surfed the long left into the bay that
begins next to the submerged reef about 60 [or] 80 yards Diamond Head of Finger Rock. I had learned about the Great Wall
of China in school, so I picked the name China Wall for that left
because when you take off and make the drop, it looks like the
China Wall.

I think we were also the first to surf Sandy Beach, the outside
left on the reef that ends by the submerged rock. No one bodysurfed the shorebreak then except one guy from Kalihi, Ken
Kahoonei. Ken was a terrific bodysurfer, and he could ride the
shorebreak without fins.

I surfed China Wall from 1948 to 1957, and during that time
we went from hollow boards to balsa boards. I made my last
balsa board in 1957 and that's when my surfing days ended, after
I finished college.

Richard Okita, November 9, 2000

My family moved to Hawai'i Kai in the early 1950s before it
was Hawai'i Kai. Kaiser hadn't developed it yet. Our house was
between the two bridges on Kalaniana'ole Highway, near the
Keāhole Street intersection, right about where Roy's is now. We
could see the surf from the house, and when it was big, we
could see the whitewater shooting up above the point when the
big sets hit the rocks. When it was big, all of us kids would go
out, and even some of the good surfers from Waikīkī would
come, like Conrad Cunha and Squirrelly Carvalho. In the early
fifties, we were riding redwood planks, hollows, and semi-

C

hollows, and in later years we went to balsa and then finally to foam boards. Sometimes we would just walk across the highway and paddle out to the point from our house. Our gang was the second generation to surf out there. The guys before us were Richard Okita and his gang, and as far as I know, they were the first to surf China Walls. They were older than us, and they were all competitive swimmers in high school, so they were really good in the water, especially bodysurfing and surfing. Another one of the regulars out there was Dale Crooker, a doctor who lived on Portlock Road.

Besides surfing China Walls, we bodysurfed, rode *paipos*, and surfed the break along the cliffs. We called it Main Point, or the Point, but we called the takeoff Deadman's Pole because it was right below a wooden pole on the rocks that marked the spot where a fisherman had died. Sometimes we would actually catch the waves at the Point by diving into them. If you timed it just right, you could run across the terrace, dive into the wave, catch it and ride it all the way to the shallow reef next to Finger Rock.

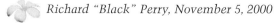 *Richard "Black" Perry, November 5, 2000*

Chocolate. Beach, Pearl Harbor O'ahu. Dark detrital or chocolate-colored sand beach that lines the shore at West Loch Naval Air Station in Pearl Harbor.

Chocolates. 1. Surf site, Hale'iwa, O'ahu. Small beginner's break on a sandbar at the mouth of Anahulu Stream. The site is inside Hale'iwa Small Boat Harbor off the Surf-n- Sea surf shop and breaks only during high surf outside the harbor. The ocean here is brown, or chocolate colored, from soil runoff into the stream after heavy rains. Also known as Inside Hale'iwa Harbor, Surf-n-Sea. 2. Surf site, Hale'iwa, O'ahu. Small beginner's break on the sandbar at the head of Kaiaka Bay that forms during high surf outside the bay. Soil runoff from the streams that empty into the bay form the beach and the sandbar and turn the water in the bay a chocolate brown.

Chun's Reef. 1. Beach, dive site, surf site, Kawailoa, O'ahu. John Ah Choy Chun (1914–1996), was the founder of Chun's Store in Hale'iwa and a member of the Honolulu Fire Department. He owned a beach home near the surf site on No Name Road, a small lane that parallels Kamehameha Highway at the 4-mile marker. Chun's children were avid surfers and beginning in the 1950s, they often surfed at this reef, their favorite surf site. A family friend, Edna Reese, coined the name Chun's Reef for the site. Also known as Kuaumania. 2. Support park (3 acres). Undeveloped park across Kamehameha Highway from Chun's Reef.

CII. Offshore fish farm. 'Ewa Beach, O'ahu, Hawai'i's first commercial underwater fish farm established in March 2000 by Randy Cates of Cates International Inc. CII has a 15 year lease on 28 acres of submerged ocean lands 1.7 miles of 'Ewa Beach. The farm consists of four large cages that rise from 150 feet to 40 feet below the surface. Hawaiian fish such as *moi (Polydactylus sexfilis)* are inserted in the cages as fingerlings, fed regularly, and harvested when they are ready for market. Each cage has the potential of producing 150,000 pounds of *moi* every eight months.

Cinder Cone. Fishing site, cinder cone, Kahuku, Hawai'i. Also known as Pu'u Hou.

City of Refuge. National historic park, Hōnaunau, Hawai'i. Site of a *pu'uhonua,* or place of refuge. Early missionaries, including William Ellis in 1823, compared the *pu'uhonua* to the ancient Hebrew cities of refuge, and "city of refuge" became the accepted definition. *Pu'uhonua,* however, were not cities, but rather safety zones that were administered by priests where war refugees or people accused or crimes could seek refuge. When the *pu'uhonua* at Hōnaunau was established as a county park in 1920, it was called the City of Refuge, and on July 1, 1961, it was established as the City of Refuge National Historical Park. The Hawaiian community, however, requested that the name be changed, and in 1978 Congress authorized its official change to Pu'uhonua o Hōnaunau National Historic Park.

CK Buoy. Fish aggregating device, Makahū'ena Point, Kaua'i. Buoy anchored at approximately 825 fathoms. Landmarks: Ninini Point, Makahū'ena Point.

Cliffhouse. Dive site, Kapalua, Maui. In Namalu Bay, south of Hāwea Point. A beach house was on the cliffs here prior to the development of Kapalua.

Cliffs. 1. Surf site, Mā'alaea, Maui. Off the small residential community on the low sea cliffs at the west end of Mā'alaea Bay. 2. Surf site, windsurf site, Diamond Head, O'ahu. An abbreviation of Kuilei Cliffs Beach Park, the name of the beach park with the three lookouts on Diamond Head Road. Also known as Diamond Head.

Clissold. Beach, Lā'ie, O'ahu. North section of Laniloa Beach adjacent to Lā'ie Point. Edward Clissold, a former director of Zion Securities, now Hawai'i Resources, had a home on the beach here for many years. Also known as 'Onini.

Cloudbreak. Surf site, Mā'ili, O'ahu. Big-wave, second-reef site outside of Green Lanterns. Deep-water surf sites are commonly called "second-reef" and sometimes "third-reef" breaks, but they are also called "cloudbreaks" because from sea level at the beach they appear to be breaking on the horizon where the clouds are. Also known as Second Reef.

Cloverleaf. Harbor, Pūkoʻo, Molokaʻi. During the 1960s, Pūkoʻo Fishpond was dredged and reconfigured into a cloverleaf-shaped harbor with three bays to accommodate a tourist resort that was never built. The harbor is now used for community-based development to farm seaweed and fish.

Clubhouse. Surf site, Kahuku, Oʻahu. Off the clubhouse at Kahuku Golf Course.

Club Lānaʻi. Dive site, recreation site, snorkeling site, Halepalaoa, Lānaʻi. Club Lānaʻi is a private 8-acre beach resort on the north shore of Lānaʻi that is used for day excursions to snorkel and dive. Charter boats from Lahaina make the 9-mile trip in forty-five minutes, bringing visitors from Maui on day excursions to sunbathe and snorkel. Also known as Makaiwa.

Cobbles. Surf site, Hawaiʻi Kai, Oʻahu. Shorebreak peak at Sandy Beach inside of Pipe Littles. Small, cobble-sized stones accumulate here on the ocean bottom.

CO Buoy. Kaʻena Point, Oʻahu. Approximately 1,010 fathoms. Landmarks: Kaʻena Point Light, Pōkaʻī Bay Light.

Cockroach. 1. Bay, cove, gulch, Hawaiʻi Kai, Oʻahu. Also known as From Here to Eternity Beach, Eternity Beach, and Hālona Cove. 2. Bay, Waimānalo, Oʻahu. Small bay at the north end of Kaupō Beach Park that is a popular novice surf site. Also known as Baby Makapuʻu, The Bay, Kumu Cove. Both sites were named for cockroach populations that were supported by litter from beachgoers.

Coconut. 1. Coast, Kapaʻa, Kauaʻi. Name introduced by the visitor industry to identify the coast from Wailua to Keālia. 2. Island, Hilo Bay, Hawaiʻi. A small, flat island in Hilo Bay that is a public park. The island is connected to the Waiākea Peninsula by a footbridge and has been a popular picnic site in Hilo since the late 1800s. Coconut trees have been on the island at least since the early 1800s. Reverend Charles Stewart, who was aboard the HMS *Blonde* when it entered Hilo Bay in 1824, identified the island as "Cocoanut [*sic*] Island" in his journal. Also known as Mokuola. 3. Island (28.8 acres, including 6.5 acres of enclosed lagoons), Kāneʻohe Bay, Oʻahu. Christian Holmes, heir to the Fleischmann Yeast fortune, bought the 12-acre island from Bishop Estate in 1933. Over the years he added 16 acres to the island, building a palatial home on it and dredging the surrounding coral reef to create lagoons, fishponds, and a small boat harbor. California businessman Edwin W. Pauley bought the island in 1946 and in 1947 invited the University of Hawaiʻi to establish a marine field station here. In 1965, Pauley donated the money to build the Hawaiʻi Institute of Marine Biology's original laboratory on the island. Although Pauley died in 1981, a generous gift from the Pauley Foundation in 1996 allowed the University Foundation to purchase the island and to build a new marine science center and laboratory, the Edwin W. Pauley Marine Laboratory. The island is landscaped with coconut trees, inspiring its popular name, and is surrounded by 64 acres of reef designated by the state as the Hawai'i Marine Laboratory Refuge. Also known as Moku o Lo'e.

Coconut Grove. 1. Bay, Kuiaha, Maui. Named for a small stand of coconut trees growing in the backshore. Also known as Kuiaha Bay. 2. Beach, Keōmuku, Lāna'i. The former village of Keōmuku now consists of an immense grove of coconut trees. The original trees were planted in 1936. 3. Beach, Kalama'ula, Moloka'i. Traditional stories say High Chief Kapuāiwa, who became Kamehameha V in 1863, lived nearby and planted the trees in the grove. The grove is located in Kiowea Park. Also known as Kapuāiwa or Kamehameha Coconut Grove. 4. Beach, Waiakāne, Moloka'i. Named for a small stand of coconut trees that grows on a narrow detrital sand beach bordering Palā'au Road. The West Moloka'i mountains meet the sea here.

Coconut Island. 1. Tower, Hilo, Hawai'i. Small concrete diving tower on Coconut Island that was constructed during World War II. It was used to train military personnel to jump off ships and swim with their equipment packs, and it is still used as a diving tower by children who swim here. 2. Park, Hilo, Hawai'i. Park on Coconut Island in Hilo Bay. The island is connected to the Waiākea Peninsula by a footbridge. 3. Lighthouse, Kāne'ohe Bay, O'ahu. At the entrance to West Lagoon on Coconut Island. 4. Small Boat Harbor, Kāne'ohe Bay, O'ahu. Private boating facility on Coconut Island.

Coconut Point. Light, Hilo, Hawai'i. Established in 1904 to mark the southwest point of Hilo Bay. The 34-foot tower built in 1975 stands at the water's edge where it is surrounded by coconut trees. Coconut Island lies offshore.

Coconuts. Surf site, Honolua, Maui. One of three sections of the surf site in Honolua Bay. Coconuts is the outermost section that breaks first at the north point of the bay. A small grove of coconut trees grows at the point.

Coco Palms. Surf site, Wailua, Kaua'i. The surf site is a shore-break on the shallow sandbar that fronts Wailua Beach. The Coco Palms Resort is across the street from the beach.

Coffin Corner. Beach, Waimea Bay, O'ahu. West end of the beach at Waimea Bay where the sand terminates against the rocks. During high surf, powerful rip currents sweep into this section of the bay, carrying swimmers into the rocks, sometimes with serious or fatal results. Also known as the Corner.

Cold Pond. Keaukaha, Hawai'i. Spring-fed inlet at the head of Puhi Bay in Keaukaha Beach Park. The springwaters are always cold, giving the pond its popular name. Also known as Lalakea Pond.

Compound. Surf site, south coast, Kaho'olawe. Off the navy's messhall/barracks building, or Montague Hall, and other associated structures that formerly comprised a military compound.

Concessions. Surf site, Ala Moana, O'ahu. Named in the early 1970s after the construction of the food concession at the west end of Ala Moana Beach Park.

Conradt's Cove. North shore, Kaho'olawe. In 1905 a survey crew on the USS *Patterson* mapped Kaho'olawe. They were unfamiliar with the island's traditional names, so they apparently named Kūheia Bay after Christian Conradt, who held the lease for the island from 1903 to 1906. Also known as Kūheia Bay, Pedro Bay.

Consistents. Surf site, Hawai'i Kai, O'ahu. On the east side of Turtles off Maunalua Bay Beach Park. The surf here breaks consistently on swells from any direction.

Cooke's Point. Lā'ie, O'ahu. In approximately 1900, the kama-'āina Cooke family built a summer home on land at the point that they leased from the Campbell Estate. Their lease expired in 1970, and the site is now Mālaekahana State Park. Also known as Kalanai Point.

Cook Point. Dive site, Ka'awaloa, Hawai'i. The general area where Captain James Cook was killed in 1779. The Captain Cook Monument marks the exact spot. The dive site off the point is a dropoff from 25 to 100 feet, with arches and lava tubes. Also known as Ka'awaloa Point.

Cooper Landing. Ho'okena, Hawai'i. Former interisland steamer landing in Ho'okena Beach Park that was named for Henry Cooper, road supervisor for South Kona from 1871 to 1880. Also known as Ho'okena Landing, Kauhakō Landing, Kupa Landing.

Coral Flats. Shore, Kawaihae, Hawai'i. Section of Kawaihae Harbor bordering Pelekane Beach. This section of the harbor is the result of an extensive landfill project. The fill material was the coral dredged out of Kawaihae Reef to create the harbor.

Coral Gardens. 1. Reef, snorkeling site, Pāpalaua, Maui. Extensive reef off the east end of Pāpalaua State Wayside Park. 2. Reef, snorkeling site, Kāne'ohe, O'ahu. Off Wailele Street on the shore of Kāne'ohe Bay and the former site of the Coral Gardens Hotel.

Coral House. Beach, residence, Kualoa, O'ahu. Narrow calcareous sand beach fronting a private beachfront home north of the old sugar mill that was built with coral from the reef offshore.

Coral Reef. Surf site, Paikō, Oʻahu. The takeoff spot for this left is next to an emergent coral reef. Also known as Tanks.

Corner. Beach, Waimea Bay, Oʻahu. Same as Coffin Corner.

Corners. Surf site, Māʻalaea, Maui. The last section of the wave at Māʻalaea where it forms a "corner" by bending toward shore.

Cornets. Surf site, Mākaha, Oʻahu. On the east side of Mauna Lahilahi and off the former Cornet Store, a landmark in Mākaha until it closed in 1997.

Cornucopia. Surf site, Waikīkī, Oʻahu. West of Canoes and off the Royal Hawaiian Hotel. Named by the early haole surfers in Waikīkī because the outline of the waves as they rolled toward shore resembled a cornucopia, the traditional horn of plenty. Waves here terminated near the mouth of ʻĀpuakehau Stream and were considered to be a beginner's surf site. Also known as Baby Royals.

Corsair. Dive site, Niu, Oʻahu. Wreck of a World War II Corsair airplane off Niu Valley at 100 feet that serves as a small artificial reef in an otherwise barren area. The plane ditched here in 1946 after running out of fuel on a training mission. A mooring buoy marks the site.

Courts. Surf site, Ala Moana, Oʻahu. Same as Tennis Courts.

Cove Park. 1. Beach, beach park, fishing site, surf site, Kīhei, Maui. At the south end of Kalama Beach Park at the site of the former Kīhei boat ramp. The ramp was built in 1963, but it was later closed and relocated to the Kīhei Ramp facility south of Kamaʻole III Beach Park. A small pocket of calcareous sand borders the former ramp and extends offshore as a shallow sandbar. The surf site is at the edge of the sandbar and is a popular site for beginners. 2. Shore, Hawaiʻi Kai, Oʻahu. East section of Maunalua Bay Beach Park, where kayakers frequently launch and land in a small cove adjacent to a small parking lot.

Coves. 1. Surf site, ʻEwa Beach, Oʻahu. West of Oneʻula Beach Park. The surf site is off a small cove in the rocky shore and was named in the early 1960s by two members of the ʻEwa Beach Surf Club, Chris Gardner and Kevin Johns. 2. Surf site, ʻŌhikilolo, Oʻahu. West end of ʻŌhikilolo Beach.

Cow Bowls. Surf site, Hawaiʻi Kai, Oʻahu. Near the intersection of Kealahou Street and Kalanianaʻole Highway. The right at Irma's.

Cow's Ass. Surf site, Poʻipū, Kauaʻi. The left at Cow's Head. The name is a play on words that was introduced some years after the original name, Cow's Head. Cow's Head is primarily a right, so going left, or in the opposite direction from the head, supposedly means a surfer is riding toward the rear end of the cow.

Cow's Head. Surf site, Po'ipū, Kaua'i. The surf site fronts a small landscaped park on a rocky point. A cow's skull, or "head," sat on a rock wall inshore of the surf site for many years. Cow's Head is the right on the reef. Cow's Ass is the left. Also known as Helicopters.

Crack 14. Surf site, Keālia, Kaua'i. A reef here is off the former Līhu'e Plantation sugar field that was called Makee 14. A large crevice, or "crack," in the reef was a popular fishing site, so fishermen named it 14 Crack. When surfers discovered that ridable waves break on this reef, they renamed it Crack 14.

Cracks. Dive site, Kailua, O'ahu. North end of Kailua Bay off Kapoho Point where there are cracks in the ocean bottom.

Crashboat Channel. Boat channel, Kāne'ohe Bay, O'ahu. Channel at the east end of Kāne'ohe Bay. It was dredged by the U.S. Navy adjacent to Mōkapu Peninsula to permit quick access to the open ocean for crash boats on the marine base to assist downed aircraft or vessels in distress. It connects to the Sampan Channel, one of the two main channels coming into Kāne'ohe Bay. The Crashboat Channel lies within a naval defensive sea area established by executive order in 1941. The area consists of a 500-yard prohibited zone around the perimeter of Mōkapu Peninsula that only authorized vessels may enter.

Crater Hill. Beach, volcanic cone, Kīlauea, Kaua'i. Crater Hill is the crater-shaped remnant of a tuff cone formed by the consolidation, or cementing, of volcanic ash. Tuff cones such as Punchbowl and Diamond Head are common on O'ahu, but Crater Hill is the only tuff cone on Kaua'i. The coastal portion of the cone became part of Kīlauea Point National Wildlife Refuge on March 8, 1988, when 91 acres of Crater Hill and 38 acres at Mōkōlea Point were added to the refuge. The Doran Schmidt family donated the Crater Hill property, and the Mōkōlea Point property was purchased from Ocean Vistas Consortium for $1.6 million. Two small isolated pockets of calcareous sand are found at the base of Crater Hill's high sea cliffs between Mōkōlea and Kīlauea Points. They are not accessible by land. The smaller beach between the sea cliff and Makapili Rock is a tombolo—a sandbar that connects the shore to an island.

Crater Lake. Pool, Kalaupapa, Moloka'i. A tongue-in-cheek name for the small blue-green pool of brackish water at the bottom of Kauhakō Crater. The depth of the crater to the pool is 450 feet, and the pool extends below sea level.

Cromwell's. Harbor, swimming site, Diamond Head, O'ahu. Small boat harbor built in 1936 by Doris Duke and her husband, James Cromwell, below their home, Shangri-La, on the west side of Black Point. Surge from high surf made the harbor unusable for boats from the beginning, but it is a popular swimming site. Also known as The Harbor, Shangri-La.

Crouching Lion. Dive site, surf site, Makaua, O'ahu. The sites are off the famous rock formation on the mountain ridge that resembles a crouching lion. The Crouching Lion Inn is at the base of the ridge below the rock formation. Built in 1928 by George F. Larsen Sr., it was a private home until 1951 when it was converted into the inn. The surf site is also known as Crouchings. The dive site is in Makaua Channel to the east of the surf site.

Crouchings. Surf site, Makaua, O'ahu. Same as Crouching Lion.

Crushers. Surf site, Mokulē'ia, O'ahu. The Keālia Rock Quarry, where blue rock was once quarried and crushed into construction grade gravel, is located onshore at the west end of Dillingham Airfield. The name Crushers comes from the rock crusher at the quarry. Also know as Quarries.

Cunha's. Surf site, Waikīkī, O'ahu. In the early 1900s, many beautiful homes on large estates lined the eastern shore of Waikīkī. Emanuel Sylvester Cunha's large two-story home was one of these, at the intersection of Kapahulu and Kalākaua Avenues. Cunha's daughter Cecily was an avid surfer and surfed the waves off her family home along with other surfers from Waikīkī and Kapahulu. Although the Cunha home was torn down after World War II, the site is still known as Cunha's. It is one of the few surf sites in Hawai'i where paipo boards are still ridden.

mo'olelo

My grandfather Emmanuel Sylvester—or E. S.—Cunha came from the Azores and reached Hawai'i on a whaling ship. He built a two-story house in Waikīkī at the corner of Kapahulu and Kalākaua that was fronted by a seawall. Surf hitting the wall would splash up on the lanai, and there were stairs in the wall to reach the beach below. I was born in 1911, and the house was built before that. Besides my dad Albert, or Sonny, E. S. had two other children, Clarence and Rosalei. He gave each of his three children a home, and the Waikīkī house went to Clarence, whose daughter Cecily was a great swimmer and surfer. She rode the old wooden boards and surfed right in front of the house. Lots of other people surfed there, too. The Waikīkī house was rented during World War II and eventually torn down.

 May Cunha Ross, April 8, 1996

Cut Mountain. Hill, Olowalu, Maui. Large hill on the shore at the west end of Awalua Beach that was severely graded, or "cut," during construction of Honoapi'ilani Highway.

Cyclones. Surf site, windsurf site, Diamond Head, O'ahu. Off the easternmost lookout in Kuilei Cliffs Beach Park. Named by windsurfers for the action of the powerful wind offshore.

CYOs. Surf site, Hau'ula, O'ahu. Off Kokololio Beach Park. The surf site is known by the acronym for the Catholic Youth Organization, CYO, that was formerly housed in the Cooke family's old beach home at the south end of the park. When the county acquired the land for a beach park, the home was razed.

Dairymens. Surf site, Kawailoa, Oʻahu. In 1897, several dairy farms on Oʻahu formed Dairymen's Association, Ltd., a cooperative to sell their milk. In 1957, the dairy farm moved from east Honolulu to Kawailoa on the North Shore, where it was located across Kamehameha Highway from Kawailoa Beach. North Shore surfers named the surf site opposite the farm Dairymens not only for its proximity, but also for its distinctive smell during offshore winds. In 1959, Dairymen's changed its name to Meadow Gold Dairies and at the same time Bishop Estate developed the Pāpaʻiloa Road subdivision on Kawailoa Beach across from the farm. As homes were built in the 1960s, neighborhood surfers shortened Dairymens to Dairies. When the dairy farm moved to Waimānalo in 1990, both names largely fell into disuse. Now the site is best known as Inside Himalayas.

Dan Uchi. Fishing site, Kealakekua, Hawaiʻi. The ocean bottom here is a series of ledges or steps that descend into deep water. Japanese *ulua* fishermen who frequent the site named it for the steps. *Dan* is Japanese for "steps" and *uchi* means "house." The name is probably short for *dan no uchi,* or "steps of a house."

Davidson's. Beach, point, surf site, Kekaha, Kauaʻi. Point fronted by a calcareous sand beach south of Kekaha Beach Park. The surf site is on the reef fronting the point. It was named for John Douglas Davidson, who built a two-story home across the street from the beach in 1922 and lived there until his death in 1949. Davidson came to Kauaʻi in 1919 and was employed by Kekaha Sugar Company. Also known as ʻOʻomano.

Dawson. Wharf, Kalaupapa, Molokaʻi. According to a Lions International plaque at the wharf, it was dedicated to the memory of P. O. Dawson, "a beloved friend of the people of Kalaupapa." Dawson was a settlement administrator for the Board of Hospitals and Settlements under Henry Kluegel and was loved by all of the Kalaupapa residents.

D

Day Star. Surf site, Mokulē'ia, O'ahu. The *Day Star* is a 73-foot long, 22-foot wide, 100-ton commercial fishing boat that was built by Carroll Hoeppner on the sand dunes inshore of the surf site. Hoeppner began construction in December 1971 and finished in August 1978. He launched the boat across the beach using a steel sled that was pushed by four bulldozers. During the seven-year construction period, surfers began calling the surf site offshore "The Boat" or "Iron Boat." When the boat's name, *Day Star*, was added during the last year of construction, the name of the surf site changed to Day Star. Hoeppner is a Baha'i, and in the Baha'i faith the day star is the sun and a symbol of the messengers of God, such as Christ, Buddha, Krishna, Mohammed, and Bahae'llah. The *Day Star* is registered in Honolulu and still owned by the Hoeppner family, who fish for albacore in the North and South Pacific. Also known as The Boat, Iron Boat.

 mo'olelo

I came to Hawai'i in 1968 to work as an engineer on the nuclear submarines in Pearl Harbor. I had fished in Alaska during college and liked it, so I decided to build a boat and fish for albacore after I retired from Pearl Harbor. During the 1970s there weren't too many boats from Hawai'i fishing for albacore. I moved to the North Shore and started building a boat on the sand dunes west of Mokulē'ia Beach Park in December 1971. The *Day Star* was completed and launched across the beach in August 1978. That's also when I left the yard at Pearl Harbor, and my family and I have been fishing ever since. The *Day Star*'s 73 feet long, 22 feet wide, weighs 100 tons, and holds 60 tons of fish in her refrigerated holds. We troll for albacore similar to the way sport fishermen troll for game fish. We usually stay out for three months at a time, going to the South Pacific in the winter and the North Pacific during the summer. The name *Day Star* comes from the writings of the Baha'i religion, my religious background. *Day Star* is a synonym for a prophet, like Christ or Moses. Surfers started using **Day Star** as the name of the surfing site after we put the name on the boat during our last year of construction.

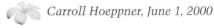 *Carroll Hoeppner, June 1, 2000*

D Buoy. Fish aggregating device, Kumukahi, Hawai'i. Buoy anchored at approximately 950 fathoms. Landmarks: Kumukahi Point Light, Kaloli Point, Leleiwi Point.

DD Buoy. Fish aggregating device, 'Opana Point, Maui. Buoy anchored at approximately 203 fathoms. Landmarks: Nākālele Point Light, Kahului Harbor Light, Pa'uwela Point Light, Opiko'ula Point.

Dead Horse. Beach, Kaluako'i, Moloka'i. Named for a dead horse that was found on the beach when the property was owned by Moloka'i Ranch. Also known as Make Horse Beach, Pōhaku Māuliuli Beach.

Deep China Walls. Dive site, Hawai'i Kai, O'ahu. Deep end of the ledge at the China Walls dive site that goes from 80 to 130 feet.

Deep Reef. Dive site, Kainaliu, Hawai'i. One of the Red Hill dive sites.

Del Monte. Beach park, Kaunakakai, Moloka'i. Adjacent to One-ali'i Beach Park. Private beach park that was originally developed by the Del Monte Corporation for its employees and that is now owned by Kawela Plantation.

Depots. Beach, surf site, Nānākuli, O'ahu. South section of Ulehawa Beach Park. An O'ahu Land and Railway (OR&L) train depot was located here before the trains stopped running in 1947. The surf site is a shorebreak.

 mo'olelo

My family moved from Kaimukī to Nānākuli in 1946, and our house was near the OR&L train depot. The depot was right on Farrington Highway near Haleakalā Avenue, directly across the street from the road that goes into the beach park. It was next to a store, Aunty Pinao's Store, which is Yuen Store today. The beach across the street was already called **Depots.** It was an excellent beach for swimming and was especially popular with the GIs who came to Camp Andrews, a military rest camp that was across the street from the beach, too. The depot was small, maybe 8 by 8 feet, with a roof on four wooden posts, and when the train came from Kahuku or Honolulu, it would stop there for passengers. The trains stopped running in 1947 and the depot was torn down by 1950, but the tracks are still there and the name Depots has lasted all these years.

When we came from Kaimukī, we brought our boards with us—hollow boards—and we made our own boards in Nānākuli, too, using railroad ties. We knew a lot of guys that worked on the trains, and they gave us ties when we needed them. We'd glue the ties together and shape them into planks—but those boards were heavy. My brother Homer and I were some of the first to surf Mākaha. In the late forties there were no cars out there and no one else around. We had a 1936 Ford station wagon, and we'd load up the boards and go. The only other surfers we'd see were George Downing, Wally Froiseth, and some of their friends.

 Henry Barrett, November 26, 2000

Desert Strip. Sand dunes, Moʻomomi, Molokaʻi. Long belt of active, largely unconsolidated dunes that extends almost completely across the northwestern corner of West Molokaʻi from Moʻomomi Beach. It was formed by the trade winds blowing sand inland from the beach. Some of the older dunes have lithified to form calcareous sandstone. Also known as Keonelele.

Devil's Rock. 1. Dive site, island, surf site, Mokulēʻia, Oʻahu. Off Mokulēʻia Polo Field. Devil's Rock is a small rock island that is 5 feet above the surface. It rests on an underwater plateau at 20 feet that drops to 70 feet on its inner side and to 90 feet on its seaward side. The surf site is a left on the north side of the rock that was first surfed in 1975 by Jack Bredin, Bob Larson, and Tom Sawicki, who lived on the beach inshore. Also known as Black Rock, Castle Rock, The Rock, Stone Island. 2. Rock awash, Hawaiʻi Kai, Oʻahu. Small rock island in the channel between Half Point and Full Point at Sandy Beach that is awash at the surface of the ocean.

Diamond Head. 1. Beach, Honolulu, Oʻahu. Narrow calcareous sand beach at the base of Diamond Head between Beach Road and Kulamanu Place. British sailors exploring the beach in 1825 found calcite crystals sparkling in the sand and believed they were diamond fragments. They named the mountain Diamond Hill, but the name was later changed to Diamond Head. *Head* is an abbreviation of headland. The crystals are still found here in the sand. 2. Beach park (1.2 acres). Between the Diamond Head Lighthouse and Beach Road to the west. Sometimes the name is incorrectly applied to Kuilei Cliffs Beach Park, the park on the east side of the lighthouse that includes the three lookouts. 3. Buoy, Honolulu, Oʻahu. Prominent navigational buoy off Diamond Head Light. 4. Light, Honolulu, Oʻahu. Established in 1899 on the seaward flank of Diamond Head at 145 feet above sea level. The concrete light tower was completed in 1918, and the light was automated in 1924. The original lightkeeper's cottage, built in 1921, has been the home of the Commander of the Fourteenth U.S. Coast Guard District since 1945. 5. Offshore mooring. Mooring site fronting the Outrigger Canoe Club. Also known as Kapua Offshore Mooring. 6. State Monument, Honolulu, Oʻahu. The state has identified Diamond Head, one of the most famous landmarks in Hawaiʻi, as a "monument." Diamond Head is a volcanic crater, a palagonite tuff cone, from the Honolulu Volcanic Series, which includes Punchbowl, Koko Crater, and Koko Head. The crater was purchased by the federal government in 1904, but most of its 500 acres, including the .7-mile hiking trail to the summit, are a state park known as Diamond Head State Monument. Also known as Kaimana Hila,

Lēʻahi. 7. Surf site, windsurf site, Honolulu, Oʻahu. Both front the three lookouts in Kuilei Cliffs Beach Park. Also known as Cliffs.

Diamond Head Ledge. Dive site, Diamond Head, Oʻahu. Off Black Point at 30 to 70 feet deep.

Diamond Head Marker. Dive site, Diamond Head, Oʻahu. At the navigational buoy off Diamond Head Light.

Dig Me. 1. Beach, Kāʻanapali, Maui. Section of Kāʻanapali Beach. 2. Beach, Waikīkī, Oʻahu. Also known as Kaimana Beach, Sans Souci Beach. Both sites were humorously named for the preening body beautifuls that frequent them. The name in Waikīkī originated in the 1980s when the beach was popular with a young professional crowd that wore the latest and briefest in swimwear. The beach is now primarily a family beach that is popular with parents of young children.

Dillingham Channel. Mokulēʻia, Oʻahu. Deep channel that leads seaward at the Mokulēʻia Polo Field. The polo field is a part of Dillingham Ranch, and the channel takes its name from the ranch. The remnants of a former pier are located here.

Dirty Ear Beach. Kīpahulu, Maui. The Hawaiian name of the beach, Pepeiaolepo, literally means "dirty ear." Also known as Pepeiaolepo Beach.

Disappearing Sands. Beach, North Kona, Hawaiʻi. Small pocket of calcareous sand on Aliʻi Drive. During periods of high surf, waves erode almost the entire beach, exposing the underlying rocks, and the beach literally "disappears" within twenty-four hours. When the high surf subsides, normal surf activity redeposits the sand on shore, covering the rocks. Also known as Magic Sands, Laʻaloa Bay Beach Park, White Sands.

Dixie Maru. Beach, surf site, Kaluakoʻi, Molokaʻi. Wide pocket of calcareous sand at the head of a small bay, with a mudflat from soil runoff in the backshore. The *Dixie Maru* was a Japanese fishing sampan that wrecked here in the early 1920s. A cowboy employed by Molokaʻi Ranch found her nameplate onshore and hung it on a pasture gate. Since that time the bay and the beach have been called Dixie Maru. The surf site is in the bay. Also known as Kapukahehu.

DK Buoy. Fish aggregating device, Anahola, Kauaʻi. Buoy anchored at approximately 700 fathoms. Landmarks: Kepuhi Point, Kāhala Point Light, and Kamilo Point.

Do Drop Inn. Dive site, ʻAnini, Kauaʻi. Vertical dropoff from 65 to 90 feet. The name is a play on words for swimming over and down, or "dropping in," over the dropoff.

Dog Bowls. Surf site, Kailua, Oʻahu. On the east side of the larger of the two Mokulua Islands. The outline of the larger island to some observers resembles a crouching dog facing east. A bowl is a curved or bowl-shaped section of a wave, so the name of the surf site is a play on words for the surfing term *bowl* and a food dish for a dog. Also known as Bowls.

Dolphin. Lagoon, South Kohala, Hawai'i. Saltwater lagoon with a calcareous sand beach that houses Atlantic bottlenose dolphins at the Hilton Waikoloa Village. It was completed in 1988 with the opening of the resort.

Domes. Dive site, Kainaliu, Hawai'i. One of the Red Hill dive sites.

Domestic Commercial Fishing Village. Fishing complex, Honolulu, O'ahu. A 16.5-acre site at Piers 36–38 in Honolulu Harbor that was completed in 2000 to consolidate the commercial fishing activities in Kewalo Basin and Honolulu Harbor. It includes a multiuser building and a 500-foot-long dock for fishing vessels.

Donkey. Beach, surf site, Keālia, Kaua'i. Wide calcareous sand beach on the north side of Paliku Point. The surf site is a shorebreak off the beach. The land here was originally part of the Makee Sugar Company until 1934 when it became part of Līhu'e Plantation in a consolidation. Līhu'e Plantation continued to grow sugarcane until 1990, when it terminated operations on its 3,300 acres of agricultural land between Keālia and Anahola. The *ahupua'a,* or land division, of Keālia, 6,700 acres in area including Keālia and Donkey Beaches, was sold by Amfac Land Company in 1998 to Keālia Plantation LLC. While the plantation was still in operation prior to 1990, donkeys were used to haul seed cane into fields that were otherwise difficult to access. When the donkeys were idle, they were pastured in the grassy field behind the beach, giving the site its popular name.

> *mo'olelo*
>
> The donkeys and mules pastured at **Donkey Beach** were used to carry seed cane into the fields, but now it's hauled in on trucks. But the donkeys and mules are still used to carry fertilizer. A truck brings in a big load, drops it on the road, then the donkeys and mules carry it into the fields where it's scattered by hand. In the old days Donkey Beach was used mostly for casting and not for swimming. Then the hippies found it in the early 1970s. They were eating the mushrooms in the pasture that grew from the animals' droppings, and they started swimming there.
>
> *George Christian, March 11, 1988*

Don's Left. Surf site, Mokulē'ia, O'ahu. Off the north end of Mokulē'ia Beach Park. Named for veteran North Shore surfer Don Rohrback, who has surfed here since the 1960s.

Doubles. Surf site, Hawai'i Kai, O'ahu. On the east side of the Kalama Stream mouth. Water from the stream meeting incoming waves creates many reformed waves, or "doubles."

Dragon Reef. Dive site, La Pérouse, Maui. South of the bay. Single underwater arch at 20–70 feet that is shaped like a dragon's back and is covered by white silver dollar-sized leather coral that resembles dragon's scales. In addition, a rock at the end of the arch looks like a dragon's head with its mouth open.

Dragon's Head. Dive site, Nāwiliwili, Kaua'i. Unusual underwater lava formation at 60–110 feet that has a dragonlike appearance.

Dragon's Teeth. Cave, 'Īlio Point, Moloka'i. A cave here at sea level is subject to the constant surge of waves. As waves roll into the cave and strike its back wall, whitewater is ejected or "spit" back out like fire from a dragon's mouth. Two pointed rocks hang from the roof of cave, resembling teeth in the dragon's mouth.

Drainpipes. Surf site, Mā'alaea, Maui. Off a drainpipe on the beach.

Drawbridge. Bridge, Honolulu, O'ahu. Bridge that connects Sand Island to O'ahu that is no longer used as a drawbridge due to the heavy traffic on Sand Island Road. Also known as the Bascule Bridge, Slattery Bridge.

Dry Cave. Hā'ena, Kaua'i. Lava tube that was once a sea cave during a higher stand of the sea. It is called the Dry Cave to differentiate it from another lava tube to the west that has water in it and is called the Wet Cave. Also known as Maniniholo Cave.

Drydock. Nāpili, Maui. During the early 1920s, David T. Fleming, the manager of Honolua Ranch, built a drydock on the north point of Nāpili Bay by cutting an opening large enough to accommodate his boat into the outer edge of the point. The drydock, however, proved dangerous and impractical. It was used once and abandoned. The family referred to it as "Fleming's Folly."

Duck Island. Hawai'i Kai, O'ahu. Small island in Hawai'i Kai Marina at the intersection of Kalaniana'ole Highway and Hawai'i Kai Drive that is home to a large population of resident and migratory ducks.

Duke's. 1. Harbor, Diamond Head, O'ahu. Small harbor at the foot of Doris Duke's estate, Shangri-La. Also known as Cromwell's. 2. Surf site, Kāhala, O'ahu. Nadine and Duke Kahanamoku's home was on the east side of Black Point overlooking the surf site. Their three-level, five-bedroom home on Royal Circle was built in 1937 on a 14,266-square-foot lot. Kahanamoku died in 1968 and his wife Nadine lived there until her death in 1997. Also known as Black's.

Duke Statue. Waikīkī Beach, O'ahu. Statue of Duke Kahanamoku in Kūhiō Beach Park. Commonly called the Duke Statue. See Kahanamoku.

Dumps. Surf site, 'Ahihi, Maui. Off the former rubbish dump that was on the shore of the 'Ahihi-Kina'u Natural Area Reserve.

Dumptrucks. Surf site, Hā'ena, Kaua'i. Outermost takeoff spot at Tunnels. The force of the waves breaking here is compared to the force of a load sliding off a dumptruck.

Eagle's Rock Point. Surf site, Pāpalaua, Maui. Off the small parking lot at the west end of Pāpalaua State Wayside Park. The silhouette of a rock formation on the mountain inland of the site resembles an eagle.

Earl's Reef. Surf site, Sunset Beach, O'ahu. Nearshore site on the east side of Val's Reef. Named for Earl Morita, a surfer who lived at Sunset Point and always surfed here. Also known as Shorebreak, Shores.

East Lagoon. Kāne'ohe, O'ahu. One of several man-made lagoons at Coconut Island created by Christian Holmes, who owned the island in the 1930s. It is connected to Kāne'ohe Bay by a 40-foot wide opening between two narrow peninsulas. The docks in East Lagoon are used for the transportation of people and equipment, and a floating bridge spanning the northern arm of the lagoon provides access to the coral reef research facilities.

East Loch. Bay, Pearl Harbor, O'ahu. Easternmost bay within Pearl Harbor. *Loch* is a Scottish word that is used to describe a bay that is almost entirely landlocked.

East Māmala Bay. Honolulu, O'ahu. Bay defined by the shore from Diamond Head to the Honolulu International Airport Reef Runway.

East Moloka'i. Section of Moloka'i east of an imaginary line approximately from Keonelele at Mo'omomi to Waiakāne on Palā'au Road. West Moloka'i is west of the line.

East Shore. O'ahu. Shore from Makapu'u Point to Kahuku Point.

E Buoy. Fish aggregating device, Leleiwi, Hawai'i. Buoy anchored at approximately 920 fathoms. Landmarks: Kumukahi Point Light, Hilo Bay Light, Leleiwi Point, Pepe'ekeo Point Light.

Eddie Hosaka. Point, fishing site, Pōhue, Hawai'i. Named for Edward Hosaka, an agronomist with the University of Hawai'i's Extension Services, who died at the point in 1961 while fishing for ulua. Also known as Hosaka Point, Pu'u Ki.

Edge of the World. Dive site, Molokini Island, Maui. Shelf that juts out and drops to 250 feet, the deepest drop-off on the backside of Molokini.

Eel Bait. Surf site, Mokulēʻia, Oʻahu. Off the west end of Army Beach. Waves here break over a shallow reef, and a bad wipe-out will cut careless surfers into "eel bait" if they are dragged across the reef.

Egusaʻs. Beach, surf site, Lāʻau Point, Molokaʻi. Northernmost section of Kamākaʻipō Beach. Kimi and Takujiro Egusa were employees of Molokaʻi Ranch. During the 1930s and 1940s, they lived in a house on the bluff above the north end of the beach and among other duties maintained the Kaupōa beach house for the Cooke family. The surf site is off the beach.

 moʻolelo

Kimi and Takujiro Egusa moved to Kamākaʻipō before World War II. When the Munros of Lānaʻi were with Molokaʻi Ranch, Egusa was one of four men they trained as beekeepers. His apiaries were at Hālena, and it was a large operation with a processing plant. His record was 160 pounds of algarroba honey in one year, but foul brood eventually wiped out the bees. Then Egusa became the poison man, clearing the pastures of kiawe, and he took care of the Kaupoa house.

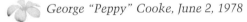 *George "Peppy" Cooke, June 2, 1978*

ʻEhukai. Beach park (1.2 acres), surf site, Sunset Beach, Oʻahu. The park provides the primary public access point to the world-famous Banzai Pipeline. The surf site ʻEhukai is off the park. Also known as Sandbars. *Lit.,* sea spray.

EK Buoy. Fish aggregating device, Hanalei, Kauaʻi. Buoy anchored at approximately 910 fathoms. Landmarks: Kīlauea Point Light, Kaʻilio Point, and Hanalei Bay.

Electric Beach. 1. Beach park, Kahe, Oʻahu. Also known as Hawaiian Electric Beach Park. 2. Dive site, Kahe, Oʻahu. Off the beach park. Also known as Kahe Point.

ʻEleʻileʻi. Bay, fishing site, Māliko, Maui. First small bay east of Māliko Bay. Also known as Watercress Bay. *Lit.,* shiny black.

Elephant Rock. Island, Moakea, Molokaʻi. The outline of the island resembles the rounded back of an elephant. Also known as Mokuhoʻoniki.

Elks Club. Private club, Waikīkī Beach, Oʻahu. The Honolulu Elks Lodge 616 was established on April 15, 1901. In 1920, the Elks purchased James Castle's four-story home Kainalu, a famous landmark in Waikīkī, for their lodge, or "club." Before Castle built his mansion here in the 1890s, it had been the home of Boki, the governor of Oʻahu, and his wife Liliha.

After Castle died in 1918, his wife offered to sell the property to the Elks. She had heard about the charitable programs they were sponsoring in the community. The purchase price was $155,000—one dollar per square foot. The former Castle home was demolished in 1958 and replaced by the present building in 1960. In addition to being a charitable organization, the Honolulu Elks Lodge also supports positive community activities, including ocean sports such as surfing, outrigger canoe paddling, and paddleboard racing.

Embassy Suites. Windsurf site, Honokowai, Maui. Off the Embassy Suites Resort. One of several west-side sites that are used as starting places to make the sail to Moloka'i.

Empty Lots. Surf site, 'Ewa Beach, O'ahu. Off the center of 'Ewa Beach Road. In the 1960s when the site was named, the beachfront lots here were undeveloped.

End of the Road. Surf site, Ka'ena, O'ahu. Off the end of the paved road where Ka'ena Point State Park begins.

Enenue Side. Dive site, Molokini, Maui. *Enenue,* or rudder fish, school on this reef that slopes from the surface to 60 feet. *Lit.,* rudder fish.

Erdman. Surf site, Mokulē'ia, O'ahu. On the north end of the reef fronting Camp Erdman. Also known as Camp Erdman, Rock-n-Roll Reef, Tigers, Tiger Reef.

Eternity. Beach, Hawai'i Kai, O'ahu. Same as From Here to Eternity Beach.

'Ewa Beach. Park (4.9 acres), 'Ewa, O'ahu. Narrow calcareous sand beach that fronts the community of 'Ewa Beach. Harry K. Ching, a former 'Ewa postmaster who was appointed in 1932, coined the name 'Ewa Beach to differentiate 'Ewa town near the former sugar mill from the growing community several miles away at the beach. When he was appointed postmaster for 'Ewa in 1932, part of his jurisdiction was known as Kūpaka, the Hawaiian word for tobacco. The original name, he said in a 1991 interview in the Honolulu Star Bulletin, was difficult for non-Hawaiians to remember and pronounce. 'Ewa Beach was easier, he said, "because you're near the beach and near 'Ewa town. I didn't want them to forget about 'Ewa town."

Fagans Beach. Pōhaku Pili, Molokaʻi. Small calcareous sand pocket beach at the head of a small bay. A narrow, sand-bottomed channel runs through the bay and terminates at the beach. Paul Fagan, a wealthy businessman from California, purchased Hālawa Valley and Puʻu o Hoku Ranch during the 1930s. The ranch included this beach, and it was named for him. Also known as Pōhaku Pili.

Falls of Clyde. Museum ship, Honolulu, Oʻahu. Part of the Hawaiʻi Maritime Center at Pier 7 in Honolulu Harbor. Built in Port Glasgow, Scotland in 1878, the *Falls of Clyde* was purchased by Captain William Matson, founder of the Matson Navigation Company. The ship carried passengers and cargo between Hawaiʻi and San Francisco until 1906, when it was converted into a sail-driven tanker, spending fourteen more years on the Hawaiʻi-California run. In 1920, the *Falls of Clyde* was dismasted and towed to Ketchikan, Alaska, where it was used as a floating fuel depot for fishing boats until the late 1950s, when it was purchased by a Seattle resident. In 1963, a Seattle bank decided that the vessel should be sold as scrap to recoup a bad mortgage, but a successful fund-raising drive in Honolulu saved the day. The ship was towed to Honolulu, where it was restored and established as a maritime museum ship. The *Falls of Clyde* is the last of the original Matson fleet, the only surviving four-masted, square-rigged ship, and the sole surviving sail-driven oil tanker. It is widely recognized as one of the most important museum ships in the world.

Family Housing. Surf site, Pacific Missile Range Facility, Kauaʻi. Off the family housing complex that was built inshore of the site in the 1970s.

Fantasy Reef. 1. Dive site, Kainaliu, Hawaiʻi. One of the Red Hill dive sites. Large open cavern with a skylight at 15–60 feet. 2. Dive site, Kāhala, Oʻahu. Series of lava ledges and arches at 40–60 feet that harbor a wide variety of marine life. Both dive sites supposedly fulfill every scuba diver's fantasy about the "perfect dive site." Veteran dive instructor Roy Damron named Fantasy Reef in Kāhala during the late 1960s.

 moʻolelo

The story of **Fantasy Reef** begins in the late 1960s when I moved to Oʻahu. While attending a Hawaiʻi Council of Dive Clubs meeting held at Hawaiʻi Mission Academy, I met a fellow named Don Bieber. He had just acquired a navy surplus liberty launch (40-footer) and was building a dive boat. He had already replaced the Bufah engine with a GMC 671 and was working on the cabin. I had always enjoyed working on boats between jobs in the Hollywood picture biz, so it was a natural to become involved with Don. Besides working on the boat, the *Scuba Belle,* we studied together and obtained our Coast Guard skipper's licenses. Then we established the first commercial dive boat in Hawaiʻi. Most of our dive trips took place off Waikīkī because the *Belle* was berthed at Ala Wai Boat Harbor. Once in a while we would get a group for an all-day charter, and if the trades were down and the ocean flat, we would go east around Diamond Head into Maunalua Bay. One evening we were studying the Geodetic Survey map of that area and noticed a shallower spot a ways offshore from the Kāhala Hilton. Next time we had a dive group there, we began slowly towing a diver back and forth. Mostly we saw flat bottom with lots of rubble. Then quite suddenly the bottom came up and showed many coral reefs, caves, and swarms of fish. We dropped anchor and spent the afternoon in our new playland. Besides lots of tropical fish, we saw several turtles and many shells. When we finally emptied all tanks, pulled anchor, and headed for the Ala Wai, I was somewhat mesmerized. I kept thinking, "What a fabulous dive site!" At that time one of the most wonderful experiences of my life was seeing Walt Disney's production, *Fantasia*. I have always been a classical music fan, so I thought, "How fitting to name the site Fantasy Reef." I'm delighted to learn that the name has endured after all these years.

Roy Damron, October 20, 1999

Father Jules Papa. Beach, Kūʻau, Maui. Pocket beach of calcareous sand fronted by a *papa*—a wide reef shelf. Father Jules Verhaeghe was a Catholic priest who was born in Belgium on March 28, 1885. He arrived in Kūʻau in 1922 to take over the Holy Rosary Church, which had been built on the hill above the beach about 1900. Only the cemetery remains now. Fishermen named the beach after him. Also known as Kūʻau Cove, Mama's.

F Buoy. Fish aggregating device, Kailua-Kona, Hawai'i. Buoy anchored at approximately 1,510 fathoms. Landmarks: Kailua Bay Light, Keauhou Bay Light, Captain Cook.

Federation Camp. Beach, camp, north shore, Lāna'i. Narrow calcareous sand beach that is a section of Shipwreck Beach. On December 25, 1925, Hilario Camino Moncado founded the Filipino Federation of America, a religious, cultural, and social organization. After Moncado's death in 1956, the Lāna'i Federation, like the federation branches elsewhere, split into two groups. The larger of the two groups on Lāna'i built a camp on the beach at Kaiolohia during this period. Also known as Kaiolohia.

Feedlots. Surf site, Campbell Industrial Park. Off the former Hawai'i Meat Packing Company feedlots at the east end of Ola'i Street.

Fence Lines. Surf site, Kalaeloa, O'ahu. Off the eastern boundary of the district where the chain-link fence intersects White Plains Beach.

FF Buoy. Fish aggregating device, Pukaulua Point, Maui. Buoy anchored at approximately 828 fathoms. Landmarks: Opiko-'ula Point, Hana Bay Light.

50-Foot Fingers. Dive site, Hawai'i Kai, O'ahu. Ridges, or "fingers," and canyons at 50 feet deep.

Finger Rock. Point, surf site, Hawai'i Kai, O'ahu. Narrow finger of rock that juts into the ocean at the foot of the Hanapēpē Loop public right-of-way. Surfers use the rock to jump into the ocean. The surf site is adjacent to the rock. Also known as Fingers.

Fingers. Surf site, Hawai'i Kai, O'ahu. Same as Finger Rock.

Fin Hole. 1. Dive site, Hawai'i Kai, O'ahu. Small overhanging ledge close to shore at Sandy Beach. 2. Dive site, Makapu'u, O'ahu. Small overhanging ledge close to shore at Makapu'u Beach. Both sites are named for underwater rock formations that trap fins lost by bodysurfers and bodyboarders. These sites also trap any other debris that is transported underwater by the nearshore currents.

Fire Department. Dive site, Sunset Beach, O'ahu. In the center of Pūpūkea Beach Park off the Sunset Beach Fire Station.

Firehouse. Surf site, Wailupe, O'ahu. Off Wailupe Beach Park. Wailupe Fire Station, the "firehouse," is on Kalaniana'ole Highway across the street from the park. Also known as Goofys, Kim's.

First Break. 1. Surf site, Po'ipū, Kaua'i. Open-ocean site off the west end of Po'ipū Beach. Named in the late 1950s after the surf site in Waikīkī because, like the Waikīkī site, it breaks only on big swells. 2. Surf site, Waikīkī, O'ahu. Outermost, or "first," of several surf sites to form seaward of Canoes during a big south swell. 3. Surf site, Kailua, O'ahu. Seaward of Flat Island. Named after the surf site in Waikīkī because it breaks only on big swells.

First Bridge. Fishing site, Hawai'i Kai, O'ahu. On the rocky ledge below the first bridge to the east of Lāna'i Lookout on Kalaniana'ole Highway. Also known as the 'Ihi'ihilaukea Bridge.

First Cathedral. Dive site, Mānele, Lāna'i. Near Pu'u Pehe Rock between Mānele and Hulopo'e Bays. The most popular dive site on the island, especially with boat tours from Maui. One of two dive sites with similar underwater features that are known as the Cathedrals, specifically First Cathedral and Second Cathedral. Several pinnacles rise from 60 feet to just below the surface. Spacious caverns in the pinnacles have a cathedral-like appearance when shafts of sunlight crisscross the interiors through skylights in the exterior walls. First Cathedral also has a boulder that resembles an altar.

First Channel. Surf site, Ka'alāwai, O'ahu. Off Kulamanu Place on the west side of Black Point. The narrow channel here is the first of several that bisect the reef off Ka'alāwai Beach between Black Point and Kuilei Cliffs Beach Park.

First Dip. Surf site, Keawa'ula, O'ahu. Off the first of several drainage swales, or "dips," in the road at the west end of Yokohama Beach.

First Ditch. Surf site, Kekaha, Kaua'i. Off the first drainage ditch in Kaumuali'i Highway west of Kekaha Beach Park.

First Flow. Dive site, fishing site, Honokua, Hawai'i. One of three lava flows from an eruption in the southwest rift zone of Mauna Kea that began on June 1, 1950. Each of the flows reached the ocean, creating small pockets of black sand on a coast of sea cliffs. Fishermen in boats use the flows as landmarks, numbering them from north to south. The dive site is a narrow shelf close to shore, with some pinnacles and canyons at approximately 40 feet and a steep dropoff to 100 feet. Also known as Honokua.

First Hole. Surf site, Ala Moana, O'ahu. Between Courts and Concessions.

First Lagoon. Swimming site, Ko 'Olina, O'ahu. From west to east, the first of four man-made lagoons at Ko 'Olina. First Lagoon is adjacent to the Ihilani Hotel.

First Reef. Surf site, Hawai'i Kai, O'ahu. Shallow reef adjoining Portlock Beach that has small waves for beginners. A sand trail through the reef, the bed of the former Portlock Pier, leads to deeper water offshore and Second Reef, another surf site.

Firsts. Surf site, Hickam Air Force Base, O'ahu. On the east side of the Hickam Harbor Channel. The surf site on the west side of the channel is known as Seconds. Firsts is also known as Fumes.

Fish Bowl. Dive site, Kukui'ula, Kaua'i. Lava terraces with ledges and holes at 50 to 80 feet. A wide variety of fish are found here, such as might be found in an aquarium or "fish bowl."

Fishermans. Fishing site, surf site, Polihale, Kaua'i. North of Queen's Pond in Polihale State Park. This section of beach fronting the park pavilion is a popular fishing site for *moi* and *pāpio* among Kekaha Plantation fishermen. The surf site is directly offshore.

Fish Rock. Dive site, southeast coast, Lāna'i. East of Mānele Bay at approximately 50 feet. The eastern side of the rock is a 40-foot wall that breaks the surface. Large schools of fish surround the rock, giving it its name.

Five Caves. Dive site, Mākena, Maui. Although there are more than five caves here, the name is a play on words for another name of the same site, Five Graves. Also known as Five Graves, Nahuna Point, Turtle Town.

Five Graves. Dive site, Mākena, Maui. The dive site is off a small graveyard at Pamolepo, a section of Nahuna Point, that belongs to the Kukahiko family of Mākena and contains five graves. Shore divers access the ocean by crossing the point near the graveyard. Also known as Five Caves, Nahuna Point, Turtle Town.

Five Needles. Sea stacks, Honopū, Lāna'i. Part of the Hawai'i State Seabird Sanctuary. Sea stacks are vertical rocks that are left standing alone when the ocean erodes the rocks that once connected them to the shore. The cluster of five sea stacks at Honopū Bay is one of the best examples of sea stacks in Hawai'i. Also known as Nānāhoa, Three Stone, Needles.

Five O'clock. Surf site, Hawai'i Kai, O'ahu. Off Queen's Beach. First site east of the former Wāwāmalu Ranch boundary wall that is frequented by afterwork surfers who do not get there until five o'clock in the afternoon. Also known as 5-O's.

5-O's. Surf site, Hawai'i Kai, O'ahu. Same as Five O'clock.

Flagpoles. Surf site, Kailua, O'ahu. Shorebreak surf site on Kailua Beach off Ka'apuni Drive. Named for the flagpole in the backyard of Lloyd Osborne's beachfront home. Osborne (1909–2001) was a decorated naval aviator, champion masters swimmer, and longtime Hawai'i business executive who in 1959 was the first manager of Ala Moana Center. On July 4, 1969, he erected a 30-foot flagpole at his home to honor his nation and his state. The flagpole is a Windward landmark and marks the spot for the surf site Flagpoles.

Flat Island. Island, surf site, Kailua, O'ahu. Small, flat limestone island one-quarter mile off the east end of Kailua Beach that is less than 10 feet above sea level. The surf site on the east side of the island is one of the most popular ones in Kailua. In addition to surfers, outrigger canoe paddlers, kayakers, wave skiers, windsurfers, and small catamaran sailors ride the waves here. The island is also known as Popoiʻa Island.

Flat Reef. Surf site, Hanalei, Kauaʻi. Middle, inside reef section of Hanalei that forms over a wide, flat reef. Also known as Flat Rock.

Flat Rock. Surf site, Hanalei, Kauaʻi. Same as Flat Reef.

Fleming. Beach park, surf site, Honokahua, Maui. Named for David Thomas Fleming (1881–1955). Born in Scotland but raised on Maui, Fleming became manager of Honolua Ranch in 1912 and was instrumental in converting the cattle ranch into a pineapple plantation. His home, Makaʻoiʻoi, completed in 1915, is now Pineapple Hill Restaurant. Maui Land and Pineapple Company provided the land for the beach park in 1975. The surf site is a shorebreak on a sandbar off the beach, but includes a board surf site on a small reef at the north end of the beach.

Flies. Surf site, Kakaʻako, Oʻahu. Off the west end of Kakaʻako Waterfront Park. The park is built on a former landfill which, when it was active, was the home of many aggressive black flies that bit the surfers and fishermen. It was named in the early 1960s by Joe Kuala who worked nearby in the Interisland Surf Shop. Flies was the closest surf site to the shop.

 moʻolelo

During the late 1950s, Roy Graham and I were working on the beach for Walter Kitazaki at Hale ʻAuʻau and at the surfboard concession in front of the Moana for 25 cents commission per board. We were only making about $8.00 a day, so when Inter Island Resorts opened the Inter Island Surf Shop in the early 1960s, we left the beach to work at the shop. The shop was in Kakaʻako on Punchbowl Street where the federal building is now. Harbor Light Café was next door. The closest spot to the shop to surf was in front of the landfill by the old incinerator, so when the surf was good, we'd close the shop and cut out for a couple of hours. It was a good wave for nose riding, and it was never crowded. It was probably about 1963 that I named that spot **Flies** for all of the flies at the landfill.

Joe Kuala, October 19, 2000

Flying Sea Cliffs. Dive site, Molokini, Maui. Shelf at 50 feet on the outer wall of Molokini that is severely undercut as it drops to 130 feet. Swimming over the edge of the drop gives divers the impression that they are "flying."

Forbidden Island. Ni'ihau. The Robinson family, the owners of Ni'ihau since 1864, made a decision in approximately 1915 to preserve the Hawaiian language and culture on the island by severely restricting access to outsiders. Entry is forbidden to anyone who is not a resident of the island, a member of the Robinson family, or an invited guest. For this reason, the island has been called the Forbidden Island.

Ford Island. Island (450 acres), Pearl Harbor, O'ahu. Dr. Seth Ford (1818–1866), a Honolulu physician, came to Hawai'i from Boston and worked at the Hawaiian Insane Asylum and the U.S. Marine Hospital from 1861 to 1866. He purchased the island, and it was named after him. Following his death the Honolulu Plantation bought the island and used it to grow sugarcane. During World War I, the army purchased it from the Li Estate for $236,000. In 1923 it was transferred to the navy and used as a landing field. In 1962 the navy decommissioned it as a landing field. In 1964 it was designated as a national historic landmark, and in 1975 it was listed on the National Register of Historic Places. Also known as Moku'ume'ume, Poka 'Ailana.

Ford Island Bridge. Pearl Harbor, O'ahu. Same as Admiral Clarey Bridge.

Fort Alexander. Historic site, Princeville, Kaua'i. On the summit of Pu'u Poa overlooking Hanalei Bay. One of two forts constructed on Kaua'i by Georg Anton Scheffer, a German who was managing Russian trading interests in the Hawaiian Islands in the early 1800s. Scheffer secretly planned to take over the islands in the name of Russia and had decided to use Kaua'i as his base of operations. In 1817, Scheffer was ordered to leave Hawai'i by King Kamehameha I. Scheffer named Fort Alexander in honor of Tsar Alexander I of Russia and named a second fort at Waimea Fort Elizabeth in honor of the tsar's consort.

Fort Armstrong. Shore, Honolulu, O'ahu. Section of Honolulu Harbor that is now Piers 1 and 2. Named for Brigadier-General Samuel Armstrong (1839–1893), a member of the Union Army who served with distinction in the Civil War.

Fort DeRussy. Beach, Waikīkī, O'ahu. The beach and the lands that comprise the fort were acquired by the federal government in 1904 and named the Kalia Military Reservation. The reservation was renamed Fort DeRussy in 1909 after Brigadier-General René Edward DeRussy (1790–1865), a member of the Engineer Corps who had served with distinction in the War of 1812 and the Civil War. Fort DeRussy is an important recreation and visitor destination site for the military. The man-made beach fronting Fort DeRussy is 1,800 feet long and 140 feet wide and covered with imported sand. The U.S. Army Museum in Battery Randolph is at the east end of the beach.

Fort Elizabeth. State historic park (17.3 acres), Waimea, Kaua'i. On the east bank of the Waimea River across from Lucy Wright Beach Park. The fort was constructed between 1815 and 1817 during an alliance between King Kaumuali'i of Kaua'i and the Russian-American Company, represented by a German named Georg Anton Scheffer. Scheffer designed the fort and directed the large Hawaiian workforce that constructed its walls. Russian occupation of the fort ended abruptly in 1817 when the Russians were expelled from Hawai'i by King Kamehameha I. Hawaiian soldiers then occupied the fort until 1864, when it was deactivated by order of the Hawaiian government. Scheffer named Fort Elizabeth in honor of the consort of Tsar Alexander I of Russia and named a second fort at Princeville Fort Alexander in honor of the tsar.

Fort Hase. Beach, surf site, Mōkapu, O'ahu. In 1918 a portion of Mōkapu Peninsula was established as an army camp called Kuwa'a'ohe Military Reservation. During World War II, the reservation was renamed Fort Hase. In 1952 the Marine Corps acquired the entire peninsula, including Fort Hase, but continued to use the name for the military housing here. The beach and the surf site front the housing area. Also known as Kuwa'a'ohe.

Fort Kamehameha. Beach, Pearl Harbor, O'ahu. Narrow calcareous sand beach fronting Fort Kamehameha housing. Fort Kamehameha was established as an army installation in 1901 to provide coastal defense at the entrance to Pearl Harbor. It was named for King Kamehameha in 1909. In 1991 the 506-acre fort, which adjoins Hickam Air Force Base and is the site of many Hawai'i Air National Guard facilities, was transferred to the Air Force.

Foster. Point, Hickam Air Force Base, O'ahu. Point and picnic pavilion at the west end of Hickam Harbor named for Lou Foster, longtime harbormaster at Hickam Harbor who helped to develop the harbor in 1957.

Four Miles. Beach park, surf site, Keaukaha, Hawai'i. The official name of the beach park is Kealoha Park, but it is best known to Big Island residents as Four Miles. When the Hilo Post Office was constructed, it was designated as the starting point for all road mileage measurements beginning in Hilo. The park is 4 miles from the post office. The surf site is off the park.

Fours. Surfing, windsurf site, Waikīkī, O'ahu. Same as Number Fours.

14 Crack. Surf site, Keālia, Kaua'i. Same as Crack 14.

Fourteenth Hole. Surf site, Mōkapu, Oʻahu. Off the fourteenth hole of the golf course on Marine Corps Base Hawaiʻi, Kāneʻohe Bay.

Fourth Lagoon. Beach, lagoon, surf site, Ko ʻOlina, Oʻahu. One of four man-made beaches and lagoons at Ko ʻOlina Resort and Marina. Adjacent to the Ko ʻOlina Marina. The surf site is offshore the lagoon.

Freddieland. Surf site, Kaunalā, Oʻahu. Between Sunset Point and Velzyland. Named for Fred Grosskreutz, a surfer from the East Coast, who lived near the beach in the 1960s and 1970s and surfed here almost exclusively, often alone. "Freddieland" was coined as an imitation of the name Velzyland, the next surf site to the east that was named in 1958. Also known as Freddie's, No Mans Land.

Freddie's. Surf site, Kaunalā, Oʻahu. Same as Freddieland.

Free Hawaiʻi. Surf site, Keaʻau, Oʻahu. Off the comfort station in the center of Keaʻau Beach Park. Named by a Waiʻanae surfer who surfed here regularly during the 1970s. He was a firm believer in alternate or "free" lifestyles.

Freight Train Lefts. Surf site, Sand Island, Oʻahu. On a good swell, the lefts at this site break as fast as a moving freight train.

Fresh Air Camp. Surf site, Haleʻiwa, Oʻahu. Off the calcareous sand beach at Kaiaka Bay Beach Park, the site of the former Fresh Air Camp. James Rath established the camp in 1915 as a support facility for Pālama Settlement, which he founded in 1906. The camp was primarily for low-income city mothers and their children, providing them an opportunity for a vacation in the country. Also known as Fresh Airs.

Fresh Airs. Surf site, Haleʻiwa, Oʻahu. Same as Fresh Air Camp.

Friendly Isle. Molokaʻi. Nickname for the island of Molokaʻi.

Frog Rock. Dive site, Kawaihae, Hawaiʻi. A large rock near the dive site looks like a sitting frog when viewed from the proper angle.

From Here to Eternity. Beach, Hawaiʻi Kai, Oʻahu. Name popularized by circle-island tour drivers for the small cove adjacent to the Hālona Blowhole. The famous love scene between Burt Lancaster and Deborah Kerr in the Columbia Pictures 1953 movie *From Here to Eternity* was filmed here. Also known as Cockroach Bay/Beach/Cove, Eternity Beach, Hālona Cove.

Front Street Park. Keaukaha, Hawaiʻi. Kalanianaʻole Highway, which borders the park, was formerly known as Front Street. Residents of Keaukaha still use the former name of the highway for the park. Also known as Keaukaha Beach Park.

Fujioka's. Surf site, Mokulēʻia, Oʻahu. The Fujioka family opened Fujioka Super Market in Haleʻiwa in 1910 and own a beachfront home here on Crozier Drive. The surf site is off their home. Also known as Fuji's.

Fujioka's Channel. Fishing site, Mokulē'ia, O'ahu. Channel through the reef that is used by fishermen as a fishing site and by surfers to access the surf site Fujioka's.

Fuji's. Surf site, Mokulē'ia, O'ahu. An abbreviation of the name Fujioka. Same as Fujioka's.

Full Point. Surf site, Hawai'i Kai, O'ahu. At the edge of the reef east of the comfort station at Sandy Beach Park. Named to differentiate it from Half Point, the surf site on the small rocky point immediately in front of the comfort station.

Fumes. Surf site, Hickam Harbor, O'ahu. Jet fumes from aircraft approaching and taking off on the Reef Runway often inundate the surf site. Also known as Firsts.

Futa Point. Fishing site, Hawai'i Kai, O'ahu. One of several fishing sites along the Koko Head sea cliffs that are favored by *ulua* fishermen. Named after a man named Futa who fished here regularly during the 1950s and 1960s.

Futures. Surf site, Hanalei, Kaua'i. Big-wave, second-reef site off Pu'u Poa Point that is so far offshore it is like surfing in the "future."

Garden Eel Cove. Dive site, Keāhole, Hawaiʻi. In Hoʻona Bay, a small bay on the north side of Keāhole Point that is known for its garden eels and manta rays. Also known as Hoʻona.

Gas Chambers. 1. Surf site, Hawaiʻi Kai, Oʻahu. At the west end of Sandy Beach. 2. Surf site, Sunset Beach, Oʻahu. On the west side of Rocky Point. Both sites are also known as Chambers. Waves at both sites are steep and wipeouts can be severe. Waves break on a shallow sandbar at Sandy Beach and on a shallow reef at Rocky Point. Both names appeared in the early1960s and are spin-offs of "taking gas," then a popular phrase for a particularly bad wipeout. The chamber is the hollow wave. The name at Rocky Point resulted as a challenge in 1961 between two Saint Louis High School students who were regular surfers at Pūpūkea, a popular site to the west. Gas Chambers was unnamed, and one surfer told the other that he would name the site and establish the name by circulating it by word-of-mouth in the surfing community. The experiment worked.

G Buoy. Fish aggregating device, Pepeʻekeo, Hawaiʻi. Buoy anchored at approximately 600 fathoms. Landmarks: Kumukahi Point Light, Pepeʻekeo Point Light, Hilo Bay Light, Leleiwi Point.

Generals. Surf site, Hawaiʻi Kai, Oʻahu. Big-wave, second-reef site that breaks off the comfort station in Sandy Beach Park. The name infers that only the best surfers ride here, the "generals."

General Store. Dive site, shipwreck site, Kalāheo, Kauaʻi. One of the three most popular dive sites on Kauaʻi. Horseshoe-shaped ledge off Makaokahaʻi Point at 60 feet, with two caverns that attract a wide variety of reef fish. The ruins of the SS *Pele*, a 165-ton interisland steamer, are here, with five large anchors. She was built in San Francisco in 1884 with a wood screw and a two-cylinder compound engine, placed in interisland plantation service in 1886, and sank here in 1895. The name General Store compares the wide variety of features at the site to that of the merchandise in a general store.

George Washington Stone. Rock, Sunset Beach, Oʻahu. Rock formation on a ridge inland of Rocky Point that resembles George Washington wearing a three-cornered hat. Also known as Kahikilani.

Gillinʻs. Beach, windsurf site, Māhāʻulepū, Kauaʻi. Narrow calcareous sand beach between Punahoa and Kamala Points, with beachrock shelves in the foreshore and vegetated dunes in the backshore. Named for Elbert Gillin, a supervisor for Grove Farm Company, the owner of the Māhāʻulepū plantation lands. Gillin arrived in Hawaiʻi in 1912 and worked on Maui, where he helped engineer the bridge over ʻOheo Stream in Kīpahulu. Moving to Kauaʻi in 1925, he was the construction superintendent of the Haʻupu Range Tunnel. The half-mile long tunnel allowed direct access for cane trucks traveling from the fields on the north side of the Haʻupu Range to Kōloa Mill on the south side. During his employment with Grove Farm, Gillin built a beach home at Māhāʻulepū, the only home on the entire beach.

GIʻs. Surf site, Waimea, Kauaʻi. Off Waimea State Recreation Pier. Named for veteran Waimea surfer George Inouye, who surfed here regularly for many years.

Glass. Beach, Port Allen, Kauaʻi. Small pocket beach covered with glass fragments on the east side of the Chevron tank farm. The glass originates from a former refuse dump nearby.

Glass Doors. Surf site, Mokulēʻia, Oʻahu. The water is often so clear here that looking through the wall of the wave is like looking through a glass door. Also known as Homelani.

Glassies. Surf site, Lāʻie, Oʻahu. Near shore in the center of Lāʻie Bay. The ocean here always seems to be calm, or "glassy," no matter how strong the trade winds are blowing.

Gloverʻs. Beach, Pōhue, Hawaiʻi. James W. Glover, founder of the general construction company James W. Glover, Ltd., was a former owner of Kahuku Ranch. After his death the ranch was sold to pay estate taxes, including inheritance taxes. Although the Samuel M. Damon Estate was the successful bidder and purchased the 158,000-acre ranch in 1958 for $1.3 million, some area residents still call the beach Gloverʻs Beach. Also known as Kahuku Beach, Pōhue Beach.

Goat. 1. Island, Lāʻie, Oʻahu. Prior to the island becoming part of the Hawaiʻi State Seabird Sanctuary, residents of Lāʻie attempted to graze goats on the island. Also known as Mokū-ʻauia. 2. Trail, Makapuʻu, Oʻahu. Narrow, dangerous trail used by *ulua* fishermen that begins at Makapuʻu Lookout on Kalaniana'ole Highway and leads to the north side of Makapuʻu

Point. In a February 1970 article in *Salt Water Sportsman* magazine, veteran fishing writer and television personality Bruce Carter identified Hawai'i's *ulua* fishermen as "mountain goats" for their ability to reach seemingly inaccessible rocky ledges at the base of sea cliffs. His description was used to name this trail.

Gold Coast. 1. Shore, Kāhala, O'ahu. Name given by the cruise boat industry to the Kāhala coast between Black Point and the Kāhala Mandarin Oriental Hotel. Homes here are among the most expensive in Hawai'i. 2. Shore, Waikīkī, O'ahu. Name given by real estate agents to the Waikīkī coast from the New Otani Kaimana Beach Hotel to the south end of Kalākaua Avenue because the real estate is considered "as good as gold." The condominiums here, built in the late 1950s and 1960s, are the only beachfront condominiums in Waikīkī.

Golden Arches. 1. Dive site, Kohanaiki, Hawai'i. One of the dive sites at Pine Trees that is known for its underwater arches. 2. Dive site, La Pérouse, Maui. South of the bay at 70 feet. The undersides of three arches are covered with gold and orange tube coral and red and yellow sponges. Both sites are known for their underwater arches, and the name is a play on words for the trademark "golden arches" of McDonald's Restaurants.

Golf Links. Plateau, Honolua, Maui. One of the first golf courses on Maui was built on the plateau above Honolua Bay. During the early 1920s, David Fleming, the manager of Honolua Ranch, converted the cattle pasture on the plateau into the West Maui Golf Course, a rugged nine-hole course. The course fell into disuse with the outbreak of World War II, but the former clubhouse still remains on the point in a stand of Norfolk Island pine trees. Also known as Kulaoka'e'a.

Goofys. Surf site, Wailupe, O'ahu. Abbreviation of *goofyfoot*, a surfing term for surfers who stand on their surfboard with their right foot ahead of their left. On big days, the waves at Goofys are primarily lefts, which favor surfers who have a goofyfoot stance. Also known as Firehouse, Kim's.

Gordieland. Surf site, Kawela, O'ahu. Off the north point of Kawela Bay. Velzyland, to the west of Kawela, was named in 1958 after California surfboard manufacturer Dale Velzy. In the 1960s, however, many of the neighborhood surfers at Kawela rode surfboards by Gordie, another California surfboard manufacturer, so they named this site Gordieland for fun. Also known as Gordie's, Pillboxes.

Gordie's. Surf site, Kawela, O'ahu. Same as Gordieland.

Grand Canyon. Dive site, south coast, Lāna'i. East of Kaunolū. Massive submarine canyon at 20 to 100 feet, with many varieties of reef fish.

G

Graveyards. 1. Surf site, Diamond Head, Oʻahu. Off the intersection of Kalākaua Avenue and Coconut Avenue. 2. Surf site, Māʻili, Oʻahu. Shallow inside reef at Hospitals. 3. Surf site, Waikīkī, Oʻahu. On the west side of The Wall, or the Kapahulu Groin. All of these surf sites break over shallow reefs and often have hollow waves on a good day. When surfers wipe out in the tube of a hollow wave, they often say they were "buried," which is the connection between the surf site and the term *graveyard.*

Gray's. 1. Beach, Waikīkī, Oʻahu. Section of Waikīkī Beach fronting the Halekūlani Hotel. Named for Gray's-by-the-Sea, a small two-story boardinghouse near the beach that was operated by La Vancha Maria Chapin Gray from 1912 to 1929. The boardinghouse was closed when Clifford Kimball bought the property to build the Halekūlani Hotel. Also known as Kawehewehe. 2. Channel, Waikīkī, Oʻahu. Natural channel through the reef off the Halekūlani Hotel that was enlarged by dredging in the early 1950s to allow catamarans to come ashore at Gray's Beach. The channel lies between two surf sites, Paradise and Number Threes.

 moʻolelo

My grandmother bought 3 acres for $7,000 in the present Halekūlani area from a man named Hall. The estate was divided between my mother and my two uncles. My oldest uncle got the Diamond Head half, my mother got the middle quarter, and my other uncle, Arthur Brown, got the Ft. DeRussy quarter. My mother put up a two-story house on the Diamond Head side of the present swimming beach, and I was born and raised there. My uncle built a beautiful home on the Ft. DeRussy side of us that later became the Halekūlani Hotel.

In 1912 my mother rented our house to Ma Gray, who used it as a boardinghouse until 1928. I never knew her first name, but because of the boardinghouse, the beach quickly became known as **Gray's Beach** and the name stuck. It was the only good sand beach in the immediate area, and people came from all over to swim there. There was coral on both sides of the beach and a natural sand-filled channel out through the reef that was called Gray's Channel. I remember when Teddy Roosevelt's daughter Alice came to Waikīkī. She was newly married to an older senator, Nicholas Longworth. They were staying at the Seaside, but she would walk up to swim at Gray's Beach. She attracted a lot of attention and was the first woman I ever saw smoke or wear lipstick.

My mother sold the property to Clifford Kimball in 1929. He developed the Halekūlani Hotel.

  J. Atherton Gilman, October 22, 1972

Green Lanterns. Surf site, Māʻili, Oʻahu. Off the mouth of Māʻiliʻili Channel. Named for the Green Lantern Restaurant that was located across the street until 1958, when it was purchased by Vickie and Anson Rego and renamed. Also known as Māʻili.

Green Sand. Beach, surf site, South Point, Hawaiʻi. One of the most unique beaches in Hawaiʻi at the base of Puʻu o Mahana, a littoral cone 3 miles east of South Point. Waves eroding the base of the cinder cone mine olivine out of the cinder and deposit it on the beach, giving it a distinctive green tint. Olivine is a greenish volcanic mineral. The surf site is a shorebreak at the beach. Also known as Mahana.

Green Tree. Surf site, windsurf site, Hoʻokipa, Maui. Off the west end of Hoʻokipa Beach Park. A beach heliotrope in the backshore is the "green tree."

Grim Reapers. Surf site, Kalaeloa, Oʻahu. Big-wave, second-reef site off the seaward end of the east runway. Death is often personified as a skeleton with a scythe and called the grim reaper. The name here is a reference to the large sharks, or "grim reapers," that are commonly seen at the site. Also known as Van Winkles.

Grotto. Dive site, northeast coast, Kahoʻolawe. Cave with a large entrance at the north end of Kanapou Bay. A grotto is a cave.

Groucho's. Surf site, Wailupe, Oʻahu. West of Wailupe Beach Park.

Guard Rail. Surf site, Olowalu, Maui. One of several sites between Ukumehame State Wayside Park and Olowalu. It is off a metal traffic barrier, or "guard rail," that lines the seaward edge of Honoapiʻilani Highway.

Guard Shacks. Surf site, Keawaʻula, Oʻahu. Off the section of Yokohama Beach fronting the guard shack for the tracking station.

Gumbys. Surf site, ʻEwa Beach, Oʻahu. Off Iroquois Beach.

Gums. Surf site, Sunset Beach, Oʻahu. At the west end of the ʻEhukai Beach Park sandbar. During the early 1970s, when most surfers were changing from longboards to shortboards, one surfer who lived nearby continued to surf here with an old longboard. One day during a bad wipeout his board struck him in the mouth and he lost his front teeth, exposing his gums. He had dentures made and continued to surf there, but had another similar wipeout and lost his dentures. From then on the regular surfers in the area called the site "Gums" to commemorate his misadventures.

Gun Point. Surf site, Kaʻaʻawa, Oʻahu. During World War II, gun emplacements were built into the cliff above Kalaeokaʻoʻio Point. Also known as Kualoa.

Haʻaheo o Hawaiʻi. Shipwreck, Hanalei, Kauaʻi. The *Haʻaheo o Hawaiʻi* was the Hawaiian monarchy's first royal yacht, an 83-foot vessel purchased in 1820 for $90,000 by King Kamehameha II. She went aground and sank on Waiʻoli Reef at the hands of an irresponsible crew. The ship was located in 1995 and excavated by a team lead by Paul Johnston, the curator of Maritime History at the Smithsonian Institution's National Museum of American History. *Lit.*, pride of Hawaiʻi.

Hāʻena. 1. Beach park, Hāʻena, Kauaʻi. Calcareous sand beach bordering the wide bay between Mākua Reef to the east and Hauwa Reef to the west, with vegetated sand dunes in the backshore. Across the road from Maniniholo Cave. 2. Point, Hāʻena, Kauaʻi. Wide point inshore of Mākua Reef to the east of Hāʻena Beach Park. Also known as Tunnels. 3. State park (230 acres), Hāʻena, Kauaʻi. Calcareous sand beach between Limahuli Stream and the end of Highway 56. Fronted by shallow reefs and backed by dunes vegetated with ironwood trees. The west end of the park, or Kēʻē Beach, is the start of the 11-mile Kalalau Trail to Kalalau Valley. Several important archaeological sites associated with the hula are located here, including Ke Ahu o Laka, a platform where the hula was performed, and Kauluapaoa Heiau, a temple dedicated to Laka, the deity of the hula. The house on the point belonged to John Allerton and was acquired by the state upon his death in 1986. *Lit.*, red-hot.

 moʻolelo

I retired from the Kauaʻi Police Department in 1975. I was born and raised at the end of the road in Hāʻena. Our home was near Limahuli Stream, and my parents named it Peʻe Kauaʻi. That means "Kauaʻi hide-a-way." The Hawaiians gave names to all the places where food was gathered. The names were important because when you were on foot, carrying gear and fishing equipment, you wanted to be sure you went to the right place and got there at the right time. When we would throw nets on the *'āpapa*, the reefs, we started at low tide with the deepest reef and then as the tide came in, we worked our way to the shallowest reef. We fished on all the reefs from Wainiha to Kē'ē.

The first reef west of **Hā'ena Beach Park** is Po'ohau, and the rocks on the beach are called Halepōhaku. Then the reef gets wider and below the Wichman's house there's a small pond, Hauwa, and a large pond, Paweaka. Paweaka gets up to waist-deep during high tide, and this is the *he'e* [octopus] ground. The surfing spot Cannons is offshore. Then there's a channel, and the reef across the channel is Pu'u Kahuaiki. The surfing spot Bobo's is offshore. The other end of the reef is Pu'u Kahuanui, a high reef that is out of the water even at high tide. The *"iki"* and *"nui"* in these names do not refer to the size of the reef, but rather to the depth. It's more like low reef and high reef. We used to call Pu'u Kahuanui the "last chance" reef because this is where we would end up last. Then there's a small reef, Puakala, and Poholokeiki, the channel where Limahuli Stream goes into the ocean. Simeon Maka told me the name Poholokeiki sometime in the 1930s. During high tide the channel current is very swift, and with the steep sandbank close to shore, you can easily lose your footing and be swept into the channel. Across the channel is the long reef at Hā'ena State Park. *Ka'īlioiki* is the first section of the reef, and *Ka'īlionui* is the second near Kē'ē. *Ka'īlionui* monk seals were frequently seen in the area up to the 1940s.

Maniniholo is the bay at Hā'ena Beach Park. We used to *hukilau* there from July to August. The first reef east of the beach park is Waikalua, then there's the big reef Makua at Tunnels. Then there's the channel at Hā'ena Point where the windsurfers go in and out. The next reef is Kanahā, and there were always big schools of *kala* on this *'āpapa*. We used to get *piliko'a* there, too. It's a green anemone that's a relative of *'ōkole*. It lives in the small holes on the reef vacated by the *ina*. We dug them out with a butter knife, cooked them, and the texture was crisp like *pualoli*. Kahaki is the next small reef, then there's Kūpopou at Camp Naue. *Kūpopou* means that the tails of fish like *nenue* would sometimes stick up out of the water when the tide was low and the fish were feeding. The old-timers used to say, *"Poupou ta 'ōkole,"* and it means to show your rear end to someone as a sign of contempt. Using *t* for *k* was common in Hā'ena and Nā Pali, like the name Waitulu at Kalalau, where water dripped on the beach below Auwē ka Manu, the top of the trail where you paused to rest after coming up from sea level. Ka'onohi is the reef at the point on the Hanalei side of the camp, and it was good for *nenue*, too. Then there's Wainiha Kū'au, the long reef from the point to Wainiha.

This reef was getting outside the areas that we always frequented, so we just called it by one name. Kūʻau means "to wade," and to us it meant that you can easily wade to all parts of the reef.

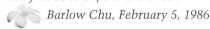 *Barlow Chu, February 5, 1986*

Haili. Rock, Hāna, Maui. Stone on the south side of Paʻiloa Bay in Waiʻānapanapa State Park that resembles two fingers forming a victory or peace sign. *Lit.,* loving memory.

Hākaʻaʻano. Fishing site, Pāpalaua, Molokaʻi. Flat, rocky peninsula on the east side of Pāpalaua Valley that is used as a fishing and camping site. Sometimes the name is extended to include the Pāpalaua shore.

Hakalau. Bay, beach, surf site, Hakalau, Hawaiʻi. Hakalau is one of the few navigable bays on the precipitous Hāmākua coast. A narrow detrital sand beach lines the head of the bay. The surf site is off the beach. The ruins of Hakalau Mill are on the shore of the bay where it was destroyed by the tsunami of 1946. *Lit.,* many [bird] perches.

Hakioawa. Bay, beach, north shore, Kahoʻolawe. Pocket beach of detrital sand at the head of a bay between two rocky points. Hakioawa has been the primary camp and ceremonial site for the Protect Kahoʻolawe ʻOhana since 1976 when members of the group first landed on Kahoʻolawe. Also known as Big Gulch. *Lit.,* breaking of [the] harbor.

Halapē. Camping site, Hawaiʻi Volcanoes National Park, Hawaiʻi. Calcareous sand beach at the head of a small cove. Keʻaʻoi Island is offshore. *Lit.,* crushed or flattened pandanus.

Hālawa. Beach, beach park, surf site, Hālawa, Molokaʻi. Hālawa is one of six coastal valleys on Molokaʻi's north shore and was formerly a fishing and commercial taro farming community. It is the only one of the valleys that is accessible by road. The tsunamis of 1946 and 1957 destroyed the taro patches and marked the end of commercial taro farming. Hālawa Beach is actually two detrital sand beaches, one on either side of the rocky point in the middle of the bay. The beach to the west of the point was called Māʻalaea and is used as an anchorage and boat launching site. The beach to the east was called Kāwili. The surf site is off the point in the center of the bay. Facilities in the beach park were built in 1968. *Lit.,* curve.

Hale. See Isaac Hale.

Hale ʻĀina. Pavilion, Keaukaha, Hawaiʻi. Abandoned structure at Kulapae in Keaukaha Beach Park that was a former social hall for the Keaukaha community. *Lit.,* eating house.

Halehaku. Bay, fishing site, point, Kaupakalua, Maui. Also known as Kakipi. *Lit.,* master's house, or overseer's house.

Haleʻiwa. 1. Beach park (15.7 acres), Haleʻiwa, Oʻahu. On the north side of Anahulu Stream. 2. Breakwater, Haleʻiwa, Oʻahu. Boulder breakwater on the seaward side of the boat harbor. 3. Channel, Haleʻiwa, Oʻahu. Natural channel off the boat harbor cut through the reef by Anahulu Stream. 4. Harbor Range Lights. Navigational lights to mark the channel into the small boat harbor. 5. Small Boat Harbor, Haleʻiwa, Oʻahu. Facilities include sixty-four berths, fifteen moorings, three ramps, and a vessel washdown area. 6. Surf center, Haleʻiwa, Oʻahu. Recreation facility in Haleʻiwa Aliʻi Beach Park. The second story of the building was added in the summer of 1999 by the Baywatch television series. Also known as the Kalili Surf Center. 7. Surf site, Haleʻiwa, Oʻahu. Off Haleʻiwa Aliʻi Beach Park. *Lit.,* home [of the] frigate bird. The *ʻiwa* is a poetic symbol for an attractive person, so the figurative meaning of the name is "home of attractive people." Haleʻiwa was originally the name of the dormitory building of the Waialua Female Seminary (1865–1882), a Protestant school built on the banks of Anahulu Stream. The name was permanently established in the area by the Haleʻiwa Hotel, a popular beach resort destination on the Oahu Railway and Land Co. train line from 1899 to 1943. When the hotel opened, the name was translated as "beautiful home."

Haleʻiwa Aliʻi. Beach park (19.3 acres), Haleʻiwa, Oʻahu. On the south side of Anahulu Stream. Haleʻiwa Aliʻi Beach Park was named after the Country Keiki Aliʻi football team, a youth team coached by Herman Soares during the 1950s. The Country Keiki Aliʻi played the Town Keiki Aliʻi in the Shriner's Football League. Prior to the development of the beach park, the country team used a portion of the site as a practice field, and the community called it Aliʻi Park. In later years when the site was developed into a beach park, "Aliʻi" was included in the name. Also known as Aliʻi Beach. *Lit.,* Haleʻiwa chiefs.

Haleʻiwa Trench. Channel, dive site, Haleʻiwa, Oʻahu. Off the west side of Haleʻiwa Aliʻi Beach Park. A 90-foot vertical drop from the shallow reef at the surf site forms the channel, or "trench."

Halekou. Fishpond, Mōkapu, Oʻahu. *Lit., kou*-wood house.

Halekūlani. Channel, Waikīkī, Oʻahu. Channel through the reef between Paradise and Number Threes surf sites that leads to the Halekūlani Hotel. Also known as Gray's Channel, Kawehewehe. *Lit.,* house befitting royalty.

Halemanō. Surf site, Kaʻalāwai, Oʻahu. The Littlejohn family has lived and surfed at Kaʻalāwai for many years. During the 1930s when Bill Littlejohn began surfing at Black Point at the east end of Kaʻalāwai Beach, he named the site Halemanō, "house [of the] shark," for the numerous sharks that he saw there. Halemanō is now commonly mispronounced "Halemanu." The surf site is off the public right-of-way on Kaikoʻo Place. Also known as Kaikoʻo.

Halemanu. Surf site, Kaʻalāwai, Oʻahu. Same as and a mispronunciation of Halemanō. *Lit.,* house [of the] birds.

Hale Mōhalu. Beach, Mākua, Oʻahu. West end of Mākua Beach. Hale Mohalu was a state institution in Pearl City, Oʻahu, for people with Hanson's Disease. It opened in 1949 and closed in 1969. Hale Mōhalu residents were taken on beach excursions to swim and bodysurf at Mākua because it was remote and used infrequently by the public on weekdays. *Lit.,* house [of] relaxation.

Hālena. Beach, camp, surf site, Hālena, Molokaʻi. Calcareous sand beach fronting the ruins of a former Boy Scout camp. George P. Cooke, the first president of Molokaʻi Ranch, was an enthusiastic scouting supporter and sponsored the construction of Camp Hālena, a cluster of small cabins and related buildings on Hālena Beach. Hālena was once noted for its gold to cream-colored beach rock that was cut into stepping-stones for footpaths and patios. The surf site is off the beach. *Lit.,* yellowish.

Haleokapuni. *Heiau,* Kawaihae, Hawaiʻi. Shrine in the ocean fronting Pelekane Beach where sharks were fed. Part of the Puʻukoholā Heiau National Park. Sharks and turtles are commonly seen here. *Lit.,* house of Kapuni. Kapuni was a high priest of the famous chief Keawe; also the name of a god.

Haleola. Spring, Kapuʻa, Hawaiʻi. Spring at which people prayed to be cured or forgiven. The ceremony included pouring water over oneself, then total immersion. *Lit.,* house [of] healing.

Hale o Lono. 1. Beach, Hale o Lono, Molokaʻi. Long, narrow calcareous sand beach to the west of the harbor. 2. Small Boat Harbor, Hale o Lono, Molokaʻi. Facilities include undesignated moorings. Construction of the harbor by Honolulu Construction and Draying Company, Ltd. (now Ameron Hawaiʻi) began in 1959 and was completed several years later. It includes an entrance channel, two breakwaters, and a turning basin. Commercial use of the harbor proved to be of marginal value due to heavy surges from seasonal high surf, and it was eventually abandoned. The harbor has been the staging area and starting line for the annual Molokaʻi to Oʻahu outrigger canoe races since 1963. Kawākiu was the site of the original start. Also known as Lono Harbor. 3. Surf site, Hale o Lono, Molokaʻi. Off the west side of the harbor. Also known as Lono's. *Lit.,* house of Lono. *Heiau* with this name for the worship of the god Lono are found on all of the islands.

89

Hale 'Opihi. Fishing site, Lā'au, Moloka'i. Low sea cliffs between Kapukuwahine and Kahalepōhaku Beaches where *'opihi* were gathered. Also known as Man-on-the-Rock, 'Opihi Road. *Lit.*, house [of] limpets.

Halepalaoa. 1. Beach, landing, Halepalaoa, Lāna'i. Narrow calcareous sand beach that was the site of a former landing for the short-lived Maunalei Sugar Plantation (1899–1901) at Keōmuku. The only evidence of the landing are a few pilings in the ocean. A narrow-gauge railroad connected the plantation to the landing. In the underbrush near the landing are the ruins of a warehouse and some remnants of the railroad, including a locomotive and its tender, a boiler, and several handcarts. 2. Monument, Halepalaoa, Lāna'i. Stone monument on Keōmuku Road south of the landing that is a memorial to the Japanese plantation workers who died at Keōmuku during the bubonic plaque of 1900. The Buddhist community on Lāna'i holds a memorial service here once a year. *Lit.*, whale house, or ivory house.

Halepōhaku. Fishing site, rock, Hā'ena, Kaua'i. Rock formation near the west end of Hā'ena Beach Park. *Lit.*, stone house.

Haleweke. Fishing site, Lā'ie, O'ahu. Section of Kokololio Beach Park where the highest sand dunes are located. *Lit.*, house [of the] goatfish.

Half Point. 1. Surf site, Hawai'i Kai, O'ahu. At the small rocky point fronting the comfort station at Sandy Beach Park. The name is a play on words to differentiate it from Full Point, a surf site farther out to sea at the edge of the reef. 2. Surf site, Hawai'i Kai, O'ahu. Approximately halfway to Portlock Point from the former Portlock Pier. Also known as Pillars, Poles.

Hāli'i. Fishing site, reef, Mālaekahana, O'ahu. Flat reef nearshore where fish congregated. *Lit.*, covered or spread.

Hāli'ilua. Spring, Kealakekua, Hawai'i. Small spring in the rocks on the shore of Ka'awaloa village in Kealakekua Bay State Historic Park. The name Hāli'ilua is etched into the rock. *Lit.*, spread twice.

Hāloa Point. Dive site, Mākena, Maui. Point that separates Po'olenalena and Palau'ea Beaches. The dive site consists of lava ridges and sand channels at 30 feet off the point. *Lit.*, long breath or long life.

Hālona. 1. Blowhole, Hawai'i Kai, O'ahu. Blowholes are narrow chimneys that connect lava terraces to sea caves or lava tubes below them. Waves rolling into the sea caves or lava tubes force a powerful rush of compressed air, spray, and whitewater through the chimneys that erupts on the terraces as spectacular fountains. Blowholes are sometimes called "spouting horns" because of the loud roaring noises created by the rushing air and water coming up the chimney. The blowhole at Hālona Point is one of Oʻahu's famous visitor attractions. 2. Cove, Hawaiʻi Kai, Oʻahu. Small cove west of the blowhole with a pocket of calcareous sand. Also known as Cockroach Bay or Gulch, From Here to Eternity Beach, Eternity Beach. 3. Point, Hawaiʻi Kai, Oʻahu. Rocky point at the west end of Sandy Beach that is a popular visitor stop for the blowhole and for viewing the island of Molokaʻi. *Lit.*, [a] lookout.

Hāmākua Poko. Point, Pāʻia, Maui. Rocky point that separates H-Poko Papa and Hoʻokipa Beach Park. Popular lookout to watch windsurfers. Also known as H-Poko Point. *Lit.*, short Hāmākua. Hāmākua is the name of two land divisions, Hāmākua Loa, "long Hāmākua," and Hāmākua Poko, "short Hāmākua."

Hāmākua Poko Papa. Beach, fishing site, Pāʻia, Maui. Small calcareous sand beach behind a reef flat to the west of Hāmākua Poko Point. Inland of the point on Holomua Road are the ruins of Hāmākua Poko Mill, constructed in 1880, and Hāmākua Poko Camp. Also known as H-Poko Papa. *Lit.*, Hāmākua Poko reef flat.

Hamburger. Rock, Keawaʻula, Oʻahu. Jagged rock in the Yokohama surf site that is exposed at low tide. If surfers wipe out on the rock and are severely lacerated, their lacerations resemble ground beef, or "hamburger."

Hammerhead Point. Dive site, Kainaliu, Hawaiʻi. One of the Red Hill dive sites. Ledge at 25 to 45 feet that drops abruptly to 100 feet. Hammerhead sharks are commonly seen here.

Hammerheads. Surf site, tow-in surf site, Mokulēʻia, Oʻahu. On the west side of Kaiaka Channel. Hammerhead sharks are commonly found in Kaiaka Bay and in the channel. Also known as Puʻuiki.

Hāmoa. Beach, surf site, Hāna, Maui. A 1,000-foot-long calcareous sand beach at the head of Mokae Cove. The surf site is a shorebreak on a sandbar. The beach lies on the shore of the land division of Hāmoa. Hotel Hāna Maui uses the backshore as a beach recreational site for its guests.

Hāna. 1. Beach park, Hāna, Maui. A 700-foot-long calcareous sand beach fronts the park between the wharf and the pilings of the former Hāna Landing. 2. Ramp and Wharf, Hāna, Maui. The 300-foot-long wharf was no longer used for interisland shipping once Hāna was connected to Kahului Harbor by road. The Hāna Highway, a 52-mile paved road, opened as a dirt road in 1927. Facilities for boaters include ten moorings, a ramp, a pier, and a vessel washdown area. *Lit.*, work or profession. The goddess Luʻukia was said to have taught tapa beating to the women of Hāna in a cave called Hāna o Lu'ukia, or the "work of Lu'ukia."

Hanaka'īlio. Beach, Kahuku, O'ahu. Calcareous sand beach between Kalaeokauna'oa and Kalaeuila Points. Also known as Big Beach, Marconi. *Lit.,* work [of] the dog.

Hanakanai'a. Bay, beach, surf site, southwest shore, Kaho'olawe. Calcareous sand beach on a small bay at the southwest point of the island. It is one of only three significant calcareous sand beaches on the island. The other two are Kanapou and Kaukaukapapa. The surf site is primarily a shorebreak that breaks on the shallow sandbar fronting the beach at Hanakanai'a Bay. During high surf, a big-wave, second-reef site forms outside the bay. The bay is an excellent anchorage during trade wind conditions. Also known as Honokanai'a, Smugglers Cove. *Lit.,* dolphin (mammal) bay. Dolphin schools are commonly seen here.

Hanaka'ō'ō. Beach park, Kā'anapali, Maui. At the southern boundary of Kā'anapali and adjacent to Hanaka'ō'ō Cemetery. The south section of Kā'anapali Beach begins here and ends at Black Rock to the north. Also known as Canoe Beach. *Lit.,* digging stick bay.

Hanakapi'ai. Beach, surf site, Nā Pali, Kaua'i. One of five beaches within Nā Pali Coast State Park. Pocket beach of calcareous sand at the mouth of Hanakapi'ai Valley fronted by a shallow sandbar. High surf during the winter erodes the beach. The surf site is a shorebreak on the sandbar. Hanakapi'ai Stream crosses the east end of the beach. At 2 miles in on the Kalalau Trail, Hanakapi'ai is one of the island's most popular day-hike destinations. *Lit.,* bay sprinkling food.

Hanakoa. Beach, Nā Pali, Kaua'i. Small pocket of calcareous sand that accretes at the base of the sea cliffs below Hanakoa Valley during the summer. *Lit.,* bay [of] *koa* trees, or bay [of] warriors.

Hanalei. 1. Bay, Hanalei, Kaua'i. Semicircle-shaped bay that is the largest on Kaua'i. A calcareous sand beach 2 miles long lines the head of the bay between the Hanalei River to the east and the Waikoko Reef to the west. Three beach parks are located on the beach: Black Pot, Hanalei Pavilion, and Wai'oli. 2. Offshore mooring, Hanalei, Kaua'i. Designated area for a hundred moorings off Hanalei Pier on a sandy bottom at a depth of approximately 35 feet. Popular summer anchorage for yachts and other large boats. 3. Pier, Hanalei, Kaua'i. The 300-foot pier at the east end of Hanalei Bay was an interisland steamer landing. The original pier was built in the 1890s and later improved with a concrete deck in the 1920s to accommodate the large quantities of rice that Hanalei farmers were shipping out of the valley. Commercial rice shipping activity ended in 1933 when California rice growers dominated the market, undercutting the price of Hawaiian rice. Since then the pier has been used as an ocean recreation facility, primarily for fishing and swimming. A surf site for beginners is on the west side of the pier. 4. River, Hanalei, Kaua'i. Hanalei River, one of the few navigable rivers in Hawai'i, is famous among Hawaiians for its native biota, including 'o'opu (goby fish), 'ōpae (shrimp), and hīhīwai (mollusks), and for providing water to the inland taro fields. The river is also popular for kayaking and outrigger canoe paddling. 5. River landing, Hanalei, Kaua'i. Boat landing on the west bank of the river adjacent to Black Pot Beach Park. Facilities include one ramp. The river mouth is normally barred by beach sand, allowing access to the ocean only for shallow-draft boats. 6. Surf site, Hanalei, Kaua'i. Off the mouth of the Hanalei River. There are three sections within the site: Impossibles (the takeoff), Flat Rock (the center), and the Bowl (the end). Also known as The Bay. *Lit.*, crescent bay.

Hanalei Pavilion. Beach park, surf site, Hanalei, Kaua'i. One of three beach parks on Hanalei Bay's 2-mile calcareous sand beach. The surf site is a shorebreak on the shallow sandbar fronting the park.

Hanaloa. Fishpond, Waipahu, O'ahu. On Waipi'o Peninsula. *Lit.*, long bay.

Hanamanioa. Light, Honua'ula, Maui. Southeast point of La Pérouse Bay. Established in 1918 to mark the southern tip of the island when lights at Kanahena and Mākena were discontinued and a 73-foot concrete tower was built on the point.

Hanamā'ulu. Beach park, Hanamā'ulu, Kaua'i. Narrow calcareous sand beach fronted by a shallow sandbar at the head of Hanamā'ulu Bay. The bay waters are normally murky from the discharge of Hanamā'ulu Stream at the south end of the beach. *Lit.*, tired [as from walking] bay.

Hananena. Beach, Kīpū Kai, Kaua'i. Calcareous sand beach between Mōlehu and Kawelikoa Points. Also known as Kīpū Kai Beach. *Lit.*, bay [of the] nena plant. *Nena* is also an alternate name for *kīpūkai* (a seaside heliotrope).

Hanapēpē. 1. Bay, beach park, Hanapēpē, Kaua'i. The beach park is at the west end of Hanapēpē Bay where it is fronted by a seawall. 2. Light, Hanapēpē, Kaua'i. Established in 1902. The light is atop a 20-foot pole. *Lit.*, crushed bay (due to landslides).

Hanauma Bay. 1. Beach, Honolulu, O'ahu. Narrow calcareous sand beach at the head of the bay. The name Hanauma Bay is used to indicate the beach as well as the bay. Residents of Hawai'i do not say Hanauma "Beach." 2. Marine life conservation district (101 acres) established in 1967. The conservation area includes the entire bay inshore of Palea and Pai'olu-'olu Points, the outer points of the bay. 3. Nature preserve. In 1998, Hanauma Bay Beach Park was renamed Hanauma Bay Nature Preserve to emphasize protecting and preserving the bay's natural resources. *Lit.*, curved bay or hand-wrestling bay.

Hanawana. Bay, fishing site, Huelo, Maui. *Lit.*, sea urchin bay.

Hanawī. Fishing site, landing, Onomea, Hawai'i. Small peninsula at the base of the sea cliffs in Onomea Bay.

Hancock Landing. Boat ramp, Hawai'i Kai, O'ahu. Private boat ramp, including a washdown area and trailer parking, on Hawai'i Kai Drive for members of the Hawai'i Kai Marina Community Association. Named for Lambreth "Handy" Hancock, Henry J. Kaiser's executive assistant during the construction of the Kaiser Hawaiian Village Hotel (now the Hilton Hawaiian Village), the Kaiser Medical Center, and the Hawai'i Kai community. The ramp was named for him when he retired in 1974 for his personal effort in establishing the administrative rules of the marina.

Haneo'o. Fishpond, Hāna, Maui. Private fishpond south of Koki Beach Park. *Lit.*, [a] strong blow.

Hanno's. Surf site, Kailua-Kona, Hawai'i. Off the Honl family home on Ali'i Drive. "Hanno's" is a mispronunciation of Honl's. Also known as Honl's.

Happy 'Ōpū. Windsurf site, Kahana, Maui. One of several westside sites that are used as starting places to make the sail to Moloka'i. A restaurant called The Happy 'Ōpū ("stomach" in Hawaiian) was on the beach here prior to the condominiums.

Hāpuna. Bay, beach, surf site, Hāpuna, Hawai'i. Flat calcareous sand beach fronted by a shallow sandbar that is the longest and widest calcareous sand beach on the island. During the summer months, the beach is 200 feet wide. A state park borders the south half of the beach, and the Hāpuna Beach Prince Hotel borders the north half. The surf site is a shorebreak on the sandbar. State law permits only bodysurfing and bodyboarding in the shorebreak. Board surfing is not allowed. Hāpuna is the island's most popular beach, with beachgoers often driving from every corner of the island on weekends and holidays. The 1.1-mile Big Island Rough Water Swim has been held here every summer since 1979. The racecourse circles the bay. *Lit.*, spring.

Hāpuna Beach. State recreation area (61.8 acres), Hāpuna, Hawai'i. Beach park at Hāpuna Beach.

Hāpuna Point. Fishing site, surf site, Hāpuna, Hawai'i. South point of Hāpuna Beach. The surf site is off the point. Also known as H Point, Kānekanaka Point.

Harbor Lefts. Surf site, Lahaina, Maui. Off the Lahaina Small Boat Harbor on the east side of the channel. The site is a left that breaks into the channel. Also known as Breakwalls.

Harbor Rights. Surf site, Lahaina, Maui. On the west side of the channel into the Lahaina Small Boat Harbor. The site is a right that breaks into the channel.

Harris Island. Ke'ehi, O'ahu. One of several small islands in Ke'ehi Lagoon on the western side of Kalihi Channel. Also known as Kahaka'aulana.

Hauanio. Point, Keaukaha, Hawai'i. Point that protects Peiwe, or Scout Island.

Hau Bush. 1. Surf site, Kekaha, Kaua'i. Big-wave, second-reef site off Davidson's Point. *Hau* trees grow on the shore here. 2. Beach, surf site, 'Ewa Beach, O'ahu. Narrow calcareous sand beach that borders Pāpipi Road between Pūpū Place and One-'ula Beach Park. Groves of *hau* trees grow along the shore here. The surf site is off the beach.

Hā'ula. Beach, Māhā'ulepū, Kaua'i. Small pocket beach of calcareous sand at the head of a large cove between Pa'o'o and Na'akea Points. A flat, rocky shelf fronts the beach and dunes up to 100 feet high line the backshore. *Lit.*, reddish.

Hauna. Fishpond, Keaukaha, Hawai'i. Fishpond within Lokowaka Fishpond. *Lit.*, fishy smell or stench.

Haunted Caves. Dive site, Honokōhau, Hawai'i. The caves were discovered on Halloween by the owners of Dive Makai and are inhabited by huge spiny pufferfish that look ghostly.

Hau'ula. Beach park (9.1 acres), Hau'ula, O'ahu. County beach park fronted by a narrow calcareous sand beach. Established in 1921, it was named after the town of Hau'ula. The *hau*, a native hibiscus *(Hibiscus tiliaceus)*, blossoms during the summer months. Its flowers are bright yellow when they open, but turn red by the time they fall to the ground. *Lit.*, red *hau* [flower].

Hauwa. Reef, Hā'ena, Kaua'i. Large reef west of Hā'ena Beach Park. The surf site on this reef is known as Cannons.

Hawai'i. Hawai'i is the largest of the eight major Hawaiian Islands (4,028 square miles). It has a population of 148,677. The highest mountain on the island is Mauna Kea, with an elevation of 13,796 feet, and the *pua lehua (Metrosideros polymorpha)* is the emblem of the island. Hawai'i's nickname is the Orchid Isle; it is also called the Big Island because it is twice the combined size of the other seven islands. The state takes its name from this island.

Hawaiian Archipelago. Chain of islands in the central Pacific Ocean that includes the eight major Hawaiian Islands: Hawai'i, Maui, Moloka'i, Lāna'i, Kaho'olawe, O'ahu, Kaua'i, and Ni'ihau. Each island is the summit of a mountain rising from the ocean floor. Beyond the eight major islands, the archipelago includes the islands and associated reefs and banks beyond Ni'ihau that are known as the Northwestern Hawaiian Islands.

Hawaiian Beaches. Park (3.6 acres), Hawaiian Beaches, Hawai'i. On the rocky shore at the seaward end of Kahakai Drive. The park is owned and maintained by the Hawaiian Beaches homeowners association.

Hawaiian Deep. Extensive moatlike depressions that form large-scale structural features on the ocean floor around the Hawaiian Islands. Six sections of the Hawaiian Deep are known individually by the names of the nearest island, including the Kaua'i Deep, O'ahu Deep, Maui Deep, Lāna'i Deep, Kaho'olawe Deep, and Hawai'i Deep. Northwest of Maui and Hawai'i, it reaches depths of nearly 18,000 feet.

Hawaiian Electric. Beach park. Wai'anae, O'ahu. Public park developed and maintained by the Hawaiian Electric Company, which owns and operates the Kahe Point Power Plant across the highway from the park. Land for the park and the power plant were acquired by the state in 1960. Also known as Electric Beach.

Hawaiian Islands Humpback Whale National Marine Sanctuary. The National Oceanic and Atmospheric Administration (NOAA) in the U.S. Department of Commerce manages national marine sanctuaries to maintain their natural beauty and diversity. The warm, shallow waters surrounding the main Hawaiian Islands constitute one of the world's most important humpback whale habitats and one of the only places in the United States where humpbacks reproduce. Scientists estimate that two-thirds of the entire North Pacific humpback whale population (approximately two to three thousand whales) migrate to Hawaiian waters to engage in breeding, calving, and nursing activities. The continued protection of humpback whales and their habitats is crucial to the long-term recovery of this endangered species. Congress, in consultation with the State of Hawai'i, recognized the importance of Hawai'i's nearshore waters to humpbacks by designating the Hawaiian Islands Humpback Whale National Marine Sanctuary on November 4, 1992. The sanctuary includes the area from the high water mark to the 100-fathom (600-foot) isobath around the islands of Maui, Molokai, and Lanai, including Penguin Bank, the Pailolo Channel, and a small area off Kīlauea Point, Kaua'i. The waters around Kaho'olawe are not included.

Hawaiian Islands National Wildlife Refuge. Wildlife refuge in Region 1, the Pacific Region of the U.S. Fish and Wildlife Service, Department of the Interior. The refuge includes the small islands and associated reefs and banks that are called the Northwestern Hawaiian Islands and more than 250,000 acres of atoll lagoons. The refuge protects millions of seabirds and the endangered Hawaiian monk seal. Landing is prohibited on all of the islands without a permit. The only island in the refuge visible from the main Hawaiian Islands is Ka'ula, 22 miles southwest of Ni'ihau.

Hawaiian Reef. Dive site, Mākena, Maui. Named by Ed Robinson of Ed Robinson's Diving Adventures for the wide variety of Hawaiian marine life found here.

Hawai'i Institute of Marine Biology. Research site, Kāne'ohe, O'ahu. An institute of the University of Hawai'i, HIMB's field research facilities are on Coconut Island and include laboratories, classrooms, administrative facilities, boat moorings, tanks, housing, and support facilities. Fields of research at Coconut Island include fish biology, coral reef research, large marine animal research, pelagic fish research, fisheries biology, aquaculture, marine ecology, environmental physiology, and developmental biology. HIMB was established on the island in 1947 when the Edwin Pauley family invited the University of Hawai'i to use an old army building as a field station.

Hawai'i Kai. 1. Boat ramp, Hawai'i Kai, O'ahu. Also known as Maunalua Bay Boat Ramp. 2. Marina, Hawai'i Kai, O'ahu. Private marina with 26 miles of waterways, inland of Kalaniana'ole Highway and administered by the Hawai'i Kai Marina Community Association. *Lit.*, Hawai'i [by the] sea. In 1959, Henry J. Kaiser and his planning staff were discussing various names for the community that he proposed to build in east Honolulu. They wanted a name that would have meaning, public appeal, be easily remembered, easily pronounced, and yet still sound Hawaiian. Kaiser himself came up with the name Hawai'i Kai. It sounds Hawaiian. It has meaning, since *kai* means "sea" in Hawaiian, and it can be interpreted as "Hawai'i by the sea." It is easy to pronounce and remember—and *kai* is also the first syllable of Kaiser, so there was a personal connection, too. Hawai'i Kai was selected.

Hawai'i Marine Laboratory Refuge. Reef, Kāne'ohe, O'ahu. A 64-acre reef that surrounds Coconut Island in Kāne'ohe Bay. The refuge designation extends 25 feet beyond the outer edges of the reef and prohibits all consumptive activities, except those by officers, faculty, students, and employees of the University of Hawai'i and licensees of the University of Hawai'i Board of Regents.

Hawai'i Maritime Center. Visitor site, Honolulu, O'ahu. Maritime center and museum at Pier 7 in Honolulu Harbor housed in a building called the Kalākaua Boat House. The center opened in 1988 and includes the museum ship *Falls of Clyde.*

Hawai'i State Seabird Sanctuary. Small state-owned islands and rocks off the eight major islands that have been established as wildlife sanctuaries for the conservation, management, and protection of seabirds. Many seabirds are ground nesters, making them easy prey for introduced animals, including dogs, cats, rats, and mongooses. These small islands offer some of the last nesting areas that are free from predators. Landing without a permit from the Department of Land and Natural Resources is prohibited on most of the islands and rocks in the sanctuary.

Hawai'i Tropical Botanical Garden. Fishing site, park, Onomea, Hawai'i. A 20-acre private park on the southwestern shore of Onomea Bay. Dan Lutkenhouse, a former California trucking and warehousing entrepreneur, purchased the property in 1978 and opened it as a botanical garden in August 1984. The garden features tropical plant and tree species from all over the world, specializing in palms, heliconia, and bromeliads. The fishing site is on the park's rocky shore.

Hawai'i Volcanoes National Park. Park (200,000 acres), Kīlauea, Hawai'i. Dedicated in 1916 as Hawai'i's first and the nation's eleventh national park. The park includes the shield volcanoes of Mauna Loa and Kīlauea and nearly 30 miles of undeveloped coast. Coastal campsites are located at Kamoamoa, 'Āpua, Keauhou, Halapē, and Ka'aha.

Hawai'i Yacht Club. Recreation site, Waikīkī, O'ahu. Private facility in the Ala Wai Small Boat Harbor that includes twenty-six slips and four visitor slips.

Hāwea. Point light, Hāwea, Maui. A 16-foot tower built 75 feet above sea level in 1912 on the south point of Oneloa Beach. Name of a legendary drum.

Hāwīni. Bay, fishing site, landing, Huelo, Maui. Small bay west of Waipi'o Bay and a former landing site.

Haycraft. Park, Mā'alaea, Maui. Small community-developed beach park at the northeast end of Mā'alaea village. The park was cleared and landscaped by Kenny Haycraft and his brother-in-law Vern Johnson, who adopted the site in 1985 as part of the county's Adopt-a-Park program.

Haywood's Lot. Surf site, Mā'alaea, Maui. Off the swimming pool of the Island Sands condominium in Mā'alaea Village. The Fred Haywood family was the former owner of the condominium property when it was undeveloped and still a "lot."

Healing Stones. Historic site, Waikīkī, O'ahu. Same as the Kapaemāhū Stones.

Heʻeia. 1. Bay, beach, dive site, surf site, Keauhou, Hawaiʻi. Small bay on the north side of Keauhou Bay with a pocket beach of pebbles and black sand. The dive and surf sites are off the bay. Heʻeia and its surfing waves are described in the song "Heʻeia," written by J. Kalahiki and published by Charles E. King in his book of Hawaiian songs. Also known as Walker Bay. 2. Fishpond, state park (19 acres), Heʻeia, Oʻahu. The park was acquired in 1977 and is on Keʻalohi Point in Kāneʻohe Bay. The 88-acre fishpond is adjacent to the park. *Lit.*, surfed, or washed [out to sea], or swept away.

Heʻeia Kea. Small boat harbor, Heʻeia, Oʻahu. Facilities include twenty-two berths, fifty-four moorings, three ramps, anchorage by permit, and a vessel washdown area. *Lit.*, white Heʻeia. The shore of Heʻeia is divided into two sections, Heʻeia Kea, or white Heʻeia, and Heʻeia Uli, or black Heʻeia. Heʻeia Kea had a white calcareous sand beach, and Heʻeia Uli a black detrital sand beach.

Heleloa. Beach, Mōkapu, Oʻahu. Calcareous sand beach and dunes that border the golf course. Also known as North Beach. *Lit.*, travels far.

Helicopters. Surf site, Poʻipū, Kauaʻi. An old helipad is inshore of the site. Also known as Cow's Head.

Hellcat. Dive site, Kīhei, Maui. Wreck of a World War II F-6-F Hellcat airplane that lies upside-down at 32 feet.

Helm's. Bay, windsurf site, Mokulēʻia, Oʻahu. David Helms, an avid windsurfer, has been a beachfront homeowner here since 1978. The bay off his home is a windsurf site in Mokulēʻia, especially when high surf precludes windsurfing at other sites. Also known as Akua House, Kawaihāpai Bay.

HH Buoy. Fish aggregating device, Pearl Harbor, Oʻahu. Buoy anchored at approximately 700 fathoms. Landmarks: Diamond Head Light, Honolulu Harbor Buoy Light, Barbers Point Light.

Hickam. 1. Beach park, Hickam Air Force Base, Oʻahu. Man-made calcareous sand beach between Kumumau Canal and the seawall fronting the restaurant. The approximately 500-foot-long beach was constructed in 1965 with the assistance of explosive ordinance detail personnel from the U.S. Marine Corps and the Hickam civil engineers. 2. Harbor, Hickam Air Force Base, Oʻahu. Department of Defense facility that includes sixteen slips, dry storage for sixty trailered boats, a ramp, a vessel washdown area, and fifteen offshore moorings. During the early 1940s, several seaplane runways were dredged in Keʻehi Lagoon. Part of this project included dredging a channel from ʻĀhua Point to Fort Kamehameha. The western remnant of that channel is Hickam Harbor. 3. Outdoor recreational facility, Hickam Air Force Base, Oʻahu. Recreation complex on the shore between the Reef Runway of the Honolulu International Airport and Fort Kamehameha Housing. The facility includes two beach parks, Honeymoon and Hickam Beach Parks, a restaurant, a small boat harbor, a mooring area, and a water-ski area. 4. Water-skiing site, Hickam Air Force Base, Oʻahu. Along with Keʻehi Lagoon, one of the two primary water-skiing sites on Oʻahu. 5. Wetland management area, Hickam Air Force Base, Oʻahu. On the shore between Hickam Harbor and Fort Kamehameha housing. The primary vegetation in the wetland is mangrove and pickleweed, two salt-tolerant species. Recreational uses of the wetland are restricted to hiking on the trails through it. Hickam Air Force Base was named for Lt. Colonel Horace M. Hickam, who was killed in an airplane accident at Fort Crockett, Texas in 1934.

Hickam Harbor Channel. Hickam Air Force Base, Oʻahu. Prior to the construction of the Reef Runway in the 1970s, boaters from Hickam Harbor used Kalihi Channel to reach the open ocean. When the Reef Runway blocked that access, a new channel, Hickam Harbor Channel, was dredged through ʻĀhua Reef directly off the harbor.

Hidden Pinnacle. Dive site, Kahakuloa, Maui. Rock formation that rises from 120 feet to the surface of the ocean.

Hidden Pinnacles. Dive site, Lahaina Pali, Maui.

Hideaway. Beach, Princeville, Kauaʻi. Below the Pali Ke Kua condominiums. Named after Hideaways, the surf site offshore. Also known as Pali Ke Kua Beach.

Hideaways. Snorkeling site, surf site, Princeville, Kauaʻi. Below the Pali Ke Kua condominiums. First surfed in the early 1960s by Nick Beck, Pat Cockett, and several other Kauaʻi residents. Cockett was a novice musician who had just learned to play the song "Hernando's Hideaway" on his guitar. During the surf session, all of them kept singing the song as they surfed. When they went in, Beck suggested they call the site "Hideaways." At that time Princeville was undeveloped, so the name was appropriate for this secret spot, hidden from public view. The snorkeling site is on the same reef as the surf site.

 moʻolelo

Hideaways is the break that runs along the reef below Pali Ke Kua at Princeville. We started surfing there when all the land above it was pastureland for Princeville Ranch. To get to it by land was really a big deal—getting keys, going through many gates— a four-wheel drive was a must. So the only way for us was a paddle from the Hanalei River mouth. I remember one day in the early sixties when I was at our beach house at Waikoko, and some of the kids came over to visit and surf the break in front of the house. It was David Goodale, his brother Ricky, Paul Lawrence, and Pat Cockett. Pat was just learning to play the guitar, and the one big new song that he could pluck was "Hernando's Hideaway." Anyway, that day was one of those perfect, glassy *kona* wind days, and every break had some waves. I could look across from our place at Waikoko and see the lines around the point off Princeville Ranch. So we packed up the boards and headed for the pier. We paddled and surfed every break until I led those kids around the point to a break that they had never surfed before. They were so stoked, and it was as good as I have ever surfed it. All the time we were surfing, I kept singing the song from Pat Cockett's guitar theme song, "Hernando's Hideaway." When we came back in, I told them not to tell anyone where I took them. I said, "Let's just say we went to Hideaways," and it is still Hideaways today. My personal name for it before that was Number Threes, because the wave reminded me of Number Threes in Waikīkī.

 Nick Beck, December 26, 1998

High Rock. 1. Rock formation, Kalaupapa, Moloka'i. Large rock formation near Kāhili Beach. 2. Fishing site, Hawai'i Kai, O'ahu. Near the breakwater at the west end of the Makapu'u sea cliffs. A large rock formation on the ledge here marks the fishing site. 3. Fishing site, point, rock formation, Kahuku, O'ahu. Large limestone rock south of Kahuku Point that is the highest rock formation on the Kahuku shore between the Turtle Bay Hilton Hotel and the Kahuku Golf Course. Also known as Kalaeuila.

Hikauhi. Fishpond, Kaunakakai, Moloka'i. Name of the daughter of Chief Ho'olehua.

Hikiau. *Heiau*, surf site, Nāpo'opo'o, Hawai'i. Shrine in Nāpo-'opo'o Beach Park on the south shore of Kealakekua Bay that was built by Kalaniopu'u. The name is related to the star Hiki-aumoana, or "Hiki that travels by the sea." This is the shrine where Captain James Cook was received by the Hawaiians and honored as the god Lono. Cook was on his third expedition into the Pacific and first anchored in Kealakekua Bay in January 1779. His expedition left the bay and sailed north, but a damaged mast soon forced their return to Kealakekua Bay, where Cook was killed in February 1779 at Ka'awaloa on the north shore of the bay. The surf site is a shorebreak on a shallow sandbar fronting the boulder beach at the base of the *heiau*. Also known as Ins and Outs. *Lit.*, moving current.

Hilo. 1. Bay, breakwater, Hilo, Hawai'i. Construction of the Hilo Breakwater across Hilo Bay was undertaken in three sections, which were completed respectively in 1910, 1911, and 1929. The third section extended the breakwater to its present length of 10,070 feet, or 1.9 miles. **2. Harbor, Hilo, Hawai'i.** Hilo Harbor was created by building the Hilo Breakwater seaward of Kūhiō Bay, a large, natural deepwater gap in the fringing reef at Waiākea, and then by enlarging the gap to form the harbor basin. A deepwater channel was dredged into the bay in 1914, and from 1925 to 1930 additional dredging operations enlarged the bay to form the present harbor basin. Piers 1, 2, and 3 were built during this period. Hilo Harbor is one of the Big Island's two deep-draft harbors; the other is Kawaihae Harbor. **3. Harbor range lights, Hilo, Hawai'i.** Navigational aids for boats entering the harbor. Name of the first night of the new moon; also a legendary navigator.

Hilo Bayfront. Park, fishing site, Hilo, Hawai'i. On the shore, or "bayfront," of Hilo Bay between the Wailuku and Wailoa Rivers and lined by a detrital black sand beach. The park is the primary outrigger canoe training and racing site in Hilo. Shore casting is a popular activity on the beach.

Hilton Hawaiian Village. Pier, Waikīkī, O'ahu. At the east end of the Hilton Hawaiian Village. The Hilton Hawaiian Village Pier is the only pier on Waikīkī Beach, making it a highly desirable site for commercial tour boat operations, its primary activity.

Hilton's. Surf site, windsurf site, Kāhala, O'ahu. Off the Kāhala Mandarin Oriental Hotel. The hotel was known as the Kāhala Hilton Hotel from 1964 to 1996. In 1996 it closed for renovations and reopened in 1998 as the Kāhala Mandarin Oriental Hotel, but the surf site is still known as Hilton's. Also known as Kāhala.

 mo'olelo

My gang started surfing **Hilton's** in the late seventies and surfed there regularly into the early nineties. Some people call it Kāhala's, but all the regulars call it Hilton's, even though the hotel is now known as the Kāhala Mandarin. It was strange because we rarely ever paddled out from the beach park. We parked our cars next to the third hole, hopped the rock wall and, holding our boards, sprinted across the golf course. Sometimes it was treacherous. If you decided to cut across the golf course on a busy weekend, you'd have to strategically sprint from tree to tree without getting bombarded by golf balls. We would wait until the last person in the foursome hit and then run like the wind to the next fairway. It must have looked like something out of *Mission Impossible* or a Bugs Bunny cartoon. Sometimes it would take us twenty minutes to cross three holes. It's amazing that we never once got yelled at or reprimanded.

There is a deep channel right in front of the hotel. On the Koko Head side of the channel is a spot called Terminal's. This is for madmen only—big and nasty. Breaks right on the reef. If you get this spot on just the right day—which is about once every decade—it is fun. When you take off, you can only go right and the face of the wave seems to stretch all the way down to Koko Head. This spot is for those who are either desperate or sick pups. The spot where we surfed was just Diamond Head of the channel. The right was big, steep, and broke quickly—no time for games. The left was just the opposite—clean, hollow, and just prime for "shredding." We would surf out here in all kinds of conditions and never complained—windy and mushy, 1-foot mush to 8-foot closeout sets. We all knew each other, and we always welcomed newcomers, pleading with them not to tell anyone about this spot. We'd surf for hours, talking story and cheering each other on. We actually looked forward to it being crowded so we could rip one another about being "chicken" for not charging a late takeoff or a "make-a" wipeout. There were never any hassles in the water. These were truly soul sessions. We knew Hilton's wasn't a great spot, but it was our spot.

 Robert Dodge Jr., November 5, 1998

Hilton Waikoloa Village Lagoon. Beach, South Kohala, Hawai'i. Private, calcareous sand beach that was constructed on the shore of a large saltwater lagoon in the Hilton Waikoloa Village in 1988. A smaller lagoon adjacent to it, the Dolphin Lagoon, houses Atlantic bottlenose dolphins.

Himalayas. Surf site, Hale'iwa, O'ahu. Second-reef, big-wave break. During the late 1950s, veteran big-wave surfers Wally Froiseth and John Kelly drove to Waimea to go surfing. The surf was so big, however, that the sets at Waimea were closing out the entire bay. They drove back to Laniākea and noticed that on the west side of the channel at Laniākea there were huge but makable waves. They paddled out and surfed for several hours. When they came in, they believed that they had surfed the biggest waves in the world, so they named the site for the highest mountain range in the world, the Himalaya Mountains.

Hoaloha. Park, Kahului, Maui. Beach park on the shore of Kahului Harbor that was developed, landscaped, and named under the guidance of Helen Toms (1910–1990). In 1970, as the charter president of the newly formed Soroptimist Club, Toms suggested to the members that the club improve the site as a community service project. They agreed, and the park was opened on Kamehameha Day, June 11, 1971. *Hoaloha* means "friends" and was chosen to recognize the united efforts of the community to create the park. *Lit.*, beloved companion.

 moʻolelo

When the Soroptimist Club was first formed, I was the charter president. At that time the land next to the Hukilau was being used as a dump, and I was tired of seeing a dump in the middle of Kahului, so I suggested that we clean up the area as a club project. The club agreed and enlisted the help of many other community organizations and private companies. The project was done with the blessing of A&B, the landowners, and began in February 1971. It was finished by Kamehameha Day, June 11, 1977, when the park was blessed and dedicated. *Hoaloha* means "friends," and we chose the name to recognize the community spirit and togetherness that went into the park's completion by all of the central Maui businesses and service organizations.

Helen Toms, February 11, 1978

Hoalua. Bay, fishing site, landing, Huelo, Maui. Small bay that was a former canoe landing.

Hobron. Point, Kahului, Maui. Site of Pier 1 in Kahului Harbor. Named after Captain Thomas Hobron, a sea captain who built the Kingdom of Hawaiʻi's first railroad in 1880 to improve transportation between Kahului Harbor and Maui's expanding sugar plantations.

HO Buoy. Fish aggregating device, Hoʻolawa Point, Maui. Buoy anchored at approximately 550 fathoms. Landmarks: Paʻuwela Point Light, Keʻanae Point, Pukaulua Point.

Hōkūloa. 1. Church, Puakō, Hawaiʻi. On the shore of Puakō. One of fourteen churches built by the Reverend Lorenzo Lyons, it was dedicated on March 21, 1859. Lyons was a noted Hawaiian linguist and composed many songs before his death in 1886. "Hawaiʻi Aloha," his most famous composition, was rediscovered during activist movements in the 1970s and has become the unofficial state anthem. 2. Church, Punaluʻu, Hawaiʻi. On a hill overlooking Punaluʻu Beach. Memorial chapel for Henry Opukahaia (1792–1818), the Hawaiian whose conversion to Christianity in Connecticut was in part responsible for the arrival of the first Christian missionaries in Hawaiʻi in 1820. Constructed by the Congregational Christian Churches of Hawaiʻi and completed on April 20, 1957. *Lit.*, morning star or Venus. Hōkūloa, or Hokuao as it is alternately known, is the morning star, which is actually the planet Venus seen in the morning. It has long been associated with the American

Protestant Mission in Hawai'i and was the name of their ship that served Micronesia.

Hole in the Head. Surf site, 'Alaeloa, Maui. At the north end of 'Alaeloa Bay. Waves here break over several shallow shelves that have been the cause of many injuries, or "holes in the head."

Hole in the Rock. Arch, Hanauma Bay, O'ahu. Naturally eroded hole or arch in a rock formation on the south terrace of the bay.

Holoholokai. Beach park, Puakō, Hawai'i. On the shore of Pauoa Bay where it adjoins the Puakō Petroglyph Archaeological Park. Dedicated in 1991. *Lit.,* [a] beach outing.

Hōlualoa. Bay, Kailua-Kona, Hawai'i. Bay with a rocky shore on Ali'i Drive. The surf site Lyman's is located at the south end of the bay at Kamoa Point. *Lit.,* long sled course.

Homelani. Surf site, Mokulē'ia, O'ahu. Off the Salvation Army's Camp Homelani on Crozier Drive. Also known as Camp Homelani, Glass Doors, Salvation Army. *Lit.,* heavenly home.

Hōnaunau. Bay, ramp, dive site, snorkeling site, Hōnaunau, Hawai'i. Pu'uhonua o Hōnaunau National Historic Park occupies the south end of Hōnaunau Bay. The one-lane boat ramp, dive site, and snorkeling site are at Kapuwai at the north end of the bay.

Honeymoon. 1. Beach, Kalalau, Kaua'i. Narrow calcareous sand beach at the foot of the sea cliffs to the east of Kalalau Valley. Named for its isolated location away from the rest of the beachgoers at Kalalau. 2. Beach park, Hickam Air Force Base, O'ahu. Small, man-made calcareous sand beach approximately 150 feet long and picnic area on the shore of Hickam Harbor adjacent to the Reef Runway. Its use is by permit only and primarily by organized groups. Named because of its isolated location away from the rest of the beachgoers at Hickam Beach Park.

Honl's. Surf site, Kailua-Kona, Hawai'i. Surf site on Ali'i Drive that is off the Honl family home. Also known as Hanno's.

Honoipu. Bay, landing, Kohala, Hawai'i. Small bay approximately 4 miles southwest of 'Upolu Point that served as a port for the Hāwī Plantation, a sugar plantation that was established in 1881 by Robert Hind. Ruins of the landing still stand on the bluff above the bay. During World War II, the federal government established a transmitting station at Honoipu that is now managed by the Coast Guard. *Lit.,* gourd bay.

Honoka'ā Landing. Fishing site, Hāmākua, Hawai'i. Remnants of the former interisland steamer landing are at the base of the sea cliffs. *Lit.,* cavern or sea cave.

Honoka'āpe. 1. Beach, Mauna Lani, Hawai'i. Also known as Honoka'ope. 2. Bay, Kōloa, Kaua'i. Also known as Kōloa Landing. Perhaps literally, headstrong bay.

Honokahua. 1. Bay, Honokahua, Maui. One of six famous West Maui bays whose names begin with the word *hono*, or bay. Collectively they are known as Nā Honoapi'ilani, the "bays acquired by Pi'ilani" (a chief). Honoapi'ilani is also the name of the West Maui coastal highway that connects the six bays. 2. Beach, Honokahua, Maui. Calcareous sand beach backed by vegetated dunes that fronts Fleming Beach Park.

Honokanai'a. Bay, beach, surf site, southwest shore, Kaho-'olawe. Calcareous sand beach on a small bay at the southwest point of the island. The surf site is primarily a shorebreak on a shallow sandbar, but a big-wave, second-reef site also forms offshore during large south swells. Also known as Hanakanai'a, Smugglers Cove. *Lit.,* dolphin (mammal) bay. Dolphin schools are common here.

Honokāne. Bay, beach, valley, North Kohala, Hawai'i. Same as Honokāne Nui. *Lit.,* (the god) Kāne's bay.

Honokāne Iki. Bay, beach, landing, surf site, valley, North Kohala, Hawai'i. Honokāne Iki Valley is one of seven isolated coastal valleys on the north side of Kohala Mountain. The small black sand beach at the head of the bay is detrital material eroded and transported to the shore by Honokāne Iki Stream. The surf site is a shorebreak on the shallow sandbar fronting the beach and is primarily for bodysurfing and bodyboarding. The lower valley behind the beach was the former home of Bill Sproat, the superintendent of the Kohala Ditch from 1928 to 1968. Material and equipment for maintenance of the ditch were landed on the east side of the bay with a boom rig. *Lit.,* small Honokāne.

 mo'olelo

I was born on February 12, 1903, in Mahiki on the Honoka'a side of Waimea. My mother's name was Clara Kalehua Ramon. Her father was a Spaniard who spoke English and Hawaiian, and her mother was a Hawaiian born in Pololū. My mother went to school at the Kohala Seminary and later became the schoolteacher in Pololū. There was still a large farming community in the valley when she taught school. During the summer months, she would go to Honolulu and this is how she met my father. After they got married, they moved to the Big Island.

About 1915 my father became the superintendent of the Kohala Ditch Trail. We had a beach home in **Honokāne Iki,** so we moved there in 1917. When I took over as superintendent from my father in 1928, I lived there with my own family. As the kids got older, though, they had to go to school, so we had to send them out of the valley. After a while, we felt we weren't spending enough time as a family, so we left the valley in 1938. I continued *as superintendent of the ditch until I retired in 1968, and we still have the lease at Honokāne Iki.*

There are seven valleys from Waipi'o to Pololū that front the ocean. All of them supported self-sufficient farming communities until the Kohala Ditch was completed in 1906. After the ditch was put in, only a few people lived permanently in the smaller valleys. The ditch cut down the water supply and people moved away when they couldn't irrigate their taro and other crops. The Keawes lived at Laupāhoehoe Nui at the base of the cliffs between Honopue and Waimanu. They were able to grow taro there, and I visited them with my mother about 1917. Kahikina and his nephew Kahele lived in a lauhala house on the small plateau outside of Honopue. They layered the leaves like shingles with the big ends down. The house looked like a chicken and was very watertight. We called Kahikina "Wawae 'Ekake" because he only had the rear half of each foot. But even with his half-feet, he was very agile, even on the shoreline boulders. Eventually, he moved out to live with other members of his family.

 William Kaneakala Sproat, August 21, 1981

Honokāne Nui. Bay, beach, valley, North Kohala, Hawai'i. Honokāne Nui Valley is one of seven isolated coastal valleys on the north side of Kohala Mountain. A small pocket of black sand lies behind the boulder beach that fronts the valley. Ironwood trees are the primary shoreline vegetation. Larger deposits of black sand front the boulder beach on the ocean bottom. The black sand is material eroded and transported to the shore by Honokāne Nui Stream. Also known as Honokāne. *Lit.*, large Honokāne.

Honoka'ope. Bay, beach, dive site, Mauna Lani, Hawai'i. Calcareous sand and lava fragment beach in a bay at the southern end of the Mauna Lani resort. Sand dunes extend inland from the backshore across an adjoining lava flow. The dive site is off the beach. Also known as Honoka'ape. *Lit.*, yellow mother-of-pearl bay.

Honoke'a. Bay, beach, valley, North Kohala, Hawai'i. Honoke'a Valley is one of seven isolated coastal valleys on the north side of Kohala Mountain. Small deposits of black sand lie behind the boulder beach that fronts the valley. Larger deposits of black sand front the boulder beach on the ocean bottom. The black sand is material eroded and transported to the shore by Honoke'a Stream. The valley marks the eastern edge of the district of Kohala. Three islands lie offshore: Pa'alaea, Paoakalani, and Mokupuku. They are also known collectively as Nāmoku, "the islands." *Lit.*, volcanic rock bay.

107

Honokeana. 1. Bay, Honokeana, Maui. One of six famous West Maui bays whose names begin with the word *hono*, or bay. Collectively they are known as Nā Honoapi'ilani, the "bays acquired by Pi'ilani" (a chief). Honoapi'ilani is also the name of the West Maui coastal highway that connects the six bays. 2. Beach, Honokeana, Maui. Small cobblestone and calcareous sand beach at the head of the bay. Also known as Ka'eleki'i. *Lit.*, cave bay.

Honokoa. 1. Bay, dive site, Kawaihae, Hawai'i. Popular scuba dive tour destination in a small bay north of Kawaihae Harbor. 2. Bay, beach, northwest shore, Kaho'olawe. The bay falls within the coastal boundaries of the *'ili*, or land division, of Honokoa. A deep, wide channel through the center of the bay ends just off the beach. In December 1875, King David Kalākaua visited Kaho'olawe, accompanied among others by a reporter from the Hawaiian language newspaper *Ka Lahui Hawai'i*. The article recounting the events of the visit states: "At 4:30 a.m. the steamer left Lahaina bearing to the east slightly south on Kaho'olawe where there is a harbor; and at 7:00 a.m. we entered the harbor of Honokoa, which is near the famous cape to the south, Kealaikahiki." The article mentions that a small Hawaiian community occupied the bay. A detrital sand beach lines the head of the bay. *Lit.*, bay [of] *koa* trees or bay [of] warriors.

Honokōhau. 1. Bay, beach, surf site, Honokōhau, Hawai'i. Long calcareous sand and lava fragment beach on the shore of the bay. The beach fronts part of the Kaloko-Honokōhau National Historical Park. The surf site is off the beach. 2. Small boat harbor, Honokōhau, Hawai'i. The original harbor was completed in 1970 and an expansion project was completed in 1980. Facilities include 262 moorings, 4 ramps, a pier, vessel washdown area, fuel facility, and harbor office. 3. Bay, dive site, surf site, Honokōhau, Maui. One of six famous West Maui bays whose names begin with the word *hono*, or bay. Collectively they are known as Nā Honoapi'ilani, "the bays acquired by Pi'ilani" (a chief). Honoapi'ilani is also the name of the West Maui coastal highway that connects the six bays. The dive and surf sites are in the bay. *Lit.*, bay drawing dew.

Honokōhau Burial Site. Historic site, Honokōhau, Maui. Precontact burial site in the sand dunes above the south end of end of Honokōhau Beach.

Honokowai. 1. Bay, beach park, Honokowai, Maui. One of six famous West Maui bays whose names begin with the word *hono*, or bay. Collectively they are known as Nā Honoapi'ilani, "the bays acquired by Pi'ilani" (a chief). Honoapi'ilani is also the name of the West Maui coastal highway that connects the six bays. A rocky shelf with small pockets of calcareous sand fronts the beach park.

Honokua. Lava flow, Honokua, Hawai'i. One of three lava flows from an eruption in the southwest rift zone of Mauna Kea that began on June 1, 1950. Each of the flows reached the ocean, creating small pockets on black sand on a coast of sea cliffs. Also known as First Flow.

Honoli'i. Bay, beach park, surf site, Hilo, Hawai'i. Detrital sand and pebble beach on the south side of Honoli'i Stream. The surf site is off the beach and one of the most popular sites on the Hilo side of the island. The beach park was dedicated in 1970. *Lit.,* small weave [of a fishnet].

 mo'olelo

I was raised in Wainaku but spent a lot of time in **Honoli'i** with my family there. We're related to the Kapahua family who lived close to the beach. The houses in the village went from the beach back under the bridge and across the river. The canoes were kept by the Kapahua's place, and that property had a spring that always had water. When there were droughts and the river dried up, everyone got their water from the spring.

The fishermen went into Hilo Bay, but they also fished in the river for *'ōpae* and *'o'opu nāwao* and gathered *wī*. Honoli'i was also known for its *limu 'ele'ele. Hō'i'o* and *'āweu* taro grew up *mauka.* The taro leaves were excellent for cooking. The community was self-sufficient and lived off the land, the river, and the sea. Before World War II, though, the young people started leaving for the big cities. They wanted more than to just subsist. Then the 1946 tidal wave wiped everyone out and broke up the community.

Elizabeth Beck, June 29, 1982

I was born and raised at Honoli'i, and Honoli'i does not mean "small harbor." For this name, *hono* means to weave like a net or a hat or to patch. *Li'i* means small, so the name means "small weave or small patch." 'Ili'ili Hele o Honoli'i is a famous name of Honoli'i's sands. It means the "traveling sands of Honoli'i." The *'ili'ili,* the sand there, disappears after heavy flooding in the river and leaves only boulders on the shore, but it always returns. There are many strange stories of Honoli'i, and many fishermen get spooked. *Ka 'oi'o* come through on the old trail, and where the *kamani* tree is on the outside point is a *kolohe* place, but Honoli'i was good for *ulua,* mullet, and *āholehole.* The Hawaiians that lived at Honoli'i moved out before World War II, and after the war only a few families remained.

 Lillian Paauhau, July 20, 1982

Honolua. 1. Bay, Honolua, Maui. One of six famous West Maui bays whose names begin with the word *hono*, or bay. Collectively they are known as Nā Honoapi'ilani, "the bays acquired by Pi'ilani" (a chief). Honoapi'ilani is also the name of the West Maui coastal highway that connects the six bays. On May 1, 1976, the first voyage of the double-hulled Hawaiian voyaging canoe *Hokule'a* began here, generating a Pacific-wide renaissance in double-hulled canoe construction and sailing. 2. Dive site, Honolua, Maui. Several dive sites are located within the bay. 3. Ramp, Honolua, Maui. Remnant of a former boat ramp at the head of the bay. 4. Surf site, Honolua, Maui. On the north point of the bay it is one of the best winter surf sites in Hawai'i. Also known as The Bay. *Lit.*, two bays or twin bays.

mo'olelo

My mother, Lucy Kuaana, and Richard Cooper Searle Jr. were married at Honolua July 30, 1905. This was my mother's second marriage, and from then on I was Lucy Kailipakalua Searle. We lived at Honolua, where Richard Cooper Searle Sr. was the first manager of Honolua Ranch from 1892 to 1912. I knew him as Grampa Searle, and he embraced me as his own grandchild. When Grampa Searle retired in 1912, David Fleming replaced him as the ranch manager and moved into the main ranch house. Fleming continued the cattle operation until it was phased out for pine and built himself a new house on the hill. His home was called Maka'oi'oi, which means "sharp-eyed."

The interisland steamers called at Honolua once a month. The boat stood offshore and goods and people came in and out on lighters. The old pier was in the center of the bay where the ramp in now. Hides that were salted and stacked were shipped out with the coffee when the steamer left. The coffee mill was next to the ranch house, but the coffee fields were in Honokahua. My uncle Willy Searle ran the mill. The whole bay was grassy and open, not overgrown like it is now. My father often surround-netted *akule* in the bay. Everyone that helped was given a *ka'au* of fish. My father would always ask if anyone had guests, and if they needed extra fish, he gave them what they needed.

My wet nurse was a woman named Hulimai. She was also the caretaker of the *heiau* in the bay, which is now on two sides of the road. Whenever I came home on vacation from Sacred Hearts in Honolulu, my mother always took me to Hulimai's house. Hulimai would chant, and I would have to respond, *"Eō,"* and draw out the final syllable. Hulimai set out the old-style fish

*basket traps off the right point of the bay near the white coral.
She gathered 'opihi and limu there, too. I believe one of the
graves in the bay is hers.*

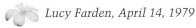 *Lucy Farden, April 14, 1979*

Honolua-Mokulēʻia Bay. Dive site, snorkeling site, marine life
conservation district (48 acres), Honolua, Maui. The MLCD
was established in 1978 and includes Honolua and Mokulēʻia
Bays.

Honolulu. 1. Landing, Puna, Hawaiʻi. One of many former ship
landings that were established around the island during the
late 1800s and early 1900s, and also one of Puna's famous 'opihi
harvesting sites. 2. Channel, Honolulu, Oʻahu. Main entrance
channel into Honolulu Harbor. The first non-Hawaiian to
negotiate what was originally a narrow gap through the reef
was Captain William Brown, who in 1794 sailed his schooner
Jackall through the channel into the harbor. 3. Harbor, Honolulu, Oʻahu. Primary deep-draft harbor in Hawaiʻi. Honolulu
Harbor is controlled by the Harbors Division, State of Hawaiʻi
Department of Transportation. Vessel communications are
coordinated through Aloha Tower, the traffic control center
for the harbor. Commercial tugs and barges based in the harbor
transship freight from Oʻahu to the neighbor islands. 4. Harbor
light, Honolulu, Oʻahu. Established in 1869 at the harbor entrance and relocated to the top of Aloha Tower when it was
built in 1926. Relocated again in 1975 to a 95-foot pole at Pier
2 when its light became indistinguishable from the lights of the
high-rise buildings inland of Aloha Tower. *Lit.*, protected bay.

 moʻolelo

The village at Honolulu was on the high ground behind the concrete building that the Board of Forestry built as a storage shed
for their equipment. There were many graves and house sites—
the platforms were still in good shape—but they were all bull-
dozed by a landowner who leveled the area for house lots.
Honolulu was used as a landing for ships, but not the interisland steamers. Schooners stopped offshore periodically to pick
up coconut, coffee, and dried 'awa, but it wasn't one of their
regular stops. McBride and McKeague owned the boats, and
canoes were used as lighters. The coffee mill was above Koaʻe,
a mauka village in the mango grove area. I used to live nearby
at Halepuaʻa, and my wife's family was from Kahuwai. Before the
shoreline sank in 1924, there was a black sand beach on the
Makuʻu side of Honolulu and an 'iliʻili beach on the Puʻu One
side. After 1924, people moved out of the shoreline areas toward

111

*the forest line, and by the thirties and forties the younger genera-
tions just moved away. They were not interested in a subsistence
lifestyle.*

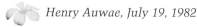

Henry Auwae, July 19, 1982

Honomalino. Bay, beach, Honomalino, Hawai'i. Calcareous and
detrital sand beach fronted by a shallow sandbar in the north
corner of the bay. An extensive coconut grove, some private
beach homes, and many habitation ruins are found in the backshore. The bay is recessed into the shore, making it one of the
most protected bays in South Kona. *Lit.,* calm bay.

Honomanu. Bay, beach, surf site, Honomanu, Maui. Honomanu
is a narrow bay with a boulder beach. During the summer
months a small sand beach may form among the boulders. The
surf site is off the beach.

Honomūni. Beach, Pūko'o, Moloka'i. Narrow calcareous sand
beach east of Pūko'o.

Hononana. Bay, dive site, Hononana, Maui. One of six famous
West Maui bays whose names begin with the word *hono,* or
bay. Collectively they are known as Nā Honoapi'ilani, the
"bays acquired by Pi'ilani" (a chief). Honoapi'ilani is also the
name of the West Maui coastal highway that connects the six
bays. The dive site is in the bay, north of Nākālele Point Light.
Lit., animated bay.

Honopū. 1. Beach, surf site, Nā Pali, Kaua'i. One of five beaches
within Nā Pali Coast State Park and the most photographed
of these beaches. The beach is actually two large pockets of
calcareous sand at the base of a sea cliff. Honopū Valley is
above the sea cliff, approximately 150 above sea level. The
pocket beaches are separated by a wave-cut sea arch approximately 65 feet high and 200 feet wide, fronted by shallow sandbars, and backed by vegetated dunes. A waterfall on the sea
cliffs falls into the backshore and runs through the arch. The
surf site is a shorebreak on the sandbars. 2. Bay, southwest
shore, Lāna'i. Site of the Nānāhoa Islands. *Lit.,* conch bay.

Honopū'e. Anchorage, bay, beach, valley, surf site, Hāmākua,
Hawai'i. Honopū'e Valley is one of seven isolated coastal
valleys on the north side of Kohala Mountain. Small deposits
of black sand lie behind the boulder beach that lines the
shore. Larger deposits of black sand front the boulder beach on
the ocean bottom. The black sand is material eroded and
transported to the shore by Honopū'e Stream. Honopū'e is the
westernmost valley in the district of Hāmākua. The bay is
used as an anchorage, and the surf site is on the east point of
the bay. *Lit.,* dune bay.

mo'olelo

Besides "rape," pu'e also means two sheer things coming together. I feel that this is the meaning—the sheer cliffs, the high valley walls that are hugging each other. There is a legend . . . that says a chief there was eaten by a shark and that his spirit is still alive in the shark. If you wanted to go to Pololū, then you threw a ti leaf in the ocean. If it sank, then you couldn't go, but if it floated, then it was okay.

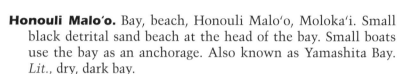 *Alfred Solomon, June 25, 1982*

Honouli Malo'o. Bay, beach, Honouli Malo'o, Moloka'i. Small black detrital sand beach at the head of the bay. Small boats use the bay as an anchorage. Also known as Yamashita Bay. *Lit.,* dry, dark bay.

Honouliuli Unit. Wildlife refuge (61 acres), Honouliuli, O'ahu. One of three satellite sections, or "units," of the Pearl Harbor National Wildlife Refuge. The Honouliuli Unit is a man-made wetland on West Loch in Pearl Harbor Naval Base that was established for the Hawaiian coot, the Hawaiian duck, the Hawaiian moorhen, and the Hawaiian stilt; it also supports migratory shorebirds and waterfowl. The other units are Kalaeloa and Waiawa. *Lit.,* dark bay.

Honouli Wai. Anchorage, bay, beach, Honouli Wai, Moloka'i. Small black detrital sand beach at the head of the bay. Small boats use the bay as an anchorage. *Lit.,* freshwater dark bay.

Honu'apo. Bay, landing, pond, Honu'apo, Hawai'i. Former interisland steamer landing on Honu'apo Bay. Ruins of the wharf are on the shore. Sugar planters deepened the bay in the 1870s and completed the wharf in 1883, but the wharf fell into disuse in the 1940s as trucks began to replace ships to transport raw sugar. The tsunami of April 1, 1946, severely damaged the wharf and it was never used again. Honu'apo Pond at the edge of the park is one of the many spring-fed ponds that were once found between Honu'apo and Punalu'u. Whittington Park is on the shore. *Lit.,* caught turtle.

Ho'okena. Beach park, dive site, landing, surf site, ramp, Ho-'okena, Hawai'i. Large pocket of white and detrital sand in the north corner of Kauhakō Bay. The foreshore is primarily rocky, but the beach is used as a landing for *'ōpelu* fishing canoes. The dive site and surf site are off the beach. Ruins of the former interisland steamer landing are on the shore of the beach park. Facilities include a ramp. Also known as Cooper Landing, Kupa Landing, Kauhakō Ramp. *Lit.,* to satisfy thirst.

Ho'okipa. 1. Beach park, Pā'ia, Maui. Pocket beach of calcareous sand beach fronted by a reef shelf. Built in 1933, the park was made famous throughout Hawai'i by Alice Johnson, a resident

H

of Kū'au and a singer with the Royal Hawaiian Band. In 1937, Johnson wrote and popularized the song "Ho'okipa Park Hula," now a hula standard. Originally a surf site, Ho'okipa became the premier windsurf site on Maui's north shore in the 1970s when the sport moved to Maui from O'ahu. Ho'okipa is now regarded as a world-class site for windsurfing competition, especially wave jumping and surfing. 2. Surf site, windsurf site, Pā'ia, Maui. Ho'okipa is the overall site name, and there are at least five individual sites off the beach park. From east to west they are: Pavilions, Middles, Green Tree, H-Poko's, and Lanes. The first two are primarily surf sites, and the last three are primarily windsurf sites. *Lit.*, hospitality.

 mo'olelo

In 1936 my family moved from Lower Pā'ia to Kū'au. I was singing with the Royal Hawaiian Band, but in 1937 I left them to come home. One day my sister and I decided to walk over to the park. We were curious to see what it looked like. A friend of ours was the park keeper, and when we arrived, she had just finished her poi lunch and had fallen asleep under the *hau* trees. The peacefulness and beauty of the entire scene inspired me to write "Ho'okipa Park Hula." The kids from Lower Pā'ia and Kū'au were already surfing here, so I mentioned surfing in the song. The '46 tidal wave destroyed the area and completely changed it. The wide beach and many of the *hau* trees were lost, and the high wall there today was built to prevent further damage.

Alice Johnson, January 27, 1978

Ho'olawa. Bay, fishing site, landing, Huelo, Maui. Small rocky bay and a former plantation landing. Ruins of a sugar mill are inland of the bay. *Lit.*, make sufficient.

Ho'olehua. Beach, salt-gathering site, Kalaupapa, Moloka'i. One of five beaches on Kalaupapa Peninsula. Wide, sloping calcareous sand storm beach on the northeast side of Kahi'u Point. The beach was created by high surf carrying sand inland over the rocky shore. A wide expanse of shallow tidal pools on the west side of Ho'olehua Beach is the traditional salt-gathering site for the residents of Kalaupapa Peninsula. *Lit.*, swift, expert, strong.

Ho'ona. Dive site, Keāhole, Hawai'i. Small bay on the north side of Keāhole Point that is known for its manta rays and garden eels. Also known as Garden Eel Cove. *Lit.*, intoxicating.

Ho'onoua. Pond, Kamilo, Hawai'i. Large, brackish-water pond with a small rock island behind the narrow calcareous sand beach at Kamilo Point.

Hoʻopaʻewaʻa. Beach, Kalaupapa, Molokaʻi. South section of Papaloa Beach where a narrow, sand-bottomed channel cuts through the reef to the beach. *Lit.,* to land a canoe.

Hoʻopuloa. Beach, Miloliʻi, Hawaiʻi. Small pocket beach of pebbles, lava fragments, and coral rubble at the edge of the 1926 lava flow that destroyed Hoʻopuloa village.

Hopeaia. Fishpond, Mauna Lani, Hawaiʻi. One of four fishponds at Mauna Lani.

Horner's. Surf site, Wailua, Kauaʻi. Off the Lae Nani condominium at the north end of Wailua Beach and named for the former Horner home that was on the same site. Albert Horner, a pioneer in Kauaʻi's pineapple industry, was the manager of Hawaiian Canneries Company from 1920 to 1953. The canning operation was started by his father in 1914 to process pineapple from the fields in Kapahi and Moloaʻa. In 1929, Horner built a twenty-room home on a 4-acre site inshore of the surf site. It remained a landmark on the shore until 1976, when Pauline and Mel Ventura purchased it. The Venturas built a condominium on the site, the Lae Nani, but rather than demolish the Horner home, they hired a house-moving company to disassemble, transport, and reassemble it on a lot near ʻOpaekaʻa Falls in Wailua. There it became their family home.

Horseshoes. Surf site, Black Point, Oʻahu. Inside section of Kaikoʻo that breaks in a semicircle on a shallow, horseshoe-shaped reef. Also known as Inside Halemanō.

Hosaka Point. Fishing site, Pōhue, Hawaiʻi. Low, flat terrace on the seaward side of Puʻu Ki, the littoral cone that forms the east point of Pōhue Bay. Named for Edward Y. Hosaka, an agronomist with the University of Hawaiʻi's Extension Services. Hosaka earned a master's degree from UH–Mānoa in 1934 and specialized in pasture management. His work took him to the Big Island's remotest areas doing work for the island's large ranches. An avid fisherman, he often fished at Puʻu Ki on the shore of Kahuku Ranch, and it was there that he suffered a stroke. Taken immediately by his companions to Hilo Hospital, he died on July 23, 1961. Since then the point has been known as Hosaka Point, or simply Eddie Hosaka. Hosaka was the author and illustrator of *Sport Fishing in Hawaiʻi,* a book he published in 1944 that is still considered a standard reference on fish and fishing in Hawaiʻi.

 moʻolelo

The area near Pōhue known as Eddie Hosaka or **Hosaka Point** is a good *ulua* grounds. My brother fished there a lot and caught a lot. One day in 1961 when he was fishing there, he had a fish on the line, but he said he felt ill and asked one of his friends to bring it in. Then he collapsed. They took him to the hospital, but he died. He was 55 years old. Eddie was recognized in Hawai'i as one of the leading authorities on pasture grasses for cattle. Ranchers paid him to look at their pastures, so he had almost unlimited access to all the big ranches and their shoreline areas as well.

 Yaichiro Hosaka, July 28, 1982

Hospitals. Surf site, Mā'ili, O'ahu. East end of Tumbleland. Many injuries have occurred on the shallow reef shelf here, sending bodysurfers, bodyboarders, and surfers to the "hospital."

Hot Pond. Pool, Pohoiki, Hawai'i. Brackish-water pool in Ahalanui Beach Park heated by a geothermal spring in a lava sink on the shore. Cooler ocean water washes into the pool over the seaward wall. Also known as Mauna Kea Pond, Millionaire's Pond.

Hotels. 1. Surf site, Diamond Head, O'ahu. Beginners break located inshore of Ricebowl. The high-rise condominiums of the Gold Coast are the "hotels." Also known as Inside Tongg's, Silver Stairs. 2. Surf site, windsurf site, Kahuku, O'ahu. Off the cove at the Hilton Turtle Bay Hotel. Also known as Bayviews, Keyholes.

Hou Point. Dive site, surf site, Kīholo, Hawai'i. Northern point of Kīholo Bay formed by a lava flow from Mauna Loa in 1859. The dive site and the surf site are adjacent to the point and within Kīholo Bay. Also known as Laehou, Kalaehou. *Lit.*, new point [of land]. Hou Point is a shortened form of Laehou or Kalaehou.

Housings. Surf site, Pacific Missile Range Facility, Kaua'i. Same as Family Housing.

H Point. Fishing site, surf site, Hāpuna, Hawai'i. The south point of Hāpuna Beach, or Kānekanaka Point, is popularly known as Hāpuna, or H Point. "H" is short for Hāpuna. The surf site is off the point.

H-Poko Papa. Beach, reef, Kū'au, Maui. Calcareous sand beach at the base of a low sea cliff fronted by a papa, or a wide reef shelf. H-Poko is an abbreviation of Hāmākua Poko, the land division in which the papa is located. Also known as Hāmākua Poko Papa. *Lit.*, Hāmākua Poko reef flat.

H-Poko Point. Fishing site, surf site, windsurf site, Kū'au, Maui. High, rocky point that separates H-Poko Papa and Ho'okipa Beach Park. Popular lookout to watch windsurfers. H-Poko is an abbreviation of Hāmākua Poko, the land division in which the point is located. Also known as Hāmākua Poko Point, H-Poko's.

H-Poko's. Point, surf site, windsurf site, Kū'au, Maui. Same as H-Poko Point.

Huakini. Bay, beach, Kaupō, Maui. Detrital sand beach on the shore of the bay.

Huelo. Island (3.1 acres), Waikolu, Moloka'i. Part of the Hawai'i State Seabird Sanctuary. *Lit.*, tail end, last.

Huialoha. Church, windsurf site, Kaupō, Maui. Constructed in 1859, the church stands alone on Mokulau Point. The congregation renovated the church during the 1970s and held a re-dedication service on Easter Sunday, March 26, 1978. The windsurf site is off the point. *Lit.*, meeting of compassion, or coming together in love.

Hui Hanalike. Park (6 acres), Hawaiian Paradise Park, Hawai'i. Park on low sea cliffs that is owned and maintained by the Hawaiian Paradise Park homeowners' association, after which it is also named. Near the seaward end of Paradise Drive. *Lit.*, association [that] works together.

Huilua. Fishpond (200 acres), Kahana, O'ahu. On the south shore of Kahana Bay. *Lit.*, twice joined.

Hukilau. 1. Beach, Lā'ie, O'ahu. In 1947, members of the Church of Jesus Christ of Latter-Day Saints in Lā'ie put on a *hukilau* as a fundraiser to replace their chapel, which had been destroyed in a fire. A *hukilau* is a traditional method of fishing that employs a large group of people to pull a long net onshore. The *hukilau* was held in Lā'ie Bay and proved to be so popular with tourists that it continued as a monthly attraction until 1971. One participant, Jack Owens, was so impressed with the event that he wrote the "Hukilau Song," which became a *hapa*-haole hula standard. Also known as Lā'ie Bay. 2. Beach park, Lā'ie, O'ahu. Private beach park owned and maintained by Zion Securities at Hukilau Beach. *Lit.*, to pull [a] rope with ti leaves [and a net attached].

Hula'ia. River, Nāwiliwili, Kaua'i. Same as Hule'ia.

Hule'ia. 1. National wildlife refuge (238 acres), Nāwiliwili, Kaua'i. Established in 1973 to include the Hule'ia Stream estuary, a habitat for endangered waterbirds, and Hule'ia Valley. The refuge protects the largest population of kōloa, or Hawaiian ducks, on Kaua'i. 2. River, Nāwiliwili, Kaua'i. Navigable river that is accessed from Nāwiliwili Harbor or Niumalu Beach Park. A kind of pumice stone.

Hulihe'e Palace. Museum, Kailua, Hawai'i. On the shore of Kailua Bay. Built as a home in 1838 by Kuakini, governor of Hawai'i and brother of Ka'ahumanu, wife of King Kamehameha I. Restored in 1927 as a museum by the Daughters of Hawai'i. *Lit.*, turn [and] flee.

Hulopo'e. 1. Bay, beach park, surf site, Mānele, Lāna'i. Long, wide crescent of calcareous sand between two rocky points. The bay offshore is part of the Mānele-Hulopo'e Marine Life Conservation District. The surf site is off the east end of the beach. The Ko'ele Company of Lāna'i developed the beach park and its facilities in 1961 in the sand dunes behind the beach. 2. Pool, Mānele, Lāna'i. Large pool in the lava terrace that forms the east point of the bay. The pool was blasted out of the terrace in 1951 to create a safe swimming site for children. Perhaps a man's name.

Hultin's. Surf site, Kawailoa, O'ahu. During the early 1960s when this site was first surfed, Fritz Hultin owned a beachfront home on the point directly inshore. An English teacher at Waialua High School, Hultin was well known in the community. His son Donald was a surfer and was among the first to surf regularly in front of their home.

Hulu. Island (1.5 acres, 80 feet high), Waihe'e, Maui. Part of the Hawai'i State Seabird Sanctuary. *Lit.,* feather.

Humuhumu. Beach, point, Ka'ū, Hawai'i. Black sand beach on the south side of Humuhumu Point at the base of a small littoral cone. At the end of Road to the Sea. *Lit.,* the trigger fish.

Hunakai. Beach, surf site, Kāhala, O'ahu. Section of Kāhala Beach at the intersection of Kāhala Avenue and Hunakai Street. The surf site is off the right-of-way. Also known as Mothers Beach. *Lit.,* sea foam. Name of a bird, the sanderling *(Crocethia alba),* a small winter migrant to Hawai'i, cinnamon brown with dark markings. The bird was thus named because it runs after receding waves in search of food.

Hyatt Reef. Dive site, Kā'anapali, Maui. Off the Hyatt Regency Maui Resort and Spa.

I Buoy. Fish aggregating device, Hālona, Kahoʻolawe. Buoy anchored at approximately 500 fathoms. Landmarks: Kākā Point, Waikahalulu Bay Light, Molokini.

Icebox. 1. Dive site, Poʻipū, Kauaʻi. 2. Dive site, springs, Pāʻia, Maui. On the north side of Pāʻia Bay. Although electric refrigerators have been in Hawaiʻi for many years, the term *icebox* is still used occasionally in Pidgin English for refrigerator. Local divers especially use the term for dive sites where there are many edible varieties of marine life concentrated in one area.

Ice Pond. Swimming site, Hilo, Hawaiʻi. Natural brackish water pond at the head of Reeds Bay on the eastern side of Waiākea Peninsula. The pond waters are a combination of salt water from the bay and springwater in the pond. During the winter months the spring water is ice-cold, giving the pond its popular name. Swimmers use several large concrete blocks at the edge of the pond as jumping platforms. These blocks are train track foundation remnants of the former Hawaiʻi Consolidated Railway. Fishermen gather a special seaweed for mullet bait from the pond. Also known as Kanākea.

ʻIhiʻihilaukea Bridge. Fishing site, Hawaiʻi Kai, Oʻahu. Bridge on Kalanianaʻole Highway between the Lānaʻi Lookout and the Hālona Blowhole that was constructed in 1931. The fishing site is at the base of the sea cliffs below the bridge and is also known as First Bridge.

Ihumoku. Rock, Hāpuna, Hawaiʻi. Rock formation on Hāpuna Beach that separates the state beach park and the Hāpuna Prince Hotel. *Lit.*, bow [of the] ship.

II Buoy. Fish aggregating device, Haleʻiwa, Oʻahu. Buoy anchored at approximately 985 fathoms. Landmarks: Kaʻena Point, Haleʻiwa Channel Buoy Light, Kahuku Point.

ʻIliʻilihele o Honoliʻi. Beach, Honoliʻi, Hawaiʻi. ʻIliʻili or pebble beach at Honoliʻi Beach Park. The beach at the river mouth disappears when the river floods after heavy rains but returns when the floodwaters subside. This is the reason for its name. *Lit.*, traveling pebbles of Honoli'i.

'Ili'iliholo. Beach, Kama'ole, Maui. When high surf erodes the beach during high surf, a pebble and cobblestone beach is exposed. The waves tumble or roll the pebbles and cobblestones, giving the beach its name. Also known as Kama'ole II Beach Park. *Lit.*, rolling pebbles or quickly moving pebbles.

'Ili'ililoa. Beach, Kamōhio, Kaho'olawe. Narrow cobble and pebble beach that lies at the base of the sea cliffs in the eastern end of Kamōhio Bay. *Lit.*, long [stretch of] pebbles.

'Īlio. Point, surf site, west coast, Moloka'i. Northwest extremity of Moloka'i, the closest point on the island to O'ahu, and one of two points that define the west end of the island. The other is Lā'au Point. The surf site is south of the point. *Lit.*, dog.

'Īliopi'i. Beach, Kalaupapa, Moloka'i. One of the five beaches on Kalaupapa Peninsula. Long crescent of calcareous sand between Kalaemilo and Kalae'a Points that was once a popular site for beach homes of Kalaupapa residents. The wreck of the SS *Ka'ala* is visible on the reef offshore where she went aground in 1932. *Lit.*, climbing dog.

Impossibles. 1. Surf site, Hanalei, Kaua'i. The outermost takeoff spot at Hanalei, from where it is almost impossible to make the wave from start to finish. Named by veteran Kauai surfer Nick Beck in the late 1950s after some children swimming by the pier asked him where he was going, and when he explained, they said it was "impossible." 2. Surf site, Sunset Beach, O'ahu. An extremely dangerous site in the middle of Waimea Point that is rarely surfed. The waves are almost impossible to ride except by expert surfers under the most ideal conditions.

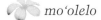 *mo'olelo*

Impossibles is the far-right point break outside the reef to the right of the pier looking out into the bay. When you take off really deep and make the wave all the way to the Bowl, it's one of the longest rides I've ever seen or surfed. When I first started surfing it in the mid- to late fifties, some kids swimming by the pier asked me where I was going. When I told them, they said, "Eh, Nick, you no can make that wave, brah. Da place is impossible fo ride." Well, on some waves—when I was getting the lineups down and on my old boards—it was, and so the name seems to have stuck till today with those who really know the lineups and ride the big waves from the peak at Impossibles.

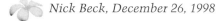 *Nick Beck, December 26, 1998*

In Betweens. 1. Surf site, Ka'alāwai, O'ahu. Between Brown's and Mansions. Also known as Backdoor. 2. Surf site, Waikīkī,

Oʻahu. Between Kaiser's and Rockpile. 3. Surf site, Waikīkī, Oʻahu. Between Rockpile and Ala Moana Bowls. All of the "in between" sites are secondary sites that are situated between two primary or more popular sites.

Incinerators. Surf site, Kakaʻako, Oʻahu. In 1930 the City and County of Honolulu built an incinerator in Kakaʻako as an alternative to using the land that is now Ala Moana Beach Park as a dump. In 1946 a new incinerator was built next to the old one, and it served the community until it, too, finally closed. In 1998 it was renovated and became the Children's Discovery Museum. During all the years that an incinerator was operational, its tall smokestack was a prominent landmark in Kakaʻako, and the surf site offshore was called Incinerators. Originally, Incinerators included several surf sites, including Point Panic, but after Point Panic was applied in the early 1960s to the site next to Kewalo Channel, Incinerators was redefined to include only the site directly in line with the incinerator.

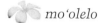 *moʻolelo*

I was born in Kakaʻako in 1916 and graduated from McKinley in 1933. I was raised near the old Iron Works. I used to surf Kakaʻako before the reef was landfilled. We rode the old wooden boards, some of them 12, 13 feet long. The reef then was shallow, and the beach was at Ala Moana Boulevard. We called the surf **Incinerators** for the old incinerator. At that time there was another place to surf in Kakaʻako that we called Armstrong's. It was in front of Fort Armstrong. The shore there was different, too—it was a shallow reef, and there were many military homes on the beach. We surfed in front of the homes. The landfill on the reef that made Piers 1 and 2 destroyed Armstrong's.

Rawlins "Sonny" Kauhane, November 5, 1998

I was born in Kakaʻako in 1922 and lived there until I was about nine. Then my dad moved our family to Nānākuli where we were some of the first homesteaders. My grandfather, Kaʻaikaula, was in charge of the city dump where Ala Moana Beach Park is today and that's where I learned to surf. We used the old redwood boards that were maybe 12 feet long, and when I got older, we made them ourselves. We surfed all the spots in front of the park, but we didn't have any names for them. We also surfed in front of the old incinerator and called it Incinerators.

 *George Keoho, June 28, 2000*

Incons. Surf site, Waiʻalae Iki, Oʻahu. Off the Board of Water Supply pumping station. Incons is an abbreviation of "inconsistent." The waves here are inconsistent, breaking only on certain south swells. Named by neighborhood surfers about 1970. Also known as Sundays.

Indicators. Surf site, Waiale'e, O'ahu. Off Kuka'imanini Island in Waiale'e Beach Park. During big west or northwest swells, surfers riding other sites to the north watch Indicators because it breaks first, indicating that a set of waves is coming their way.

Infinities. 1. Surf site, Pākala, Kaua'i. Fronting the village of Pākala in Makaweli, where many Ni'ihau residents live while they are on Kaua'i. The surf site is on the west end of the wide, shallow fringing reef off the village. The village and the lands surrounding it are part of the Gay and Robinson sugar plantation, and several members of the Robinson family have beach homes next to the village. The name Infinity—now Infinities—was given to the surf site in 1962 by Randy Wier, a member of one of the Robinson families who have homes there. Wier, then a teenage surfer from Kailua High School on O'ahu, spent his summers surfing the waves at Pākala, where the rides are so long that he compared them to surfing into infinity. Also known as Pākala. 2. Surf site, Mokulē'ia, O'ahu. Second-reef break outside of Crushers that provides an "infinitely" long ride.

 mo'olelo

After my parents were divorced in 1962, my father stayed in Kailua and my mother moved to my grandfather's big house on the beach at Pākalā. So that's when I first surfed it, in 1962, with some other surfers from Kailua—John Day, Mike McCormick, and Mike MacPherson. I graduated from Kailua High School in 1963. No one else surfed at all there, and the Hawaiians in Pākalā village considered us an oddity. The other guys and I named it **Infinity** because of the extremely long rides. It was like surfing into infinity.

 Randy Wier, December 20, 1988

Inikiwai. Point, Kahalu'u, Hawai'i. South end of Pāokamenehune, or the Menehune Breakwater. *Lit.*, piercing water.

Inoa'ole. Stream, Waimānalo, O'ahu. Stream that separates Bellows Field Beach Park and Waimānalo Bay Beach Park. *Lit.*, nameless, unnamed.

Ins and Outs. 1. Surf site, Nāpo'opo'o, Hawai'i. Shorebreak on the shallow sandbar fronting the boulder beach at Nāpo'opo'o Beach Park. When incoming waves strike the boulders, the backwash reforms into smaller waves going back out to sea. Bodysurfers and bodyboarders can, therefore, ride in and out. Also known as Hikiau. 2. Surf site, Waikīkī, O'ahu. Off the seawall in Kūhiō Beach Park. When incoming waves strike the seawall, the backwash reforms into smaller waves going back out to sea. Surfers can, therefore, ride in and out. Also known as Baby Cunha's.

Insanities. 1. Surf site, Kahului, Maui. Big-wave, second-reef break on a small reef near the entrance to Kahului Harbor. 2. Surf site, La Pérouse Bay, Maui. 3. Surf site, Hawai'i Kai, O'ahu. Off the rocks at the west end of Sandy Beach. 4. Surf site, Sunset Beach, O'ahu. Between Off the Wall and Rockpiles. All sites are named because they are dangerous, and the surfers who attempt to ride the waves there are "insane."

Inside Avalanche. Surf site, Hale'iwa, O'ahu. Reform break on a shallow reef inshore of Avalanche, a deepwater surf site.

Inside Castles. Surf site, Waikīkī, O'ahu. Deepwater site between Natatoriums and Castles that breaks only during big south swells. It is inshore of Castles, a big-wave, second-reef surf site. Also known as No Name, No Place.

Inside Chun's. Surf site, Hale'iwa, O'ahu. Inside section at the west end of Chun's Reef that often breaks as a distinct surf site.

Inside Hale'iwa Harbor. Surf site, Hale'iwa, O'ahu. Beginner's break inside the harbor off Surf-n-Sea surf shop. Also known as Chocolates, Surf-n-Sea.

Inside Halemanō. Surf site, Black Point, O'ahu. Inside section of Halemanō. Also known as Horseshoes.

Inside Himalayas. Surf site, Kawailoa, O'ahu. Inside section of Himalayas. Also known as Dairymens.

Inside Pua'ena Point. Surf site, Hale'iwa, O'ahu. Shallow reef break between Pua'ena Point and the Hale'iwa Channel that is a popular beginner's break.

Inside Tongg's. Surf site, Diamond Head, O'ahu. Beginners break located inshore of Tongg's. Also known as Hotels, Silver Stairs.

Inters. Surf site, Kekaha, Kaua'i. Off the intersection of Kaumuali'i Highway and 'Akialoa Street. Inters is an abbreviation of "intersection."

Irma's. Surf site, Hawai'i Kai, O'ahu. During the 1960s, Irma and Willy Akima owned and operated Irma's Lunchwagon here. Surfers who frequented the surf site offshore named it after the lunchwagon.

 mo'olelo

The surf spot **Irma's** was named for Irma's Lunchwagon. Irma and Willy Akima owned the lunchwagon, and they used to park it on Kalaniana'ole Highway right where the Kealahou Street intersection is now. Irma was from Germany, and Willy was from Kahalu'u. They met and got married in Germany when Willy was stationed there in the army. When they came back to Hawai'i, Willy worked as a janitor at Kailua High School. They lived on Hilu Street in the beach lots in Waimanalo and kept the lunchwagon there when *they weren't using it. Sometimes the lunchwagon didn't run too good, so I towed them down to the beach and back with my pickup truck. Irma's regular stew and curry stew were outstanding, and she always gave generous portions to everyone.*

Haywood Kalima, July 6, 2000

Iron Boat. Surf site, Mokulē'ia, O'ahu. Same as Day Star.

Iron Bridge. Surf site, Hilo, Hawai'i. Off the steel ("iron") bridge that spans the mouth of the Wailuku River in Hilo. Also known as Bayfront.

Ironwood. Beach, surf site, Kapalua, Maui. Wide, straight calcareous sand beach between Hāwea and Makāluapuna Points. The public right-of-way to the beach at its north end is near the Ironwood Villas. The surf site is off the beach. Also known as Oneloa Beach.

Ironwood Park. Windsurf site, Spreckelsville, Maui. East end of Spreckelsville Beach where the dunes in the backshore are low, permitting easy access to the beach for windsurfers. A large stand of ironwood trees lines the beach.

Iroquois. 1. Beach, 'Ewa Beach, O'ahu. Calcareous sand beach fronting Capehart Housing, the navy housing at Keahi Point. Named for Iroquois Drive, the main road along the shore in the subdivision. 2. Beach park, 'Ewa Beach, O'ahu. Small beach park for military personnel at the west end of Capehart Housing. 3. Lagoon, lagoon yacht club, 'Ewa Beach, O'ahu. Military facility in Pearl Harbor at the east end of Capehart Housing. Facilities include fifty slips and fifteen moorings. Visitor moorings are restricted to vessels with a Pearl Harbor permit. 4. Point, 'Ewa Beach, O'ahu. West point of Pearl Harbor Channel. Also known as Keahi Point.

Iroquois Point. Dive site, 'Ewa Beach, O'ahu. On the west side of the Pearl Harbor Channel. Named for Iroquois Drive, the main road in Capehart Housing on the point.

Issac Hale. Beach park, Pohoiki, Hawai'i. Small beach park with a rocky shore on the eastern point of Pohoiki Bay. Named in 1951 for Issac Hale, who was killed in the Korean War. Hale was a member of the Hawaiian family whose home on Pohoiki Bay is adjacent to the park. The park is also the site of Pohoiki Ramp, the only boat ramp in the district of Puna. *Hale* means "house."

Iwi Kupuna. Memorial, Waikīkī, O'ahu. Memorial and burial vault established in 2001 at the corner of Kapahulu and Kalakaua Avenues in Kapi'olani Regional Park. The memorial provides a site where the bones of native Hawaiians can be re-interred if they are unearthed during construction projects in Waikīkī. *Lit.,* bones [of the] ancestors.

Jackie's Mountain. Dive site, Hawai'i Kai, O'ahu. Off Palea Point at Hanauma Bay. A rock shaped like a mountain that begins at 90 feet and rises to 15 feet below the surface. It was named for Jackie James, who opened Aloha Dive Shop in Hawai'i Kai in 1970. Born in Georgia, James came to Hawai'i in 1968 when she was 35 years old. She took a dive class and enjoyed it so much that she became a certified instructor in 1969, opened her own shop a year later, and never quit diving. One of her favorite dive sites is the underwater mountain at Hanauma Bay, which was named for her by one of her boat captains.

James C. Campbell National Wildlife Refuge. See Campbell National Wildlife Refuge.

James Kealoha Beach Park. See Kealoha Beach Park.

Japanese Cemetery. Fishing site, Kahuku, O'ahu. North end of Kahuku Golf Course. Before the Kahuku Sugar Mill closed in 1971, the plantation maintained two cemeteries for its workers, the Japanese cemetery for Buddhists at the north end of the golf course and the Christian cemetery at the south end.

Jaws. Tow-in surf site, windsurf site, Pe'ahi, Maui. Jaws was first surfed and named in 1975 by three Maui surfers, John Roberson, John Lemus, and John Potterick. While they were surfing it for the first time, the surf changed abruptly from small, fun waves to huge, dangerous waves. They compared their experience to the unpredictability of an encounter with "jaws," or a shark. The movie *Jaws*—the story of a big shark that terrorizes a small coastal vacation town—was released the summer before they surfed the site. Directed by Steven Spielberg, the movie heightened shark awareness nationwide, including in Hawai'i. Jaws was first surfed regularly in the early 1990s by windsurfers from Ho'okipa, and in 1993 Laird Hamilton and Buzzy Kerbox —who with Darrick Doerner had pioneered tow-in surfing on O'ahu's North Shore in 1992—moved to Maui and introduced tow-in surfing at Jaws. Jaws is now regarded as one of the pre- **125**

mier tow-in surf sites in the world, where surfers ride waves 25 to 50 feet high after being towed into the takeoff by motorized personal watercraft. These craft are launched at the boat ramp in Māliko Bay. Also known as Pe'ahi.

 mo'olelo

In the 1970s, I bought some property in Kaupakalua Gulch and built a house there. When **Jaws** is really big, I can see the left from my second story. Originally we called it Domes for Mike Kalas' geodesic dome-shaped house that marked the turnoff to the spot, but even though we had a name for it, we just watched and didn't try to ride it. Then one winter day in 1975, a big north swell started rolling in and it was perfect big-wave surf—glassy, no wind, and ridable at about 8 to 10 feet. Three of us—John Lemus, John Potterick, and me—decided to go for it. We were good friends who rode Ho'okipa big together all the time, so we walked down the hill and paddled out. The boards we were riding then were like eight-foot pintails with no leashes. We surfed it for an hour and a half, and then suddenly—within about fifteen minutes—it changed radically and turned mean. It got giant, wind-blown, and totally out of control. We said, " f—— this" and went in. The shore there is solid boulders, huge, slippery ones, and with the waves pounding it's almost impossible to get out of the water. We got thrashed, and John Potterick ended up with six stitches on his eye socket.

When we got out, we stood on the cliff and looked back where these massive 15-foot plus waves were spitting like the Pipeline. They had really worked us, and we thought the whole session was like a nasty "jaws" encounter. Sharks are totally unpredictable —they will get you if you don't watch out, and it had been the same situation out there for us. We changed the name that day from Domes to Jaws. We found out that Jaws isn't really a paddle-in place unless you catch it on a good day when it's just coming up. We tried it, got nailed, named it, and never surfed it again.

After that day, we told every big-wave rider we knew about Jaws, including some of the guys who were riding the second-reef breaks on the North Shore of O'ahu, but as much as we tried to convince them to try it, none of them came. The real credit for pioneering Jaws goes to the windsurfers, who were the first ones to ride it consistently.

John Roberson, November 24, 2000

I first heard about Jaws from John Roberson about 1975. He and a couple of other guys were the first to surf it, and we surfed it after them. With the big boulders onshore, it's too hard to get in and out over the rocks, so we used my boat and *launched out of Māliko Bay. We rode it with no leashes, but only up to maybe 15 feet. When it's that big and you paddle in, you're going uphill before you drop in, and when you drop in, it's a total elevator drop—really radical. We had some pretty memorable days, but there's no paddle-in surfers out there now. The tow-in guys pretty much own it.*

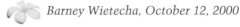

               Barney Wietecha, October 12, 2000

J Buoy. Fish aggregating device, Kamōhio, Kahoʻolawe. Buoy anchored at approximately 900 fathoms. Landmarks: Kākā Point, Waikahalulu Bay Light.

Jetty, The. 1. Breakwater, fishing site, surf site. Kalaeloa, Oʻahu. Boulder groin fronting the Coast Guard Air Station Barbers Point, which is within the Kalaeloa Community Development District. The groin protects a sewer outfall. The surf site is off the jetty and is also known as Swabbieland. 2. Surf site, Waimānalo, Oʻahu. Off a small, largely destroyed beachrock jetty at the mouth of Inoaʻole Stream that separates Waimānalo Bay Beach Park from Bellows Beach Park.

Jizo. 1. Statue, Hawaiʻi Kai, Oʻahu. Jizo is one of the best known of Buddhist guardian deities, and one of his manifestations is as the guardian of dangerous waterways and coastlines. In 1935, members of the Honolulu Japanese Casting Club purchased a statue of Jizo from Japan and placed it above Bamboo Ridge as part of a community service project to identify fishing sites around Oʻahu where shorecasters had drowned. Their project also included placing less expensive warning markers on a number of other dangerous ledges. The sides of the markers, which were concrete or wooden posts, were painted with the Japanese character *abunai*, or "danger." During World War II the statue at Bamboo Ridge was destroyed, but following the war it was replaced with an image of Jizo carved into a stone. 2. Statue, Mokulēʻia, Oʻahu. In 1913, Shunkichi Yamaguchi carved a statue of Jizo and placed it on the shore of Kawaihāpai Bay to protect swimmers, divers, and shorecasters from dangerous currents and shark attacks here and along the entire Mokulēʻia coast. Yamaguchi was born in Niigata Prefecture in Japan, where he learned stone carving, but came to Hawaiʻi to work on the sugar plantations. He carved the statue while he was working for Waialua Sugar Company and living in Kawaihāpai Camp. The camp was opposite the statue on the inland side of Farrington Highway. The Ryusenji Soto Mission in Wahiawa maintains the statue. Both statues are also known by variations of the name Jizo, such as Jizobosatsu, Jizosan, O-jizo, O-jizosama, and O-jizosan.

mo'olelo

The April 22, 1962 edition of the *Advertiser* has a good article about the Honolulu Japanese Casting Club. My husband was one of the original members. In 1935 he and the other club members put up the warning markers at the Blowhole and at other places around the island. They also put up a statue of Ojizo-san above Bamboo Ridge. Ojizo-san is a protective figure on all dangerous coasts and waterways where people may drown. He gives warning and serves as a guardian. The original statue was a carved figure that was purchased by the club from Japan. At the start of World War II, the head was broken off because it was a statue of the "enemy," and the body was eventually broken as well. After the war the costs to replace the statue were too high, so the club members had Ojizo-san carved into a stone which still stands today on the site of the original statue.

 Mrs. Yasukei Tsutsumi, September 22, 1972

JJ Buoy. Fish aggregating device, Waiale'e, O'ahu. Buoy anchored at approximately 960 fathoms. Landmarks: Ka'ena Point, Hale'iwa Channel Buoy Light, Kahuku Point.

Jocko's. 1. Surf site, 'Āina Haina, O'ahu. Left at Ledges. Neighborhood surfers from 'Āina Haina named this site in the 1970s for the resemblance of the waves here to those at Jocko's on O'ahu's North Shore. 2. Surf site, Kawailoa, O'ahu. During the 1960s and 1970s, Jock Sutherland was one of the most creative and fearless surfers on the North Shore at Pipeline, Sunset, and Waimea. A natural goofyfoot, he is one of the most accomplished switchfoot surfers in the world. Sutherland's family home has been on the rocky point inshore of the site since 1961, and he was the first to surf here in the preleash era.

 mo'olelo

We moved to the North Shore in August 1954, and Jock started surfing at Chun's Reef. He was six. In August 1961, I bought my home on Pōhakuloa Way and that's when Jock started surfing in front of the house at **Jocko's,** although we never called Jock or the spot by that name. There were no leashes then, so no one else would surf there because of the rocks onshore. But I would watch Jock while he surfed and get his board when he wiped out before it hit the rocks. When other surfers saw Jock out there, they started calling it Jocko's.

Audrey Sutherland, January 12, 1997

John Brown's. Bay, surf site, Kawailoa, O'ahu. Bay off Pāpa'iloa Road. John Brown (1948–1983) was an avid surfer from Sydney,

Australia, who moved to Hawai'i in the late 1960s. He began surfing here in the early 1970s, and it became one of his favorite spots. It has been known as John Brown's since his ashes were scattered there in 1983. Also known as Brown's Bay.

John Jack. Bay, surf site, Kahuku, O'ahu. Off the east end of Kaihalulu Beach and adjacent to Kalaeokauna'oa, or Kahuku Point. The surf site is in the bay. John "John Jack" McCandless had a small beach home here in the early 1900s. McCandless and his two brothers, Jim and Lincoln, were well drillers. They arrived in Hawai'i in the late 1800s and over a period of fifty-five years drilled more than seven hundred artesian wells. In 1906 they constructed one of Honolulu's first office buildings, the McCandless Building, at the corner of Bethel and King Streets. Also known as Punapālaha.

John's. Surf site, 'Ewa Beach, O'ahu. Off the west end of One'ula Beach Park between Sand Tracks and Coves. Named for veteran surfer John Sadowski from 'Ewa Beach, who was the first to surf here in 1962. Sadowski, a 1965 graduate of Waipahu High School, and his three brothers, Lui, George "Bumbum," and Stanley helped to found the 'Ewa Beach Surf Club in 1958.

> *mo'olelo*
>
> The story of **John's,** or John's Beach, takes place during the summer of 1962. A bunch of 'Ewa Beach surfers—Lester Enomoto, Winnie Medeiros, Barney Silva, my brother John, and I —took in a day of surfing at Sand Track. We checked out Hau Bush first, but the waves weren't that great. We scanned over to Sand Track, and the waves were breaking pretty good. John noticed a good bowl with outstanding right breaks further west towards Barbers Point and decided to try it out; thus, "John's Beach," which is what us guys on the beach called it as we watched him ride the waves.
>
> *Lui Sadowski, September 6, 2000*

JR's. Fishing site, Pōhue, Hawai'i. On the seaward side of Pu'u Ki, the littoral cone that forms the east point of Pōhue Bay. Named for Emilio Molcilio Jr., a retired employee of Kahuku Ranch. Molcilio worked for the ranch from January 1952 until January 2000 and has always been known as Junior or JR. He began fishing for *ulua* on the east side of Pu'u Ki in the late 1950s, and the spot has since been known as JR's.

Jump City. Surf site, windsurf site, Kailua, O'ahu. Big-wave, second-reef site north of Popoi'a Island in Kailua Bay. Named by the first windsurfers in the 1970s who discovered the waves here are a good jump site.

Jump Rock. Island, Waimea Bay, O'ahu. Large lava island in the ocean at the west end of the beach that is a popular jumping site.

Juniors. Surf site, Hawai'i Kai, O'ahu. Off Portlock Beach. Where younger or "junior" surfers learned to surf before moving over to Seconds, a site for intermediate and advanced surfers.

Ka'ā. Fishpond, Keōmuku, Lāna'i. One of two precontact fishponds on the shore of the former Keōmuku village. *Lit.*, the [*a'ā*] lava, or the fiery burning one.

Ka'a'awa. 1. Beach park (2 acres), Ka'a'awa, O'ahu. Julie Judd Swanzy donated the land for the park in 1921. 2. Point, Ka'a-'awa, O'ahu. Point adjoining the west end of Swanzy Beach Park. Also known as Pūlā'ī. *Lit.*, the wrasse [*'a'awa*] fish.

Ka'a'awa Channel. Surf site, Ka'a'awa. Big-wave, second-reef site located outside of the channel into Kaiaka Bay off Kalae'ō'io Beach Park. Also known as Outside Rainbows, Phantoms.

Ka'a'awa Lefts. Surf site, Ka'a'awa, O'ahu. Left at the east end of the reef off Puakenikeni Street.

Ka'aha. Camping site, Hawai'i Volcanoes National Park, Hawai'i. Pocket of black sand in a small inlet in on a wide, flat rocky point at the intersection of the Kālu'e and Hilina Pali Trails. *Lit.*, the assembly.

Ka'aka'aniu. Beach, reef, Kaua'i. Narrow calcareous sand beach fronted by a long, wide, shallow reef. The reef is one of the island's famous seaweed harvesting sites for *limu kohu*, or *Asparagopsis taxiformis*. This prized edible seaweed is found elsewhere in Hawai'i, but local consumers believe the best *limu kohu* comes from Kaua'i and specifically from the reefs at 'Aliomanu, Ka'aka'aniu, and Pīla'a. Commercial harvesting on these reefs has for generations been the domain of a small group of Hawaiian families from Anahola and Moloa'a, the communities closest to these reefs. *Limu kohu* grows at the edge of the reef where there is a constant flow of water from breaking waves. After it is harvested and cleaned, it is soaked overnight in fresh water to reduce its iodine flavor, drained, and lightly salted. If it is to be sent to market, it is rolled into tight balls. Hawaiians differentiate between *limu kohu līpehe*, a milder flavored, light red variety, and *limu kohu koko*, a stronger flavored, dark red variety. *Lit.*, rolling coconut. **131**

Ka'akaukukui. Point, reef, Honolulu, O'ahu. Reef that was filled in to create Kaka'ako Waterfront Park and the rest of lower Kaka'ako, seaward of Olomehani Street. *Lit.,* the right (or north) light.

Ka'aku'u. Beach, north coast, Ni'ihau. Calcareous sand beach between Pu'u Kole and Kaunuokahe Points. The backshore consists of dunes covered primarily by *pōhinahina,* or beach vitex, while small patch reefs and rocky shoals front the foreshore. Lehua Landing is at the south end of the beach, where a deep sand channel comes ashore.

Ka'alaea. Beach, point, Kawailoa, O'ahu. Narrow calcareous beach fronted by several large limestone rock formations, one of which is Alligator Rock. *Lit.,* the ocherous earth.

Ka'alāwai. Beach, springs, Honolulu, O'ahu. Section of Diamond Head Beach between Kulamanu Place and Kuilei Cliffs Beach Park. Probably named for the springs on the beach and among the rocks at the east end of the beach. *Lit.,* the water [basalt] rock.

Ka'alu'alu. Bay, landing, surf site, Wai'ōhinu, Hawai'i. One of the few protected bays in Ka'ū, Ka'alu'alu served as the major landing in the district for shipping sugar and cattle. Many ruins, including a cattle-loading chute, are found on the shore of the bay. An extensive tidal flat lies at the head of the bay. The surf site is off the cattle-loading chute. *Lit.,* the wrinkle. From a boat offshore, fissures in the rock look like wrinkles.

Ka'amola. Point light, Kamalō, Moloka'i. Established in 1968 to mark Kamalō Harbor, a small, shallow natural harbor east of Kaunakakai Harbor that is used primarily by small boats. *Lit.,* loose, unsteady.

Kā'anapali. 1. Beach, Kā'anapali, Maui. Wide, calcareous sand beach fronting the Kā'anapali resort complex. Pu'u Keka'a, a cinder cone more commonly known as Black Rock, divides the beach into two sections. The center of the south section between Hanaka'o'o Beach Park and Black Rock is also known as Dig Me Beach. The north section between Black Rock and Honokowai Point is also known as North Beach. 2. Landing, Kā'anapali, Maui. Ruins of the landing Pioneer Mill Company built to ship processed sugar from Maui to O'ahu are on the north side of Black Rock. The landing was abandoned shortly before World War II, but Pioneer Mill continued the sugar operations it began in 1895 until 1999. 3. Offshore moorings, Kā-'anapali, Maui. Undesignated mooring areas for private sailing vessels off Kā'anapali. *Lit.,* Kā'ana cliff.

Ka'apuna. Lava flow, Ka'apuna, Hawai'i. One of three lava flows from an eruption in the southwest rift zone of Mauna Kea that began on June 1, 1950. Each of the flows reached the ocean, creating small pockets of black sand on a coast of sea cliffs. Fishermen offshore use the flows as landmarks. Also known as Third Flow. *Lit.*, wipe pumice (as in cleaning gourd containers).

Ka'awaloa. 1. Cove, dive site, snorkeling site, Kealakekua, Hawai'i. At the north end of Kealakekua Bay. One of the most sheltered natural anchorages on the Kona Coast and one of the most popular commercial dive and snorkeling tour destinations on the Big Island. The dive site is off the ruins of Ka'awaloa village and the Captain Cook Monument in Kealakekua Bay State Historical Park. 2. Point, Ka'awaloa, Hawai'i. Westernmost point of Kealakekua Bay. Also known as Cook Point. *Lit.*, the distant 'awa plant. Runners were sent to Waipi'o and Puna to get *'awa* (kava) plants to make the narcotic drink *'awa* for chiefs at Ka'awaloa.

Ka'ehu. Bay, beach, Wai'ehu, Maui. Narrow detrital sand beach on a small bay that fronts Paukūkalo Marsh. *Lit.*, the sea spray.

Ka'elehuluhulu. Beach, Mahai'ula, Hawai'i. Calcareous sand and lava fragment beach on the south point of Mahai'ula Bay. *Lit.*, frayed [outrigger canoe] hull.

Ka'eleki'i. Beach, point, Honokeana, Maui. Cobblestone and calcareous sand beach at the head of Honokeana Bay. *Lit.*, the image blackness.

Ka'elua. Island (.9 acres, 40 feet high), Ke'anae, Maui. *Lit.*, the two.

Kaemi. Island (2.5 acres, 120 feet high), Kahakuloa, Maui. *Lit.*, the ebbing [tide].

Ka'ena Point. 1. Fishing site, Ka'ena, Lāna'i. 2. Dive site, Ka'ena, O'ahu. Off the north side of the point among large boulders at 20 to 45 feet. 3. Natural area reserve, Ka'ena, O'ahu. 4. Passing light, Ka'ena, O'ahu. The original Ka'ena Point Light, a 65-foot high lighthouse built in 1920, was eventually reduced to a solar-powered light atop a pole and renamed the Ka'ena Point Passing Light because it aids interisland traffic passing the point. It was relocated to the Ka'ena Point Tracking Station on Kuaokalā Ridge above the point in 1987 where it is visible for 15 miles. At 931 feet above sea level, it is among the highest lighted navigational aids in the world. 5. State park (778.6 acres), Ka'ena, O'ahu. Largely undeveloped coastal park that includes Ka'ena Point, the western end of the island. The walk around the point from gate to gate is 2.7 miles. 6. Surf site, Ka'ena, O'ahu. Big-wave, second-reef site on the Wai'anae side of the point that is rarely surfed. *Lit.*, the heat.

Kaha'akolu. Reef, Kawailoa, O'ahu. Reef fronting the public right-of-way on Pāpa'iloa Road. Also known as The Point. *Lit.*, the three marks or the third mark.

Kahaka'aulana. Island, Ke'ehi, O'ahu. One of several small islands in Ke'ehi Lagoon on the western side of Kalihi Channel. Also known as Harris Island. *Lit.,* the floating swimmers pass by (perhaps named for fishermen and their floating containers).

Kahakahakea. Beach, fishing site, surf site, Pōhue, Hawai'i. Narrow calcareous sand storm beach fronted by boulders and lava. Lava fragments are mixed with the sand, giving it a salt-and-pepper appearance. A small brackish-water pond is in the backshore, along with several natural wells. The surf site is off the beach. *Lit.,* a small white stone.

Kahaki. Reef, Hā'ena, Kaua'i. Small reef on the east side of Hā'ena Point. *Lit.,* the break.

Kahakuloa. Beach, dive site, Kahakuloa, Maui. Boulder beach fronting the isolated community of Kahakuloa. The dive site is off the beach. *Lit.,* the tall lord or the tall overseer.

Kāhala. 1. Point light, Anahola, Kaua'i. Light atop a 22-foot pole on the low sea cliffs south of Anahola Beach Park. 2. Artificial reef, Kāhala, O'ahu. Approximately a mile off the Kāhala Mandarin Oriental Hotel. 3. Beach, Honolulu, O'ahu. Narrow calcareous sand beach between the Kāhala Mandarin Oriental Hotel and Black Point. The section of beach fronting the hotel, its saltwater lagoon, and its offshore island are man-made. They were created in 1963 during construction of the hotel, which opened as the Kāhala Hilton Hotel in January 1964. The hotel was renovated and reopened as the Kāhala Mandarin Oriental Hotel in March 1996. 4. Beach park. Popular but officially incorrect name for Wai'alae Beach Park. 5. Channel. Natural channel at Wai'alae Beach Park cut through the reef by Kapakahi Stream. *Lit.,* amberjack fish.

Kāhala Barge. Dive site, Kāhala, O'ahu. A 200-foot interisland barge off the Kāhala Mandarin Oriental Hotel with its pilothouse intact that was sunk at the Kāhala Artificial Reef at 80 feet. Fish species seen here include the *kāhala,* or amberjack.

Kāhalahala. Beach, Lumaha'i, Kaua'i. East end of Lumaha'i Beach. Popular swimming site during the summer months. *Lit.,* the complaint.

Kahālau. Island, (.3 acres), Ha'ikū, Maui. *Lit.,* the large house.

Kahalepōhaku. Beach, Kaluako'i, Moloka'i. One of four long, wide calcareous sand beaches between Lā'au Point and Hale o Lono Harbor. *Lit.,* the stone house.

Kahaloa. Beach, Waikīkī, O'ahu. Section of Waikīkī Beach between the Royal Hawaiian and Halekūlani Hotels that was noted for its fragrant *limu līpoa,* a seaweed. *Lit.,* long place.

Kahaloko. Beach, Mākaha, O'ahu. Center section of Mākaha Beach. A former wetland created by Wai'ele Stream and adjacent to the beach here was filled in when the railroad bed for the Oʻahu Land and Railway Company route was built. *Lit.*, pond place.

Kahaluʻu. 1. Bay, beach park, dive site, snorkeling site, surf site, North Kona, Hawaiʻi. Calcareous sand and lava fragment beach partially protected by a wall of boulders in the ocean off the beach. The wall is known as the Menehune Breakwater. The park was dedicated in 1953 when the county leased the site from Bishop Estate. Fee simple title was acquired in 1966. The park is the most popular nearshore snorkeling site in Kona. The dive site is in deeper waters offshore. The surf site is at the end of the breakwater. 2. Regional park (2.7 acres), Kahaluʻu, Oʻahu. *Lit.*, diving place.

Kahamanini. Beach, Wailea, Maui. Calcareous sand beach now known as Wailea Beach. *Lit.*, place [of the] surgeon fish.

Kahana. 1. Beach, Kahana, Maui. Narrow calcareous sand beach that lies within the boundaries of the land division of Kahana. 2. Bay, beach park, surf site, Kahana, Oʻahu. Calcareous sand beach between the mouth of Kahana Stream and the Kahana Boat Ramp. The surf site is a shorebreak on the shallow sandbar fronting the beach. A second surf site identified by the same name is a big-wave, second-reef break off the north point of the bay. 3. Boat ramp, Kahana, Oʻahu. Facilities include a ramp and a vessel washdown area. Also known as Kapaʻeleʻele. 4. State park, Kahana, Oʻahu. *Lit.*, cutting or turning point.

 moʻolelo

I was born in Papaʻakoko in 1890. Papaʻakoko is in Kaluanui near Pat's at Punaluʻu. I had sixteen older sisters. My father died the day I was born, so my mother moved to Hauʻula near the *muliwai* in the park and then to Kahana. When I was a teenager I was a musician, and my friends and I used to play at the Haleʻiwa Hotel for three dollars a night. I also used to serenade the girls here in the valley. I would tie a thread to a common pin and stick it in the wall of the girl's bedroom. Then I would trail the thread back to my house, and tie the other end to another common pin and stick it in the string bridge on the sound box of my guitar. Then I would play slack key using the *kiʻi wahine* tuning and the music would travel back to the girl's room and serenade her. Only slack key would carry across the thread.

When the boat ramp was built, I blessed it and named it Kapaʻeleʻele. That's the old name for that point. The next little point is Keaniani, and the last little point is Kaluapulehu. Kulaa-hulili is the flat, open area beyond Kahana. It was used for horse racing. Going towards Kaʻaʻawa, there's Wailua, the small stream in the grove near Kapaʻeleʻele. *Wailua* means "water from the hole." And then there's Huilua, the fishpond near the big stream. *Huilua* means "two get together." Pu'u Mahie is the last point. *Mahie* means "pleasant connotations, no harm."

 Peter Kau, November 22, 1972

Kahanamoku. 1. Beach, lagoon, Honolulu, O'ahu. Man-made beach and lagoon dredged out of the reef in 1955 by Henry J. Kaiser, developer of the Kaiser Hawaiian Village Hotel, now the Hilton Hawaiian Village. Kaiser enhanced the beach and the lagoon by importing calcareous sand. 2. Beach park (.4 acres), Waikīkī, O'ahu. The beach, the lagoon, and the park were named for Duke Paoa Kahanamoku (1890–1968), former Olympic swimming star and for many years sheriff of Honolulu. Duke was named for his father, who was named by Bernice Pauahi Bishop to commemorate the visit of the Duke of Edinburgh to Hawai'i in 1869. The beach and the lagoon were named for Kahanamoku in 1958 to recognize the area where he learned to swim. Also known as Kālia.

Kahapapa. Fishpond, 'Anaeho'omalu, Hawai'i. One of two fishponds behind 'Anaeho'omalu Beach. Perhaps literally, reef place.

Kahauloa. Cove, dive site, Hawai'i Kai, O'ahu. Rocky cove on the west side of the Lāna'i Lookout on Kalaniana'ole Highway. Kahauloa is the name of the crater across the highway that houses the Koko Head Shooting Complex. Also known as Lāna'i Lookout, Rifle Range. *Lit.,* the tall *hau* tree.

Kahawai. Support park, Sunset Beach, O'ahu. Across Kamehameha Highway from the beach between Ke Iki and Ke Waena Roads. *Lit.,* stream.

Kāhe'a. Cove, Hāmākua Poko, Maui. First large, rocky cove east of Ho'okipa Beach Park. Also known as Turtle Bay. *Lit.,* the red stains or streaks (as at dawn).

Kahekili. Beach park, dive site, Kā'anapali, Maui. At the north end of the Kā'anapali Resort. The park is one of West Maui's most popular dive and snorkeling sites. Kahekili was a famous Maui chief who ruled for twenty-seven years on Maui until 1782 and then for nine years on O'ahu. *Lit.,* the thunder.

Kahekili's Leap. Sea cliff, Mōkapu, O'ahu. Kahekili, a king of O'ahu whose son Kalanikupule fought Kamehameha I in the famous battle at Nu'uanu Pali, is said to have jumped from the cliff into the ocean. Also known as Pali Kaholo.

Kahemanō. Beach, Kahemanō, Lāna'i. Narrow detrital sand beach at the seaward end of the 'Awehi Trail, which intersects the Munro Trail on the summit of Maunalei. The reef offshore attracts small schools of sharks, but what brings them here is unknown. *Lit.*, school [of] sharks.

Kahe Point. Beach park (4.5 acres), dive site, Wai'anae, O'ahu. The beach park is on the low sea cliffs at Kahe Point. The dive site is off Hawaiian Electric Beach Park to the west and focuses on the two submerged discharge pipes from the power plant. The dive site is also known as Electric Beach. *Lit.*, flow.

Kahikilani. Rock, Sunset Beach, O'ahu. Kahikilani was a legendary surfer whose wife gave him a *lehua* lei every day. One day he returned wearing an *'ilima* lei given to him by another woman. Angered, his wife called upon her *'aumakua*, or family god, and Kahikilani was turned to stone. His head is visible on the ridge inland of Rocky Point. The rock formation is also known as the George Washington Stone. *Lit.*, the arrival [of the] chief.

Kāhili. 1. Beach, quarry, Kīlauea, Kaua'i. Long calcareous sand beach at the head of Kīlauea Bay. Vegetated dunes line the backshore and Kīlauea Stream crosses the west end of the beach. The beach was named for the Kāhili Quarry at the eastern point of the bay. The 400-foot boulder revetment at the point was completed in 1971 to protect the quarry equipment from high surf. 2. Beach, Kalaupapa, Moloka'i. One of five beaches on Kalaupapa Peninsula. Long, wide, steep strip of coral rubble and calcareous sand on the west side of the airport pavilion. Kāhili is a storm beach that was created by high surf carrying the beach material inland over the rocks between the beach and the ocean. Kāhili is probably short for Kāhili'opua, a chiefess of the former village at 'Īliopi'i, who lived in the present airport area with only female retainers. From a rock chair called Kanohopōhaku o Kāhili'opua, she acted as an intermediary for men seeking wives or companions. The rock is near the airport gate. *Lit.*, the feather standard.

Kahinapōhaku. Fishpond, Hālawa, Moloka'i. *Lit.*, stone carving.

Kahinihini'ula. Pool, Honokōhau, Hawai'i. Freshwater pool inland of Honokōhau Beach in Kalako-Honokōhau National Historic Park. Also known as the Queen's Bath. *Lit.*, the red moss.

Kahiolo. Point, Punalu'u, Hawai'i. At the east end of Punalu'u Beach and the site of Punalu'u Boat Ramp. The ruins of the former Punalu'u Landing and precontact ruins, including a *heiau* and a sacrificial stone, are also here. *Lit.*, the collapse, or the defeat.

Kahi'u. Point, Kalaupapa, Moloka'i. Northernmost point on Kalaupapa Peninsula. *Lit.*, the fish tail.

Kaholo Pali. Sea cliff, southwest shore, Lāna'i. At 1,000 feet, Kaholo Pali is the highest sea cliff on Lāna'i and also the highest south-shore sea cliff in Hawai'i. Although there are higher sea cliffs in Hawaiʻi, they are located on the northern sides of the islands. Also known as Pali Kaholo. *Lit.*, landslide cliff.

Kahoʻohaʻihaʻi. Beach, cove, fishing site, Hawaiʻi Kai, Oʻahu. Small pocket beach at the head of the cove and the adjoining rocky shore on the west side of the small breakwater at Queen's Beach. *Lit.*, the breaking of waves.

Kahoʻolawe. 1. Island, Maui County. The smallest of the eight major Hawaiian Islands (about 45 square miles). The highest point on the island is 1,477 feet above sea level. The emblem of the island is the *pua hinahina (Heliotropium anomalum).* 2. Island reserve, Maui County. In 1993, the Hawaiʻi State Legislature passed Chapter 6K Hawaiʻi Revised Statutes, which established the Kahoʻolawe Island Reserve to include the island of Kahoʻolawe and the submerged lands and waters extending 2 miles from its shore. Under the law, the island is to be used exclusively for the following purposes: "a. preservation and practice of all rights customarily and traditionally exercised by native Hawaiians for cultural, spiritual, and subsistence purposes; b. preservation and protection of its archaeological, historical, and environmental resources; c. rehabilitation, re-vegetation, habitat restoration, and preservation; and d. education." Commercial uses are strictly prohibited. Chapter 6K also provides for the eventual transfer of the Kahoʻolawe Island Reserve to the sovereign native Hawaiian entity as follows: "Upon its return to the State, the resources and waters of Kahoʻolawe shall be held in trust as part of the public land trust; provided that the State shall transfer management and control of the island and its waters to sovereign native Hawaiian entity upon its recognition by the United States and the State of Hawaiʻi. In the interim, the island is managed by the Kahoʻolawe Island Reserve Commission." 3. Point light, Kealaikahiki, Kahoʻolawe. Established in 1928 at Kealaikahiki Point. A 20-foot skeleton tower approximately 100 feet above sea level. *Lit.*, the carrying away [by currents].

 *moʻolelo*

I bought my first sampan in 1933 and started commercial fishing to supplement my income from Wailuku Sugar. I fished all around **Kahoʻolawe** and mingled with the old Hawaiians who fished and hunted there. I learned the names on the island from them, but not everyone used the Hawaiian names. Hanakanaʻia was Smuggler's. Several families on Maui were in on the opium smuggling. The contraband was brought by boat from the Orient and landed on Kahoʻolawe. Then it was taken to Maui and then to Oʻahu on the old interisland steamers. Honokoa was called

Tickman Bay. He lived in Waikapū and wrecked his boat there in the late 1920s. There's a big rock in the middle of the bay, and boats going in have to keep right. At the other end of the island, Ule Point was good for *ehu,* and Kanapou was good for *'ōpelu.* But you had to watch out for the *kākū* [barracuda]; there were plenty of them and they would attack. The old-time Japanese commercial fishermen called Kanapou "Obake." The wind and currents were bad sometimes and came out of nowhere, but it's a good *kona* storm anchorage. A lot of *koa'e* lived on Pu'u Koa'e, but the Hawaiians called it Kaho'olaweli'ili'i. In English it's called Little Kaho'olawe.

 Louis Hubbard, June 14, 1978

Kaho'olaweli'ili'i. Dive site, island (13 acres, 378 feet high), south coast, Kaho'olawe. Small island with steep sides west of Kamō-hio Bay. The shape of the island was said to resemble that of Kaho'olawe, so it was called "Small Kaho'olawe." Also known as Li'ili'i, Pu'u Koa'e. *Lit.,* small Kaho'olawe.

Kahue. Beach, Kahue, Lāna'i. Narrow calcareous sand beach that is a section of Shipwreck Beach. *Lit.,* the gourd.

Kahuku. 1. Beach, Pōhue, Hawai'i. Small calcareous sand beach on Pōhue Bay. The property surrounding the beach has been owned for many years by Kahuku Ranch, so some area residents call the beach Kahuku Beach. Also known as Glover's Beach, Pōhue Beach. 2. Beach, Kahuku, O'ahu. Calcareous sand beach and dunes fronting Kahuku Golf Course. Also known as Keone'ō'io. 3. Point, Kahuku, O'ahu. Northernmost point on O'ahu. Also known as Kalaeokauna'oa. *Lit.,* the projection.

Kahuku Ledge. Dive site, Kahuku, O'ahu. Ledge three-quarters of a mile off Kahuku Point at 70 feet and parallel to shore.

Kahului. 1. Beach, Kahului, Maui. Narrow detrital sand beach between Kahului Beach Road and Pier. 2. Harbor, Kahului, Maui. Maui's only deep-draft harbor. First used as a commercial landing in 1879 by Maui sugar planters. By 1910, the Kahului Railroad Company had completed an 1,800-foot long breakwater, dredged a turning basin, and constructed a 200-foot wharf. Facilities now include a 2,315-foot breakwater to the west, a 2,760-foot breakwater to the east, a 600-foot wide entrance channel, and two commercial piers. 3. Harbor range lights, light, Kahului, Maui. A light was established on the Kahului waterfront in 1905. Kahului Light, the 32-foot skeleton tower on the east breakwater, was built in 1917. 4. Ramp, Kahului, Maui. Constructed in 1963 in Kahului Breakwater Park, the park on the west breakwater of the harbor. Facilities include a ramp, a dock, and a vessel washdown area. Perhaps *lit.*, the winning.

Kahului Breakwater. Park, Kahului, Maui. Except for Kahului Ramp, an otherwise undeveloped park on the west breakwater of Kahului Harbor that is a large landfill.

Kahului Harbor. Surf site, Kahului, Maui. On a shallow reef inside the harbor off Kahului Ramp.

Kahuwai. 1. Bay, Kaʻūpūlehu, Hawaiʻi. Small bay with a deep channel into Kaʻūpūlehu Beach fronting the Kona Village Resort. 2. Beach, Puna, Hawaiʻi. Black sand beach that formed in 1960 at the end of the Kapoho eruption. This eruption destroyed the nearby village of Kapoho and entered the ocean to the east of Kahuwai. Steam explosions from the interaction of the molten lava and the ocean created the cinder, or "black sand," and the prevailing currents transported it to Kahuwai. Also known as Orr's Beach. *Lit.*, caretaker [of the] water.

 moʻolelo

I was born at Laupāhoehoe but raised by my grandparents at Koaʻe in Puna where the old county dirt road and the paved road meet. There were many *koaʻe* that nested at Kīpū, a sea cliff below us, but the cliff was wiped out with most of the village by the 1960 lava flow. Kahuwai, Waʻawaʻa, Honolulu, and Makuʻu were the villages to the north, and they were connected by trails, *ala hele*, that were paved with *pohaku ʻala*. At one time all the villages were canoe landings with black sand beaches, but the shoreline dropped in 1924, and it took away the sand and changed the shoreline. People began moving away.

There were many *hala* trees nearby at Waiʻeli, and we planted dryland taro around them and jokingly called it our *pū hala* taro patch. Hau was important to us, too, and we used the bark for cordage and for sandals—*pale wāwae*. The Hawaiians didn't go around barefoot like everyone thinks, and my grandfather showed me how to make sandals. He also made sandals out of the *ule hala*—the *hala* root—for going along the ocean. The *ule hala* sandals didn't slip on wet rocks.

Kahuwai was the name of a legendary person. It was a canoe-building village, but the logs came from Nanawale. The Kelas were the last family to live there.

Minnie Kaawaloa, June 24, 1982

My wife and I started visiting the Big Island in the 1950s, staying in the Kapoho Beach Lots. One day we picnicked nearby on the Hilo side of Cape Kumukahi. I took a walk along the shore and found the beach. There was no sand there until after the 1960 lava flow and the ocean currents brought the cinder in. We decided that we wanted to build a house on the cliff above the beach, but it was Bishop Estate land, so we talked to Arthur Lyman at Kapoho. His brother Richard was one of the Bishop Estate trustees and with his help we got a lease in 1963 and built our home. That's when people started calling it Orr's Beach.

The Hawaiian name for this area is **Kahuwai,** and at one time it was an extensive village. The missionary William Ellis mentions it in his journal of 1823. The village is well preserved because no agricultural work or land clearing was done in this part of Puna. Whales come in close to the sea cliffs, and we've seen them mating. They lie side-by-side, belly-to-belly, with their pectoral flukes skyward. Turtles have found the beach and occasionally lay their eggs in the sand.

 John Orr, June 23, 1982

Kai'ae. Beach, surf site, Mokulē'ia, O'ahu. Last section of Mokulē'ia Beach west of Camp Erdman. The surf site is off the Lyman home of the same name, Kai'ae, and is also known as Kimo's, Lyman's, and Lone Tree. Kai'ae was the site of a small fishing village west of the Lyman home that was sustained by a perched spring, Kawaiaka'aiea, the same spring that provides water for the Lymans. *Lit.,* edge [of the] sea.

Kai'ahulu. 1. Bay, beach, beach retreat, Mokulē'ia, O'ahu. Calcareous sand beach that is a section of Mokulē'ia Beach. The beach retreat named Kai'ahulu is for the use of employees of Castle and Cooke. Edward Tenney, a longtime employee, gave it to the firm. *Lit.,* foamy sea.

Kaiaka. 1. Bay, channel, Hale'iwa, O'ahu. Bay with a narrow black detrital sand beach on the west side of Kaiaka Bay Beach Park. The waters of Kaukonahua and Paukauila Streams flow through the bay into the ocean and have cut a wide channel through the reef offshore. 2. Bay, Ka'a'awa, O'ahu. Off Kalae-'ō'io Beach Park. *Lit.,* shadowy sea.

Kaiaka Bay Beach Park. (52.8 acres), Hale'iwa, O'ahu. Calcareous sand beach and beach park on the northeast point of Kaiaka Bay. The former site of Fresh Air Camp, the park contains a famous historic pedestal rock called Pōhaku Lāna'i.

Kaiehu. Beach, point, Mo'omomi, Moloka'i. Long calcareous sand beach that adjoins Kaiehu Point and that borders the sand dunes of Keonelele. *Lit.,* sea spray.

Ka'ie'ie Waho. Channel between O'ahu and Kaua'i. Also known as Kaua'i Channel. *Lit.,* the outside high [waves].

Kaihalulu. 1. Bay, beach, Hāna, Maui. Ka'ūiki Head separates Hāna Bay to the north from Kaihalulu Bay to the south. Kaihalulu Beach is a red sand beach on the south side of Ka'ūiki Head at the head of Kaihalulu Bay. Also known as Ka'ūiki

Beach, Red Sand Beach. 2. Beach, Kahuku, Oʻahu. Calcareous sand beach between the Turtle Bay Hilton Hotel and Kahuku Point. *Lit.*, roaring sea.

Kaikoʻo. Surf site, Kāhala, Oʻahu. Off the public right-of-way at the end of Kaikoʻo Place. Kaikoʻo was the name of an estate here that belonged to the wife of former governor George R. Carter. The estate bordered the sea and was subdivided in the early 1950s. Also known as Halemanō, Halemanu. *Lit.*, strong sea.

Kaʻiliʻili. 1. Beach, Olowalu, Maui. Narrow detrital sand and pebble beach east of Hekili Point at Olowalu. Popular roadside snorkeling site. 2. Beach, fishing site, Hawaiʻi Kai, Oʻahu. Calcareous sand beach fronted by a low lava bench between the former Wāwāmalu Ranch boundary wall and Kaloko Point. Also known as Queen's Beach. *Lit.*, the pebble.

Kāʻilikiʻi. Beach, surf site, Kahuku, Hawaiʻi. Green sand beach with a foreshore of pebbles at the head of a small bay. The surf site is off the beach. The beach and the surf site take their name from Kāʻilikiʻi, a former fishing village and landing. When outrigger canoes were still the primary mode of transportation, Hawaiians traveling from Kona to Kaʻū normally did not paddle or sail past Ka Lae, or South Point, with its powerful winds and dangerous currents. They landed at Kāʻilikiʻi and then walked east. *Lit.*, seize [the] wooden image.

Kaʻīlio. Point, reef, Hāʻena, Kauaʻi. Point and reef on the west side of Limahuli Stream. Two sites are known here as Kaʻīlioiki and Kaʻīlionui. Also known as Reefers. *Lit.*, the dog.

Kailua. 1. Bay, pier, Kailua, Hawaiʻi. On April 4, 1820, the first company of Congregational missionaries from New England landed on the shore of the bay at the site of the pier. The pier is used by commercial and privately owned boats and is internationally known as the start and finish of the swim portion of the Ironman Triathlon since 1980 and as the weigh-in site for the Hawaiian International Billfish Tournament since 1959. Also known as Kailua-Kona Wharf. 2. Bay entrance light, light, Kailua, Hawaiʻi. The Kailua Light was established in 1909 at Kukaʻilimoku Point on the north side of Kailua Bay. The light tower was built in 1915. The Kailua Bay Entrance Light is a 25-foot pole with a light on Kailua Pier. 3. Bay, Kailua, Maui. Small bay with a rocky shore in East Maui. 4. Bay, beach, beach park (35.2 acres), boat ramp, windsurf site, Kailua, Oʻahu. The bay and the 2.5-mile calcareous sand beach that lines it are between Alāla and Kapoho Points. The beach park is at the south end of the beach, where it is bisected by Kaʻelepulu Canal. The boat ramp is at the south end of the beach park in the lee of Alāla Point. The windsurf site is off the beach park. *Lit.*, two seas (probably two currents).

 *moʻolelo*

I was born in Kailua at our family home Mahulua in 1892. *Mahulua* means "two vapors," and it was where the Liberty House parking lot is today. We also owned property at the end of the beach park. My dad named our home there Kalapawai, "the rascal water," for one of the best fishermen in Kailua. I put up a sign that said "Kalapawai" near Kalaheo Avenue, and the Wong family used the name for their store. The old-timers called the Mokulua Islands Moku Nui and Moku Iki. These names were used very commonly. The point inshore was Popoʻo, not Wailea. Wailea was a small *muliwai* [pool] on the Kailua side of the point. We also called the pond in the middle of the beach park the *muliwai*, too. *Mōkōlea* means "plover island." During the day, Kula o ʻAlele, the plains of Kailua, would be covered with them, and at night they flew by the hundreds to Mōkōlea.

 Louis Mahoe, August 28, 1972

Kailua Bay. Offshore mooring, Kailua, Hawaiʻi. Boat mooring site in Kailua Bay.

Kailua-Kona. 1. Coastal district, Kailua-Kona, Hawaiʻi. The islands of Hawaiʻi, Maui, and Oʻahu each have a town named Kailua. This situation created a mail delivery problem, primarily between the two larger Kailua towns on Hawaiʻi and Oʻahu, so in 1957 the U.S. Postal Service changed the postal designation of Kailua on Hawaiʻi to Kona, the name of the district. Members of the Kona Civic Club, however, believed that the name Kailua should be preserved. They successfully petitioned for the name Kailua-Kona, which was officially adopted on July 13, 1957. This change solved the mail delivery problem but also has resulted in the town often being called Kailua-Kona instead of Kailua. 2. Wharf, Kailua, Hawaiʻi. Facilities in-clude eleven recreational berths, anchor mooring in the bay adjacent to the wharf, a ramp, and a vessel washdown area. Also known as Kailua Pier.

Kailua Reef. Dive site, Kailua, Hawaiʻi. Reef in Kailua Bay with ledges at 30 to 60 feet.

Kaimana. 1. Beach, Waikīkī, Oʻahu. Pocket of calcareous sand that is a section of Waikīkī Beach between the War Memorial Natatorium and the New Otani Kaimana Beach Hotel. The name Kaimana for the beach came from its proximity to the hotel. Also known as Dig Me Beach, Sans Souci. 2. Channel, Waikīkī, Oʻahu. Channel through the reef fronting Kaimana Beach. This channel is the beginning of the Waikīkī Rough-water Swim corridor and is used daily by open ocean swimmers to access the deeper waters beyond the reef. *Lit.*, diamond (English).

Kaimana Hila. Crater, Waikīkī, Oʻahu. British sailors originally called Diamond Head "Diamond Hill." Hawaiians pronounced it "Kaimana Hila." *Lit.*, diamond hill (English).

Kaimū. Beach Park, Kaimū, Hawaiʻi. Once the site of Hawaiʻi's most famous and most photographed black sand beach, the beach and park were overrun by lava flows from Kīlauea in 1990. The flows also filled the bay that fronted the beach, destroying several surf sites. The park's shore is now rocky, with small pockets of black sand. *Lit.*, gathering [at the] sea [to watch surfing], or silent sea.

Kainaliu. Beach, Kainaliu, Hawaiʻi. Small storm beaches of calcareous sand on the low sea cliffs in Kainaliu. *Lit.*, bail the canoe bilge.

Kāināʻohe. Fishpond, Kamalō, Molokaʻi. *Lit.*, cast with the bamboo.

Kaiona. Beach park (4.3 acres), boat ramp, surf site, Waimānalo, Oʻahu. Small beach park at the south end of Waimānalo Beach. The boat ramp is only for small boats and was built by the community in 1999. Also known as Waimānalo Boat Ramp. The surf site is at the north end of the reef off the beach park. The name of a legendary person, a relative of Pele, goddess of the volcano.

Kaiser Channel. Waikīkī, Oʻahu. Boat channel dredged through the reef in 1955 by Henry J. Kaiser during the development of the Kaiser Hawaiian Village Hotel, now the Hilton Hawaiian Village.

Kaiser's. Surf site, Waikīkī, Oʻahu. In 1954, Henry J. Kaiser and Fritz Burns purchased 8 acres of Waikīkī beachfront property from the John Ena Estate and several adjoining properties, including the Niumalu Hotel. Their intent was to build the first self-contained visitor resort in Waikīkī. In mid-1955 the first increment of the Kaiser Hawaiian Village Hotel opened for business. Kaiser then dredged a channel, the Kaiser Channel, through the reef to allow access to the beach for commercial catamaran tours. The surf site is on the west margin of the Kaiser Channel. In 1961, Conrad Hilton bought the resort for $21.5 million. It is now called the Hilton Hawaiian Village, but the name Kaiser's for the surf site has not changed.

Kaiwi. 1. Dive site, point, Honokōhau, Hawaiʻi. One of the most popular dive sites on the Big Island. Besides being the name of an individual dive site south of Honokōhau Small Boat Harbor at Kaiwi Point, Kaiwi is also an area name that includes other individual sites, such as Kona Cathedrals. 2. Channel, Oʻahu. A 25-mile-wide channel between the west end of Molo-

ka'i and the east end of O'ahu. 3. Coast, shore, Hawai'i Kai,
O'ahu. Same as Ka Iwi. *Lit.*, the bone.

Ka Iwi. Coast, scenic shoreline park, shore, Hawai'i Kai, O'ahu.
In 1987, the Sea Grant Extension Service at the University of
Hawai'i–Mānoa convened a task force of concerned citizens
to determine if the shore lands and parks from Hanauma Bay
to Makapu'u Beach Park could be integrated into a single state
or national park to protect the area from further development.
Task force member John Clark suggested the name Kaiwi for
the new park. He noted that the Kaiwi or Moloka'i Channel
was a common element to the individual properties and parks.
It touched each of them, unifying all of them. The task force
adopted the name, elected to spell it as two words, Ka Iwi, and
then called themselves the Ka Iwi Scenic Shoreline Park Ini-
tiating Committee. On April 1, 1988, under the leadership of
Marion Kelly, the committee was successful in introducing a
resolution in the State Legislature that encouraged all of the
concerned parties to work together to establish the unified
park. Although a single, unified park was never established in
the years that followed, the name Ka Iwi has been perpetuated
on O'ahu's east end as either the Ka Iwi Coast or the Ka Iwi
Shoreline. Also known as Queen's Beach, Wāwāmalu.

Ka Iwi o Pele. Cinder cone, Hāna, Maui. Cinder cone of the
Hāna Volcanic Series on the north end of Leho'ula Beach. *Lit.*,
the bone of Pele. Bones of Pele, the goddess of the volcano,
were left here after a battle with her sister, Nā Maka o Kaha'i.

Kaiwi Point. 1. Dive site, Honokōhau, Hawai'i. Off Kaiwi Point
between Old Kona Airport State Park and Honokōhau Small
Boat Harbor. Lava tubes, arches, pinnacles, and dramatic dropoffs at approximately 40 feet. 2. Fishing site, Keawaiki, Hawai'i.
On the point at the south end of Keawaiki Bay.

Kaka'ako 1. Peninsula, O'ahu. Land seaward of Ala Moana
Boulevard between Kewalo Basin and Honolulu Harbor. The
eastern half of the peninsula is the result of a reclamation
project that began in 1948 with the construction of a massive
seawall 10 feet high, 10 feet wide, and 30 feet wide at its base.
The wall began on the reef near Olomehani Street and followed
the Kewalo Channel to the present site of the University of
Hawai'i's Pacific Biomedical Research Center. Then it was
extended west to Fort Armstrong. With the completion of the
seawall, the city began a reclamation project on the reef to
create new industrial land. The shallow reef enclosed by the
seawall was used as a landfill for noncombustible materials
from the nearby incinerator and for other municipal refuse.
The western half of the peninsula is the result of an earlier
landfill to create Fort Armstrong and Piers 1 and 2 in Hono-

lulu Harbor. 2. Waterfront park (35 acres), Oʻahu. State park at the seaward end of the Kakaʻako Peninsula that was completed in 1992. *Lit.,* dull, slow.

 moʻolelo

My family came from Nāpōʻopoʻo in 1939. Our first home was in Squattersville near Kewalo Basin, and at that time the shoreline was at Olomehami Street. The water came up to a low stone wall. The reef was a good *limu* ground, and many Japanese from Kakaʻako came to pick *ogo*. There was also a lot of *wana,* squid, and fish. We made our own goggles by carving *hau* branches and inserting pieces of glass. We used strips of inner tube for the head straps. There was good surf on the reef, too, and we surfed on the old redwood planks. In 1948 the city decided to make a dump for the new incinerator, and they built a boulder seawall along the boat channel and across the reef. It surrounded a wreck, a PT boat called the *La Putita.* The boat was our playground and we often camped on it, but by 1956 the boat and the reef were covered over by fill.

James "Kimo" Kalua, October 19, 1975

In 1948 I was working for the Roads Division, and at that time the Roads and Refuse Divisions were together. I was the superintendent for the Kewalo seawall job. It started in August at the Otani Fishcake Factory and followed the boat channel out to where the UH research center is now. The boulders for this section and around the point 150 feet towards Waiʻanae came from Wailupe, where they were clearing to build ʻĀina Haina. The boulders for the rest of the wall came from Punchbowl, where James W. Glover, Ltd., was putting in the access road and clearing the crater floor for the national memorial cemetery. We completed the wall in 1949.

 Hamilton Rodrigues, October 25, 1975

Kakahaiʻa. Beach park, national wildlife refuge, Kakahaiʻa, Molokaʻi. Small roadside beach park named for a pond on the inland side of Kamehameha V Highway. A narrow detrital sand beach bordering a shallow reef flat fronts the park. The Kakahaiʻa National Wildlife Refuge is a 42-acre refuge that includes a freshwater pond and marsh with dense thickets of bulrush. Native birds such as the Hawaiian coot and Hawaiian stilt are found here, along with migratory seabirds and waterfowl. Also known as Rice Patch. Perhaps lit., shallow place in the sea [where there are] fish.

Kakaihala. Fishing site, reef, Hauʻula, Oʻahu. North of Kaipapaʻu Point.

Kākalaioa. Rock, Makapuʻu, Oʻahu. Rock in the sea off Makapuʻu. *Lit.*, gray nickers (a rough bramble; the rocks here are as sharp as *kākalaioa* thorns).

Kākā Point. Dive site, east shore, Kahoʻolawe. *Lit.*, to hew.

Kākela. Beach, Kaipapaʻu, Oʻahu. The north half of Kokololio Beach Park was once the estate of the Castle family of Honolulu. The estate, with its two-story house, was known as Kākela, or "castle." In 1953, Zion Securities, the business branch of the Mormon Church, purchased the estate and maintained it as a private campsite for members of the church. The city acquired the property in 1988 and converted it into Kokololio Beach Park. *Lit.*, castle (English).

Kākiʻo. Beach, fishing site, Kahuku, Hawaiʻi. Small pocket of calcareous sand in the otherwise rocky shore of the 1887 lava flow. *Lit.*, skin rash or sore.

Kākipi. Bay, fishing site, Kaupakalua, Maui. Gulch inland of Halehaku Bay that is also used by some fishermen as the name of the bay. Also known as Halehaku Bay.

Kalaʻa. Point, Kalaupapa, Molokaʻi. One of two points that borders ʻĪliopiʻi Beach. *Lit.*, the rocky point.

Ka Lae. Fishing site, light, point, Kahuku, Hawaiʻi. Ka Lae is the southernmost point in the United States and a famous historic fishing site. The light was established in 1906 approximately 63 feet above sea level and automated in 1949. The 32-foot pole with the light atop was erected in 1972. Also known as South Point. *Lit.*, the point.

Kalaehou. Same as Hou Point. *Lit.*, the new point.

Kalaehuku. Beach, Kamaʻole, Maui. Also known as Kamaʻole I Beach Park. *Lit.*, the protruding point.

Kalaeloa. 1. Harbor, point, Keawanui, Molokaʻi. Kalaeloa is the point between Keawanui and Mikiawa fishponds. The harbor was named after the point. Although it is the largest and best-protected harbor on this coast, it is used only by shallow-draft boats because of its shallow entrance channel. 2. Regional park (120 acres), Kalaeloa, Oʻahu. On July 2, 1999, Barbers Point Naval Air Station was turned over to the state, although the navy retained a number of housing units with a commissary and exchange. Part of the conveyed property included this beach park between White Plains Beach and the runways. 3. Community development district. Name given to the former Barbers Point Naval Air Station when it was turned over to the state on July 2, 1999. On July 13, 2000, the U.S. Board on Geographic Names approved the BPNAS Redevelopment Commission's application to apply the name Kalaeloa to the surplus land that was conveyed to various state and county agencies for public purposes. The name change to Kalaeloa was consistent with a State of Hawai'i 1995 legislative resolution requesting that Kalaeloa, the traditional Hawaiian name for the area, be used instead of Barbers Point. 4. Point, Kalaeloa, O'ahu. Southwesternmost point on O'ahu. Also known as Barbers Point. *Lit.,* long point. Probably named for the view of the point from the east (Diamond Head) end of Mamala Bay, from which it appears to be an extremely long point.

Kalaeloa Barbers Point. Harbor, Kalaeloa, O'ahu. The harbor was known as Barbers Point Harbor until July 1999 when Barbers Point Naval Air Station was turned over to the state and Kalaeloa, the Hawaiian name of the point, was reintroduced. The state then renamed the harbor Kalaeloa Barbers Point Harbor. Developed in the 1980s, it became fully operational in July 1990 and includes an entrance channel, a harbor basin, a barge basin, several piers, storage yards, and an adminstration building.

Kalaeloa Unit. Wildlife refuge (37 acres), Kalaeloa, O'ahu. One of three satellite sections, or "units," of the Pearl Harbor National Wildlife Refuge. The unit is in the Kalaeloa Community Development District. The other units are Honouliuli and Waiawa. *Lit.,* the long point.

Kalaemilo. Point, Kalaupapa, Moloka'i. On the west shore of the peninsula and the site of the Ocean View Pavilion. Perhaps lit., the milo tree point or the twisting point.

Kalae'ō'io. Beach park (.8 acres), point, Ka'a'awa, O'ahu. Small, landscaped roadside park named after the point to the east. Kalae'ō'io Point is the coastal boundary between the districts of Ko'olaupoko and Ko'olauloa. *Lit.,* the point [of the] bonefish.

Kalaeokai'a. Estate, point, Kahana, Maui. Beachfront estate of the Robinson family in Kahana Bay. The name is from a legend of two men from Kahana who fished together in the bay. *Lit.,* the point of the fish.

Kalaeokamanu. Point, Kahuku, O'ahu. On the east side of the swimming cove adjacent to the Turtle Bay Hilton Hotel. *Lit.,* the point of the bird.

Kalaeokauna'oa. Point, Kahuku, O'ahu. Northernmost point on O'ahu. Also known as Kahuku Point. *Lit.,* the point of the native dodder or the point of the tube snail. Tube snails are mollusks that attach themselves to rocks and build a hard tube-shaped shell.

Kalaeokaunu. Point, Kahuku, O'ahu. Point on which the Turtle Bay Hilton Hotel was built. Also known as Kuilima Point. *Lit.,* the point of the altar.

Kalaeokūpaoa. Beach, point, Hale'iwa, O'ahu. Calcareous sand beach and point at Kaiaka Bay Beach Park, and the site of

Pōhaku Lāna'i, a famous pedestal rock. Also known as Kūpaoa. *Lit.,* the point of the octopus lure stone.

Kalaeopa'akai. Gathering site, point, Mākua, O'ahu. Point at the west end of 'Ōhikilolo Beach. Artificial depressions in the rocks here were used to produce salt by evaporating water from the ocean. *Lit.,* the point of salt.

Kalaeuila. Fishing site, point, Kahuku, O'ahu. Also known as High Rock Point. *Lit.,* the lightning point.

Kalāheo. Beach, Kalāheo, Kaua'i. Small flat pocket of calcareous sand fronted by boulders at the head of Kalāheo Gulch. Also known as Kawaihaka.

Kalāhiki. Beach, Ho'okena, Hawai'i. The former village of Kalāhiki is at the south end of Kauhakō Bay in Ho'okena on a low, wide lava peninsula that terminates at Limukoko Point. A long, wide calcareous sand, lava fragment, and coral rubble storm beach lines the point. The beach is fronted by a shallow fringing reef. Ruins of the village are in the vegetation inland of the beach. *Lit.,* the sunrise.

Kalāhuipua'a. Fishpond, shore, Mauna Lani, Hawai'i. Francis H. I. Brown (1892–1976), a part-Hawaiian businessman, politician, and sportsman, purchased the land division of Kalāhuipua'a in 1932 and used the site as his home. It includes Kalāhuipua'a Fishpond and three others—Waipuhi, Hopeaia, and Manoku—and a large coconut grove on the shore. Hawaiian composer Helen Desha Beamer, a family friend, immortalized Brown and his home in her song Ke Keawaiki Hula. In 1972 Brown sold his estate to the development company that built the Mauna Lani resort. Also known as Mauna Lani Beach. *Lit.,* the herd [of] pigs.

Kalakala. Fishing site, Kahuku, O'ahu. Finger of submerged rocks off the west end of Hanaka'ilio Beach. *Lit.,* rough, craggy.

Kalākaua Boat House. Maritime center, Honolulu, O'ahu. Kalākaua Boat House is the name of the building that houses the Hawai'i Maritime Center and museum at Pier 7 in Honolulu Harbor. The building was named for King David Kalākaua (1836–1891), an avid supporter of ocean sports.

Kalalau. 1. Beach, camping site, surf site, Nā Pali, Kaua'i. One of five beaches within Nā Pali Coast State Park. Long, wide calcareous sand beach on the shore of Kalalau Valley, fronted by a sandbar and backed by low vegetated dunes. During the summer, sand accretes to the west, extending into the large sea caves at the end of beach. The campsites border the beach. The surf site is a shorebreak on the sandbar. 2. Trail, Nā Pali, Kaua'i. Kalalau is the most famous coastal wilderness hiking destination in Hawai'i. The Kalalau Trail is an 11-mile hiking trail that begins at Kē'ē Beach in Hā'ena State Park and ends in Kalalau Valley in the Nā Pali Coast State Park. Between Kē'ē and Kalalau, the trail follows the sea cliffs, dropping down to sea level only at Hanakāpī'ai, 2 miles in from the start. *Lit.*, the straying.

Kalama. 1. Beach park (36.4 acres), surf site, Kīhei, Maui. The park was named for Samuel E. Kalama (1869–1933), chairman of the Maui Board of Supervisors from 1913 to 1933. The position of chairman of the board then was equivalent to the position of mayor today. Land for the park was acquired in 1939. The surf site is off the south end of the park and is also known as Kalama Point. 2. Beach, Kailua, O'ahu. Center section of Kailua Beach fronting Kalama Beach Club. In 1925, Harold Kainalu Long Castle opened the first housing tract in Kailua. He named it Kalama in honor of Queen Kalama, wife of Kamehameha III, who had previously owned the land division of Kailua. Castle set aside a large oceanfront parcel for the use of the tract residents as a private beach park. In 1928, a clubhouse and pavilion were built on the property, and it was named the Kalama Beach Club. The beach fronting the clubhouse has been known since as Kalama Beach. 3. Beach park (4.3 acres), Kailua, O'ahu. In 1978, the City and County of Honolulu purchased the Boettcher Estate on Kailua Beach for use as a community center and beach park. The acquisition included the Boettcher home, a historically significant building designed by architect Vladimir Ossipoff and constructed by Charles Boettcher II in 1936. The Boettcher Estate was part of the Kalama subdivision, so it was renamed Kalama Beach Park. *Lit.*, the torch.

Kalama Park. Dive site, Kīhei, Maui. Off the south end of Kalama Park.

Kalama Point. Surf site, Kīhei, Maui. Off the south end of Kalama Park. Also known as Kalama.

Kalama'ula. Shore, Kalama'ula, Moloka'i. In 1920 Congress passed the Hawaiian Homes Commission Act to provide public lands for Hawaiians who were "not less than one-half part of the blood of the races inhabiting the Hawaiian Islands previous to 1778." Provisions were made for a commission to administer the lands, and in 1925 Kalama'ula became the first Hawaiian homestead subdivision in the islands. Among the first residents there were Marcelus and Emma Kala Dudoit. Fronting their home was a large stone that had a natural etching of a sun and five rays, and it was from this stone called Kalama'ula that the area took its name. Mrs. Dudoit wrote a song entitled "Kalama'ula" in honor of her home. The song is now a Hawaiian falsetto standard. *Lit.*, the red torch.

mo'olelo

I was born in Kaka'ako on August 20, 1918, and I was the second youngest of the eight children in our family. My brother John was the youngest. My parents, Emma Kala and Marcellus Dudoit, moved to Kalama'ula in 1922. The Kalama'ula stone was right in our driveway, but we didn't know it was a famous stone. My dad wanted to get rid of it, so John and I tried with a sledgehammer, but we couldn't break it. Then we found out that it was the stone that Kalama'ula was named for, so we left it where it was. It has five natural veins in it, and the legend is that it's the handprint of a young woman. My mother wrote the song "Kalama'ula" about the beauty of the area and our home there. She died when I was five, so my sister, Hannah, later copyrighted the song on her behalf.

 Valentine Dudoit, September 22, 2000

Kalanai Point. Mālaekahana, O'ahu. Point dividing Mālaeka-hana and Lā'ie Bays.

Kalanipū'ao. Dive site, rock, Kalāheo, Kaua'i. Same as Lani-pū'ao Rock. *Lit.*, the enmeshed sky.

Kalaoa. Beach, surf site, east coast, Ni'ihau. The high south-eastern sea cliffs between Po'ooneone Beach and Pueo Point contain a series of narrow stream-cut valleys, some of which contain small pocket beaches of calcareous sand. Kalaoa Beach is the most prominent of these pocket beaches. The backshore is primarily a mudflat, and a shallow sandbar lies off the beach. The surf site is a shorebreak on the sandbar. *Lit.*, the choker (as a stick for catching eels).

Kalapaki. Beach, surf site, Nāwiliwili, Kaua'i. Calcareous sand beach at the north end of Nāwiliwili Harbor fronted by a shallow sandbar. The surf site is a shorebreak on the sandbar. Kalapaki is one of Kaua'i's most popular family beaches.

Kalapawai. Beach, Kailua, O'ahu. Solomon Mahoe, a resident of Kailua during the early 1900s, lived at the north end of Kailua Beach Park and named his home Kalapawai. He put the name on a sign at his front gate. The Wong family, the original owners of Kalapawai Store at the intersection of Kailua Road and Kalāheo Avenue, perpetuated it by using it as the name of their store. *Lit.*, the rippling water or the shining water.

Kalauhaehae. Beach, Niu, O'ahu. Calcareous sand beach at the end of the channel through the reef on the east side of Niu Peninsula. *Lit.*, the torn leaf.

Kalaupapa. 1. Dive site, Kalaupapa, Moloka'i. One of several dive sites on the leeward side of the peninsula. 2. Harbor, Ka-laupapa, Moloka'i. Small harbor on the southwest side of the

151

peninsula where supplies for the village are delivered by tug and barge twice a year. Improvements made in 1967 included a 144-foot-long rubblemound breakwater, a turning basin, and an entrance channel through the reef. Also known as Dawson Wharf. 3. Light, Kalaupapa, Moloka'i. Same as Moloka'i Light. 4. Peninsula, Kalaupapa, Moloka'i. Broad, low basaltic shield volcano that became a peninsula when lava from Kauhakō Crater flowed against the great sea cliffs of East Moloka'i. Although the peninsula consists of three land divisions—Kalaupapa, Makanalua, and Kalawao—it is known as Kalaupapa Peninsula. Kalaupapa has been the permanent settlement on the peninsula since the 1930s. In 1866, the Board of Health selected the peninsula to be the site of an exile colony for Hansen's Disease patients. Father Damien arrived in 1873 as the first resident Catholic priest and died there in 1889. 5. Trail, Kalaupapa, Moloka'i. The historic 3-mile cliff trail with twenty-six switchbacks begins 1,664 feet above sea level in Pala'au State Park and descends to 'Awahua Beach on the west side of the peninsula. *Lit.*, the flat plain or the broad, flat reef.

mo'olelo

I'm the minister of the church in Hālawa, but I was the administrator at Kalaupapa from 1947 to 1974. I was always interested in the old things, so I spoke to the Hawaiians and talked to the old residents. Ke One Ne'e o 'Awahua, "the sliding sands of 'Awahua," is the correct title of the black sand beach near the trail. 'Awahua was someone's name. My wife Abigail was a nurse, and when the patients had babies, she would carry them up the trail when they were several weeks old and accompany them to Honolulu. This was one of the hardest things for the patients, that there were no children in the settlement. The plateau to the left of the beach is Nihoa. Papaloa is the beach below the cemetery. The old-timers said this was the garden area of the settlement, and they grew watermelons there in the 1920s. Ocean View pavilion was Spud Patois' home. He ran the laundry, but he wasn't assigned a house in the settlement, so he used the beach house as his home. The '46 tidal wave took his house, and Ocean View was built on the foundation about 1952. 'Īliopi, the "stingy dog," is the next beach and a former village. You can still see many old walls. Kāhili is a beach that was named for a woman, Kāhili'opua, a chiefess from 'Īliopi. She moved to the airport area and had only female retainers. If someone wanted a wife or a helper, a *kōko'olua*, she acted as an intermediary. Her place of operation was Kanohopohaku o Kāhili'opua, the rock chair near the airport gate. One always went to her with gifts, *"hele no a lako."* Ho'olehua is the last sand beach on the point. Turtles laid their eggs there because it was easy for them to get in over the rocks, and from the airport to Ho'olehua was the place to gather salt.

 Elmer Wilson, May 31, 1978

Kalehuawehe. Surf site, Waikīkī, O'ahu. Site of the biggest surf in Waikīkī and the south shore of O'ahu. *Lit.,* the removed *lehua* lei. A legend tells of Pi'ikoi, who went to Waikīkī wearing a *lehua* lei and gave it to a chiefess who surfed with him. Also known as Castle's.

Kalei's Island. Reef, Kawela, O'ahu. Small island-shaped *papa,* or reef, at the west point of Kawela Bay that is awash at high tide but emergent at low tide. Named for Nancy Kalei Espinda Fernandez (1908–1989), a longtime Kawela Bay resident whose home was on the point inshore of the reef from the 1950s to the 1980s. Fernandez, who lived alone, often walked on the reef at low tide to gather *limu,* or seaweed, so the Kawela community regarded the reef as her "island." Following her death in December 1989, her children scattered her ashes here. Also known as Auntie Kalei's Island.

Kalelepā. Beach, Punalu'u, O'ahu. Section of Punalu'u Beach at the Kaluanui Stream bridge. The name refers to one of the adventures of the demigod Kamapua'a in which he was being pursued and jumped a fence here. *Lit.,* the fence jumper.

Kalepeamoa. Island, Kapu'a, Hawai'i. Small rock island fronting the beach at Kapu'a. The island marked the landing at Kapu'a for incoming fishing and voyaging canoes. *Lit.,* the cock's comb. The outline of the island is said to resemble a cock's comb against the setting sun.

Kalepolepo. Beach, beach park, fishpond, Kīhei, Maui. Calcareous sand beach in and on either side of Kalepolepo Fishpond. The small landscaped beach park borders the inner edge of the pond. The fishpond is also known as Ko'ie'ie. *Lit.,* the dirt. Possibly for the large dust storms that once swept through this area.

Kālia. Beach, Waikīkī, O'ahu. Section of Waikīkī Beach that includes Kahanamoku Beach and Lagoon, which is the shore fronting the Hilton Hawaiian Village.

Kalihi Channel. Honolulu, O'ahu. Main channel into Ke'ehi Lagoon and Ke'ehi Small Boat Harbor; a secondary channel into Honolulu Harbor. *Lit.,* the edge.

Kalihiwai. Bay, beach, surf site, Kaua'i. Wide pocket of calcareous sand fronted by a shallow sandbar at the head of the bay. Ironwood trees line the backshore. Surf sites are found at the small point at the west end of the beach, in the shorebreak on the sandbar, and at the outside point at the east end of the beach. *Lit.*, Kalihi [with a] stream. *Kalihi* means "the edge."

Kalili Surf Center. Recreation facility, Hale'iwa, O'ahu. Ocean recreation center and office building in Hale'iwa Ali'i Beach Park dedicated on September 11, 1976, to John K. Kalili, who died on July 1 that year. Kalili, a lifelong Hale'iwa resident, was a captain in the Honolulu Fire Department until he retired in 1946. He was an excellent waterman and made many high-surf rescues in the days when no other professional rescue assistance was available. He devoted his entire life to helping others on the North Shore and was a tireless volunteer for his church and other organizations. In 1974, he received an award from the *Honolulu Star-Bulletin* for his outstanding community service. Also known as the Hale'iwa Surf Center.

Kalohi Channel. Moloka'i. Channel 9 miles wide between Lāna'i and Moloka'i. *Lit.*, the slowness.

Kaloko. 1. Fishpond (11 acres), Honokōhau, Hawai'i. At the north end of Honokōhau Beach and part of the Kaloko-Honokōhau National Historical Park. The fishpond is a natural bay that was closed off with the construction of a 750-foot long boulder wall. 2. Point, pond, shore, Hawai'i Kai, O'ahu. Point and pond at the mouth of Kalama Stream, Hawai'i Kai, O'ahu. *Lit.*, the pond.

Kaloko'eli. Fishpond, Kaunakakai, Moloka'i. *Lit.*, the dug pond.

Kalokohanahou. Fishpond, Kāne'ohe, O'ahu. *Lit.*, the repaired pond.

Kaloko-Honokōhau National Historical Park. (1,161 acres), Honokōhau, Hawai'i. The park was established on November 10, 1978, and includes Kaloko and 'Aimakapā Fishponds, Queen's Bath, a section of the Māmalahoa Trail, petroglyphs, other archaeological sites, Honokōhau Beach, and 'Ai'ōpio Fishpond at the south end of the beach.

Kalokoiki. Beach, cove, Kahuku, O'ahu. Calcareous sand beach in a cove that forms the Turtle Bay Hilton Hotel's swimming area between Kalaeokaunu and Kalaeokamanu Points. 'Ō'io Stream formerly emptied into the cove but was rerouted to the east during the construction of the hotel in the early 1970s. The stream probably helped to shape the cove and the channel to the open ocean. Also known as the Keyhole. *Lit.*, the small pond.

Kalou. 1. Landing, Nu'u, Maui. At the east end of Nu'u Beach where an interisland steamer landing was located. 2. Marsh, Waiale'e, O'ahu. Inland of Waiale'e Beach. *Lit.*, the hook.

Kalua. Beach, reef, Waiehu, Maui. Narrow calcareous sand beach and shallow reef fronting Waiehu Beach Park. *Lit.*, the pit.

Kaluaapuhi. Fishpond, southwest coast, Moloka'i. *Lit.*, the pit of [the] eel.

Kaluahe'e. Rock, Pāhoehoe, Hawai'i. Small rock island near Pū'o'a Point. *Lit.*, the octopus hole.

Kaluahine. Waterfall, Kukuihaele, Hawai'i. Falls over a 1,000-foot sea cliff near the Waipi'o Valley Lookout that has a 620-foot cascade. One of several major waterfalls on the Big Island, with Hi'ilawe Falls in Waipi'o and 'Akaka Falls in Honomū. *Lit.*, the old lady.

Kaluahole. 1. Beach, Diamond Head, O'ahu. One of the former fisheries of Waikīkī that included the small pocket of calcareous sand at Mākālei Beach Park and the adjoining shore east to Beach Road. The name comes from a legend of 'Ai'ai, the son of Kū'ulakai, the god of fishermen. During his travels around O'ahu, 'Ai'ai placed a brown and white rock in the ocean here that attracted *āhole* fish. 2. Fishing site, Kahuku, O'ahu. Between Kahuku Golf Course and the Ki'i section of the James C. Campbell National Wildlife Refuge. *Lit.*, the pit [of the] adult *āhole* fish. Kaluahole is an abbreviation of Kaluaāhole.

Kaluakauwā. Pond, Hau'ula, O'ahu. Brackish-water pond on the north side of the Hau'ula Fire Station that was a *muliwai* —a pond separated from the ocean by a sandbar—before the construction of Kamehameha Highway. It was the home of a supernatural eel. *Lit.*, the pit [of the] servant.

Kaluako'i. Shore, west coast, Moloka'i. Shore of the Kaluako'i *ahupua'a*, or land division, that includes the Kaluako'i Resort and Kepuhi Beach. *Lit.*, the adze pit. There are adze pits nearby at Maunaloa and Mo'omomi.

Kaluanui. Beach, channel, Kaluanui, O'ahu. Calcareous sand beach fronting the land division of Kaluanui, the site of Sacred Falls, and a channel through the reef off the beach. *Lit.*, the big pit. The name is from the adventures of the demigod Kamapua'a in this area.

Kaluao'aihakoko. Beach, Kama'ole, Maui. Calcareous sand beach that fronts Kama'ole III Beach Park. In *Ruling Chiefs of Hawai'i*, Hawaiian historian Samuel Kamakau wrote: "Kiha a Pi'ilani killed 'Aihakoko's personal attendant in the sea. That was why 'Aihakoko lamented grievously at sea. He landed at Kapa'ahi in Kama'ole, Kula, and that place was given the name Ka Lua o 'Aihakoko." Also known as Kama'ole III Beach Park, Young's Beach. *Lit.*, the pit of 'Aihakoko.

Kaluapuhi. Fishpond, Mōkapu, O'ahu. Salt evaporation ponds were also found here near the fishpond. The surf site Zombies is offshore of the sluice gate, or *mākaha*, of the fishpond. *Lit.*, the eel pit (an eel-shaped rock was in a cave here).

Kaluapūleho. Point, Kahana, Oʻahu. The outermost point on the north side of Kahana Bay. *Lit.*, the pit [of the] cowrie shell.

Kamāhuʻehuʻe. Fishpond, Kamalō, Molokaʻi. *Lit.*, the openings.

Kamakahonu. Beach, Kailua, Hawaiʻi. Small pocket of calcareous sand fronting King Kamehameha's Kona Beach Hotel. This area was the last home of King Kamehameha I, who in 1810 became sole ruler of the Hawaiian Islands. In 1812, Kamehameha moved his royal residence from Honolulu to Kailua. His residential complex on the shore of Kailua Bay at Kamakahonu included thatched and stone houses and Ahuʻena Heiau. The king conducted personal and governmental matters here until his death on May 8, 1819. The U.S. Department of the Interior designated the complex a National Historic Landmark in 1964. *Lit.*, the turtle eye. A rock formation resembling a turtle was formerly on a lava outcrop at the south end of the beach. It was buried under the concrete used to construct Kailua Pier.

 moʻolelo

All my life I wanted to know the deep and beautiful things about Hawaiʻi and my Hawaiian people. This is one of their riddles:

> *Ua hanau ia o ka lani i nuna o Kamakaokahonu.*
> *Ua hanai ia o ka lani i nuna o Kamakaokahonu.*
> *Ua make o ka lani nui i nuna o Kamakaokahonu.*

In English it means:

> The king was born above Kamakaokahonu.
> The king was raised above Kamakaokahonu.
> The great king died above Kamakaokahonu.

The answer is Kamehameha the Great. At each of these times in his life, he was near a place called Kamakaokahonu. In the first two lines he is called *ka lani,* "the king," because he was a baby and a boy. In the last line he is called *ka lani nui,* "the great king," because when he died, he was the ruler of all the islands.

John Lane, July 17, 1981

There is a place—Kamakaokahonu in Kohala—that was a famous canoe landing for going [to] and coming from Maui.

Alfred Solomon, June 25, 1982

We moved to Honokāne Iki in 1917, after my dad took over as superintendent of the Kohala Ditch, but before that we lived in ʻAwini where my dad grew taro. Other families were farming there, too. Kamakahonu was the place in ʻAwini where Kamehameha was raised. Of course, I know where it is, but it's really overgrown now and kind of hard to describe if you haven't been up *mauka.*

Bill Sproat. July 14, 1982

There were two canoe landings in Kailua, one at the little sand beach next to Hulihe'e Palace and one at the beach at Makahonu. The turtle at Makahonu was outlined in the *pāhoehoe* under the old wharf. It was lying down, looking at the cove, and could be seen best at low tide. It was covered up by the new pier.

Bill Upchurch, September 29, 1981

I was born in 1909, and our family property was in the center of Kailua town about where the bend in the road is on Ali'i Drive. I lived there until I got married when I was nineteen. There was a lot of white sand around the pier, and we used to swim under it. I remember the stone under the pier that resembled a turtle, and that's why that place was called Makahonu. Our family and others kept their boats and canoes there.

 Agnes Kaelemakule Winsley Dairo, April 17, 1983

Kamāka'īpō. Beach, Lā'au, Moloka'i. Calcareous sand beach north of Lā'au Point approximately a mile long and fronted by a rock shelf. Low vegetated sand dunes comprise the backshore. Five sections of the beach have individual place names: Sam Wight's, Keo Nakama, Soda Pop Pool, Aholehole Flats, and Egusa's. *Lit.*, the night guard.

Kamalino. Bay, beach, surf site, southwest coast, Ni'ihau. Small bay with a pocket of calcareous sand. The surf site is off the north point of the bay and is also known as Antennas. *Lit.*, the calm.

Kamalō. Harbor, Kamalō, Moloka'i. Narrow detrital sand beach bordering a wide, shallow fringing reef. A natural opening in the reef serves as a harbor. *Lit.*, the dry place. The name was originally Kamalō'o and is now abbreviated to Kamalō.

Kama'ole. Beach parks, dive sites, surf sites, Kīhei, Maui. Kama-'ole is a land division that includes three beach parks: Kama-'ole I (2.9 acres acquired in 1938), also known as Kalaehuku; Kama'ole II (2.1 acres acquired in 1938), also known as 'Ili'iliholo; and Kama'ole III (5.9 acres acquired in 1947), also known as Kaluao'aihakoko, Young's Beach. The beach parks are on South Kīhei Road between Kīhei and Wailea. The surf sites are shorebreaks that form on the sandbars fronting the beaches. The dive sites are off parks II and III. *Lit.*, childless.

Kamehame. Beach, fishing site, littoral cone (50 feet), Pāhala, Hawai'i. Black sand and olivine beach approximately 400 feet long at the base of the littoral cone. As the only elevated feature on an otherwise barren shore of low sea cliffs, the cone has served for many years as a landmark for travelers from Puna to Ka'ū. Boaters use the cone as a triangulation mark for their *ko'a*, or offshore fishing sites, and shore fishermen use it as a base camp. *Lit.*, the *mehame* tree.

Kamehameha Coconut Grove. Kalama'ula, Moloka'i. Named for High Chief Kapuāiwa, who became Kamehameha V in 1863. Traditional stories say the king once lived nearby and planted the trees in the grove. The grove is located in Kiowea Park. Also known as Coconut Grove, Kamehameha V Coconut Grove.

Kamehameha Iki. Park, Lahaina, Maui. Small beach park at 525 Front Street, with a canoe repair and storage building. A detrital sand beach that terminates at Lahaina Small Boat Harbor fronts the park. *Lit.*, small Kamehameha.

Kamehameha I Birthsite Memorial. Historic park (.5 acres), Kokoiki, Hawai'i. Boulders said to mark the birthplace of Kamehameha I, who in 1810 became the first king to unify all of the Hawaiian Islands. Historians are not in agreement on the exact year of his birth, but sometime during the 1750s or 1760s seems to be generally accepted. *Lit.*, the lonely one.

Kamilo. Beach, beachcombing site, fishing site, point, Wai'ōhinu, Hawai'i. Narrow calcareous sand beach lining a rocky point. Ocean currents deposit a great deal of debris here, making the beach a popular beachcombing site. Fishing for *ulua* is common along the point. Ho'onoua Pond, a large brackish-water pond, is inland of the beach. *Lit.*, the twisting [of ocean currents].

Kamilomilo. Beach, Keawa'ula, O'ahu. West end of Keawa'ula Beach. *Lit.*, the twisting [of ocean currents].

Kamisugi's. Surf site, Kawailoa, O'ahu. North of Chun's Reef and off the Kamisugi beach house on Kamehameha Highway. The Kamisugi family has surfed here since Sunao "Flash" Kamisugi bought the property in 1963.

Kammieland. Surf site, Sunset Beach, O'ahu. Same as Kammie's.

Kammie's. Surf site, Sunset Beach, O'ahu. Off Kammie's Market on Kamehameha Highway that was opened in 1961 by Gladys and Henry Buck Chon Kam (d. 1998). Kam, who came to Hawai'i from China at the age of fifteen, was known as Mr. Kammie. Also known as Kammieland.

Kamoamoa. Beach, campground, Hawai'i Volcanoes National Park, Hawai'i. The black volcanic sand beach fronting the campground was formed in 1988 by lava flows from Kūpaianaha in Kīlauea Volcano's East Rift Zone. Steam explosions from the molten lava interacting with the ocean created the cinder, or black sand, which was transported to Kamoamoa by the prevailing currents.

Kamōhio. Bay, south shore, Kaho'olawe. One of two large bays with high sea cliffs on the south shore of Kaho'olawe. Pu'u

Koaʻe Island is off this deep bay's western headland. *Lit.*, the gust [of wind].

Kamokuʻākulikuli. Island, Honolulu, Oʻahu. Also known as Sand Island. *Lit.*, the *ʻākulikuli* plant island.

Kanahā. 1. Beach park (66 acres), gathering site, windsurf site, Kahului, Maui. Narrow calcareous sand beach on an eroding shore. The beach is a traditional seaweed-gathering site. The park takes its name from adjacent Kanahā Pond and is also known as Naska. The windsurf site is at the north end of the park and is also known as Kooks Beach. 2. Pond, Kahului, Maui. Large pond that was designated a wildlife refuge in 1952 and a Registered National Natural History Landmark in 1971. 3. Island (1.2 acres, 100 feet high), Moakea, Molokaʻi. Part of the Hawaiʻi State Seabird Sanctuary. Built by the posterosional eruption that created Mokuhoʻoniki Island; eventually divided into a second island by wave erosion. 4. Channel, reef, Hāʻena, Kauaʻi. Wide reef at Hāʻena Point separated from Mākua Reef (Tunnels) by a sand-bottomed channel. *Lit.*, the shattered [thing].

Kanaio. Beach, shore, Honuaʻula, Maui. Kanaio is a land division on the south side of Haleakalā, where its shore lies approximately between Kamanamana and Pōhakueaea Points. The several small rocky beaches here are known collectively as Kanaio Beach. *Lit.*, the false sandalwood tree.

Kanaka Umi. Fishing site, Oneʻula, Oʻahu. Rocky shore beyond the west end of Oneʻula Beach Park. During the early 1900s when Japanese fishermen from ʻEwa Plantation came here to fish, they did not know the Hawaiian name of the area, so they called it Kanaka, their word for Hawaiians, and Umi, the Japanese word for ocean. Several Hawaiian fishermen lived here, so the name translates roughly as "[the place where] Hawaiians [lived on the] ocean."

Kanākea. Bay, pond, Hilo, Hawaiʻi. Bay on the east side of the Waiākea Peninsula. The brackish-water pond at the head of the bay is also known as Ice Pond. The bay is also known as Reed's Bay. *Lit.*, the goby fish.

Kanaloa. Dive site, Kanaio, Maui. At Kanaloa Point between La Pérouse and Nuʻu Bays. Kanaloa is the name of one of the four primary gods.

Kanalukaha. Beach, Hale o Lono, Molokaʻi. One of four long, wide calcareous sand beaches between Hale o Lono Harbor and Lāʻau Point. Also known as Puʻu Hakina Beach. *Lit.*, the passing wave.

Kanapou. 1. Bay, east shore, Kahoʻolawe. The bay borders the coastal boundaries of the *ʻili*, or land division, of Kanapou. It is the widest bay on the island, with a width of 2 miles between Ule and Hālona Points, and is an excellent anchorage during *kona* (southerly) winds. 2. Beach, east shore, Kahoʻolawe. On the shore of Kanapou Bay. One of only three significant calcareous sand beaches on the island. The other two are Hanakanaiʻa and Kaukaukapapa. Sand dunes line the backshore and a great deal of trade wind debris accumulates in the foreshore. 3. Surf site, east shore, Kahoʻolawe. The surf site is a shorebreak on the shallow sandbar fronting the beach. Also known as Beck's Cove, Keanapou, Obake Bay. Kanapou is probably a contraction of Keanapou, which literally means "the canoe cave."

Kāneakua. 1. Island, Kaunolū, Lānaʻi. Small island off the former village of Kaunolū. 2. Bay, fishing site, Kahuku, Oʻahu. Small, rocky bay on the north side of Kalaeuila. *Lit.,* Kāne [the] god.

Kāneana. 1. Beach, Mākua, Oʻahu. Western section of ʻŌhikilolo Beach. The name is from nearby Kāneana Cave. Beachgoers park on the seaward side of Farrington Highway across from the cave to access a trail to the beach. 2. Cave, Mākua, Oʻahu. The cave is a lava tube that was enlarged as a sea cave during a former stand of the sea when the ocean stood higher than it does now. It is said to have been the home of the demigod Nanaue, who could assume the form of a man or a shark. Also known as Mākua Cave. *Lit.,* Kāne's cave. Kāne is the name of one of the four major gods.

Kāneʻāpua. Island (.9 acres, 50 feet high), Kaholo, Lānaʻi. Kāneʻāpua was a fish god and a trickster. *Lit.,* Kāne [of the] fish trap.

Kāneʻilio. Point, Waiʻanae, Oʻahu. A *heiau* (shrine) on the point was dedicated to Kūʻilioloa, a demigod who could take the form of either a man or dog. Also known as Black Rock. *Lit.,* Kāne [of the] dog form.

Kānekanaka. 1. Dive site, point, Hāpuna, Hawaiʻi. Also known as H Point and Hāpuna Point. 2. Sea arch, Wailea, Hawaiʻi. Natural sea arch eroded in one of the small points at the south end of Kānekanaka Point. *Lit.,* Kāne [of the] human form.

Kanenelu. 1. Fishing site, Kaʻaluʻalu, Hawaiʻi. Off the tidal flat at the head of Kaʻaluʻalu Bay. 2. Fishing site, Punaluʻu, Hawaiʻi. Between Punaluʻu and Kamehame. 3. Beach, Kaʻaʻawa. The land inland of Kamehameha Highway from the beach was a former marsh. *Lit.,* the marsh.

Kāneʻohe. 1. Bay, Kāneʻohe, Oʻahu. Largest sheltered bay in the Hawaiian Islands and one of the finest estuaries in the state. It lies between Kualoa Point and Mōkapu Peninsula. 2. Bay offshore mooring area, Kāneʻohe, Oʻahu. There are sixty-six moorings in the southwestern corner of the bay. 3. Beach park (1.1 acres), Kāneʻohe, Oʻahu. Small landscaped park that borders the mudflats of Kāne'ohe Bay at the end of Waikalua Road. Also known as Nāoneala'a. 4. Yacht club, Kāne'ohe, O'ahu. Private recreation facility that includes 190 slips, 3 visitor slips, and dry mooring. *Lit.*, bamboo husband. According to legend, a woman compared her husband's cruelty to the cutting edge of a bamboo knife.

Kāne'ohe Bay Naval Defensive Sea Area. Zone, Marine Corps Base Hawai'i, Kāne'ohe Bay, O'ahu. A 500-yard prohibited zone around the perimeter of Mōkapu Peninsula where only authorized vessels may enter. It was established by executive order in 1941.

Kānoa. Fishpond, Kaunakakai, Moloka'i. *Lit.*, bowl [for *'awa*].

Kanohopōhaku o Kāhili'ōpua. Rock, Kalaupapa, Moloka'i. Kāhili'ōpua, a chiefess of the former village at 'Īliopi'i, lived in the present airport area with only female retainers. From a rock chair called Kanohopōhaku o Kāhili'ōpua, she acted as an intermediary for men seeking wives or companions. The rock chair is near the airport gate. *Lit.*, the rock chair of Kāhili'ōpua.

Kanonone. Pond, Pōhue, Hawai'i. Large rectangular brackish-water pond encircled by coconut and pandanus trees on the western margin of Pōhue Bay. A storm beach of calcareous sand, lava fragments, and coral rubble fronts the pond.

Kanuha. Beach, Kailua, Hawai'i. Small pocket of calcareous sand on Kailua Bay on the north side of Hulihe'e Palace. Named for the Kanuha family of Kona, who once owned land near the beach.

Kanukuawa. Fishpond, Kamalō, Moloka'i. *Lit.*, the harbor entrance.

Ka'ō. Fishing site, reef, Hau'ula, O'ahu. Between Kaipapa'u Point and Waipilopilo Stream. *Lit.*, the thrust.

Ka'ohana. Beach, Lā'ie, O'ahu. Calcareous sand beach at the north end of Kahuku Beach fronting the Japanese cemetery. *Lit.*, the family.

Ka'ōhao. Beach, Lanikai, O'ahu. Legendary name of Lanikai Beach. *Lit.*, the tying.

Ka'ohe. Beach, Ka'ohe, Hawai'i. 'Ili'ili, or pebble, beach on the shore of the Kona Paradise Properties subdivision. The beach and the subdivision are in the land division of Ka'ohe. Also known as Pebble Beach. *Lit.*, the bamboo.

Kāohikaipu. Island (11 acres, 40 feet high), Makapu'u, O'ahu. Part of the Hawai'i State Seabird Sanctuary. Volcanic cinder cone of red and black cinders with a *pāhoehoe* lava flow on its western side. Although the cinder cone is an island now, it appears to have formed on dry land during a lower stand of the sea. If it had erupted through salt water, it would have been a tuff cone like its neighbor Mānana (Rabbit) Island. Also known as Black Rock. *Lit.*, the container that gathers (flotsom collects here).

Ka'ōpala. Cove, Kahana, Maui. Prevailing currents deposit rubbish in this small cove. *Lit.*, the rubbish.

Ka'ōpapa Ledges. Dive site, Hōnaunau, Hawai'i. Perhaps lit., the smooth, floorlike flat (as *pāhoehoe* lava).

Ka'opeahina. Fishpond, Hālawa, Moloka'i. *Lit.*, the bundle of Hina.

Kapa'a. 1. Dive site, park, North Kohala, Hawai'i. The park is on low sea cliffs where it provides a good view of Maui. The dive site is off the park. 2. Beach park, landing, Kapa'a, Kaua'i. Narrow calcareous sand beach fronting a wide, shallow reef. The interisland steamer landing was at the south end of the beach. *Lit.*, the solid or the closing.

Kapa'ele'ele. Fishing shrine, ramp, Kahana Bay, O'ahu. The ramp is at the north end of Kahana Beach. The ramp was blessed and named by former Kahana Valley resident Peter Kau for Kapa'ele'ele fishing shrine on the hill above the ramp. *Lit.*, black border.

Kapaeloa. Shore, Kawailoa, O'ahu. Former land division west of Waimea Bay that was incorporated into the Kawailoa land division. *Lit.*, the long [canoe] landing.

Kapaemāhū. Stones, Waikīkī, O'ahu. Four large rocks in Kūhiō Beach Park that represent four ancient kahuna who were renowned for their wisdom and healing powers: Kapaemāhū, Kahaloa, Kapuni, and Kīnohi. Also known as the Healing Stones, Wizard Stones. *Lit.*, the homosexual row.

Kapahulu Groin. Seawall, Waikīkī, O'ahu. Seawall, or groin, that extends an underground drainage culvert into the ocean at the intersection of Kalākaua and Kapahulu Avenues, with pedestrian access over it. The wall was completed in July 1951 by James W. Glover, Ltd., as part of the Waikīkī Beach Improvement Project. Also known as Kuekaunahi, The Wall. *Lit.*, the worn-out soil.

 mo'olelo

I was born on June 13, 1923, and when I was young, my family lived on Makini Street in Kapahulu. I started surfing at Waikīkī about 1935 when I was twelve years old. We were using the old solid redwood boards. We kept them at home and they were heavy for us to carry all the way to the beach. At that time there was a wide, open ditch that went from Pākī Avenue along Kapahulu Avenue to the beach. The zoo wasn't built and there was only black sand there. At the Kapahulu-Kalākaua intersection, the ditch went under the road and ended at a small jetty. The ocean came all the way up the ditch to Pākī, so that's where we put our boards in the water, and we paddled to Waikīkī. Sometimes we surfed at the jetty, but we usually went to Queen's or Canoes.

 Daniel Kapuniai, September 28, 2000

Kapaka. Beach, Hauʻula, Oʻahu. Section of Kaluanui Beach in the land division of Kapaka east of Mākao Road. *Lit.*, the raindrop.

Kapālama Basin. Harbor, Honolulu, Oʻahu. West section of Honolulu Harbor that fronts the mouth of Kapālama Stream. *Lit.*, the *lama* wood enclosure.

Kapalaoa. 1. Beach, ʻAnaehoʻomalu, Hawaiʻi. Calcareous sand, lava fragment, and olivine beach approximately 800 feet long with low vegetated dunes in the backshore and an anchialine pond behind the dunes. On the south point of ʻAnaehoʻomalu Bay. 2. Bay, beach, point, Hauʻula, Oʻahu. Off Hauʻula Elementary School. The Oʻahu sites are associated with the legend of Mākuakaumana, a man who was carried away from the beach here by a whale. *Lit.*, the whale or the whale tooth.

 mo'olelo

I was born in Kalaoa in 1906, and I used to fish commercially at most of the beaches in North Kona, mostly for *akule* and *ʻōpelu*. Before the Magoon's were at Mahaiʻula, John Kaelemakule lived there with his nets and canoes. We'd go up to a *koʻa* near Keāhole for *ʻōpelu*, then dry and sell them for seventy-five cents a *kaʻau* at John's store in Kailua. Other people lived there, too, like the Kuemaka family. Sometimes I fished with them on their four-man canoe, and we hardly ever paddled. We sailed, but not with the old-style claw sail. An old interisland steamer sank at Mahaiʻula and Kuemaka dived on it for gunnysacks whenever he needed them.

About 1929 I bought Kaelemakule's two six-man fishing canoes and nets and started fishing on my own. I went for *ʻōpelu* and *akule,* and I would *hukilau* for inshore fish. About 1930 I moved my operation to **Kapalaoa,** where the Alapai family lived. They hauled their fish out by mule to Kawaihae, but I worked out a deal with the captains of one of the interisland steamers, the *Humuʻula,* to stop offshore to pick up my fish. They gave me a dollar per pound, then sold them elsewhere. I also sold fish at Kawaihae when I went there for supplies, but they only paid fifty cents a pound. The *hukilau* fish I sold cheap to the coffee plantation laborers.

When the ocean was too rough to fish outside, we would go to Keawaiki to spear and throw net. We used thick 24-gauge fence wire for our spears that we sharpened with a barb. We made our goggles out of *hau,* glass, and strips of tire tubes, *which is what we also used to shoot the spears. We didn't have any fins, just light tabbies, but there were plenty of fish in 10 feet of water. Three of us speared and two of us bagged. We'd leave the bags on the rocks and pick them up on the way back.*

In 1933 we cut down one of the two canoes I bought from Kaelemakule and made it into a racing canoe for the first races at Nāpōʻopoʻo. We named it the Kaimalino, *and now it's Kaiʻopua's* koa *boat.*

Bill Upchurch, September 29, 1981

Kapalawai. Beach, Makaweli, Kauaʻi. Narrow calcareous sand beach between Pākala village and Waimea River. The famous surf site Pākala, or Infinities, is off the southeast end of the beach. *Lit.*, the *palawai* seaweed or the bottom lands.

Kapalilua. Land division, South Kona, Hawaiʻi. Coastal area from Honokua to Manukā. Named for a cliff with two sides, one facing the ocean and one facing north. *Lit.*, the double cliff.

Kapaliokamoa. Sea cliff, Hawaiʻi Kai, Oʻahu. Site of a small breakwater built by Henry J. Kaiser. A rock formation here above the breakwater is known as the Balancing Rock, Pele's Chair, and Rebel Rock. *Lit.*, the cliff of the chicken.

Kapalua. Beach park, dive site, snorkeling site, surf site, Kapalua, Maui. Crescent calcareous sand beach between two rocky points. One of West Maui's most popular family beaches for swimming and snorkeling, especially during the winter high surf season. It is not subject to high surf. The dive and snorkeling sites are off the beach. The surf site is at the edge of the outermost reef. *Lit.*, two borders.

Kapanaiʻa. Bay, beach, landing, surf site, North Kohala, Hawaiʻi. One of the most protected bays on the Kohala Coast, formerly used as an interisland steamer landing during periods of southerly storms at Māhukona. A narrow black sand beach lines the head of the bay. The surf site is off the beach on the east side of the bay. Kapanaiʻa was the site of a public access lawsuit in which the public's traditional right of access to the bay was reconfirmed in March 1982 in a settlement between Hui Māmalahoa, a group of Kohala citizens, and the landowner. *Lit.*, the bow-spear fishing.

Kapapa. Dive site, island (14 feet high), surf site, Kāneʻohe, Oʻahu. Low, flat, sparsely vegetated island in Kāneʻohe Bay that is a popular picnic, camping, and fishing site. A large wedge-tailed shearwater colony nests here from March to November. The dive site is on a fringing reef adjacent to the island at approximately 15–25 feet. The surf site is on the north side of the island. Also known as Kīpapa. *Lit.,* the flat surface or the reef.

Kāpī. Fishpond, Kawela, Oʻahu. Same as Punaulua. *Lit.,* sprinkle with water [or salt].

Kapiʻolani. Regional park (154.7 acres), Waikīkī, Oʻahu. One of Honolulu's most heavily used urban parks that includes the Honolulu Zoo, the Kapiʻolani Park Bandstand, the Waikīkī Aquarium, the Waikīkī Shell, the War Memorial Natatorium, and the section of Waikīkī Beach from the Kapahulu Groin to the New Otani Kaimana Beach Hotel. Dedicated as a public park on Kamehameha Day (June 11) in 1877 by King Kalākaua and named in honor of his wife, Queen Kapiʻolani. *Lit.,* the heavenly arch.

Kapoho. 1. Fishing site, surf site, Naha, Lānaʻi. Also known as Stone Shack. 2. Point, Kailua, Oʻahu. Point at the north end of Kailua Beach. Also known as Castle's. *Lit.,* the depression.

Kapoho Tide Pools. Fishing site, swimming site, Kapoho, Hawaiʻi. A low-lying lava flat on the shore of the Kapoho Beach Lots and Vacationland contains many large interconnected tidepools that are popular swimming and snorkeling sites. Fishing for *ulua,* or crevalle fish, is common along the outer edge of the lava flat.

Kapoʻikai. Pond, Makalawena, Hawaiʻi. Also known as ʻŌpaeʻula Pond. *Lit.,* the sea breaking.

Kapoli. Beach park, Māʻalaea, Maui. Unimproved park on the low cliffs southwest of Māʻalaea Small Boat Harbor. *Lit.,* the bosom. Kapoli is the name of a former spring in the area.

Kapoʻo. Rock formation, Sunset Beach, Oʻahu. The rocky center section of Pūpūkea Beach Park seaward of the Sunset Fire Station and between Sharks Cove and Three Tables. *Lit.,* the depression or the cavity.

Kapua. 1. Beach, Waikīkī, Oʻahu. One of the former fisheries of Waikīkī that includes the beach adjacent to the War Memorial Natatorium. Also known as Kaimana Beach, Sans Souci Beach. 2. Offshore mooring, Waikīkī, Oʻahu. Mooring site off the Outrigger Canoe Club. Also known as Diamond Head Offshore Mooring. *Lit.,* the fish spawn or the fry.

Kapuʻa. Beach, historic complex, Honomalino, Hawaiʻi. Small calcareous sand, coral rubble, olivine, and lava fragment beach at the head of a small inlet. The historic complex includes the ruins of the former village of Kapuʻa, the most famous site of which is ʻĀhole Hōlua to the south at Puʻu Hinahina Bay, the best-preserved precontact sled run in Hawaiʻi. *Lit.,* the whistle.

Kapuaikea. Point, Mākena, Maui. Small rocky point at Paipu, the south section of Poʻolenalena Beach.

Kapuāiwa Coconut Grove. Beach park, Kalama'ula, Moloka'i. Traditional stories say that High Chief Kapuāiwa, who became Kamehameha V in 1863, once lived nearby and planted the trees in the grove. Also known as Coconut Grove, Kamehameha Coconut Grove. *Lit.*, mysterious taboo.

Kapueokahi. Bay, beach, Hāna, Maui. Bay and calcareous sand beach at Hāna Beach Park. *Lit.*, the lone owl.

Kapukaamāui. Rock, Kailua, Maui. Rock formation with a large hole through it on the north point of Makaīwa Bay. Many seabirds nest here. *Lit.*, the hole [made] by Māui.

Kapukahehu. Beach, Kaluako'i, Moloka'i. Pocket of calcareous sand at the head of a small bay. Also known as Dixie Maru.

Kapukawa'a. Island, Miloli'i, Hawai'i. Rock island between Miloli'i and Ho'opuloa.

Kapukuwahine. Beach, Lā'au, Moloka'i. One of four long, wide calcareous sand beaches with a low sea cliff in the backshore between Hale o Lono Harbor and Lā'au Point. *Lit.*, the gathering place [of] females.

Kapuna. Springs, Waihe'e, Maui. Springs in the ocean in a small bay near the mouth of Waihe'e Stream. *Lit.*, the spring.

Kapuni. Beach, Waikīkī, O'ahu. Section of Waikīkī Beach fronting the Duke Kahanamoku statue and the name of one of the four kahuna who were associated with the Kapaemāhū stones near the statue. *Lit.*, the fine-meshed net.

Kapuwai. Inlet, snorkeling site, Hōnaunau, Hawai'i. Inlet on the shore of Hōnaunau Bay near Pu'uhonua o Hōnaunau National Historic Park off the Hōnaunau Ramp. The snorkeling site is in the bay near the boat ramp. *Lit.*, freshwater restriction. Springs here were reserved for chiefs.

Kaua'i. Kaua'i is the fifth largest (552.3 square miles) of the eight major Hawaiian Islands and with Ni'ihau and its offshore islands comprises Kaua'i County. It has a population of 58,303. The highest mountain on the island is Kawaikini with an elevation of 5,243 feet, and Wai'ale'ale at 5,148 feet is one of the wettest spots on earth, with an average annual rainfall of 444 inches. The *pua mokihana* fruit *(Pelea anisata)* is the emblem of the island, and Kaua'i's nickname is the Garden Isle.

Kaua'i Channel. Channel 72 miles wide between O'ahu and Kaua'i. Also known as Ka'ie'ie Waho.

Kaua'i Express. Current, Mākaha, O'ahu. Powerful longshore current that runs from Mākaha Point toward Ka'ena Point and beyond toward Kaua'i. The term *express* compares the speed of the current to an express train.

Kauakio. Bay, surf site, Koali, Maui. Off the cliffs in the bay. *Lit.*, the rain pool; mock warfare or sham battle.

Kauale. Spring, Nīnole, Hawai'i. One of two springs that supply Pūhau, a pond on the shore at Nīnole.

Kauapea. Beach, Kīlauea, Kaua'i. A 3,000-foot long, 75-foot wide calcareous sand beach fronted by a wide sandbar on the west side of Kīlauea Point. Also known as Secret Beach.

Kauapo. Beach, channel, Waiehu, Maui. Section of beach and channel through the reef near the sixth hole of the Waiehu Golf Course where a boulder retaining wall was built to protect the golf course from erosion. Remnants of an old wharf that was destroyed by the tsunami of April 1, 1946, are here. *Lit.*, the wharf. *Uapo* is the Hawaiianization of the English word *wharf.*

Kauhakō. 1. Landing, ramp, Ho'okena, Hawai'i. Former inter-island steamer landing at Ho'okena Beach Park on Kauhakō Bay. Facilities include a ramp. Also known as Cooper Landing, Ho'okena Ramp, Kupa Landing. 2. Crater, Kalaupapa, Moloka'i. The crater that formed the broad, low shield volcano that is Kalaupapa Peninsula. It is more than 450 feet deep, and its blue-green pool of brackish water extends below sea level. *Lit.*, highly esteemed.

Kauhala. Beach, fishing site, Kahuku, O'ahu. Easternmost section of Kaihalulu Beach next to Kalaeokauna'oa, or Kahuku Point.

Kauhola. 1. Point light, Hala'ula, Hawai'i. Established in 1897 and automated in 1951. The light tower was built in 1933 and stands 86 feet high. It is identical in size and design to the Nāwiliwili Light tower. 2. Surf site, Hala'ula, Hawai'i. The surf site is on the west side of Kauhola Point in Keawa'eli Bay. *Lit.*, to open or unfold.

Kauikeaouli. Stone, Keauhou, Hawai'i. Memorial for Kauikeaouli, or King Kamehameha III. In 1814, High Chiefess Keopuolani, the highest-ranking wife of King Kamehameha I, gave birth to her third child, a son, Kauikeaouli, in a house on the shore of Keauhou Bay. According to tradition he was stillborn, but he was revived by Kapihe, a kahuna from Kalapana who happened to be at Keauhou. Kapihe took the infant, placed him on a nearby boulder and recited a chant for the living. Kauikeaouli revived and eventually ruled the kingdom as Kamehameha III from 1825 until his death in 1854. On March 17, 1914, the Daughters of Hawai'i conducted a ceremony at Keauhou to mark the hundredth anniversary of Kauikeaouli's birth and placed a bronze plaque on the boulder. Queen Lili'uokalani and Prince Kūhiō were among the dignitaries who attended. In 1925, the Daughters of Hawai'i acquired title to the small parcel of land containing the Kauikeaouli Stone, perpetuating the site as a memorial. *Lit.,* one who is placed in the blue vault of heaven.

Ka'uiki. 1. Beach, Hāna, Maui. Same as Kaihalulu Beach or Red Sand Beach. 2. Head. Cinder cone, Hāna, Maui. Cinder cone of the Hāna Volcanic Series on the shore of Hāna Bay. *Head* is an abbreviation of *headland. Lit.,* the glimmer or twinkle.

Ka'uiki Head Light. Hāna, Maui. Established in 1909 on the summit of Pu'uki'i, a small island at the base of Ka'uiki Head that is connected to shore by a natural rock bridge. The 14-foot concrete tower was built in 1914.

Kaukalā. Reef, Waiehu, Maui. Reef fronting the eighth hole on the Waiehu Golf Course. *Lit.,* the sun sets.

Kaukamoku. Bay, beach, north shore, Kaho'olawe. Detrital sand beach that lines the shore of Kaukamoku Bay. *Lit.,* boarding a ship.

Kaukaukapapa. Beach, southwest shore, Kaho'olawe. Long, wide calcareous sand beach with a moderately steep slope into the ocean just north of Kealaikahiki Point. It is one of only three significant calcareous sand beaches on Kaho'olawe. The other two are Hanakanai'a and Kanapou. The name Kaukaukapapa first appeared on Harold Stearn's 1939 geologic map of Kaho'o-lawe. It is likely that Stearns learned the name from Jack Aina, a former ranch foreman on Kaho'olawe, who was Stearn's guide during his 1939 trip to the island. Also known as Twin Sands Beach.

Ka'ula. Island (540 feet in high), City and County of Honolulu. Tuff cone island 22 miles southwest of Ni'ihau. Ka'ula is part of the Hawai'i State Seabird Sanctuary. Also known as Ka'ula Rock. Perhaps lit., the red-tailed tropicbird. Tropicbirds are also known as bosun birds for their shrill screams, which sounded like bosun's whistles to sailors.

Kaulahao. Beach, reef, Kū'au, Maui. Small calcareous sand beach fronted by a rocky shelf at the west end of Kū'au Bay. *Lit.,* the iron chain.

Kaula'inaiwi. Island (.35 acres, 40 feet high), Hilo, Hawai'i. Sea-ward of Mokuola, or Coconut Island, in Hilo Bay. *Lit.,* dry the bones (bones of chiefs were dried here).

Kaulakahi. Channel between Kaua'i and Ni'ihau. *Lit.,* single cord.

Kaulana. 1. Bay, ramp, Kahuku, Hawai'i. Small bay a mile east of Ka Lae, or South Point. The only boat ramp in the district of Ka'ū is in Kaulana Bay, a 20-foot-wide, single-lane ramp on land leased from the Hawaiian Homes Commission. 2. Bay, northeast shore, Kaho'olawe. The bay lies within the coastal boundaries of the *'ili,* or land division, of Kaulana. From approximately 1830 to 1850 the bay was the site of a penal colony for men who were transported here from Lahaina, Maui. In an article entitled "Kahoolawe an Early Place of Banishment" in his *Hawaiian Almanac and Annual for 1903*, editor Thomas Thrum noted that the prisoners were sent to "Kaulana, a small bay, where with some residents they numbered 80 or more." *Lit.*, [boat] landing or resting place.

Ka'ula Rock. 1. Island, City and County of Honolulu. Same as Ka'ula. 2. Light, Ka'ula. Navigational light established on the summit of the island in 1932 but discontinued in 1948.

Kaumaha'ole. Point, Kahalu'u, Hawai'i. North end of Pāokamenehune, or the Menehune Breakwater. *Lit.*, weightless.

Kaumalapau. 1. Harbor, Kaumalapau, Lāna'i. In 1922, James Dole purchased most of the island of Lāna'i for $1.1 million to turn it into the world's largest pineapple plantation. He designated Kaumalapau as the site of a harbor where harvested pine would be shipped by tug and barge to the cannery in Honolulu. Hawaiian Dredging completed the project in 1926. It included a 400-foot concrete wharf, a 250-foot breakwater, and a turning basin with a depth of 30 feet. On July 10, 2000, the state took over ownership of the harbor. 2. Light, Kaumalapau, Lāna'i. Originally a private light established in 1924 at approximately 66 feet above sea level during the construction of Kaumalapau Harbor. 3. Offshore mooring, Kaumalapau, Lāna'i. State mooring site off the harbor. *Lit.*, soot placed [in] gardens. The original name was Kaumalapa'u.

Kaumanamana. Fishpond, Kaunakakai, Moloka'i. *Lit.*, place branching out.

Kaumaui. Point, Keaukaha, Hawai'i. Point that houses the picnic pavilions in Leleiwi Beach Park.

Kaunakakai. 1. Beach park, Kaunakakai, Moloka'i. Undeveloped park where Kaunakakai Wharf intersects the shore. 2. Harbor, Kaunakakai, Moloka'i. The 530-foot-wide channel and the turning basin were dredged in 1934, creating the principal port on the island. The harbor, however, cannot accommodate deep-draft vessels, so freight for the island is transshipped from Honolulu by tug and barge. 3. Harbor range lights, Kaunakakai, Moloka'i. Originally established in 1880 by Rudolph Meyer, a Moloka'i businessman, at the request of the monarchy. 4. Offshore mooring, Kaunakakai, Moloka'i. State mooring site off the wharf. 5. Small boat harbor, Kaunakakai, Moloka'i. Facilities include twenty-nine berths/moorings, two docks, a ramp, a pier, and a vessel washdown area. The ramp is the only public boat ramp on Moloka'i. 6. Wharf, Kaunakakai, Moloka'i. The original wooden wharf across the shallow reef flats was constructed in 1898. A concrete wharf replaced it in 1929. *Lit.*, beach landing. Kaunakakai is an abbreviation of Kaunakahakai.

Kaunala. 1. Beach, Kaunalā, Oʻahu. Calcareous sand beach on the shore of the land division of Kaunalā. Also known as Velzyland. 2. Beach, reef, Lāʻie, Oʻahu. Section of Lāʻie Bay on the north side of Lāʻie Point. Also known as Temple Beach. *Lit.,* the calm.

Kaunalā. Beach, Kaluakoʻi, Molokaʻi. Calcareous sand pocket beach with a mudflat from soil runoff in the backshore. *Lit.,* the rising sun.

Kaunaʻoa. Beach, Kawaihae, Hawaiʻi. Long calcareous sand beach with a shallow sandbar that fronts the Mauna Kea Beach Hotel. Also known as Mauna Kea Beach. *Lit.,* tube snail mollusk or native dodder.

Kauna Point. Dive site, Manukā, Hawaiʻi. Off the prominent point between Manukā and Road to the Sea. Narrow shelf with canyons, lava tubes, arches, and dropoffs to 100 feet. *Lit.,* placed or suspended.

Kaunolū. Bay, historical site, Lānaʻi. Site of a well-preserved precontact fishing village with many ruins, including house sites, shelters, animal pens, fishing shrines, and temples. Someone trying to improve the freshwater well that served the village in 1895 apparently destroyed it. The ocean off the village was a favorite fishing site of King Kamehameha I. The village was registered as a National Historic Landmark in 1963.

Kaununui. Dive site, point, surf site, northwest shore, Niʻihau. North point of Kauwaha Beach. *Lit.,* the large altar.

Kaupō. 1. Bay, beach, historic complex, Kapuʻa, Hawaiʻi. Small pocket of calcareous sand and coral rubble at the head of a small bay in the lee of Kākiʻo Point. Habitation ruins are clustered around two brackish-water wells, and several trails paved with stepping-stones converge here. 2. Beach park (8.2 acres), peninsula, Waimānalo, Oʻahu. Narrow park that includes the south end of Waimānalo Beach and Makai Research Pier. It is on the seaward edge of Kaupō Peninsula, one of the youngest lava flows on Oʻahu. *Lit.,* boarding [of canoes at] night.

Kaupoa. Bay, beach, campsite, Kaupoa, Molokaʻi. Wide pocket beach of calcareous sand below Puʻu Kaheu, a knoll overlooking Kaupoa Bay. George P. Cooke, the first president of Molokaʻi Ranch, lived at Kalaʻe but built a beach house at Kaupoa in 1933. When he died, the house reverted to the ranch and was used by shareholders as a private beach retreat until September 10, 1995, when it was destroyed by fire. In 1998 Molokaʻi Ranch developed a private campsite on the site of the former Kaupoa house.

Kaupō Landing. Fishing site, Kaupō, Maui. At the remnants of a former interisland steamer landing.

Ka'ūpūlehu. Beach, Ka'ūpūlehu, Hawai'i. Calcareous sand and lava fragment beach with the Kona Village Resort on Kahuwai Bay at its north end and the Four Seasons Resort Hualālai at its south end. *Lit.,* the roasted breadfruit. Ka'ūpūlehu is a contraction of Ka'ulupūlehu. Pele, the goddess of the volcano, met two girls here who were roasting breadfruit, but only one shared. That night Hualālai erupted and the lava flow destroyed the entire village except for the home of the girl who shared her breadfruit.

Kauwaha. Bay, beach, northwest coast, Ni'ihau. Wide bay between Kaununui and Kalanaei Points bordered by a calcareous sand beach approximately 2 miles long. The backshore consists of low, vegetated dunes, and the foreshore is lined with beachrock and small rocky points. A dune system parallels the beach, extending several hundred yards inland.

Kauwalu. Island (.3 acres, 40 feet high), Ke'anae, Maui.

Kāwā. Bay, beach, surf site, Ka'ū, Hawai'i. Black sand, olivine, and pebble beach at the head of Kāwā Bay. Hīlea Stream crosses the east end of the beach. Kāwā was the site of a public access lawsuit in which the public's traditional right of access to the bay was reconfirmed in October 1980 in a settlement between the Sportsman's Club of Ka'ū, a group of Ka'ū citizens, and the landowner. The surf site is off the beach on a shallow sandbar and is also known as Windmills. *Lit.,* distance or a length of time.

Kawa'a'ele'ele. Point, Keawa'ula, O'ahu. Next to the last point before the east end of Keawa'ula Beach. *Lit.,* the black canoe.

Kawa'aloa. Bay, beach, Mo'omomi, Moloka'i. Long, wide calcareous sand beach at the head of a large bay. The Del Monte Corporation built a beach home here on a bluff above the beach for its white-collar employees. *Lit.,* the long canoe.

Kawaiaka'aiea. 1. Bridge, fishing site, Hawai'i Kai, O'ahu. Bridge on Kalaniana'ole Highway between the Lāna'i Lookout and the Hālona Blowhole that was constructed in 1931. The fishing site is at the base of the sea cliffs below the bridge and is also known as Second Bridge. 2. Beach, spring, Ka'ena, O'ahu. Perched spring on the mountainside at approximately 700 feet above sea level that was said to be one of four along this otherwise arid coast. Also known as Waiaka'aiea. *Lit.,* the water of the 'aiea tree. 'Aiea are all species of the endemic *Nothocestrum,* a small tree that thrives in dry, rocky areas.

Kawai'ele. Wildlife sanctuary (30 acres), Kekaha, Kaua'i. Wetlands for endangered waterbirds such as Hawaiian stilts, coots, and gallinules. The site was deliberately sandmined by the State Department of Land and Natural Resources to expose the water table and create additional waterbird habitat, including nesting islets, shallow-water feeding areas, and moats. *Lit.*, the black water.

Kawaihae. 1. Bay range lights, light, Kawaihae, Hawai'i. A navigational light was established in 1869. The 36-foot light tower was built in 1915. 2. Harbor, Kawaihae, Hawai'i. Construction of the harbor complex, one of the island's two deep-draft harbors, was completed in 1959. Coral dredged from the harbor basin and entrance channel was deposited on the south side of the harbor, creating a massive landfill and stockpile of spoil material. Erosion of the landfill has created several artificial beaches within the harbor that are used for various ocean recreation activities. 3. Small boat harbor (north), Kawaihae, Hawai'i. At the north end of Kawaihae Harbor. Facilities include eleven moorings, a ramp, and a pier. 4. Small boat harbor (south), Kawaihae, Hawai'i. At the south end of Kawaihae Harbor. Facilities include forty moorings and a vessel washdown area. 5. Surf site, Kawaihae, Hawai'i. On the reef between the south small boat harbor and the entrance channel. *Lit.*, the wild, raging water (for the wind and rain that come with a fury).

Kawaihaka. Beach, Kalāheo, Kaua'i. Shore of Kalāheo Gulch where a spring, Kawaihaka, once flowed from the slope of the gulch into the ocean. Also known as Kalāheo.

Kawaihāpai. Bay, beach, Mokulē'ia, O'ahu. Bay with a calcareous sand beach, primarily on the points of the bay, that is a section of Mokulē'ia Beach. The center of the bay has suffered serious erosion and consists of seawalls protecting the homes behind them. A Japanese fishing shrine called Jizo was erected on the shore of the bay by residents of the former Kawaihāpai Camp. Also known as Akua House. *Lit.*, the carried water. A cloud carried water here in answer to the prayers of two chiefs.

Kawaihoa. 1. Point, Ni'ihau. Tuff (consolidated volcanic ash) cone 550 feet high that forms the southernmost point of the island. Also known as South Point. 2. Point, Hawai'i Kai, O'ahu. Easternmost point of Maunalua Bay. Also known as Portlock Point. *Lit.*, the setting aside.

Kawaiku'i. Beach park (4.1 acres), spring, Honolulu, O'ahu. Formerly well known spring on the shore at the east corner of the park. Once a small, deep pool, but now filled in, it still produces freshwater seeps that are visible at low tide. At the recommendation of an advisory group made up of area residents, Kawaiku'i became the official name of the beach park in 1976, replacing the name 'Āina Haina. *Lit.*, the united water. Fresh and salt water unite at the spring.

Kawailoa. 1. Beach, Māhā'ulepu, Kaua'i. Narrow calcareous sand beach that is a section of Māhā'ulepu Beach. 2. Beach, Kawailoa, Oʻahu. Calcareous sand beach between Pōhaku Loa Way and Puaʻena Point. The beach takes its name from Kawailoa, the *ahupuaʻa* (land division) that begins on the shore at Anahulu Stream and ends at Waimea Bay. Kawailoa Beach is an older name that is now divided into three sections: Laniākea, Pāpaʻiloa, and Police Beaches. 3. Beach park, Kawailoa, Oʻahu. Two adjacent residential lots on the point inshore of Chun's Reef. 4. Beach, Kailua, Oʻahu. South half of Kailua Beach Park. *Lit.*, the long stream.

Kawainui. 1. Canal, Kailua, Oʻahu. Long canal in Kailua that connects Kawainui Marsh to the ocean at Kapoho Point, the north point of Kailua Bay. 2. Marsh (830 acres), Kailua, Oʻahu. Important historical site, wildlife refuge, and flood basin for Maunawili, Kahanaiki, and Kapaʻa Streams. The marsh drains into the ocean at the north end of Kailua Beach through Kawainui Canal. It attracts migratory seabirds and is home to four species of endangered waterbirds: the Hawaiian stilt *(aeʻo)*, the Hawaiian coot *(ʻalae keʻokeʻo)*, the Hawaiian gallinule *(ʻalaeʻula)*, and the Hawaiian duck *(kōloa maoli)*. The marsh sits in a basin that is the center of the former Koʻolau volcano caldera. A thick mat of floating vegetation covers approximately three-quarters of its acreage. *Lit.*, the large [flow of] fresh water.

Kawākiu. Bay, beach, Kaluakoʻi, Molokaʻi. Wide calcareous sand beach at the head of Kawākiu Bay. The first Molokaʻi to Oʻahu outrigger canoe race was started here on October 27, 1952, with three entries. Kukui o Lanikaula Canoe Club of Molokaʻi won, crossing the finish line at the Moana Hotel after eight hours and fifty-five minutes. Successive races were held here until the starting venue was moved to Hale o Lono Harbor in 1963. *Lit.*, the place or time to observe secretly.

🌺 *moʻolelo*

I worked for Molokaʻi Ranch from 1934 to 1938, and that's when I got the idea for a Molokaʻi to Oʻahu canoe race. All the races then were flat-water races, and I wanted to race in the open ocean. I tried to get George Cooke of Molokaʻi Ranch to sponsor it, but I couldn't interest him or anyone else until 1952. That year two friends of mine, John Lind and Vance Faucett, were involved with Aloha Week, and they got the committee [to agree] to sponsor the race if I could get three teams to enter. Waikīkī Surf Club was the first to enter with their canoe the *Malia*. The second team was a crew from Kukui o Lanikaula Canoe Club of Molokaʻi. They used a 30-foot canoe I had picked up at Nāpōʻopoʻo. The third team was a bunch of guys from Ala Moana Park, and they used a 30-foot canoe owned by Dad Center. Each team had a six-man crew. We set the race for October 27 and decided it would start at Kawākiu and end at the Moana Hotel.

I got Albert Kahinu, the superintendent of roads on Moloka'i, to truck the boats to the beach at Kawākiu, but we had to carry them the last 400 yards from the end of the road. We all slept there that night. In the morning we had a service, and then I went out on the point. The surf was really big, and I signaled with a towel between sets to get the boats in the water. When the three boats were out, I started the race, then flew back to O'ahu. In the channel, the *Malia's* lashing broke three times. Surf Club had also rigged a plywood keel to the bottom of the *ama* that they thought would help them track better in the open ocean. They sawed it off in mid-channel. And none of the canoes had splash covers, so they all had to bail the whole race. Surf Club had the *Malia*, the best boat, and they probably should have won, but all of their problems slowed them down. Moloka'i won in eight hours and fifty-five minutes, Surf Club was second, and the guys from Ala Moana Park were third. They all finished within eighteen minutes of each other. Francis Brown had put up $500 for first place and the Aloha Week committee had put up $300 for second and $100 for third.

 A. E. "Toots" Minneville, November 30, 1977

Kawākiuiki. Bay, beach, Kaluako'i, Moloka'i. Primarily rocky beach with small pockets of calcareous sand north of Kawākiu Bay. *Lit.*, small Kawākiu.

Kawehewehe. Beach, channel, Waikīkī, O'ahu. Small pocket of calcareous sand on the east side of the Halekūlani Hotel. The channel goes through the reef between Paradise and Number Threes surf sites. The beach is also known as Gray's Beach. The channel is also known as Gray's Channel, Halekūlani Channel. *Lit.*, the removal. The sick were bathed here to "remove" their sickness.

Kawela. Bay, beach, dive site, snorkeling site, surf site, windsurf site, Kawela, O'ahu. Calcareous sand beach on the shore of Kawela Bay, the most protected bay on O'ahu's North Shore. Residents of the bay were evicted in 1986 to make way for a resort that was never built. Development of the resort was to include public access to the bay, so without the development there is no public access. The dive and snorkeling sites are inside the bay, and several surfing and windsurf sites are outside. *Lit.*, the heat.

Kāwili. 1. Channel, Waiehu, Maui. Channel through the reef off the westernmost beach homes in Waiehu. 2. Beach, Hālawa, Moloka'i. Easternmost of the two beaches in Hālawa Valley.

Lit., twist. The Maui site was named for the *wiliau*, or rip current, that runs through the channel.

Kāwililīpoa. Beach, gathering site, Kīhei, Maui. Narrow calcareous sand beach between Welakahao and Līpoa Streets. *Līpoa* and other varieties of seaweed were gathered here. *Lit.*, twisting [of] *līpoa* seaweed.

Kawiʻu. Fishpond, Kamalō, Molokaʻi. *Lit.*, the entanglement.

K-Bay. Bay, Kāneʻohe, Oʻahu. Same as Kāneʻohe Bay.

K Buoy. Fish aggregating device, Palaoa, Lānaʻi. Buoy anchored at approximately 319 fathoms. Landmarks: Palaoa Point Light, Keanapapa Point.

K. D. Greens. Surf site, Sunset Beach, Oʻahu. In 1965 two Rocky Point neighbors, Kevin Cole and Dennis Brown, began bodysurfing and board surfing an unnamed site between Rocky Point Rights and Gas Chambers. The landmark they used to line up the takeoff spot was a green house, so they decided to name the site using the initials of their first names and the color of their landmark. K. D. Greens means Kevin and Dennis' spot in front of a green house.

Keaʻalau. Fishpond, Kāneʻohe, Oʻahu. *Lit.*, the many roots.

Keaʻau. 1. Beach, Keaʻau, Hawaiʻi. Small pocket of detrital and calcareous sand at the head of an inlet in an otherwise rocky shore. Also known as Shipman Beach. 2. Beach park (38 acres), Keaʻau, Oʻahu. West of Mākaha Point in the land division of Keaʻau. Primarily rocky shore with a calcareous sand beach at its west end. 3. Dive site, Keaʻau, Oʻahu. Off the beach park on a long ledge parallel to shore at 35 to 70 feet. The site includes arches, lava tubes, and overhangs. Also known as Stars. 4. Surf site, Keaʻau, Oʻahu. At the west end of the beach park. *Lit.*, the rippling of the sea.

Keahi. Point, ʻEwa Beach, Oʻahu. West point of Pearl Harbor Channel. Also known as Iroquois Point. *Lit.*, the fire.

Keāhole. 1. Cable station, Keāhole, Hawaiʻi. Fiber-optic submarine cables were installed here by the University of Hawaiʻi for neutrino research off Keāhole Point. 2. Point light, Keāhole, Hawaiʻi. Established in the 1880s, it was the first navigational light on the Big Island. The 33-foot light tower was built in 1915. *Lit.*, the *āhole* fish.

Keāhole Cove. Dive site, Keāhole, Hawaiʻi. North of Keāhole Point at approximately 50 feet. Also known as Keāhole Point.

Keāhole Point. Dive site, Keāhole, Hawaiʻi. Same as Keāhole Cove.

Kealaikahiki. Channel, point, Kahoʻolawe. Westernmost point on Kahoʻolawe and the western boundary of the ʻili (land division) of Kealaikahiki. The largest land division on the island, its coastline stretches from the western edge of Kamōhio Bay to the point. Legendary and contemporary navigators of Hawaiian voyaging canoes have acknowledged Kealaikahiki Point as an indicator that points the way to other Polynesian islands south of Hawaiʻi. Kealaikahiki Channel is the channel between Kahoʻolawe and Lānaʻi. In *Hawaiian Antiquties,* David Malo writes: "When Kila was grown up he in turn sailed on an expedition to Tahiti, taking his departure, it is said, from the western point of Kahoolawe, for which reason that cape is called to this day Ke-ala-i-kahiki (the route to Tahiti)." The point is also known as Lae Paki. *Lit.,* the way to foreign lands, or Tahiti, or south.

Kealakekua Bay. 1. Bay, Kealakekua, Hawaiʻi. A mile-wide bay with Nāpoʻopoʻo on its south end, Kaʻawaloa on its north end, and Pali Kapu o Keoua, a high sea cliff approximately 1.5 miles long, between them. The bay is one of the most protected anchorages on the island. 2. State historical park, Kealakekua, Hawaiʻi. Undeveloped state park that consists of three sections: Nāpoʻopoʻo, including Nāpoʻopoʻo Beach Park; Pali Kapu o Keoua, including several pastures on top of the *pali;* and Kaʻawaloa, including the Captain Cook Monument and the ruins of Kaʻawaloa village. 3. State underwater park, Kealakekua, Hawaiʻi. The 315-acre marine life conservation district is also known as a state underwater park. 4. Dive site, Kealakekua, Hawaiʻi. Any of several dive sites within the bay, but especially in Kaʻawaloa Cove. 5. Marine life conservation district (315 acres), Kealakekua, Hawaiʻi. In 1969 the state set aside the entire bay as a marine life conservation district. The MLCD is inshore of a straight line between Kaʻawaloa Point and the north end of Nāpoʻopoʻo Beach Park. 6. Offshore mooring, Kealakekua, Hawaiʻi. Off Nāpoʻopoʻo. *Lit.,* pathway [of] the god (a contraction of Kealakeakua).

Kealakīpapa. Trail, valley, Hawaiʻi Kai, Oʻahu. Coastal trail that went around the east end of Oʻahu prior to the construction of Kalanianaʻole Highway in the early 1930s. The highway probably followed the trail. Kealakīpapa is also the name of the valley between the Hawaiʻi Kai Golf Course and Makapuʻu Head. The trail is also known as the King's Highway. *Lit.,* the paved trail.

Keālia. 1. Beach, Hoʻokena, Hawaiʻi. Narrow calcareous sand and coral rubble beach on a low, wide lava bench fronting the beach homes at Keālia. 2. Beach, landing, surf site, Keālia, Kauaʻi. Long, wide calcareous sand beach fronted by a sandbar. Several shorebreak surf sites are on the sandbar. A small jetty at the north end of the beach marks the former interisland steamer landing. Keālia Stream crosses the south end of the beach. Keālia was originally part of the Makee Sugar Company until 1934, when it became part of Līhu'e Plantation in a consolidation. Līhu'e Plantation continued to grow sugar until 1990, when it terminated operations on its 3,300 acres of agricultural land between Keālia and Anahola. The *ahupua'a* of Keālia (6,700 acres), including Keālia and Donkey Beaches, was sold by Amfac Land Company in 1998 to Keālia Plantation LLC. 3. Surf site, Mā'alaea, Maui. Off Keālia Pond at the east end of the Mā'alaea Bay. 4. Bay, beach, Keālia, O'ahu. Section of Mokulē'ia Beach. Calcareous sand beach on a bay near the west end of Dillingham Airfield that is within the land division of Keālia. *Lit.,* the salt bed.

Keālia Pond. National wildlife refuge, Mā'alaea, Maui. A 300-acre saltwater marsh at the head of Mā'alaea Bay that was designated as a refuge in 1953. The marsh supports large populations of indigenous waterbirds, including Hawaiian stilts, Hawaiian coots, Hawaiian ducks, and black-crowned night herons. Many migratory shorebirds and waterfowl are also found here. At the turn of the century the pond was 6–8 feet deep, but it has since been filled in by soil runoff from the surrounding sugarcane fields. Today it is only 1–2 feet deep.

Kealoha. Park, Hilo, Hawai'i. Named in 1963 for James Kealoha, a former Hawai'i County chairman and the first elected lieutenant governor of the State of Hawai'i. The son of a grocer, Kealoha was born in 1908 and graduated from Hilo High School in 1926. He entered politics in 1934 and held a number of offices until 1962. He died on August 24, 1983. Also known as Four Miles.

Ke'alohi. Point, He'eia, O'ahu. Site of He'eia State Park. *Lit.,* the shine or the brightness.

Keamano. Bay, beach, north coast, Ni'ihau. Wide, calcareous sand beach backed by low vegetated dunes at the head of a large bay between Kīkepa and Kamakalepo Points. Northernmost beach on the island.

Keana. Fishpond, Kāne'ohe, O'ahu. *Lit.,* the cave.

Ke'anae. 1. Park, Ke'anae, Maui. On the rocky shore next to historic Lanakila 'Ihi'ihi o Iehowa Ona Kaua Church, a Congregational church built in 1860. 2. Ramp, Ke'anae, Maui. Constructed in 1961 on the leeward side of Ke'anae, it is used primarily during the summer months. Facilities include a single 12-foot paved landing area. *Lit.,* the mullet. Ke'anae, one of the most famous taro-producing areas on Maui, is said to have been the name of a royal taro patch.

Keanahaki. Anchorage, bay, beach, southeast coast, Ni'ihau. Bay on the windward side of Kawaihoa, the southernmost point on the island, that is used as an anchorage during *kona* (southerly) weather. A large pocket of calcareous sand fronted by a low rocky shelf lies at the head of the bay. *Lit.,* the broken or split cave.

Keanakaulehu. Cave, Kalaupapa, Moloka'i. One of a series of sea caves on the north side of Kalaupapa Peninsula.

Keanakauwapa. Cave, Kalaupapa, Moloka'i. One of a series of sea caves on the north side of Kalaupapa Peninsula.

Keanakeiki. Point, west shore, Kaho'olawe. *Lit.,* the child's cave.

Keanakoninanahu. Cave, Kalaupapa, Moloka'i. One of a series of sea caves on the north side of Kalaupapa Peninsula.

Keanakuinu. Cave, Kalaupapa, Moloka'i. One of a series of sea caves on the north side of Kalaupapa Peninsula.

Keananoio. Cave, Kalaupapa, Moloka'i. One of a series of sea caves on the north side of Kalaupapa Peninsula. Also known as Ananoio. *Lit.,* the cave [of the] noddy terns.

Keanaonāluahine. Cave, Kalaupapa, Moloka'i. One of a series of sea caves on the north side of Kalaupapa Peninsula. Also known as Anakaluahine. *Lit.,* the cave of the old women.

Keanapapa. Fishing site, point, west coast, Lāna'i. South of Polihua Beach. Marked by an old water tank. *Lit.,* the flat cave.

Keanapou. Bay, beach, east shore, Kaho'olawe. Keanapou is the name given for Kanapou in Abraham Fornander's *Collection of Hawaiian Antiquities and Folklore,* in which three legends refer to the bay as Keanapou. Kanapou, the present name of the bay, is probably a contraction of Keanapou. *Lit.,* the vaulted cave.

Keanapuka. Anchorage, sea arch, Pāpalaua, Moloka'i. Small bight used as an anchorage by boaters. *Lit.,* the cave [with] entrances.

Keaniani. Point, Kahana, O'ahu. Small point in Kahana Bay north of the boat ramp. *Lit.,* the transparence.

Keaoi. Island, Hawai'i Volcanoes National Park, Hawai'i. Small, barren island off the Halapē campsite. Part of the Hawai'i State Seabird Sanctuary.

Keauhou. 1. Beach, campsite, Hawai'i Volcanoes National Park, Hawai'i. The beach consists of small pockets of black sand in several inlets on a rocky point. The campsite is inland of the beach. 2. Bay, beach, North Kona, Hawai'i. Small pebble beach at the head of one of the most protected bays in South Kona. 3. *Hōlua,* Keauhou, Hawai'i. This sled run was built by King Kamehameha I in honor of the birth of his son, Kauikeaouli (1814–1854), who eventually became King Kamehameha III. The *hōlua* was constructed at Keauhou, the site of Kauikeaouli's birth, on the steep hill above the bay. Depressions were filled with earth and stones, and the entire course covered with *pili* grass to provide a slick surface on the downhill course. Sleds *(papa hōlua)* were 12 to 18 feet long and fitted with hardwood runners. 4. Light, Keauhou, Hawai'i. Light atop

a 30-foot pole that was erected in 1967 on the shore of Keauhou Bay. 5. North and south offshore moorings, Keauhou,
Hawai'i. In Keauhou Bay. 6. Small boat harbor, Keauhou,
North Kona, Hawai'i. Facilities include twelve moorings, a
double-lane ramp, a pier, and a vessel washdown area. *Lit.,* the
new era or the new current.

Keauhou Bay. Dive site, Keauhou, Hawai'i. Several sites in the
outer bay at approximately 30 to 80 feet. Also known as Kona
Surf.

Keaukaha. Beach park, Keaukaha, Hawai'i. On the rocky shore
of Puhi Bay fronting the community of Keaukaha. Keaukaha
is one of the oldest Hawaiian Homes Commission settlements
in the state, second only to Kalama'ula on Moloka'i. Congress
passed the Hawaiian Homes Commission Act in 1920 to provide public lands to be assigned to citizens of "not less than
one-half part of the blood of the races inhabiting the Hawaiian
Islands previous to 1778." In 1925, the newly formed commission designated Keaukaha as homestead land and by 1930 more
than 200 house lots had been assigned. Also known as Front
Street. *Lit.,* the desolate one.

Keaulana's. Surf site, Nānākuli, O'ahu. Off Keaulana Avenue,
one of four streets in Nānāikapono Subdivision, a Department
of Hawaiian Home Lands subdivision developed in the early
1920s. Keaulana Avenue was named for John Keaulana, one of
the original Hawaiian homesteaders in the subdivision and
the uncle of veteran surfer Richard "Buffalo" Keaulana. John
Keaulana lived on the point during the 1930s and 1940s when
the surf site first became popular for bodysurfing, *paipo* board
riding, and surfing.

 moʻolelo

Keaulana's was named for my father, John K. Keaulana. After he
and my mother, Florence Kawaiahaʻo Kekai, were married, they
moved to Nānākuli in the early 1920s and built their home on
the point. The ocean provided us with many things. We gathered
Hawaiian salt from the rocks, and it was very clean. We picked
limu from the *papa, līpeʻe, wawaiʻiole,* and *manauea,* and gathered *haʻukeʻuke* and *ʻopihi.* That area was the best fishing ground
and was especially good for *ʻūʻū,* and there was white crab and
Kona crab, too. In those days, people only took what they
needed for their families, so there was always plenty.

The bay next to the point is surrounded by a reef, and there's
a little sand beach inside the reef. As other people moved in, they
began calling it Keaulana's Beach. Another one of the first families
there was the Zablans, and they built their home around the
other side of the point near the beach park. This sandy beach

was called Zablan Beach, so when you wanted to meet at either area, you would say, "Keaulana's" or "Zablan's." Keaulana's was known for surfing, and Zablan's was known for swimming. The surf spot Keaulana's was in front of our house, and the first surfer I remember there was our cousin Bla Williams. He lived nearby and was an excellent surfer. When he died, his ashes were scattered there.

Originally, that entire area was all *kiawe* trees, but as the neighborhood grew, roads were built and one of them was named Keaulana Avenue. My dad worked for the City and County road department, and he was well known in the community. He was called Uncle John, and everyone knew him because he had just one hand. When he died in the late 1950s, his ashes were scattered in the ocean in front of our house on the point.

Yvette Lahaina Keaulana Jackman, November 29, 2000

I moved to Nānākuli in 1946 when I was twelve, and I lived there with my relatives. My dad's brother, my Uncle John Keaulana, lived on the point at Keaulana's. That spot was named for him. He was there from the twenties and was still there in the forties. Keaulana's is where the kids in the neighborhood learned to surf—Vernon Taylor, Henry Preece, and all the rest of us. Even Rabbit used to come down. His family, the Kekai's, lived across the street from my uncle. We used to surf before school, and if the surf was good, the parents had to come down and throw rocks to get us out of the water.

Richard "Buffalo" Keaulana, October 24, 2000

My family moved to Nānākuli in 1939 when I was three. My grandmother owned a home right there on the point next to Buffalo's uncle, John Keaulana, and I started surfing at Keaulana's in the forties. The waves were always good, and we used to *paipo* and bodysurf, too. Some of the other families that lived there were the Lakes, the Williams, the Kamealohas, and the Victors. I'll always remember the 1946 tidal wave. The water came right into the house and flooded the dining room while we were eating breakfast. My brothers got excited and before my mother could stop them, they grabbed their boards and ran down the road to go surfing at Keaulana's. But when they saw all the fish on the road, they stopped to pick them up and never did go in the water.

 Vernon Taylor, October 24, 2000

Ke'awa'awaloa. Bay, beach, fishing site, Kahuku, O'ahu. Small bay and narrow calcareous sand beach north of the Ki'i section of the James C. Campbell National Wildlife Refuge. *Lit.*, the place where chiefly remains were placed.

Keawaʻeli. Bay, Kohala, Hawaiʻi. Bay on the west side of Kauhola Point. The surf site in the bay is known as Kauhola. *Lit.,* the dug-out harbor.

Keawaiki. 1. Beach, dive site, Kaʻū, Hawaiʻi. Wide, flat lava shelf covered with large rocks and tidal pools. Brackish-water ponds and small pockets of coral rubble and green sand line the backshore of the shelf. The ruins of a former fishing village are between the shelf and Na Puʻu a Pele, two littoral cones at the end of Road to the Sea. The dive site is a narrow underwater shelf with canyons and dropoffs to 100 feet. 2. Bay, beach, dive site, surf site, North Kona, Hawaiʻi. Wide bay that is lined primarily with black sand and pebbles. A small pocket of white and black sand approximately 600 feet long at the south end of the beach is partially protected by a shallow reef. The dive and surf sites are near the reef. The most prominent landmark at Keawaiki is the 15-acre estate of Francis Hyde Ii Brown (1892–1976). Brown, a part-Hawaiian businessman, politician, and sportsman, acquired the property in the 1920s. He used the site, which includes a fishpond and a large coconut grove, as a retreat for himself and his friends, many of whom were celebrities of the day. Hawaiian composer Helen Desha Beamer, a family friend, immortalized Brown and his home in her song "Ke Keawaiki." 3. Beach, Hāna, Maui. Small *iliʻili* beach in a cove on the north side of Paʻiloa Bay in Waiʻānapanapa State Park. 4. Cove, Keawaʻula, Oʻahu. In the rocky shore west of Mākua Beach. 5. Bay, beach, Mākaha, Oʻahu. Small bay on the west side of Mauna Lahilahi with a wide calcareous sand beach. Also known as Papaoneone, Turtle Beach. *Lit.,* the small harbor.

Keawakapu. Artificial reef, beach, surf site, Keawakapu, Maui. The artificial reef was established in August 1962 when 150 car bodies were dumped 400 yards off Keawakapu Beach in 80 feet of water. The beach is one of five calcareous sand beaches that front the Wailea resort complex. The public right-of-way to the beach at its east end was donated to the County of Maui by Wailea Resorts. The surf site is a shorebreak on the sandbar fronting the beach. *Lit.,* the sacred or forbidden harbor.

Keawalaʻi. Beach, church, cove, Mākena, Maui. Small pocket of calcareous sand at the head of a cove formed by two points of lava. The cove fronts Keawalaʻi Church, a Congregational church built in 1855 from coral blocks cut from nearby reefs. Across the street from the church, a comfort station with paved parking and showers accommodates beachgoers using Maluaka Beach to the east. *Lit.,* the peaceful harbor.

Keawanaku. Beach, Honuaʻula, Maui. Small pocket of detrital sand east of Hanamanioa Light at La Pérouse Bay. *Lit.,* the agitated water harbor.

Keawanui. 1. Cove, Mākena, Maui. Small cove with *'ili'ili,* or pebbles, near the south end of Po'olenalena Beach. 2. Beach, fishpond, Kamalō, Moloka'i. Narrow calcareous sand beach and fishpond near the Smith and Bronte Monument. 3. Bay, beach, surf site, northwest coast, Ni'ihau. Large bay between Pali-koa'e and Kaununui Points bordered by a wide, calcareous sand beach approximately 3.5 miles long, the longest beach on the island. The backshore is covered primarily by *pōhinahina,* or beach vitex, and the foreshore is fronted by patch reefs and sandbars. An extensive dune system parallels the beach, varying in width from 300 feet at its northern end to over 2,000 feet at its southern end, where the dunes are 100 feet high. Keawanui Beach is one of the sites where island residents gather Ni'ihau shells. The surf site is at the north end of the beach near Palikoa'e. *Lit.,* the big harbor.

Keawa'ula. 1. Bay, beach, Ka'ena Point State Park, O'ahu. Wide calcareous sand beach in Keawa'ula Bay, the last sand beach on the Wai'anae Coast before Ka'ena Point. Also known as of Yokohama Bay. 2. Cable station, Keawa'ula, O'ahu. Keawa'ula Beach is the landing site for a number of fiber-optic submarine cables. *Lit.,* the red harbor. The bay was named for the great schools of squid that once came to this area. From shore the schools appeared reddish brown in color.

Kē'ē. Beach, snorkeling site, Hā'ena, Kaua'i. Westernmost section of the calcareous sand beach fronting Hā'ena State Park. A small sand-bottomed lagoon off the beach is protected by a reef and provides one of the most popular snorkeling sites on Kaua'i's north shore. Several important archaeological sites associated with the hula are on the hill above the beach. These include Ke Ahu o Laka, a platform where the hula is still performed by modern hula *hālau,* and Kauluapaoa Heiau, a shrine dedicated to Laka, the goddess of the hula. *Lit.,* a hula master who is invited to access another's students.

Ke'ehi. 1. Lagoon, Honolulu, O'ahu. Large bay between Sand Island and the Honolulu International Airport that is popularly called a lagoon. 2. Lagoon canoe facility competition center, Honolulu, O'ahu. Section of Ke'ehi Lagoon Park dedicated in 1991 to outrigger canoe paddling, Hawai'i's official ocean team sport. 3. Lagoon park (72 acres), Honolulu, O'ahu. On the west shore of Ke'ehi Lagoon, with a man-made calcareous sand beach fronting the canoe facility competition center. 4. Marine center. Private marine facility that includes 160 slips and a boat repair yard. 5. Offshore mooring, Honolulu, O'ahu. There are 202 moorings in the lagoon. 6. Salt works, Honolulu, O'ahu. Evaporation pond remnants of the last commercial Hawaiian crude salt operation in Hawai'i that was discontinued in the

1970s. 7. Small boat harbor, Honolulu, O'ahu. Facilities include 389 berths, 2 ramps, and a vessel washdown area. 8. Triangle, Honolulu, O'ahu. Mooring site in the lagoon. *Lit.*, tread upon.

 mo'olelo

Stephen Lee and I have known each other since the 1950s. We were classmates at Jefferson Elementary School in Waikīkī, and then again as freshmen at St. Louis High School in 1960. It was about that time that Stephen's dad, Joseph, bought a Hawaiian salt operation on the shore of Ke'ehi Lagoon. The complex consisted of several large ponds and about a dozen small evaporation pans that were used for making *pa'akai,* or crude salt. The pans were made out of clay that the old-timers called poi *lepo.*

The Lees named their business the Hawaiian Pa'akai Company and set out to make Hawaiian salt. Salt is a low-priced commodity with a small profit margin, so to minimize costs Mr. Lee put Stephen in charge of the operation, and Stephen hired three of his teenaged friends as laborers—Buzzy Kneubuhl, Craig Williams, and me. So during our high school summers, the four of us worked in the salt mines, three of us for slave wages. As our good friend, the son of the owner, and our boss, Stephen took a lot of good-natured teasing about our pay, our working conditions, and his position as the Chinese *luna* over three *hapa-haole* laborers. Stephen really earned his money when the surf was good, and he'd have to convince us that we should be spending our mornings laboring in the hot Kalihi sun instead of riding waves at Ala Moana. All of us surfed then, and still do now.

Salt making is a summertime project that is dependent on extended periods of dry weather and hot sun. Rain dilutes or completely dissolves the drying salt. The first step in the process was to pump ocean water from Ke'ehi Lagoon into the large ponds that were used to increase the salinity of the natural ocean water. As the water level in the ponds dropped from evaporation, we pumped in more ocean water until the desired salinity was reached. Then we pumped the pond water into the shallow evaporation pans where it was allowed to evaporate completely. After several days, only the crystallized salt was left. Using push "brooms" with wooden blades instead of bristles, we pushed the salt into the center of the beds, or into the corners if they were higher, and briefly allowed it to drain. Then we shoveled it into wheelbarrows and dumped it on the floor of a wooden shed, where it was protected from the rain and allowed to dry completely. From the floor of the shack we shoveled it into burlap bags, or gunnysacks, and hauled the 100-pound bags to the warehouse in a pickup truck where we processed the salt for the market.

The processing consisted of spreading the salt out on long Formica tables and removing the impurities by hand. Coming from the shore of Ke'ehi Lagoon, the salt contained a lot of miscellaneous items, such as crabs, pebbles, leaves, and bird feathers, and these all had to be painstakingly removed. We hated the boredom of the production line, but Stephen cracked the whip and kept us at it. Once the salt was cleaned, we bagged it, boxed the bags, and delivered the boxes to the markets.

In addition to the white *pa'akai*, we also made red or *'alaea* salt. In Hawai'i, *'alaea*—or *'alae* as it is commonly pronounced—is a red, water-soluble, colloidal clay that is added to evaporated salt, coloring it red. In addition to being used as a salt for food, *'alaea* salt is traditionally valued as a medicine and a component of mixtures used in purification ceremonies. Most of the *'alaea* in Hawai'i comes from certain riverbanks on Kaua'i, the locations of which are closely guarded secrets. These caches of clay are often in remote areas where they have been found by pig hunters. Among the four of us, Stephen was the only one who made the *'alaea* salt. It took a delicate touch, and he was the one who had it. The clay was baked to remove the moisture and pulverized into a fine powder to mix with the salt. Then the salt was sprayed with a water mist to moisten it, which allowed the *'alaea* powder to stick to the salt crystals. This was the tricky part, the spraying and the mixing. Too much water would melt the salt and ruin it.

During the 1970s, the Lees stopped making evaporated salt, ending the last commercial *pa'akai* production operation in Hawai'i.

John Clark, December 1, 2000

Ke'ehuku'una. Beach, Lā'ie, O'ahu. Calcareous sand beach on the north side of Kōloa Stream. Section of Pounders Beach. *Lit.*, sea foam where nets are set.

Ke'ei. Beach, dive site, surf site, Ke'ei, Hawai'i. Calcareous sand and lava fragment beach between Palemano Point and the beach homes at Ke'ei. The surf site is on the wide, shallow reef off the beach. The dive site is at the edge of the reef, with some pinnacles and canyons at approximately 35 feet.

Kehena. Beach, Kehena, Hawai'i. Black sand beach at the base of Kehena's low sea cliffs that was created by the lava flow at the east end of the beach during the eruption of 1955. In 1979 the beach dropped nearly three feet after a severe earthquake shook the Puna District. *Lit.*, place where refuse is thrown and burned.

Kei Kei Caves. Dive site, Kawaihae, Hawai'i. Caves and lava tubes with many large puffer fish. Kei Kei is a phonetic spelling of *kēkē*, the Hawaiian word for *pot-bellied*, and a reference to the "pot-bellied" puffer fish.

Ke Iki. Beach, surf site, Sunset Beach, O'ahu. Section of Sunset Beach that borders Ke Iki Road. The surf site is a shorebreak on the beach. *Lit.,* the small one.

Keiki Corner. Surf site, Makapu'u, O'ahu. East end, or "corner," of Makapu'u Beach where surf conditions are often smaller and safer for younger bodysurfers and bodyboarders—the *keiki,* or children.

Keiki Pool. Beach, Makapu'u, O'ahu. Section of beach at Kaupō Beach Park that is a popular swimming site for families with young children. Several shallow, sand-bottomed pools on the otherwise rocky shore offer protected swimming sites.

Keka'a. Hill, point, Kā'anapali, Maui. Cinder cone in the center of Kā'anapali Beach that separates the two sections of the beach. Also known as Black Rock, Pu'u Keka'a. *Lit.,* the rumble.

Kekaha. Beach park, Kekaha, Kaua'i. On the shore of Kekaha, the westernmost town on Kaua'i, and at the south end of the 15-mile-long calcareous sand beach that borders the Mānā Coastal Plain from Polihale to Kekaha. *Lit.,* the place.

Kekaha Kai. State park, North Kona, Hawai'i. Largely undeveloped coastal park north of Keāhole Airport that includes Mahai'ula and Manini'ōwali Beaches. Same as Kona Coast State Park. *Lit.,* seaward Kekaha.

Kekepa. Island, Kāne'ohe, O'ahu. Part of the Hawai'i State Seabird Sanctuary. Off the north end of Mōkapu Peninsula near Pyramid Rock. Also known as Turtle Island, Turtleback Island. *Lit.,* to snap at, or a style of bonito fishing.

Keko'a. Point, Nāpo'opo'o, Hawai'i. Informal community gathering site adjacent to Nāpo'opo'o Landing. *Lit.,* the coral, the fishing shrine, or the fishing grounds.

Keku. Fishing site, point, One'ula, O'ahu. On the east side of the Kalaeloa Community Development District boundary fence. Named for a Hawaiian fisherman who lived alone here during the 1920s and 1930s.

Kekuanohu. Fort, Honolulu, O'ahu. Fort on the shore of Honolulu Harbor at Pier 12 that was built in 1816 during the reign of King Kamehameha I with coral blocks quarried from the reef offshore. It measured 336 feet by 277 feet and had walls 12 feet high. When it was dismantled in 1857, the coral blocks were used for retaining walls along the waterfront. A few of these blocks may still be seen in a loose pile in the water fronting Pier 12. Fort Street in downtown Honolulu is named after this fort. Also known as Kepapu. *Lit.,* the thorny back (for the guns on the outer wall of the fort).

Kēōkea. Beach park (7 acres), landing, Niuli'i, Hawai'i. Beach park in the east corner of a large bay that was a former boat landing site. The predominantly rocky shore has a small sandy inlet behind a boulder breakwater. The breakwater was built as a community service project between the residents of Niuli'i and the Kohala Corporation shortly before sugar operations were phased out in October 1975. *Lit.,* the sound of white [caps].

Keolonāhihi. State historical park (12 acres), North Kona, Hawai'i. Site of a surfing heiau, or shrine, bathing pools, and a rock grandstand for spectators to watch surfing here at Kamoa Point at the south end of Hōlualoa Bay. The contemporary name of the surf site is Lyman's. *Lit.,* the tangled *olonā* plant. Keolonāhihi is the name of the *heiau* that was constructed by order of Chiefess Keakealani.

Keōmuku. 1. Beach, dive site, Keōmuku, Lāna'i. A narrow, 6-mile-long detrital sand beach that stretches from Kahōkūnui to Halepalaoa. The dive site is off the former village. 2. Village, Keōmuku, Lāna'i. Former fishing village that was briefly transformed into a plantation town in 1899 when Talula and Frederick Hayselden established the Maunalei Sugar Company at Keōmuku. Five hundred Japanese laborers were brought in to work the cane fields, a pier was constructed at Halepalaoa, and a narrow-gauge railroad was laid out between the pier and the village. The plantation folded by March 1901 after the bubonic plague of 1900 decimated its workforce and the freshwater sources for its irrigation turned brackish. 3. Whaleboats, Keōmuku, Lāna'i. Three abandoned whaleboats seaward of Ka Lanakila o Ka Malamalama Church (1903) in Keōmuku village. The boats mark the location of the shore in 1935. The present shore is approximately 500 feet seaward of the boats, the result of soil erosion and runoff into the ocean. *Lit.,* the shortened sand. The *o* in Keōmuku is a contraction of *one,* or "sand."

Keo Nakama. Beach, Kamāka'ipō, Moloka'i. Section of Kamāka-'ipō Beach with a narrow channel through the rocky shelf that lines the beach. On September 29, 1961, local resident Keo Nakama waded through the channel and swam to O'ahu, becoming the first swimmer to successfully make the crossing. He landed on the beach at Hanauma Bay after 15.5 hours.

Keone. Bay, fishing site, Kaupakalua, Maui. Fishing site for surround-netting *akule,* or big-eyed scad. *Akule* congregate here over a large pocket of sand on the bottom of the bay. Also known as Black Sand, Uaoa Bay. *Lit.,* the sand.

Keone'ele. Beach, Pu'uhonua o Hōnaunau National Historical Park, Hawai'i. Small pocket of calcareous sand on the shore of the royal residence within the park. As a former royal canoe landing, Keone'ele was a sacred site. Park regulations, therefore, discourage recreational activities, including swimming and snorkeling, at the beach. *Lit.*, the black sand.

Keoneʻeleʻele. Bay, beach, trail, Punaluʻu, Hawaiʻi. Small black sand beach at the head of the first large bay northeast of Punaluʻu. A historic stepping-stone trail paved with smooth, flat, waterworn stones, or *paʻalā*, crosses the *aʻā* from Kāneʻeleʻele Heiau at Punaluʻu to Keoneʻeleʻele Bay. The stepping-stone trail is part of the Ala Kahakai National Historic Trail. *Lit.*, the black sand.

Keonekani. Sand dunes, ʻŌhikilolo, Oʻahu. High, vegetated sand dunes at the west end of ʻŌhikilolo Beach and one of three sites in Hawaiʻi that have been identified as acoustical sands. Also known as Barking Sands. *Lit.*, the sounding sand.

Keonekani o Nohili. Sand dunes, Nohili, Kauaʻi. High, vegetated sand dunes at the west end of the Pacific Missile Range Facility at Nohili Point and one of three sites in Hawaiʻi that have been identified as acoustical sands. Also known as Barking Sands. *Lit.*, the sounding sand of Nohili.

Keonelele. Sand dunes, Moʻomomi, Molokaʻi. Extensive, active belt of largely unconsolidated dunes that extends from Moʻomomi Beach almost completely across the western corner of West Molokaʻi. The belt was formed by the trade winds blowing sand inland from the beach. Some of the older dunes have lithified to form calcareous sandstone. Also known as the Desert Strip. *Lit.*, the flying sand.

Keoneloa. Beach, petroglyph site, Poʻipū, Kauaʻi. Calcareous sand beach between Makawehi and Makahūʻena Points that is mostly fronted by a rocky shelf. Petroglyphs were carved into the soft beachrock shelves here and to the east at Māhāʻulepū, but they are exposed only during intense periods of high surf that scour the sand off the shelves. Also known as Shipwreck Beach. *Lit.*, the long sand [beach].

Ke One Neʻe o ʻAwahua. Kalaupapa, Molokaʻi. One of five beaches on the Kalaupapa Peninsula. Long, wide detrital sand beach at the foot of the Kalaupapa Trail on the west side of the peninsula. Also known as ʻAwahua Beach, Black Sands Beach. *Lit.*, the shifting sands of ʻAwahua.

Keonenui. Beach, ʻAlaeloa, Maui. Pocket of calcareous sand fronting the Kahana Sunset condominium. Also known as Yabui Beach. *Lit.*, the big sand [beach].

Keoneʻōʻio. 1. Bay, beach, Honuaʻula, Maui. Small pockets of calcareous sand and coral rubble on the shore of an otherwise rocky bay. Also known as La Pérouse Bay. 2. Beach, Kahe, Oʻahu. Calcareous sand beach west of Kahe Point. Also known as Tracks Beach Park. 3. Beach, channel, Kahuku, Oʻahu. Calcareous sand beach and sand channel fronting the Kahuku Golf Course. Also known as Kahuku Beach. *Lit.*, the bonefish sand. *'Ō'io*, or bonefish, is a popular food fish that forages in pockets of sand and is found at all three sites.

Keonepūpū. Shore, Keaukaha, Hawai'i. Large, open grassy field on the shore of Lehia Park. *Lit.*, the sand [beach with] shells. Keonepūpū was a legendary person, one of the wives of Leleiwi.

Keone'ula. Beach, 'Ewa Beach, O'ahu. Same as One'ula. *Lit.*, the reddish sand.

Keōpuka. Island (1.7 acres, 120 foot high), Honomanu, Maui. State-owned island off Moiki Point on the north side of Honomanu Bay. Part of the Hawai'i State Seabird Sanctuary. *Lit.*, the perforated sand. The *o* is short for *one.*

Kepapu. Fort, Honolulu, O'ahu. Same as Kekuanohu. *Lit.*, the gun wall.

Kepuhi. 1. Point, Hā'ena, Kaua'i. Long, broad point between Waini̇ha and Hā'ena bordered by a calcareous sand beach. 2. Beach, Kaluako'i, Moloka'i. Long calcareous sand beach fronting the Sheraton Moloka'i Hotel and its golf course, both of which opened in 1977. 3. Point, Mākaha, O'ahu. Off the west end of Mākaha Beach Park. Probably named for the blowhole at the point. Also known as Mākaha Point. *Lit.*, the blowhole.

Kewalo. 1. Basin, Honolulu, O'ahu. Small boat harbor constructed by the U.S. Navy in 1945 and later given to the Territory of Hawai'i. The 126-slip harbor is used exclusively for commercial boats, primarily cruise, charter fishing, and commercial fishing boats. The land surrounding the harbor was created by landfill projects. 2. Channel, Honolulu, O'ahu. Entrance channel to Kewalo Basin that is 200 feet wide, 2,000 feet long, and 20 feet deep. 3. Peninsula, Honolulu, O'ahu. Site of Kewalo Basin Park on the east side of the harbor. *Lit.*, the resounding.

Kewalo Basin Marine Mammal Laboratory. Research facility, Kewalo Basin, O'ahu. Internationally renowned laboratory for conducting dolphin and humpback whale intelligence research, including their sensory perceptions and language. Established by Louis Herman in 1975, the lab is part of the Dolphin Institute, an organization that provides opportunities for students and researchers to work with captive dolphins. The Kewalo facility has four bottlenose dolphins in a tank on one-quarter acre of land.

Kewalo Basin Park. Honolulu, O'ahu. State park on the east side of Kewalo Basin, a harbor primarily for commercial boats.

Kewalo Reef. Dive site, Honolulu, O'ahu. On the east side of Kewalo Channel at 30 to 40 feet. Introductory dive site with some ledges.

Kewalo's. Surf site, Honolulu, O'ahu. On the east side of Kewalo Channel off Kewalo Basin Park.

Keyhole. 1. Swimming, snorkeling site, Hanauma Bay, O'ahu. Largest sand pocket in the reef at Hanauma Bay that looks like a keyhole when viewed from the cliffs above. Military personnel who established a camp here in World War II used dynamite to create a coral-free swimming zone. 2. Cove, Kahuku, O'ahu. The keyhole-shaped cove used as a swimming and snorkeling site on the north side of the Turtle Bay Hilton Hotel between Kalaeokaunu and Kalaeokamanu Points. Also known as Kalokoiki.

Keyholes. 1. Surf site, Hanauma Bay, O'ahu. Beyond the reef outside of the Keyhole. Also known as Skulls. 2. Surf site, Kahuku, O'ahu. Off the Keyhole, or swimming area, at the Turtle Bay Hilton Hotel. Also known as Bayviews, Hotels.

KH Buoy. Fish aggregating device, Kehena, Hawai'i. Buoy anchored at approximately 940 fathoms. Landmarks: Pohoiki Light, Hākuma Point.

Kiddies. 1. Surf site, Hanalei, Kaua'i. On the west side of Hanalei Pier. Beginners break surfed primarily by young children, or "kiddies." 2. Beach, surf site, Mākaha, O'ahu. Cove with a small calcareous sand beach between 'Upena and Moua Streets. Popular place for neighborhood children to swim. The surf site is a shorebreak on the beach. Also known as Aki's Beach.

Ki'eki'e. Beach, southwest coast, Ni'ihau. Calcareous sand beach approximately 1.25 miles long between Paliuli and Halawela. A cluster of small rock islands lies off the south end of the beach, the largest of which is Kūakamoku. Ki'eki'e is also the name of the Ni'ihau Ranch headquarters, which is on a rise inland of the beach. *Lit.*, lofty.

Kihaloko. Fishpond, Hālawa, Moloka'i. *Lit.*, Chief Kiha's pond.

Kīhei. 1. Landing, Kīhei, Maui. Landing ruins at the north end of Mai Poina 'Oe I'au Beach Park. About 1890, Maui Sugar Plantation owners and farmers selected this site for a landing in Mā'alaea Bay. A 200-foot-long wharf was constructed and used by interisland steamers to land freight and ship produce. About 1915, the interisland steamers stopped calling because severe sand accretion prevented them from reaching the wharf, but smaller boats continued to use it until 1952 when Mā'alaea Small Boat Harbor was constructed. Now only a few pilings and a rubblemound remain. 2. Offshore mooring, Kīhei, Maui. State mooring site off the old landing. 3. Ramp, Kīhei, Maui. State boat launching facility south of Kama'ole III Beach Park. Facilities include three ramps, two docks, and a vessel washdown area. *Lit.*, shawl, cape, cloak.

Kīhei Memorial Park. Kīhei, Maui. Same as Mai Poina 'Oe Ia'u Beach Park.

Kīhewamoku. Island, Mālaekahana, O'ahu. Part of the Hawai'i State Seabird Sanctuary. One of five islets visible from Lā'ie Point that were created when the demigods Kana and Nīheu cut up the body of a *mo'o,* or legendary lizard, and threw the pieces into the sea.

Kīholo. 1. Bay, dive site, surf site, Kīholo, Hawai'i. One of the Big Island's largest bays at 2 miles in width. Black sand and pebble beaches line the shore of the bay. The surf site and primary dive site are on the reef in the center of the bay off the large coconut grove. Wainānāli'i Pond at the north end of the bay is a unique lagoon that is an important habitat for sea turtles. Kīholo Bay is also known as Turtle Bay. 2. Special fisheries management area. This designation for Kīholo Bay prohibits the use of gill nets to protect the turtles that feed and rest here. Gill nets trap and drown turtles. The rules still permit pole and throw-net fishing. Kīholo Bay, including Wainānāli'i Pond, is one of the major habitats on the island for green sea turtles and hawksbill turtles. 3. Trail, Kīholo, Hawai'i. Historic stepping-stone trail paved with smooth, flat, waterworn stones, or *pa'alā,* across the *a'ā* on the shore of Kīholo Bay to Nāwaikulua Point. Part of the Ala Kahakai National Historic Trail. *Lit.,* large fishhook or net.

 *mo'olelo*

In the 1890s my grandfather, Robert Hind, and Eben Lowe acquired the lease for Pu'u Wa'awa'a Ranch. **Kīholo** was the cattle shipping point for the ranch because there was no circle-island road. They herded the cattle *makai,* tied them to lighters, and loaded them on the steamers like the *Kīna'u,* the *Hawai'i,* and the *Humu'ula.* The landing was the black sand beach at the south end of the bay towards Luahinewai. It has a sharp drop-off, so the lighters could get in close. They called it Shipping Pen Beach. In 1932, a narrow, partially paved road was completed to Hu'ehu'e Ranch, and within a few years they stopped shipping cattle and started trucking them to Kailua.

There was also some lesser commercial activity at Kīholo. Until 1915 or so a man named Muller had a saltpan operation near Shipping Pen Beach. He used a windmill to pump salt water into the pans and took the salt to Kona to trade. His tomb is there, a caved-in concrete structure. There are also natural *kāheka* [salt pans] in the rocks at Kalaemano, and we would always go after big westerly surf because it would fill the *kāheka.* At home we would mix the salt with *'alae* from Kaua'i.

Kīholo had some big goat drives, one about 1910 that netted

10,000 goats using the Boy Scouts, the National Guard, and everyone else around. The goats were slaughtered for their skins, and the carcasses were thrown into the ocean. Sharks came in huge numbers and sat in the shallow water facing the beach, waiting for the discarded bodies. We raised pigs, and during the kiawe *bean season, we'd fatten about seventy-five head of cattle at Kīholo for about three months. We also harvested about 1,000 pounds of* moi *and* awa *annually from the ponds, which paid for the caretaker and the maintenance of our beach house. My grandfather built it about 1905. The pond operations continued until the 1960 tidal wave. The '46 wave moved the houses off their foundations, but the '60 wave wiped out everything.*

 Robert L. Hind Jr., October 11, 1981

Kiʻi. Bay, landing, northwest shore, Niʻihau. Kiʻi and Lehua are the two landings on the north end of the island. Niʻihau Ranch uses the landings to haul livestock, equipment, passengers, food, dry goods, and other necessities to the island from Makaweli Landing on Kauaʻi. Kiʻi Landing is an alternate site that is used when high surf precludes the use of Lehua Landing. *Lit.,* [carved, wooden] image.

Kiʻi Unit. Wildlife refuge, Kahuku, Oʻahu. A 164-acre wetland that is one of two sections, or "units," of the James Campbell National Wildlife Refuge at Kahuku Point. The refuge attracts both native and migratory waterbirds.

Kīkīaola. Small boat harbor, Poʻipū, Kauaʻi. Completed in 1959 to provide a small boat harbor for West Kauaʻi. Facilities include four moorings, a ramp, and a vessel washdown area. *Lit.,* spouting springs of Ola. Kīkīaola is the name of an inland watercourse that is also known the Menehune Ditch. Chief Ola ordered the *menehune,* a legendary people, to build the watercourse, and they completed the project in one night.

Kikila. Beach estate, Lāʻie, Oʻahu. In 1885 Cecil Brown, a prominent resident of Honolulu, purchased some beachfront property in Lāʻie Maloʻo and built a country home on it. The home was called Kikila, or Cecil, for him. The portion of the estate on the seaward side of Kamehameha Highway is now Lāʻie Beach Park. The remainder of the estate on the inland side of the highway is owned by his descendants and still known as Kikila. *Lit.,* Cecil (English).

Kīlauea. 1. Volcano, Puna, Hawaiʻi. One of the five volcanoes that make up the island of Hawaiʻi, and the most active volcano in the state. 2. Point light, Kīlauea, Kauaʻi. Established in 1913 on the northernmost point on the island. The 52-foot concrete light tower is approximately 217 feet above sea level. In 1976 the Coast Guard deactivated the light tower and replaced it with a light atop a 14-foot pole that stands in front of the tower. The tower and point are part of Kīlauea Point National Wildlife Refuge. 3. Bay, Kīlauea, Kaua'i. Large bay east of Mōkōlea Point off Kīlauea Stream. *Lit.,* spewing, much spreading (on Hawai'i, referring to volcanic eruptions).

Kīlauea Point. National wildlife refuge (160 acres), Kīlauea, Kaua'i. The refuge was established in 1974 when the U.S. Fish and Wildlife Service took over a 31-acre Coast Guard Reservation at Kīlauea Point. The Coast Guard used the site to maintain Kīlauea Light. The refuge includes the sea cliffs at Mōkōlea Point, Crater Hill, and Kīlauea Point and is home to at least seven species of seabirds, including wedge-tailed shearwaters, red-footed boobies, brown boobies, Laysan albatrosses, red-tailed and white-tailed tropic birds, and great frigate birds. The refuge is one of the few places in the world where the public can see nesting colonies of Central Pacific seabirds. The visitor center is on the point.

Kilia. Channel, reef, surf site, Hau'ula, O'ahu. On the north side of Hau'ula Beach park. The surf site is also known as Suddenlys. Perhaps lit., a type of wave.

Kīloa. Wharf, Nāpo'opo'o, Hawai'i. Also known as Nāpo'opo'o Landing or Wharf. *Lit.,* long ti plant or to put away objects for safekeeping.

Kiloi'a. Point, Lā'ie, O'ahu. Limestone point on Lā'ie Malo'o Bay that separates Pounders and Kokololio Beaches. Fish spotters used the point to watch for schools of fish in the bay and to direct fishermen in canoes with surround nets. Also known as Pali Kiloi'a. *Lit.,* fish spotter.

Kimo's. Surf site, Mokulē'ia, O'ahu. Veteran surfer Kimo Lyman was one of the first to surf this site and still surfs here regularly. His family home, Kai'ae, built in 1938 and now the only house beyond Camp Erdman, is on the hill inshore of the surf site. Also known as Kai'ae, Lone Tree, Lyman's.

Kim's. Surf site, Wailupe, O'ahu. Off Wailupe Beach Park. Named for an 'Āina Haina surfer named Kim who was one of the first to surf here regularly in the 1970s. Also known as Firehouse, Goofys.

Kina'u. Cape, Honua'ula, Maui. Point that is part of the 'Āhihi-Kīna'u Natural Area Reserve. *Lit.,* flaw.

King's Highway. 1. Trail, North Kona and South Kohala, Hawai'i. Remnant of a coastal trail that formerly circled most of the Big Island. 2. Trail, Hawai'i Kai, O'ahu. Coastal trail that went around the east end of the island prior to the construction of

Kalaniana'ole Highway in the early 1930s. Also known as Kealakīpapa.

King's Landing. Beach, Papa'i, Hawai'i. Narrow crescent of black and green sand fronting a coconut grove and the ruins of the former fishing village of Pāpa'i. It was here in 1793 that King Kamehameha I led a small raiding party in an attack on the village. During the skirmish, a fisherman struck him over the head with a canoe paddle. This incident later resulted in the now legendary Law of the Splintered Paddle. The site was named King's Landing because Kamehameha's raiding party landed here in canoes. Also known as Pāpa'i.

King's Pillars. Historic site, Kumukahi, Hawai'i. Stone cairns near the Cape Kumukahi Light that were nearly overrun by the 1960 Kapoho lava flow. The reason the cairns were built here is unknown and probably not related to their English name.

King's Pond. Pond, Kūki'o, Hawai'i. On the grounds of the Four Seasons Resort Hualālai. Private, man-made, 2.5 million gallon, spring-fed anchialine pond 16 feet deep, stocked with Hawaiian tropical fish and designed for snorkeling and scuba diving.

Kinikini. Surf site, windsurf site, Pacific Missile Range Facility, Kaua'i. Kinikini is the section of the shore that includes the drainage canal that empties into the ocean at the south end of the runway. Also known as Airports. *Lit.,* abundant.

Kinney. Reef, Pā'ia, Maui. Off the Lime Kiln at the west end of Pā'ia Bay. Claude Kinney, a Hawai'i Commercial and Sugar Co. employee, lived next to the Lime Kiln.

Kiowea. Park, Kalama'ula, Moloka'i. West of Kaunakakai and fronted by a narrow detrital sand beach. The park is the site of a famous coconut grove known as the Kapuāiwa or Kamehameha Coconut Grove. *Lit.,* bristle-thighed curlew (a large, brown, migratory seabird). The May 9, 1863, edition of the Hawaiian language newspaper *Ka Nūpepa Kū'oko'a* offered the following description of the *kiowea,* also spelled *kioea:* "This bird is about the size of a wild pigeon with a pointed head, a straight beak, dark feathers, and long legs. When he flies, his legs swiftly point back and whip up under his tail. He is an expert bird at fishing and his flesh is very delicious. This bird was named because of his cry, which is like calling out kioea. This is no other bird-cry like it."

Kīpapa. 1. Fishpond, Kamalō, Moloka'i. *Lit.,* placed prone (referring to slain corpses). 2. Island, Kāne'ohe Bay, O'ahu. Common mispronunciation and misspelling of Kapapa, the correct name of the island. *Lit.,* paved. 3. Fishpond, Niu, O'ahu. Fishpond fronting Niu Valley that was filled to create Niu Peninsula. *Lit.,* paved.

Kīpū. Beach, salt gathering site, Hōnaunau, Hawai'i. Between Pu'uhonua o Hōnaunau National Historical Park and Ke'ei. Salt was made in the depressions of large stones on the shore. *Lit.,* to remain, as mist or rain.

Kīpū Kai. Beach, dive site, snorkeling site, surf site, Kīpū Kai, Kaua'i. Kīpū Kai is a coastal valley in the Hā'upu Range that lies between Māhā'ulepu and Nāwiliwili. The valley has been privately owned and operated as a cattle ranch for many years. John T. Waterhouse, the last owner of the 1,096-acre ranch, died on February 20, 1984. In 1977, Waterhouse deeded the entire ranch to the state, but stipulated that the state's ownership is to take effect only upon the deaths of his four nieces and one nephew. The valley shore is approximately 2 miles long and consists of four calcareous sand beaches separated by low rocky points. The long calcareous sand beach between Kawelikoa and Mōlehu Points is Kīpū Kai Beach. It is also known as Hananena and Long Beach. The backshore is lined with vegetated dunes. The surf site is a shorebreak on the sandbar at the south end of the beach, and the snorkeling site is off the north end of the beach at Mōlehu Point. The dive site is northeast of Kawelikoa Point. *Lit.,* seaward Kīpū.

Kite. Beach, Kahului, Maui. Section of Kanaha Beach Park that is dedicated to kite surfing, or windsurfing with a kite, a sport that was pioneered in Hawai'i in the late 1990s.

KK Buoy. Fish aggregating device, Waimea, Kaua'i. Buoy anchored at approximately 960 fathoms. Landmarks: Kokole Point, Waimea Channel Marker, Pū'olo Point.

Klausmeyer's. Surf site, Mākaha, O'ahu. Off the beachfront home of David Klausmeyer.

Knob Hill. Dive site, Lāna'i. Lava ridges, arches, and small caves at 60 feet. The "knob" is a shallow rock with a hollow underside that houses many invertebrates.

Ko'a Heiau Holomoana. *Heiau,* Māhukona, Hawai'i. *Heiau,* or shrine, dedicated to navigation on the hillside above Māhukona Harbor. Upright boulders at the site represent specific islands in the Pacific and the paths across the ocean to reach them. Contemporary voyaging canoe navigators continue to visit the site. *Lit.,* shrine [for those who] travel the open ocean.

Koai'e. Cove, village, Lapakahi, Hawai'i. A former precontact fishing village in Lapakahi State Historical Park, Koai'e was inhabited until the late 1800s and is now a center for *lā'au lapa'au,* the use of herbs and native medicine to heal the sick. The cove off the village is a marine life conservation district. *Lit.,* a tree *(Acacia koaia)* that has a particularly pleasant fragrance. Allusion to the *koai'e* in poetry sometimes refers to love.

Kohala Estates. Dive site, Kohala, Hawai'i. In Waiaka'īlio Bay, which is below the Kohala Estates subdivision. Also known as Ulua Cave.

Kohanaiki. Beach, Kona, Hawai'i. Calcareous sand and coral rubble beach at Wāwahiwa'a Point. Also known as Pine Trees. *Lit.*, small barreness, slightly naked, or alone.

Kohelepelepe. Crater, Hawai'i Kai, O'ahu. In a legend of Pele, the goddess of the volcano, her sister threw her vagina to this spot where it became the crater. Also known as Koko Crater. *Lit.*, vagina labia minor.

Koholālele. Fishpond, Kualoa, O'ahu. Also known as Mokoli'i. *Lit.*, breaching whale.

Ko'ie'ie. Fishpond, Kīhei, Maui. Ancient fishpond at Kalepolepo Beach in Kīhei. *Ke Au 'Oko'a*, a Hawaiian language newspaper, reported in December 1869 that Kamehameha I had ordered the pond rebuilt during his reign. Also known as Kalepolepo. *Lit.*, rapid, rushing water or current.

Kōke'e Beach Right-of-Way. Beach park (.5 acres), Hawai'i Kai, O'ahu. Streets in the Koko Kai subdivision are named after places on Kaua'i. The right-of-way, actually a minipark, is on the low sea cliffs bordering Kōke'e Place. *Lit.*, to bend or to wind.

Koki. Beach park, surf site, Hāna, Maui. Small calcareous sand beach on the south side of Ka Iwi o Pele, a cinder cone of the Hāna Volcanic Series. The beach park was developed during the late 1960s as a community service project by Hāna Post 3860 of the Veterans of Foreign Wars (VFW) and their women's auxiliary. The surf site is a shorebreak on a sandbar. *Lit.*, successful or the epitome.

Koko. Crater, head, Hawai'i Kai, O'ahu. Koko Crater and Koko Head are two prominent volcanic tuff cones at the east end of Maunalua Bay. Koko Crater is also known as Kohelepelepe. *Lit.*, blood. Both the crater and the headland took their name from a former canoe landing named Koko at Portlock Beach. In one legendary account, blood washed ashore here from the victim of a shark attack.

Koko Craters. Dive site, Hawai'i Kai, O'ahu. Popular boat dive site, with many turtles and fish at 35 to 45 feet deep and four underwater mooring buoys.

Koko Head Regional Park and Nature Preserve. Park, Hawai'i Kai, O'ahu. A 1,265-acre county park that extends from Sandy Beach to Koko Head and includes Sandy Beach Park, Hālona Blowhole, Koko Crater Botanical Garden, Koko Crater, Koko Head Shooting Complex, Hanauma Bay, Koko Head, and Koko Head District Park.

Kokoiki. North Kohala, Hawai'i. Birthplace of Kamehameha I (1758?–1819) and one of many sites in Hawai'i associated with the life of the king who unified the Hawaiian islands. *Lit.*, little blood (for the afterbirth).

Koko Kai Beach Right-of-Way. Beach park (.6 acres), Hawai'i Kai, O'ahu. The right-of-way, actually a minipark, is on the sea cliffs at Hanapēpē Place in the Koko Kai subdivision. It is the primary access to several surf sites, including China Walls, off the sea cliffs. Koko Kai includes the homes between Portlock Road and Kawaihoa Point. *Lit.*, seaward Koko.

Kokole. Light, Mānā, Kaua'i. Light atop a pole approximately 58 feet above sea level on the dunes south of the Pacific Missile Range Facility. *Lit.*, raw.

Kokololio. Beach, beach park (15.5 acres), Hau'ula, O'ahu. Calcareous sand beach on either side of Kokololio Stream. During the early 1900s two prominent island families, the Castles and the Cookes, bought adjacent lots here and built country homes on them. In 1953 the Castles sold their home to the Zion Securities Company, the business branch of the Mormon Church, who used the area as a campsite. The Cookes eventually sold their home to the Catholic Youth Organization (CYO), which also used the area as a campsite. In 1988 and 1991 respectively, the City and County of Honolulu bought the two parcels of land to create Kokololio Beach Park. The beach park is on the south side of Kokololio Stream. Also known as Kākela. *Lit.*, gusty, or rapidly flowing water.

Koko Marina. Shopping center, Hawai'i Kai, O'ahu. Shopping center on the east side of Hawai'i Kai Marina. Many people incorrectly use the name of the shopping center, Koko Marina, as the name of the marina.

Kōlea. Rock, Mākena, Maui. Small rock island in Mākena Bay. *Lit.*, plover.

Kōlealea. Point, reef, Mākua, O'ahu. Near the west end of Mākua Beach. A child's ditty in which *"kōlealea"* is the refrain.

Kolekole. Park, North Hilo, Hawai'i. On the ocean at the mouth of Kolekole Stream, but swimming is possible only in the stream. 'Akaka Falls, one of the most famous waterfalls in Hawai'i, is situated on the stream approximately 4 miles inland of the town of Honomū. A picnic pavilion in the park is named after former County Supervisor Elias P. (Epy) Yadao. *Lit.*, raw.

Kolo. 1. Beach, Kolo, Moloka'i. Narrow calcareous sand beach that borders Pālā'au Road. 2. Cliffs camp, Kolo, Moloka'i. Private campsite on the hillside above the beach that is owned and operated by Moloka'i Ranch. 3. Wharf, Kolo, Moloka'i. In 1923, Libby, McNeill and Libby leased some land at Maunaloa from Moloka'i Ranch and began growing pineapples. The dirt road to Kaunakakai was in poor condition, so they dredged a channel through the reef and built a wharf below Maunaloa at Kaumanamana to service the plantation. The wharf was named Kolo for a nearby gulch because Libby felt that Kolo would be easier to pronounce than Kaumanamana. Kolo Wharf remained the major shipping point for pineapple on the island until the early 1950s when the road to Kaunakakai was improved and shipping operations were moved to Kaunakakai Wharf. *Lit.*, to crawl.

Kōloa. Beach, Punalu'u, Hawai'i. Pebble or *'ili'ili* beach between Punalu'u and Nīnole where birth pebbles are said to occur. Traditional stories say that the pebbles, or *'ili'ili hānau*, reproduce themselves and give birth to smaller pebbles. *Lit.*, long [grass] cane, or to roar.

Kōloa Landing. Dive site, snorkeling site, Po'ipū, Kaua'i. Former interisland steamer landing established by and named for Kōloa Plantation, a former sugar plantation. The dive and snorkeling sites are in the small bay off the landing at approximately 25 feet deep. They are among the most popular dive and snorkeling sites on the island. Dive instructors bring their students here for introductory and certification dives.

Kolo Rock. Fishing site, Pāhoehoe, Hawai'i. Small rock island about 20 feet from the base of the sea cliffs here that is accessed by a cable and a cable chair. Kolo Rock is one of the Big Island's famous *ulua* fishing sites.

Kona Cathedrals. Dive site, Honokōhau, Hawai'i. Large room at 60 feet under a lava dome with natural skylights that allow light to filter through, producing a "cathedral" effect. Six divers can fit under the dome, which also harbors many varieties of fish. Also known as Kaiwi.

Kona Coast. State park, Kona, Hawai'i. Largely undeveloped coastal park north of Keāhole Airport that includes Mahai'ula and Manini'ōwali Beaches, which are connected by a 4.5-mile trail on the shore. Also known as Kekaha Kai State Park.

Kona District. Ancient name given to the leeward districts of five of the eight major islands: Hawai'i, Kaua'i, Moloka'i, Ni'ihau, and O'ahu. Only Hawai'i retains the name today in its North Kona and South Kona Districts. The former Kona District on O'ahu, including the land divisions from Maunalua to Moanalua, was renamed the Honolulu District in 1859 and is now called the City of Honolulu. *Lit.*, leeward.

Kona Reef. Surf site, North Kona, Hawai'i. Off the Kona Reef condominium.

Kona Surf. Dive site, Keauhou, Hawai'i. Off the Kona Surf Hotel. Also known as Keauhou Bay.

Kona Village. Beach. Ka'ūpūlehu, Hawai'i. Calcareous sand and lava fragment beach at the head of Kahuwai Bay fronting the

Kona Village Resort. The resort was built by a wealthy businessman named Johnno Jackson and completed in June 1964. Originally Jackson Village, the name was changed to the Kona Village Resort when Jackson sold his interests. Also known as Ka'ūpūlehu.

Kooks. Beach, windsurf site, Kahului, Maui. Wide, calcareous sand beach north of Kanahā Beach Park. The dictionary defines *kook* as someone who is silly, eccentric, or crazy, but among surfers and windsurfers a kook is someone who is incompetent in the water and constantly gets in the way. Originally a surfing term coined by California surfers in the 1960s, *kook* was applied here in the 1970s with the introduction of windsurfing to Maui because this beach is the primary beginner's site on Maui's north shore. Also known as Alahao Airport Park.

Ko'olina. Beaches, lagoons, Ko 'Olina, O'ahu. Ko'olina is the original spelling of Ko 'Olina. The variant spelling Ko 'Olina was adopted by the Ko 'Olina Resort and Marina as its official name. *Lit.,* delightful, lovely.

Ko 'Olina. 1. Beaches, lagoons, Ko 'Olina, O'ahu. Four man-made lagoons with calcareous sand beaches. Collectively they are known as the Ko 'Olina Lagoons and individually from west to east as First, Second, Third, and Fourth Lagoons. 2. Marina, Ko 'Olina, O'ahu. Private marina that opened in March 2000. Facilities include 267 slips, a fuel dock, 33 trailer parking stalls, dry storage, and a public ramp. Also known as Ko'olina. *Lit.,* delightful, lovely.

Kou. Fishing site, reef, Mālaekahana, O'ahu. Flat, nearshore reef where seaweed and fish congregated. *Lit., kou* tree.

Kua Bay. 1. Bay, beach, Manini'ōwali, Hawai'i. Kua Bay, the bay off Manini'ōwali Beach, is often used as the name of the beach because it is easier to pronounce than Manini'ōwali. 2. Dive site, Manini'ōwali, Hawai'i. Off Pāpiha Point at the north end of Manini'ōwali Beach at approximately 40 feet. *Lit.,* back, or shortened form of *akua* [god].

Kuahonu. Beach, Kīpū Kai, Kaua'i. Small calcareous sand beach inshore of Kuahonu Point. The Kīpū Kai ranch house is on a grassy knoll above the beach. *Lit.,* turtle back.

Kūakamoku. Island, (1.1 acres, 4 feet high), reef, Ki'eki'e, Ni'ihau. Largest of a cluster of small rock islands on a reef off the south end of Ki'eki'e Beach. Kūakamoku Island is in the center of the reef and 1,500 feet offshore. *Lit.,* resembling the island, or to rule the land.

Kualaka'i. Beach, Kalaeloa, O'ahu. Calcareous sand beach at the east end of the Kalaeloa Community Development District. Also known as White Plains Beach. Name of a sea cucumber *(Aplysia dachylomela* or *A. Juliana).*

Kualoa. 1. Artificial reef, Kualoa, Oʻahu. A mile off Kualoa Regional Park in approximately 90 feet of water. The state deposited material to establish the reef in 1972, and it now includes a barge that was sunk in 1994 and 400 concrete fish habitats that were dropped in 1999. 2. Point, Kualoa, Oʻahu. Also known as Kalaeʻōʻio Point. 3. Point range lights, Kualoa, Oʻahu. Navigational lights off Kualoa Regional Park that mark the channel into Kāneʻohe Bay. 4. Regional park (153.4 acres), Kualoa, Oʻahu. This park is listed in the National Register of Historical Places because of its traditional cultural importance. Young chiefs were brought here to be schooled in the arts of war and other political matters. Also known as ʻĀpua. 5. Surf site, windsurf site, Kualoa, Oʻahu. Off Kalaeʻōʻio Point. Also known as Gun Point, Kanenelu, Kūloa. *Lit.*, long back or ridge.

Kuamaka. Fishpond, Hāna, Maui. Privately owned pond south of Kōkī Beach Park. *Lit.*, to have offspring.

Kuapā. Fishpond, Hawaiʻi Kai, Oʻahu. Huge fishpond that was converted into Hawaiʻi Kai Marina by Henry J. Kaiser in the 1950s. The original pond covered 523 acres, and its longest wall extended 5,000 feet. *Lit.*, fishpond wall.

Kūʻau. 1. Windsurf site, Kūʻau, Maui. In the center of the Kūʻau community at the public right-of-way on ʻAleiki Place. Access to the open ocean is through a narrow channel in the rocks known as Ako Channel. 2. Rock, Mōkapu, Oʻahu. At the north end of Pyramid Rock Beach. Also known as Pyramid Rock. *Lit.*, shank of a fishhook.

Kūʻau Bay. Beach, surf site, Kūʻau, Maui. Calcareous sand beach on the west side of the Kūʻau community. The beach is also known as Kaulahao, and a cove within the bay is also known as Lamalani. The surf site is adjacent to the point and is also known as Tavares Bay.

Kūʻau Cove. Beach, Kūʻau, Maui. Small calcareous sand beach on the east side of the Kūʻau community fronting Mama's Fish House. Also known as Father Jules Papa, Mama's.

Kuaumania. Beach, reef, Kawailoa, Oʻahu. Calcareous sand beach and the wide, shallow reef fronting it to the north of Pōhakuloa Way. Also known as Chun's Reef.

Kuekaunahi. Stream, Waikīkī, Oʻahu. Small stream that paralleled Kapahulu Avenue and crossed Waikīkī Beach at the intersection of Kalākaua and Kapahulu Avenue. It was eventually enclosed in a culvert and at the shore its waters were channeled into the ocean through the Kapahulu Groin. Perhaps *lit.*, to remove scales from fish.

Kuʻemanu. *Heiau*, Kahaluʻu, Hawaiʻi. Ruins of a surfing *heiau*, or shrine, on the shore of Kahaluʻu Bay. Chiefs prayed for surf here and rinsed off after surfing in a nearby pool. A popular surf site, Kahalu'u, is located off the *heiau*. Perhaps lit., to attract and net petrel birds.

Kūheia. Bay, beach, north shore, Kaho'olawe. The bay lies within the coastal boundaries of the *'ili* (land division) of Kūheia. A horseshoe-shaped bay, it has two pocket beaches of detrital sand separated by a rocky bluff. A narrow channel through the north side of the bay leads to the beach. Beginning in 1858, Kaho'olawe was leased a number of times to individuals who attempted to use the island as a sheep, goat, and cattle ranch. When King Kalākaua visited the island in 1875, the Hawaiian newspaper *Ka Lāhui Hawai'i* reported that he and his entourage found two men, two women, two children, two dogs, four houses, and ten horses at Kūheia. The newspaper also reported that the island was home to hundreds of goats and twenty thousand sheep. By 1909 the foraging of these animals had severely denuded the island of vegetation, creating a serious soil erosion problem. In 1917, Angus MacPhee, a cowboy from Wyoming and a former manager of 'Ulupalakua Ranch on Maui, secured the lease. Although he was never able to completely exterminate the goats and sheep, he greatly reduced their numbers. In 1922, MacPhee established Kaho'olawe Ranch with the financial assistance of Harry A. Baldwin and reintroduced cattle to the island. As the other lessees before him had done, MacPhee established his ranch headquarters at Kūheia. He continued his ranching operations until the attack on Pearl Harbor on December 7, 1941. At that time, MacPhee and Baldwin gave over their lease for use of the island to the federal government for as long as necessary. Although MacPhee's lease was good until 1953, the island was never returned to him when the war ended in 1945, and the federal government continued to use it as a bombing range. The ruins of the ranch buildings and several corrals are inland of the beach. Also known as Pedro Bay. *Lit.,* stand entangled.

Kūhiō. 1. Bay, Hilo, Hawai'i. Large, deep, natural gap, or "bay," in the fringing reef at Waiākea that was dredged from 1925 to 1930 to form the present harbor basin. The basin, or bay, was named for Prince Jonah Kūhiō Kalaniana'ole. When Kūhiō's mother died shortly after his birth in 1871, he and his two older brothers were adopted by his mother's sister, Kapi'olani. Kapi'olani and her husband, Kalākaua, had no children of their own, so when Kalākaua became king of Hawai'i in 1874, he gave each of the boys the title of prince. Prince Kūhiō went on to become a delegate to Congress from 1902 until his death in 1922. He is best remembered for his efforts to establish the Hawaiian Homes Commission Act, which resulted in certain public lands being made available to Hawaiians on five of the eight major islands. 2. Beach park (3.4 acres), Waikīkī, Oʻahu. Prince Jonah Kūhiō Kalanianaʻole lived the final years of his life here at Pualeilani, his home on the beach at Waikīkī. Upon his death, Pualeilani was given to the city and eventually dedicated as a public park. The park was named for him in 1940.

Kuhulu. Rock, Pāhoehoe, Hawaiʻi. Small rock island near Pūʻoʻa Point.

Kuʻi. Channel, Hawaiʻi Kai, Oʻahu. Also known as the Hawaiʻi Kai Channel. *Lit.,* to strike.

Kuʻia. Dive site, shoal, southwest shore, Kahoʻolawe. Extensive shallow reef that extends approximately 1.5 miles off Kealaikahiki Point and is as little as 6 feet below the surface of the ocean. *Lit.,* obstructed.

Kuiaha. Bay, Paʻuwela, Maui. Bay with a boulder beach and a small coconut grove in the backshore. Kuiaha was the site of two protest marches in November 1977 led by Leslie Kuloloio and Charles Maxwell to gain public access to the shore. Also known as Coconut Grove, Puniawa.

Kuilei Cliffs. Beach park (10.6 acres), Honolulu, Oʻahu. On Diamond Head Road between the Diamond Head Lighthouse and the first home to the east at Kaʻalāwai. Popular viewpoint with three lookouts on Diamond Head Road. A fishery below the sea cliffs here was called Kuilei. A paved trail in the park from Diamond Head Road to the beach provides the primary access for surfers and windsurfers to the shore below. Also known as Diamond Head Beach Park, Diamond Head Lookouts. *Lit.,* to string lei.

Kuilima. Point, Kahuku, Oʻahu. When the Turtle Bay Hilton Hotel opened in May 1972, it was named the Kuilima Hotel, and the point on which the hotel is situated was named Kuilima Point. Also known as Kalaeokaunu. *Lit.,* joining hands.

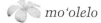 *moʻolelo*

I was born in the Marconi area on May 10, 1887. My maiden name was Kainanui, and my father was a former chief of the village. The only good swimming area at Kahuku was Kalokoiki, the cove next to the hotel. All of the old-timers went there. The point the hotel is on is called **Kuilima Point** now, but Kuilima is an inland name for the plains area around the highway bridge that says "Kuilima." The correct name of the point is Kalaeokaunu. The smaller point on the other side of the cove is Kalaeokamanu. I composed a song entitled "Kuilima" that mentions some of the special places in Kahuku, including Kalokoiki, but it hasn't been recorded. *Kuilima* means "to walk hand-in-hand."

 Emily Blanchard, February 9, 1973

Kū'ilioloa. *Heiau,* Wai'anae, O'ahu. Shrine with three terraces on the south point of Pōka'ī Bay. One of the few *heiau* remaining on the shore of O'ahu. *Lit.,* long dog Kū. Kū'ilioloa was a *kupua,* a demigod, who could assume the form of a man or dog. He was a protector of travelers.

Kūkae'ōhiki. Beach, Kawailoa, O'ahu. Calcareous sand beach between Pōhaku Loa Way and the Lauhulu Stream bridge. Also known as Laniākea Beach. *Lit.,* ghost crab excrement. Ghost crabs, popularly known as sand crabs, are common on this beach, where they dig their holes and forage for food. On occasion, as part of their foraging, they mold damp sand grains into small, compact balls. These balls are what were called *kūkae,* or "excrement."

Kūka'imanini. Island, Waiale'e, O'ahu. Small vegetated rock island off Waiale'e Beach Park. *Lit., manini* fish school.

Kūki'i. Point light, Nāwiliwili, Kaua'i. A 22-foot light tower approximately 47 feet above sea level at the north end of Nāwiliwili Harbor. *Lit.,* appearance of an image.

Kūki'o. Beach, dive site, surf site, Kūki'o, Hawai'i. Long calcareous sand beach fronted by a rocky shelf between Kīkaua Point and a finger of the 1801 lava flow from Hualālai. A sandy cove enclosed by lava at the south end of the beach has an unusual rock formation with an arch at its base. The rock formation was a legendary woman, Kahawaliwali, who was turned into stone. Several brackish-water ponds are found in the backshore. The dive site is north of Kīkaua Point at approximately 35 feet. The surf site is off the south end of the beach. *Lit.,* small pool of water.

Kūki'o/Ka'ūpūlehu Fishery Management Area. Conservation area, North Kona, Hawai'i. This area includes the nearshore waters at Kūki'o and Ka'ūpūlehu and is managed using traditional Hawaiian fishing restrictions to provide sustainable yields of marine resources for anyone at these sites. Establishment of the area was a joint effort between the resorts and the community. Signs are posted on the public accesses to the beach identifying the area and the suggested bag limits for certain species, such as *he'e, pualu, 'ōmilu, kole, mū,* and *kūmū.*

Kukuihaele. 1. Fishing site, landing, Kukuihaele, Hawai'i. Established in 1883, Kukuihaele Landing was one of eight interisland steamer wire landings along the Hāmākua Coast. The fishing site is at the ruins of the former landing, which are adjacent to the light. 2. Light, Kukuihaele, Hawai'i. Established in 1905. The 34-foot light tower was built in 1937. *Lit.,* traveling lights. Night marchers were seen here.

Kukuiho'olua. Island, Lā'ie, O'ahu. Part of the Hawai'i State Seabird Sanctuary. One of five islets visible from Lā'ie Point that were created when the demigods Kana and Nīheu cut up the body of a *moʻo*, a legendary lizard, and threw the pieces into the sea. This islet is directly off the point. The hole in the island was a sea cave until 1946, when the tsunami of April 1 broke the back wall of the cave, creating the hole. *Lit.,* oven-baked candlenut.

Kukuipalaoa. Island (3.6 acres, 50 feet high), north shore, Molokaʻi. *Lit.,* whale [bone] lamp.

Kukuiʻula. Small boat harbor, surf site, Kukuiʻula, Kauaʻi. Facilities include eight moorings, a ramp, and a vessel washdown area. The surf site is on the reef off the breakwater. *Lit.,* red light.

Kulaʻalamihi. Fishpond, Hālawa, Molokaʻi. *Lit.,* crab container.

Kulalua. Point, Sunset Beach, Oʻahu. Wide, flat rocky point with a cluster of large boulders on the north side of Shark's Cove.

Kulaokaʻeʻa. Plateau, Honolua, Maui. Plateau above Honolua Bay where one of the first golf courses on Maui was built. During the early 1920s, David Fleming, the manager of Honolua Ranch, converted the cattle pasture on the plateau into the West Maui Golf Course, a rugged nine-hole course. The course fell into disuse with the outbreak of World War II, but the former clubhouse still remains on the point in a stand of Norfolk pine trees. Also known as Golf Links. *Lit.,* plain of dust.

Kulapae. Point, Keaukaha, Hawaiʻi. Eastern section of Keaukaha Beach Park where the ruins of Hale ʻĀina, a former public pavilion for the Keaukaha community, are located. *Lit.,* [canoe] landing plain.

Kuliʻouʻou. Beach park (3.2 acres), Honolulu, Oʻahu. Narrow calcareous sand beach between the park and the shallow reef flat offshore. *Lit.,* sounding knee. The name refers to a small drum that was tied to the knee and played while performing the hula.

Kuloa. Surf site, Kaʻaʻawa, Oʻahu. The surf site is off Kalaeʻōʻio Point but is commonly called Kualoa Point. Surfers have shortened Kualoa to Kuloa. Also known as Gun Point, Kanenelu. *Lit.,* long back or ridge.

Kūmakani. Beach, reef, Kawailoa, Oʻahu. Calcareous sand beach and a wide, shallow reef off No Name Lane, a small lane that parallels Kamehameha Highway on the west side of Waimea Bay. Also known as Leftovers. *Lit.,* stand [against the] wind, or a windbreak.

Kumimi. Point, fishing site, Waialua, Molokaʻi. Also known as Maurice Point. Name of a type of crab.

Kumu. Cove, surf site, Waimānalo, Oʻahu. At the north end of Kaupō Beach Park. This small bay was once a good spearfishing site for *kumu* and other reef fish. Also known as Baby Makapuʻu, The Bay. *Lit.,* red goatfish.

Kumuku. Beach, Mākaha, Oʻahu. South section of Mākaha Beach. Perhaps lit., school of red goatfish.

Kumukahi. 1. Light, point, Puna, Hawaiʻi. Easternmost point of the Big Island and, therefore, of the Hawaiian Islands. Small black sand storm beaches, or pockets of cinder on the sea cliffs, are found here. Some of these are green sand beaches, or black sand mixed with olivine. Lava from the 1960 Kapoho eruption added 3 miles of new shore at Kumukahi and nearly overran the light, stopping only a few feet away. 2. Channel, Niʻihau. The channel between Lehua and Niʻihau. *Lit.*, first beginning or origin.

Kumumau. Canal, Hickam Air Force Base, Oʻahu. Drainage canal at the south end of Hickam Beach Park. The beach adjacent to the canal is a landing site for small, nonmotorized craft such as kayaks and outrigger canoes. *Lit.*, eternal source.

Kunanunu. Reef, Ukumehame, Maui. Small reef fronting Makaʻohai to the south of Ukumehame Beach Park.

Kupa. Landing, Hoʻokena, Hawaiʻi. Former interisland steamer landing in Hoʻokena Beach Park that was named for Henry Cooper, the road supervisor in South Kona from 1871 to 1880. *Kupa* is the Hawaiianized version of "Cooper." The landing was immortalized in a traditional Hawaiian song called "Kupa Landing." Also known as Cooper Landing, Hoʻokena Landing, Kauhakō Landing. *Lit.*, Cooper (English).

Kūpaka. Beach, ʻEwa Beach, Oʻahu. Shore where ʻEwa Beach Park is now. *Lit.*, to kick or thrash in anger (as a child's temper tantrum).

Kūpaoa. Beach, point, Haleʻiwa, Oʻahu. Calcareous sand beach and point at Kaiaka Bay Beach Park. Site of Pōhaku Lānaʻi, a famous pedestal rock. Also known as Kalaeokūpaoa. *Lit.*, strong fragrance, or stone sinker of an octopus lure.

Kūpeke. Fishpond, Hālawa, Molokaʻi. *Lit.*, stunted.

Kūpikipikiʻo. Point, Diamond Head, Oʻahu. Southernmost point on the island. Also known as Black Point. *Lit.*, rough [sea], or agitated [wind or storm].

Kūpopou. Reef, Hāʻena, Kauaʻi. Off Camp Naue. *Lit.*, to bend forward. When certain reef fish feed in shallow water, their tails may stick out of the water as they "bend forward."

Kuʻualiʻi. Fishpond, ʻAnaehoʻomalu, Hawaiʻi. One of two fishponds behind ʻAnaehoʻomalu Beach.

Kuwaʻaʻohe. Beach, Mōkapu, Oʻahu. Narrow calcareous sand beach on the east side of Ulupaʻu Crater. Also known as Fort Hase Beach.

La'aloa Bay. Beach park, North Kona, Hawai'i. Large pocket of calcareous sand between two rocky points on Ali'i Drive. The shorebreak on the beach is the most popular bodysurfing and bodyboarding site in Kona. A board surf site is off the south point of the beach. Also known as Disappearing Sands, Magic Sands, White Sands. *Lit.,* very sacred.

La'aloa Lava Tube. Dive site, North Kona, Hawai'i. Off the 4-mile marker on Ali'i Drive at approximately 40 feet.

Lā'au Point. 1. Cape, Lā'au, Moloka'i. Southwest extremity of Moloka'i and one of two points that define the west end of the island. The other is 'Īlio Point. 2. Point light, Lā'au, Moloka'i. Established by the monarchy in 1881 and automated in 1912. The 20-foot steel pole supporting the light stands approximately 132 feet above sea level. 3. Landing, Lā'au, Moloka'i. Former landing in a small inlet on the north side of the point that was used to service the lighthouse when it was manned. A boom extended over the inlet to unload the lighters that came ashore from the interisland steamers. Only a few concrete foundation blocks remain. *Lit.,* wood or tree.

LA Buoy. Fish aggregating device, Lahaina, Maui. Buoy anchored at approximately 110 fathoms. Landmarks: Lahaina Light, McGregor Point Light, Molokini, Mānele Bay Light.

Lady Land. Surf site, Ukumehame, Maui. At Ukumehame Park. Popular longboard surf site for women, or "ladies."

Lady Pua'ena Stone. Rock, Hale'iwa, O'ahu. Same as Pua'ena Stone.

Lae Hī. Point, Keōmuku, Lāna'i. Wide limestone hill on the shore that is crossed by Keōmuku Road. Also known as White Rock. *Lit.,* casting [for fish] point.

Laehou. Point, Kīholo, Hawai'i. Same as Hou Point. *Lit.,* new point.

Laenani. Neighborhood park (1.4 acres), Kāne'ohe, O'ahu. On Wailau Point in Kāne'ohe Bay. *Lit.,* beautiful point [of land].

Lae o Hālona. Point, southeast shore, Kahoʻolawe. *Lit., hālona* point, or peering place point.

Lae o Kākā. Point, southeast shore, Kahoʻolawe. *Lit., kākā* point, or point to fish with the *kākā* technique.

Lae o Kuikui. Point, northeast shore, Kahoʻolawe. Northernmost point on the island. Also known as Lae o Kukui. *Lit., kuikui* point, or point of light. *Kuikui* is a variant of *kukui.*

Lae o Kukui. Point, northeast shore, Kahoʻolawe. Same as Lae o Kuikui. *Lit., kukui* point, or point of light.

Lae Pakī. Point, southwest shore, Kahoʻolawe. Westernmost point on the island. Also known as Kealaikahiki. *Lit.,* point [where the water] splashes.

Lagoon. Swimming site, Spreckelsville, Maui. Natural pool, or "lagoon," on the east side of Wawau Point formed by a large section of beach rock on the beach. The pool is a popular swimming site for families with little children.

Lagoon Rights. Surf site, Kīholo, Hawaiʻi. Beginners break at the north end of Kīholo Bay adjacent to Wainānaliʻi Pond, the "lagoon."

Lahaina. 1. Light, Lahaina, Maui. Established on the Lahaina waterfront in 1840, the first lighted navigational aid in Hawaiʻi. In 1917, a 39-foot concrete tower with an automatic light replaced the previous structure. 2. Roadstead, Lahaina, Maui. Undesignated moorings off the Lahaina Small Boat Harbor. 3. Small boat harbor, Lahaina, Maui. Facilities include sixteen berths, eighty-three moorings, a pier, and a fuel facility. 4. Yacht club, Lahaina, Maui. Private club. Facilities include ten moorings. *Lit.,* cruel sun (from the old pronunciation, Lāhainā).

Lahaina Breakwater. Surf site, Lahaina, Maui. On the east side of the harbor entrance channel off the breakwater that protects the small boat harbor. Also known as Lahaina Lefts.

Lahaina Harbor. Surf site, Lahaina, Maui. On the west side of the harbor entrance channel. Also known as Lahaina Rights.

Lahaina Lefts. Surf site, Lahaina, Maui. On the east side of the harbor entrance channel. Also known as Lahaina Breakwater.

Lahaina Rights. Surf site, Lahaina, Maui. On the west side of the harbor entrance channel. Also known as Lahaina Harbor.

Lahaina Pali. Sea cliffs, Pāpalaua, Maui. Sea cliffs southwest of Māʻalaea Bay that were called Lahaina Pali because they are the only sea cliffs on the road to Lahaina. The original stretch of road to Lahaina along these cliffs was 4 miles long and had 115 sharp curves. The present highway and the 315-foot-long tunnel were completed in July 1951. Also known as ʻAalaloloa, Pali. *Lit.,* Lahaina cliffs.

Lahilahi. 1. Beach, Mākaha, Oʻahu. Same as Mauna Lahilahi. 2. Express, Mākaha, Oʻahu. Powerful longshore current that runs from Mākaha Point toward Lahilahi Point. The term *express* compares the speed of the current to an express train. *Lit.,* thin.

Lahilahi Point. Surf site, Mākaha, Oʻahu. On the west side of Mauna Lahilahi.

Lāʻie. 1. Bay, beach, Lāʻie, Oʻahu. Calcareous sand beach on Lāʻie Bay, the wide bay between Lāʻie and Kalanai Points. 2. Beach park (4.5 acres), Lāʻie, Oʻahu. Calcareous sand beach on Lāʻie Maloʻo Bay between Pali Kiloiʻa and Kōloa Stream. Also known as Pahumoa, Pounders. 3. Landing, Lāʻie, Oʻahu. Remnants of the former interisland steamer landing at the north end of Lāʻie Beach Park. 4. Point, Lāʻie, Oʻahu. Long limestone point in the center of Lāʻie. Also known as Laniloa. *Lit., ʻie* vine leaf. *Lāʻie* is short for *lau ʻie.* The vine is a symbol of royalty. All of the Lāʻie sites were named for a beautiful legendary princess, Lāʻie, who was hidden as a child in a secret chamber in a riverbank. The chamber was accessible only through an underwater entrance.

Lāʻieikawai. Pools, Keaukaha, Hawaiʻi. Cluster of sand-bottomed, brackish-water pools that are used as swimming pools in Lehia Park. Lāʻieikawai was a legendary person, a wife of Leleiwi. *Lit., ʻie* vine leaf of the fresh water.

Lāʻie Maloʻo. Bay, Lāʻie, Oʻahu. Bay fronting Lāʻie and Kokololio Beach Parks. *Lit.,* dry Lāʻie. Lāʻie Maloʻo is one of three sections in Lāʻie: Lāʻie Maloʻo (dry Lāʻie), Lāʻie, and Lāʻie Wai (wet Lāʻie).

Lāʻie Point. Fishing site, state wayside park (1.4 acres). Small undeveloped park established in 1990 at the seaward end of Naupaka Street on Lāʻie Point. The park is a popular scenic lookout for circle-island travelers and a popular fishing site, especially for *ulua.*

Lalakea. Pond, Keaukaha, Hawaiʻi. Spring-fed inlet at the head of Puhi Bay in Keaukaha Beach Park. The springwaters are always cold, giving the pond its popular name, Cold Pond. Name of a kind of shark.

Lalaland. Surf site, Kalaeloa, Oʻahu. Nonsensical name for a big-wave, second-reef break outside of White Plains Beach.

Lalilali. Landing, point, Molokini, Maui. South point of Molokini island. The landing was on the wave-cut terrace within the crescent of the island. *Lit.,* shiny.

Lamalani. Cove, Kūʻau, Maui. Small cove in the east corner of Kūʻau Bay. *Lit.,* royal torch.

Lamaloa. Beach, Mākua, Oʻahu. Section of Mākua Beach crossed by Mākua Stream. *Lit.,* tall *lama* tree or torch.

LaMariana Sailing Club. Small boat harbor, Keʻehi, Oʻahu. Private facility on the shore of Keʻehi Lagoon that includes eighty slips.

Lāna'i. 1. Island. Lāna'i is the sixth largest (140.6 square miles) of the eight major Hawaiian Islands and one of four islands in Maui County. It has a population of 3,193. The highest mountain on the island is Lāna'i Hale with an elevation of 3,370 feet, and the *pua kauna'oa (Cuscuta sandwichiana)* is the emblem of the island. Lāna'i's original nickname was the Pineapple Isle; another nickname is the Secluded Isle. 2. Lookout, Hawai'i Kai, O'ahu. On Kalaniana'ole Highway east of Hanauma Bay, with a view of the island of Lāna'i across the Kaiwi Channel. *Lit.,* day [of] conquest.

Lāna'i Lookout. Dive site, Hawai'i Kai, O'ahu. In the cove on the west side of the Lāna'i Lookout. Also known as Kahauloa Cove, Rifle Range.

Lanakila. Church, Hau'ula, O'ahu. Across Kamehameha Highway from Hau'ula Beach Park. Ruins of a Congregational church built on the summit of the hill in 1853. Coral blocks for the church walls were cut from the semicircular reef fronting the beach park. About 1897, the church was dismantled and the wood was used to built another church several miles away in Hale'aha. Later, however, a new church constructed of wood was built next to the original church. *Lit.,* victory.

Landing Craft. Dive site, Hawai'i Kai, O'ahu. Wreck of a World War II Navy LCM (landing craft mechanized) at 40 feet deep, straight out from the Hawai'i Kai Channel. After Hurricanes 'Iwa (1982) and 'Iniki (1992), only pieces of the wreck remain.

Land of Oz. Dive site, Mākaha, O'ahu. West of Kepuhi Point at 20 to 70 feet. This site was pioneered as a commercial dive site by an Australian, or an "Ozzie" (a variant pronunciation of *Aussie*). Also known as Outer Mākaha.

Lanes. Surf site, windsurf site, Ho'okipa, Maui. One of five surfing and windsurf sites at Ho'okipa Beach Park. Lanes is off the west end of the park.

Laniākea. 1. Beach, Kawailoa, O'ahu. Section of Kawailoa Beach between the Lauhulu Stream bridge and Pōhaku Loa Way. Also known as Kūkae'ōhiki. 2. Spring, Kawailoa, O'ahu. Laniākea is the name of a freshwater spring on the beach at the northeast end of Pōhaku Loa Way. During the 1920s a cottage built on the property above the spring was named Laniākea, and a sign with that name was placed on the side of the cottage, where it remained for many years. 3. Surf site, Kawailoa, O'ahu. In November 1955, veteran surfers Pat Curren, Buzzy Trent, Peter Van Dyke, Fred Van Dyke, George Downing, and Wally Froiseth drove up to then unnamed Laniākea. Bud Browne, surfing's first movie producer, accompanied them. The waves were huge and breaking so far out that Browne started searching for an elevated vantage point for his camera.

In the rear of the homes on Pōhaku Loa Way he found an old three-story steel-frame observation tower that had supported an antiaircraft gun during World War II. After the surf session, the seven of them discussed possible names for the new spot. Browne mentioned that a cottage near the tower he had climbed to film the surf session was called Laniākea and suggested they use the name. Everyone agreed, and they named it Laniākea. 4. Support park (3 acres). Undeveloped park across Kamehameha Highway from Laniākea. *Lit.*, wide sky.

L

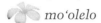 *moʻolelo*

My husband is pure Japanese, but he was raised by a Hawaiian, Hoʻokala, and speaks Hawaiian. His parents were very close to Hoʻokala and his wife, so they gave them their baby, and he was raised as a Hawaiian of a fishing family. When he was young, he fished with all of the old Hawaiians in the area. When he got older, he went to court and had his name legally changed to Hoʻokala. His *hanai* father is the Hoʻokala mentioned in McAllister's book on Oʻahu as an authority in the Waialua District. I'm from Makalawena on the Big Island, but I learned the names from my husband and the other Hawaiians here. Mokumana is the first big rock down from the small islands at Waimea. It looks whole from the front, but is divided on the back. That's why it's named Mokumana, "divided island." Kaʻalaea is the point in front of our home. Kumakani is the next big reef. It's in front of the road that's off to the side of Kam Highway. It means "stand against the wind." Kipa is the name of the big rock on the Waimea side of the Paty's house. Kuaumania is the reef and the point at Chun's Reef. Laniākea is the name of the freshwater spring on the Waimea side of the next big point. Sheriff Rose made his home there and called it **Laniākea** after the spring.

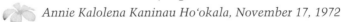 *Annie Kalolena Kaninau Hoʻokala, November 17, 1972*

Lanikai. 1. Boat ramp, Kailua, Oʻahu. Ramp in Kailua Beach Park that is also known as Kailua Ramp. 2. Beach, Lanikai, Oʻahu. Calcareous sand beach between Alāla and Wailea Points that is considered to be one of the best swimming beaches on Oʻahu. Also known as Kaʻōhao. 3. Lighthouse, Lanikai, Oʻahu. When Charles R. Frazier named and developed Lanikai in 1924, he erected a concrete monument on Alāla Point at the entrance to the subdivision. The monument was constructed to resemble a New England lighthouse, but has never housed a light, navigational or otherwise. 4. Reef, Lanikai, Oʻahu. Long, wide reef off Lanikai Beach. *Lit.*, sea heaven. *Lanikai* was intended to mean "heavenly sea," which it would have if the word order was in English. In Hawaiian, however, the qualifier normally follows the noun, so "heavenly sea" should have been *kailani.*

Lanikai Reef. Surf site, Lanikai, Oʻahu. At the east end of Lanikai Reef.

Lanikūhonua. Estate, ʻEwa, Oʻahu. Alice Kamokila Campbell was one of four daughters of wealthy landowner James Campbell. In 1939 she built a weekend retreat on an 11-acre beachfront parcel that was part of her father's estate. Located on the western edge of the ʻEwa Plain, she named it Lanikūhonua. Campbell died in 1971, but Lanikūhonua is still owned by Campbell Estate and used as a spiritual retreat for Oʻahu's hula *hālau. Lit.,* where the heavens meet the earth.

Laniloa. Beach, point, Lāʻie, Oʻahu. Laniloa is the long limestone point that is also known as Lāʻie Point. Laniloa Beach is the calcareous sand beach between the point and Lāʻie Beach Park. *Lit.,* tall majesty.

Lanipūʻao. Dive site, rock, Kalāheo, Kauaʻi. Lone pinnacle surrounded by sand that rises from 35 feet to approximately 5 feet below the surface of the ocean. The dive site is at the pinnacle. A navigational buoy marking the rock is known as Pālama Buoy. Also known as Kalanipūʻao Rock, Oasis Reef. *Lit.,* womb sky.

Lapaiki. Beach, Lapaiki, Lānaʻi. Narrow calcareous sand beach that is a section of Shipwreck Beach. *Lit.,* small ridge.

Lapakahi. Marine life conservation district (146 acres), state historical park (262 acres), North Kohala, Hawaiʻi. Lapakahi is a large *ahupuaʻa* (land division) that measures approximately a mile along the ocean and extends 4 miles inland. The historical park focuses on Koaiʻe, a fishing village that was inhabited until the late 1800s and is now a center for *lapaʻau*, the use of herbs and native medicine to heal the sick. Two small coral rubble beaches are in Koaiʻe Cove at the foot of the village. In 1979 the state created the Lapakahi Marine Life Conservation District to protect the marine life and geological features in the cove. *Lit.,* single ridge.

La Pérouse. Bay, Honuaʻula, Maui. After Captain James Cook's third expedition returned to England, news of his discoveries, including the location of the Hawaiian Islands, spread throughout Europe. In August 1785, France mounted its own expedition, consisting of two ships, *La Boussole* and *L'Astrolabe*, under the command of Captain Jean François de Galaup, Comte de La Pérouse. On May 29, 1786, the expedition reached Hawaiian waters and found themselves looking for an anchorage along the south shore of Haleakalā. They finally found shelter from the severe trade winds in a bay protected by a wide lava flow and anchored for the night. The following day Captain La Pérouse and a landing party went ashore, the first non-Hawaiians to set foot on Maui. The anchorage became known as La Pérouse Bay. Also known as Keone'ō'io. 2. Dive site, surf site, windsurf site, Honua'ula, Maui. The dive site is in the bay, the surf site is off the south end of the bay, and the windsurf site is outside the bay.

La Pérouse Pinnacle. Dive site, La Pérouse Bay, Maui. Rock formation in the middle of the bay that rises from 60 feet to 10 feet below the surface.

L

Larsen's. Beach, Ka'aka'aniu, Kaua'i. Narrow calcareous sand beach fronted by a long, wide shallow reef called Ka'aka'aniu. Named for L. David Larsen (1886–1944), a Kīlauea Plantation manager and later C. Brewer and Co. executive who had a beach home here for many years. Ka'aka'aniu Reef is one of the island's famous gathering sites for *limu kohu,* a highly prized edible seaweed. Also known as Ka'aka'aniu.

Last Break. Surf site, Kualoa, O'ahu. Last surf site, or "break," on the reef heading south before Kāne'ohe Bay. Also known as Sugar Mills.

Last Sands. Surf site, Hanapēpē, Kaua'i. Last sand beach heading south past Olokele Mill before Salt Pond Beach Park. The surf site is off the beach.

Laukīnui. Beach, Mākaha, O'ahu. Cove with a small calcareous sand beach between 'Upena and Moua Streets. Also known as Aki's. *Lit.,* large ti leaf.

Laulaunui. Island, Pearl Harbor, O'ahu. Uninhabited island in West Loch. Also known as Monkey Island. *Lit.,* large leaf food bundle.

Laulauwa'a. Beach, Mākaha, O'ahu. Calcareous sand beach at Mauna Lahilahi Beach Park, Wai'anae, O'ahu. *Lit.,* canoe paddle blade.

Launiupoko. State wayside park, surf site, Launiupoko, Maui. The park is on the shore of the land division of Launiupoko. A boulder seawall at the park forms a large wading pool for children. The surf site is off the park. *Lit.,* short coconut leaf.

Launiupoko Park. Dive site, Launiupoko, Maui. Off Launiupoko State Wayside Park.

Laupāhoehoe. 1. Ramp, surf site, North Hilo, Hawai'i. Laupāhoehoe is a rocky peninsula with a boat ramp on its eastern side. The surf site is off the ramp. 2. Monument, Laupāhoehoe, Hawai'i. At the eastern edge of Laupāhoehoe Point Park above the ramp. The monument is a memorial to the students of Laupāhoehoe School who were killed in the tsunami of April 1, 1946. 3. Point light, Laupāhoehoe, Hawai'i. Established in

1890 at the seaward end of the peninsula. The light is on a 20-foot pole that was erected in 1975 approximately 39 feet above sea level. A breakwater light was established in 1989 on the eastern side of the point to mark the boat ramp and the huge concrete tetrahedrons that protect it. *Lit.*, smooth lava flat/tip.

 moʻolelo

L

I arrived in Laupāhoehoe in the last week of August 1945 from Cincinnati, Ohio. I came over on the *Matsonia* shortly after VJ Day, and it was carrying many of the local Japanese who had been held in the internment camps in California. I was one of six new teachers who were assembled in Hilo and then caravanned off to their respective school assignments. I lived with three other teachers—Fay Johnson, Dorothy Drake, and Helen Kingseed—in one of the teachers' cottages, which were at the end of the point, and I taught arts and crafts in the morning and PE for girls in the afternoon.

On April 1, 1946, Mr. Akiona, one of the Hawaiians who lived nearby, knocked on our cottage door and told us to come see the tidal wave. We figured if the Hawaiians weren't running from it, there was no danger. The first wave was very low and mild, and we said, "That's it?" and started to walk back. But the waves got progressively bigger and started to recede farther out. The fourth wave or so washed the *naupaka* off the point, but the school kids were already arriving, so we continued back to the cottage to change. The children were dropped off early because most of their parents were plantation workers. The next wave washed fish into the schoolyard, and the kids rushed to pick them up.

I put on blue jeans, a blouse, saddle shoes, and a bandana and then went out on the porch with Fay. We stood there wishing a bigger wave would come. It did. The next wave kept building and building and building. We ran into the cottage and met Dorothy and Helen at the back door, all of us trying to escape. By then water was already covering the cottage, fighting to get in. The roof collapsed. Fay and I managed to grab on, using the roof like a raft, and climbed up to the cone. We tried to hold Helen, but couldn't, and Dorothy, who had grabbed a corner of the roof, lost her grip. The water receded swiftly, and we watched the principal's car tossed end over end like a feather.

The roof caught on the rocks of the outer point and hung up. Fay and I figured we'd better get off and run. We had barely taken a few steps when the next wave struck. Fay disappeared and I took a deep breath. I managed to surface and breathe again, and then I was slammed into the ocean bottom. When I surfaced again, I was floating past the lighthouse. I could only see the top of it. I felt like every bone in my body was broken, and I tried to

swim. I couldn't. I grabbed a piece of wreckage and hung on. As
the current pulled me towards Kohala, I kept changing rafts in all
the wreckage. I could see cars starting to line the cliffs.

One of the major setbacks to the rescue operation was that
all of the boats had been destroyed, but one was finally located
in Kamuela—a pond boat. It was hauled to Laupāhoehoe, where
the plantation carpenters had to rebuild the stern so it could hold
the only motor they had found. All of this took hours and it got
late, but Libert Fernandez, the plantation doctor at Laupāhoehoe
Hospital, insisted on going out because from the cliffs they could
see people floating. They managed to launch the boat and made
their way out. I was rescued before dark. As we returned, the
entire line of cliffs was edged with families waiting to see who
had been rescued.

 Marsue McShane, June 27, 1980

Laupāhoehoe Nui. Peninsula, surf site, Kohala, Hawai'i. Vegetated peninsula at the base of the sea cliffs north of Waimanu
Valley. The surf site is off the north end of the peninsula. *Lit.,*
big smooth lava flat/ tip.

Laupāhoehoe Point. Park, North Hilo, Hawai'i. Park that is the
site of the former Laupāhoehoe School, where on the morning
of April 1, 1946, a powerful tsunami struck the peninsula and
overran the school grounds, killing thirty-two students and
faculty.

Laupapa. Reef, Kalaupapa, Moloka'i. Reef on the north side of
Kalaupapa Wharf that was leaf-shaped prior to the construction of the wharf. *Lit.,* broad, flat reef.

Laupapa'ōhua. Reef, Punalu'u, Hawai'i. Long, flat reef shelf on
the west side of Punalu'u Beach Park where many *'ōhua,* or
juvenile fish, congregate. *Lit.,* broad, flat reef [where] *'ōhua* [are
found].

Lāwai. Beach, snorkeling site, Po'ipū, Kauai. Lāwai is the name
of a small coastal valley to the west of the beach between Kalāheo and Kōloa, but commercial snorkeling and dive operators
have applied the name to this beach. Also known as Beach
House, Longhouse.

Lāwai Kai. Beach, surf site, Lāwai Kai, Kaua'i. Lāwai is a valley
between Kalāheo and Kōloa. Lāwai Kai is the portion of the
valley on the ocean and the site of the Pacific Tropical Botanical Garden. A calcareous sand beach fronted by a sandbar
borders Lāwai Kai. The surf site is a shorebreak on the sandbar. Also known as Allertons. *Lit.,* seaward Lāwai.

L Buoy. Dive site, Polihale, Kaua'i. North of Polihale, fronting
Halemanu River at approximately 15 feet.

L

Lead City. Dive site, Kaloko, Hawai'i. Off Wāwahiwa'a Point. The ocean bottom at the site is littered with lead from *ulua* fishermen onshore who cast into this site.

Lē'ahi. 1. Hill, southwest coast, Ni'ihau. Small hill on the shore approximately 2 miles from Kawaihoa, the south point of the island, that is said to resemble Lē'ahi, or Diamond Head, on O'ahu. 2. Beach park (1.3 acres), Honolulu, O'ahu. Small community park at the base of Diamond Head that is between two beachfront homes and bordered by a seawall. A small pocket of calcareous sand adjoins the west end of the park. 3. Crater, Honolulu, O'ahu. *Lit.*, forehead [of the] *'ahi* fish. The 760-foot high crest of the crater's west rim, formed by the trade winds when it erupted approximately one hundred thousand years ago, resembles the forehead and dorsal fin of an *'ahi* (yellowfin tuna) when viewed from the east, especially from offshore in the Kaiwi Channel. This profile was compared in legend by the goddess Hi'iaka to the brow of the *'ahi*. Also known as Diamond Head.

Ledge. Fishing site, North Shore, O'ahu. Ledge that closely follows the 40-fathom (240-foot) contour line between Kahuku and Ka'ena Points. Fishing boats troll the Ledge, especially for *ono*. Also known as Ono Ledge.

Ledges. Surf site, 'Āina Haina, O'ahu. Off Calvary-by-the-Sea Lutheran Church. Named in the early 1970s by surfers from 'Āina Haina for the vertical reef ledge that causes waves to break here.

> *mo'olelo*
>
> When we were surfing outside the park in the 1960s and 70s, the spot called Signs was also called Steve's after Steve Sullam, who would go there when Secret's was too crowded. Secret's is mainly the right break, but if you go left, it is Secret's Left, and a nearly unknown name of the left is Spoon Meat. This name came in the early 1970s as a bunch of us were sitting around between surf sessions, spooning out soft coconut meat and watching an exceptionally good left reel off out at Secret's. That was the same day we named **Ledges,** for the reef ledge in front of the spot, and this name has stuck. I can't remember who came up with the names, but we jointly agreed on them that day.
>
> *Mark Magelssen, February 14, 1999*

Left Lefts. Surf site, Lanikai, O'ahu. Last surf site at the east or left end of Lanikai Reef. The waves here are primarily ridden to the left, so the reduplication of "left" in Left Lefts is a humorous way of reinforcing the primary direction that the wave is surfed and its location at the left end of the reef.

Leftovers. Surf site, Kawailoa, O'ahu. In the 1960s, surfers going to the "country," or North Shore, from "town," or Honolulu, usually checked out the surf sites starting with Hale'iwa and then worked their way north past Laniākea and Chun's Reef. Leftovers was considered to be a "leftover" or second-choice site at the end of the line of the more famous and often more crowded sites before Waimea Bay. The name is also a play on words because Leftovers is a left—a wave that surfers ride to their left. Also known as Kūmakani.

Left Point. Surf site, Hawai'i Kai, O'ahu. Off Queen's Beach. Two sites on the west side of Kalama Stream are named Left Point and Right Point. Left Point is also known as A. D.'s and Alan Davis.

Lefts. 1. Surf site, Kaunakakai, Moloka'i. Surfers ride primarily to their left on the north side of Kaunakakai Wharf. 2. Surf site, Wailupe, O'ahu. Surfers ride primarily to their left on the west edge of Wailupe Channel. Also known as Lunch Breaks.

Lehia. Park, Hilo, Hawai'i. Coastal park at Leleiwi Point at the east end of Kalaniana'ole Avenue. The shore is rocky, consisting of low lava sea cliffs. Two sections of the park are known as Keonepūpū and Lā'ieikawai. Also known as Pu'u Maile. *Lit.,* skilled.

Leho'ula. Beach, Hāna, Maui. Small pocket beach of calcareous sand on the north side of Ka Iwi o Pele, a cinder cone of the Hāna Volcanic Series. Kū'ula, the god of Hawaiian fishermen, made his home in Hāna. He asked his son, 'Ai'ai, to travel throughout the islands and teach the people the ceremonies and techniques of fishing. When 'Ai'ai was ready to leave Hāna, Kū'ula gifted him with a red cowrie shell, a *leho'ula.* Leho'ula Beach was named for this gift. *Lit.,* red cowrie.

Lehua. 1. Island (291 acres, 710 feet high), Lehua, Ni'ihau. Part of the Hawai'i State Seabird Sanctuary. Large tuff (cemented volcanic ash, basalt, and limestone) island approximately three-quarters of a mile off the north end of Ni'ihau. The south side of the island is steep sea cliffs, and the north side is a large, crescent-shaped bay. 2. Landing, Ka'aku'u, Ni'ihau. Lehua and Ki'i are the two landings on the north end of Ni'ihau. Ni'ihau Ranch uses the landings to haul livestock, equipment, passengers, food, dry goods, and other necessities to the island from Makaweli Landing on Kaua'i. Lehua Landing is named for its proximity to Lehua Island. 3. Rock light, Lehua, Ni'ihau. The original light, completed in 1931, was replaced in 1989 by a light atop a 10-foot fiberglass pole. At 704 feet above sea level, it is among the highest lighted navigational aids in the world. Ni'ihau is a privately owned island, and its owners have elected not to have any navigational lights on the island, so Lehua

L

Rock Light establishes the locations of Lehua and Ni'ihau. *Lit., lehua* flower. Hi'iaka, sister of Pele, the goddess of the volcano, left a *lehua* flower on the island.

Leinaaka'uhane. Ka'ena, O'ahu. Large limestone rock near Ka'ena Point that was said to be a *leinaaka'uhane*, a place where souls of the dead left the earth. Also known as White Rock. *Lit.*, leaping place of the soul.

Leleiwi. Beach park, Keaukaha, Hawai'i. Rocky shore consisting of ponds, inlets, and coves fronted by small rock islets. The park is the site of Richardson Ocean Center, an outdoor recreation and interpretive center that was developed cooperatively by the county, state, and University of Hawai'i. *Lit.*, bone altar (poetically, a symbol of disaster or anger). The name suggests a graveyard, or the scaffold on which bodies of human sacrifices (the bones) were left exposed.

Lelekawa. Point, Pā'ia, Maui. On the north side of Pā'ia Bay. *Lit.*, [sport of] jumping from a high place into the water.

Lenalena. Landing, Kalaupapa, Moloka'i. *Lit.*, yellow.

Lepeamoa Rock. Dive site, Honokua, Hawai'i. South of the Honokua lava flow. The rock has an elevation of 95 feet and is the crescent-shaped remnant of a former crater. *Lit.*, cock's comb.

Lighthouse. 1. Dive site, south coast, Lāna'i. Northwest of Kaunolū. 2. Surf site, Mā'alaea, Maui. Off the McGregor Point Light. Also known as McGregor Point. 3. Beach, Moloka'i. Four coves of calcareous sand in the low sea cliffs below the Lā'au Point Light. 4. Surf site, Diamond Head, O'ahu. Named in the late 1950s by surfers from Ka'alawai because it is off the Diamond Head Lighthouse.

Li'ili'i. Dive site, island, south coast, Kaho'olawe. An abbreviated form of Kaho'olaweli'ili'i. *Lit.*, small.

Li'ilioholo. Offshore mooring, Kīhei, Maui. State mooring site. Perhaps a misspelling of 'Ili'iliholo, the name of the beach at Kama'ole II Beach Park.

Likelike. Dive site, wreck, Keawe'ula, Hawai'i. An interisland steamer bound for Māhukona with a hold full of coal for the Kohala Sugar Company Railway, the *Likelike* sank in 1897 and was rediscovered by scuba divers in 1976. A 592-ton wooden steamer built in 1877 by Dickie Brothers, a San Francisco shipbuilder, she was named for Princess Miriam Likelike Cleghorn (1851–1887), who was her sponsor and a passenger on the maiden voyage to Honolulu. Princess Likelike was married to Archibald Cleghorn, and they were the parents of Princess Ka'iulani.

Lilipuna. Pier, Kāne'ohe, O'ahu. A 1.4-acre state-owned parcel on Lilipuna Road that includes a guardhouse, parking lot, and pier. These facilities support the shuttle boat service to and from Coconut Island.

Liliʻuokalani Gardens. Park, Hilo, Hawaiʻi. On the shore of Waiā-kea Peninsula and named after Queen Liliʻuokalani (1838–1917), the last queen of the Hawaiian monarchy. The Yedo-type gardens were designed by landscape architect Kinsaku Nakane of Kyoto University in Japan and are reportedly the largest of their kind outside Japan. *Lit.*, smarting of the high-born one. At the time of Liliʻuokalani's birth, her foster mother's aunt, Kīnaʻu, was suffering from eye pain; hence the name.

Lime Kiln. Beach, fishing site, Pāʻia, Maui. Section of calcareous sand beach at the west end of Pāʻia Bay. The lime kiln inland of the beach was a Hawaiian Commercial and Sugar Company facility that was constructed in the 1920s. The lime powder produced from beach sand was bagged and sent to the sugar mills, where it was used in processing sugarcane. After the cane was crushed, the lime was added to the juice to prevent deterioration and to aid in clarification, the removal of impurities.

Limu Make o Hāna. Point, Kīpahulu, Maui. Site of *limu make,* or *Palythoa toxica,* a toxic seaweed. Although the point is at Mūʻolea in Kīpahulu, the seaweed is commonly identified as being from Hāna. *Lit.*, deadly seaweed of Hāna.

Lions. Beach, ʻEwa Beach, Oʻahu. Section of Oneʻula Beach fronting the Kālia Lions Clubs International beach house.

Līpoa. Beach, Kīhei, Maui. Narrow calcareous sand beach at the end of Līpoa Street. *Lit.*, *līpoa* seaweed.

Little. Beach, Mākena, Maui. Pocket of calcareous sand at the base of Puʻu Ōlaʻi, a littoral cone at the north end of Mākena State Park. A transient hippie community that lived at Puʻu Ōlaʻi from 1968 to 1972 popularized the names Little Beach and Big Beach for the two beaches in Mākena State Park. Although nudity is prohibited in state parks, Little Beach is used as a nudist beach. Also known as Puʻu Ōlaʻi Beach.

Little Beach. Snorkeling site, surf site, Mākena, Maui. The snorkeling site is along the rocky point between Big Beach and Little Beach. The surf site is a shorebreak on the sandbar fronting Little Beach.

Little Cape St. Francis. Surf site, Māʻalaea, Maui. Off the low sea cliffs at the southwest end of Māʻalaea Bay. Named after the Cape St. Francis surf site in Africa that was immortalized in Bruce Brown's 1964 surfing movie, *The Endless Summer.* Also known as The Cliffs.

L

Little Glass Shacks. Surf site, Princeville, Kaua'i. Off Sea Lodge Beach. The name is a play on words of the song written in 1933 called "My Little Grass Shack in Kealakekua Hawai'i." The "glass shack" at the surf site is actually a large home with many windows on the sea cliff above the beach.

Little Mākaha. Surf site, 'Alaeloa, Maui. Waves here resemble those at Mākaha on O'ahu.

Little Sunset. Surf site, Kawailoa, O'ahu. Waves here resemble those at Sunset several miles to the north. Also known as Alligators.

LL Buoy. Fish aggregating device, Hau'ula, O'ahu. Buoy anchored at approximately 1,140 fathoms. Landmarks: Kahuku Point, Lā'ie Point, Pyramid Rock.

Loading Zone. Surf site, Mā'alaea, Maui. Northeast of Mā'alaea Village and off a high-walled concrete building in the backshore. The truck delivery area for the building is stenciled with the words "Loading Zone." The name is also a play on words for a popular phrase in the 1970s for smoking marijuana, "getting loaded." Surfers would park here and get loaded before going in the water.

Lobster Rock. Dive site, Kaunolū, Lāna'i. Rock awash east of Kaunolū, with a lava tube that opens at both ends at 40 to 60 feet and that harbors lobsters and many species of fish. Also known as Wash Rock.

Log Cabins. Surf site, Sunset Beach, O'ahu. Off a beachfront home built here in 1964 that is a log cabin.

Lō'ihi. Seamount, Ka'ū, Hawai'i. Undersea volcano 20 miles off the southeast coast of the Big Island that is considered to be the next Hawaiian island. Dredge samples and underwater photographs taken in 1980 confirmed its location. The University of Hawai'i monitors activity at the volcano with instruments on its summit, approximately 3,000 feet deep. The instruments are connected by fiber-optic submarine cable to a cable station in Whittington Beach Park in Ka'ū. *Lit.*, long.

Lokoea. 1. Fishpond, Hale'iwa, O'ahu. 2. Fishpond, Waipahu, O'ahu. *Lit., ea* pond. *Ea* means "rising."

Lokoeo. Fishpond, Pearl Harbor, O'ahu. *Lit., eo* pond. The meaning of *eo* is unknown.

Lokowaiaho. Fishpond, Pearl Harbor, O'ahu. *Lit., waiaho* pond. *Waiaho* means "fishline water."

Lokowaka. Fishpond, Keaukaha, Hawai'i. At 60 acres, the largest of the fourteen fishponds on the shores of Waiākea and Keaukaha. Lokowaka is owned by the state but leased to private interests. Across the highway from Kealoha Park, the pond is famous for its mullet. *Lit.*, Waka's pond. Waka, a demigod who could assume the form of a giant lizard or a woman, dove into the pond to escape the wrath of Pele.

Lone Palm. Dive site, pond, 'Anaeho'omalu, Hawai'i. L-shaped, spring-fed anchialine pond and swimming site with good water clarity. It is on the shore, approximately one-quarter mile south of Kapalaoa Beach. The dive site is off the pond. A single coconut palm tree, the "lone palm," marks the site of the pond. Also known as 'Akahi Kaimu.

Lone Pine. Surf site, Ukumehame, Maui. A single ironwood tree, the "lone pine," is inshore of the site. Ironwoods in Hawai'i are commonly called pine trees because their seeds resemble miniature pinecones. Also known as Pine Tree.

Lone Tree. Surf site, Mokulē'ia, O'ahu. A single beach heliotrope tree, the "lone tree," stands in the backshore and is used by surfers to mark the lineup. Also known as Kai'ae, Kimo's, and Lyman's.

Long. Beach, Kīpū Kai, Kaua'i. Longest of the calcareous sand beaches at Kīpū Kai. Also known as Hananena, Kīpū Kai Beach.

Longhouse. Beach, Kukui'ula, Kaua'i. Small pocket of calcareous sand on the west side of the Beach House Restaurant. The first restaurant here was called the Tahiti Longhouse. Also known as Beach House Beach.

Long Lava Tube. Dive site, Kainaliu, Hawai'i. One of the Red Hill dive sites.

Long Sands. Beach, Mākena, Maui. The 3,300-foot-long calcareous sand beach fronting Mākena State Park. Also known as Big Beach, Mākena Beach, Oneloa.

Lono. Harbor, Hale o Lono, Moloka'i. Same as Hale o Lono Harbor. After the god Lono.

Lono's. Surf site, Hale o Lono, Moloka'i. Off Hale o Lono Harbor. Also known as Hale o Lono.

Look Laboratory In-Water Test Range. Artificial reef, Kewalo, O'ahu. The University of Hawai'i's J. K. K. Look Laboratory test range consists of two artificial reefs on the west side of Kewalo Basin Channel in approximately 40 feet of water. One is constructed of automobile tires and one is constructed of concrete blocks. Several flat platforms nearby are used for mounting instruments for ocean engineering tests.

Lōpā. Beach, fishpond, surf site, Lāna'i. Narrow calcareous sand beach fronting one of the four fishponds on Lāna'i. Lōpā Fishpond, the only one with a *mākaha* (sluice gate) that connects it to the ocean, is also a bird sanctuary. The surf site is on the shallow reef offshore. *Lit.,* tenant farmer.

Loretta's. Dive site, Kīholo Bay, Hawai'i. Black sand, rock patches, and ledges in 15–25 feet of water at the south end of Kīholo Bay. Off the circular-shaped beachfront home built by country-western singer Loretta Lind but sold in 1999 to Dr. Earl E. Bakken, owner of another Kīholo Bay beachfront home.

Love Rock. Island, Waimea, O'ahu. Westernmost of the Wānanapaoa Islands off the west point of Waimea Bay. During the summer months and other periods of calm surf, surfers occasionally use the island as a site for romantic interludes.

Lower Kanahā. Windsurf site, Kanahā, Maui. Same as Lowers.

Lowers. Windsurf site, Kanahā, Maui. Farthest downwind site off Kanahā Beach Park, as opposed to Uppers, an upwind site. One of the best places for windsurfers to learn wave riding on Maui. Also known as Lower Kanahā.

Low Point. Fishing site, Hawai'i Kai, O'ahu. Small point at the base of the Koko Head sea cliffs west of Hanauma Bay, it is the nearest (lowest) point to the surface of the ocean among those favored by *ulua* fishermen here. Their campsite nearby is at a higher elevation.

Luaawa. Fishing site, reef, Lā'ie, O'ahu. Small reef at the north end of Lā'ie Bay near Kalanai Point. *Lit., awa* fish hole.

Luahinewai. Beach, dive site, pond, Kīholo, Hawai'i. Large spring-fed pond bordered by a small coconut grove adjacent to a black sand beach approximately 600 feet long at the south end of Kīholo Bay. The dive site is off the beach in 15–25 feet of water and consists of black sand, rock patches, and some ledges. Luahinewai was a famous rest stop during canoe voyages along the coast and is mentioned by Samuel Kamakau in *Ruling Chiefs of Hawai'i* and John Papa Ii in *Fragments of Hawaiian History. Lit.,* old woman's water.

Lualualei. Beach park (17.8 acres), Wai'anae, O'ahu. On the low sea cliffs at the south end of Wai'anae town.

Luamoi. Fishing site, Mākena, Maui. In Mākena Bay near Keawala'i Church. *Lit., moi* fish hole.

Lucy Wright. See Wright.

Luhi. Beach, Waimea, Kaua'i. Calcareous sand beach below the Russian Fort where, according to Captain Cook's journal, one of his crew members killed a Hawaiian, the first Hawaiian killed by a westerner. *Lit.,* tired.

Lumaha'i. 1. Beach, Lumaha'i, Kaua'i. Long, wide calcareous sand beach at the base of heavily vegetated sea cliffs; one of the widest beaches on Kaua'i. Lumaha'i Stream crosses the north end of the beach. Noted for its beauty, Lumaha'i has been the subject of many paintings and photographs and has provided the background for many advertisements, commercials, and movies, the best known of which was *South Pacific* in 1958. Also known as Nurses Beach. 2. Estuary, stream, Lumaha'i, Kaua'i. The stream and estuary are at the north end of the beach and are noted for their waterbirds and *'o'opu,* or native goby fish. *'O'opu* spawn in mountain streams and their larvae are washed into the sea, where they spend the early part of their juvenile phase. The fish return to the mountain streams, where they grow into adulthood and live the rest of their lives. In addition to being one of the few freshwater fish that spends part of its life in the ocean, the goby is the only fish in the world that makes its way upstream by swimming *and climbing.* Gobies have suction disks on their chests that allow them to hold onto rocks while their back fins propel them upward.

Lunch Breaks. Surf site, Wailupe, O'ahu. During low tides, especially during the spring, the shallow reef inshore of this site is emergent for long periods of time. Surfers would leave their lunches on the highest rocks while they surfed and still find them intact when they returned. The name is also a play on words with the word *break.* Surf sites are also known as surfing breaks. Also known as Lefts.

Lydgate. State park, windsurf site, Wailua, Kaua'i. Narrow calcareous sand beach fronted by a large, man-made saltwater pool. The pool was created in 1970 by building a semicircular boulder wall off the beach. The park was named for the Reverend John M. Lydgate (d. 1922), a prominent civic leader and pastor of Līhu'e Union Church and Kōloa Church. His foresight resulted in many of the island's historical sites being established as parks. Lydgate State Park is a windsurf site during *kona* or south winds.

Lyman's. 1. Surf site, Hōlualoa, Hawai'i. Adjacent to Kamoa Point in Hōlualoa Bay. Named for the beachfront home of Barbara and Howard Lyman, a landmark on the bay since it was built in 1956. The Lyman family and their home are immortalized in "Laimana," a song written by Lei Collins, a former curator of Hulihe'e Palace. *Laimana* is the Hawaiianized version of Lyman. 2. Surf site, Mokulē'ia, O'ahu. Off Kimo Lyman's family home on Farrington Highway. Also known as Kai'ae, Kimo's, Lone Tree.

Māʻalaea. 1. Bay, beach, Māʻalaea, Maui. Māʻalaea Bay is an important part of the Hawaiian Islands Humpback Whale National Marine Sanctuary. Although humpbacks are seen throughout the islands, they concentrate in the waters between the four islands of Maui County, where they calve, nurse, and mate. Māʻalaea Beach is a narrow calcareous sand beach approximately 3 miles long and backed by low dunes at the head of the bay. The northeast end of the beach is also known as Sugar Beach. 2. Small boat harbor, Māʻalaea, Maui. Constructed in 1952. Facilities include eighty-nine berth/moorings, a ramp, a drydock, and a vessel washdown area. 3. Surf site, Māʻalaea, Maui. On the northeast side of the entrance channel to the small boat harbor. The steep, hollow, plunging waves here form one of the longest and fastest rides in Hawaiʻi and possibly in the world. *Surfer Magazine* (established in 1960) has rated it as one of the ten best waves in the world and the fastest-breaking right in the world. Also known as Māʻalaea Pipeline, Pipeline. 4. U.S. Coast Guard station. On the shore of the small boat harbor. 5. Beach, Hālawa, Molokaʻi. The westernmost of the two beaches in Hālawa Valley that is used as an anchorage and boat launching site. *Lit.*, ocherous earth beginnings. Māʻalaea is a contracted form of Makaʻalaea.

Māʻalaea Ebesu Kotohira Jinsha. Shrine, Māʻalaea, Maui. Traditional Shinto fishing shrine on the shore of Māʻalaea Small Boat Harbor that was originally on the site of the adjacent Maui Ocean Center. The present shrine was completed in 1999 and is a replica of the original shrine built in 1914 by Reverend Masaho Matsumura. The first service in the present shrine was held in January 2000 and was conducted by Reverend Torako Arine, who takes care of the Māʻalaea Ebesu Kotohira Jinsha and the Maui Jinsha in Wailuku. The words in shrine's name are *Ebesu*, one of seven lucky deities and the guardian god of fishermen and merchants; *kotohira*, or fishermen; and *jinsha*, or shrine. Fishermen believed that by honoring the god they would have good luck at sea and a safe return home. Although the shrine is Shinto, the congregation now is multiracial and multicultural, including commercial and recreational fishermen, surfers, and other people of the sea.

Māʻalaea Lefts. Surf site, Kahuku, Oʻahu. On the north side of the Turtle Bay Hilton Hotel. During big west or northwest swells, the long lefts here resemble the famous long rights at Māʻalaea on Maui.

Māʻalaea Pipeline. Surf site, Māʻalaea, Maui. The steep, hollow waves at this surf site are compared to those at the world-famous Banzai Pipeline on Oʻahu's North Shore. Same as Māʻalaea.

MacKenzie. 1. State recreational area (13.1 acres), fishing site, Malama, Hawaiʻi. Established in 1934, but named in 1939 to honor Albert J. W. MacKenzie, a forest ranger from 1917 until his death on June 28, 1938. MacKenzie worked extensively on planting projects in the Puna and Kaʻū Districts, including the planting of the ironwood trees in this park. The low sea cliffs fronting the park are a popular but dangerous fishing site. Many fishermen have been swept off the rocky ledges here by high surf. 2. Monuments, Malama, Hawaiʻi. When the park was named for MacKenzie in 1939, a monument was erected here for him. Family members erected a second monument, a stone drinking fountain, to honor the memory of MacKenzie's wife, Catherine, after her death in 1952.

moʻolelo

The MacKenzie family came from the MacKenzie Highlands in Scotland and moved to Nova Scotia. My father left home and arrived in Hawaiʻi in the late 1890s when he was sixteen. On the Big Island, he became a stage driver for tourists visiting the volcano. He met my mother at the Volcano House. My mother was the daughter of Peter Lee, the Volcano House manager, and they eventually got married when she was sixteen. All of us were born in Volcano—ten children—two boys and eight girls. I was the youngest and graduated from Hilo High in 1938.

My dad was a forest ranger for many years. He was involved with the reforestation of many areas that were destroyed by fire. He worked extensively in Puna and Kaʻū and planted eucalyptus as windbreaks and the ironwoods in the park that's named for him. I traveled and camped in many places with my dad, and I remember the ironwoods in the park being very small when I was still small. That area is called Malama, and it supposedly has night marchers, but my dad attributed the sounds to the *waves washing into the caves under the sea cliffs. My dad died in 1938 mauka of Waiʻohinu in an auto accident while he was inspecting a project.*

 Aileen MacPherson, December 16, 1982

Magic Island. 1. Beach park, Ala Moana, Oʻahu. Easternmost and outermost section of Ala Moana Regional Park. Magic Island is a man-made peninsula that was constructed on the shallow reef at the east end of Ala Moana Regional Park. Completed in 1964, it was originally named Magic Island by its developers, who intended it to be the site of a resort complex. Also known as the ʻĀina Moana section of Ala Moana Regional Park. 2. Dive site, Ala Moana, Oʻahu. Off the east end of Magic Island from 0–40 feet. A heavily used introductory dive site because of its close proximity to Waikīkī, it is one of the three most popular dive sites on the island. Also known as Rainbow Reef. 3. Lagoon, Honolulu, Oahu. Swimming area, or "lagoon," at the seaward end of Magic Island that is protected from the open ocean by several boulder islands. 4. Surf site, Ala Moana, Oʻahu. Off the west end of Magic Island. Also known as Bomboras.

Magic Sands. Beach, dive site, surf site, North Kona, Hawaiʻi. During periods of high surf, waves erode almost the entire beach, exposing the underlying rocks, and the beach "magically" disappears within twenty-four hours. When the surf subsides, normal surf activity redeposits the sand on shore, covering the rocks, and the beach "magically" reappears. The dive site is off the beach. The surf site is a shorebreak on the sandbar bordering the beach. During periods of high surf a big-wave, second-reef site forms off the south point of the beach. Also known as Disappearing Sands Beach, Laʻaloa Bay Beach Park, White Sands.

Magnums. Surf site, Waimānalo, Oʻahu. On the north side of a small channel through the reef off Pāhonu, the beachfront residence where the CBS television series *Magnum, P.I.* was filmed from 1980 to 1988. Also known as Pāhonu.

Mahaiʻula. Bay, beach, dive site, surf site, Mahaiʻula, Hawaiʻi. Calcareous sand beach at the head of a large bay that was opened to the public in 1992 as a section of Kekaha Kai State Park. The dive site is in the center of the bay at approximately 45 feet. The surf site is at Kāwili Point, the north point of the bay. Mahaiʻula is the former estate of Alfred Kapala Magoon, a prominent part-Hawaiian businessman. Magoon purchased the property during the 1930s, and it remained in his family until it was acquired by the state. Hawaiian composer Helen

Desha Beamer, a family friend, immortalized Magoon, his wife Puanani, and their home in her song "Mahai'ula." Perhaps the name of a type of reddish banana.

Mahakea. Beach, estate, Lā'ie, O'ahu. North section of Kokololio Beach between Kokololio Stream and Pali Kiloi'a, the limestone point at the north end of the beach. Mahakea is the name of a beach estate that is used as a retreat by Hawaiian Electric Company executives. The house and land were purchased in 1952. The beach took its name from the estate. *Lit.,* fallow fields.

Mahana. Beach, Kahuku, Hawai'i. Green sand beach at the base of Pu'u o Mahana, a littoral cone formed during an ancient eruption of Mauna Loa. Also known as Green Sand Beach. *Lit.,* warmth.

Māhā'ulepū. Beach, petroglyph site, windsurf site, Māhā'ulepū, Kaua'i. Narrow, 2-mile calcareous sand beach between Punahoa and Pa'o'o Points. Most of the recreational activity, including windsurfing, is concentrated at Pa'o'o Point. The center of the beach is known as Gillin's Beach, where petroglyphs carved into the soft beach-rock shelves are exposed only during severe high-surf storms that scour the sand off the shelves. The petroglyphs are also known as the Rainbow Petroglyphs.

Mahi. Dive site, Wai'anae, O'ahu. One of the three most popular dive sites on O'ahu. The *Mahimahi* was a 165-foot navy minesweeper sunk in 1982 as an artificial reef at 90 feet. The name of the ship is commonly shortened to *Mahi. Lit.,* dolphin fish.

Mahikea. Island (1 acre, 40 feet high), Hilo, Hawai'i.

Mahinanui. Island (.6 acres, 40 feet high), Kahakuloa, Maui. *Lit.,* large moon or large plantation.

Mahinauli. Beach, Makaweli, Kaua'i. Section of beach fronting the village at Pākala next to Robinson Landing.

Mahinui. Fishpond, Mōkapu, O'ahu. *Lit.,* great strength.

Mahoney's. Surf site, Ka'alawai, O'ahu. Off the former beachfront home of Fred Mahoney (1912–1969) who built the Breakers Hotel in Waikīkī after World War II and operated it until 1969. Mahoney built his home at Ka'alawai in 1954 and his family lived there until 1993. Mahoney's sons, Frederick and Dennis, were avid surfers who often surfed off their home with other neighborhood surfers.

Māhukona. 1. Beach park, dive site, harbor, landing, snorkeling site, Māhukona, Hawai'i. Māhukona Harbor was developed as a port for the sugar plantations in Kohala and as a landing for interisland steamers. Raw sugar manufactured in the Kohala mills was bagged, transported by rail to Māhukona, and stored in warehouses until the arrival of a freighter. When a freighter moored offshore, lighters carried out the bags. Although port operations terminated in 1956, ruins of the port structures remain on the shore of the harbor. In addition, railroad and other industrial remnants litter the floor of the harbor where they provide unique viewing opportunities for snorkelers and scuba divers. Māhukona Beach Park is on the south shore of the harbor, where a chain hoist is used to launch and land small boats. 2. Light, Māhukona, Hawai'i. Established in 1889. The 22-foot light tower was built in 1915 approximately 42 feet above sea level. *Lit.*, leeward steam or vapor.

Mailekini. *Heiau*, Kawaihae, Hawai'i. Shrine at Pelekane Beach that is part of the Pu'ukoholā Heiau National Site. *Lit.*, many *maile* vines.

Maile Point. Landing, Kāne'ohe, O'ahu. Southwestern tip of Coconut Island where the University of Hawai'i's Hawai'i Institute of Marine Biology has traditionally allowed recreational boaters to land and picnic.

Mā'ili. 1. Beach park (39.6 acres), Mā'ili, O'ahu. Park on the shore that fronts most of Mā'ili, from Mā'ili Point to Mā'ili'ili Stream. 2. Point, Mā'ili, O'ahu. Rocky, undeveloped point that separates the communities of Nānākuli and Mā'ili. Also known as Obake Point. *Lit.*, lots of little pebbles. Mā'ili is a contracted form of Mā'ili'ili and is commonly mispronounced "Maile."

Mā'ili Cove. Surf site, Mā'ili, O'ahu. On the east side of the Mā'ili Cove apartments.

Mā'ili Point. Surf site, Mā'ili, O'ahu. On the west side of the point.

Main Hawaiian Islands. Eight major islands in the Hawaiian Archipelago: Hawai'i, Maui, O'ahu, Kaua'i, Moloka'i, Lāna'i, Ni'ihau, and Kaho'olawe. The remainder of the islands and shoals in the archipelago are called the Northwestern Hawaiian Islands.

Mai Poina 'Oe Ia'u. Beach park, Kīhei, Maui. When the park property was acquired in May 1951, it was called Kīhei Memorial Park. The name Mai Poina 'Oe Ia'u was introduced at the park's dedication ceremony on August 3, 1952. Both names are still used. A sign in the park reads: "Dedicated to all those who sacrificed their lives to preserve our freedom for all humanity." Also known as Veterans Park. *Lit.*, do not forget me.

Major's Bay. Surf site, windsurf site, Pacific Missile Range Facility, Kaua'i. Off Recreation Area #3. Former base commanders held the rank of major and their quarters were on the north point of the bay. During the 1970s, a new home for the base commanders and a family housing complex were constructed at another site on the shore. The home on the point was converted to quarters for visiting dignitaries, but the surf site is still known as Major's Bay.

Maka'alae. 1. Bay, beach, point, northwest shore, Kaho'olawe. Bay with a detrital sand beach south of Maka'alae Point. 2. Beach, landing, Hāna, Maui. Narrow detrital sand beach at the head of Pōhakuloa Bay in the land division of Maka'alae. The bay was a former interisland steamer landing. *Lit.,* mud hen's eyes or face.

Mākaha. 1. Beach, Mākaha, O'ahu. Calcareous sand beach on the shore of Mākaha Valley. 2. Beach park (20.6 acres), Mākaha, O'ahu. 3. Cable Station, Mākaha, O'ahu. Mākaha Beach is the landing site for a number of transpacific and interisland fiber-optic submarine cables. The first transpacific cable was installed in 1964 and the cables that followed are buried in a trench across the beach. Communications technicians staff the cable station twenty-four hours per day. 4. Point, Mākaha, O'ahu. At the west end of the beach. Also known as Kepuhi Point. 5. Surf site. World-famous surf site off the beach park. In 1954 Mākaha was the site of Hawai'i's first international surfing meet, the Mākaha International Surfing Contest. *Lit.,* fierce.

Mākaha Canyons. Dive site, Mākaha, O'ahu. One of O'ahu's most popular dive sites. Series of arches, caverns, and over-hanging ledges at 20–50 feet, south of Kepuhi Point.

Mākaha Caverns. Dive site, Mākaha, O'ahu. Same as Mākaha Canyons.

Mākaha Caves. Dive site, Mākaha, O'ahu. Same as Mākaha Canyons.

Makahoa. 1. Point, Mālaekahana, O'ahu. Northwest point of Mālaekahana Bay. 2. Point, Hanalei, Kaua'i. North point of Hanalei Bay. *Lit.,* friendly, or a companion.

Makahonu. Fishing site, point, reef, surf site, Ka'a'awa, O'ahu. Point with a small stand of ironwood trees alongside Kamehameha Highway and the reef off the point. Both are between Kalae'ō'io Point and Kalae'ō'io Beach Park. The surf site is off the reef and is also known as Rainbows. *Lit.,* turtle eye or face.

Makahū'ena. Point light, Po'ipū, Kaua'i. Established in 1908. A light atop a 20-foot pole approximately 60 feet above sea level. *Lit.,* very angry eyes or face.

Maka'i. Fishing site, Waipi'o, Maui. At the base of the sea cliffs at the north end of Waipi'o Bay.

Makai Pier. Research facility, Waimānalo, O'ahu. 1. Same as Makai Research Pier. 2. Dive site, snorkeling site, surf site, Waimānalo, O'ahu. The dive and snorkeling sites are on the north side of the pier. They are popular shore dive sites with commercial tour companies. The surf site is at the east end of the reef off Makai Research Pier and is also known as Avalanche, Submarines. *Lit.,* toward the ocean.

Makai Research Pier. Research facility, Waimānalo, Oʻahu. Privately operated ocean research facility built in the late 1960s that includes a 600-foot long, L-shaped pier protected by a breakwater, a 200-by-200-foot boat basin, and an entrance channel. Also known as Makai Pier. *Lit.*, toward the ocean.

Makaiwa. 1. Bay, beach, dive site, Mauna Lani, Hawaiʻi. Manmade, calcareous beach at the south end of the bay. The dive site is off the beach. 2. Surf site, Kapaʻa, Kauaʻi. Makaiwa is the name of an ancient surf site here that is mentioned by historian Abraham Fornander is his account of Moikeha, a famous voyager, who landed nearby at Wailua. 3. Beach, point, Halepalaoa, Lānaʻi. Calcareous sand beach at Makaiwa Point, the site of Club Lānaʻi. 4. Bay, fishing site, landing, Kailua, Maui. Former canoe landing and a fishing site noted for *akule*, or big-eyed scad. 5. Beach, landing, Punaluʻu, Oʻahu. Site of the former Punaluʻu Landing near Punaluʻu Stream. *Lit.*, mother-of-pearl eyes (as in an image).

 moʻolelo

Moʻikeha was a famous voyaging *aliʻi* whose name is attached to Kauaʻi. He arrived there from Tahiti and was drawn by the beauty of two women, Hoʻoipoikamalanai and Hinauʻu, as they went surfing at Wailua in the district of Puna. They were also attracted to him and told their father, the paramount *aliʻi* of Kauaʻi, that they would have him for their mate. The mating of two women with one man was not an unusual custom in those days. (Some folks contend that it was only one woman with two names.)

In time, Moʻikeha became paramount *aliʻi* of Kauaʻi, but he had left a son, Laʻamaikahiki, in Tahiti whom he longed to see once more as he got to an advanced age. He decided to send one of his sons that had been born to him on Kauaʻi to fetch him from Tahiti. He held a contest to determine which of his sons was best suited for the task and chose Kila to navigate to the south to retrieve Laʻamaikahiki.

On his way south, Kila stopped at the different Hawaiian islands to pick up the crewmembers who had accompanied his father on the initial voyage north to Hawaiʻi. They had been left on the other islands to follow their fortunes. As Kila greeted each of these people, they would ask him, "Is Moʻikeha then still living? What is he doing?" Kiha would answer, "He is dwelling at ease on Kauaʻi where the sun rises and sets; where the surf of **Makaīwa** curves and bends; where the *kukui* blossoms of Puna change; where the waters of Wailua stretch out. He will live and die on Kauaʻi."

Today, when Hawaiʻi and Hawaiians are being inundated

229

with floods of immigrants from other places, the land is being covered up with their businesses, homes, and activities. Part of this colonizing process is that they are placing their names on the land. Naming is claiming, and surfers are an integral part of this process. Although there are numerous Hawaiian names for surfing sites, the prevalent trend is to call them by the foreign names that have been attached in the last forty or so years. Witness the well-known names like Sunset, Banzai Pipeline, or the more esoteric ones like Acid Drop and Heroins on Kaua'i's south shore. The examples are too numerous to recount. Often, surf spots are still sort of Hawaiian in that they are named after a place like Waimea Bay, Hanalei, or the peculiar adding of s to places like Pākalās. However, few if any of the surf sites are called by their specific Hawaiian names.

Some Hawaiians are now looking for the old names, which hold much meaning by way of the stories attached to these places by ancestors who surfed them for many centuries. Maka-īwa is one such spot. Here, the name has been restored and is being used by the general surfing population. Although most of them have no idea of the history, meaning, and background of the name, it warms the hearts of those of us whose ancestors lived here long before Europeans and Asians came to this place to hear the sound of our ancestral language attached to the surf that still "curves and bends; where the *kukui* blossoms of Puna change; where the waters of Wailua stretch out."

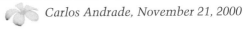
Carlos Andrade, November 21, 2000

Makalawena. Beach, dive site, surf site, Makalawena, Hawai'i. Calcareous sand beach with a series of rock outcrops that create small coves. Vegetated sand dunes occupy the backshore. The dive and surf sites are off the north end of the beach. Makalawena was the site of Kaikalia Church and a Hawaiian fishing village that was inhabited until the destructive tsunami of April 1, 1946, displaced the last residents. *Lit.*, release [of] glow.

Makaleha. Beach park (27 acres), Mokulē'ia, O'ahu. Undeveloped county beach park on the north side of the Mokulē'ia Polo Field. The park is crossed by Makaleha Stream, which originates in Makaleha Valley in the Wai'anae Mountains. A public-right-of-way connects Farrington Highway with the beach. *Lit.*, eyes looking about in wonder or admiration.

Mākālei. Beach park (.7 acres), Honolulu, O'ahu. Small community park at the base of Diamond Head at the intersection of Mākālei Place and Diamond Head Road. *Lit.*, fish trap, or the name of a supernatural tree that attracted fish.

Makaliʻi. Beach, point, Punaluʻu, Oʻahu. Narrow calcareous sand beach on the point north of Kahana Bay. *Lit.,* tiny, or Pleiades constellation.

Makaloaka. Island (.39 acres, 80 feet high), Keʻanae, Maui.

Makani Kai. Marina, Kāneʻohe Bay, Oʻahu. Private marina. Named after the Makani Kai subdivision. Facilities include eighty slips. *Lit.,* sea wind.

Mākao. Bay, beach, surf site, Hauʻula, Oʻahu. Calcareous sand beach on the bay south of Hauʻula Beach Park. Chinese farmers lived and grew rice here. Ships traveling from China to Hawaiʻi often sailed out of Macao near Canton, and the name was associated with the former Chinese farming community. The surf site is at the edge of the reef on the south side of the bay. *Lit.,* Macao.

Makaʻohai. Fishing site, Ukumehame, Maui. West of Ukumehame Beach Park. *Lit.,* bud [of the] *ʻōhai* plant *(Sesbania tomentosa).*

Makapili. Rock, Kīlauea, Kauaʻi. Small island off Crater Hill that is part of the Kīlauea Point National Wildlife Refuge and connected to the base of the sea cliffs by a sandbar, or tombolo. Two other tombolos are found on Kauaʻi: one at Poʻipū Beach Park that joins the beach to Nukumoi Point and one at Kīpū Kai that joins Kīpū Kai Beach to Mōlehu Point. *Lit.,* squinting eyes (nearly closed).

Makapuʻu. Bay, beach park (46.9 acres), dive site, head, point, surf site, Waimānalo, Oʻahu. Pocket of calcareous sand on the bay between Mānana (Rabbit) Island and Makapuʻu Point. The beach is in the lee of Makapuʻu Head (647 feet), the headland that is the easternmost point of Oʻahu and marked by a light at Makapuʻu Point. *Lit.,* bulging eyes. A stone on the point below the light was said to have had eight protrusions resembling human eyes. The stone, a *kinolau*—the physical manifestation of a legendary woman named Makapuʻu—is no longer there.

Makapuʻu Point. Dive site, light, state wayside park (38.2 acres), Waimānalo, Oʻahu. The dive site is off the point. The light was established on the point in 1909 at 395 feet above sea level in a 35-foot concrete tower. It was automated in 1924. Makapuʻu Point State Wayside Park is a scenic park on the sea cliffs above the point that includes Makapuʻu Point Light. At 500 feet above sea level, the park is one of the best whale watching sites on Oʻahu and a popular day hike. The park is accessed by following the mile-long paved Coast Guard road from Kalanianaʻole Highway to the light.

Makaua. Beach park (.1 acre), channel, Kaʻaʻawa, Oʻahu. Undeveloped roadside park north of Kaʻaʻawa. Makaua Channel is a wide, natural channel off the beach park that was cut through the reef by Makaua Stream. The nearshore section of the channel is used as a small boat anchorage. *Lit.*, unfriendly.

Makaweli. Landing, Makaweli, Kaua'i. Ni'ihau Ranch operates a private ferry service between Makaweli Landing at Pākala on Kaua'i and Lehua Landing on Ni'ihau. The ferry, a navy LCM (landing craft mechanized), carries livestock, passengers, food (including poi), dry goods, and other necessities to Ni'ihau. Also known as Robinson Landing. *Lit.*, fearful features.

Make Horse. Beach, surf site, Kaluako'i, Moloka'i. Prior to 1977 when the Sheraton Moloka'i Hotel opened, the property here was under the control of Moloka'i Ranch. After an old horse fell from the cliff at Pōhaku Māuliuli and died from the fall, the cowboys called the beach Make Horse. *Make* is the Hawaiian word for dead, so the name means "dead horse." Also known as Pōhaku Māuliuli Beach.

Mākena. 1. Bay, Mākena, Maui. Wide bay with several beaches east of Wailea and the site of Mākena Landing. 2. Beach, state park (164.4 acres), Mākena, Maui. Long calcareous sand beach adjoining Pu'u 'Ola'i at the east end of Mākena Bay. The park is undeveloped except for paved parking. Also known as Big Beach, Long Sands, Oneloa. *Lit.*, abundance.

Mākena Bay. Offshore mooring, Mākena, Maui. State mooring site off the former landing.

Mākena Beach. Dive site, Mākena, Maui. Off Mākena State Park.

Mākena Landing. Dive site, beach park, Mākena, Maui. From the 1850s to the 1920s, Mākena was one of the busiest ports on Maui, first for shipping sugar from the Makee Sugar Mill and later for shipping cattle from Ulupalakua Ranch. With the development of a deep-draft harbor at Kahului, however, many of the interisland steamer landings such as the one here fell into disuse. The ruins of the landing are in the north corner of the bay. The army dismantled the former pier while it occupied the area for training during World War II. Mākena Landing Beach Park is fronted by of two small pockets of calcareous sand.

Mākila. Beach, Lahaina, Maui. Also known as Puamana Beach Park. *Lit.*, needle (the Maui word for *mania*, or "needle").

Mākole. Beach, Polihale, Kaua'i. Same as Treasure Beach. *Lit.*, red-eyed.

Mākole'ā. 1. Beach, Keāhole, North Kona, Hawai'i. Black sand beach on the shore of the 1801 lava flow from Hualālai. Several small brackish-water ponds are in the backshore. 2. Beach, Keauhou, North Kona, Hawai'i. Calcareous sand, black sand, pebble, and coral rubble beach at the head of a small cove fronting the Kona Lagoon Hotel. A wide tidal flat of *pāhoehoe* lines the foreshore of the beach. Mākole'ā is the name of a legendary woman who lived here and who was said to be the most beautiful woman in Hawai'i. *Lit.*, glowing red eye.

Mākua. Beach, cave, dive site, surf site, Mākua, O'ahu. Calcareous sand beach that fronts Mākua Valley and that is part of Ka'ena State Park. Mākua Cave is a large lava tube on Farrington Highway near the south end of the beach. It is also known as Kāneana Cave. The dive site is off the south end of the beach and includes a ridge, two small pinnacles, and a channel at 45 feet. The surf site is also off the south end of the beach. *Lit.*, parent.

Mākua Point. Fishing site, Mākua, O'ahu. Limestone point at the south end of Mākua Beach. Also known as Po'ohuna Point.

Māla. 1. Offshore mooring, Lahaina, Maui. State mooring site off the former wharf. 2. Ramp, Lahaina, Maui. On the west side of the former wharf. Facilities include two ramps, a pier, two docks, and a vessel washdown area. 3. Wharf, Lahaina, Maui. Dedicated on April 5, 1922, by Governor Wallace R. Farrington, the wharf was built specifically to accommodate interisland steamers instead of having them anchor offshore in the Lahaina Roadstead. However, after strong currents and heavy surf damaged several steamers, they reverted to anchoring offshore and the wharf was never used again as a major interisland passenger and cargo terminal. Smaller boats continued to use it until 1950. *Lit.*, garden.

Mālaekahana. Bay, beach, dive site, state recreation area (110 acres), Lā'ie, O'ahu. Long calcareous sand beach on Mālaekahana Bay between Makahoa and Kalanai Points. Mālaekahana State Recreation Area is a beach park at Kalanai Point. Moku-'auia Island is off the point, where it is accessible at low tide by wading. The dive site is adjacent to the island. Mālaekahana is the name of a legendary person, the mother of Lā'ie.

Malaeola. Island (.09 acres, 80 feet high), Hāna, Maui.

Malama Flats. Fishing site, Malama, Hawai'i. On the sea cliffs in the land district of Malama. Ledges here in the cliffs are the "flats." *Lit.*, month or moon.

Māla Wharf. Dive site, surf site, Lahaina, Maui. The dive site is off the ruins of Māla Wharf. The surf site is a long left on the east side of the ruins.

Māliko. 1. Bay, ramp, Māliko, Maui. Narrow bay with steep sides and a small boulder beach at the head of the bay. The bay is named after Māliko Gulch, the long, deep gulch that originates above Makawao and ends here on the shore. A single-lane ramp was constructed in 1976. Although the bay is subject to high winter surf, the ramp is still well used because of the great distances between public ramps on Maui. 2. Beach,

Punalu'u, O'ahu. Section of Punalu'u Beach at the south end of Punalu'u Beach Park. Possibly named after one of the original land court awardees here. *Lit.*, budding.

Maluaka. Beach, beach park, Mākena, Maui. Small calcareous sand beach near the Maui Prince Hotel that lies within the boundaries of the land division of Maluaka. Support facilities for the beach park, including paved parking, showers, and a comfort station, are not in the park, but are nearby across from Keawala'i Church. Also known as Pu'u One.

Mamalu. Bay, Punalu'u, O'ahu. Bay off the former Punalu'u Landing near the mouth of Punalu'u Stream. *Lit.*, shady.

Mama's. Beach, windsurf site, Kū'au, Maui. Small pocket of calcareous sand fronting Mama's Fish House. In 1973 Floyd Christenson bought the restaurant and leased it to Hilda Costa, the original "Mama," who ran it as a family venture until 1976. The windsurf site is off the beach. Also known as Father Jules Papa, Kū'au Cove.

Mānā. Plain, Mānā, Kaua'i. Coastal plain from Kekaha to Polihale fronted by a calcareous sand beach approximately 15 miles long, one of the longest beaches in Hawai'i. The cliff along the inner edge of the plain is an ancient sea cliff and the composition of the plain is a combination of lagoon deposits, calcareous beach and dune sand, and alluvium. *Lit.*, arid.

Mānā Crack. Dive site, Mānā, Kaua'i. Named for a large crevice, or "crack," on the ocean floor. The dive site is off the Mānā Plain, the coastal plain between Kekaha and Polihale.

Mana'e. Coast, east end of Moloka'i. *Mana'e* is a direction, like *mauka* or *makai*, that means "to the east." The term is used almost exclusively on Moloka'i, where—because of the island's geography—travel is primarily east or west. "Going *mana'e*" means traveling east. Moloka'i residents also use Mana'e as a proper name to mean the east end of the island.

Manahoa. Island (.35 acres, 40 feet high), Ke'anae, Maui.

Mānana. Island (67 acres, 200 feet high), Waimānalo, O'ahu. Part of the Hawai'i State Seabird Sanctuary. Tuff cone built around two vents, each marked by a crater. Tuff forms when hot magma encounters seawater and the explosion caused by the rapidly expanding steam blows the magma apart, forming a spray of ash. The ash quickly cements to form a firm rock called tuff. Also known as Rabbit Island. *Lit.*, buoyant.

Manantan's. Surf site, Kuli'ou'ou, O'ahu. Off Kuli'ou'ou Beach Park. Robert "Bobby" Kalaukoa Manantan, a former resident of 'Āina Haina, was one of the first regular surfers here in the late 1960s and early 1970s. This surf site breaks behind a well-developed reef that is emergent at low tide, making it a dangerous spot to ride. Surfers have to complete their ride quickly and get out of the wave before they hit the reef. This was especially challenging in the preleash days of the 1960s when every wipeout meant that loose boards went onto the rocks. During the 1970s, the westernmost of two peaks at this site was named Tunas, while the name Manantan's remained at the east peak.

 moʻolelo

I'm a 1972 grad of Kalani High. I lived in ʻĀina Haina and started surfing around fifth or sixth grade, first outside of ʻĀina Haina and then anywhere I could. My friends next door, Brian and Dennis Okamura, had a car. When Dennis got his license, Dennis, Brian, George Luhe, Jason Uehara, Edwin Onaga, and I would load up the boards and head to Ala Moana or Waikīkī frequently and then occasionally. Gas was a main factor, as all of us who were involved were unemployed. About 1967–1968 is when I met Chris Yoza while attending Niu Valley Intermediate. It was about then that we started surfing Kuliʻouʻou simply because Chris and his brother David lived right next to the park.

As far as **Manantan's** is concerned—and I don't even know if that's how it's spelled now—Chris is the one who came to me one day after surfing Pillars and said that they named a spot after me. I really thought he was kidding and didn't think much about it until maybe months later when I overheard a couple guys talking about surfing here and there, and then I heard "Manantan's," and of course I had to *nīele* [be inquisitive]. So I asked them the name of that place, and one guy said, "Manantan's." I said, "Where is it?" and he said, "Outside Kuliʻouʻou." I said, "Oh," smiled and walked away, saying to myself, "Sucking Chris, I thought you was joking." Why they felt so moved to do such a thing is beyond me. I was nobody special, I was just like the rest of them—love to laugh, love to have fun with my friends, but most of all . . . love to surf! Now I'm working for Walt Disney World in Florida as a musician at the Polynesian Resort and also as a professional massage therapist. I left Hawaiʻi in 1976 for Disney, twenty-four years ago. A long time ago, but the beach boy is still in me.

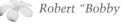 *Robert "Bobby" Kalaukoa Manantan, July 22, 2000*

Manawai. Landing, Waipiʻo, Maui. Landing for fishing canoes on the boulder beach in Waipiʻo Bay. *Lit.*, water branch. The stream splits into two branches.

Mānele. Bay, bay light, cattle chute, saltpans, small boat harbor, Mānele, Lānaʻi. Mānele Bay, the most protected bay on the island, is the site of Mānele Small Boat Harbor. Constructed in 1965 in the west corner of the bay with a 570-foot rubblemound breakwater, its facilities include twenty-eight berths, a ramp, a pier, a dock, and a vessel washdown area. Mānele Bay Light was established in 1965 during the construction of the harbor. Ruins of a cattle-loading chute constructed in 1921 by the Kahului Railroad Company for the Lānaʻi Company are found on the west point of the bay. Two concrete slabs for making salt were also constructed in 1921 on top of the sea cliffs above the old cattle-loading chute. Water pumped into the pans from the ocean below was allowed to evaporate, and the resulting salt was used to make salt licks for the cattle. The residents of Lānaʻi also used the salt during World War II when salt and other staples were scarce. *Lit.*, sedan chair.

Mānele-Hulopoʻe. Marine life conservation district (309 acres), Mānele, Lānaʻi. Established in 1976 to include Mānele and Hulopoʻe Bays.

Manini. Beach, point, surf site, Nāpoʻopoʻo, Hawaiʻi. Storm beach of coral rubble at Manini Point across the bay from Nāpoʻopoʻo Landing. The surf site is at the point. The beach and point took their name from Manini Road, the access road to the point. Also known as Pahukapu. *Lit.*, convict tang fish.

Manini Castle. Surf site, Kakaʻako, Oʻahu. Off Kakaʻako Waterfront Park. Waves break over a shallow rock formation, the "castle," that attracts schools of *manini*, or convict tang fish. Also known as Flies.

Maniniholo. Cave, Hāʻena, Kauaʻi. Lava tube several hundred feet long at Hāʻena Beach Park that was once a sea cave when the level of the ocean was higher than it is now. Waves striking the sea cliff enlarged the mouth of the cave to its present size. Also known as the Dry Cave. *Lit.*, traveling *manini* (convict tang fish).

Maninikaʻi. Fishing site, Waipiʻo, Maui. At the base of the sea cliffs between Hawini and Hoʻolawa Bays. *Lit.*, netted *manini* fish.

Maniniʻōwali. 1. Beach, dive site, surf site, Maniniʻōwali, Hawaiʻi. Section of Kekaha Kai State Park. Calcareous sand beach at the head of Kua Bay that is approximately 600 feet long and fronted by a shallow sandbar. Low, vegetated sand dunes and a small brackish-water pond are in the backshore at the north end of the beach. The surf site is a shorebreak on the sandbar, primarily for bodysurfing and bodyboarding. Maniniʻōwali is a "disappearing" sand beach like the one at Laʻaloa Beach Park on Aliʻi Drive. During periods of high surf, waves erode almost the entire beach, exposing the underlying rocks, and the beach "disappears" within twenty-four hours. When the surf subsides, normal surf activity redeposits the sand on shore, covering the rocks, and the beach reappears. The dive site is off

Pāpiha Point at the north end of the beach. Also known as Kua Bay. 2. Trail, Maniniʻōwali, Hawaiʻi. Part of the Ala Kaha-kai National Historic Trail. Historic stepping-stone trail paved with smooth, flat, waterworn stones, or *paʻalā*, across the *aʻā* at Pāpiha Point between Maniniʻōwali Beach and Kākāpa Bay to the north. *Lit.*, weak *manini* fish. Maniniʻōwali is the name of a legendary girl who was turned into a rock at the beach.

Manner's. Beach, Kahe, Oʻahu. During World War II, the navy constructed a small recreational complex at the west end of Kahe Beach. After the war, in 1946, Francis J. Manner of Waiʻanae leased the land and the buildings from Campbell Estate, and that section of the beach was called Manner's Beach.

M

Manny Jhun Point. Fishing site, Makapuʻu, Oʻahu. *Ulua* fishing site on the north side of Makapuʻu Point that is accessed from the Goat Trail, which originates at Makapuʻu Lookout on Kalanianaʻole Highway. The point was named for veteran *ulua* fisherman Manuel "Manny" Jhun (1916–2000), who pioneered fishing here in the 1970s when Bamboo Ridge and other sites to the west began to get crowded.

Manoku. Fishpond, Mauna Lani, Hawaiʻi. One of four fishponds at the Mauna Lani resort.

Man on the Rock. Fishing site, Lāʻau, Molokaʻi. Large vertical rock on the low sea cliff between Kapukuwahine and Kahale-pōhaku Beaches that suggests a man standing upright. Fishermen use it as a landmark to triangulate their fishing sites offshore. Also known as Hale ʻOpihi, ʻOpihi Road.

Manō Point. Dive site, fishing site, salt gathering site, Kīholo, Hawaiʻi. The dive site consists of ledges, canyons, and caverns in depths of 25–75 feet off the point between the Kona Village Resort and Kīholo Bay. The fishing site is on the rocks at the point. Natural depressions in the rocks here are traditional gathering sites for evaporated salt. *Lit.*, shark point.

Manta Ray. Beach, Honokōhau, Hawaiʻi. Calcareous sand beach at the entrance to Honokōhau Small Boat Harbor. Manta rays are common here. Also known as ʻAlula Beach.

Manta Ray Beach. Dive site, Honokōhau, Hawaiʻi. Off Manta Ray Beach at approximately 30 feet.

Manta Reef. Dive site, Keaweʻula, Hawaiʻi. Reef near the north point of Keaweʻula Bay. Manta rays, in addition to humpback whales and spinner dolphins, are common here during the winter months.

Mantokuji. Bay, beach, Pāʻia, Maui. The Pāʻia Mantokuji Mission is on the shore of the bay, where it was founded in 1906 by Sokyo Ueoka. Ordained in Tokyo in the Soto Zen sect, Ueoka came to Hawaiʻi to minister to plantation workers. The present temple was completed in 1921 on land that the congregation purchased, which included 3 acres for a cemetery. A small calcareous sand beach is on the seaward side of the mission. Also known as Otera Bay.

Manukā. 1. Beach, dive site, fishing site, historic complex, Manukā, Hawaiʻi. Calcareous sand, coral rubble, and lava fragment beach at the head of a small bay. Manukā is an undeveloped state park with a road to the shore that is for four-wheel drive vehicles only. The fishing site is at the beach. The dive site off the beach is a narrow shelf with a dropoff to 40 feet. The historic complex includes the ruins of a former village, a temple, a *holua* slide, and a trail system. Manukā marks the boundary between the districts of Kaʻū and South Kona. It lies in South Kona. 2. Fishing site, Kahuku, Hawaiʻi. At ʻĀwili Point and known to fishermen as Manukā, although it is actually in Kaʻū and not in South Kona. Also known as Road to the Sea, Smoking Rock. *Lit.*, lagging. The name of a legendary person.

Manuʻōhule. Dive site, Lahaina Pali, Maui. Also known as Wash Rock. *Lit.*, bird [of the] whitewash.

Mapulehu. Beach, mango orchard, Mapulehu, Molokaʻi. Narrow detrital sand beach bordering a mango orchard developed by the Hawaiian Sugar Planters Association (HSPA). Founded in 1895, the HSPA was dedicated to improving the sugar industry in Hawaiʻi. It has since become an internationally recognized research center and in 1996 changed its name to Hawaiʻi Agriculture Research Center (HARC) to reflect its expanding scope to encompass research in forestry, coffee, forage, vegetable crops, tropical fruits, and many other diversified crops in addition to sugarcane. The former HSPA Mapulehu Nursery of Mango Trees is the largest mango orchard in Hawaiʻi, with the most varieties of mangoes. It was established on 40 acres of Mapulehu beachfront property in 1940 and contains 2,000 trees, 500 of which are Hayden and Joe Welsch mangoes. The remaining 1,500 trees are other superior varieties of mangoes that were collected from around the world. The HSPA discontinued active maintenance of the orchard in 1983.

Marconi. Beach, surf site, Kahuku, Oʻahu. Calcareous sand beach between Kalaeokaunaʻoa, or Kahuku Point, and Kalaeuila, or High Rock. The beach and the surf site were named after the small community immediately inland. The American Marconi Company set up wireless operations in Hawaiʻi in 1902 and built their transpacific receiving station here at Kahuku in 1915. Since then the community that developed around the station has been known as Marconi. The beach is also known as Hanakaʻīlio Beach.

Marijuanas. Surf site, Kawailoa, Oʻahu. In the early 1970s when illegal drugs were widely prevalent on the North Shore, surfers from California lived here in a beach house rental. They often smoked marijuana before surfing and named the site. Also known as Rights off the Reef.

Marina Hale. Ramp, Hawaiʻi Kai, Oʻahu. Private boat ramp in Hawaiʻi Kai Marina for Marina Hale community residents. *Lit.,* marina house.

Marine Corps Base Hawaiʻi, Kāneʻohe Bay. Marina, Mōkapu, Oʻahu. Private marina in the lee of Mōkapu Peninsula for military personnel only.

Marineland. Surf site, Ala Moana, Oʻahu. On the shallow reef off the Kewalo Basin Marine Mammal Laboratory, or "marineland," at the east end of Kewalo Basin Park. Marineland is the left on the reef and Shallows is the right.

Mariners Cove Bay Club. Boat ramp, Hawaiʻi Kai, Oʻahu. Private boat ramp for the residents of Mariners Cove.

Maui. Maui is the second largest (727.3 square miles) of the eight major Hawaiian islands and one of four islands in Maui County. It has a population of 117,644. The highest mountain on the island is Haleakalā, with an elevation of 10,023 feet, and the *pua lokelani*, or rose, is the emblem of the island. Maui's nickname is the Valley Isle. The County of Maui includes four islands: Maui, Molokaʻi, Lānaʻi, and Kahoʻolawe. Named for the demigod Māui.

Maui Lu. Surf site, Kīhei, Maui. Off the Maui Lu Hotel, built by J. Gordon Gibson on the shore of Kīhei.

Maui Ocean Center. Aquarium, Māʻalaea, Maui. Ocean center and aquarium at Māʻalaea Harbor that opened in March 1998. It features over a hundred species of marine life in several exhibits, including a 750,000-gallon ocean tank with a 54-foot-long acrylic tunnel. Built at a cost of $20 million, the ocean center is one of five worldwide operated by Coral World International, with other centers in Israel, the U.S. Virgin Islands, and two in Australia.

Maui Sunset. Windsurf site, Kīhei, Maui. Off the Maui Sunset condominium.

Mauiwai. Beach, well, Mākena, Maui. Small pocket of calcareous sand and a former well south of Oneloa Beach. *Lit.,* Maui's water.

Mauliola. Island, Honolulu, Oʻahu. Same as Sand Island. Name of deity of health.

Mauna Kea. 1. Beach, beach park, surf site, Kawaihae, Hawaiʻi. Long calcareous sand beach with a shallow sandbar that fronts the Mauna Kea Beach Hotel. The hotel opened on July 24, 1965, the first of the large coastal resorts between Kailua and

Kawaihae. It is named after Mauna Kea, the highest mountain on the Big Island and in Hawai'i at 13,796 feet above sea level. The surf site is normally a shorebreak on the sandbar, but during high surf another surf site develops in the middle of the bay. The beach park is at the south end of the beach. Also known as Kauna'oa Beach. 2. Pond, Poho'iki, Hawai'i. Geothermally heated brackish-water pond in Ahalanui Beach Park. The name is from a former owner of the property. Also known as Hot Pond, Millionaire's Pond. *Lit.*, white mountain (probably for the snow on its summit during the winter).

Mauna Kohala. Cove, gathering site, Hāmākua Poko, Maui. Second large, rocky cove east of Ho'okipa Beach Park. *'Opihi* gathering site. Also known as Blockhouse. *Lit.*, Kohala mountain.

Mauna Lahilahi. Beach park (8.7 acres), mountain, Wai'anae, O'ahu. The beach park is on the south side of Mauna Lahilahi, which is also known as Black Rock. The beach is also known as Laulauwa'a. *Lit.*, frail mountain.

Mauna Lani. Beach, surf site, Mauna Lani, Hawai'i. Calcareous sand beach bordering a wide, sandy cove surrounded by small outcrops of lava. The surf site is off the beach. Francis Hyde Ii Brown (1892–1976), a part-Hawaiian businessman, politician, and sportsman, acquired the land division of Kalāhuipua'a in 1932 and later developed the site as his home. In 1972 Brown sold his estate to the development company that built the Mauna Lani resort. The name Mauna Lani, meaning "heavenly mountain," was suggested by Emma de Fries, a Hawaiian scholar, who noted the strong sense of volcanic presence at Kalāhuipua'a in its central position among four of the Big Island's most prominent volcanoes—Hualālai, Kohala, Mauna Loa, and Mauna Kea—and, across the 'Alenuihāhā Channel, Haleakalā on Maui. The development company adopted the name in 1980 and opened the Mauna Lani Bay Hotel on February 1, 1983. Also known as Kalāhuipua'a. *Lit.*, heavenly mountain.

Mauna Lani Reef. Dive site, Mauna Lani, Hawai'i. Off Mauna Lani Beach.

Maunalua. Bay, offshore mooring, Honolulu, O'ahu. Maunalua Bay is the wide bay in East Honolulu between Koko Head and Diamond Head. The artificial reef is off the Kāhala Mandarin Oriental Hotel. The offshore mooring is near the Hawai'i Kai Marina bridge over Kalaniana'ole Highway. *Lit.*, two mountains (probably for Koko Head and Koko Crater, the two prominent mountains at the east end of the bay).

Maunalua Bay. 1. Artificial reef, Kāhala, O'ahu. First artificial reef built by the Department of Land and Natural Resources in 1961 approximately 1.5 miles off Kāhala at a depth of 80 feet.

2. Beach park (5.4 acres), ramp, windsurf site, Hawai'i Kai, O'ahu. Man-made beach park created by deposition of material dredged from the bay during the developed of Hawai'i Kai. Henry J. Kaiser donated the park to the City and County of Honolulu in 1960. Maunalua Bay Ramp is in the park at the intersection of Hawai'i Kai Drive and Kalaniana'ole Highway and includes two ramps and a vessel washdown area. It is also known as Hawai'i Kai Boat Ramp. The windsurf site is at the east end of the beach park, where it is ridden only during strong southwesterly winds.

Maunawai. Beach, Sunset Beach, O'ahu. Calcareous sand beach between Waimea Point and Pūpūkea Road. Also known as Three Tables, a section of Pūpūkea Beach Park. *Lit.*, water mountain.

Maurice Point. Beach park, fishing site, Moanui, Moloka'i. Named for Maurice Dudoit Sr. (1898–1964) who lived across the highway from the point. Dudoit and his four brothers moved from Honolulu to Moloka'i in the 1920s, and he established his home on the shore here in 1930. He was a member of the Kamehameha Lodge and an honorary deacon of the Waialua Congregational Church. A well-known east end Moloka'i family, the Dudoits trace their roots to Jules Dudoit (1803–1866), a sea captain and coffee plantation manager. He served as French consul from 1837 to 1848 and helped found the Catholic mission in Hawai'i. In 1970, the Moloka'i Junior Chamber of Commerce (JCs) improved the beachfront property next to Maurice Point and turned it into a beach park. The fishing site is the rocky point adjacent to the park. Also known as Kumimi.

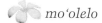 *mo'olelo*

My dad was one of five brothers and eventually they all moved to Moloka'i, but my dad was the only one on homestead land. Besides my dad, there was Adrian, Abraham, Peter, and Maurice. My Uncle Maurice was the youngest and the tallest of the brothers, and he made his home at the East End. **Maurice Point** was named for him. He lived right across the street from the point and used to fish there for *ulua* and *'ū'ū*. At that time there were a lot of fish off the point—which is actually called Kumimi—but almost no one else fished there. My uncle's family still lives on the original property across the street, and the point is still called Maurice Point.

Valentine Dudoit, September 22, 2000

My father, Maurice Dudoit Sr., came to Moloka'i in the 1920s and settled in Moanui. I'm the youngest of his fifteen children, and I own the business that he started, Dudoit's Bus Service.

We provide school bus service for the communities on the east and west ends of the island. The point across the street from our family home was named Maurice Point after my father. In Hawaiian it's called Kumimi, and it's always been a good fishing area. People still fish there now and on the reef nearby. In the early days, my dad was a Catholic, but my mom, Rachel Lahela Puaa Dudoit, was a Protestant, so later my dad changed the whole family over to Protestant. When he passed away on October 19, 1964, his service was held at Waialua Congregational Church, but he was buried on the family property.

 Moana Dudoit, December 26, 2000

Mau'umae. Beach, South Kohala, Hawai'i. Large pocket of calcareous sand with low vegetated dunes in the backshore. The beachfront estate above this secluded beach was for many years the home of Lurline Matson Roth, daughter of Captain William Matson, the founder of the Matson Navigation Company. *Lit.,* wilted grass.

Māwae. Anchialine ponds, Punalu'u, Hawai'i. Series of narrow fissures with anchialine ponds in the low sea cliffs between Punalu'u and Kamehame. *Lit.,* cleft.

M Buoy. Fish aggregating device, Hāna, Maui. Buoy anchored at approximately 438 fathoms. Landmark: Hāna Bay Light.

MC Buoy. Fish aggregating device, Palaoa, Lāna'i. Buoy anchored at approximately 575 fathoms. Landmarks: Keanapapa Point, Palaoa Point Light, Mānele Bay Light.

McGregor. Landing, point, point light, Mā'alaea, Maui. Landing for interisland steamers that was discovered at the foot of the sea cliffs to the southwest of Mā'alaea Bay by Captain Daniel McGregor (1857–1887). A wharf constructed at the landing was eventually dismantled. The ruins of the landing below the Federal Aviation Agency blockhouse include only a few concrete foundations and a cleat embedded in the rock. McGregor Point Light was established in 1906 to replace the discontinued Mā'alaea Bay Light. The 20-foot concrete pyramidal tower is on a site 48 feet above sea level.

 mo'olelo

McGregor's Landing was named for my grandfather, Daniel McGregor. He was a ship's captain on the interisland ships before his death in 1887. The story of the naming was told to me by my Tutu Paika Kanakaole. He was my step-grandfather who had married my father's mother, and he lived with us in his declining years. He was quiet and said very little, but one night he overheard the family talking about the landing. He told us he had been a member of the crew, which surprised all of us, *and then he told us the story of how they had found the landing.*

That night had been extremely stormy, and the rain was pouring down. They had been heading up the coast from Lahaina for Māʻalaea, their intended destination, but it was too rough. Captain McGregor, however, was determined to make a safe landing that night. He brought the ship close to shore and had the crew line the sides of the deck to take soundings, and, of course, they were all soaked. Finally, between two or three in the morning, they found a place that was sheltered and deep enough, but just barely, and they dropped anchor. The next morning they were all surprised to see that they had anchored next to a high sea cliff. Later a landing was constructed at the bottom of the cliff, and it was called McGregor's Landing.

My dad was only two when my grandfather died, so he never got the story firsthand. Hauʻula on Oʻahu was a common stopping point for the ships going around the island, and one day there my grandfather was involved in a fight with some sailors. He died shortly after in Honolulu on April 4, 1887, and was buried at Kawaiahaʻo.

 Marion Lee Loy, September 12, 1977

McGregor Point. Dive site, surf site, Māʻalaea, Maui. The dive site is off the former landing. The surf site is northeast of McGregor Point along the low sea cliffs. Also known as Lighthouse.

Menehune Breakwater. Dive site, seawall, Kahaluʻu, Hawaiʻi. One of the most striking features at Kahaluʻu Beach Park is the ruin of a great boulder wall or breakwater. It was originally a semicircle 3,900 feet long that enclosed the bay, forming a large fishpond. Traditional stories say the wall was built in one night by the *menehune,* a mythical people who were known for their public works projects. The dive site is off the breakwater. Also known as Pāokamenehune.

Menehune Fishpond., Nāwiliwili, Kauaʻi. Pond created by the construction of a 2,700-foot boulder wall that cut off a bend in the Hulēʻia River near Nāwiliwili Harbor. Construction of the pond is attributed to the *menehune,* a mythical people who reputedly inhabited the islands before the arrival of the Hawaiians. They often constructed public works projects, completing them in one night or abandoning them forever. Also known as Alekoko.

Menehune Reef. Dive site, Kīhei, Maui. North of Kalepolepo (or Koʻieʻie) Fishpond.

Menpachi Cave. Dive site, south coast, Lānaʻi. East of Kaunolū. A 100-foot-long lava tube wide enough for two divers side-

243

by-side at 40–60 feet. *Lit.*, squirrel fish cave. Squirrel fish, commonly known to Hawaiian fishermen by their Japanese name, *menpachi*, are found throughout the cave.

Mentaloafs. Surf site, Hawai'i Kai, O'ahu. On the west side of the Kalama Stream mouth. A steep, dangerous wave that breaks on a shallow ledge fronting a rocky shore, the name is a play on words—*mental* ("stupid") and *oaf* ("idiot")—to describe anyone who would attempt to surf here.

Mesh Piles. Surf site, Niu, O'ahu. In June 1958 a charter fishing boat named *Mizpah* went aground here, and this surf site was named for it. Mesh Piles is a corruption of Mizpah. Also known as Mizpah.

Middle Break. Surf site, Lā'ie, O'ahu. Off Hukilau Beach Park in the middle of Lā'ie Bay.

Middle Loch. Bay, Pearl Harbor, O'ahu. The centermost, or "middle," bay in Pearl Harbor.

Middle of the Bay. 1. Surf site, 'Anaeho'omalu, Hawai'i. Big-wave, second-reef site that breaks approximately one-quarter mile offshore in the middle of 'Anaeho'omalu Bay. 2. Surf site, Kīholo, Hawai'i. In the middle of Kīholo Bay off the beach-front home of Dr. Earl E. Bakken, inventor of the pacemaker. Also known as Kīholo, Pacers. 3. Surf site, Hanalei, Kaua'i. Big-wave, second-reef site that breaks approximately in the middle of Hanalei Bay, terminating at Wai'oli Channel. Also known as Middles, Wai'oli. 4. Surf site, Kawela, O'ahu. Big-wave, second-reef site that breaks approximately in the middle of Kawela Bay. Also known as The Bay, Kawela, Middles.

Middle Peak. Surf site, Hawai'i Kai, O'ahu. The peak in the middle of Sandy Beach that breaks outside of the shorebreak during big swells.

Middle Reef. Surf site, Kailua, O'ahu. General name for several peaks in the middle of the reef off Lanikai Beach.

Middles. 1. Surf site, Ho'okipa, Maui. One of several surfing and windsurf sites off Ho'okipa Beach Park. Middles is off the middle of the park, between the concrete pavilion at the east end of the park and Hāmākua Poko Point at the west. 2. Surf site, Sand Island, O'ahu. Off the middle of the beach in Sand Island State Park. 3. Surf site, Mokulē'ia, O'ahu. Between (in the middle of) two more prominent surf sites, Park Rights and Day Star. Also known as The Box, Straight Outs. 4. Surf site, Hanalei, Kaua'i. Alternate name for Middle of the Bay. 5. Surf site, Kawela, O'ahu. Alternate name for Middle of the Bay.

Mid Pacs. Surf site, Kailua, O'ahu. At the west end of Lanikai Reef off the main entrance to Mid-Pacific (Mid Pac) Country Club. The country club was incorporated on May 5, 1926 as an amenity of Charles Frazier's new subdivision, Lanikai. Its

18-hole championship golf course, designed by golf course, designed by golf course architect Seth Raynor, opened in 1928 with the first nine holes. Also known as Right Rights.

Mid Reef. Dive site, Molokini, Maui. Wide, extensive reef that is in the middle of Molokini's crescent.

Miki. Fishing site, point, Kalaeloa, Oʻahu. Rocky point near the east boundary of Campbell Industrial Park. Named after a Japanese fisherman from ʻEwa Plantation.

Mikiawa. Fishpond, Keawanui, Molokaʻi. *Lit.*, round milkfish.

Mile 4. Dive site, North Kona, Hawaiʻi. Off the 4-mile marker on Aliʻi Drive, the coastal road between Kailua and Keauhou.

Miller's Hill. Littoral cone, Mākena, Maui. Miller was an English whaler who lived in the late 1800s at Paʻako near Puʻu Ōlaʻi, the littoral cone at the north end of Mākena State Park. Little is known about Miller, but his son Alexander and granddaughter Sara Miller Makaiwa are buried in the family graveyard at Paʻako. Also known as Puʻu Ōlaʻi.

Millionaire's Pond. Pool, Pohoʻiki, Hawaiʻi. Geothermally heated brackish-water pond in Ahalanui Beach Park. The name is for a former owner of the property. Also known as Hot Pond, Mauna Kea Pond.

Milokukohi. Fishpond, Mauna Lani, Hawaiʻi. West of the hotel.

Miloliʻi. 1. Beach park, dive site, light, ramp, Miloliʻi, Hawaiʻi. Large sandy lot bordered by a seawall on a low, flat, rocky point in the center of Miloliʻi village. Facilities include a ramp and a fish hoist. Miloliʻi Light is a light atop a 20-foot pole that is 44 feet above sea level. The dive site is off the beach park. 2. Beach, dive site, park, surf site, Nā Pali, Kauaʻi. One of five calcareous sand beaches in Nā Pali Coast State Park. The beach borders a long, narrow coastal flat at the base of high sea cliffs. Miloliʻi Valley is at the south end of the flat. A large fringing reef fronts the beach and vegetated dunes line the backshore. The dive site is off the reef at approximately 35 feet. A boat channel cuts through the reef at the north end of the beach. The surf site is off the reef on the south side of the channel. *Lit.*, fine twist. Miloliʻi village on Hawaiʻi was noted for its excellent sennit, or coconut husk fiber cord, which is made by twisting the fiber. An alternate translation is "small twisting," as a current.

Mine Fields. Surf site, Māʻili, Oʻahu. On the west side of Māʻili Point near Hoʻokele Street. Most of the reef and many of the rocks in the ocean here are emergent even at high tide, making it a dangerous site to surf. Dodging the rocks is like trying to avoid mines in a minefield.

Missouri. Memorial, Pearl Harbor, Oʻahu. Same as Battleship *Missouri* Memorial.

Mizpah. Surf site, Niu, Oʻahu. On June 9, 1958, the 58-foot, 31-ton charter fishing boat *Mizpah* ran aground in high surf on the reef off Niu Peninsula. It was eventually completely destroyed, but its engine still remains on the bottom of Niu Channel near the surf site. Also known as Mesh Piles.

MM Buoy. Fish aggregating device, Mōkapu Point, Oʻahu. Buoy anchored at approximately 1,355 fathoms. Landmarks: Pyramid Rock, Makapuʻu Point Light.

Moana. Hotel, Waikīkī, Oʻahu. The first large tourist hotel in Hawaiʻi and now the oldest. Opened on March 11, 1901 at Ulukou on the shore of Waikīkī Beach, it is now known as the Sheraton Moana Surfrider. *Lit.,* open ocean.

Moi Bay. Fishing site, Mānele, Lānaʻi. Small bay west of Kaluakoʻi Point, the western boundary of the Mānele-Hulopoʻe Marine Life Conservation District. *Moi,* or threadfish *(Polydactylus sexfilis),* are caught here.

Moi Hole. 1. Fishing site, Keawaʻula, Oʻahu. Off the rocks beyond the west end of Yokohama Beach. 2. Fishing site, Mākua, Oʻahu. The "hole" is actually a small cave in the low sea cliffs off Kāneana Cave, a large cave on Farrington Highway. *Moi,* or threadfish *(Polydactylus sexfilis),* are caught at both sites.

Moikeha. Canal, Waipouli, Kauaʻi. Drainage canal with a small jetty at Waipouli Beach. One of several canals in Waipouli and Kapaʻa that were built to drain the inland marshes to make the land suitable for agriculture. A large pool in the reef off the canal was the result of successive dredging operations, first by Līhuʻe Plantation for road fill material and then again by the county for a proposed natatorium. Name of an early navigator.

Mokae. Cove, landing, Hāna, Maui. Site of a former interisland steamer landing for the Reciprocity Plantation. The landing and warehouse were situated on the north point of the cove. Hāmoa Beach is at the head of the cove. *Lit.,* a sedge-like plant.

Mōkapu. 1. Beach, snorkeling site, surf site, Wailea, Maui. One of five calcareous sand beaches fronting the Wailea resort complex. The beach was named for a small rock island called Mōkapu. During World War II, however, the island was almost entirely destroyed by the military during combat demolition exercises. Today it is indistinguishable from the other submerged rocks off the north end of the beach. The surf site is off the beach. The reefs at Mōkapu are considered to be among the best snorkeling sites on Maui. 2. Island (3.6 acres, 360 feet high), Kalaupapa, Molokaʻi. Part of the Hawaiʻi State Seabird Sanctuary. One of two sea stacks on the east side of Kalaupapa Peninsula. 3. Native Hawaiian burial dunes, Mōkapu, Oʻahu. In the backshore of North Beach at the edge of the Klipper

Golf Course on Marine Corps Base Hawai'i, Kāne'ohe Bay. The dunes contain the precontact burials of native Hawaiians. 4. Peninsula, Mōkapu, O'ahu. Wide point of land that separates Kāne'ohe and Kailua Bays and includes two large volcanic cones, Ulupa'u and Pu'u Hawai'iloa. The peninsula has been a military base since the 1930s and has been occupied by Marine Corps Base Hawai'i, Kāne'ohe Bay since 1952. In precontact times, it was a meeting place for Hawaiian chiefs. 5. Beach, Wailea, Maui. Fronting the Renaissance Wailea Beach Resort. *Lit.*, sacred district *(mō* is short for *moku).*

Mokauea. Island, Ke'ehi, O'ahu. Largest of several small islands in Ke'ehi Lagoon. In July 1978, the state and the Mokauea Fishermen's Association entered into a long-term, low-rent agreement, allowing members of the association to live on the island as they and their families had done in the past.

Mōke'ehia. Island (4.5 acres, 160 feet high), Kahakuloa, Maui. State-owned island that is part of the Hawai'i State Seabird Sanctuary. Off Hakuhe'e Point. *Lit.*, trodden island *(mō* is short for *moku).*

Mokes. 1. Surfing, windsurf site, Mokulē'ia, O'ahu. Surfing and windsurf sites that front Mokulē'ia Beach Park. "Mokes" is an abbreviation of Mokulē'ia. 2. Islands, Kailua, O'ahu. Two islands off Wailea Point in Lanikai. "Mokes" is an abbreviation of Mokulua, the Hawaiian name for the two islands.

Mōkoholā. Island (.36 acres, 50 feet high), Pelekunu, Moloka'i. *Lit.*, cut whale *(mō* is short for *moku,* cut).

Mōkōlea. 1. Point, Kīlauea, Kaua'i. Part of Kīlauea Point National Wildlife Refuge. On March 8, 1988, 91 acres of Crater Hill and 38 acres at Mōkōlea Point were added to the refuge. The Doran Schmidt family donated the Crater Hill property, and the Mōkōlea Point property was purchased from Ocean Vistas Consortium for $1.6 million. 2. Dive site, point, Kahakuloa, Maui. At Mōkōlea Point north of Kahakuloa. 3. Island (.46 acres, 50 feet high), Pelekunu, Moloka'i. 4. Island, Kailua, O'ahu. Solitary island at the north end of Kailua Bay that is part of the Hawai'i State Seabird Sanctuary. Also known as Bird Island, Black Rock. *Lit.*, plover island *(mō* is short for *moku).*

Mokoli'i. 1. Fishpond, Kualoa, O'ahu. Also known as Koholālele. 2. Island, Kualoa, O'ahu. Approximately 500 yards off Kualoa Regional Park, the island was said in legend to be the tail of a giant lizard named Mokoli'i who was killed by Hi'iaka, the sister of Pele, the goddess of the volcano. Also known as Chinaman's Hat, Pake Papale. *Lit.*, little lizard (a rare use of *moko* for *mo'o).*

Moku'ae'ae. Island (.3 acres, 104 feet high), Kīlauea, Kaua'i. Part of the Hawai'i State Seabird Sanctuary. The island is directly off Kīlauea Point where it is an important nesting site for the refuge's bird colonies. *Lit.,* fine [small] island.

Mokuālai. Island (.74 acres, 10 feet high), Lā'ie, O'ahu. Part of the Hawai'i State Seabird Sanctuary. Island remnant east of Lā'ie Point that is now a rock awash. One of five islands visible from the point that were created when the demigods Kana and Nīheu cut up the body of a *mo'o,* a giant lizard, and threw the pieces into the sea. *Lit.,* island that obstructs or blocks.

Mokū'auia. Island (25 acres, 10 feet high), Lā'ie, O'ahu. Part of the Hawai'i State Seabird Sanctuary and an important nesting site for wedge-tailed shearwaters. One of five islets visible from Lā'ie Point that were created when the demigods Kana and Nīheu cut up the body of a *mo'o,* a giant lizard, and threw the pieces into the sea. Also known as Goat Island. *Lit.,* island that was cast aside.

Mokuhala. Island (.18 acres, 40 feet high), Ke'anae, Maui. One of two state-owned islands near Pauwalu Point. Part of the Hawai'i State Seabird Sanctuary. *Lit.,* pandanus tree island or island passed by.

Mokuhano. Island, Hāna, Maui. Off Ka'uiki Head. *Lit.,* majestic island.

Mokuholua. Island (.18 acres, 40 feet high), Ke'anae, Maui. *Lit., holua* [sled] island.

Mokuho'oniki. Dive site, island (10.6 acres, 203 feet high), Moakea, Moloka'i. Part of the Hawai'i Seabird Sanctuary. One of two islands that were built by a posterosional eruption and eventually divided into two islands by wave erosion. Kanahā is the second island. Mokuho'oniki was used as a bombing target by the military until 1958 when Moloka'i residents' complaints about noise and concerns about safety were finally heeded. The dive site off the island includes pinnacles and dropoffs at 30 to 100 feet. Also known as Elephant Rock. *Lit.,* pinch island (as a lover pinches).

Mokuhuki. Fishing site, island (.35 acres, 40 feet high), Nāhiku, Maui. On the north side of Waiohue Bay. A large pocket of flat sand here is a fishing site for akule. *Lit.,* pulling island.

Moku Iki. 1. Island (9 acres), Kailua, O'ahu. Smaller of the two Mokulua Islands off Wailea Point. The larger is Moku Nui. Also known as Baby Moke, One Hump. 2. Island, Pearl Harbor, O'ahu. Smaller of two rock islands off Ford Island near the USS *Arizona* Memorial. The larger is Moku Nui. *Lit.,* small island.

Mokulau. Beach, islands, landing, point, Kaupō, Maui. Many small rock islands are located in the ocean off the cobblestone beach lining the north side of the point. Huialoha Church, constructed in 1857 on the otherwise barren point, has an active congregation. The ruins of Mokulau Landing are located across the bay from the church. *Lit.,* many islands.

Mokulēʻia. 1. Beach, snorkeling site, Honolua, Maui. Large calcareous sand pocket beach at the foot of the sea cliffs. Part of the Honolua-Mokulēʻia Bay Marine Life Conservation District established in 1978. Also known as Slaughterhouse Beach. 2. Beach, Mokulēʻia, Oʻahu. A 6-mile-long calcareous sand beach between Kaiaka Bay and Camp Erdman. The beach passes through four land divisions in the Waialua District—Mokulēʻia, Kawaihāpai, Keālia, and Kaʻena—but is known only as Mokulēʻia Beach. 3. Beach park (38.5 acres), Mokulēʻia, Oʻahu. Section of Mokulēʻia Beach near Dillingham Airfield. 4. Dive site, Mokulēʻia, Oʻahu. Off the beach park. 5. Surf site, windsurf site, Mokulēʻia, Oʻahu. Off the beach park. Also known as Mokes, Park Rights. *Lit.,* district of abundance.

Mokulēʻia Army Beach. Mokulēʻia, Oʻahu. Section of Mokulēʻia Beach opposite Dillingham Airfield, Mokulēʻia, Oʻahu. Same as Army Beach.

Mokulua. Islands (24.1 acres, 225 feet high), Kailua, Oʻahu. Collective name for two islands approximately three-quarters of a mile off Wailea Point in Lanikai. Both are part of the Hawaiʻi State Seabird Sanctuary and primary nesting sites for wedge-tailed shearwaters and Bulwer's petrels. The calcareous sand beach in the lee of Moku Nui, the larger island, is a popular landing site for boaters, kayakers, and surfers. Both islands are also known as the Mokuluas, Mokes, and Twin Islands. The larger island is also known as Big Moke, Moku Nui, and Two Humps. The smaller island is also known as Baby Moke, Moku Iki, and One Hump. *Lit.,* two islands.

Mokumana. 1. Island (.7 acres, 40 feet high), Keʻanae, Maui. One of two state-owned islands near Pauwalu Point. Part of the Hawaiʻi State Seabird Sanctuary. Also known as Bird Island. 2. Island, Kawailoa, Oʻahu. Small island adjoining the shore west of Waimea Bay. Also known as The Point. *Lit.,* branched island. The seaward side of the Oʻahu island divides, or branches, into two small points.

Mokumanu. 1. Island (2.87 acres, 150 feet high), Pelekunu, Molokaʻi. Part of the Hawaiʻi State Seabird Sanctuary. 2. Dive site, island (16.6 acres, 225 feet high), Mōkapu, Oʻahu. Large island off Ulupaʻu Head with a narrow, shallow passage through its center. Mokumanu is part of the Hawaiʻi State Seabird Sanctuary and is an eroded remnant of Ulupaʻu Head, the volcanic tuff cone on the shore of Mōkapu Peninsula. The dive site on the north side of Mokumanu includes a sea cave and is noted for its tiger sharks. *Lit.,* bird island.

Mokunaio. Island, Kaunolū, Lāna'i. Part of the Hawai'i State Seabird Sanctuary. *Lit.,* false sandalwood tree island.

Mokunoio. Island, Hāna, Maui. *Lit.,* noddy tern island.

Moku Nui. 1. Island (13 acres), Kailua, O'ahu. Larger of the two Mokulua Islands off Wailea Point in Lanikai. Also known as Big Moke, Two Humps. 2. Island, Pearl Harbor, O'ahu. Larger of two small rock islands off Ford Island near the USS *Arizona* Memorial. *Lit.,* large island.

Mokuoeo. Island, Ke'ehi Lagoon, O'ahu. One of several small islands in Ke'ehi Lagoon on the western side of Kalihi Channel that was mostly destroyed by the dredging of the seaplane runways in the 1940s.

Mokuokaha'ilani. Island (.9 acres, 40 feet high), Ho'ōpūloa, Hawai'i. *Lit.,* island of Kaha'ilani (a chief).

Mokuokau. Island (.18 acres, 40 feet high), Ha'ikū, Maui.

Mokuola. Island, Hilo, Hawai'i. Prior to its development as a park, the island was visited by Hawaiians who wanted to be cured of diseases. The water around the island was believed to heal those who swam in it. Also known as Coconut Island. *Lit.,* healing island.

Moku o Lo'e. Island, Kāne'ohe Bay, O'ahu. Also known as Coconut Island. *Lit.,* island of Lo'e. Lo'e was a legendary woman who is said to have lived on the island.

Moku'opihi. Island, Maku'u, Hawai'i. Small rock island off Maku'u. Also known as 'Opihi. *Lit.,* limpet island.

Mokupala. Island (.18 acres, 40 feet high), Kīpahulu, Maui. *Lit,* rotten island (probably referring to seaweed).

Mokupapapa. Island (.72 acres, 50 feet high), Hālawa, Moloka'i. *Lit.,* flat island.

Mokupipi. Island (1.08 acres, 80 feet high), Hāna, Maui. *Lit.,* pearl oyster island.

Moku Pōpolo. Island, Hāna, Maui. Small cluster of rocks behind the prominent rock called Haili in Pa'iloa Bay in Wai'ānapanapa State Park. *Lit.,* black nightshade plant island.

Mokupuku. Island (1.5 acres, 40 feet high), North Kohala, Hawai'i. Part of the Hawai'i State Seabird Sanctuary. One of three islands off Honoke'ā Valley on the north side of the Kohala Mountains. The islands are sea stacks—rocks isolated from the main island by erosion. The island has a large hole through it above sea level. *Lit.,* contracted island.

Moku'ume'ume. Island, Pearl Harbor, O'ahu. Also known as Ford Island and Poka 'Ailana. *Lit.,* sexual game island.

Mōlehu. Beach, point, Kīpū Kai, Kaua'i. Point connected to a small calcareous sand beach by a tombolo, a sandbar that joins two islands. Two other tombolos are found on Kaua'i, one at Crater Hill that joins the base of the hill to Makapili Island, and one at Po'ipū Beach Park that joins the beach to Nukumoi Point. *Lit.,* twilight.

Mōli'i. Fishpond, Hakipu'u, O'ahu. *Lit.,* small section.

Moloa'a. Bay, beach, Kaua'i. Calcareous sand beach at the head of Moloa'a Bay. Both ends of the beach terminate at high bluffs. Moloa'a Stream crosses the north end of the beach. *Lit.,* matted roots. The wauke, or paper mulberry, once grew so thickly here that the roots of the trees were interwoven, or matted.

 *mo'olelo*

I'm retired from the Kaua'i Police Department, and I was raised at Moloa'a. I went to Ko'olau School, which was next to the graveyard on Ko'olau Road. The graveyard is near the right-of-way to Larsen's Beach, and my parents are buried there. When the *nalu* [surf] comes into the bay, there's a strong rip current. It comes in from the east point, sweeps across the entire swimming area, and then makes a sharp U-turn straight out the center of the bay. I lost an uncle there, and I also made some rescues myself of my own family members. If there's no surf, there's good swimming and diving all over the bay.

My dad was deputy sheriff of the Hanalei District, and when he went to work, I would pick *limu* with my mother, my aunties, and others in my family. Our *limu* expeditions took us from **Moloa'a** to Pīla'a and back. Ka'aka'aniu is the reef that's good for *limu kohu* on the west side of the bay. The *kohu* here is very red, but has more *'opala* to clean than the *kohu* at Pīla'a, which is lighter but has less *'opala*. To pick, you need a calm day, but with some waves playing over the *limu*. If [there are] no waves, the sun burns the *limu* and turns it white. We would try to break the *limu* off above the *kumu,* the base, before putting it in the bag. And we always kept the storage bag in the water or the *limu* would get *palahe'e* [overripe].

Lepeuli is the little bay with a freshwater stream before Kepuhi Point. We would get *piliko'a* there. It was dark maroon with a greenish hue, and to prepare it, you just boil it, and you can also add *limu 'opihi*.

 Bill Huddy, February 5, 1986

Moloka'i. 1. Island. Moloka'i is the fifth largest (260 square miles) of the eight major Hawaiian Islands and one of four islands in Maui County. It has a population of 7,404, many of whom are of Hawaiian ancestry. The highest mountain on the island is Kamakou, with an elevation of 4,970 feet, and the *pua kukui*

flower is the emblem of the island. Moloka'i's nickname is the Friendly Isle. 2. Light, Kalaupapa, Moloka'i. Established in 1906 and automated in 1966. The 132-foot light tower was completed in 1909 and its base is approximately 100 feet above sea level. Also known as the Kalaupapa Light. 3. Reef, Papa'i, Hawai'i. Reef bordering the channel into the beach at Papa'i that was used as a canoe landing. 4. Reef, Hanalei, Kaua'i. In Hanalei Bay off the mouth of Wai'oli Stream. The reef is the site of a shipwreck, the *Ha'aheo o Hawai'i*, a historic ship that sank here in 1820. The ship was located in 1995 and excavated by a team led by Paul Johnston, the curator of Maritime History at the Smithsonian's National Museum of American History.

Moloka'i Express. Current, Hawai'i Kai, O'ahu. Powerful current that runs from Koko Head toward Moloka'i, traveling in the opposite direction of the prevailing currents and trade winds. In November 1983, four men night-diving at Portlock Point were caught in this current and towed 4 miles into the Kaiwi Channel before they were rescued off Sandy Beach. The term *express* compares the speed of the current to an express train.

Molokini. 1. Dive site, snorkeling site, Molokini, Maui. The most popular dive site in Maui County and rated as one of the top ten dive sites in the world, with both snorkeling and scuba diving opportunities at 10–80 feet. Many individual dive sites with individual names are located around the island. 2. Island, Molokini, Maui. Crescent-shaped palagonite tuff cone formed by an eruption in the ocean on the southwest rift zone of Haleakalā. The island lies in the 'Alalākeiki Channel between Maui and Kaho'olawe. The ocean within the island's crescent is a marine life conservation district (MLCD) and is the destination of daily snorkel and dive tours on a variety of boats from Maui, including custom dive boats, inflatable boats, and glass-bottomed boats. 3. Light, Molokini, Maui. Established in 1911 on the southwest summit of the cone at approximately 173 feet above sea level. 4. State seabird sanctuary. The state-owned island is part of the Hawai'i State Seabird Sanctuary. Landing on the island is prohibited. *Lit.*, many ties.

Molokini Shoal. Marine life conservation district (200 acres). Established in 1977. The marine life conservation district surrounds the island, following the 30-fathom or 180-foot contour line. The shallow inner cove of Molokini, or the shoal, harbors a wide diversity of marine life and is one of Hawai'i's most popular snorkeling and scuba diving destinations.

Monkey. Island, Pearl Harbor, O'ahu. Large island in West Loch in Pearl Harbor. The military constructed a monkey farm here and conducted experiments on the monkeys, subjecting them to doses of radar impulses. Also known as Laulaunui Island.

Monolith. Dive site, south coast, Lāna'i. East of Kaunolū. Plateau that begins at 40 feet and then drops abruptly to 110 feet. The face of the wall at the dropoff is the "monolith."

Monster Mush. Surf site, Sunset Beach, O'ahu. *Mush* is surfing slang for sloppy, poorly formed waves that spill when they break instead of plunge. During the winter months, large ("monster-sized") waves here are mushy during strong on-shore winds.

Monuments. Surf site, Mā'ili, O'ahu. On the east side of Mā'ili Point and off the warning marker, or "monument," on the rocky ledge. In 1935, members of the Honolulu Japanese Casting Club began a community service project to identify fishing sites around O'ahu where shorecasters had drowned. Their project included placing warning markers on a number of dangerous ledges, including this one at Mā'ili Point. The sides of the markers were painted with the Japanese character *abunai,* or "danger." Also known as Olympic Point.

Mo'oheau. Park, Hilo, Hawai'i. On the waterfront at the foot of downtown Hilo. Name of a chief whose father, Ho'olulu, is said to have hidden the bones of Kamehameha I.

Mo'okini. *Heiau,* 'Upolu, Hawai'i. Massive *heiau,* or shrine, with 30-foot-high walls forming a rectangle approximately 250 by 125 feet. Tradition says the *heiau* was built about A.D. 500 by the High Priest Kuamo'o Mo'okini and rebuilt by Pā'ao, a priest from Tahiti, about A.D. 1000. According to legend and genealogical chants of the Mo'okini family, the *heiau* is the only one in Hawai'i with a continuous family line of guardianship since its beginning. It was designated as Hawai'i's first national historic landmark in 1963. *Lit.,* many *mo'o* or many lineages.

Mo'omomi. 1. Bay, beach, dive site, recreation center, surf site, Mo'omomi, Moloka'i. Narrow calcareous sand beach at the head of Mo'omomi Bay fronting the Hawaiian Home Lands recreation center. The dive site and surf site are off the pavilion. 2. Coast, Mo'omomi, Moloka'i. General name for the 3 miles of calcareous sand beaches from the Hawaiian Home Lands recreation center to the sea cliffs at Keonelele. 3. Conservation area. Established in 1993 by Hui Malama o Mo'omomi, a group of Moloka'i residents who were concerned over the serious depletion of the ocean resources at Mo'omomi, especially fish, lobster, and *'opihi.* The conservation area is not a Department of Land and Natural Resources' Natural Area Reserve or Marine Life Conservation District. Mo'omomi Bay is in the center of the area that extends east to Nihoa near the base of the Kalaupapa Trail and west to 'Īlio Point.

 *moʻolelo*

I've lived on Molokaʻi and fished at **Moʻomomi** all my life. During the 1980s was when I really started to notice the loss of our resources there, the serious depletion of the fish species, the lobster, and the *ʻopihi*. Moʻomomi was noted for its *kumu,* but not now. The commercial activity especially really hit the area hard, so in 1993, Wade Lee and I put a conservation program together called Hui Malama o Moʻomomi, and I've been working on it ever since. The program encourages traditional fishing methods that go hand-in-hand with a subsistence lifestyle. We estimate that at least 15 percent of the Molokaʻi residents do some type of subsistence fishing, and this program is to help ensure that they will always have fish. The program discourages the use of technology, and the only commercial activities that are allowed are trolling, bottom fishing, and surround netting for *akule* and *taʻape*. We also discourage the use of scuba gear unless it's used to free nets from the coral so the coral isn't broken. Although there are several good places to surf, we only have one designated surfing spot. It's off the north point of Moʻomomi Bay. We discourage surfing at the other spots because the waves are breaking on papa where the fish feed.

The area that we've designated as the conservation area is from Moʻomomi Bay north to Nīhoa, which is just before the foot of the Kalaupapa Trail, and from Moʻomomi Bay south to ʻĪlio Point. We included the rocky areas past the sand beaches because those are our *ʻopihi* grounds. Our area is not part of any of the State's natural area reserves or conservation districts, but we have been caretakers there for generations, so the word is out and people are respectful of our system and our lifestyle. Anyone can come down and fish as long as they follow the rules. And what's important is that the system works, and now people can see the results. The fish, the lobster, and the *ʻopihi* are coming back.

 Mac Poepoe, November 25, 2000

Moorings. Mooring site, Barbers Point, Oʻahu. Roadstead where oil tankers anchor to discharge their cargoes for the two refineries at Campbell Industrial Park.

Mormon Pond. Tide pool, Kalaupapa, Molokaʻi. At the base of the low sea cliffs at Judd Park fronting Waiʻaleʻia Valley, where the Mormons baptized their converts.

Mothers. 1. Beach, Kāhala, Oʻahu. Section of Kāhala Beach at the intersection of Kāhala Avenue and Hunakai Street. Several small pockets of sand in the reef here provide protected swimming and wading opportunities for little children, making it a popular place for mothers to bring their children. 2. Beach, surf site, Sunset Beach, O'ahu. On the west side of Sunset Point. Popular place for mothers to bring their children during the summer and other periods of no surf. The surf site is a beginner's site off the beach.

Mudflats. Surf site, Mā'alaea, Maui. Northeast of Haycraft Park in Mā'alaea Village. The backshore inland of the surf site is undeveloped and consists of shallow mudflats that pond after heavy rains.

Mū'olea. Point, Kīpahulu, Maui. Site of the *limu make,* or "deadly seaweed." An article dated March 8, 1884, about Kihapi'ilani in the *Kū'oko'a* newspaper states: "They reached the cape of Paa at Muolea, the place where the houses of King Kalākaua stand. It is also the place where the poisonous seaweed grows until this day." *Limu make (Palythoa toxica)* was collected from Mū'olea and studied at the Hawai'i Institute of Marine Biology on O'ahu. Studying its chemical composition resulted in an important scientific discovery—the potent biotoxin, palytoxin. Palytoxin has been found to help in the treatment of some types of cancer. Perhaps a variation of *mu'ele'a,* or "thoroughly bitter."

Naha. Beach, fishpond, surf site, Naha, Lānaʻi. Narrow detrital sand beach at the end of Keōmuku Road. The beach is the site of a former fishing village, one of the four fishponds on Lānaʻi, and the seaward end of the Naha Trail, a trail that connects Pālāwai Basin to the ocean. The surf site is off the beach. *Lit.,* bent or curved.

Nāhiku Landing. Scenic point, Nāhiku, Maui. Site of the Nāhiku Rubber Plantation, incorporated on January 24, 1905, the first rubber plantation on American soil. High-quality rubber trees had been planted in Nāhiku as early as 1899 to determine if they would grow well and be commercially productive. Planting and tapping operations continued until 1916, when high labor costs forced the company to close. The landing was constructed in 1903 and abandoned in 1916. The 3-mile road from Hāna Highway to the ruins of the landing passes many rubber trees and the remains of a coral flume. *Lit.,* the seven (districts of the area).

Nahuna Point. Dive site, Mākena, Maui. Off the north point of Mākena Bay. Also known as Five Caves, Five Graves, Turtle Town.

Nākālele. 1. Point, Hāmākua Poko, Maui. Small point separating Father Jules Papa and Hāmākua Poko Papa. 2. Blowhole, dive site, fishing site, point light, Nākālele, Maui. Established on the northernmost point of West Maui in 1910, at a site 150 feet above sea level, the light was automated in 1922. The blowhole is on a lava terrace at the water's edge. The fishing site is on the rocks near the light. The dive site is off the rocks. *Lit.,* the supports.

Nāmāhana. Point, Mākua, Oʻahu. West end of Mākua Beach, where the sand is fronted by rocks at the water's edge. *Lit.,* the twins.

Nāmoku. 1. Islands, Honokeʻa, Hawaiʻi. Collective name for the three islands off Honokeʻa: Mokupuka, Paʻalaea, and Paoakalani. The islands are sea stacks—rocks left by the collapse of an arch or isolated from the main island by erosion. 2. Island (.09 acres, 50 feet high), Kalaupapa, Moloka'i. *Lit.*, the islands.

Nā Mokulua. Islands, Kailua, O'ahu. Two islands off Wailea Point in Lanikai. Also known as the Mokulua Islands. *Lit.*, the two islands.

Nānāhoa. Sea stacks, Honopū, Lāna'i. Part of the Hawai'i State Seabird Sanctuary. Sea stacks are vertical rocks that are left standing alone when the ocean erodes the rocks that once connected them to the shore. The cluster of five sea stacks at Honopū Bay is one of the best examples of sea stacks in Hawai'i. Also known as Five Needles, Three Stone, Needles. Name of a legendary man who was a symbol of sexuality.

Nānaku. Pond, Punalu'u, Hawai'i. Large spring-fed pond adjoining the east end of Punalu'u Beach. *Lit.*, bulrushes. The pond was formerly filled with bulrushes.

Nānākuli. Beach park (39.6 acres), Nānākuli, O'ahu. Calcareous sand beach 500 feet long and 125 feet wide between two limestone points fronting the beach park. Also known as Zablan Beach. *Lit.*, to look at the knee.

Nānākuli Beach. Dive site, Nānākuli, O'ahu. Off Nānākuli Beach Park.

Nānākuli Sand Dunes. Surf site, Kahe, O'ahu.

Nānākuli Tracks. Surf site, Kahe, O'ahu. Also known as Tracks.

Nānāwale. Park (78 acres), Nānāwale, Hawai'i. The park is situated on a littoral cone approximately 150 feet high that was formed when a lava flow from Kīlauea entered the sea here in May 1840. The flow destroyed the coastal village of Nānāwale and created the littoral cone of cinder, or "sand," during the explosive interaction of the molten lava and the cold water of the ocean. A large grove of ironwood trees covers the littoral cone, which is also known as Pu'u One, or Sand Hill. *Lit.*, just look around.

Nāniuokāne. Rocks, Hāna, Maui. Small rock islands in Hāna Bay. *Lit.*, the coconuts of Kāne.

Nanuku. Cove, Mauna Lani, Hawai'i. Shallow, sandy cove at Mauna Lani Beach that is surrounded by small lava islands.

Nāoneala'a. Beach, Kāne'ohe Bay, O'ahu. Beach at Kāne'ohe Beach Park. Where High Chief La'amaikahiki landed after a voyage from Tahiti in the 1200s and built three *heiau. Lit.*, the sands of La'a.

Nāpaia. Fishing site, Hawai'i Kai, O'ahu. Rocky shore between the mouth of Kalama Stream and the breakwater. *Lit.*, the walls.

Nā Pali. Coast state park (6,500 acres), Nā Pali, Kaua'i. Some 15 miles of isolated shore between Kē'ē and Polihale Beaches that includes sea cliffs and coastal valleys. Five significant sand beaches are located within the park at Hanakāpīʻai, Kalalau, Honopū, Nuʻalolo Kai, and Miloliʻi. The first two are accessible from the Kalalau Trail, and the remaining three are accessible only from the ocean. *Lit.*, the cliffs.

Nāpili. Bay, beach, surf site, Nāpili, Maui. Wide calcareous sand beach between two rocky points. A small rock island is off the center of the beach. The surf site is off the north point of the bay. *Lit.*, the joinings or the *pili* grass.

Nāpoʻopoʻo. 1. Beach park (6 acres), surf site, Nāpoʻopoʻo, Hawaiʻi. Pebble and boulder beach at the base of Hikiau Heiau. The surf site is a shorebreak on the shallow sandbar that fronts the rocky beach. The foreshore and backshore of the beach were covered with boulders during Hurricane ʻIniki in 1992. 2. Landing, Nāpoʻopoʻo, Hawaiʻi. One of many former landings around the Big Island for interisland steamers. The concrete ruin is used to launch and land kayaks and other small watercraft. It is a popular swimming site among neighborhood residents. Also known as Kīloa, Nāpoʻopoʻo Wharf. 3. Light, Kaʻawaloa, Hawaiʻi. Nāpoʻopoʻo Light was established in 1908 at Kaʻawaloa on the north side of Kealakekua Bay, but apparently named for Nāpoʻopoʻo Landing on the south side of the bay. The 22-foot light tower was built in 1922. 4. Wharf, Nāpoʻopoʻo, Hawaiʻi. Same as Nāpoʻopoʻo Landing. *Lit.*, the holes.

Nā Puʻu a Pele. Littoral cones, Keawaiki, Hawaiʻi. The two highest of a group of littoral cones at the bottom of Road to the Sea, an access road to the ocean. According to legend, these two hills were once chiefs of Kahuku who were chased and overrun by Pele, the goddess of the volcano, just inland of Keawaiki. Also known as Two Mountains. *Lit.*, the hills of Pele.

Naska. Beach, Kahului, Maui. Name for Kanahā Beach Park that originated during World War II. As part of the war effort, the U.S. Navy took over the airport area, including the park, and in March 1943 established Naval Air Station Kahului, or NASKA. The acronym became another name for the beach.

Natatorium. 1. Swimming pool, Waikīkī, Oʻahu. Same as the War Memorial Natatorium. 2. Surf site, Waikīkī, Oʻahu. On the reef off the War Memorial Natatorium. Also known as Nats.

Nats. Surf site, Waikīkī, Oʻahu. An abbreviated name for Natatorium.

Natural Energy Lab of Hawaiʻi. Research site, Keāhole, Hawaiʻi. Research facilities established at Keāhole Point in 1974 that use cold, deep ocean water for environmentally suitable development, including agriculture, marine biotechnology, freshwater generation, industrial cooling/air conditioning, and electrical power generation.

Naue. Coastal plain, Hāʻena, Kauaʻi. Shore area around Camp Naue that was famous for its large grove of *hala*, or pandanus trees. The grove is mentioned in many chants and songs. *Lit.*, to move.

Naupaka. Beach, Mākena, Maui. Dark detrital sand beach on the north side of Puʻu Ōlaʻi. A small patch of *naupaka* once grew at the south end of the beach, so neighborhood fishermen called the beach Naupaka. Also known as Oneuli Beach, Onouli Beach.

Navy. Bay, North Kohala, Hawaiʻi. Small circular bay at ʻAkoʻakoʻa Point. "Navy" is a popular mispronunciation of Neue, the Hawaiian name of the bay. Also known as Neue Bay.

Nawawa. Bay, beach, landing, Kainaliu, Hawaiʻi. On the south side of Puʻu Ohau. Small bay with a pocket of black sand that was formerly used as a canoe landing.

Nāwiliwili. Bay, harbor, light, offshore mooring, park, small boat harbor, Nāwiliwili, Kauaʻi. Nāwiliwili Harbor is the principal port on Kauaʻi, and one of two deep-draft harbors on the island. When it was completed on July 22, 1930, the *Hualālai*, an interisland steamer, was the first vessel in the harbor. Nāwiliwili Light was established in 1897 at Ninini Point and automated in 1953. The 86-foot light tower was built in 1933, approximately 30 feet above sea level. The offshore mooring in the bay is near the small boat harbor. Nāwiliwili Park is on the shore at the north end of the harbor, where it is fronted by a concrete seawall. Facilities in the small boat harbor include eighty-two berths, five multihull moorings, three piers, a two-lane ramp, a vessel washdown area, a loading dock, and a fish hoist. *Lit.*, the *wiliwili* trees.

N Buoy. Fish aggregating device, Hālawa, Molokaʻi. Buoy anchored at approximately 236 fathoms. Landmarks: Lamaloa Head, Kalaupapa Peninsula Light.

Needles. Dive site, sea stacks, west coast, Lānaʻi. Sea stacks are vertical rocks that are left standing alone when the ocean erodes the rocks that once connected them to the shore. The Needles are a cluster of five sea stacks and are one of the best examples of sea stacks in Hawaiʻi. They are a well-known landmark to boaters. The dive site is off the sea stacks. Also known as Nānāhoa, Three Stone.

Neill's. Beach, surf site, ʻŌhikilolo, Oʻahu. Caroline and Alika Neill lived on the beach here with their family for many years. The surf site is offshore of the beach. Also known as Waikomo.

Nēnēleʻa. Shore, Kaʻena, Oʻahu. Calcareous sand dunes and storm beach at Kaʻena Point facing Pōhaku o Kauaʻi, or the "Stone of

Kauaʻi." *Lit.*, playful *nēnē.* The name suggests that seabirds resembling the Hawaiian goose, the *nēnē,* were common in ancient times.

Neneʻu. Beach, Waiʻanae, Oʻahu. Calcareous sand beach fronting Pōkaʻī Bay Beach Park.

Neue. Bay, North Kohala, Hawaiʻi. Small circular bay at ʻĀkoʻakoʻa Point. Also known as Navy Bay.

Nīʻaupala. Fishpond, Hālawa, Molokaʻi. *Lit.*, yellow coconut leaf midrib.

Niʻihau. 1. Niʻihau is the seventh largest (69.5 square miles) of the eight major Hawaiian Islands and with Kauaʻi is one of two islands in Kauaʻi County. It has a population of 160, the majority of whom are of Hawaiian ancestry. The highest mountain on the island is Paniʻau with an elevation of 1,281 feet, and the *pupu Niʻihau,* or Niʻihau shell, is the emblem of the island. Niʻihau's nickname is the Hawaiian Island. The island is privately owned and operated by the Robinson family as a sheep and cattle ranch. Residents there produce charcoal for commercial sale, and Niʻihau Ranch runs a small hunting business, flying hunters to the island by helicopter to shoot trophy sheep and boars. Residents also collect the prized Niʻihau shells and string them into leis for commercial sale. Also known as the Forbidden Island. 2. Dive site, north shore, Niʻihau. Dive tour operators from Kauaʻi dive at several sites that they call "Niʻihau" between the north point of the island and Lehua Island.

Nimitz. Beach, cove, Kalaeloa, Oʻahu. Long calcareous sand beach fronting the central and western shore of the Kalaeloa Community Development District. After Barbers Point Naval Air Station was commissioned on April 15, 1945, the beach along the rocky shore was named for Fleet Admiral Chester W. Nimitz (1885–1966), commander-in-chief of the Pacific Forces during World War II. Nimitz Cove is the beach fronting Coast Guard Air Station Barbers Point at the west end of the district.

Nimitz Lefts. Surf site, Kalaeloa, Oʻahu. Off the west end of Nimitz Beach. Primarily a left-breaking wave.

Ninini. Beach, surf site, Nāwiliwili, Kauaʻi. Two pockets of calcareous sand at Ninini Point, the north point of Nāwiliwili Harbor. The surf site is a shorebreak on the larger beach and primarily for bodysurfing and bodyboarding. Also known as Running Waters Beach. *Lit.*, pour. Ninini was the name of a *heiau,* or shrine, that stood near the lighthouse at the point.

Nīnole. Beach, cove, Punaluʻu, Hawaiʻi. Nīnole Cove is a small beach park seaward of the Seamountain Golf Course. The rocky shore has several small inlets, some of which have small pockets of black sand, and a spring-fed pond, Pūhau. On April 2, 1868, an extremely violent earthquake in Ka'ū generated a local tsunami that destroyed the coastal villages of Punalu'u, Nīnole, Kāwā, and Honu'apo. At Nīnole a man named Holoua and his wife escaped from their home and ran for higher ground, but as they ran Holoua remembered that he had money in the house. He turned and ran back to get it. As he entered his house, a wave of the tsunami struck, first carrying the house a short distance inland and then out to sea as it receded. Holoua ripped a plank from the collapsing structure, jumped into the ocean with it, and surfed the next incoming wave to shore and safety, the only person to have ever surfed a tsunami wave. The villagers on the hillside witnessed his ride, and it was reported in the April 29, 1868, edition of the *Hawaiian Gazette. Lit.,* bending.

Niu. Channel, peninsula, Niu, O'ahu. A natural, unmarked channel cuts through the reef on the east side of Niu Peninsula and leads to an anchorage off the beachfront homes on the peninsula. The peninsula was created by filling in a former fishpond. *Lit.,* coconut.

Niumalu. 1. Beach, Kailua, Hawai'i. Small pocket of calcareous sand on the north side of Hulihe'e Palace. Also known as Kanuha Beach. 2. Beach park, ramp, Nāwiliwili, Kaua'i. Small beach park fronted by mudflats at the mouth of Hule'ia Stream. The ramp is used only for small, shallow-draft boats. The community of Niumalu is best known as the home of Paul Puhiula Kalakua Kanoa (1802–1885), governor of Kaua'i from 1847 to 1877. Kanoa planted an Indian Banyan tree on the two-acre parcel where he lived, a tree that is on Kaua'i County's list of exceptional and therefore protected trees. *Lit.,* shaded coconut trees.

Niu'ō'ū. Beach, South Kona, Hawai'i. Storm beach of calcareous sand, lava fragments, olivines, and coral rubble on a low section of *pāhoehoe* between Kaupō and Manukā. A large stand of *kiawe* or mesquite trees lines the backshore, the only trees on the otherwise barren coast. Niu'ō'ū was the site of a famous coconut grove, the last surviving trees of which died in the early 1950s. *Lit.,* coconut perch.

NL Buoy. Fish aggregating device, Nu'u, Maui. Buoy anchored at approximately 664 fathoms. Landmarks: Apole Point (Nu'u Landing), Nakaohu Point, Puhilele Point.

No Can Tell. Surf site, Waimānalo, O'ahu. On the reef opposite Waimānalo Stream, approximately one-half mile offshore. During the late 1950s, several surfers from Lanikai were spearfishing from a boat in Waimānalo when they saw some small, ridable waves on the reef near them. They realized that the site was so far offshore that no one could tell how good it was until they actually got out there, so they named it "No Can Tell," giving the name a humorous touch of pidgin English.

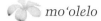 *mo'olelo*

The nearest I can place the date of discovery is the early 1970s—probably 1973 or 1974. Kenny Olds, Collin Perry, and I were skindiving some coral heads just inside the reef there. The water was not very clear, and, as usual, there were no lobsters to be found. I started swimming towards the reef when I saw some *uhu* in the area, but they were wild, and I soon gave up the chase. A non-productive day was at hand. While I was snorkeling on the inside corner of the reef, I noticed that some nicely shaped waves were breaking on the outside corner of the reef. I said "Laters" to the diving, got Kenny and Collin, and the three of us spent the rest of our "dive" bodysurfing on some really nice, uncrowded waves.

We were all part of a fairly close-knit group of individuals that hung around together, the Lanikai Canoe Club gang, and as time passed, we would occasionally go out to the reef with our gang and surf or bodysurf these waves. We used my old wooden flat-bottom boat and later on my Boston Whaler to get there. However, the surf spot was so far offshore, we never could tell how good the waves were until we actually got there. One day a group of us were partying in Kenny's yard on the beach, and we were looking at the spot. We were commenting that one could never tell whether the waves were good or not, and someone coined the name **"No Can Tell."** But who coined the name, no one can really remember. In those days we partied a lot! It was probably Kenny or me.

 *Douglas Hooper, October 1, 2000*

Nohili. Barking sands, point, point light, Mānā, Kaua'i. The famous Barking Sands of Kaua'i are the high sand dunes at Nohili Point. Hawaiians called these sites *keonekani*, or "the sounding sands," and this site is often referred to as Keonekani o Nohili in chants and songs. Nohili Point Light is atop a pole approximately 100 feet above sea level on the dunes at the west end of the Pacific Missile Range Facility. *Lit.*, tedious, slow.

No Mans. Surf site, Diamond Head, O'ahu. Same as No Mans Land.

No Mans Land. 1. Surf site, Kaunala, O'ahu. Between Sunset Point and Velzyland. Also known as Freddieland. 2. Surf site, Diamond Head, O'ahu. On the west side of the Diamond Head Lighthouse between Lighthouse and Sleepy Hollows. This site breaks only during big south swells and is rarely surfed. Also known as No Mans. 3. Surf site, Waikīkī, Oʻahu. Off the Outrigger Canoe Club between Ricebowl and Old Mans. This site only breaks on certain big swells and is in "no-man's-land" on the seaward side of an emergent reef.

Nōmilu. Crater, fishpond, Nōmilu, Kauaʻi. One of the most unusual fishponds in Hawaiʻi. The fishpond is a 20-acre saltwater lake in the crater of Nōmilu Cone, a volcanic cinder cone. Water in the lake is fed by springs, but its level rises and falls with the tides. In the early 1900s, a tunnel was cut through a crater wall to connect the lake to the ocean and improve its circulation. Nōmilu Fishpond is privately owned by the Pālama family of Kauaʻi. Perhaps lit., whirlpool, as of water draining.

No Name. Surf site, Waikīkī, Oʻahu. Off the War Memorial Natatorium. Deepwater site between Natatoriums and Castles that only breaks during big south swells and therefore has "no name." Also known as Inside Castles, No Place.

No Name Bay. Dive site, south coast, Lānaʻi. Same as No Name Paradise.

No Name Paradise. Dive site, south coast, Lānaʻi. East of Kaunolū. Also known as No Name Bay.

Nonopapa. Beach, landing, surf site, southwest coast, Niʻihau. Calcareous sand beach approximately 2 miles long between Nonopapa and Makahūʻena Points. The backshore consists of dunes covered with *pōhinahina*, or beach vitex. The former landing for interisland steamers is at Nonopapa Point, the site of a warehouse, several corrals, and a grove of coconut trees. The surf site is also at the point, and during especially high surf a second-reef site forms approximately a mile offshore. *Lit.*, invalid.

No Place. 1. Surf site, Sand Island, Oʻahu. Off the tower at Sand Island State Park. Named in the early 1960s by surfers from Waikīkī who, when asked by other surfers where they were going surfing, answered "no place." 2. Surf site, Waikīkī, Oʻahu. Off the War Memorial Natatorium. Deepwater site between Natatorium and Castles that only breaks occasionally during big south swells. The site is not associated with any channel, reef, or landmark and therefore is "no place." Also known as Inside Castles, No Name.

North. 1. Bay, Kāneʻohe, Oʻahu. Northernmost section of Kāneʻohe Bay. 2. Beach, Kāʻanapali, Maui. Northernmost section of Kāʻanapali Beach between Black Rock and Kahekili Beach Park. 3. Beach, surf site, Mōkapu, Oʻahu. Calcareous sand beach on the north end of Mōkapu Peninsula between Ulupaʻu Crater and the runway. Also known as Heleloa. 4. Lagoon, Kāneʻohe, Oʻahu. One of several man-made lagoons at Coconut Island that were created by Christian Holmes, who owned the island in the 1930s. It is used primarily for recreational swimming. 5. Shore, Moloka'i. Coast of Moloka'i from Hālawa to Kalaupapa. 6. Shore, O'ahu. Coast of O'ahu from Kahuku Point to Ka'ena Point. These boundaries are used by the North Shore Neighborhood Board to define their area of responsibility. For most surfers, the "North Shore" is the 10 miles of shore from Kahuku Point to Kaiaka Bay that includes eight world-class surf sites: Velzyland, Sunset, Rocky Point, Pipeline, Waimea, Chun's Reef, Laniakea, and Haleiwa. The remainder of the coast from Kaiaka Bay to Ka'ena Point is called Mokulē'ia.

North Beach. Surf site, Mōkapu, O'ahu. At the edge of the wide sandbar that fronts North Beach.

Northern Lights. Dive site, Kainaliu, Hawai'i. One of the Red Hill dive sites.

Northwestern Hawaiian Islands. The small islands, associated reefs, and banks northwest of the eight Main Hawaiian Islands that comprise the rest of the Hawaiian Archipelago. They include Nīhoa, Necker Island, French Frigate Shoals, Gardner Pinnacles, Maro Reef, Laysan Island, Lisianski Island, Pearl and Hermes Atoll, Midway Atoll, and Kure Atoll.

Nu'alolo Kai. Beach, dive site, snorkeling site, Nā Pali, Kaua'i. One of five beaches within Nā Pali Coast State Park. Nu'alolo Kai is a narrow coastal flat at the base of high sea cliffs. Nu'alolo Valley is above the cliffs. A narrow calcareous sand beach lies along the eastern half of the coastal flat in the lee of Alapi'i Point, where it is fronted by an extensive reef, one of the best examples of an actively growing, pristine fringing reef in Hawai'i. Commercial tour boat companies who bring in groups of snorkelers and scuba divers anchor in a deep channel on the western edge of the reef. The snorkeling and dive sites are in the channel. *Lit.*, seaward Nu'alolo.

Nukoli'i. Beach park, Kaua'i. Narrow calcareous sand beach fronted by a rocky shelf. The beach park was completed in 1986 on the site of the former Nukoli'i Dairy.

Nukumoi. Point, Po'ipū, Kaua'i. Sandy point at the west end of Po'ipū Beach Park that is an example of a tombolo—a sandbar that joins two islands. Two other tombolos are found on Kaua'i, one at Crater Hill that joins the base of the hill to Makapili Island and one at Kīpū Kai that joins Kīpū Kai Beach to Mōlehu Point.

Number Fours. Surf site, windsurf site, Waikīkī, O'ahu. The fourth surf site from east to west on the reef that begins off the Sheraton Waikīkī Hotel and ends at the Kaiser Channel. The three surf sites that precede it are Populars, Paradise, and

Number Threes. Windsurfers use the site during *kona* or southerly winds. Also known as Fours.

Number Threes. Surf site, Waikīkī, Oʻahu. Number Threes is the third surf site from east to west on the reef that begins off the Sheraton Waikīkī Hotel and ends at the Kaiser Channel. The two surf sites that precede it are Populars and Paradise. During the late 1950s, young surfers from the Outrigger Canoe Club "discovered" the site and named it Number Threes. The club was then in the center of Waikīkī Beach at the site of the Outrigger Waikīkī Hotel. Also known as Threes.

Number Twos. Surf site, Waikīkī, Oʻahu. The second surf site from east to west on the reef that begins off the Sheraton Waikīkī Hotel and ends at the Kaiser Channel. The surf site that precedes it is Populars. Also known as Paradise, Twos.

Nurses. Beach, Lumahaʻi, Kauaʻi. East end of Lumahaʻi Beach. Part of the 1958 movie *South Pacific,* starring Rossano Brazzi and Mitzi Gaynor, was filmed here, and Lumahaʻi Beach became Nurses Beach. In this lavish Hollywood version of Rodgers and Hammerstein's classic musical, Nurses Beach was where Nurse Nellie Forbush sang her famous song, "I'm Going to Wash That Man Right Out of My Hair."

Nuʻu. Bay, beach, dive site, landing, Nuʻu, Maui. Detrital sand beach on the shore of Nuʻu Bay that is the largest beach in the district of Kaupō. The ruins of the landing are on the point on the east side of the bay. The landing was a shipping point for cattle from Kaupō Ranch. The dive site is off the landing. *Lit.,* height.

Nuʻupia. Fishpond, Mōkapu, Oʻahu. *Lit.,* arrowroot heap.

Oʻahu. Oʻahu is the third largest (597.1 square miles) of the eight major Hawaiian islands. It has a population of 876,156 (U.S. Census figures for 2000 indicate that Oʻahu's population makes up 72.3 percent of the state's total of 1,211,537 residents). The highest mountain on the island is Kaʻala with an elevation of 4,003 feet, and the *pua ʻilima (Sida fallax)* is the emblem of the island. Oʻahu's nickname is the Gathering Place. The island of Oʻahu is also known as the County of Honolulu.

Oasis Reef. Dive site, Nōmilu, Kauaʻi. Lone pinnacle surrounded by sand that rises from 35 feet to approximately 5 feet below the surface of the ocean. The pinnacle is an "oasis" for thousands of reef fish. Also known as Lanipūʻao Rock, Pālama Buoy.

ʻOawapalua. Bay, beach, southwest shore, Kahoʻolawe. Two parallel gulches open onto a sand beach on the shore of the bay. *Lit.,* double gulch.

Obake. 1. Bay, east shore, Kahoʻolawe. Local Japanese commercial fishermen formerly fished here for *akule* and *ʻōpelu,* pelagic schooling fish that frequent large bays and harbors. This bay is subject to abrupt changes in ocean and weather conditions. High surf, powerful currents, and strong winds seem to come out of nowhere, creating unexpected hazards for boats in the bay. The fishermen called the bay Obake (Japanese for "ghost") for the mysterious appearance of these dangerous conditions. Also known as Kanapou Bay. 2. Point, Māʻili, Oʻahu. Local Japanese shore fishermen believed the point was haunted. Also known as Māʻili Point. *Lit.,* ghost (Japanese).

O Buoy. Fish aggregating device, Kalaupapa, Molokaʻi. Buoy anchored at approximately 600 fathoms. Landmarks: Kalaupapa Peninsula Light, ʻĪlio Point.

Oceanarium. Dive site, Hāʻena, Kauaʻi. Tall pinnacles and sheer drop-offs to 140 feet, with so many varieties of fish that it is like an ocean aquarium, or oceanarium.

Oceanic Institute. Research site (50 acres), Waimānalo, Oʻahu. Founded in 1960 on the grounds of Sea Life Park by Taylor "Tap" Prior. The nonprofit institute specializes in using advanced technology to increase aquaculture production in Hawaiʻi as part of the state's economic diversification.

Ocean View Pavilion. Recreation site, Kalaupapa, Molokaʻi. Homesite at Kalaemilo Point of the man who ran the Kalaupapa Laundry until April 1, 1946, when a tsunami washed his house out to sea. In 1952 the Kalaupapa Lions built a community picnic pavilion here.

Oea. Beach, Kapuʻa, Hawaiʻi. Small beach of calcareous sand, lava fragments, olivine, and coral rubble at the head of a small inlet. Habitation ruins are *mauka* of the inlet. The name of a star.

Off the Wall. 1. Surf site, Māʻalaea, Maui. Off the end of the east breakwater and adjacent to the channel at Māʻalaea Small Boat Harbor. Off the Wall breaks directly off the breakwater, or the "wall." 2. Surf site, Sunset Beach, Oʻahu. Off a high, vertical concrete retaining wall fronting a beachfront home.

ʻŌhaiʻula. Beach, South Kohala, Hawaiʻi. Small calcareous sand beach in Spencer Beach Park. *Lit.,* red *ʻōhai* shrub.

ʻOheʻo. Stream, Kīpahulu, Maui. Stream containing seven waterfall plunge pools that meets the ocean in Seven Pools Park. The park is named after the pools.

ʻOhepuʻupuʻu. Trail, Kapuʻa, Hawaiʻi. Trail that connected the coastal village of Kapuʻa to Māmalahoa Highway.

ʻŌhikilolo. Beach, ʻŌhikilolo, Oʻahu. Calcareous sand beach between Keaʻau Beach Park and Mākua Valley that borders the land division of ʻŌhikilolo. Also known as Barking Sands. *Lit.,* sand crab.

ʻŌhūkai Road. Windsurf site, Kīhei, Maui. Off the public right-of-way on ʻŌhūkai Road. *Lit.,* ocean swell (specifically, a wave that does not break).

ʻŌhumu. Fishing site, Waipiʻo, Maui. At the base of the sea cliffs at the north end of Waipiʻo Bay. *Lit.,* complain.

O-jizo. Statues, Hawaiʻi Kai, Mokulēʻia, Oʻahu. Same as Jizo. O-jizo, O-jizosama, and O-jizosan are honorific variations of Jizo.

ʻŌkala. Island (2.15 acres, 400 feet high), Waikolu, Molokaʻi. Part of the Hawaiʻi State Seabird Sanctuary. One of two sea stacks on the east side of Kalaupapa Peninsula. *Lit.,* bristling.

Okoe. Beach, Kapuʻa, Hawaiʻi. Detrital sand beach on the south side of Hanamalo Point. Habitation ruins include a deep well with a stone-lined shaft and several stepping-stone trails. The name of a legendary woman.

Old Airport. Beach, dive site, park, surf site, Kailua, Hawai'i. An abbreviation of Old Kona Airport State Recreation Area. The dive site is off the north end of the beach and is also known as Pāwai. The surf site is off the center of the park.

Old Kona Airport. Marine life conservation district (217 acres), state recreation area (103.7 acres), Kailua, Hawai'i. The Kona Airport, constructed in the 1940s at the edge of Kailua town and closed in 1970, was converted into a state park. Although its official name is the Old Kona Airport State Recreation Area, most Kona residents call it Old Airport. The park is fronted by a long, wide calcareous sand beach behind a wide rocky shelf. The marine life conservation district off the park was established in 1992. A surf site off the center of the beach is called Old Airport. Pāwai Bay at the north end of the beach is a snorkeling and nearshore scuba site.

Old Lady's. Surf site, Pāpalaua, Maui. First surf site at the west end of Lahaina Pali, or Pali. Waves here are gentle enough for even an "old lady" to ride.

Old Lady's Cave. Cave, Kalaupapa, Moloka'i. Sea cave on the north side of the peninsula. The name is the translation of the cave's Hawaiian name. Also known as Anakaluahine.

Old Man's. Surf site, Waikīkī, O'ahu. Off the Kaimana Channel. This site was first surfed regularly by Albert "Oscar" Teller (1909–1995). He came to Hawai'i in 1932 and learned to surf in Waikīkī. A bodybuilder with an excellent physique, the beachboys immediately named him "Oscar" after the statuette given out for the Academy Awards in Hollywood, and that was the name he used for the rest of his life. In 1958, Teller moved into a cottage behind the Sans Souci condominium and started surfing Old Man's. During the early 1960s, Ralph Sallee and Floyd Bendickson, two younger friends who surfed with him, began calling the site Old Man's and the name stuck. Teller surfed here regularly until 1984, when he finally stopped surfing at the age of 75. His ashes were scattered at Old Man's in 1995.

mo'olelo

In 1959, my wife Harriett and I decided to move to Hawai'i, so we left our two children with a babysitter and came to Honolulu to look for a house. When we didn't have any luck finding something we liked, Harriett left early to get back to the kids, and I spent my last day in Waikīkī. As I walked on the beach in front of the Royal, Charlie Amalu came up to me and asked if I'd like to help him paddle an outrigger canoe. I'd never been in one before, so I said yes. Charlie was one of the old-time beachboys, and he was helping to show some condominium units in the

Sans Souci, which had just been built. He had a couple he wanted to take there by canoe, and he needed an extra paddler. We paddled to the former pier at Sans Souci Beach, and I walked through the building with them. Until then we hadn't thought about living in a condo, but when I saw the view and the surf off-shore, I told Charlie I would buy two units. He couldn't believe it.

In 1960, Harriett, my two sons, Bob and Phil, and I started surfing the spots off the Sans Souci and soon met Floyd Bendickson, who lived nearby in the Tropic Seas. Floyd and I became surfing buddies, and we often surfed Tongg's and **Old Man's,** although it wasn't named yet. At that time, there was a surfer named Oscar Teller who was always out there, and he would sit for hours, often from morning till night, waiting for the best waves. Sometimes he carried a plastic bag of bananas with him, so he wouldn't have to come in for lunch. Oscar was a wonderful guy, a quiet, calm, and gentle person, and he rode a long hollow board. He was older than us, so Floyd referred to him as the "old man," and if we were out at Tongg's and we'd see Oscar, Floyd would always say, "That's the old man's surf." Naturally, we started calling the spot Old Man's, but that was pretty much just our name until 1964. That's when the Outrigger Canoe Club moved from its old location on Waikīkī Beach to its present one. When the Outrigger surfers heard us calling the spot Old Man's, they picked up the name and started using it themselves, and that's when the name Old Man's was really established.

 Ralph Sallee, November 4, 2000

Old Sugar Mill. Beach, Kualoa, Oʻahu. Between 1860 and 1880 five sugar plantations were started in the windward district of Koʻolaupoko, but all were unprofitable and soon abandoned. The only evidence of their existence is the collapsing ruin of the Kualoa Plantation sugar mill, commonly known as the Old Sugar Mill, alongside Kamehameha Highway. It closed in 1871.

Olowalu. Dive site, landing, snorkeling site, surf site, Olowalu, Maui. Olowalu Plantation was a sugar plantation started in 1876 by Philip Milton and Goodale Armstrong. Olowalu Landing supported the plantation, and its ruins are on Olowalu Point. The dive site is off the landing. The primary snorkeling site is on the shallow reef south of Olowalu Point bordering Honoapiʻilani Highway. The surf site west of the landing is called Olowalu Point, and the surf site on the west side of Olowalu along Honoapiʻilani Highway is called Olowalu. *Lit.,* many hills.

Olympic Point. Surf site, Māʻili, Oʻahu. Big-wave site at the east end of Māʻili Point that was first surfed and named in the winter of 1979 by Brian Keaulana and James "Bird" Mahelona. Like the Olympics, which take place only every four years, the conditions that make it possible to surf here also occur infrequently. Also known as Monuments.

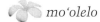 *mo'olelo*

Bird Mahelona and I first surfed **Olympic Point** in the winter of 1979. We'd always watched it, but it was never ridable until one day that winter. The conditions were perfect—the wind, the tide, the swell direction, and the wave heights. The waves have to be at least 20 feet or bigger for it to work. We didn't have any guns of our own, so we borrowed two from Rell Sun—a 9'0" and a 9'6". We jumped in between sets near the monument and caught the backwash out. When the swell is working out there, you're surfing almost parallel to Farrington Highway, so when we were riding, we were looking right into the cars going by. People driving by who were looking at us couldn't believe it, and they started stopping their cars on the highway to watch. Pretty soon there was a major traffic jam, so the police came, the fire department came, and then they finally called my dad to come down and get us out of the water. But by the time he got there, I had broken my leash, so we were already onshore. We named it Olympic Point because it rarely breaks good, kind of like the Olympics—maybe once every four years. All the conditions have to be perfect, and that doesn't happen very often.

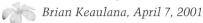 *Brian Keaulana, April 7, 2001*

Oneali'i. Beach park, Kaunakakai, Moloka'i. Narrow calcareous sand beach bordering a shallow reef flat. The park site was purchased from Moloka'i Ranch, Ltd., in 1959 and developed as a county beach park. It was named after a precontact fishpond on the shore near the park. *Lit.*, royal sands.

Oneawa. Beach, Kailua, O'ahu. North end of Kailua Beach. Oneawa was a famous fishery off the beach for *awa*, or milkfish, and *'ō'io*, or bonefish. *Awa* are surface feeders that eat seaweed, while *'ō'io* are bottom feeders that forage in calcareous sand, especially for crabs. Both fish are eaten raw or used to make fish cakes. *Lit.*, milkfish sand.

One Hump. Island, Kailua, O'ahu. An alternate name for the smaller of the two Mokulua Islands. From a distance the outline of the island's summit resembles the back of a single-humped camel.

100-Foot Hole. Dive site, Waikīkī, O'ahu. Off the Kaimana Channel in 80 feet of water, although it has always been called the 100-Foot Hole. The "hole" is actually a massive coral head with an overhang that divers can swim under. Half of the overhang was destroyed during Hurricane 'Iniki in 1992.

Onekahakaha. Beach park, Keaukaha, Hawai'i. Large, calcareous sand-bottomed cove that is protected from the open ocean by a breakwater. This small sheltered beach is one of the most popular family beaches on the Hilo side of the island. *Lit.,* drawing [pictures] sand.

Oneloa. 1. Beach, surf site, windsurf site, Kapalua, Maui. Wide, straight calcareous sand beach between Hāwea and Makāluapuna Points. The surfing and windsurf sites are off the beach. Also known as Ironwood Beach. 2. Beach, Mākena, Maui. Calcareous sand beach 3,300 feet long at Mākena State Park. Also known as Big Beach, Long Sands, and Mākena Beach. *Lit.,* long [stretch of] sand.

One'ula. Beach park (30 acres), 'Ewa Beach, O'ahu. Narrow calcareous sand beach at the west end of Pāpipi Road. *Lit.,* red sand.

Oneuli. Beach, dive site, Mākena, Maui. Dark detrital sand beach on the north side of Pu'u Ōla'i in Mākena. The dive site is off the beach. Also known as Naupaka Beach, Onouli Beach. *Lit.,* dark sand.

'Ōnini. Beach, channel, reef, Lā'ie, O'ahu. North section of Laniloa Beach adjacent to Lā'ie Point. The smaller of two sand pockets on Laniloa Beach that are good for swimming. Also known as Clissold Beach. *Lit.,* slight breeze.

Ono Ledge. Fishing site, North Shore, O'ahu. Ledge that follows the 40-fathom (240-foot) contour line between Kahuku and Ka'ena Points. Fishing boats troll the ledge, especially for *ono,* or wahoo. *Ono,* pelagic fish with an average weight of about 40 pounds, feed on small fish, shrimp, and squid and are excellent eating. Also known as The Ledge.

Onomea. One of the few navigable bays on the precipitous Hāmākua Coast and the site of the Hawaiian Tropical Botanical Garden. In 1995 an agreement between the state, the owner of the botanical garden, and the community established public access to the bay over an old government road leading through the garden to the mouth of Onomea Stream.

 mo'olelo

I was born in Onomea on May 23, 1894, about 2 miles above the bay. My father was the section boss for Onomea Sugar Company. He came to Hawai'i in 1888 and was one of the many Scots who worked in the sugar plantations on the Hāmākua Coast. There were so many of them that for years it was known as "the Scottish coast of Hawai'i." In 1889, my father sent some money back for his girlfriend, my mother, and she came to Hawai'i with her brother, William. They were married at George Chalmer's home.

Hanawī was the flat area in **Onomea Bay,** and the old landing was on the Pepe'ekeo end of it. The steamers tied up offshore and the passengers and cargo came in on lighters. When the boats pulled up to the rocks, everyone had to have good timing to throw the cargo onshore and for the passengers to jump. The Hawaiians who rowed the boats were tough, and there was a friendly competitiveness among them in all phases of their work. There were also many Hawaiians living at Hanawī. They were independent farmers who grew taro and bananas on their *kuleana's*.

A stage ran back and forth to Hilo, and freight along the Hāmākua Coast was hauled on wagons with at least a four-horse team. At that time many of the streams had covered bridges. The walls were made of 1-by-12-inch boards, and they had corrugated iron roofs. The walls and roofs were designed to protect the bridges from rain and to increase the longevity of the big beams and prevent them from rotting.

 John Moir, April 19, 1984

Onomea Arch. Fishing site, Onomea, Hawai'i. Bay, Onomea, Hawai'i. North point of Onomea Bay where a former sea arch collapsed on May 24, 1956, when it cracked in the center, buckled upward, and fell.

Onouli. Beach, Mākena, Maui. Dark detrital sand beach on the north side of Pu'u Ōla'i in Mākena. Onouli is a regional pronunciation of Oneuli (*lit.*, dark sand). Also known as Naupaka Beach, Oneuli Beach.

Oofie's. Island, Ke'ehi, O'ahu. Outermost of several small islands in Ke'ehi Lagoon on the western side of Kalihi Channel and at the east end of the Reef Runway. Ke'ehi boat owner Eric Schladermundt used the island to exercise his live-aboard black Labrador retriever, Oofie (pronounced like "goofy" without a *g*), beginning in 1994 when she was six weeks old. As a live-aboard dog, she was trained not to get off the boat, so she had to be picked up and carried off the boat to go ashore. "Oof" is the sound she made whenever she was picked up.

O'ohope. Fishpond, He'eia, O'ahu. *Lit.*, late maturity.

'Ō'ō'ia. Fishpond, Kaunakakai, Moloka'i. *Lit.*, pierced.

'Ō'ōmanō. Point, Kekaha, Kaua'i. Also known as Davidson's Point. *Lit.*, shark spear.

Ōpae'ula. Pond (12 acres), Makalawena, North Kona, Hawai'i. Important wetland for native and migratory waterbirds behind the dunes of Makalawena Beach. Also known as Kapo'ikai

Pond. *Lit.*, red shrimp. Fishermen here and elsewhere in Kona caught *'ōpae'ula* and mixed them with their chum when netting *'ōpelu,* or mackerel scad.

'Opihi. Island, Maku'u, Hawai'i. Small rock island off Maku'u. Also known as Moku'opihi. *Lit.,* limpet.

'Opihi Road. Fishing site, Lā'au, Moloka'i. Low sea cliffs between Kapukuwahine and Kahalepōhaku Beaches where *'opihi* were gathered. Also known as Man-on-the-Rock, Hale 'Opihi.

Orr's Beach. Puna, Hawai'i. Black sand beach that formed at Kahuwai in 1960 at the end of the Kapoho eruption. This eruption destroyed the nearby village of Kapoho and entered the ocean to the east of Kahuwai. Steam explosions from the interaction of the molten lava and the ocean created cinder or "black sand," and prevailing currents transported it to Kahuwai. In 1963 John Orr leased 5 acres at Kahuwai and built his home on a bluff above the beach. Since then the beach has been known as Orr's Beach. Also known as Kahuwai.

OT Buoy. Fish aggregating device, Waikoloa, Hawai'i. Buoy anchored at approximately 714 fathoms. Landmarks: Kawaihae Light, Māhukona, Keāhole Point.

OTEC. Beach, Keāhole, North Kona, Hawai'i. Calcareous sand beach near the Natural Energy Lab of Hawai'i that was established at Keāhole Point in 1974. OTEC is an acronym for Ocean Thermal Energy Conversion, an alternate-energy project conducted at the lab. OTEC uses the temperature difference between warm water on the surface and cold water from the depths to generate electricity. Also known as Wawaloli.

Otera. Bay, Pā'ia, Maui. Same as Mantokuji Bay. *Lit.,* temple (Japanese). The Mantokuji Mission temple is on the shore of the bay.

Outer Mākaha. Dive site, Mākaha, O'ahu. Same as Land of Oz.

Outer Spreckelsville. Tow-in surf site, Spreckelsville, Maui. Big-wave, second-reef site outside of Spreckelsville.

Outrigger Canoe Club. Private club, Waikīkī Beach, O'ahu. Founded on the beach at Waikīkī in 1908 for the purpose of preserving and promoting surfing on surfboards and canoes. The club was originally at the site of the Outrigger Waikīkī Hotel and moved to its present site at the east end of Waikīkī in 1964, a site leased from the Honolulu Elks Lodge in 1956.

Outside. Surf site, Honolua, Maui. One of three sections of the surf site at Honolua Bay. Outside is the second section between Coconuts at the point and the Cave on the inside reef.

Outside Alligators. Surf site, tow-in surf site, Kawailoa, O'ahu. Big-wave, second-reef site outside of Alligators.

Outside Hau'ula. Surf site, Hau'ula, O'ahu. Big-wave, second-reef site off the north end of Hau'ula Beach Park.

Outside Kāhala. Surf site, Kāhala, Oʻahu. Big-wave, second-reef site off Waiʻalae Beach Park.

Outside Kahana. Surf site, Kahana, Oʻahu. Big-wave, second-reef site off the north point of Kahana Bay.

Outside Kaikoʻoʻs. Surf site, Diamond Head, Oʻahu. Big-wave, second-reef site off Kaikoʻoʻs at Black Point.

Outside Log Cabins. Surf site, tow-in surf site, Sunset Beach, Oʻahu. Big-wave, second-reef site off Log Cabins on Ke Iki Road.

Outside Mānele. Dive site, Mānele, Lānaʻi. Off Mānele Bay at approximately 30 feet.

Outside Marijuanas. Surf site, tow-in surf site. Haleʻiwa, Oʻahu. Big-wave, second-reef site.

Outside Pipeline. Surf site, Sunset Beach, Oʻahu. Big-wave, second-reef site outside of the Pipeline.

Outside Puaʻena Point. Surf site, Haleʻiwa, Oʻahu. Big-wave, second-reef site between the point and Police Beach.

Outside Rainbows. Surf site, Kaʻaʻawa, Oʻahu. Big-wave, second-reef site off Kalaeʻōʻio Beach Park and to the north of Rainbows. Also known as Kaʻaʻawa Channel, Phantoms.

Outside Reef. Surf site, ʻEwa Beach, Oʻahu. Big-wave, second-reef site outside Beach Parks at ʻEwa Beach Park.

Outside Velzyland. Surf site, windsurf site, Waialeʻe, Oʻahu. Big-wave, second-reef site off the north end of Kaunalā Beach.

Outside Wilds. Surf site, Kahuku, Oʻahu. Big-wave, second-reef site off Wild Beach.

Over the Reefs. Surf site, Ala Moana, Oʻahu. West end of Magic Island. Primarily a bodyboarding site that breaks on a shallow reef with coral heads exposed at low tide.

Owen's Retreat. Beach, Mokulēʻia, Oʻahu. Section of Mokulēʻia Beach fronting Owen's Retreat. The retreat is a complex of five beach vacation rentals that was established by Philo and Ok Soon Owen in the mid 1960s. It is adjacent to the west end of Mokulēʻia Beach Park.

Pa'akea. Fishpond, Pearl Harbor, O'ahu. *Lit.*, coral bed, limestone.

Pa'akō. Coastal area, Mākena, Maui. Where Miller of Miller's Hill made his home. *Lit.*, dry lowland plain.

Pa'alaea. Island (.16 acres, 40 feet high), North Kohala, Hawai'i. One of three islands, including Mokupuku and Paoakalani, off Honoke'a Valley on the north side of the Kohala Mountains. The islands are sea stacks—rocks isolated from the main island by erosion.

Pā'auhau Landing. Fishing site, Pā'auhau, Hawai'i. One of the few former interisland steamer landing sites on the Hāmākua Coast. Remnants include the concrete footing of the landing at the base of the sea cliffs and an inclined railroad bed that leads to the top of the bluff. *Lit.*, tribute enclosure.

Pacers. Dive site, surf site, Kīholo, Hawai'i. In the center of Kīholo Bay off the beachfront home of Dr. Earl E. Bakken, inventor of the pacemaker. Bakken is the founder of Medtronics, Inc., a company that specializes in electrical medical devices. Pacers is an abbreviation of pacemaker. Also known as Middle of the Bay.

Pacific Missile Range Facility. Military base, Mānā, Kaua'i. Multipurpose naval installation on the shore of the Mānā Coastal Plain that is an important center for the detection of aircraft and vessels in the Pacific. Public access is permitted to the long calcareous sand beach that fronts the facility. Also known as PMRF.

Pahe'e o Lono. Point, Molokini, Maui. North point of Molokini island. *Lit.*, (the god) Lono's slide.

Pahiomu. Fishpond, Kamalō, Moloka'i.

Pāhoehoe. 1. Beach park, dive site, North Kona, Hawai'i. Tiny pocket of calcareous sand and coral rubble on a rocky shore. A low seawall lines the seaward edge of the park. The former village of Pāhoehoe was located near the park. The dive site is off the beach. 2. Lava flow, Pāhoehoe, Hawai'i. One of three lava flows from an eruption in the southwest rift zone of Mauna Kea that began on June 1, 1950. Each of the flows reached the ocean, creating small pockets of black sand on a coast of sea cliffs. Boaters use the flows as landmarks. Also known as Second Flow. *Lit.,* smooth lava.

P

Pāhonu. Beach, fishpond, residence, surf site, Waimānalo, Oʻahu. At the south end of Waimānalo Beach. Remnants of a fishpond called Pāhonu are off the beach. Turtles were kept in the pond for a chief of the district. The beachfront residence named Pāhonu inland of the pond was used from 1980 to 1988 as the base of operations for the popular television series, *Magnum P.I.* The surf site borders a small channel through the reef and is also known as Magnums. *Lit.,* turtle enclosure.

Pahu Iʻa. Surf site, Kūkiʻo, Hawaiʻi. Off the Pahu Iʻa Restaurant on the shore of the Four Seasons Resort Hualālai. *Lit.,* aquarium.

Pahukapu. Beach, Nāpoʻopoʻo, Hawaiʻi. Also known Manini Beach. *Lit.,* sacred drum.

Pahulu. *Heiau,* Kualoa, Oʻahu. Shrine formerly onshore but now in the ocean due to shore erosion and consisting of a cluster of stones at the edge of the beach. Near the old sugar mill and visible at low tide. Name of the god of nightmares.

Pahumoa. Beach, Lāʻie, Oʻahu. Calcareous sand beach fronting Lāʻie Beach Park. Named for Pahumoa, a fisherman from Lāʻie Maloʻo in the late 1800s and early 1900s who lived here and kept his nets on the beach adjacent to Kōloa Stream. He was well known in Lāʻie for his generosity and gave fish to everyone in the village, especially to those who could not fish for themselves. Pahumoa conducted many *hukilau,* a method of community net fishing. Also known as Lāʻie Beach Park, Pounders.

Pahuula. Fishing site, Lāʻie, Oʻahu. Cluster of three rocks nearshore on the shallow reef in the center of Laniloa Beach. Resident fishermen kept lobsters live here in traps. *Lit.,* lobster box.

Pāʻia. Bay, beach park, surf site, Pāʻia, Maui. Calcareous sand beach with dunes in the backshore that was a former rubbish dump. The site was cleared and converted into a park in 1934 as a community service project of the Outdoor Circle. The surf site is offshore the beach park and the bodysurf site is a shorebreak. *Lit.,* noisy.

Paiāhaʻa. Bay, surf site, Paiāhaʻa, Hawaiʻi. Small green sand, pebble beach at the head of a small bay west of Kaʻaluʻalu. The surf site is off the beach. *Lit.,* lift and sway [of waves].

Paikō. Beach, lagoon, peninsula, Kuliʻouʻou, Oʻahu. Narrow calcareous sand beach fronting Paikō Drive and Paikō Peninsula. The peninsula is an undeveloped sand spit that separates Paikō Lagoon from the open ocean. It is also known as Sand Point and Stubenberg's Island. The lagoon was designated a wildlife sanctuary on March 30, 1974. It is an important resting and nesting site for the Hawaiian stilt and other native shorebirds. Named for Manuel Paikō, who made his home here until his death on April 8, 189. His property remained in the family until the death of his grandson, Joseph Paikō Jr., who died childless in 1947.

Paikōs. Surf site, Kuli'ou'ou, O'ahu. Off the center of Paikō Drive. Also known as Shoulders.

Pa'iloa. Beach, Hāna, Maui. Pebble beach at the head of Pa'iloa Bay in Wai'ānapanapa State Park.

Pailolo. Channel between Maui and Moloka'i. *Lit.*, lift and shift (a contraction of *pai* and *oloolo*).

Pai'olu'olu. Point, Hanauma Bay, O'ahu. West point of the bay. *Lit.*, lifted gently.

Pāipu. Beach, Mākena, Maui. South end of Po'olenalena Beach. Also known as Chang's Beach. *Lit.*, calabash.

Pākala. 1. Beach, landing, surf site, Pākala, Kaua'i. Narrow calcareous sand beach fronting the village of Pākala in Makaweli, where many Ni'ihau residents live while they are on Kaua'i. The surf site is on the west end of the wide, shallow fringing reef off the beach and is also known as Infinities. A public right-of-way to the beach is next to the A'akukui Stream Bridge on Kaumuali'i Highway. The landing in the village accommodates the boat that takes Ni'ihau residents to and from the island. 2. Beach, Olowalu, Maui. Narrow calcareous sand and cobble beach on the east side of Hekili Point. *Lit.*, the sun shines.

 mo'olelo

One of the beauties of the Hawaiian language is its ambiguity. I have always been intrigued by the name Pākala and searched for meaning in it. I spent some time with Apelahama Nizo, a Ni'ihauan who has since passed away. He was the first Ni'ihauan to become a certified pastor and was a man of wisdom and knowledge, both of the secular as well as the sacred. He was a musician, a surfer, as well as a workingman on Ni'ihau before he moved to Kaua'i after he retired. Most importantly, he was a native speaker of Hawaiian.

He told me that there were several perspectives on the name, without fully committing to singling out one as being "right." **Pākala** with only one *kahako* on the first *a* could be translated as an enclosure for the unicorn fish known as *kala*. Pākalā, with *kahako* over the first and last *a*'s, has to do with the shining *(pā)* of the sun *(ka lā)*. Pākalā is in the lee of Kaumakani, where the clouds and wind stop and rest, and till this day the onshore wind that is common to Pākalā on especially clear mornings has to do

P

with the shining of the sun at this place, heating the land and causing convective winds to come in off the sea even on days when the trades are strong on the east side of Kaua'i. Apela also told me that if the name were pronounced with all three *a*'s covered by the *kahako*, it could mean "money field." The sugar-cane plantation of the Robinson's is legendary for its production of sugar in pounds per acre. A combination of lots of sunshine and abundant water from the Waimea, Hanapēpē, and Olokele Valleys makes this possible. It is one of the last surviving sugar plantations because of these phenomena. Close to what is the little village of Pākālā today are the most productive of the fields, according to Apela, of the entire plantation. Hence the possibility of "money field," the fields that produced the most profit.

After explaining, Apela just looked at me with a gleam of amusement in his eyes and left it at that. He was my teacher in a lot of things about the language, but never assumed to be an authority. So now I leave you as he left me, to make a choice, or maybe not to choose and thereby live with the rich diversity and ambiguity that makes Hawaiian language and people unique and special.

 Carlos Andrade, November 8, 2000

Pākanaka. Fishpond, Kaunakakai, Moloka'i. *Lit.*, touched [by] commoners (it could be used by commoners).

Pākē Pāpale. Island, Kualoa, O'ahu. An alternate name for China-man's Hat coined by circle-island tour drivers who pass the island and point it out daily. *Lit.*, Chinese hat.

Pāko'a. Fishing site, Ukumehame, Maui. Also known as Ukume-hame Beach Park. *Lit.*, coral fence.

Palahemo. Hole, Kahuku, Hawai'i. Deep hole inland of the sea cliffs at Ka Lae, or South Point, in which water rises and falls with the tide. Traditional stories say a layer of fresh water for-merly floated on top of the salt water, providing a source of drinking water at the otherwise arid point. Eight cairns sur-round the top of the hole. *Lit.*, loose dab of excreta.

Pālama. Beach, buoy, surf site, Kalāheo, Kaua'i. Calcareous sand beach fronted by a rocky shelf on the east side of Nōmilu Cone. The cinder cone contains a natural salt water lake, Nōmilu Fishpond, one of the most unusual fishponds in Hawai'i. The pond has been owned for many years by the Pālama family of Kaua'i. They maintain the site as a family recreation area. Pālama Beach adjoining the fishpond is named for them. The surf site is at the point. The buoy is a navigational aid off Pālama Beach that marks Lanipū'ao Rock, a small, submerged rock islet. *Lit.*, *lama* wood enclosure.

Pālama Buoy. Dive site, Kalāheo, Kaua'i. Off Pālama Beach at Lanipū'ao Rock, a small, submerged rock islet that is marked by a navigational buoy called Pālama Buoy.

Palaoa. Point Light, Palaoa, Lāna'i. *Lit.,* whale.

Palau'ea. Beach, surf site, Palau'ea, Maui. Calcareous sand beach south of the Wailea resort complex that is located in the land division of Palau'ea. The surf site is a shorebreak that forms on the sandbar fronting the beach. In a historic ceremony at Palau'ea Beach on May 7, 1984, the U.S. Navy returned the island of Kaho'olawe to the State of Hawai'i. With Kaho'olawe visible across the channel, Governor John Waihee received the title transfer documents from Deputy Assistant Secretary of the Navy William Cassidy Jr. *Lit.,* reddish brown sweet potato.

Palea Point. Dive site, Hanauma Bay, O'ahu. East point of the bay. *Lit.,* brushed aside.

Pali. Sea cliffs, Pāpalaua, Maui. Same as Lahaina Pali.

Pali Kaholo. 1. Sea cliff, southwest shore, Lāna'i. At 1,000 feet, this is the highest sea cliff on Lāna'i and also the highest south-shore sea cliff in Hawai'i. Although there are higher sea cliffs in Hawai'i, they are located on the northern sides of the islands. Also known as Kaholo Pali. 2. Sea cliff, Mōkapu, O'ahu. On the seaward side of Ulupa'u Crater. Also known as Kahekili's Leap. *Lit.,* cliff [of] the landslide.

Pali Ke Kua. Beach, Princeville, Kaua'i. Two pockets of calcareous sand separated by a rocky point below the Pali Ke Kua and Pu'u Poa condominiums. A shallow reef lies offshore. Tropical almond trees, or *kamani,* and pandanus trees, or *hala,* line the backshores. Also known as Hideaway Beach. *Lit.,* the back is a cliff. Part of a proverb said of handsome persons: *Pali ke kua, mahina ke alo* ("The back is a cliff, the front is a moon").

Pali Kiloi'a. Fishing site, point, Lā'ie, O'ahu. Limestone point on Lā'ie Malo'o Bay that separates Pounders and Kokololio Beaches. Fish spotters used the point to spot schools of fish in the bay and direct the efforts of fishermen in their canoes with their surround nets. Also known as Kiloi'a. *Lit.,* fish-spotter cliff.

Palikū. Sea cliff, Waipi'o, Maui. Highest sea cliff on the shore of Waipi'o Bay. *Lit.,* vertical cliff.

Pali'ukea. Fishing site, Mākena, Maui. Near Nahuna Point, the north point of Mākena Bay.

Paliuli. Point, west coast, Ni'ihau. Large basalt point bisected into twin sea cliffs by a small pocket of calcareous sand. The point separates Pu'uwai and Ki'eki'e Beaches and fronts Pu'uwai village, the only inhabited village on the island. *Lit.,* green cliff. A legendary land of plenty and joy.

Pamolepo. Point, Mākena, Maui. Site of a small graveyard between Nahuna Point, the north point of Mākena Bay, and the south end of Poʻolenalena Beach. The graveyard belongs to the Kukahiko family from Mākena.

Pānāhāhā. Fishponds, Kamalō, Hālawa, Molokaʻi. *Lit.,* broken wall.

Panics. Surf site, Kakaʻako, Oʻahu. Same as Point Panic.

Paoakalani. Island, North Kohala, Hawaiʻi. Part of the Hawaiʻi State Seabird Sanctuary. One of three islands, including Mokupuku and Paʻalaea, off Honokeʻa Valley. The islands are sea stacks—rocks isolated from the main island by erosion. *Lit.,* the royal perfume.

Pāokamenehune. Breakwater, Kahaluʻu, Hawaiʻi. One of the most striking features at Kahaluʻu Beach Park is the ruin of a great boulder wall, or breakwater. Originally a semicircle 3,900 feet long that enclosed the bay to form a large fishpond, it extended from Kaumahaʻole on the north to ʻInikiwai on the south. Traditional stories say the wall was built in one night by the *menehune,* a legendary people who were known for their public works projects. Also known as Menehune Breakwater. *Lit.,* wall of the *menehune.*

Pāpaʻa. Bay, beach, Kauaʻi. Calcareous sand beach at the head of a small bay in the sea cliffs. A wide, sand-bottomed channel runs through the bay into the beach. *Lit.,* secure enclosure.

Papaʻakea. Reef, Hauʻula, Oʻahu. Shallow reef on the north side of Kaipapaʻu Point. Also known as Papapiapia. *Lit.,* gray coral.

Pāpaʻamoi. Island, reef, Kahuku, Oʻahu. Small island and wide reef off the north point of Kawela Bay. *Lit.,* scorched thread fish.

Papaʻaula. Fishing site, reef, Lāʻie, Oʻahu. At the north end of Kokololio Beach fronting the Mahakea beach estate. *Lit.,* lobster enclosure.

Pāpā Bay. Dive site, Pāpā, Hawaiʻi. The dive site is in the bay. *Lit.,* forbidden.

Papaʻeleʻele. Beach, Kalaupapa, Molokaʻi. North section of Papaloa Beach that is fronted by a low, flat shelf of lava with many tidal pools. *Lit.,* black flat.

Pāpaʻi. Beach, Puna, Hawaiʻi. Narrow, crescent black and green sand beach fronting a coconut grove and the ruins of the former fishing village of Pāpaʻi. It was here in 1793 that King Kamehameha I lead a small raiding party in an attack on the village. Leading his warriors, Kamehameha leaped out of his canoe and gave chase to several fishermen, but as he ran, he stepped in a crevice in the lava, catching his foot. One of the fishermen picked up a canoe paddle and broke it over Kamehameha's head. By this time other men from the village were arming themselves and were coming to assist, so Kamehameha's warriors freed him, and they retreated. Years later, after Kamehameha had successfully united all the Hawaiian Islands, he visited the town of Hilo. Members of his retinue, still incensed that a commoner had struck the king and had not been punished, rounded up the fishermen at Pāpaʻi who had attacked Kamehameha, brought them before the king, and demanded their execution. Kamehameha answered these demands with a pardon in the form of the now legendary decree known as the Law of the Splintered Paddle.

> *E nā kānaka,*
> *E mālama ʻoukou i ke akua.*
> *A e mālama hoʻi ke kanaka nui a me kanaka iki.*
> *E hele ka ʻelemakule, ka luahine, a me ke kama*
> *A moe i ke ala,*
> *ʻAʻohe mea nana e hoʻopilikia.*
> *Hewa no. Make.*

> *O my people,*
> *Honor thy gods.*
> *Indeed, respect men great and small.*
> *Where old men, old women, and children go*
> *and lie down on the roadside,*
> *Let no man cause harm.*
> *Disobey, and die.*

As the king, he chose to forgive rather than to punish, admitting his fault in attacking innocent people, and showed his respect for human rights by proclaiming the Law of the Splintered Paddle. This story shows why Kamehameha I was one of Hawaiʻi's most beloved rulers. Also known as King's Landing. Perhaps lit., crab.

 moʻolelo

Pāpaʻi was a village and a canoe landing, and people lived there until the mid-1930s. The name does not mean "crab," but refers to something flat. Before 1924, it was very different, and the ocean bottom and the entrance channel are completely changed. Before, we could launch and land even during rough seas, and we used it as a hiding place if the ocean became rough quickly. When we landed on the sand, we pulled the canoes up on *hau* rollers and set them in stands carved of *milo* wood.

Molokaʻi was a big *papa*, very flat, on the Keaukaha side of the entrance channel. Canoes could pull right up and off-load people before landing on the sand beach. This is where *the famous incident with Kamehameha took place. His canoe pulled up to Molokaʻi, he jumped out, and in the fight his foot got stuck in a crack.*

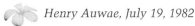

Henry Auwae, July 19, 1982

P

Pāpaʻikou. Beach, surf site, Pāpaʻikou, Hawaiʻi. Small black sand beach near the former Pāpaʻikou sugar mill. The surf site is off the beach. *Lit.*, hut [in a] *kou* tree [grove].

Pāpaʻiloa. Beach, Kawailoa, Oʻahu. Calcareous sand beach between Police Beach and Laniākea Beach fronting Pāpaʻiloa Road. Bishop Estate developed Pāpaʻiloa Road and began leasing house lots here in 1960. Also known as Kawailoa Beach. *Lit.*, long hut.

Papaka Iki. Bay, beach, northwest shore, Kahoʻolawe. The bay lies within the *ʻili* or land division of Papaka. A detrital sand beach lines the shore of the bay. Also known as Santos Bay. *Lit.*, small Papaka [drops].

Papaka Nui. Bay, beach, northwest shore, Kahoʻolawe. The bay lies within the *ʻili* or land division of Papaka. A detrital sand beach lines the shore of the bay. Also known as Water Tank Bay. *Lit.*, large Papaka [drops].

Papakōlea. Beach, Kaʻū, Hawaiʻi. Area name that has been used as a Hawaiian name for Green Sand Beach. *Lit.*, plover flats.

Papakuewa. Beach, reef, Mākena, Maui. Small pocket of calcareous sand at Mākena Landing Park between the former cattle holding pen and the beachfront homes. The reef is a small patch reef off the beach. *Lit.*, wandering reef.

Pāpalaua. 1. State wayside park, Pāpalaua, Maui. Narrow calcareous sand beach that borders Honoapiʻilani Highway on the west side of Lahaina Pali. The beach and the park are on the shore of Pāpalaua, the gulch on the opposite side of the highway. Also known as Thousand Peaks. 2. Beach, Pāpalaua, Molokaʻi. Boulder beach at the mouth of the one of the six coastal valleys on Molokaʻi's north shore. Pāpalaua Falls at the head of the valley is one of the highest waterfalls in the Hawaiian Islands. Also known as Hākaʻaʻano. *Lit.*, rain fog.

Papaloa. 1. Island (.4 acres, 40 feet high), Hāna, Maui. 2. Beach, Kalaupapa, Molokaʻi. One of five beaches on the Kalaupapa Peninsula. Long calcareous sand beach on the western side of the peninsula with low vegetated sand dunes in the backshore and a rocky shelf along the water's edge that fronts the settlement and a large graveyard. 3. Reef, Mākua, Oʻahu. Off Poʻohuna Point. *Lit.*, long shelf.

Papamoku. Reef, Waiheʻe, Maui. Off the sixth hole of the Waiehu Golf Course.

Papanui. Surf site, Waikīkī, Oʻahu. One of the outermost surf sites in Waikīkī that was named in 1930 by Duke Kahanamoku to honor the big boards that were ridden there. Papanui is in line with Castles but to the west of it and breaks primarily on big south swells from the west. Also known as Bluebirds. *Lit.,* big [surf] board.

Papanui o Kāne. Island (3.13 acres, 40 feet high), fishing site, Haʻikū, Maui. Large, flat island off the west point of Uaoa Bay that is part of the Hawaiʻi State Seabird Sanctuary. The island is known for its schools of *āhole, enenue,* and *moi. Lit.,* great flat of [the god] Kāne.

Papaoneone. Beach, Mākaha, Oʻahu. Wide calcareous sand beach on the west side of Mauna Lahilahi. Also known as Keawaiki, Turtle Beach. *Lit.,* sandy shelf or reef.

Papapiapia. Reef, Hauʻula, Oʻahu. Shallow reef on the north side of Kaipapaʻu Point. Also known as Papaʻakea. *Lit.,* unwashed genitals reef.

Papawai. 1. Beach, North Kona, Hawaiʻi. Several small pockets of calcareous sand and coral rubble used as a shore campsite by Liliʻuokalani Trust, the property owners, for its beneficiaries. Queen Liliʻuokalani (1838–1917), the last monarch of the Kingdom of Hawaiʻi, established the trust to help orphaned children, especially those of Hawaiian ancestry. The trust began making improvements at Papawai in 1975 after the opening of the Queen Kaʻahumanu Highway. Also known as Bean's Beach, Pāwai. 2. Dive site, Papawai, Maui. Off Papawai Point at Lahaina Pali. *Lit.,* water stratum.

Pāpipi. Beach, Mākena, Maui. Small pocket of calcareous sand at Mākena Landing Park fronting the former cattle holding pens. The pens were used during cattle-loading operations when interisland steamers stopped at Mākena. *Lit.,* cattle fence.

Pāpōhaku. Beach, beach park, Kaluakoʻi, Molokaʻi. Calcareous sand beach over 2 miles long and 300 feet wide that is the largest beach on Molokaʻi. It lies between two headlands, Puʻu Koaʻe to the south and Puʻu o Kaiaka to the north. From the early 1960s to 1975, this massive cache of sand was the site of the largest sand-mining operation in the state. A concrete tunnel at the south end of the beach is all that remains of the former mining activities. Pāpōhaku Beach Park is at the north end of the beach on Kaluakoʻi Road. It is the site of the Molokaʻi Ka Hula Piko, a noncompetitive hula festival that is held annually in May. *Lit.,* stone fence.

Paradise. 1. Surf site, Wailua, Maui. Open ocean site off the end of the road to the shore in Wailua. 2. Cove, snorkeling site, surf site, Ko ʻOlina, Oʻahu. Small pocket beach of calcareous sand in an otherwise rocky shore. The snorkeling and surf sites are off the beach. Paradise Cove Luau is the name of a popular visitor attraction on the shore behind the beach. 3. Surf site, tow-in surf site, Ke'ehi Lagoon, O'ahu. Big-wave, second-reef site off Mokauea Island on the east side of Kalihi Channel. 4. Surf site, Waikīkī, O'ahu. Off the Halekūlani Hotel. Also known as Number Twos, Twos. 5. Surf site, Hale'iwa, O'ahu. Big-wave, second-reef site to the west of Avalanche.

Parallels. Surf site, Hawai'i Kai, O'ahu. West of the small breakwater at Queen's Beach. High surf from the east breaks parallel to shore here rather than rolling in to shore. Surfers going left, or riding the wave to their left, are actually surfing out to sea.

Parker Ranch. Beach, 'Anaeho'omalu, Hawai'i. John Palmer Parker established Parker Ranch in Waimea in 1847. By the twentieth century it covered 300,000 acres, primarily in the districts of Hāmākua and South Kohala. During the 1960s Richard Smart, Parker's heir, sold 31,000 acres of land for development, including the property surrounding 'Anaeho'omalu Beach, but a 10-acre parcel at the south end of 'Anaeho'omalu Beach was maintained by the ranch for its employees. After Smart's death in 1992, estate trustees sold some ranch properties to pay the $25 million that was due in federal and state estate taxes. The Parker Ranch Beach site was sold in October 1998 to John Hoffee of California.

Park Rights. Surf site, Mokulē'ia, O'ahu. Off Mokulē'ia Beach Park. The primary direction that surfers ride is to their right. Also known as Beach Parks.

Patterson's. Surf site, Diamond Head, O'ahu. Off Ka'alāwai Beach fronting the Isles at Diamond Head, the site of the former Patterson Cottages. The Pattersons were from Scotland and operated beach cottage rentals at Ka'alāwai until they sold their property in 1986.

Paty's Shorebreak. Surf site, Kawailoa, O'ahu. Off William Paty's beachfront home on Kamehameha Highway on the north side of Chun's Reef. Paty, a former Waialua Sugar Company executive and chairman of the State Board of Land and Natural Resources, bought a lot and built his home here in 1957.

Pauka'a. Point light, Pauka'a, Hawai'i. Established in 1869. The 145-foot concrete light tower was built in 1929.

Paukūkalo. Beach, surf site, Paukūkalo, Maui. Rocky boulder beach that borders the Hawaiian homestead community of Paukūkalo. The surf site is off the beach. *Lit.*, taro piece.

Pauley Marine Laboratory. Research site, Kāne'ohe, O'ahu. Laboratory on Coconut Island that was funded by the Edwin W. Pauley Foundation and completed in 1997.

Paumalū. Beach, Sunset Beach, O'ahu. Calcareous sand beach that fronts the land division of Paumalū and includes Sunset

Beach Park. *Lit.*, taken by surprise. The name comes from a legend of a woman fishing here who caught more octopuses than the number that was permitted for this reef. As she made her way to shore, a large shark, the guardian of the reef, attacked and killed her. After the incident, the area was called Paumalū. *Lit.*, taken secretly.

Pauoa. Bay, surf site, Mauna Lani, Hawai'i. Small bay at the west end of the Mauna Lani Resort property and the site of Holoholokai Beach Park. The surf site is in the bay.

Pā'ūonu'akea. Island (.72 acres, 50 feet high), north shore, Moloka'i. *Lit.*, sarong of Nu'akea.

Pauwalu. Harbor, Waialua, Moloka'i. Narrow detrital sand beach bordering a wide, shallow fringing reef. A natural opening in the reef serves as a harbor. *Lit.*, eight destroyed. A shark demigod killed seven children in a family. The eighth child was set out as bait, and the shark was caught and killed.

Pa'uwela. Point light, Pa'uwela, Maui. Established in 1910 and automated in 1921. The 48-foot skeleton tower is approximately 120 feet above sea level. *Lit.*, hot soot.

Pa'uwela Point. Dive site, Pa'uwela, Maui. Off the point.

Pavilions. Surf site, Pā'ia, Maui. One of five surfing and windsurf sites off Ho'okipa Beach Park. Pavilions is off the concrete pavilion at the east end of the park.

Pāwai. Bay, snorkeling site, scuba site, North Kona, Hawai'i. Several small pockets of calcareous sand and coral rubble at the head of a small bay at the border of the Old Kona Airport State Recreation Area and the Lili'uokalani Trust's campsite, Papawai. Although this bay is commonly known as Pāwai, research by the Lili'uokalani Trust has determined that Pāwai is an abbreviation of Papawai. The trust uses the name Papawai. Also known as Bean's Beach. *Lit.*, water stratum.

PB4Y. Dive site, Kīhei, Maui. Wreck of a navy bomber that was ditched on June 26, 1944. In 1987, Doug Niessen and Ed Robinson discovered the four-engine aircraft at 200 feet.

P Buoy. Fish aggregating device, Penguin Bank, Moloka'i. Buoy anchored at approximately 286 fathoms. Landmarks: Diamond Head Light, Honolulu Harbor Buoy Light, Lā'au Point Light.

PCC. Surf site, Lā'ie, O'ahu. PCC is off the Polynesian Cultural Center (PCC), a cultural tourist attraction started in 1963 by the Church of Jesus Christ of Latter-Day Saints to provide job opportunities for students attending Brigham Young University–Hawai'i. The 42-acre complex features the seven groups of islanders that are native to Polynesia: Fijians, Hawaiians, Maoris, Marquesans, Samoans, Tahitians, and Tongans.

Peace Park. Kīhei, Maui. South section of Kamaʻole III Beach Park that is an open, grassy field for kite flying and a "peaceful" place for families.

Peʻahi. Tow-in surf site, windsurf site, Peʻahi, Maui. Also known as Jaws. *Lit.,* beckon.

Peaks. Surf site, Waikīkī, Oʻahu. Off Kaimana Beach on the west side of the Kaimana Channel. The wave is a single peak and a short ride.

Pearl Harbor. 1. Harbor, South shore, Oʻahu. The harbor was discovered by Captain Nathaniel Portlock in 1789 but was not developed as a military facility until after annexation in 1898. A congressional appropriations act of May 13, 1908, authorized establishing the Pearl Harbor Navy Yard. Dredging of the entrance channel was completed in 1912, and construction of the first drydock was completed in 1919. In 1939 an executive order established the harbor as a naval defensive sea area, thereby restricting entry to only those vessels approved by the base commander. Most Americans remember the harbor for the attack on Sunday, December 7, 1941, by aircraft of the Imperial Japanese Navy. The attack engaged the United States in World War II. In 1964 Pearl Harbor was named a national landmark and was subsequently placed on the National Register of Historic Places. It is still, however, an active naval facility. The harbor was named for the pearl oysters that were abundant in its mudflats through the 1800s, but pollution in the harbor has since killed them all. 2. Channel, Pearl Harbor, Oʻahu. Channel into Pearl Harbor that was first dredged in the early 1900s to allow large vessels through the reef into the inner lochs. 3. Historic trail, Pearl City, Oʻahu. Hiking trail on the harbor shore that follows the right-of-way of the former Oʻahu Railway and Land (OR&L) train tracks. OR&L discontinued its service in 1947. 4. National wildlife refuge. The refuge consists of three satellite sections, or "units," including the Honouliuli Unit on the shore of West Loch in Pearl Harbor, the Kalaeloa Unit in the Kalaeloa Community Development District, and the Waiawa Unit near the mouth of Waiawa Stream. 5. Park, Pearl City, Oʻahu. City park on the shore of the harbor at the foot of Kaʻahumanu Street. 6. Yacht Club, Pearl Harbor, Oʻahu. Private yacht club in ʻAiea Bay in East Loch. Pearl Harbor consists of three large lochs, or landlocked bays: East Loch, Middle Loch, and West Loch. Access to all of the lochs is restricted to military vessels, including ʻAiea Bay in East Loch, which is only for privately owned boats belonging to military personnel.

Pebble. 1. Beach, Kaʻohe, Hawaiʻi. Pebble or *ʻiliʻili* beach on the shore of the Kona Paradise Properties subdivision. Also known as Ka'ohe Beach. 2. Beach, Mōkapu, O'ahu. Small cove of white sand at the east end of North Beach below Pond Road on Marine Corps Air Station–Kāne'ohe Bay. Erosion of an adjacent lava flow from Ulupa'u Crater deposits pebbles on the beach.

Pedro. Bay, north shore, Kaho'olawe. Manuel Pedro was the foreman of Kaho'olawe Ranch and the only permanent resident of the island during the final years of the ranching period. He was born in 1875 in the Azores, a group of islands off the coast of Portugal, and came to Hawai'i with his family in 1878. When Angus MacPhee started a cattle ranch on Kaho'olawe in 1922, Pedro was the ranch foreman. Although he had a wife and four children on Maui, Pedro lived alone on the island most of the year, maintaining water troughs, repairing fences, hunting goats, and tending the cattle. His family stayed with him during the summer months at Kūheia, the ranch headquarters. He was a well-known figure to fishermen and hunters who named Kūheia "Pedro Bay" for him.

 mo'olelo

In August 1975 I went on hunting trip to Kaho'olawe with four friends of mine, Charlie Maxwell, Adrian Naeua, Paul Fujishiro, and Albert de Rego. I'd been hunting for goats and fishing there since the late sixties. While we were camped at **Pedro Bay,** we began discussing the possibility of getting Kaho'olawe back and using it as a test case for Hawaiian lands controlled by the federal government. We decided to do a demonstration-type landing to attract attention to the island. We would drop the demonstrators off on the island, return to Mā'alaea, and then notify the navy. The navy would pick everyone up and that would get the issue into the courts. We decided that the demonstrators all had to be part Hawaiian.

Back on Maui, Charlie came up with a list of names and contacted them. On January 4, 1976, about thrity-five people on boats started out for Kaho'olawe from Maui, but the navy got word of the invasion and warned everyone from a helicopter to return to Maui. The boats returned to Mā'alaea, but later the same day nine of them succeeded in landing on the island. They were arrested and taken off the island. That was the beginning of the Protect Kaho'olawe 'Ohana.

 Herbert Santos, June 25, 1978

Pe'ewē. Island, Keaukaha, Hawai'i. Small, flat rock island off Kealoha Park. Also known as Peiwē, Scout Island. *Lit.*, drupe shell.

Peiwē. Island, Keaukaha, Hawai'i. Alternate spelling of Pe'ewē.

Pelekane. Beach, Kawaihae, Hawai'i. Small calcareous sand and coral rubble beach fronting Mailekini Heiau. Pelekane Beach is part of the Pu'ukoholā Heiau National Historic Site and is regarded as a sacred area. There is no sunbathing, swimming, picnicking, or camping permitted here. *Lit.*, British. Possibly for John Young, an Englishman who served as an advisor to Kamehameha I. Young lived near the *heiau* until his death in 1835.

P

Pelekunu. Beach, landing, surf site, Pelekunu, Moloka'i. Boulder and black detrital sand beach at the mouth of one of the six coastal valleys on Moloka'i's north shore. Formerly the site of a fishing and commercial taro farming village that was abandoned by 1917, although one family remained until 1932. The tsunami of April 1, 1946, completely destroyed the taro patches and the ruins of the village. The ruins of the landing are on the rocky terrace on the west side of the bay. The surf site is a shorebreak on a sandbar fronting the beach. *Lit.*, smelly [for lack of sunshine].

Pele's Chair. Rock, Hawai'i Kai, O'ahu. Rock formation at the west end of Makapu'u Head above the small breakwater built by Henry J. Kaiser. The profile of the rock viewed from Kalaniana'ole Highway near the entrance to the Hawai'i Kai Golf course resembles a chair. The reference here to Pele, the goddess of the volcano, is unknown. Also known as Balancing Rock, Rebel Rock.

Penguin Bank. Fishing site, La'au Point, Moloka'i. Broad, flat shoal, or "bank," at 30 fathoms (180 feet,) that is an underwater extension of West Moloka'i. The bank extends 28 miles west southwest from La'au Point and drops abruptly to 100 fathoms along its north, west, and south edges. It is one of the most heavily fished sites in Hawai'i, especially for *opakapaka, onaga, 'ula'ula,* and other popular commercial bottom fish. Penguin Bank is one of a series of coalesced volcanoes, including Haleakalā, West Maui, Kaho'olawe, Lana'i, East Moloka'i, and West Moloka'i that three to four hundred thousand years ago were one large island—Maui Nui. The shallow saddles between the volcanoes are now flooded by the ocean and form the four islands of Maui County. Penguin Bank was discovered on July 20, 1897, by the HMS *Penguin*, a 1,130-ton British surveying ship that was under the command of Captain Arthur Mostyn Field (1855–1950). Commissioned in 1890 for service in the Pacific, the *Penguin*, with a crew of 137, was one of a half dozen ships tasked to conduct deep-sea soundings for the British, who were interested in connecting their possessions of Canada and Australia by a telegraph cable. In July 1897, the *Penguin* was four months out of Sydney and on her way for a layover in Honolulu Harbor when she discovered the bank. The edition of the *Pacific Commercial Advertiser* for Thursday, July 22, 1897, described the discovery in an article entitled "Struck Shoal":

> Although the officers aboard the Penguin were loath to give any information, it has been learned that at about 10 o'clock on Tuesday night and while about 30 miles off the Island of Oahu, the "tell-tale" of the ship showed that a shoal 26 fathoms below the surface of the water, had been struck. There was great excitement aboard as nothing of the kind had ever been reported and the discovery was noted for the first time. The Penguin will return to the place as soon as possible to make a full investigation into the matter and a British man-of-war will have the credit of discovery.

The *Penguin* left Honolulu Harbor for Fanning Island on August 13, but revisited the bank to complete its survey before departing Hawaiian waters on August 15.

 moʻolelo

In 1989 I was undertaking a project about native Hawaiian fishing rights. We (myself—a marine biologist—an anthropologist/ archaeologist, and a lawyer) had to do a lot digging in old records to establish just where the Hawaiians were fishing in the ancient days, the older days, and the modern era. In order to get a feeling for what the various archives contained, I signed up for a one-day orientation session about the library at the Bishop Museum. As I recall, I was looking through some old stuff—I think some samples of what the library contained—when I thought, "Wait a minute. What's that?" "That" turned out to be a chart made by the HMS *Penguin* after it sounded **Penguin Bank** in 1897. The reason the information got into the *Star Bulletin's* "Kokua Line" column in 1989 was because a reader had asked the columnist why Penguin Bank was named Penguin Bank. I saw the article and provided the information.

Robert Iverson, December 8, 2000

Pentagon. Dive site, ʻAnaehoʻomalu, Hawaiʻi. Reef, arches, and caverns from 25 to 50 feet. Marked by a mooring buoy. Also known as Pentagon Arches, Pentagon Pukas, and Penthouse.

Pentagon Arches. Dive site, ʻAnaehoʻomalu Bay, Hawaiʻi. Same as Pentagon.

Pentagon Pukas. Dive site, ʻAnaehoʻomalu Bay, Hawaiʻi. Same as Pentagon.

Penthouse. 1. Dive site, 'Anaeho'omalu Bay, Hawai'i. Same as Pentagon. 2. Fishing site, Makapu'u, O'ahu. Ledge below Makapu'u Light, but above the terrace at sea level that is used as a fishing site when high surf washes over the terrace below.

Pepe'ekeo. Beach, point light, surf site, Pepe'ekeo, Hawai'i. Small detrital sand beach at the base of the sea cliffs in Pepe'ekeo. The surf site is off the beach. The light was established in 1905, automated in 1917, and is atop a 75-foot skeleton light tower. *Lit.,* the crushed food, as by warriors in battle (from the former pronunciation of Pepe'ekeo with a macron over the *o*).

Pepeiaolepo. 1. Beach, Kīpahulu, Maui. Long, wide detrital sand beach at the base of high sea cliffs that is visible from the coastal trail above the last of the pools in Seven Pools Park and is the only sand beach in the district of Kīpahulu. Also known as Dirty Ear Beach. 2. Point, Mākena, Maui. Rocky point at the seaward end of the ridge that includes the Po'olena-lena rock formation. *Lit.,* dirty ear. The name in Kīpahulu is from a legend of Kamapua'a, the demigod who could assume the form of either a man or pig. Kamapua'a got mud in his ear while diving in a stream nearby.

Pepe Sands. Surf site, Hanapēpē, Kaua'i. Between Olokele Mill and Salt Pond Beach Park. Pepe is an abbreviation of Hanapēpē.

Phantoms. 1. Surf site, Ka'a'awa, O'ahu. Big-wave, second-reef site outside of Kaiaka Bay at Kalae'ō'io Beach Park. This site is called Phantoms because it does not break often—usually only when the North Shore is completely closed out. Also known as Ka'a'awa Channel, Outside Rainbows. 2. Surf site, tow-in surf site, windsurf site, Sunset Beach, O'ahu. Big-wave, second-reef site north of Sunset Point named by windsurfers. Waves breaking on this isolated reef appear like phantoms, seemingly out of nowhere.

Piddleys. Surf site, Kawailoa, O'ahu. Left at Chun's Reef on the north side of the reef. *Piddle* is a child's word for "urinate." Veteran surfer Robbie Rath was part of a group of neighborhood surfers here in the early 1960s that paddled up and down the coast, surfing all the spots off their homes. One day Rath noted to his friends that the waves here piddled, or dribbled, off of those at Chun's Reef, and described the site as "a piddley little wave." Also known as Backdoor Chun's.

Pier 1. Tow-in surf site, Kahului, Maui. Off Pier 1 in Kahului Harbor.

Pi'ilanihale. *Heiau,* 'Ula'ino, Maui. On a rocky shore with a small pebble beach. The largest *heiau* (shrine) in the Hawaiian Islands. *Lit.,* house [of] Pi'ilani [a famous Maui chief].

Piko. Point, Hāmākua Poko, Maui. Also known as Hāmākua Poko Point. *Lit.,* navel, umbilical chord.

Pīlaʻa. Beach, reef, surf site, Kauaʻi. Two pockets of calcareous sand beach divided by a low rocky point and fronted by a long, wide, shallow reef. The surf site is at the east end of the reef. A small spring and coconut grove are in the backshore of the easternmost pocket of sand. Pīlaʻa Stream crosses the western end of the beach, and a wide channel runs through the reef. The reef is one of the island's famous seaweed harvesting sites for *limu kohu,* or *Asparagopsis taxiformis.* This prized edible seaweed is found elsewhere in Hawaiʻi, but local consumers believe the best *limu kohu* comes Kauaʻi and specifically from the reefs at ʻAliomanu, Kaʻakaʻaniu, and Pīlaʻa. Commercial harvesting on these reefs has for generations been the domain of a small group of Hawaiian families from Anahola and Moloaʻa, the communities closest to the reefs. *Limu kohu* grows at the edge of the reef where there is a constant flow of water from breaking waves. After it is harvested and cleaned, it is soaked overnight in fresh water to reduce its iodine flavor, drained, and lightly salted. If it is to be sent to market, it is rolled into tight balls. Hawaiians differentiate between *limu kohu līpehe,* a milder flavored light red variety, and *limu kohu koko,* a stronger flavored dark red variety. The Mary N. Lucas Trust has owned the *ahupuaʻa* (land division) of Pīlaʻa—2,882 acres that extend from the mountains to the sea—since the early 1900s.

Pillars. Surf site, Hawaiʻi Kai, Oʻahu. Off Kōkeʻe Beach Right-of-Way. In 1959 when Henry J. Kaiser began planning Hawaiʻi Kai, he built a home for himself on 7.2 acres at the end of Portlock Road. Koko Kai, the subdivision between his estate and Portlock Point, was still vacant land. The seaward end of the Kaiser Estate included a large boathouse. To protect the boathouse, Kaiser dredged a small harbor and built a breakwater, and to access the boathouse from the ocean, he dredged a channel through the reef. The waves at the surf site terminate at the edge of the channel, and the tall pipes that serve as the channel markers are the "pillars." Also known as Half Point, Poles.

Pillboxes. 1. Surf site, Sand Island, Oʻahu. 2. Surf site, Kawela, Oʻahu. Also known as Gordieland, Gordie's. 3. Surf site, Haleʻiwa, Oʻahu. On the north side of Puaʻena Point. All three sites are named for the World War II concrete observation posts, or "pillboxes," that are inshore on the beaches. This type of fortification was developed and named during World War I when pills were kept in small wooden boxes that were the same shape as the fortifications. Most of the pillboxes on Hawaiʻi's shores were built during the 1920s and 1930s during the military's efforts to install coastal defenses to protect beaches and airfields.

Pinballs. Surf site, Waimea, O'ahu. In Waimea Bay alongside the boulders between the north end of the beach and the point. This site is surfed when waves are breaking only alongside Waimea Point as opposed to outside of the point. Wipeouts here often mean that surfboards and surfers bounce off the boulders like pinballs bouncing off the bumpers in a pinball machine.

Pineapple Isle. Former nickname of Lāna'i. By the early 1920s, Castle and Cooke acquired more than 98 percent of the island and established a 16,000-acre pineapple plantation. Pineapple production was discontinued in the early 1990s when new corporate ownership of the island chose to pursue tourism as the island's primary industry instead of agriculture. Also known as the Secluded Isle.

Pine Tree. Surf site, Ukumehame, Maui. A single ironwood tree is onshore. Ironwoods in Hawai'i are commonly called pine trees because their seeds resemble miniature pinecones. Also known as Lone Pine.

Pine Trees. 1. Beach, dive site, surf site, Kohanaiki, Hawai'i. Calcareous sand and coral rubble beach and several brackish-water ponds at Wāwahiwa'a Point. The largest of the ponds is filled with a tall, dense thicket of mangrove. From a distance the mangroves can be imagined to resemble a stand of ironwood or "pine" trees, giving the site its popular name. The dive and surf sites are off the beach. Pine Trees is also used as an area name that includes other dive sites such as Aquarium, Golden Arches, and Pyramid Pinnacles. Pine Trees is one of the most popular dive sites on the Big Island. Also known as Kohanaiki. 2. Beach park, surf site, Hanalei Bay, Kaua'i. One of three beach parks on Hanalei Bay's 2-mile calcareous sand beach. The surf site is a shorebreak on a shallow sandbar and is one of the island's popular contest sites. A stand of ironwood trees in the park gives the site its popular name. Ironwoods in Hawai'i are commonly called pine trees because their seeds resemble miniature pinecones. Also known as Wai'oli Beach Park.

Pinnacle Point. Dive site, La Pérouse Bay. South of the bay. Pinnacle lava formations and arches from 10 to 60 feet.

Pinnacles. 1. Dive site, 'Anaeho'omalu Bay, Hawai'i. Reef, arches, caverns, and rocky pinnacles. 2. Dive site, Pāhoehoe, Hawai'i. Same as Second Flow.

Pioneer Reef. Dive site, Kawaihae, Hawai'i. Off Kawaihae Harbor and the now defunct Pioneer Lumber Company.

 mo'olelo

Kohala Divers Ltd. was founded in May of 1986 as the only full-service dive center on the Kohala Coast, and we have since become a PADI Five-Star Dive Center. Of course, the dive sites were already there, so we chose the names from identifiable shoreline features.

Frog Rock is one of several dive sites with permanent moorings. These moorings were paid for, installed, and maintained through the joint efforts of concerned dive operators on the Kona/Kohala Coast for the preservation of our reefs in 1988. Near this site is a large rock, which—at the proper angle and the sufficient absorption of nitrogen—looks like a frog sitting.

Kei-Kei Caves is sometimes known as Horseshoe because of its semicircular formation. This site has a wonderful variety of caves and lava tubes. As we understand it, the name Kei Kei implies "potbelly." There are a number of big puffer fish at the site, which we describe as "potbelly puffer fish." There are two mooring buoys at this site. The south mooring is at a large cave that you access underwater near shore. The cave brings you into a lava tube that is fed with fresh water, and the lava tube ends up as a sinkhole onshore. We, of course, call this site Freshwater Cave.

Pioneer Reef is a beautiful reef located just out of the channel to Kawaihae Harbor. Our boat lineup consisted of a small water tower, the red harbor entrance light, and the third window of the now defunct Pioneer Lumber Company.

 Turner Lett, October 23, 2000

Pipe. Surf site, Sunset Beach, Oʻahu. Same as the Pipeline.

Pipeline. 1. Surf site, Sunset Beach, Oʻahu. The Pipeline, one of the most famous surf sites in the world, was first surfed successfully in December 1961 by Phil Edwards, recognized then as one of the best surfers in the world. California surfing movie producer Bruce Brown was with Edwards on the North Shore and filmed his historic rides. After Edwards returned to the beach, he and Brown and another California surfer, Mike Diffenderfer, were discussing an appropriate name for the site. Coincidentally, a construction project for the repair of an underground pipeline was in progress on Kamehameha Highway. As they drove past the project, Diffenderfer looked into the open trench and suggested that they name the surf site the Pipeline. They all agreed. Brown introduced the name to the surfing world in his fourth surfing movie, *Surfing Hollow Days* (1961). Also known as Banzai Pipeline, Pipe. 2. Surf site, Māʻalaea, Maui. Same as Māʻalaea.

 moʻolelo
In the second part of the film, there's a sequence of Phil Edwards being the first to ride the **Pipeline.** We'd looked at the break for

years, but nobody had ever tried it. Phil went out, rode a couple of waves, I got some great shots, he came up on the beach, and we thought, "We've got to think of a name for it." It was Phil Edwards, myself, and Mike Diffenderfer. Mike's the one who said, "How about the Pipeline?" We said, "That's great!" It's been the name ever since.

(Bruce Brown in his 1990 introduction to the
video version of his fourth surfing movie,
Surfing Hollow Days, *filmed in 1961)*

P

In the early 1960s I used to live inshore of the Pipeline with Pat Curren, but no one surfed it. Everyone went to Pūpūkea. One day I was driving Phil Edwards and Bruce Brown around looking for waves for Bruce to film. I drove to my house, and we watched it for about thirty minutes. Phil said he would go out and try it. He caught a couple of waves and came in. Bruce said that since it had never been surfed before, it needed a name. As we drove back out on Kam Highway, we passed an open trench where the Board of Water Supply was repairing a broken water main. I looked in the trench and said, "Why don't we call it the Pipeline?" We all agreed that it was a perfect name.

 Mike Diffenderfer, June 14, 2000

Pipe Littles. Surf site, Hawai'i Kai, O'ahu. On the west side of Half Point, the point fronting the comfort station in Sandy Beach Park. On a good day, waves here are a miniature or "little" version of the Pipeline on O'ahu's North Shore.

Pipes. 1. Surf site, Pākala, Kaua'i. On the east side of Pākala reef. A pipe sticks out of the reef inshore of the surf site. 2. Surf site, Mālaekahana, O'ahu. Off Castles Beach at Makahoa Point. On a good day, waves here resemble those at the Pipeline on O'ahu's North Shore.

Pipi'o. Fishpond, Hālawa, Moloka'i. *Lit.,* arched.

Pitchers. Surf site, Wailea, Hawai'i. In the center of Wailea Beach on the south side of the small rock island. Oceanographers classify waves as either plunging (steep) or spilling (not steep). Waves at Pitchers "pitch," or plunge, rather than spill.

PK's. Snorkeling site, surf site, Kukui'ula, Kaua'i. PK's is an acronym that stands for Prince Kūhiō. The snorkeling site is in a small bay off Prince Kūhiō Park. The surf site is off the Beach House Restaurant. Prior to the development of the restaurant and the adjacent condominiums, Prince Kūhiō Park was the only landmark on the shore.

Plane Wreck Point. Dive site, Keāhole, Hawai'i. Remnants of a Twin Beechcraft lying on the sand at 115 feet served as a small artificial reef, but little remains of it now.

PMRF. Beach, Barking Sands, Kaua'i. Calcareous sand beach fronting the Pacific Missile Range Facility, or PMRF.

Pō'aiwa. Beach, petroglyphs, Pō'aiwa, Lāna'i. Narrow calcareous sand beach that is a section of Shipwreck Beach. Pō'aiwa is the site of one of the two remaining shipwrecks on Shipwreck Beach, a mud barge that appeared mysteriously in 1960, and the site of a former lighthouse and some petroglyphs. *Lit.,* ninth night.

Pōhaku. Park, Honokeana, Maui. Small roadside park on a low sea cliff that overlooks S-turns, a surf site. In 1992 Maui Land and Pine donated the strip of land that comprises the park to the county. Also known as S-turns. *Lit.,* rock. The park's shore is primarily rocky.

Pōhaku 'Īlio. Rock, Kalaupapa, Moloka'i. Flat rock on Papaloa Beach that was associated with the legend of 'Īliopi'i Beach to the west. *Lit.,* dog rock.

Pōhaku Kikēkē. Rock, Mākaha, O'ahu. West of Mākaha Beach near the intersection of Lawai'a Street and Farrington Highway. A rock that resounded if it was struck with another rock like the Bell Stones at Wailua, Kaua'i; Kahakuloa, Maui; and Kaimukī, O'ahu. *Lit.,* knocking rock.

Pōhaku Ku'ihili. Rock, Kapu'a, Hawai'i. Large rock behind the beach at Kapu'a that village fishermen used as a mortar. To prolong the life of their nets, the fishermen periodically soaked the net fibers in a dye made from the bark of the *kukui*, or candlenut tree. The bark was first pounded into a powder on Pōhaku Ku'ihili and then mixed with water. *Lit.,* rock to pound bark.

Pōhaku Kūla'ila'i. Beach, rock, Mākua, O'ahu. Limestone rock at the south end of Mākua Beach that is a popular jumping rock. Legend says that a demigod, a woman who could also assume the form of a *mo'o*, a supernatural lizard, combed her hair on Pōhaku Kūla'ila'i after bathing in a spring nearby. Also known as Pray for Sex Beach. *Lit.,* rock [where waves are] dashed to pieces.

Pōhaku Lāna'i. Rock, Hale'iwa, O'ahu. In Kaiaka Bay Beach Park. Legendary limestone pedestal or "balancing" rock that was said to have floated ashore from the distant land of Kahiki. *Lit.,* day [of] conquest rock, or Lāna'i [island] rock.

Pōhakuloa. 1. Point light, Pōhakuloa, Lāna'i. Established in 1968 on Shipwreck Beach, the light marks the northernmost point on the island. 2. Point, Hāmākua Poko, Maui. Rocky point with low sea cliffs at the east end of Ho'okipa Beach Park. 3. Point, Pōhakuloa, Moloka'i. Rocky point between Honouli Wai and Honouli Malo'o Bays. Also known as Rock Point. *Lit.,* long stone.

297

Pōhakulua. Island, 'Anaeho'omalu, Hawai'i. In 'Anaeho'omalu Bay. *Lit.,* double stone.

Pōhaku Maluhia. Fishing site, rock, Waiehu, Maui. Large rock in the ocean off Waiehu that is only visible from shore at low tide when the ocean is calm. During the 1920s a subdivision here was named the Maluhia Beach Lots after the rock, and the church in the middle of the subdivision was called Maluhia Church. *Lit.,* peaceful rock.

Pōhaku Malumalu. Rock, Pīla'a, Kaua'i. Natural, wave-cut stone arch on the shore that marks the boundary between the land divisions of Pīla'a and Waiakalua. *Lit.,* sheltering stone.

Pōhaku Manu. Rock, Kalaupapa, Moloka'i. Large rock in the backshore of 'Awahua Beach near the foot of the Kalaupapa Trail. *Lit.,* bird rock.

Pōhaku Māuliuli. Beach, surf site, Kaluako'i, Moloka'i. Two pockets of calcareous sand at the base of Pōhaku Māuliuli, a large cinder cone north of Kepuhi Beach. The surf site is a shorebreak on the sandbar fronting the beach. Also known as Make Horse Beach. *Lit.,* dark stone.

Pōhaku o Lama. Rock, Mahai'ula, Hawai'i. Rock in the ocean near shore that was a stone fish goddess. Fishermen brought offerings here to ensure their luck. During the spring, "red tides" of tiny marine organisms called dinoflagellates occur at Mahai'ula and appear as a brownish red plume drifting in the bay. Fishermen believed that the plume was the deity menstruating. *Lit.,* stone of Lama.

Pōhakupaea. Island (.18 acres, 40 feet high), Mākena, Maui. *Lit.,* stone that lands [ashore].

Pōhakupili. Bay, beach, Pōhakupili, Moloka'i. Pocket of calcareous sand at the head of a small bay. A stone called Pōhakupili is located on the hill above the bay. Also known as Fagans Beach. *Lit.,* joined stone.

Pōhakupule. Beach, rock, Punalau, Maui. Calcareous sand and coral rubble beach backed by a stand of ironwood trees. Pōhakupule is a large black rock on the shallow reef off the beach. People who needed to cleanse or purify themselves spiritually came to the beach inshore of the rock and prayed for absolution. Also known as Punalau Beach and Windmill Beach. *Lit.,* prayer rock.

Pōhakus. Surf site, Hawai'i Kai, O'ahu. Right at Full Point at Sandy Beach. This site is surfed infrequently because it breaks over many shallow coral heads. *Pōhaku* means "stone," but the pluralized name, Pōhakus, is slang for "many coral heads."

Pohoiki. Bay, bay light, ramp, surf site, warm spring, Pohoiki, Hawai'i. Pohoiki Bay is the site of Issac Hale Beach Park and a boat ramp, the only one in the district of Puna. A vessel wash-down area adjoins the ramp. The bay light is atop a pole erected in 1979 when the breakwater was constructed. The surf site is off the boat ramp. The warm spring is a pool of volcanically warmed fresh water in a lava sink on the shore of Pohoiki Bay. It is also known as Waiwelawela. *Lit.,* small depression.

Poholokeiki. Channel, Hāʻena, Kauaʻi. Sand-bottomed channel cut through the reef by Limahuli Stream.

Pōhue. Bay, beach, dive site, petroglyphs, surf site, Kaʻū, Hawaiʻi. Small calcareous sand beach at the head of Pōhue Bay. An extensive petroglyph field and other archaeological sites are located on the eastern margin of the bay between the beach and Puʻu Kī, the littoral cone that forms the east point of the bay. The dive site is west of Puʻu Kī at approximately 55 feet. The surf site is off the beach. Also known as Glover's Beach and Kahuku Beach. *Lit.,* gourd.

Poi Bowls. Surf site, Campbell Industrial Park, Oʻahu. West of the public right-of-way on Kaomi Loop and named for the curved or bowl-shaped section in the wave. The name is a play on words between the surfing term *bowl* and a bowl used to either mix or serve poi.

Poinciana. Point, Hōlualoa, Hawaiʻi. Small point on the shore of Hōlualoa Bay with many poinciana trees.

Point, The. 1. Surf site, Pāʻia, Maui. One of the surfing and wind-surf sites off Hoʻokipa Beach Park. The Point is off Hāmākua Poko Point, or H-Poko Point, at the west end of the park. 2. Surf site, swimming site, Hawaiʻi Kai, Oʻahu. Waves at Kawai-hoa, or Portlock Point, break along a low sea cliff as they wrap around the point. The surf site is also known as Walls. During calm, no-surf days, swimmers jump off the multiterraced sea cliff and swim below it. 3. Surf site, Kawailoa, Oʻahu. Off the public right-of-way on Papaʻiloa Road. The wide reef here forms a point on the beach. Also known as Kahaʻakolu. 4. Surf site, Kawailoa, Oʻahu. Near Waimea Bay and off Mokumana, the small rock island that is the "point." Also known as The Spot. 5. Surf site, Makapuʻu, Oʻahu. Off the rocky point at the north end of Makapuʻu Beach. 6. Common abbreviation for many points throughout the islands.

Point Panic. Ocean waters, surf site, Kewalo, Oʻahu. The surf site is off the east end of Kakaʻako Waterfront Park fronting the University of Hawaiʻi's Pacific Biomedical Research Center and is only for bodysurfers and bodyboarders. Point Panic is an exclusive bodysurfing administrative area per Hawaiʻi Administrative Rules, Part III, Ocean Waters, Navigable Streams and Beaches (effective February 24, 1994), State Division of Boating and Ocean Recreation. The name was inspired in the early 1960s by a popular instrumental surfing song called "Point Panic" by the Surfaries. They introduced the song on their "Surf Party" album by saying, "It's about surfing where you shouldn't." Waves here terminate against a high boulder seawall that was completed in 1949. In the preleash days of the 1960s and before board surfing was banned, surfers "panicked" if they lost their boards. Also known Panics.

Poʻipū. Beach, beach park, snorkeling site, windsurf site, Poʻipū, Kauaʻi. Calcareous sand beach between Poʻipū Beach Park to the east and the Sheraton Kauaʻi Resort to the west. Poʻipū Beach Park is the most popular beach park on the island's south shore. Nukumoi Point in the beach park is an example of a tombolo, a sandbar that joins two islands. The snorkeling site is off the west end of the beach park, and the windsurf site is off the west end of the beach near the Sheraton. *Lit.*, completely overcast or crashing [as waves].

Poka ʻAilana. Island, Pearl Harbor, Oʻahu. Poka ʻAilana is the Hawaiianization of the name Ford Island. Also known as Mokuʻumeʻume. *Lit.*, Ford Island (English).

Pōkaʻī Bay. 1. Anchoring site, Waiʻanae, Oʻahu. This site was formerly Pōkaʻī Bay Small Boat Harbor, but the harbor was closed except for anchoring by permit, and its facilities were relocated to Waiʻanae Small Boat Harbor at the west end of the bay. 2. Beach park (15.5 acres), Waiʻanae, Oʻahu. City beach park on the east shore of the bay. Also known as Neneʻu. 3. Dive site, Waiʻanae, Oʻahu. Off the breakwater. 4. Surf site, Waiʻanae, Oʻahu. At the west end of the bay off the Waiʻanae Army Rest Camp. Also known as Rest Camp. *Lit.*, night [of] the supreme one. Pōkaʻī, a legendary voyaging chief, is said to have planted the first coconut tree in Hawaiʻi. He brought it from Kahiki on one of his voyages and planted it in Waiʻanae where in time it gave rise to a famous grove, Ka Ulu Niu o Pōkaʻī—the Coconut Grove of Pōkaʻī.

Pokohulu. Beach, Hāna, Maui. Small *ʻiliʻili* sand beach in Paʻiloa Bay north of Paʻiloa Beach.

Pōkole. Fishpond, Kahaluʻu, Oʻahu. *Lit.*, short.

Pōleho. Beach, northeast coast, Niʻihau. Calcareous sand beach between Kaʻali and Kiʻi Landing approximately 2.5 miles long. The backshore consists of low dunes covered primarily with *kiawe*. The foreshore is rocky, but shallow sandbars front several large sandy coves. An extensive dune system extends inland from the beach into the base of the cliff at Kaʻali. Kiʻi Landing is at the north end of the beach. *Lit.*, cowry night.

Poles. Surf site, Hawaiʻi Kai, Oʻahu. The poles mark the channel into the small harbor at the former Kaiser Estate. Also known as Half Point, Pillars.

Police. Beach, Kawailoa, O'ahu. In 1975 the Honolulu Police Relief Association (HPRA) leased some beachfront property at Pua'ena Point from the Kamehameha Schools Bishop Estate. The site is used for camping and ocean recreation by members of the Honolulu Police Department and has been known since as Police Beach.

Police Beach. Surf site, Kawailoa, O'ahu. Off Police Beach. Also known as Blockhouse.

Polies. Surf site, Mokulē'ia, O'ahu. Between Camp Mokulē'ia and Mokulē'ia Beach Park. Polies is a slang abbreviation of Polipoli, the name on the bridge of the intermittent stream that crosses the beach here. The name was etched into the concrete of the historic Farrington Highway bridge when it was constructed, but was obscured when a steel traffic barrier was tied into the bridge. Also known as Polipoli.

Polihale. Surf site, state park (137.7 acres), windsurf site, Polihale, Kaua'i. Polihale is at the north end of the one of the longest calcareous sand beaches in Hawai'i. The 15-mile-long beach borders the Mānā Coastal Plain and is widest at 300 feet at Polihale where it is fronted by a long, wide sandbar. Extensive dunes between 50 and 100 feet high line the backshore and are especially high toward Nohili Point. The dunes are known as the Barking Sands. The surf site is off the sandbar at the west end, and the windsurf site is off Queen's Pond, a swimming site in the middle of the beach. *Lit.,* house bosom.

Polihua. Beach, surf site, west shore, Lāna'i. Long, wide calcareous sand beach that was once a famous nesting site for green sea turtles. The surf site is off the north end of the beach. *Lit.,* eggs [in] bosom.

Polipoli. Beach, surf site, Mokulē'ia, O'ahu. Calcareous sand beach between Camp Mokulē'ia and Mokulē'ia Beach Park. The surf site is off the beach. Polipoli is the name on the bridge over an intermittent stream that crosses the beach here. Like all of the other historic bridges built in to the late 1920s and early 1930s on O'ahu, the name was etched into the concrete of the bridge when it was constructed; it was obscured when a steel traffic barrier was tied into the bridge. Also known as Polies. *Lit.,* polishing stone.

Polo. Beach, surf site, Wailea, Maui. One of five calcareous sand beaches fronting the Wailea resort complex. The surf site is a shorebreak that forms on the sandbar fronting the beach. In 1971 Maui historian Inez Ashdown identified this beach as Ke One o Polo, "the sand of Polo," in her book *Ke Alaloa o Maui.* When Wailea was developed, the name was shortened to Polo.

Pololū. Beach, beachcombing site, surf site, valley, North Kohala, Hawai'i. Pololū Valley is one of seven isolated coastal valleys on the north side of Kohala Mountain. A black sand beach with a wide, shallow sandbar offshore and high vegetated dunes in the backshore front the valley. Ironwood trees are the primary dune vegetation. The surf site is a shorebreak on the sandbar, and the beach is a popular beachcombing site. The black sand is detrital material eroded and transported to the shore by Pololū Stream. *Lit.*, long spear.

P

  mo'olelo

I was born on September 15, 1905, and I'm a cousin of Bill Sproat. When I was young, I spent a lot of time in Pololū and Honokāne Nui. In the middle of the surf at **Pololū,** there is a *wiliau*—a swirling current. The old folks always told us never to swim there. It's near shore where the waves are and then goes back out to sea. You can see the whitewater trail in the channel next to the *wiliau*.

I have two *papa paepō* in my artifact collection. They're two small concave boards about ¼-inch by 1 foot by 3 feet made of *wiliwili,* and they were used for spying. The spies selected a night with rough seas and then surfed in to gather information about various activities. The boards were easily concealed. I heard this from the old people, and they said that's why the boards were called *paepō,* "night landing."

In 1916, I went on a fishing trip with my uncles. Outside of Pololū there's a small flat rock with holes in it. One of my uncles jumped out and grabbed some *he'e pali*—small brown squids— between waves as they washed over the rock. Then we paddled towards the big island. About midway there's a sandy area, and we stopped, skinned the squid, and cut it for bait. Then we dropped fifteen hooks off either side of the canoe and used long, narrow *pohaku 'alā* that we picked off the beach for sinkers and *hau* floaters. We caught some huge *onaga* in about 65 feet of water. Then we went to visit Kahikina who was living on the point at Honopu'e, and traded him fish for bananas. He left after the '46 tidal wave.

On the Niuli'i side of Pololū, there are conch and other shells along the rocks. My grandmother ate the conch meat. There are also small brown eels there that the women caught by using red streamers that the eels would bite and get tangled in. There are huge *'ōkole* there, too, reddish, that we boiled to eat. We also ate the *he'e pali,* but only raw. It was considered the best squid for [eating] raw and was never cooked.

Alfred Solomon, June 25, 1982

I was born and raised in Pololū. The *wiliau* at the beach is a circling current—it comes with the waves and circles back out through the surf. You swim to the side to get out of it. On calm days, the beach is good for *moi* and *'ō'io*. You can tell what's offshore by the shells on the beach. The *moi* eat *'ōpaelolo,* and the *'ō'io* eat *polipoli,* and what they spit out comes in. The old-timers could look at what's on the beach and know where to cross-net and what they were going to catch, and they picked up plenty.

Kahikina at Honopu'e was the very last of the old-timers to leave the inside valleys. There were large communities there and at Honoke'ā, and the people lived *mauka* and *makai.*

 Tommy Solomon, July 8, 1982

Pomokupā. Beach, Mākaha, O'ahu. South section of Mākaha Beach between Kumuku and Kahaloko.

Po'ohuna. Fishing site, point, Mākua, O'ahu. Point at the south end of Mākua Beach. *Lit.,* hidden head.

Po'ohuna Point. Dive site, Mākua, O'ahu. Off the point seaward of Kaneana Cave. Also known as Mākua Point. *Lit.,* hidden head point.

Po'olau. Beach, Kaluako'i, Moloka'i. Small pocket of calcareous sand lined by boulders at the water's edge. Also known as Bomb Bay.

Po'olenalena. Beach, beach park, rock, Mākena, Maui. Calcareous sand beach between two rocky points. The beach park is a small undeveloped parcel at the west end of the beach. Po'olenalena is the name of a large rock on the fairway of the fifth hole of the Wailea Blue Golf Course. The lava rock has natural yellow streaks on its side. The beach across the street took its name from the rock. Also known as Chang's Beach. *Lit.,* yellow head.

Pools. Surf site, Lahaina, Maui. Off the community center swimming pool in the Puamana subdivision.

Po'ooneone. Beach, point, southeast coast, Ni'ihau. Calcareous sand beach between 'Ō'iamoi Point and the sea cliffs at Pā'ia that is approximately 2.5 miles long. The foreshore of the beach is lined with a rocky shelf, and the backshore consists of vegetated dunes. Po'ooneone is a 50-foot-high point of eolianite, or lithified dunes, covered with a veneer of calcareous sand that is in the middle of the beach. It is one of the most prominent landmarks on this coast. *Lit.,* sandy head.

Po'opo'o. Island (.5 acres, 40 feet high), Huawai, Lāna'i. Part of the Hawai'i State Seabird Sanctuary. *Lit.,* hollow.

Poop Shoots. Surf site, Mōkapu, O'ahu. The surf site fronts a shallow reef in a little bay off the rifle range on the marine base. Debris ("poop") accumulates in the bay and the surfers must ride ("shoot") through it.

Popoiʻa. Island (4 acres), Kailua, Oʻahu. Low, flat limestone island one-quarter mile off Kailua Beach Park. Part of the Hawaiʻi State Seabird Sanctuary and nesting site during the summer months for wedge-tailed shearwaters. Also known as Flat Island. *Lit.,* fish rot. The name probably refers to offerings of fish that were left at a fishing shrine on the island. The shrine was destroyed by the tsunami of April 1, 1946.

Popoki. Fishing site, Mākena, Maui. North of Pamolepo, the small graveyard that belongs to the Kukahiko family of Mākena. *Lit.,* short or thick (a variation of *pokipoki*).

Popoʻokaʻala. Point, Lanikai, Oʻahu. Also known as Wailea Point.

Pops. Surf site, Waikīkī, Oʻahu. Same as Populars.

Populars. Surf site, Waikīkī, Oʻahu. Off the Sheraton Waikīkī Hotel. Helumoa is the section of Waikīkī where the Sheraton and other hotels are now. Prior to its high-rise resort development, it was an area where many Hawaiians lived. They surfed directly offshore and named the site because it was the most popular place for them to surf. Also known as Pops.

Port Allen. 1. Airport, Hanapēpē, Kauaʻi. Landing field for small airplanes and helicopters at Pūʻolo Point, the west point of Port Allen Harbor. 2. Harbor, Hanapēpē, Kauaʻi. One of two deep-draft harbors on Kauaʻi. Named for Samuel C. Allen, a partner in Allen and Robinson, a chandlery and lumber business on the waterfront of Honolulu Harbor. Allen hoped to develop the site, then known as ʻEleʻele Landing, into Kauaʻi's principal port, but its distance from Honolulu Harbor proved too great an obstacle. In 1909, the Kauaʻi Railway Company, the owner of the shipping terminal, renamed the landing in honor of Allen. 3. Small boat harbor, Hanapēpē, Kauaʻi. Facilities include thirty-four berths, six moorings, a two-lane ramp, two piers, a fish hoist, and a vessel washdown area. 4. Surf site, Hanapēpē, Kauaʻi. Near Port Allen on the west point of Hanapēpē Bay.

Portlock. 1. Beach, Hawaiʻi Kai, Oʻahu. Shore from the Hawaiʻi Kai Marina Bridge at Kalanianaʻole Highway to the end of Portlock Road. Most of the narrow calcareous beach is concentrated between the bridge and the first section of homes on Portlock Road. The remainder of the shore is vertical seawalls with only a few pockets of sand between some of the walls. 2. Point, Hawaiʻi Kai, Oʻahu. Southwest point of Koko Head. Also known as Kawaihoa. In 1786, two British trading ships anchored in the lee of Koko Head to take on food, water, and other provisions for their voyage to Canton, China. Captain George Dixon commanded the *Queen Charlotte,* and Captain Nathaniel Portlock commanded the *King George.* In 1936, when Bishop Estate converted some pastureland at the base of Koko Head into a subdivision, Albert F. Judd, Bishop Estate trustee and Hawaiian historian, named the subdivision after Captain Portlock. Kawaihoa Point was then also named Portlock Point.

Portlock Point. Dive site, surf site, Hawai'i Kai, O'ahu. The surf site is a long left with many sections at Kawaihoa, or Portlock Point, that begins with a steep takeoff next to a submerged rock. The name Portlock Point comes from the Portlock community, which for thirty years, beginning in the 1930s, was the only community at the base of Koko Head until the development of Koko Kai in the 1960s. The surf site is also known as China's, China Walls. The dive site is along the low sea cliffs that form the point.

Pouhala. Fishpond, marsh, Pearl Harbor, O'ahu. A 70-acre marsh between Waipahu Depot Road and West Loch that is a wetland habitat for birds. *Lit.,* pandanus tree post.

Pounders. Beach, surf site, Lā'ie, O'ahu. Named in 1955 by the first students at Church College of Hawai'i (now Brigham Young University–Hawai'i) for the pounding shorebreak waves at this popular bodysurfing and bodyboarding site. Also known as Lā'ie Beach Park.

Power Plants. Surf site, Kahe, O'ahu. Off Kahe Point Beach Park. Hawaiian Electric Company's Kahe Power Plant is opposite the park.

PP Buoy. Kōloa, Kaua'i. Fish aggregating buoy at approximately 950 fathoms. Landmarks: Port Allen Light, Makahū'ena Point.

Pray for Sex. Beach, dive site, rock, surf site, Mākua, O'ahu. In the 1960s, the words "Pray for Sex" were painted on Pōhaku Kūla'ila'i, a large limestone rock at the east end of Mākua Beach, and the phrase has since remained a popular name for the beach. The phrase was a play on words for "Pray for Surf," a popular saying among surfers in the 1960s. The dive site and the surf site are off the rock.

Prince Kūhiō Park. Historical site, Kukui'ula, Kaua'i. Park on the shore of Hō'ai Bay that commemorates the birthplace of Prince Jonah Kūhiō Kalaniana'ole. When Kūhiō's mother died soon after his birth, he and his two brothers were adopted by his mother's sister Kapi'olani and her husband Kalākaua, who had no children of their own. When Kalākaua became king of the Hawaiian Islands in 1874, he gave each of the boys the title of prince. Prince Kūhiō served as Hawai'i's delegate to Congress from 1902 until his death in 1922. He is probably best remembered as the Mākua 'Āina Ho'opulapula, or "father of the homestead lands." It was largely through his efforts that Congress passed the Hawaiian Homes Commission Act, establishing homestead lands for native Hawaiians on five of the eight major Hawaiian Islands.

Princess Cove. Pool, Kahuku, Oʻahu. Small natural pool within a rock formation on Kaihalulu Beach.

Princeville. Coast, Princeville, Kauaʻi. Princeville is a 2,000-acre resort and residential community along the sea cliffs between 'Anini Beach to the east and Hanalei Bay to the west. The name Princeville came from Robert Wyllie (1798–1865), a Scottish physician who served as foreign minister under Kamehameha IV and Kamehameha V. Wyllie owned the property here in 1860 when Kamehameha IV and his wife Queen Emma visited with their two-year-old son, the prince Ka Haku o Hawaiʻi. Wyllie named his home Princeville in honor of this visit by the young prince.

Prindle. Beach, Kāʻanapali, Maui. North section of Kāʻanapali Beach where double-hulled sailboats such as Prindle catamarans are common in the backshore.

Psychos. Surf site, Waiʻanae, Oʻahu. In Pōkaʻī Bay near Kaupuni Channel. *Psychos* was a slang term in the 1970s that was applied to this site for fun.

Puaʻena. 1. Point, stone, Haleʻiwa, Oʻahu. Puaʻena was a legendary woman who came to Hawaiʻi with Pele, the goddess of the volcano. A stone on a small beach in the lee of the point named for her was famous for its curative powers, and Hawaiians came from all parts of Oʻahu to visit it. It was also known as the Lady Puaʻena Stone. Puaʻena was also the name of a beach home at the point that belonged to William Holt. He built it in the late 1800s and used it through the 1930s. 2. Surf site, Haleʻiwa, Oʻahu. Two distinct sites here are known as Inside Puaʻena Point and Outside Puaʻena Point. *Lit.*, issue hot.

Puahi. Beach, Kalaupapa, Molokaʻi. Black sand beach at the foot of the Kalaupapa Trail. Also known as 'Awahua Beach. *Lit.*, hill [of] fire.

Puakahīnano. Point, Keaukaha, Hawaiʻi. East point at Leleiwi Beach Park that forms the bay. Perhaps lit., the male pandanus flower.

Puakō. 1. Bay, beach, Puakō, Hawaiʻi. Narrow calcareous sand beach on the long rock bench that lines the bay. Six public rights-of-way lead to the beach from Puakō Road. 2. Ramp, Puakō, Hawaiʻi. Facilities include a ramp and loading dock, a pier, and a vessel washdown area. 3. Petroglyph archaeological park, Puakō, Hawaiʻi. The 233-acre petroglyph park, with some three thousand individual rock carvings, is one of the three largest on the Big Island. The other large fields are 'Anehoʻomalu at Waikoloa Resort and Puʻuloa in Hawaiʻi Volcanoes National Park. Puakō Petroglyph Archaeological

Park is accessed through Holoholokai Beach Park. *Lit.,* sugar-cane blossom.

Puakō Bay. Offshore mooring, Puakō, Hawai'i. State mooring site.

Puakō Ramp. Surf site, Puakō, Hawai'i. On the north side of Puakō Bay adjacent to 'Ōhai Point. Surfers access the site from Puakō Ramp.

Puakō Reef. Dive site, Puakō, Hawai'i. Many dive sites at approximately 40 feet along the rock bench that parallels Puakō Beach.

Pū'āla'a. Beach Park (1.3 acres), 'Opihikao, Hawai'i. Dedicated in 1993, the park property was purchased by the county to provide a beach park for Puna residents after the loss of Kaimū Beach Park and Harry K. Brown Park in Kalapana to lava flows in 1990. The park is the site of a precontact fishing village on the boundary of the land divisions of Pū'āla'a and Laepao'o and includes a swimming pool fed by warm springs. *Lit., 'āla'a (Planchonella)* tree (said to be common here but rare elsewhere).

Puamana. 1. Beach park, Lahaina, Maui. Puamana was the family home of Annie Kahalepouli Shaw Farden and Charles Kekua Farden. Their large two-story home, built in 1915, was located on Front Street. When the Fardens purchased the half-acre lot, it was already named Puamana. They agreed to keep the name for their home, translating it to mean the home that holds its members close. Puamana is probably best known to Hawai'i's residents through the song of the same name. Irmgard Farden Aluli, one of the twelve Farden children, composed it in 1935. Puamana Beach Park and Puamana subdivision adjacent to the park took their name from the Farden's family home. Also known as Mākila. 2. Surf site, Lahaina, Maui. Off the beach park.

 mo'olelo

Puamana was the name of our home in Lahaina. It was a six-bedroom, two-bath, two-story house, and we moved in 1915 when I was four. One day my dad had the yardman dig nine holes in the ground behind the seawall. Then he had each of us children plant a coconut tree. The other children that followed also planted trees when they were old enough, and other trees were planted to fill the gaps, but each child knew his own tree, and we often compared them when we returned home from attending school in Honolulu.

In 1935 I was teaching school on Moloka'i, and I returned home for a visit. I sat down at the piano and a tune just came to me. I decided that it would be a song for our family home. Five of my sisters were home, so I called all of them and played it. They liked it. When my dad came home for lunch, I played it for him,

P

and he liked it, too, so we all asked him how to say different descriptive things in Hawaiian, and he translated. I wanted to have one verse about the coconut trees, so he told me a few phrases: *ku'u home i ka ulu niu* (my home surrounded by coconut trees), *kū kilakila* (trees that stand straight and tall), *napenape malie* (the coconut leaves flutter in the calm of the evening). The last phrase we all especially liked. Our family often took a large mat outside on quiet, moonlight nights, and everyone sang while the breeze rustled the coconut leaves, the moonlight danced on the water, and the surf foamed white offshore.

 *Irmgard Aluli, July 16, 1978*

Puanui. Fishing site, Kahuku, O'ahu. East of Kalaeuila. *Lit.*, many flowers.

Puau. Beach, Keawa'ula, O'ahu. Center of Keawa'ula Beach inland of the surf site called Yokohama.

Publics. Surf site, Waikīkī, O'ahu. Named for the former Public Baths, a recreation facility on the shore of Kapi'olani Regional Park directly inshore of the surf site from 1908 until the early 1950s. The facility included showers, dressing rooms, lockers for men and women, and a refreshment stand. The surf site was originally called Public Baths, but the name was shortened to Publics after the recreation facility was demolished.

Pūehuehu. Beach, Lā'ie, O'ahu. North section of Laniloa Beach near Lā'ie Point. The larger of two sand pockets on Laniloa Beach that are good for swimming. *Lit.*, scattered. Goatfish and other bottom feeders scatter or stir up sand with their barbels in search of food. This activity was called *pūehu* or *pūehuehu*.

Pueo. 1. Bay, beach, surf site, Keawaiki, Hawai'i. Small bay formed by the 1859 lava flow from Mauna Loa with a coral rubble and pebble beach. The surf site is off the beach. 2. Point, east coast, Ni'ihau. The prominent easternmost point of the island approximately midway along the high sea cliffs between Po'o-oneone and Pōleho Beaches. *Lit.*, owl.

Pūhala. 1. Bay, fishing site, Māliko, Maui. Small bay east of Māliko Bay. A small grove of *hala* (pandanus) trees lies in the backshore of the bay. 2. Beach, fishing site, Ka'a'awa, O'ahu. Between Kalae'ō'io and Makahonu Points. Once the site of many *hala* trees in the backshore alongside Kamehameha Highway. *Lit.*, pandanus tree.

Pūhāloa. Fishpond, Kamalō, Moloka'i. *Lit.*, bursting forth long.

Pūhau. Pond, spring, Nīnole, Hawai'i. Spring-fed pond on the shore, partially filled by erosion runoff. The pond is named after one of two springs, Pūhau and Kauale, that supply the pond. *Lit.*, ice spring.

Puhi. Bay, Keaukaha, Hawaiʻi. Keaukaha Beach Park is on the shore of the bay. The bay was named for a blowhole on the western side of the bay that fronted the sewage treatment plant. Construction of the outfall destroyed the blowhole. *Lit.,* blowhole.

Puhi Anenue. Bay, southeast shore, Kahoʻolawe.

Puhilele. Navigational light site, Kalaeloa, Oʻahu. Location of the Barbers Point Light. *Lit.,* leaping eel.

Puhikūkae. Fishing site, Kahuku, Oʻahu. East end of Hanaka-ʻīlio Beach. *Lit.,* eel excrement.

Puhi Rock. Fishing site, Kīpāhoehoe, Hawaiʻi. At Kīpāhoehoe where an *ulua* fisher caught a 76-pound eel, or *puhi. Lit.,* moray eel.

Pukano. Point, reef, Keawaʻula, Oʻahu. At the east end of Keawaʻula Beach.

Puka Pants. Beach, surf site, Nānākuli, Oʻahu. Section of Ulehawa Beach Park across from Hakimo Road that is a popular swimming area for families with young children. *"Puka* pants" is slang for torn or tattered pants which some swimmers prefer instead of manufactured swim wear. *Puka* means "hole."

Pukihae. Beach, Hilo, Hawaiʻi. Small pocket of black sand below the highway bridge at Pukihae.

Pūkoʻo. Beach, harbor, landing, surf site, Pūkoʻo, Molokaʻi. Narrow detrital sand beach bordering the wide, shallow fringing reef. A natural opening in the reef serves as a harbor. In the early 1900s, the former village here was the county seat on Molokaʻi. The surf site is on the reef offshore. *Lit.,* support hill.

Pūkoʻo Lagoon. Anchorage, Pūkoʻo, Molokaʻi. Three-fingered boat anchorage with a private entrance channel that was dredged out of the former Pūkoʻo fishpond.

Pūlāʻī. Point, Kaʻaʻawa, Oʻahu. Point adjoining the west end of Swanzy Beach Park. Also known as Kaʻaʻawa Point. The name of a legendary person.

Pulemoku. Island, Lāʻie, Oʻahu. Part of the Hawaiʻi State Seabird Sanctuary. One of five islands visible from Lāʻie Point that were created when the demigods Kana and Nīheu cut up the body of a *moʻo,* a giant lizard, and threw the pieces into the sea. *Lit.,* broken prayer.

Puna Coast Trail. Hawaiʻi Volcanoes National Park, Hawaiʻi. Trail on the shore that connected the coastal villages in Puna to the village of Punaluʻu in Kaʻū, an important interisland steamer landing until the 1940s.

Punahoa. Beach, spring, Olowalu, Maui. East of Olowalu and marked by a single ironwood tree on the shore. *Lit.,* companion spring.

Punahoʻolapa. Marsh, Kahuku, Oʻahu. A 100-acre wetland preserve and habitat for endangered Hawaiian waterbirds such as coots, gallinules, ducks, and stilts within the Links at Kuilima, an eighteen-hole championship golf course at the Turtle Bay Hilton Golf and Tennis Resort.

Punalau. 1. Beach, Punalau, Maui. Calcareous sand beach fronted by a shallow reef. Also known as Pōhakupule Beach, Windmill Beach. 2. Fishpond, Kaunakakai, Moloka'i. *Lit.*, many springs. Freshwater springs were common along the beach at both sites.

Punalu'u. 1. Beach park, ramp, landing, Punalu'u, Hawai'i. Black sand beach 800 feet long fronting a spring-fed pond at the head of a small bay. The boat ramp is on Kahiolo Point at the east end of the beach, a former landing for interisland steamers. The beach park is on Pu'umoa Point at the west end of the beach. *Lit.*, spring [water] dived for. 2. Beach park (2.8 acres), Punalu'u, O'ahu. Calcareous sand beach fronting a narrow park on Kamehameha Highway. The park is in the land division of Punalu'u. *Lit.*, coral dived for.

 mo'olelo

I was born in Punalu'u in 1923, and I've lived here my entire life. I'm Chinese-Hawaiian, married to a fisherman, and our house is near the restaurant parking lot. We still fish the *ko'a ahi* and *'ōpelu* offshore. Kahiolo is the left point of the bay. There's a *heiau* on top of it and a sacrifice stone in the bushes. It's a big rock slab. Pu'umoa is the right point of the bay where the picnic pavilions are located. Offshore are all the little *moku* that protect the beach. **Punalu'u** is the general name for the beach and the pond behind it. When I was young, the beach used to be from half way out to the boat ramp, but it has always eroded, even before sand was hauled away by the county and other people.

Kōloa is the shore beyond the park. It used to be covered with *'ili'ili* called *'ili'ili hānau*, or "maternity stones," but there's very few left now. Most of them were hauled away for various construction projects. Further down at Nīnole there used to be two springs in a big pond, Kauale and Pūhau. Kauale was the female spring, and Pūhau was the male spring, but they were covered in 1979 and 1980 by floods that brought down a lot of mud and rock.

 Jeanette Howard, September 21, 1981

Punamanō Unit. Wildlife, refuge, Kahuku, O'ahu. A 38-acre natural, spring-fed wetland that is one of two sections in the James Campbell National Wildlife Refuge at Kahuku Point. The refuge attracts both native and migratory waterbirds. *Lit.*, shark spring.

Punapālaha. Bay, beach, spring, Kahuku, O'ahu. Section of Kaihalulu Beach near Kalaeokauna'oa, or Kahuku Point, where the rocks were smooth and slippery from the seepage of fresh water. Also known as John Jack Bay. *Lit.*, slippery spring.

Punaulua. Spring, Kawela Bay, O'ahu. Freshwater spring on the west shore of the bay said to be connected to the ocean through an underwater passage. *Ulua*, or crevalle fish, were attracted to the upwelling of the fresh water in the ocean, giving the spring its name. Also known as Kapī. *Lit.*, crevalle fish spring.

Puniawa. 1. Bay, point, Ha'ikū, Maui. Bay with a boulder beach adjacent to Pa'uwela Light. Also known as Coconut Grove, Kuiaha. 2. Bay, fishing site, Huelo, Maui. Small bay at the end of Honopou Stream.

Pu'ōkole. Point, reef, Keawa'ula, O'ahu. At the east end of Keawa'ula Beach. *Lit.*, anus hill (named for *'ōkole*, anus-shaped anemones that were gathered here for food).

Pūpūkea. 1. Beach park (36.6 acres), Sunset Beach, O'ahu. Sections of the park are also known as Kapo'o, Sharks Cove, Three Tables. 2. Marine life conservation district (25 acres), Pūpūkea, O'ahu. Established in 1983 off Pūpūkea Beach Park. Includes both Sharks Cove and Three Tables. 3. Surf site, Sunset Beach, O'ahu. On the southwest side of Rocky Point. John Severson, a surfer from California who was in the army and worked in the map department at Schofield Barracks, named the site during the winter of 1957. Severson and other California surfers living on the North Shore at that time knew the entire beach as Banzai Beach, but believed this popular surf site should have an appropriate Hawaiian name. Severson utilized the resources in his office but could not find any beach names in the area, so he selected Pūpūkea, the name of the land division that includes the surf site. Discharged in 1958, Severson went on to produce six surfing movies and found *Surfer Magazine.* He continues to create his now internationally famous surf art from his home on Maui. He was voted into the Surfing Hall of Fame in 1993, the Walk of Fame at Huntington Beach in 1995, and given a lifetime achievement award by the Surf Industry Manufacturers' Association as Waterman of the Year in 1997. *Lit.*, white shell. All of the Pūpūkea sites are located in the land division of Pūpūkea.

Pu'u. Spring, Holualoa, Hawai'i. On the shore of Holualoa Bay, where it marks the end of a canoe-hauling road called Ke Ala o Wa'a. The road is associated with a canoe-making *heiau* about a mile inland called Ke Ala Ko Wa'a.

Pu'uahi. Beach, Lā'ie, O'ahu. Southeast section of Lā'ie Bay. Also known as Temple Beach. *Lit.*, hill [of] fire. Cooking fires were built on the dunes here in anticipation of fishermen returning with their catches.

Pu'u Hakina. Beach, surf site, Hale o Lono, Moloka'i. Long, wide calcareous sand beach at the base of Pu'u Hakina. Also known as Kanalukaha Beach. *Lit.,* broken hill.

Pu'u Hinahina. Bay, beach, , Kapu'a, Hawai'i. Calcareous sand, coral rubble beach at the head of Pu'u Hinahina Bay. Āhole Hōlua, the best-preserved *hōlua* (sled ramp) in Hawai'i, terminates at the beach. *Lit.,* hill [of the] *hinahina* [plant].

Pu'uhonua o Hōnaunau. National historical park (182 acres), Hōnaunau, Hawai'i. Site of a *pu'uhonua,* or place of refuge, on the shore of Hōnaunau Bay. *Pu'uhonua* were safety zones administered by priests where war refugees, defeated warriors, or people accused breaking a *kapu*—a law against the gods—could seek refuge. In addition to the *pu'uhonua,* the park includes a royal residence, the former villages of Hōnaunau and Ki'ilae, a small beach, Keone'ele, and other historical sites. Pu'uhonua o Hōnaunau was designated as a national historical park in 1961 and is one of the Big Island's most popular visitor destinations. Also known as City of Refuge.

Pu'uhonua o Mālaekahana. Cultural site, Mālaekahana, O'ahu. Part of Mālaekahana State Park, Kahuku Section that is used for Hawaiian cultural activities and events. *Lit.,* place of refuge at Mālaekahana.

Pu'u Hou. Beach, littoral cone (240 feet), surf site, Ka'ū, Hawai'i. Largest littoral cone in Hawai'i that was formed when lava flows from the 1868 eruption of Mauna Loa entered the ocean here west of Ka Lae, or South Point. Three green sand beaches lie at the base of the cone. The easternmost of the three beaches also has red cinder mixed in with the black cinder and olivine, a unique combination of beach sands. The surf site is off the beaches. Also known as Cinder Cone. *Lit.,* new hill.

Pu'uiki. 1. Beach, Mokulē'ia, O'ahu. Section of Mokulē'ia Beach between the west point of Kaiaka Bay, the site of the Pu'uiki Cemetery, and Pu'uiki Beach Park. 2. Beach park, Mokulē'ia, O'ahu. Private beach park on Mokulē'ia Beach that was originally owned and maintained by the Waialua Sugar Company for its employees. 3. Cemetery. Behind the beach on the west side of Kaiaka Bay. Waialua Sugar Company established the cemetery for its employees. 4. Surf site, Mokulē'ia, O'ahu. Off Pu'uiki Beach Park. Also known as Hammerheads. *Lit.,* small hill.

Pu'u Kahuaiki. Reef, Hā'ena, Kaua'i. Large reef to the east of Limahuli Stream. The surf site Bobo's is on this reef. *Lit.,* small site hill.

Pu'u Kahuanui. Reef, Hā'ena, Kaua'i. Large reef on the east side of the channel cut through the reef by Limahuli Stream. Also known as Winchells. *Lit.*, large site hill.

Pu'u Kapukapu. Hill (1,050 feet), Hawai'i Volcanoes National Park, Hawai'i. Hill on the *pali* that separates the coastal camping sites of Halapē and Ka'aha. *Lit.*, regal hill.

Pu'u Keka'a. Headland, Kā'anapali, Maui. Cinder cone in the center of Kā'anapali Beach. The Sheraton Maui was completed on its summit in January 1963. Also known as Black Rock. *Lit.*, rumbling hill.

Pu'u Kī. Littoral cone, fishing site, Pōhue, Hawai'i. Littoral cone that forms the east point of Pōhue Bay. Also known as Eddie Hosaka, Hosaka Point. *Lit.*, ti plant hill.

Pu'uki'i. Island (1.5 acres, 72 feet high), Hāna, Maui. Small state-owned island that is part of the Hawai'i State Seabird Sanctuary. The island is at the base of Ka'uiki Head, where it is connected to shore by a natural rock bridge. Ka'uiki Head Light is located on its summit. Also known as Pu'ukū. *Lit.*, image hill. Tradition says 'Umi erected a huge wooden image on the hill to frighten attackers.

Pu'u Koa'e. 1. Island (13 acres, 378 feet high), south coast, Kaho'olawe. Small island with steep sides west of Kamōhio Bay. Also known as Kaho'olaweli'ili'i. 2. Hill, point, Kahakuloa, Maui. One of West Maui's most prominent coastal landmarks. Pu'u Koa'e (636 feet) is a volcanic cinder cone that has been cut by wave erosion. *Lit.*, tropicbird hill.

Pu'ukoholā. *Heiau*, national historic site (86 acres), Kawaihae, Hawai'i. The *heiau*, or shrine, was built by Kamehameha I and completed in 1791. Kamehameha had acted upon the advice of a priest who had predicted he would successfully unify the Hawaiian Islands if he built a *heiau* to Kūka'ilimoku, his war god, on Pu'ukoholā, a prominent hill overlooking Kawaihae Bay. The unification was completed in 1810 and the Hawaiian monarchy lasted for 83 years until 1893. Pu'ukoholā was designated as a historical landmark in 1928 and a national historic site on August 17, 1972. *Lit.*, whale hill.

Pu'ukū. Island, Hāna, Maui. Off Ka'uiki Head. State-owned island that is part of the Hawai'i State Seabird Sanctuary. Also known as Pu'uki'i. *Lit.*, upright hill.

Pu'u Kuili. Cinder cone (342 feet), Manini'ōwali, Hawai'i. One of North Kona's most prominent coastal features. Manini'ōwali Beach is near its base.

Pu'uloa. Salt works, 'Ewa Beach, O'ahu. Commercial salt operation established near Keahi Point, the west point of Pearl Harbor Channel, by Isaac Montgomery in partnership with King Kamehameha III. In 1849 Montgomery purchased the *'ili*, or land division, of Puʻuloa in which the ponds were located. Salt production continued on into the early 1900s. *Lit.,* long hill.

Puʻuloa USMC Range Facility. Firing range, ʻEwa Beach, Oʻahu. U.S. Marine Corps range facility on the shore between ʻEwa Beach Park and Iroquois Beach. Public access in the waters offshore is restricted when the range is in active use. The military flies red flags to warn boaters. Also known as Rifle Range.

Puʻu Māhana. Littoral cone, Kaʻū, Hawaiʻi. The cone and the lava around it are replete with olivine. The olivine is freed by waves eroding the cinder and rock and then deposited on the beach at the base of the cone. The beach is known as Green Sand Beach. Perhaps lit., warm hill.

Puʻu Maile. Shore, Keaukaha, Hawaiʻi. Puʻu Maile Home was a tuberculosis sanitarium that was first built in 1912 at the site of what is now the old terminal of the Hilo Airport. It was named for a nearby cinder cone called Puʻu Maile. During the 1930s the cinder cone was leveled to provide fill for the airport's runways. In 1939 a new facility, Puʻu Maile Hospital, was completed at the end of Kalanianaʻole Avenue adjacent to Lehia Park, and the old facility at the airport was demolished. The hospital remained at the end of the road until 1951, when it was relocated to the grounds of the Hilo Hospital. Nothing remains of the former building except its long concrete seawall at the edge of Lehia Park. Although the hospital has been gone since 1951, many Big Island residents still call the area Puʻu Maile. *Lit., maile* vine hill.

 moʻolelo

Puʻu Maile was a large hill where the old airport is that was maybe 50 or 60 feet high and 100 by 200 feet. It was located where Slim Holt and Hertz have their lots. Puʻu Maile Hospital was there, but when construction of the airport started, it was relocated to Leleʻiwi. The old wooden hospital was leveled and burned, and the hill, Puʻu Maile, was leveled for runway fill. The hospital took its name along and that's how the name Puʻu Maile came to Leleʻiwi. The new buildings there were completed in 1939.

When the '46 wave struck, I was called within an hour after the destruction to open the road through Keaukaha to Puʻu Maile. The authorities wanted to evacuate the people on the shore and the patients in the hospital. I was a heavy equipment operator, so I took a D-8 bulldozer to do the job. One section of the road was washed out so badly that I had to pull some trucks with the dozer to get them through. People were still up in the trees, many of them half naked. There were bodies everywhere. Colonel Kupihea of the National Guard was in charge of the operation, so he had soldiers walk in front of me to clear the dead out of the way. Moses Serrao assisted me, too. At the hospital I had patients riding on the dozer, and we even tied stretchers down on the front of the 'dozer. We made continuous trips until nine that night before we evacuated everyone out.

Later we helped in the Waiākea area. I ran the cranes to lift the heavy concrete slabs and the like to extricate the dead. They also brought down the prisoners at Kūlani to help, and they did more than their fair share. But they were never given any credit for assisting.

 Henry Auwae, July 19, 1982

Puʻumoa. Point, surf site, Punaluʻu, Hawaiʻi. Site of Punaluʻu Beach Park. The surf site is off the west end of Punaluʻu Beach, adjacent to the point. *Lit.,* chicken hill.

Puʻu Nao. Point, Kailua, Oʻahu. Small limestone point at the north end of Kailua Beach with a private residence on it. *Lit.,* wave-cut hill.

Puʻunoa. Beach, point, Lahaina, Maui. Calcareous sand beach at Puʻunoa Point at the west end of Lahaina. *Lit.,* hill freed of taboo.

Puʻunoa Point. Dive site, Lahaina, Maui. Off the point and south of Māla Wharf.

Puʻu Ohau. Cinder cone (230 feet), Kainaliu, Hawaiʻi. The most conspicuous coastal landmark on the low sea cliffs between Kealakekua and Keauhou Bays, Puʻu Ohau marks the boundary between North and South Kona. Also known as Red Hill.

Puʻu o Kaiaka. Littoral cone (110 feet elevation), Kaluakoʻi, Molokaʻi. Hill separating Kepuhi and Pāpōhaku Beaches. Also known as Big Rock. *Lit.,* hill of Kaiaka (a legendary man).

Puʻu Ōlaʻi. 1. Beach, Mākena, Maui. Calcareous sand beach at the base of Puʻu Ōlaʻi in Mākena State Park. Also known as Little Beach. 2. Littoral cone, Mākena, Maui. A 360-foot-high littoral cone from the Hāna Volcanic Series on the southwest rift zone of Haleakalā. At the north end of Mākena State Park. Also known as Millers Hill, Red Hill, Round Mountain. *Lit.,* earthquake hill.

Puʻu One. 1. Littoral cone, Nānāwale, Hawaiʻi. Nānāwale Park is situated on a littoral cone approximately 150 feet high that was formed when a lava flow from Kīlauea entered the sea here in May 1840. The flow destroyed the coastal village of Nānāwale and created the littoral cone of cinder, or "sand," during the explosive interaction of the molten lava and the cold water of the ocean. Also known as Nānāwale, Sand Hill. 2. Beach, Mākena, Maui. The name here refers to the sand dunes in the backshore. Also known as Maluaka Beach. *Lit.,* sand hill.

Pu'u Pehe. 1. Cove, Mānele, Lāna'i. Pocket of calcareous sand in a cove at the seaward end of the headland that separates Mānele and Hulopo'e Bays. Also known as Sharks Bay, Sharks Cove. 2. Rock, Mānele, Lāna'i. A sea stack at the seaward end of the headland that separates Mānele and Hulopo'e Bays. It is part of the Hawai'i State Seabird Sanctuary. A legendary woman named Pehe was killed here by heavy storm surf. Also known as Sweetheart Island, Sweetheart Rock. *Lit.,* Pehe's hill.

Pu'u Pili. Fishing site, littoral cone (50 feet), storm beach, Pāhala, Hawai'i. Black sand storm beach at the base of the littoral cone on top of a low Pāhoehoe shelf. Pu'u Pili is northeast of Kamehame, the most prominent littoral cone on this shore. *Lit., pili* grass hill.

Pu'u Poa. Beach, marsh, point, Princeville, Kaua'i. Calcareous sand beach on Hanalei Bay between the Sheraton Princeville Hotel and the Hanalei River. A wide fringing reef lies offshore. Tropical almond trees, or *kamani,* and ironwood trees line the backshore. The marsh is inland of the beach. The beach and the marsh are named after Pu'u Poa Point, the east point of the bay.

Pu'uwai. Beach, surf site, west coast, Ni'ihau. Narrow calcareous sand beach between Kalanaei and Paliuli Points. Low vegetated dunes line the backshore, and patch reefs and sandbars front the beach. The surf site is off the beach. Pu'uwai, the only inhabited village on the island, is at the south end of the beach. *Lit.,* heart.

Pyramid Pinnacles. Dive site, Kohanaiki, Hawai'i. One of the Pine Trees dive sites. Two tall pinnacles rise from 20 feet to just below the surface, with a series of lava tubes and arches. Fish here include several large schools of butterflyfish and false Moorish idols.

Pyramid Rock. Beach, dive site, light, rock formation, surf site, Mōkapu Peninsula, O'ahu. The Pyramid Rock lava formation is part of the point at the north end of the beach. It once resembled a pyramid, but the pointed upper half of the "pyramid" was leveled in 1941 to accommodate Pyramid Rock Light, a navigational light. The calcareous sand beach extends from the point to the edge of the runway. The dive site and the surf site are adjacent to the point. Also known as Kū'au.

Pyramids. Surf site, Mokulēʻia, Oʻahu. During World War II, the military conducted demolition training on the beach here, including constructing and destroying tank traps on the near-shore reef. The tank traps were concrete pyramids, some with pieces of train rails sticking out of them, and were intended to simulate the landing craft obstructions that American troops in the Pacific were encountering during invasions of Japanese-held islands. Many of the concrete pyramids still sit on the shallow reef off the Kōnane Kai apartment building, while others are found scattered to the north. Also known as ʻĀweoweo.

Q Buoy. Fish aggregating device, Pa'uwela Point, Maui. Buoy anchored at approximately 382 fathoms. Landmarks: Nākālele Point Light, Kahului Harbor Light, Pa'uwela Point Light, Nānu-'alele Point Light.

QQ Buoy. Fish aggregating device, Maku'u, Hawai'i. Buoy anchored at approximately 990 fathoms. Landmarks: Leleiwi Point, Kumukahi Point Light.

Quarries. Surf site, Mokulē'ia, O'ahu. The Keālia Rock Quarry, where blue rock was once quarried and crushed into construction grade gravel, is at the west end of Dillingham Airfield. The surf site is offshore. Also know as Crushers.

Queen's. 1. Beach, Hawai'i Kai, O'ahu. During the early 1960s when Henry J. Kaiser began developing Hawai'i Kai, one of his dreams was to build a mixed-use community at the eastern end of the island. He named the 1,800-acre project Queen's Beach, and it was to include single-family residences, schools, parks, commercial facilities, a golf course in Kalama Valley, and a visitor resort complex with hotels, restaurants, and a golf course in Kealakīpapa Valley on the ocean side of Kalaniana'ole Highway. On the shore the project extended from the old Wāwāmalu Ranch boundary wall to the breakwater at the west end of Makapu'u Head. Although the resort complex was never built, this shore is still known as Queen's Beach. Also known as Alan Davis, Ka Iwi Coast or shore, Wāwāmalu. 2. Beach, Waikīkī. Section of Waikīkī Beach in Kapi'olani Regional Park between the Waikīkī Aquarium and the Kapahulu Groin. The area near the large comfort station was the site of the former Queen's Surf restaurant, which was named after the surf site in Waikīkī. The restaurant opened in 1949, closed in 1971, and the land was cleared for park use. The name is also a play on the word *queen,* which is slang for "gay." This area is frequented by gay men. Also known as Queen's Surf Beach. 3. Surf site, Waikīkī, O'ahu. One of Waikīkī's most famous surf sites. Named about 1900 by two surfers, Larry Kerr and Edward "Dude" Miller, because it fronted Queen Lili'uokalani's beach home with its well-known pier. The Queen's property is now part of Kūhiō Beach Park. Also known as Queen's Surf. 4. Surf site, Kawela, O'ahu. Inside Kawela Bay along the north point of bay. Waves here resemble those at Queen's in Waikīkī.

Queen's Bath. 1. Swimming site, Honokōhau, North Kona, Hawai'i. Inland of Honokōhau Beach and part of the Kaloko-Honokōhau National Historical Park. Shallow, spring-fed pool surrounded by rock cairns. Also known as Kahinihini'ula. 2. Swimming site, Princeville, Kaua'i. Large tidepool on a rocky ledge at the base of the Princeville sea cliffs. Named for Queen Emma, wife of Kamehameha IV, who with the king visited here in 1860. Princeville was named after their two-year-old son. 3. Swimming site, Kailua, O'ahu. Large, partially enclosed pool on the seaward side of the larger of the two Mokulua Islands off Lanikai. A rock formation here resembles the profiles of a queen and king.

Queen's Beach Breakwater. Hawai'i Kai, O'ahu. One of Henry J. Kaiser's dreams was to develop a visitor resort complex at Queen's Beach that would include a boat harbor and several protected lagoons lined with imported sand. During the early 1960s he initiated the project by constructing a small break-water at the west end of Makapu'u Head and by cutting a shallow experimental lagoon near the mouth of Kalama Stream. After Kaiser died in 1967, work on the resort complex was never resumed. Also known as Kapaliokamoa.

Queen's Pond. Surf site, swimming site, windsurf site, Polihale, Kaua'i. Swimming site near the east end of Polihale State Park that is partially protected by rocks and often covered by sand. Surfers and windsurfers enter and exit the ocean adjacent to the pond. One account says the pond was named for Leilani, a legendary queen, who often swam here.

Queen's Surf. 1. Beach, Waikīkī, O'ahu. Same as Queen's Beach. 2. Surf site, Waikīkī, O'ahu. Same as Queen's.

 mo'olelo

Dude Miller and I started surfing in front of the Queen's home as kids in 1900. We considered it our break, and we were the ones who named it **Queen's Surf.** *At that time we were the only ones who rode it standing up. Canoes was named for the old koa canoes. They were heavy and couldn't ride the steeper waves at Queen's Surf, so they stayed at Canoes. About 1904 we were asked to surf for about an hour by a firm called Rice and Perkins. They filmed us for a promotion they were trying to do for the world's fair, but apparently none of the pictures came out. We*

often bodysurfed at Queen's Surf, too. The style then was to hold both your hands between your legs, palms to the rear, and to keep your head up. There's a famous picture of a Hawaiian in a *malo* on Waikīkī Beach, holding a small board behind his back. That was Charles Kauha, and we considered him to be the original Waikīkī beachboy, before us and the Duke.

Larry Kerr, September 4, 1975

I was born in Waikīkī on October 12, 1913. My dad was Daniel Kaeo, and he was a clerk for the City and County District Court. We lived on Lemon Road. My mother was Louisa Puuohao, and I was the youngest of the children. My mother picked the name Aloha for me. I started surfing at Queen's when I was in grade school. We used redwood boards, some of them 12 feet long. We bodysurfed at Queen's, too. The style then was to swim, catch the wave, then put your hands under your body or hold your arms tight against your side. We did a lot of diving in Waikīkī, especially for squid, *uhu*, and *pānūnū*. We made our own goggles from *hau,* pieces of glass, and inner tube straps. We didn't have fins then. I started with the lifeguards in 1956 and retired in 1983. I met Pauline in Waikīkī and we got married on Sunday, September 1, 1963. We used to snorkel for bottles and found a lot in front of the Moana Hotel where the old pier used to be and in the Halekūlani Channel.

 Aloha Kaeo, August 18, 2000

Rabbit Island. 1. Island, Waimānalo, Oʻahu. In the 1880s John Cummins, the first owner of Waimānalo Plantation, decided to raise rabbits. He released them on Mānana Island, where a colony survived for approximately 100 years. The last of the rabbits were trapped and removed when the state determined that they were competing with the seabirds that nest there. The island is part of the Hawaiʻi State Seabird Sanctuary. Also known as Mānana Island. 2. Surf site, Waimānalo, Oʻahu. Off the north side of the island.

Radicals. Surf site, Waikīkī, Oʻahu. Off the south end of Kalākaua Avenue between Graveyards and The Winch. Dangerous or "radical" surf site that breaks on a very shallow reef.

Radio Bay. Small boat harbor, surf site, Hilo, Hawaiʻi. Small boat harbor in the easternmost corner of Hilo Harbor between the breakwater and Pier 1. The U.S. Coast Guard maintains its Big Island headquarters here. The bay was named for the U.S. Naval Radio Station communication complex that was formerly on the shore here. The surf site is off the breakwater.

Rainbow Bay. Marina, Pearl Harbor, Oʻahu. Private marina in ʻAiea Bay for military personnel who are members of the Pearl Harbor Yacht Club. Facilites include 128 permanent slips, 7 transient slips, and 30 moorings.

Rainbow Petroglyphs. Rock carvings, Māhāʻulepū, Kauaʻi. On January 7, 1980, a severe winter storm accompanied by high surf struck the south shore and began eroding Gillin's Beach at Māhāʻulepū. By January 9 the storm had removed over 6 vertical feet of sand, exposing three large shelves of beachrock, each covered with many petroglyphs. Among the first visitors to the previously unrecorded petroglyph site were several native Hawaiians who said that they were guided here by a rainbow. This incident gave the site its name, the Rainbow Petroglyphs. Within two weeks of the storm, the sand accreted and the beach rock was buried again.

R

Rainbow Reef. Dive site, Ala Moana, Oʻahu. Popular introductory dive site at 10–40 feet on a spur-and-groove reef on the east side of Magic Island. Rain from Mānoa Valley commonly creates rainbows that are visible from Magic Island. Also known as Magic Island.

Rainbows. 1. Surf site, Kaʻaʻawa, Oʻahu. Off Kalaeʻōʻio Beach Park. Also known as Makahonu. 2. Surf site, Kawela, Oʻahu. An unusual horseshoe-shaped wave on the north side of Kawela Bay. Also known as The Wedge. 3. Surf site, Keʻehi, Oʻahu. Big-wave, second-reef break on the east side of Kalihi Channel. 4. Surf site, Kāʻanapali, Maui. Off Honokowai Point.

Rainbow Tower Mural. Ceramic mural, Waikīkī, Oʻahu. On the seaward side of the Rainbow Tower in the Hilton Hawaiian Village, bordering Kahanamoku Beach. Millard Sheets, an artist from southern California, designed the mural to be seen by travelers arriving and departing Honolulu by sea or air. At 286 feet high and 26 feet wide, it is the tallest ceramic mural in the world. The mural consists of 8,046 pieces of ceramic tile that were hand painted in Los Angeles using seventeen non-reflective colors. Conrad Hilton and Fritz Burns dedicated it on November 8, 1968. An identical mural is located on the inland side of the Rainbow Tower.

Ranch. Surf site, ʻŌhikilolo, Oʻahu. Off the large concrete bridge on Farrington Highway. The name is from ʻŌhikilolo Ranch, which is located on the inland side of the highway.

Rangers. Surf site, Mokulēʻia, Oʻahu. Big-wave, second-reef site on the west side of Dillingham Channel. In 1974 Jack Bredin, Bob Larsen, and Tom Sawicki discovered it while paddling from site to site, or "ranging," across the Mokulēʻia reefs during different swells, looking for new places to surf. They considered themselves to be "reef rangers," and Larsen applied the name to the site.

Ratchet Sound. Fishing site, Hawaiʻi Kai, Oʻahu. One of several small points along the Koko Head sea cliffs that is favored by *ulua* fishermen. Named in the late 1950s by veteran *ulua* fisher Manuel "Manny" Jhun (1916–2000) for the sound of the ratchet on a fishing reel indicating a strike.

Razorblades. Surf site, Kaʻaʻawa, Oʻahu. On the south side of Makaua Channel. Waves here break on a shallow, razor-sharp reef. Also known as Razor Reef, Razors.

Razor Reef. 1. Surf site, Kaʻaʻawa, Oʻahu. Same as Razorblades. 2. Surf site, Kāhala, Oʻahu. On the west side of Kāhala Channel. Also known as Suicides. Waves at both these sites break over a shallow, razor-sharp reef.

Razors. 1. Surf site, Ka'a'awa, O'ahu. Same as Razorblades. 2. Surf site, Mokulē'ia, O'ahu. Off the west end of the Camp Mokulē'ia property. Also known as Camps.

R Buoy. Fish aggregating device, Mākaha, O'ahu. Buoy anchored at approximately 460 fathoms. Landmarks: Lahilahi Point, Pōka'ī Bay Light, Ka'ena Point Light.

Rebel Rock. Rock, Hawai'i Kai, O'ahu. Rock formation at the west end of Makapu'u Head above the breakwater. The profile of the rock viewed from Kalaniana'ole Highway near the entrance to the Hawai'i Kai Golf course resembles a Confederate Army or "rebel" cap. Also known as Balancing Rock, Pele's Chair.

Red Hill. 1. Cinder cone, dive site, Kainaliu, Hawai'i. Pu'u Ohau, the 230-foot cinder cone between Kealakekua and Kealahou Bays, is primarily red lava, so fishermen, divers, and other boaters call it Red Hill. The dive site Red Hill is an area name that includes many individual sites between Keikiwaha and Keawakāheka Points, with a variety of large caverns and lava tubes at 25 to 70 feet: Boatwreck Reef, Deep Reef, Domes, Fantasy Reef, Hammerhead Point, Long Lava Tube, Northern Lights, Spiral Lava Tube, and White Tip Condos. 2. Dive site, North Kohala, Hawai'i. Off Pu'u 'Ula'ula at 40 feet, north of Waiaka'īlio Bay. Pu'u 'Ula'ula means "red hill." 3. Point, Pīla'a, Kaua'i. East point of Pīla'a Beach. Soil erosion on the point has exposed large sections of red dirt, giving the point its popular name. 4. Dive site, littoral cone, Mākena, Maui. Pu'u Ōla'i at the north end of Mākena State Park is called Red Hill for the red cinder on its slopes. The dive site is off the base of the hill at 40 feet. 5. Point, Kahului, Maui. The small point near the west end of the Maui Country Club. The ocean is eroding the point, which is primarily red dirt.

Red Sand. Beach, Hāna, Maui. The south side of Ka'uiki Head, a cinder cone of the Hāna Volcanic Series, is primarily red cinder. The ocean has eroded the cinder to form a red sand beach in a cove at the base of the cone. Also known as Kaihalulu Beach, Ka'uiki Beach.

Red Tank. Fishing site, north coast, Lāna'i. Seacliffs near Polihua Beach. The ruins of a red water tank are on the sea cliffs.

Reed's. Bay, landing, Hilo, Hawai'i. Small natural bay on the eastern side of Waiākea Peninsula that is used as a public mooring site. Named after William H. Reed, a prominent Big Island businessman, who died in 1880. Reed's Landing, a former landing on the western side of the peninsula, and Reed's Island in the Wailuku River were also named after him. Reed arrived in the islands during the 1840s and specialized in the construction of landings, wharves, bridges, and roads. His other business interests included ranching, coastal trading, and commercial retailing. In 1868 he married Jane Stobie Shipman, the widow of Reverend William C. Shipman, and became the stepfather of her three children, William H. Shipman (1854–1943), Oliver Taylor Shipman (1857–1942), and Margaret Clarissa Shipman (1859–1891). Also known as Kanākea.

Reed's Bay. 1. Offshore mooring, Hilo, Hawai'i. Accommodations include twenty-two moorings. 2. Park, Hilo, Hawai'i. Public park on the shore of Reed's Bay on the eastern side of Waiākea Peninsula. The coral rubble and calcareous sand that comprise the beach were deposited here between 1925 and 1930, the spoil material from dredging operations to enlarge the Hilo Harbor basin.

Reefers. Surf site, windsurf site, Hā'ena, Kaua'i. At the edge of the reef at Ka'īlio Point fronting Hā'ena State Park. The name is a play on words. The site is on the reef, but during the 1970s when it was named, many of the surfers here were from Taylor Camp onshore, where marijuana cigarettes or "reefers" were common.

Reef Runway. 1. Dive site, Honolulu, O'ahu. Off the runway. 2. Fishing site, Honolulu, O'ahu. The fishing site is the entire perimeter of the Reef Runway at the Honolulu International Airport, but primarily its west point. The perimeter is accessed at the seaward end of Lagoon Drive by a public trail along the security fence. 3. Lagoon, Honolulu, O'ahu. A 200-acre, sand-bottomed, brackish-water lagoon that was created by the construction of the Reef Runway in the 1970s. The construction enclosed a portion of a boat channel that connected Ke'ehi Lagoon to Fort Kamehameha.

Reef's End. Dive site, Molokini, Maui. Terraced reef that is an underwater extension of the crater rim. The reef begins at the surface and drops beyond recreational diving depths.

Regulars. 1. Surf site, Ala Moana, O'ahu. Off the east end of Kewalo Basin Park. Also known as Marineland. The site is surfed regularly during all sizes of surf. 2. Surf site, Sand Island, O'ahu. Off Sand Island State Park. This is the most regularly surfed of the Sand Island surf sites.

Rennick's. Surf site, Kewalo, O'ahu. On the east side of Kewalo's. Named for Renwick Miura, who surfed here regularly in the 1980s. "Rennick" is a mispronunciation of Renwick. Also known as Right Next.

Rest Camp. Surf site, Wai'anae, O'ahu. The surf site is off the Wai'anae Kai Military Reservation in Pōka'ī Bay, which is commonly known as the Wai'anae Rest Camp. Also known as Pōka'ī Bay.

Revelations. Surf site, tow-in surf site, windsurf site, Waialeʻe, Oʻahu. In 1975 a small group of surfers started surfing here regularly. They realized that this site was the last major surf site on the North Shore to be named, so they named it Revelations for the last book in the Bible. Also known as Revies and Waialeʻe.

 moʻolelo

In the early 1970s, I owned the last house on the Kahuku side of the beach at Velzyland. During big swells we'd watch the waves outside the point, but no one ever surfed them. One day during the winter of 1974, we finally decided to paddle out and ended up surfing some great waves. That night we were sitting around having a few beers and talking about the spot outside the point. We figured that it was the last spot on the North Shore that didn't have a name before you went around the point up to Kawela. So we decided to call it **"Revelations"** for the last book in the bible.

Mike Jewett, January 25, 1999

Reverses. Surf site, Niu, Oʻahu. Off Niu Peninsula. A Niu surfer in the early 1960s believed that the waves here on a good day were a miniature version of those at the world-famous Pipeline on Oʻahu's North Shore. This site, however, is a right and not a left like the Pipeline, so he called it Reverse Pipeline. The name is now shortened to Reverses.

 moʻolelo

My friends and I would often paddle our boards west as far as Wailupe and east to Portlock, pioneer surfing any and every spot that had makable waves or openings in the reef. It was not uncommon to spend six hours or more out in the water. I'd often take deer jerky out in a plastic sandwich bag to feed the gang in our quest for new surf. Magic days. Off Paikō there is Coral Reef to the right and Shoulders to the left. Zeros is the deep-water outside break that only works in very big surf. Mizpah is the channel spot named after the *Mizpah*, a cabin cruiser that grounded and broke up on the reef in 1959. The engine still sits in the middle of the channel. The channel was marked by poles my dad put up on the reef on the Koko Head side to show the way in for our boat and other boats. Next to the channel on the Diamond Head side is Beaver's Reef, named after Steve "The Beaver" Saunders, a fellow young resident of Niuiki Circle who loved to surf that spot on his tanker. Further down is **Reverse.** I named that spot because its right break can be a quick, intense, hollow tube *which seemed to me a mini version of the Banzai Pipeline. Reverse Pipeline was its original name because its prevailing break is usually a right instead of a left. After Reverse was Blue Hole, Snipes, and Toes. These names all originated over the period in the late 1950s and early 1960s. This was an era that was truly magical and filled with mana. For many of us, surfing in those days shaped a natural, inner spirituality that influenced how our lives unfolded.*

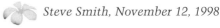 *Steve Smith, November 12, 1998*

R

Revies. Surf site, windsurf site, Waiale'e, O'ahu. Same as Revelations. Revies is an abbreviation of Revelations.

Ricebowl. 1. Surf site, Diamond Head, O'ahu. Named by members of the Tongg family in the 1950s for the curved or bowl-shaped section at the east end of the wave. 2. Surf site, Kahuku, O'ahu. Named by Kahuku surfers for the curved or bowl-shaped section at the north end of the wave. The name at both sites is a play on words between the surfing term *bowl* and a bowl for rice.

Rice Patch. Beach park, pond, surf site, Kākāhai'a, Moloka'i. Kākāhai'a Pond on the inland side of Kamehameha V Highway was formerly used to grow rice, but it is now a national wildlife refuge for native and migratory birds. Moloka'i residents still call the area Rice Patch. The surf site is directly offshore. Also known as Kākāhai'a Beach Park.

Richardson Ocean Center. Educational site, Hilo, Hawai'i. Ocean recreation and marine studies center that was developed cooperatively by the Hawai'i County Parks Department, the State Department of Business, Economic Development and Tourism, and the University of Hawai'i Sea Grant Extension Service. The building housing the center is the former home of Elsa and George Richardson. Also known as Richardson's.

Richardson's. Bay, beach, snorkeling site, surf site, Keaukaha, Hawai'i. Small pocket of black sand adjacent to the Richardson Ocean Center in Leleiwi Beach Park. The snorkeling and surf sites are off the ocean center.

Rifle Range. 1. Surf site, Mānā, Kaua'i. Off a former rifle range at Kokole Point, south of the Pacific Missile Range Facility. Also known as Targets. 2. Beach, surf site, 'Ewa Beach, O'ahu. Narrow calcareous sand beach fronting the Pu'uloa USMC Range Facility. The surf site is offshore. 3. Cliff jumping site, dive site, fishing site, Hawai'i Kai, O'ahu. Across Kalaniana-'ole Highway from the Koko Head Rifle Range, a public firing range that is part of Koko Head Regional Park. Also known as Kahauloa Cove, Lana'i Lookout. 4. Dive site, surf site, Mōkapu,

O'ahu. Off the firing range on the marine base. Also known as Poop Shoots.

Right Bay. Surf site, Ka'ena, O'ahu. Small bay near the gate at the north entrance to Ka'ena Point State Park with a right break in it.

Right Next. Surf site, Kewalo, O'ahu. This site is a right on the east, or right side, of Kewalo's and is also "right next" to it. The name is also a play on words of the original name, Renwick's, which is now pronounced "Rennick's."

Rightovers. Surf site, Kawailoa, O'ahu. A play on words with the name Leftovers to describe the right at Leftovers.

Right Point. Surf site, Hawai'i Kai, O'ahu. Off Queen's Beach. Two sites on the west side of Kalama Stream are named Left Point and Right Point.

Right Rights. Surf site, Kailua, O'ahu. At the west end of Lanikai Reef off the main entrance to Mid-Pacific (Mid Pac) Country Club. The name Right Rights is a humorous imitation of the name Left Lefts, the surf site at the east end of Lanikai Reef. Also known as Mid Pacs.

Rights. 1. Surf site, Kaunakakai, Moloka'i. Right on the right, or south side, of Kaunakakai Wharf. 2. Surf site, Ala Moana, O'ahu. Right at Kewalo's fronting Kewalo Basin Park.

Rights off the Reef. Surf site, Hale'iwa, O'ahu. Also known as Marijuanas.

Rise. Beach, Ala Moana, O'ahu. Elevated section in the center of Ala Moana Beach with steps leading onto the sand.

Rivermouth. Surf site, Waimea, Kaua'i. Off the mouth of the Waimea River.

RN Buoy. Fish aggregating device, Pālima Point, Hawai'i. Buoy anchored at approximately 733 fathoms. Landmarks: 'Āpua Point, Nīnole Cove.

Road to the Sea. Beach, fishing site, shore, Manukā, Hawai'i. Road to the Sea is a 7-mile-long cinder road that begins between the 79- and 80-mile markers on Hawai'i Belt Road and ends at Humuhumu Point. The largest concentration of littoral cones in Hawai'i is found between Humuhumu and 'Āwili Points, creating one of the most unique sections of volcanic shore in the islands. There are green and black sand beaches, rocky points, and tide pools, and a network of trails connects all brackish-water ponds at the bases of the littoral cones. Fishing, especially for *ulua*, is common here. The fishing site is also known as Manukā, Smoking Rock.

 *mo'olelo*
I was born on the Hilo bayfront on the Waiākea side of the
Wailuku Stream bridge. As a boy, I spent all my time on the

ocean, around the rivers, and on the breakwater, fishing and diving. The railroad passed right behind our house, so we would put nails on the tracks, then bend them into the shapes we wanted for our hooks after the trains flattened them. One of my favorite fishing spots now is **Road to the Sea,** which we also call Manukā. On the maps it's 'Āwili Point. In 1977, I set the Hilo Casting Club record there for the most *ulua* ever caught in one night of fishing—twenty-three—and over that entire day, a Saturday, I ended up with thirty-three *ulua*. The older-timers always told me that every seventh year there is a warm current there that really makes the fish bite. That night the ocean was rough, the wind was cold, but the water was warm.

Roy Ogata, July 6, 1982

Robinson. 1. Landing, Makaweli, Kaua'i. Small private boat harbor at Pākala village. Ni'ihau Ranch operates a private ferry service between Robinson Landing and Lehua Landing on Ni'ihau. The ferry, a Navy LCM (landing craft mechanized), carries livestock, passengers, food (including poi), dry goods, and other necessities to Ni'ihau. Also known as Makaweli Landing. 2. Bay, Kahana, Maui. The Robinson family has a beachfront estate here named Kalaeokai'a. Also known as Ka'ōpala.

Rock. Point, Pōhakuloa, Moloka'i. Rocky headland between Honouli Wai and Honouli Malo'o Bays. At the tip of the point, a large rock formation stands alone on the seaward side of Kamehameha V Highway. This is the "rock" of Rock Point.

Rock, The. Island, surf site, Mokulē'ia, O'ahu. Same as Devil's Rock.

 mo'olelo

I grew up in Florida near the beach and became obsessed with surfing pretty young. I can't remember exactly when, but sometime during my youth, like every surfer, I decided to get to Hawai'i to ride the big ones. In June 1974, I joined the navy as a boiler technician with the agreement that they would station me in Hawai'i. In November of that year I was here, stationed at Pearl on the tender *Bryce Canyon.*

The only person I knew in the Islands was my sister, Linda, who just happened to be going to school at UH, but she didn't surf and didn't have a car, so my first day in Hawai'i I got on the bus with my fins and headed to Sandy Beach. As I rode the bus, I wondered what it was going to be like getting in the water in Hawai'i for the first time, and I was nervous about going to a place where I knew no one. When I got off the bus and saw Sandy Beach for the first time, I was stoked—

spitting hollow shorebreak with crystal water and all sand bottom!

As I swam out through the shorebreak, I saw a long, gangly body swimming across the outside and thought, "That looks like Bob Larson, can't be, but what are the odds of running into somebody in Hawai'i with a body like Bob's?" Bob, a friend of mine from Florida, was 6-foot-5 and as long and gangly a guy as I had ever seen. I knew it couldn't be him, but I had to swim over to get a closer look at this Hawaiian Bob. As I approached, the mystery swimmer turned toward me, and it was Bob! I said, "Bob, is that you? What are you doing here?" He said that he had joined the army and was stationed at Schofield. He'd only been there a couple of months and was trying to get a place on the North Shore. We were happy to see each other, and I had a friend in Hawai'i.

Bob soon rented a house in Mokulē'ia, and to his delight he discovered an unridden break in front of his house. It was a left that peaked on an exposed rock jutting out of the water about a half-mile from shore. Bob showed the break to me and our other surfing buddy, Tom Sawicki, a surfer from Maryland, and the three of us went out together to try it during the winter of 1975. We couldn't believe it. Here we were in Hawai'i, just the three of us surfing with nobody around as far as the eye could see. We were stoked.

As the three of us surfed it over the years, we found that it was a fickle spot that sometimes only got good a few times a winter. We had it to ourselves until Tom and Bob moved to the Big Island to make their fortunes, and left me to surf it alone. During the years that followed, another friend of mine from New Mexico, Larry Engwal, was the only guy that surfed it with me. I was always amazed by Larry, who would fly in from New Mexico in February after not surfing all year and say, "Let's go to the Rock." The two of us rode it alone for the next ten years, and some of the most memorable days of my surfing life come from those days at the Rock, with no one around but me, Larry, and the fish.

In 1990 another Florida surfer, Dusty Welsch, discovered the Rock and began to surf it. He heard there was someone else who surfed there, and when he mentioned this to shaper Tommy Nellis, our mutual friend, Tommy told Dusty he knew who that must be, and hooked me and Dusty up. We've been surfing together ever since. Dusty introduced me to his close surfing friends, and now a small group, including Dusty, Cole Doeh, Porter Turnbull, Toby Collins, and myself make the Rock our regular spot. Dusty rides it at any size with complete abandon, and has become acknowledged by the other Rock surfers as the "King of the Rock."

R

When we first started surfing it, we didn't think about giving it a name. We just referred to it as the big left by the rock, and then just **The Rock.** In the early days I heard other people call it Castle Rock, but I didn't hear the name Devil's Rock until the nineties. When Dusty and Cole started surfing there, we used The Rock. None of us had any other important rocks in our lives to be mixed up with The Rock, so the name was sufficiently descriptive for us to know where we meant and at the same time nondescript enough that people other than us did not know what we were talking about. We liked it. It was our name. The Rock is a special place, and the best part of surfing it is the friends I've met there. It is an awesome spot with an aura all it's own.

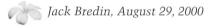 *Jack Bredin, August 29, 2000*

Rocket Reef. Surf site, Mānā, Kaua'i. At the west end of the Pacific Missile Range Facility, off the pad that has been used since 1964 to launch rockets that test military defensive technologies.

Rockies. 1. Surf site, Hawai'i Kai, O'ahu. Small bay at the east end of Sandy Beach Park with many rocks in the lineup. The rocks here are emergent even at high tide, making it a dangerous and infrequently surfed site. 2. Channel, surf site, Wailupe, O'ahu. Many coral heads, or "rocks," are in and around the channel, which is to the west of Wailupe Beach Park. 3. Surf site, Sunset Beach, O'ahu. Same as Rocky Point.

Rock-n-Roll Reef. Surf site, Mokulē'ia, O'ahu. Name used by military personnel for this site that is best when the waves are big. The name comes from the phrase, "Let's rock-n-roll" which means, "Let's go for it." The phrase is used here to mean catching or "going" for big waves. Also known as Camp Erdman, Erdman, Tiger Reef.

Rockpile. 1. Surf site, Waikīkī, O'ahu. Named for the shallow reef, or "rockpile," in the center of the site that is partially emergent during minus tides. The site on the west side of the rockpile is called Rock Pile Lefts. The site on the east side of the rock pile is called Rock Pile Rights. 2. Surf site, Sunset Beach, O'ahu. Named for a large lava rock formation inshore at the edge of the beach. Legendary diver and big-wave rider Jose Angel (1934–1976) made his home inshore of the site in 1962 and was the first to surf here regularly. Also known as Banzai Rocks.

Rock Point. Surf site, Pōhakuloa, Moloka'i. When the road around the point at Pōhakuloa was constructed, a large rock formation was left isolated on the seaward side of the road. This formation is the "rock" of Rock Point. The surf site is offshore.

Rock Quarry. Surf site, Kīlauea, Kaua'i. In Kīlauea Bay adjacent to Mōkōlea Point. Named for Kāhili Quarry, which was operational at the point from 1900 through the 1970s.

Rocky Point. Beach, surf site, Sunset Beach, O'ahu. Section of Sunset Beach near the center of Ke Nui Road. A cluster of limestone rocks on the beach and a wide, shallow reef mark the point. Local area residents named the point before it was surfed, and surfers applied the name to the surf site on the north side of the point in the late 1960s. During the early 1960s, when it was first surfed, it was known as Arma Hut. Also known as Rockies, Rocky Point Lefts, Rocky Point Rights.

Rocky Point Lefts. Surf site, Sunset Beach, O'ahu. Left at Rocky Point, the prevailing direction that the site is surfed.

Rocky Point Rights. Surf site, Sunset Beach, O'ahu. Right at Rocky Point, the less-frequent direction that the site is surfed because the wave ends on the shallow reef at the point.

Roger Rights. Surf site, Mokulē'ia, O'ahu. Same as Roger's.

Roger's. 1. Surf site, Kawela, O'ahu. Inside Kawela Bay along the west point of the bay. Named after Roger Allan, whose family home was on the point. 2. Surf site, Mokulē'ia, O'ahu. West of the public right-of-way on Crozier Drive. A surfer named Roger lived near the right-of-way in the 1960s and frequently surfed this site.

Round Mountain. Littoral cone, Mākena, Maui. Pu'u Ōla'i, at the north end of Mākena State Park, is called Round Mountain for its dome-shaped outline.

Rowland's Pond. Wetland, Kalaeloa, O'ahu. Artificial wetland on the shore of the Chevron Hawai'i Refinery in Campbell Industrial Park. Chevron developed the 5-acre pond as an emergency catch basin for oil spills, but refinery crews noticed the endangered *ae'o*, or Hawaiian stilt, nesting here in the early 1990s. Chevron contacted the U.S. Fish and Wildlife Service and agreed to designate the pond as a permanent wetland habitat for the birds. When the refinery opened in 1960, the original catch basin was named Rowland's Pond after Robert H. Rowland (1916–1999), the refinery's first manager. Rowland was born in Bartlesville, Oklahoma, and went to work for Chevron in 1938. From 1958 to 1960, he was part of a team in San Francisco that planned and designed the Hawaiian Refinery, now the Chevron Hawai'i Refinery. He moved to Hawai'i in August 1960 and managed the refinery until 1966. He then managed refineries in Iran and Belgium before he retired to Carmel Valley, California, in 1973.

Rubber Duckies. Surf site, Sunset Beach, O'ahu. On the north side of Three Tables Beach. This site is surfed only when the waves are small. During the summer and other no-surf periods,

R

it is a popular family swimming beach where little children play with water toys, including rubber duckies.

Ruddle's. Surf site, Puakō, Hawai'i. Off the 7.4-acre Ruddle estate at the south end of Puakō Road. Annabelle Ruddle visited Paniau in 1937 at the suggestion of Francis Brown, a personal friend who lived nearby at Kalahuipua'a. She came by sampan looking for a beach home for her family. She found a beautiful site on the ocean with a natural bathing pool and house foundations of the original Puakō village. She returned to Hilo and convinced her husband Albert to trade some Ruddle property in Hilo for 7.5 acres at Paniau. They built several homes on the property, which was known to the community as the Ruddle Estate for many years.

Running Waters. 1. Beach, Nāwiliwili, Kaua'i. Prior to 1987 the land above the beach was a Līhu'e Plantation Company sugarcane field. Irrigation runoff from the field drained or "ran" across the beach into Nāwiliwili Harbor. 2. Fishing site, Hawai'i Kai, O'ahu. On the sea cliffs below the Lumaha'i Street right-of-way. Receding water from waves sweeping across the rock terraces here drains or "runs" back into the ocean.

Russian Fort Elizabeth. State historical park (17.3 acres), Waimea, Kaua'i. On the east bank of the Waimea River where the river intersects the beach. Russian Fort Elizabeth is the ruin of a fort built between 1815 and 1817 during an alliance between members of the Russian-American Company and King Kaumuali'i of Kaua'i. Russian occupation of the fort ended in 1817 when King Kamehameha I expelled them from Hawai'i. Hawaiian soldiers occupied the site until it was deactivated in 1864.

Sacred Spots. Surf site, Hauʻula, Oʻahu. Deepwater, second-reef site off Sacred Falls State Park. The waterfall in the park is called Sacred Falls because of its association with Kamapuaʻa, the demigod who could assume the shape of a man or pig. The surf site was named after the falls.

Sailboat Keel Reef. Dive site, Hawaiʻi Kai, Oʻahu. Long ledge at 25 to 35 feet deep straight out from the Hawaiʻi Kai Channel. The lead keel of a wreck lies on the bottom.

Sailor Hat. Crater, southwest shore, Kahoʻolawe. In April 1965, the navy simulated an atomic explosion to the southeast of Hanakanaiʻa by detonating 500 pounds of TNT to test the effect of nuclear-sized blasts on warships nearby. The test, Operation Sailor Hat, created the crater and destroyed the decommissioned and unoccupied ship *Atlanta* that was anchored offshore. After the test, the newly formed crater was called Sailor Hat.

Saint Anthony. Dive site, Wailea, Maui. Wreck of the *St. Anthony*, a 65-foot longline fishing boat that ended up as a derelict in Honolulu Harbor. She was towed to Maui and sunk at 70 feet on the Keawakapu Artificial Reef.

Saint Peter's Catholic Church. Scenic point, Kahaluʻu, Hawaiʻi. Small, simple, clapboard building on the shore of Kahaluʻu Bay with a covered entrance porch and a tall spire with louvered windows that is often photographed by visitors.

Saint Teresa's. Surf site, Kekaha, Kauaʻi. Off St. Teresa's Catholic Church in Kekaha.

Salt Pond. 1. Beach park, surf site, windsurf site, Hanapēpē, Kauaʻi. Calcareous sand beach with a natural wall of rocks that creates a large inshore pond. The surfing and windsurf sites are off the wall of rocks. The park is named for a nearby complex of shallow ponds where rock salt is produced by evaporating seawater. Most of the ponds are supervised by Hui Hāna Paʻakai, a group whose members are permitted by the state to manufacture salt here. Many of the group's members are continuing family traditions that have changed little for generations. Salt making is a summer activity that is dependent on extended periods of dry weather and hot, sunny days. The ponds are idle during the winter months. 2. Gathering site, Mā'ili, O'ahu. Natural depressions in the rocks at Mā'ili Point where families from Mā'ili gathered salt for home consumption.

Sampan Channel. Boat channel, range lights, Kāne'ohe Bay, O'ahu. Channel on the east side of Kāne'ohe Bay dredged during the early 1940s. Range lights to mark the channel were installed in 1943. The channel is approximately .85 miles north of Mōkapu Peninsula. Sampans, or commercial tuna boats, from Honolulu that formerly came to Kāne'ohe Bay to catch baitfish used this channel. As the channel comes into Kāne'ohe Bay, it forms a "Y" with one branch going toward the Kāne-'ohe Yacht Club and the other going toward He'eia Kea Pier.

Sam Wight's. Beach, Lā'au, Moloka'i. Southernmost section of Kamāka'ipō Beach near the lighthouse. Sam Wight, an assistant manager of Moloka'i Ranch under George P. Cooke, the first president of the ranch, maintained a fishing shack on the rise above the beach during his tenure from 1923 to 1932.

Sandbar. Island (3.1 acres, awash at high tide), Kāne'ohe Bay, O'ahu. Large sandbar in the center of Kāne'ohe Bay that is emergent at low tide, awash at high tide, and a popular picnic site for boaters. Also known as Ahuolaka.

Sandbars. 1. Surf site, Sunset Beach, O'ahu. Surf here normally breaks on a wide sandbar fronting 'Ehukai Beach Park. 2. Surf site, Waikīkī, O'ahu. Off Kaimana Beach and east of Old Man's. Waves here form on a line of sand boils, which is the "sandbar."

Sand Dunes. Surf site, Kahe, O'ahu. On the west side of Tracks.

Sand Hill. Littoral cone, Nānāwale, Hawai'i. Nānāwale Park is situated on a littoral cone approximately 150 feet high that was formed when a lava flow from Kīlauea entered the sea here in May 1840. The flow destroyed the coastal village of Nānāwale and created the littoral cone of cinder or "sand" during the explosive interaction of the molten lava and the cold water of the ocean. Also known as Nānāwale Park, Pu'u One.

Sand Island. 1. Island (500 acres), Honolulu, O'ahu. A man-made island that protects Honolulu Harbor from seasonal high surf and storm surf. It was built by depositing material dredged from the harbor on the shallow reef seaward of the harbor, which originally included a small sand spit or "island" adjacent to the harbor entrance. 2. Bridge, Honolulu, O'ahu. Bridge that joins Sand Island and O'ahu. 3. Marine training facility, Honolulu, O'ahu. On the west end of Sand Island adjacent to the bridge. The facility provides boat building and repair training opportunities for students from Honolulu Community College and houses the University of Hawaiʻi's outdoor recreation program classes in sailing, windsurfing, and water safety. 4. Ramp, Honolulu, Oʻahu. Adjacent to the Sand Island Marine Training Facility. Facilities include four ramps and a vessel washdown area. The facilities were dedicated in July 1995. 5. State recreation area (140 acres), Honolulu, Oʻahu. Large park on the seaward side of Sand Island with a calcareous sand beach. 6. Surf site, Sand Island, Oʻahu. Off the park.

Sandman's Patch. Dive site, Hanauma Bay, Oʻahu. Shallow pocket of sand inshore of the Cable Channel where James Sand conducted a reef topography study for the University of Hawaiʻi's Marine Option Program.

Sand Point. Peninsula, Kuliʻouʻou, Oʻahu. Undeveloped sand spit that separates Paikō Lagoon from the open ocean. Also known as Paikō Peninsula, Stubenberg's Island.

Sand Tracks. Surf site, ʻEwa Beach, Oʻahu. Off Oneʻula Beach Park. Fishermen and surfers have driven through the sand here for many years, leaving tire tracks in the sand.

Sandy. 1. Beach, Honouli Maloʻo, Molokaʻi. Small calcareous sand pocket beach on Kamehameha V Highway north of Honouli Maloʻo. 2. Beach park (22.6 acres), surf site, Hawaiʻi Kai, Oʻahu. Prior to 1931, fishermen followed a trail along the sea cliffs from Hanauma Bay to the Hālona Blowhole in this area. They called the beach at the east end of the cliffs Sand Beach. When Kalanianaʻole Highway replaced the trail in 1933 and people began driving through the area, the name changed to Sandy Beach. A number of surf sites are located at Sandy Beach, including those in the shorebreak, those at Half Point, and those at Full Point. Also known as Sandys.

Sandys. Beach, Hawaiʻi Kai, Oʻahu. Same as Sandy Beach.

Sans Souci. Beach, Waikīkī, Oʻahu. Section of Waikīkī Beach between the Outrigger Canoe Club to the east and the War Memorial Natatorium to the west. In 1884, Allen Herbert bought the land where the New Otani Kaimana Beach Hotel is located. He opened a lodging house that he named Sans Souci, French for "without a care," after the palace of Frederick the Great in Potsdam. The beach was named after Herbert's lodging house. Also known as Dig Me, Kaimana, Kapua.

Santos Bay. Kahoʻolawe. In 1965 two cousins, Rodney and Herbert Santos, were anchored at Papaka Iki Bay. During the night their boat broke its mooring and wrecked onshore. The men were picked up the next day by another fishing boat, but the incident inspired the name Santos Bay. Also known as Papaka Iki.

S Buoy. Fish aggregating device, Pōka'ī Bay, O'ahu. Buoy anchored at approximately 460 fathoms. Landmarks: Ka'ena Point Light, Pōka'ī Bay Light, Barbers Point Light.

Scenic Lookout. Dive site, Lahaina Pali, Maui. Off the scenic lookout on Honoapi'ilani Highway.

Scout. Island, Keaukaha, Hawai'i. Small, flat rock island off Kealoha Park that was formerly a popular camping site for Keaukaha residents and for the Big Island's Boy Scouts. Also known as Pe'ewē, Peiwē.

Sculptured Reef. Dive site, Po'ipū, Kaua'i. Coral formations that comprise the reef appear to have been trimmed, or "sculptured," by a gardener.

Sea Life Park Hawai'i. Marine park, Waimānalo, O'ahu. Private park near Makapu'u Beach that offers exhibits and programs about marine life and the ocean environment. The Hawaiian Reef tank is a 300,000-gallon aquarium with hundreds of fish and other sea creatures.

Sea Lodge. Beach, Princeville, Kaua'i. Pocket of calcareous sand at the base of the sea cliffs below the Sea Lodge condominiums. Tropical almond trees, or *kamani*, line the backshore.

Seaplane. Dock, Ke'ehi, O'ahu. On Lagoon Drive. Facility for commercial seaplanes operating in Ke'ehi Lagoon.

Seaplane Triangle. Channels, Ke'ehi, O'ahu. Three channels in Ke'ehi Lagoon that form a triangle. They were dredged out of the inner reef in the early 1940s as runways for seaplanes.

 mo'olelo

After I graduated from the UH in 1938, I went to work for Standard Dredging as a civil engineer. In 1941, we were land-filling in the Māpunapuna and airport areas, dredging the inner reefs in Ke'ehi Lagoon and pumping the fill material onshore. The Damon family controlled the fishing rights in the lagoon—no one could fish there without permission—so those were some of the most productive reefs I've ever seen. All kinds of crabs—especially white crabs—and slipper lobsters would come up with the fill material, and there were mullet by the thousands. Lots of hammerheads, too; we'd see them chasing the mullet into the shallow water. At the outer edge of the reef, fish like *ulua*, *pāpio*, and *nenue* swarmed around Mokauea Island.

Our dredge, the *Jefferson*, worked like a brace and bit. The bit rotated and cut the coral. A big pump behind it pumped the fill material onshore through a steel pipeline supported by pontoons, and the fill material went into a levee where the water was allowed to drain through spillways back into the ocean. After the

war broke out on December 7, the Army Corps of Engineers contracted Standard Dredging to use the *Jefferson* to dredge the seaplane runways in the lagoon that are still there now.

 George V. Clark, March 25, 1984

Seaplane Wreck. Dive site, Wai'anae, O'ahu. North of the *Mahi*
and directly off Pōka'ī Bay. The wreck is a twin-engine Beechcraft seaplane that was sunk at 90 feet as an artificial reef.

Sea Shell Pool. Swimming site, Kūki'o, Hawai'i. Large saltwater
pool with a calcareous sand beach in the rocky terrace bordering the Four Seasons Resort Hualālai.

Sea Tiger. Artificial reef, Ala Moana, O'ahu. A 200-foot vessel that
was sunk on June 24, 1999, at 110 feet off Ala Moana Beach
Park. Also known as Voyager Artificial Reef.

Sea Walls. Surf site, 'Ewa Beach, O'ahu. Off the seawalls that line
the beachfront homes at the west end of Pūpū St.

Secluded Isle. Marketing nickname for the island of Lāna'i.

Second Bridge. Fishing site, Hawai'i Kai, O'ahu. On the rocky
ledge below the second bridge to the east of Lāna'i Lookout on
Kalaniana'ole Highway. Also known as Kawaiaka'aiea Bridge.

Second Cathedral. Dive site, Mānele, Lāna'i. One of two dive
sites with similar underwater features that are known collectively as Cathedrals and individually as First Cathedral and
Second Cathedral. Several pinnacles rise from 60 feet to just
below the surface. Spacious caverns in the pinnacles have a
cathedral-like appearance when shafts of sunlight crisscross
the interiors through skylights in the exterior walls.

Second Ditch. Surf site, Kekaha, Kaua'i. Off the second drainage
ditch in Kaumuali'i Highway west of Kekaha Beach Park.

Second Flow. Dive site, fishing site, lava flow, Pāhoehoe, Hawai'i.
One of three lava flows from an eruption on the southwest
rift zone of Mauna Kea that began on June 1, 1950. Each of the
flows reached the ocean, creating small pockets of black sand
on a coast of sea cliffs. Fishermen offshore use the flows as
landmarks, numbering them from north to south. The dive
site is a narrow shelf close to shore, with large pinnacles and
canyons between the second and third flows. Also known as
Pāhoehoe, Pinnacles.

Second Hole. Surf site, Ala Moana, O'ahu. Between Courts and
Concessions.

Second Lagoon. Beach, lagoon, Ko 'Olina, O'ahu. One of four
man-made beaches and lagoons at Ko 'Olina Resort and Marina.

Second Reef. Surf site, Mā'ili, O'ahu. Big-wave, second-reef site
outside of Green Lanterns. Also known as Cloudbreak.

Seconds. 1. Surf site, Hawaiʻi Kai, Oʻahu. The former Portlock Pier crossed a shallow inshore reef, First Reef, and ended at a deepwater swimming area at the edge of the reef. A second shallow reef seaward of the swimming area was called Second Reef. Surfers eventually shortened the name to Seconds. 2. Surf site, Hickam Air Force Base, Oʻahu. On the west side of Hickam Channel.

 moʻolelo

As far as China Walls goes, I've always called that spot Portlock Point. The first photo ever published of that place, as far as I know, was by me in a 1965 issue of *Surfer Magazine*. I always thought China Walls referred to the break right next to the wall, but I guess it makes sense that the break beyond the boil would be called China Walls, based on how long the wave is. The spot off Kaiser's old Portlock mansion we used to call Half Point, sometimes Poles, and another favorite spot off Portlock was Junior's, which is just to the left, looking out to sea, of **Seconds.** It's a fast tubular left that goes off when the waves are big. Seconds, or Second Reef, is outside of First Reef. That's where the Portlock swimming pier used to be and that's where I learned to surf when I was eleven years old.

 Mark Coleman, January 30, 1999

Secret. 1. Beach, surf site, Kalāheo, Kauaʻi. Small pocket of calcareous sand at the mouth of a small gulch west of Kalāheo Gulch. The surf site is a shorebreak on the beach. 2. Beach, surf site, Kīlauea, Kauaʻi. A 3,000-foot-long, 75-foot-wide calcareous sand beach fronted by a wide sandbar on the west side of Kīlauea Point. The beach can only be seen on land from Kīlauea Point, so until the point was opened to the public in 1974 as Kīlauea Point National Wildlife Refuge, the existence of the beach was a "secret," known only to island residents. The surf site is a shorebreak on the sandbar. Also known as Kauapea Beach. 3. Island, Kualoa, Oʻahu. On the outer edge of Mōiliʻi Fishpond. A small calcareous sand beach that accreted here against the outer wall of the fishpond has created a secluded "island." Kualoa Ranch, the owner of the fishpond, named the beach and uses it as a private beach club.

Secret's. 1. Surf site, Māhukona, Hawaiʻi. 2. Surf site, ʻĀina Haina, Oʻahu. Off Kawaikuʻi Beach Park. 3. Surf site, Kahuku, Oʻahu. Off the concrete blocks that mark the old Marconi sewer line at Hanakaʻīlio Beach. All of the Secret surf sites were "secret" spots when they were named.

Sergeant Major Reef. Dive site, southeast coast, Lānaʻi. Near Kamaiki Point between Naha and Mānele. Three parallel lava ridges with a cave and an arch at 15 to 50 feet. Several large schools of sergeant major damselfish are found here.

Sergeant Minor Reef. Dive site, southeast coast, Lāna'i. North of Sergeant Major Reef at 50 feet, but not as spectacular. The name is a play on the word *major* in sergeant major.

Seven Pools. Park, Kīpahulu, Maui. Coastal section of Haleakalā National Park that contains a series of waterfall plunge pools in 'Ohe'o Stream. The stream empties into the ocean below the lowest pool.

Seventh Hole. Surf site, Kahuku, O'ahu. Off the seventh hole of Kahuku Golf Course.

Sewers. Surf site, Wai'anae, O'ahu. Off the Wai'anae Sewage Treatment Plant.

Shacks. 1. Surf site, Kapoho, Hawai'i. East of Kaimū. 2. Surf site, Kahuku, O'ahu. Off Hanaka'īlio Beach. Shacks on the shore were once found at both sites.

Shallows. 1. Surf site, Ala Moana, O'ahu. Off the east end of Kewalo Basin Park. 2. Surf site, Sand Island, O'ahu. Both of these sites break over a reef that is very shallow at low tide.

Shangri-La. Small boat harbor, Black Point, O'ahu. Doris Duke was the only child of American Tobacco Company founder James Buchanan Duke and became one of the wealthiest women in the world upon the death of her father. At the time of her death in 1993, her estate was worth about $1.2 billion. She fell in love with Hawai'i on her honeymoon in 1935, and in 1936 she and her husband James Cromwell began building a fortresslike home on a 4.9-acre parcel on the west side of Black Point. The state's first $1 million home, Duke named it Shangri-La, after the mythical valley in James Hilton's novel *Lost Horizon,* where people never grow old. Over the next fifty years, Duke used the home as a personal retreat and sanctuary, working on it constantly and filling it with thousands of pieces of art and cultural artifacts. The home is maintained by the Doris Duke Foundation of Islamic Art. In addition to the home, Duke constructed a small boat harbor on the rocky shore by building two boulder breakwaters. The harbor, however, is subject to heavy surge, and except for a brief period after its construction, it was never used for its original purpose. It is a popular public swimming area that is also known as Cromwell's and The Harbor.

Shark. Island, Mākaha, O'ahu. Small rock island on the east side of Mauna Lahilahi.

Shark Bay. Surf site, Mānele, Lāna'i. Pocket calcareous sand beach in a cove at the seaward end of the headland that separates Mānele and Hulopo'e Bays. The surf site is off the beach. Also known as Pu'u Pehe, Sharks Bay, Sweetheart Rock.

Shark Condos. Dive site, Molokini, Maui. Series of shelves at 130 feet that create shallow caves, or "condos" (condominiums), that are resting habitats for white tipped sharks.

Shark Country. Surf site, 'Ewa Beach, O'ahu. Off Pūpū Place. Named in the early 1960s by the members of the 'Ewa Beach Surf Club who were among the first to surf here. Sharks were common, especially hammerheads.

Shark-Fin Rock. Dive site, south coast, Lāna'i. Northwest of Kaunolū. A large rock formation that resembles a shark's fin protrudes above the surface of the ocean. A vertical wall that harbors many species of fish and invertebrates drops from the surface to 60 feet.

Shark Hole. Fishing site, Pa'uwela, Maui. Deep cove on the lava terrace below the Pa'uwela Light. In 1924 a group of men began fishing for sharks here, stretching a line with baited hooks across the cove. They lifted the sharks they caught out of the cove with a boom constructed on the terrace. The shark hunters also dug the steps and the two caves in the cliff behind the terrace.

Shark Pit. 1. Surf site, Hawai'i Kai, O'ahu. On the west side of Hawai'i Kai Channel. Sharks are commonly seen here on the shallow reef flat. Also known as Channels. 2. Dive site, Kā'anapali, Maui. 3. Surf site, Lahaina, Maui. Off Puamana subdivision. Shark sightings are common here.

Shark Rock. Mooring buoy site, Kailua-Kona, Hawai'i. Day-use mooring buoy site within the Old Kona Airport Marine Life Conservation District. The buoy is anchored at 40 feet off Shark Rock, a large rock in the water at the edge of the beach.

Sharks. 1. Bay, cove, Mānele, Lāna'i. Pocket beach of calcareous sand in a cove at the seaward end of the headland that separates Mānele and Hulopo'e Bays. Also known as Shark Bay, Pu'u Pehe, Sweetheart Rock.

Sharks Cove. Dive site, snorkeling site, Sunset Beach, O'ahu. One of the most popular dive and snorkeling sites on O'ahu. The cove is situated in the rocky northeast section of Pūpūkea Beach Park. The underwater caves outside of the cove are among the most popular cave dive sites on the island. Sharks Cove has been part of the Pūpūkea Marine Life Conservation District since it was established in 1983. It was named for the outline of the underwater reefs and ledges that are thought to resemble a shark's head from the hill above the cove.

Sheraton. Dive site, snorkeling site, Kā'anapali, Maui. The Sheraton Maui, completed in 1963, is on the summit of Pu'u Keka'a, a cinder cone in the center of Kā'anapali Beach. The dive and snorkeling sites are on the seaward side of the hill. Also known as Black Rock.

Sheraton Caverns. Dive site, Poʻipū, Kauaʻi. One of the most popular dive sites on Kauaʻi. A 30- to 60-foot site with three large parallel lava tubes 80–120 feet long offshore that are the island's most popular cave dives. The dive site is off the Sheraton Kauaʻi Resort, which opened in 1968 and was Kauaʻi's first resort managed by a national chain. Severely damaged by Hurricane ʻIniki in 1992, the resort reopened in 1997. Also known as Sheraton Caves.

Sheraton Caves. Dive site, Poʻipū, Kauaʻi. Same as Sheraton Caverns.

Sheraton Reef. Dive site, Waikīkī, Oʻahu. Off the Sheraton Waikīkī Hotel at 50 feet. Introductory boat dive site with eels and turtles.

Sherwood Forest. Beach park, surf site, Waimānalo, Oʻahu. During the late 1950s, *Robin Hood,* starring Richard Greene, was a popular television series in Hawaiʻi. At the same time a gang of thieves used the ironwood forest that is now part of the beach park to strip cars and to fence stolen property. The gang was compared to Robin Hood and his Merry Men in England, and the ironwood forest was named Sherwood Forest. The forest is now part of Waimānalo Bay Beach Park. The surf site is a shorebreak on the sandbar fronting the park and is also known as Sherwoods.

Sherwoods. Surf site, Waimānalo, Oʻahu. Same as Sherwood Forest.

Shinmachi Tsunami Memorial. Monument, Hilo, Hawaiʻi. Monument erected in Wailoa State Recreation Area on the shore of Hilo Bay in memory of those who have died during tsunami, especially the tsunami of April 1, 1946 and May 23, 1960.

Shipman. Beach, Keaʻau, Hawaiʻi. Small pocket of detrital and calcareous sand at the head of an inlet in an otherwise rocky shore. The Shipman Estate is inland of the beach. William H. Shipman (1854–1943) purchased the property in the late 1800s and made his home here. His heirs own the land. Also known as Keaʻau Beach.

Shipwreck. 1. Beach, surf site, windsurf site, Poʻipū, Kauaʻi. The shipwreck that gave the beach its name was an unidentified wooden boat that lay on the sand at the water's edge for many years. Hurricane ʻIwa in 1982 destroyed what little of the wooden structure remained but left its heavy, rusted engine. The engine is buried in the sand, where it is occasionally exposed when high surf erodes the beach. The shorebreak is one of Kauaʻi's most popular bodysurfing and bodyboarding sites. The windsurf site is offshore of the beach. Also known as Keoneloa. 2. Beach, Lānaʻi. Some 8 miles of narrow calcareous sand beaches from Polihua to Kahōkūnui. Included are the following individual beaches: Awalua, Lapaiki, Kahue, Yamada, Pō-ʻaiwa, and Federation Camp. In former times, this shore was the site of many intentional shipwrecks. Boats that were no longer of any value were deliberately run aground on the offshore reefs and left to the destructive forces of the ocean. These boats included interisland steamers, pineapple barges, and assorted pleasure craft. The two shipwrecks still visible are a shipyard oil tanker at Awahua and a concrete mud barge at Pōʻaiwa. Shipwreck Beach is also known for its excellent beachcombing opportunities.

Shorebreak. 1. Beach, surf site, Kailua, Oʻahu. Section of Kailua Beach north of Kalama Beach. Named for the shorebreak waves that break on the shallow sandbars here. 2. Surf site, Sunset Beach, Oʻahu. Shorebreak on the east side of Valʻs Reef. Also known as Shores.

Shores. Surf site, Sunset Beach, Oʻahu. Shores is an abbreviation of shorebreak. Same as Shorebreak.

Shoulders. Surf site, Kuliʻouʻou, Oʻahu. Waves here form more of a shoulder than a wall. Also known as Paikōs.

Shriners. Beach, Waimānalo, Oʻahu. Section of beach at the south end of Waimānalo Beach fronting the Shriners Beach Club. The club was built in 1931 and is managed by the Aloha Temple in Honolulu.

Signs. Surf site, ʻĀina Haina, Oʻahu. Off Kawaikuʻi Beach Park. During the 1960s, a tall pipe with a small metal plate, the "sign," stood in the reef where the waves at this site terminate. Now only several feet of the pipe remain, visible only at low tide.

Silver Channel. Beach, surf site, Mokulēʻia, Oʻahu. "Silver" is a mispronunciation of "Sylva." Also known as Sylvaʻs Channel.

Silver Stairs. Surf site, Waikīkī, Oʻahu. The shore here consists of vertical seawalls protecting the condominiums of the Gold Coast. A set of silver-colored metal stairs in one of the walls provides pedestrian access to the shallow reef below. Also known as Hotels, Inside Tonggs.

Six Fingers. Dive site, Hawaiʻi Kai, Oʻahu. Spur-and-groove formation that has six ridges, or "fingers," at 50 feet.

Sixth Hole. Dive site, Mauna Lani, Hawaiʻi. Off the sixth hole of the golf course.

68s. Surf site, Wailea, Hawaiʻi. One of four surf sites off Wailea Beach that are named after the numbers on nearby utility poles. 68s is in the center of the beach on the north side of the small rock island.

69s. Surf site, Wailea, Hawaiʻi. One of four surf sites off Wailea Beach that are named after the numbers on nearby utility poles. 69s is at the south end of the beach off Wailea Point. Many surfers consider it to be the "Pipeline" of the Big Island.

67s. Surf site, Wailea, Hawai'i. One of four surf sites off Wailea Beach that are named after the numbers on nearby utility poles. 67s is at the north point of the beach.

67s Shorebreak. Surf site, Wailea, Hawai'i. One of four surf sites off Wailea Beach that are named after the numbers on nearby utility poles. 67s Shorebreak is at the north end of the beach, inshore of 67s.

Skulls. Surf site, Hanauma Bay, O'ahu. Beyond the reef outside of the Keyhole. A rock formation in the cliff face on the east side of the bay resembles a skull. Also known as Keyholes.

Slattery Bridge. Honolulu, O'ahu. Bridge that connects Sand Island to O'ahu. A bascule, or drawbridge, it was completed at a cost of $3 million in May 1962 and named for Colonel John Rudolph Slattery, an engineer with the U.S. Army Corps of Engineers, Pacific Ocean Division. It spans 400 feet of the Kalihi Channel and provides a second entrance into Honolulu Harbor. It is no longer used as a drawbridge due to the heavy traffic on Sand Island Road, and the control tower in the center of the bridge is no longer manned.

Slaughterhouse. 1. Beach, dive site, snorkeling site, Honolua, Maui. During the early 1900s, Honolua Ranch built two sheds on the sea cliffs above the beach. One was used as a slaughterhouse and the other as a storehouse for hides. The sheds were torn down in the mid-1960s, but the beach is still called Slaughterhouse Beach. The dive and snorkeling sites are off the beach. Also known as Mokulē'ia Beach. 2. Surf site, Ki'eki'e, Ni'ihau. Near Kūakamoku Reef off Ki'eki'e Beach. A former slaughterhouse is onshore.

Slipper Island. Ke'ehi Lagoon, O'ahu. Long, narrow island directly off Ke'ehi Small Boat Harbor. Slippers washed overboard from the boats in the harbor invariably end up on shore here. Also known as the Berm.

Slippery Rock. Surf site, Mā'ili, O'ahu. West end of Tumbleland. Primarily a bodysurfing and bodyboarding site that washes over a "slippery rock" shelf.

Slippery Wall. Seawall, Waikīkī, O'ahu. Low seawall, or cribwall, that joins the west side of the Kapahulu Groin and parallels the length of Kūhiō Beach Park. The algae that grows on its surface makes it slippery when wet.

Sloping Waters. Reef, Mokulē'ia, O'ahu. Shallow section of reef inshore of Devil's Rock that causes an unusual "sloping" movement of waves passing over it.

Slot, The. 1. Channel, Mōkapu, O'ahu. Channel between Moku Manu and Ulupa'u Crater. 2. Channel, Hanauma Bay, O'ahu. Narrow channel that was dynamited throught the west end of the reef to accommodate the submarine communication cable from California to Hawai'i. 3. Channel, Moloka'i. Channel between Moloka'i and Lāna'i.

Small Bay. Beach, Kaunalā, Moloka'i. Small pocket of calcareous sand immediately south of Kaunalā Beach.

Smith's. Point, Lanikai, O'ahu. Point that separates Lanikai from Bellows Field Air Force Station. Named for Helen and Alvin Smith, who purchased 1.6 acres on the point in 1936 and built their home here. Also known as Wailea Point.

Smoking Rock. Fishing site, Manukā, Hawai'i. Named in 1986 by Chuck Johnson, editor of the *Hawai'i Fishing News*, when he joined a group of *ulua* fishermen at Road to the Sea during the Second Annual Kona Casting Club Fishing Tournament. The ocean was rough, and waves were pounding against a large rock at the fishing site. As the waves rose above the rock, the wind would blow their tops off. Watching the wind whip the waves reminded Johnson of trolling in the open ocean on a stormy day. When the wind is really strong and blows the tops of the waves, boaters on the radio say, "It's really smoking out here." Johnson suggested the name Smoking Rock and published a picture of it in the September issue of *Hawai'i Fishing News*. Also known as Manukā, Road to the Sea.

Smugglers Cove. Bay, beach, surf site, Hanakanai'a, Kaho'olawe. During the 1800s and early 1900s, ships from the Orient smuggling opium into Hawai'i would land their cargoes on remote beaches such as Hanakanai'a. The opium would then be picked up by fishing boats from Maui and transshipped to Honolulu. Hanakanai'a was a natural site for this illegal activity because of its excellent anchorage, long sand beach, and isolated location. In June 1898, the captain of the Schooner *Labrador* was arrested on Kaho'olawe and charged with unlawfully importing opium. He was sentenced to eighteen months hard labor and fined $500. In her book *Born in Paradise* (1940), Armine Von Tempski wrote: "As suspected, opium was still being landed on Kaho'olawe for distribution. Mac [Angus MacPhee, who leased the island from 1917 to 1941 as a cattle ranch] and Yamaichi ran into a cache sufficient enough to take care of most of his debts—if he didn't turn it over to authorities. He did." Smugglers Cove was a fitting name to describe this illegal activity. The surf site is a shorebreak on the sandbar. Also known as Hanakanai'a, Honokanai'a.

Snipes. Surf site, Niu, O'ahu. Short for *snipers*, a military term for marksmen. Named in the early 1960s by surfers from Niu.

Snug Harbor. Pier 45, Honolulu Harbor, O'ahu. Site of the University of Hawai'i's School of Ocean and Earth Science and Technology (SOEST) Marine Center. The center's research vessels are berthed here.

Soda Pop Pool. Beach, Lāʻau, Molokaʻi. Section of Kamākaʻipō Beach with a natural pool in the rocky ledge that lines the beach. Foaming waves spilling into it gave the pool its name. The pool is the only swimming site on the otherwise rocky beach.

South. 1. Lagoon, Kāneʻohe, Oʻahu. One of several man-made lagoons at Coconut Island that were made by Christian Holmes, who owned the island in the 1930s. South Lagoon is primarily used for research vessels and private boats. 2. Point, fishing site, mooring site, Kahuku, Hawaiʻi. Southernmost point in the United States. The mooring site is at the base of the sea cliffs at the end of the point. The deep waters off South Point are a famous fishing site, especially for ʻahi, or yellowfin tuna. Also known as Ka Lae. 3. Point, Niʻihau. South end of the island. Also known as Kawaihoa. 4. Shore, Oʻahu. Shore from Makapuʻu Point to Barbers Point.

South Bay. Anchorage, Kāneʻohe, Oʻahu. Section of Kāneʻohe Bay between Coconut Island and the Kāneʻohe Yacht Club.

South Oʻahu Dredged Material Ocean Disposal Site. South of Oʻahu at latitude 21 degrees 15′10″ North and longitude 157 degrees 56′50″ West. The site was established by the Environmental Protection Agency in September 1980. Since its designation approximately 2.5 million cubic yards of dredged material have been discharged at the side with 1.6 million cubic yards (63%) from navy locations in Pearl Harbor.

South Point. 1. Complex, Kahuku, Hawaiʻi. Important group of archaeological features at Ka Lae, or South Point, including approximately eighty canoe-mooring holes drilled through the rocks below the navigational light. Hawaiian fishermen apparently used the holes to help anchor their canoes. 2. Dive site, park, Kahuku, Hawaiʻi. Park on the low sea cliffs at South Point. The dive site is off the park. 3. Light, Kahuku, Hawaiʻi. Navigational light at the point.

South Shore Ocean Safety Operations and Training Center. Ocean safety facility, Honolulu, Oʻahu. Substation and training center for the Ocean Safety and Lifeguard Division of the Honolulu Emergency Services Department of the City and County of Honolulu. The facility is located in the former food concession building on the ʻEwa side of Ala Moana Beach Park. It was dedicated on March 13, 2001.

Spartan. Reef, Pāʻia, Maui. Wide reef off Spreckelsville Beach.

Spencer. Beach park, Kawaihae, South Kohala, Hawaiʻi. Large, flat pocket of calcareous sand on the shore below Puʻukoholā Heiau National Historical Site. The park was named for Samuel Mahuka Spencer (1875–1960), county chairman (the equivalent of mayor at that time) from 1924 to 1944. The beach is also known as ʻŌhaiʻula Beach.

Spiral Lava Tube. Dive site, Kainaliu, Hawai'i. One of the Red Hill dive sites.

Spitting Cave. Cliff jumping site, fishing site, sea cave, Hawai'i Kai, O'ahu. On the seaward side of Koko Head, east of the Lumaha'i Street Beach right-of-way. The cave is at sea level, where it is subject to the constant surge of waves. As waves roll into the cave and strike its back wall, whitewater is ejected or "spit" back out of its mouth. Cliff jumpers jump into the ocean here from several small terraces above the cave, and *ulua* fishermen fish on either side of it.

Split Reef. Dive site, La Pérouse Bay. South of the bay at 50 feet, the reef is an extension of the last lava flow on Maui, which splits underwater.

Spot, The. Surf site, Kawailoa, O'ahu. This is "the spot" or the place to be when the waves are good. Also known as The Point.

Spouting Horn. Beach park, blowhole, snorkeling site, Kukui-'ula, Kaua'i. Blowholes are narrow chimneys that connect lava terraces to sea caves or lava tubes below them. Waves rolling into the sea caves or lava tubes force a powerful rush of compressed air, spray, and whitewater through the chimneys that erupts on the terraces as spectacular fountains. Blowholes are also called spouting horns because of the loud roaring noises created by the rushing air and water coming up the chimney. Spouting Horn is one of Hawai'i's most famous blowholes. The shore of the beach park is primarily rocky except for a small pocket beach of calcareous sand west of the lookout. This beach is a "disappearing" sand beach, where high surf may temporarily erode the entire beach. The snorkeling site is off the beach.

Spouting Horn Reef. Dive site, Kukui'ula, Kaua'i. Near Spouting Horn Beach Park.

Spreckelsville. 1. Beach, Spreckelsville, Maui. Calcareous sand beach with vegetated dunes in the backshore between Papa'ula Point to the west and Wawau Point to the east. The runways of Kahului Airport are immediately inland of the dunes. 2. Windsurf site, Spreckelsville, Maui. Off Spreckelsville Beach and accessed from Stables Road on the east side of Kahului Airport. Also known as Ironwood Park. Claus Spreckels was a sugar refiner from San Francisco. In 1878 he founded the Spreckelsville Plantation on Maui. Henry P. Baldwin later purchased the plantation and changed its name to the Hawaiian Commercial and Sugar Company (HC&S Co.), now the largest and one of the last sugar plantations in the state. The community of Spreckelsville is a cluster of homes at the end of Spreckelsville Beach Road.

SS Buoy. Fish aggregating device, ʻĀpua Point, Hawaiʻi. Buoy anchored at approximately 515 fathoms. Landmarks: ʻĀpua Point, Keauhou Point.

SS *Kaʻala*. Shipwreck, Kalaupapa, Molokaʻi. In 1932 the SS *Kaʻala*, an interisland steamer, was making her way at night from ʻĪlio Point to Kalaupapa and went aground on the reef at ʻĪliopiʻi Beach. Part of the vessel is still visible above water.

Statue of Liberty. Rock, Keʻanae, Maui. Pinnacle rock off Keʻanae between the point and Mokumana, or Bird Island. The outline of the rock closely resembles the Statue of Liberty, including its upraised arm with the torch.

Stone Island. Island, Mokuléʻia, Oʻahu. An alternate name for Devil's Rock used primarily by commercial fishermen.

Stone Shack. Surf site, Naha, Lānaʻi. Approximately a mile west of the end of the road at Naha on a shallow rocky shelf. The walls of a fishing shack on the rocky beach here are made of small boulders or "stones." Also known as Kapoho.

Stone Zone. Surf site, windsurf site, Sunset Beach, Oʻahu. Secondary surf site between Rocky Point and Monster Mush. The name implies that surfers or windsurfers here are stoned, or high on drugs. Also known as Arma Hut.

Straight Outs. 1. Surf site, Ala Moana, Oʻahu. Off, or "straight out from," Kewalo Basin Park. 2. Surf site, Mokuléʻia, Oʻahu. Off, or "straight out from," Owen's Retreat at the west end of Mokuléʻia Beach Park. Also known as Middles, The Box.

Stubenberg's Island. Peninsula, Kuliʻouʻou, Oʻahu. Undeveloped sand spit at the east end of Paikō Drive that was owned from 1948 to 1973 by Arthur F. Stubenberg, a former director of Castle and Cooke, Inc. Also known as Paikō Peninsula, Sand Point.

S-turns. Park, surf site, Honokeana, Maui. Small roadside park on a low sea cliff overlooking the surf site. The "S-turns" are the turns in the road bordering the park. Also known as Pōhaku Park.

Submarine Point. Fishing site, Hawaiʻi Kai, Oʻahu. Below the Lānaʻi Lookout on Kalanianaʻole Highway. The outline of the point from the east resembles the bow and conning tower of a submarine. The submarine is easiest to see driving from Sandy Beach toward the lookout.

Submarines. Surf site, Makapuʻu, Oʻahu. At the east end of the reef off Makai Research Pier. Minisubs for research purposes are stored at the pier. Also known as Avalanche, Makai Pier.

Suddenlys. Surf site, Hauʻula, Oʻahu. At the north end of Hauʻula Beach Park. Waves here come out of deep water and appear "suddenly" on a shallow reef. Also known as Kilia.

Sugar. Beach, windsurf site, Kīhei, Maui. Kīhei section of the long, narrow calcareous sand beach at the head of Māʻalaea Bay between Māʻalaea village and Kīhei. The sand here is said to be as fine as sugar. The windsurf site off the beach allows windsurfers to sail parallel to the beach and is the site of Maui's speed-sailing contests in the powerful Māʻalaea winds.

Sugar Mills. Surf site, Kualoa, Oʻahu. Off the ruins of the old sugar mill on Kamehameha Highway in Kualoa. Also known as Last Break.

Sugi's. Surf site, Ala Moana, Oʻahu. Between Big Rights and Shallows. Named for the fishing line, or *sugi*, stuck on the reef here.

Suicide Point. Fishing site, Hawaiʻi Kai, Oʻahu. Large, prominent point at the base of Koko Head's sea cliffs immediately west of Hanauma Bay. *Ulua* fishermen named the point because it is dangerous, or "suicidal," to fish here during periods of high surf when waves wash over the point.

Suicide Rock. Fishing site, Ka Lae, Hawaiʻi. Small rock island off the sea cliffs at Ka Lae, or South Point. *Ulua* fishermen named the rock because it is dangerous, or "suicidal," to fish here during periods of high surf when waves wash over the rock.

Suicides. 1. Surf site, Diamond Head, Oʻahu. Off Mākālei Beach Park on Diamond Head Road. 2. Surf site, Kāhala, Oʻahu. On the west side of Kāhala Channel. Also known as Razor Reef. 3. Surf site, Kawailoa, Oʻahu. Off the Pāpaʻiloa Road right-of-way. 4. Surf site, Makapuʻu, Oʻahu. Off Sea Life Park Hawaiʻi. Also known as Baby Makapuʻu. 5. Surf site, Wailupe, Oʻahu. Off Wailupe Penninsula. 6. Surf site, Waimea, Oʻahu. Off Waimea Point. All sites are named for the dangerous or "suicidal" waves breaking over a shallow reef or terminating against a rocky point.

Suisan. Fish market, Hilo, Hawaiʻi. At Wailoa Sampan Basin, site of Hilo's famous daily fish auction.

Summer Break. Surf site, Hanalei, Kauaʻi. Near the channel in the reef in front of the Princeville Hotel. This site breaks only during the summer, when waves from south swells wrap into Hanalei Bay from the west.

Sundays. Surf site, Waiʻalae Iki, Oʻahu. Off the Board of Water Supply booster station. Also known as Incons.

Sunset. 1. Beach, Sunset Beach, Oʻahu. Calcareous sand beach between Pūpūkea Beach Park and ʻOʻopuola Street. The beach took its name from Sunset Tract, the housing development bordering the beach, where lots were first offered for sale in 1919. 2. Beach park, Sunset Beach, Oʻahu. On Kamehameha Highway between Ke Nui Street and Sunset Point. Also known as Paumalū. 3. Beach support park (2.1 acres), Sunset Beach, Oʻahu. Small park on the inland side of Kamehameha Highway across from Sunset Beach Park. Dedicated in June 1999, it provides the facilities for the beach park. 4. Point, Sunset Beach, Oʻahu. Section of Sunset Beach from the beach park to ʻOʻopuola Street. 5. Surf site, Sunset Beach, Oʻahu. Off Sunset Beach Park. Sunset is one of the best surf sites in the world, especially for waves over 10 feet high. It is the home of the Triple Crown of Surfing, one of the premier events on the professional surfing tour, and is the preferred site for many other surfing competitions.

Sunset Point. 1. Beach park (.9 acres), Sunset Beach, Oʻahu. 2. Surf site, windsurf site, Sunset Beach, Oʻahu. Off the west side of Sunset Point.

Surf-n-Sea. Surf site, windsurf site, Haleʻiwa, Oʻahu. Small beginner's break on a sandbar inside Haleʻiwa Small Boat Harbor and off the Surf-n-Sea surf shop. It is also an excellent beginner's windsurf site. The shop was named Surf-n-Sea when it first opened in 1965 as a general sports store. When Joe Green became the sole owner in 1985, he and his wife retained the name but refocused the shop on surfing and scuba diving. Also known as Chocolates, Inside Haleʻiwa Harbor.

Swabbieland. Surf site, ʻEwa, Oʻahu. Off Coast Guard Air Station Barbers Point, which is within the Kalaeloa Community Redevelopment District. This site was originally surfed primarily by navy and coast guard personnel. Enlisted navy personnel are known as swabbies because one of their duties aboard ship is to mop, or "swab," the decks. Also known as The Jetty.

Swanzy. Beach park (4.8 acres), Kaʻaʻawa, Oʻahu. Named for Julie Judd Swanzy in 1950 in recognition of her donation of the lands for Swanzy Beach Park, Kaʻaʻawa Beach Park, and Kaʻaʻawa Elementary School in 1921.

Sweetheart Rock. Island (1.1 acres, 50 feet high), Mānele, Lānaʻi. Sea stack at the seaward end of the headland that separates Mānele and Hulopoʻe Bays. A traditional legend says that a young warrior from Lānaʻi brought a beautiful girl, Pehe, to Lānaʻi as his wife. Fearing he would lose her, he kept her hidden in a sea cave. Then a great storm struck and high surf surged into the cave, killing her. The warrior buried her on top of Sweetheart Rock and jumped to his death below. Also known as Puʻu Pehe, Sweetheart Island.

Sylva's Channel. Beach, channel, surf site, Mokulēʻia, Oʻahu. Named for Edward N. Sylva (1903–1977), a lawyer and former Territory of Hawaiʻi attorney general from 1953 to 1956. In the mid-1960s, he built two homes on his family property at the west end of Crozier Drive. During the late 1960s when the surf site off his home was "discovered," surfers began calling it Sylva's Channel. Also known as Kaiʻahulu, Silver Channel.

mo'olelo

My grandmother owned the property on Crozier Drive inshore of **Sylva's Channel** for many years. We started going out there in the 1950s, but no one surfed there. My dad, Edward Sylva, built two small houses on the property in the 1960s, and he lived there from 1965 to 1977. His sister lived in the house next door. When my dad died in 1977, I inherited the property and rented out the houses until I sold the property in 1998. I was a surfer, and I used to surf there myself. At 6 to 8 feet on a *kona* wind day, it's one of the best lefts around. No one else really surfed there until the late sixties, and it was about 1968 when it was "discovered." That's when we first started hearing the name Sylva's Channel.

 Richard Sylva, January 24, 1999

S

Taʻape Ridge. Dive site, south coast, Lānaʻi. East of Kaunolū. Schools of blue-lined snappers, or *taʻape,* are common here. *Taʻape* are from the Marquesas and were first introduced to Hawaiian waters in 1958 and again in 1961. They are now well established throughout Hawaiʻi and often school in great numbers.

Tables. Surf site, Mokulēʻia, Oʻahu. West of Camp Erdman off the highest bluff on the shore. The peak here shifts constantly, breaking over a number of patch reefs, or "tables," on the ocean bottom.

Tako Flats. Dive site, Molokini, Maui. Flat-bottomed sand channel adjacent to Mid Reef, with coral heads and coral rubble. Octopus, or *tako,* are commonly found here. *Lit.,* octopus (Japanese).

Tank and Landing Craft. Dive site, Mākena, Maui. Off Maluaka Beach in Mākena Bay at 60 feet. Two amphibious tractors (amtracs) are on the sandy ocean floor, one that looks like a tank with its mortar turret and one that was fitted as an armored personnel carrier.

Tanks. Surf site, Kuliʻouʻou, Oʻahu. Off the center of Paikō Drive. Surfers here often ride old longboards (surfboards over 9 feet long), or "tankers." *Tanks* is an abbreviation of tankers. Also known as Coral Reef.

Tank Traps. Surf site, ʻEwa Beach, Oʻahu. On the west side of Pearl Harbor Channel, off Capehart Housing. During World War II, anti-landing craft devices, or "tank traps," were erected on the reef here.

Targets. Surf site, Mānā, Kauaʻi. Off the old rifle range south of the Pacific Missile Range Facility and named for the targets on the rifle range. Also known as Rifle Range.

Tavares Bay. Surf site, Kūʻau, Maui. Named for Antone F. (A. F.) Tavares, a well-known resident of Kūʻau who lived on the bay. Also known as Lamalani, Kūʻau Bay.

Taylor Camp. Hā'ena, Kaua'i. Property on the west bank of Lima-huli Stream that was owned by Howard Taylor, brother of actress Elizabeth Taylor, and that is now part of Hā'ena State Park. During the late 1960s, Taylor made his property available to "hippies," transients from the mainland in their late teens and twenties who were experimenting with alternate lifestyles. During its peak, the camp was home to approximately 150 residents living in tents, tree houses, and shacks. The state took possession of the property in 1977.

T Buoy. Fish aggregating device, Makapu'u, O'ahu. Buoy anchored at approximately 365 fathoms. Landmarks: Makapu'u Point Light, Mōkapu Point.

Techniques. Surf site, Waikīkī, O'ahu. Big-wave, second-reef break between Publics and Cunha's. During the 1930s, surfers were still riding heavy redwood boards that were difficult to turn, but in 1935 Tom Blake introduced the lighter, hollow board, which was more maneuverable. Younger surfers of the day were then able to maneuver the hollow boards instead of just riding in one direction. They were able to "slide left" or "slide right." In the surfing slang of the day, this maneuvering was called "making technique." Techniques was a site where surfers had to maneuver, or "make technique," to ride from Publics to Cunha's on a big wave.

Tech Reef. Dive site, Kahe Point, O'ahu. Shallow reef at 10–20 feet off the south end of Kahe Point Beach Park. *Tech* is an abbreviation of technical; there is enough ambient light here for photographers.

Temple. Beach, Lā'ie, O'ahu. Section of Lā'ie Beach at the intersection of Kamehameha Highway and Hale La'a Road. The Mormon Temple is visible at the opposite end of Hale La'a Road. The beach is a popular site for baptisms, weddings, and sunrise services. Also known as Pu'uahi.

Tennis Courts. Surf site, Ala Moana, O'ahu. Off the tennis courts in Ala Moana Beach Park. Also known as Courts.

Terminals. Surf site, Kāhala, O'ahu. Dangerous site on the east side of the Kāhala Mandarin Oriental Hotel that is rarely surfed. The waves are almost impossible to ride except under big, ideal conditions by expert surfers. A mistake on the emergent reef here may be "terminal."

Terrors. Surf site, Waimānalo, O'ahu. Second-reef break on the east side of Makai Research Pier. The name Terrors was introduced for fun by surfers from Waimānalo in the 1960s for this surf site that breaks only during periods of high surf outside of The Bay.

Third Dip. Fishing site, surf site, Keawa'ula, O'ahu. Counting from east to west, off the third drainage ditch, or "dip," in Farrington Highway at the west end of Yokohama Beach in Ka'ena Point State Park.

Third Ditch. Surf site, Kekaha, Kaua'i. Off the third drainage ditch in Kaumuali'i Highway west of Kekaha Beach Park.

Third Flow. Fishing site, Pāhoehoe, Hawai'i. One of three lava flows from an eruption in the southwest rift zone of Mauna Kea that began on June 1, 1950. Each of the flows reached the ocean, creating small pockets of black sand on a coast of sea cliffs. Fishermen offshore use the flows as landmarks, numbering them from north to south. Also known as Ka'apuna.

Third Lagoon. Beach, lagoon, Ko 'Olina, O'ahu. Third of four man-made beaches and lagoons at Ko 'Olina Resort and Marina.

Third Pocket. Surf site, Mā'ili, O'ahu. Center of Mā'ili Beach Park and the third opening in the vegetation.

Third Tank. Dive site, Mākena, Maui. Off Mākena Beach at 80 feet on a sandy ocean floor. The dive site is a World War II amphibious tractor (amtrac) that looks like a tank with its mortar turret. It is called Third Tank because there are two other similar tanklike amtracs off Mākena Landing at Tank and Landing Craft.

Thousand Peaks. Surf site, Pāpalaua, Maui. During periods of high surf, there are numerous—"thousands"—of surf sites, or "peaks," along this beach fronting Pāpalaua State Wayside Park. Hundreds of coral heads make up an extensive submerged reef offshore, creating the numerous surf sites. Also known as Pāpalaua State Wayside Park.

Threes. Surf site, Waikīkī, O'ahu. Threes is the third surf site from east to west on the reef that begins off the Sheraton Waikīkī Hotel and ends at the Kaiser Channel. The two surf sites that precede it are Populars and Paradise. During the late 1950s, young surfers from the Outrigger Canoe Club "discovered" the site and named it Number Threes. The club was then still in the center of Waikīkī Beach at the site of the Outrigger Waikīkī Hotel. *Threes* is an abbreviation of Number Threes. Also known as Number Threes.

Three Sisters. Rocks, Ala Wai Channel, O'ahu. Three limestone rocks on the shallow reef flat inshore of Ala Moana Bowls that mark the eastern edge of the channel for boaters.

Three Stones. Sea stacks, west shore, Lāna'i. Sea stacks are vertical rocks that are left standing alone when the ocean erodes the rocks that once connected them to shore. This cluster is one of the best examples of sea stacks in Hawai'i. Although there are five of them, from a distance it appears that there are only three, giving rise to their popular name among local residents. Also known as Nānāhoa, Needles.

Three Tables. Beach, dive site, reef, Sunset Beach, Oʻahu. Small pocket beach in the southwest section of Pūpūkea Beach Park that is fronted by a flat reef that is emergent at low tide. The reef is broken into three tablelike sections, inspiring the name. The dive site beyond the tables includes large rock formations, caverns, and ledges at 15–60 feet.

Thurston Small Boat Harbor. Kailua, Hawaiʻi. Private harbor in the 10-acre oceanfront Thurston Estate on the west side of Kailua Bay.

Tickman Bay. Kahoʻolawe. Name given to Honokoa Bay by fishermen for a man from Maui whose boat wrecked here in the 1920s.

Tiger Reef. Surf site, Mokulēʻia, Oʻahu. Tiger sharks are commonly seen here. Also known as Camp Erdman, Erdman, Rock-n-Roll Reef, Tigers.

Tigers. 1. Surf site, Makaweli, Kauaʻi. Big-wave, second-reef site outside of Pākala, or Infinities. The site was first surfed in the early 1970s by Carlos Andrade, Kaleo Hookano, and Tiger Espere, and initially named for Espere. The name has been reinforced over the years by numerous sightings here of tiger sharks. 2. Surf site, Mokulēʻia, Oʻahu. Same as Tiger Reef.

moʻolelo

Between 1970 and 1975, Tiger Espere lived for a while on the north shore of Kauaʻi. On a big southeast swell, early in the morning before the trades began to blow, we decided to paddle out on the Hanapēpē side of the point at Pākala. The channel between Pipes, or Mahinauli, and the right off Pākala Point was closing out on the sets. I paddled out to the left at Pipes, and Tiger paddled out to the right. He was riding the inside, which has this incredible boil toward the end of the wave, and doing his trademark arches, coming from behind the boil and pulling right up into it.

A friend of mine from Waimea, Kaleo Hookano, then paddled out as I was crossing the channel to check out the rights. There were waves breaking about 200 yards or more outside and farther up the point from where Tiger was sitting. I asked Kaleo if he wanted to go check out the outside cloud break. He was game, so we went for it. When we got out there, the waves were breaking on a line of boils. They were peeling so perfectly but so fast that by the time you got to your feet, the wave would be reeling off too fast to get around the corner of the fall line and make it into the wall. We managed to get a couple of good long ones, but the best ones were going too fast to catch and make. Kaleo broke his board in half, and shortly after, I took a wipeout that broke all the buttons on my surf trunks. Luckily, I caught them around my ankles. No leashes those days, so we both made the long swim in, me with my trunks around my neck so I wouldn't lose them. Kaleo and I called the outer break "Clouds" because when you observe it breaking from Pākalā proper, it looks like a cloud break, but most of the younger kids call it **"Tigers."** The spot is now used mostly by tow-in guys, as they have the speed to get the wave at its very beginning and go all the way through.

The name Tigers had also been perpetuated by many shark sightings there, most of which have been tiger sharks. The water on that side of the reef is very dirty, more so than at Pākalā, and seems to attract them. One surfer sitting on his longboard was suddenly lifted out of the water and fell off his board. He had been lifted by a huge shark, which surfaced right under him. He fell on one side of the shark, and the board fell on the other side. He was eyeball-to-eyeball with the shark and said that the eyeball was about as big around as the bottom of a beer can. He has never been back there surfing. Last summer as I paddled back out to the point after riding a wave at Pākalā, a bodyboarder who was sitting right in the middle of a pack of about 10–12 board surfers suddenly started paddling furiously toward the reef. He paddled right by me, eyes bugging out to the max, and when I questioned him as he blazed by, he said that a shark had just taken the swim fin off his foot. Luckily, he didn't lose his foot.

Carlos Andrade, October 15, 2000

Tiny Bubbles. Surf site, Kailua, Oʻahu. Off the northwest end of Lanikai Beach fronting the home of island entertainer Do Ho. "Tiny Bubbles" has been Ho's signature song since he first introduced it in 1965 and is the name of the surf site off his family home. The name is a play on words because breaking waves generate foam, or tiny bubbles, as does the wine in Ho's song. One of several sites also known as Middle Reef.

Toes. Surf site, windsurf site, Niu, Oʻahu. In 1962, veteran surfer and Triple Crown of Surfing producer Randy Rarick lived on the beach directly inshore of the site. He and his neighbors were the first to discover that the waves on the shallow reef here could be ridden and that they were good for nose riding. They called the site Toes Reef after a then popular surfing phrase, "Toes on the Nose." The name is now usually shortened to Toes. At high tide, windsurfers use the channel on the west side of the site to access the open ocean and to surf the lefts here. Also known as Toes Reef.

 moʻolelo
In 1962, my family moved from Kaimukī to a house on the beach at Niu Valley. It was the first house on the Koko Head side of what

T

is now Kawaikuʻi Beach Park. **Toes** was straight out from the house, but we didn't think you could surf it because the reef is so shallow, especially at low tide. So for the first year we lived there, I walked a half-mile down the beach and surfed ʻĀina Haina. But one day in 1963 I was standing there watching it and I thought, "You know, that looks pretty surfable." So I started surfing it with the Value brothers, Rick and Todd. At that time we only rode longboards, and nose riding, or getting your toes on the nose, was a big part of surfing. One day a friend of mine named Scott Morey took off on this wave, ran up and got his toes on the nose. I yelled, "You got toes! You got toes!" And to this day the spot is called Toes Reef.

 Randy Rarick, February 24, 2000

Toes Reef. Surf site, windsurf site, Niu, Oʻahu. Same as Toes.

Toilet Bowl. 1. Reef, Haleʻiwa, Oʻahu. Hole in the reef off Haleʻiwa Aliʻi Beach Park. Surfers try to avoid the swirling water in the hole as they ride past it. Inlet, Hanauma Bay, Oʻahu. Small pool at the head of an inlet at Palea Point on the east side of the bay. The water from incoming surf rises and falls like the filling and flushing of a toilet, giving the site its colorful name. Swimmers floating in the pool ride up and down with the movement of the water. 3. Underwater tunnel, Lāʻie Point, Oʻahu. Named for the movement of the water as it surges through the tunnel.

Tombstones. Surf site, Honoliʻi, Hawaiʻi. East of Honoliʻi Beach Park. The building in which tombstones are made for ʻAlae Cemetery on top of the sea cliffs is the landmark for the surf site.

Tongg's. Surf site, Diamond Head, Oʻahu. Named for Ruddy Fah Tongg, an island businessman, who had a beachfront home here from 1946 to 1961. His sons Michael and Ronnie were avid surfers, and their home was a focal point for the neighborhood surfing community.

Topside. North shore, Molokaʻi. Name used by residents of Kalaupapa to describe the rest of the island. From their vantage point on the peninsula at the base of Molokaʻi's high sea cliffs, the rest of the island appears to be on top of the cliffs.

Towers. Surf site, Sand Island, Oʻahu. Off the high tower in Sand Island State Park.

Tracks. 1. Beach park (14.3 acres), Waiʻanae, Oʻahu. The development of the beach park resulted from a lawsuit filed in 1976 by the Nānākuli Surf Club when the Hawaiian Electric Company (HECO) destroyed a surf site by constructing a hot water outfall into the ocean. In a federal court judgment, HECO was fined, and the money and the interest from the fine were eventually used to build the park facilities. The park was created in 1987 when HECO gave the city a twenty-five-year lease on the site for $1 per year and Campbell estate donated 2 acres of beachfront at the west end of the site. The beach park takes its name from the surf site. 2. Surf site, Wai'anae, O'ahu. Named by surfers in the 1950s for the railroad tracks in the backshore that were used by trains belonging to the former O'ahu Railway and Land (OR&L) Company. The trains stopped running in 1947, but the tracks here were never removed. Also known as Keone'ō'io.

Trains. Surf site, Hawai'i Volcanoes National Park, Hawai'i. Big-wave, second-reef break on the west side of 'Āpua Point. A left and a right originate from a single peak and break at high speed. Traveling away from each other, the wave sections look like two trains going in opposite directions, the flying spray resembling trailing smoke. Also known as 'Āpua.

Treasure Beach. Polihale, Kaua'i. Small pocket of calcareous sand fronting Makole Valley between Miloli'i and Polihale that appears only during the summer months. High surf during the winter erodes the sand, leaving only a boulder beach. When the sand is "in," it is considered a good beach for beachcombing for "treasure" from the sea. Also known as Mākole.

Tree Stumps. Surf site, 'Ewa Beach, O'ahu. West of One'ula Beach Park. Named after the *kiawe* tree stumps in the underbrush onshore.

Triangle. 1. Windsurf site, Kanahā, Maui. Off Kanahā Beach Park on a reef where intersecting waves come from all angles. Triangle is an abbreviation of Bermuda Triangle. Also known as Bermuda Triangle. 2. Dive site, Hanauma Bay, O'ahu. Triangle-shaped pocket of sand off the center of the beach.

TT Buoy. Fish aggregating device, Manukā, Hawai'i. Buoy anchored at approximately 700 fathoms. Landmarks: Miloli'i, Kaunā Point.

Tumbleland. Surf site, Mā'ili, O'ahu. A rock shelf on the shore is slippery, causing people to tumble and fall. Tumbleland was primarily a bodysurf site until short boards made their appearance in the 1970s. Longboards cannot make the drop. The east end of the site is known as Hospitals and the west end as Slippery Rock.

Tuna Bowls. Surf site, Kuli'ou'ou, O'ahu. Same as Tunas. The bowl is the curved or bowl-shaped section at the start of the wave.

Tunas. Surf site, Kuli'ou'ou, O'ahu. During the early 1970s, some of regular surfers at Manantan's included Stanley Ogino, Les Sasaki, and Charlie Takaesu, who graduated from Kaiser High

T

School in 1974. During big south swells, a steep peak that breaks dangerously close to the reef develops to the west of Manantan's. Sometimes Charlie would paddle over and attempt to surf it, but usually with disastrous results, especially in those preleash days. During the same period, StarKist Tuna was running a series of commercials featuring a cartoon character named Charlie the Tuna. Charlie first appeared in 1961 and over the years always tried his best to be selected as a Star-Kist tuna, but even after eighty-five commercials, he never was ("Sorry, Charlie"). Television viewers loved him because no matter how many times he was rejected, he never gave up. After watching Charlie Takaesu wipe out one day at the steep peak west of Manantan's, his friends compared him to Charlie the Tuna. From then on the site was known as Tunas. For fun, Stanley Ogino also started calling it Akus, a play on words with the Hawaiian word for tuna *(aku)*. And as for Charlie the Tuna, he continues to be the supermarket symbol for StarKist and the star of their website. Also known as Akus, Aku Bowls, Tuna Bowls.

Tunnels. 1. Beach, dive site, snorkeling site, reef, surf site, windsurf site, Hāʻena, Kauaʻi. Calcareous sand beach at Hāʻena Point that is fronted by a massive, hook-shaped reef. The reef forms a lagoon within its hook that is a summer anchorage, a snorkeling site, and a dive site. Surfing and windsurf sites are outside of the reef. Surfers use a variety of phrases to describe riding inside a wave as it breaks over them, including being *in the barrel, in the pipe, in the tube,* and *in the tunnel.* The first surfers here in the 1950s were excited about discovering a site with long inside-the-wave rides, so they named it Tunnels. The name now includes the reef, beach, and point inshore of the surf site. Also known as Mākua. 2. Surf site, Kaluakoʻi, Molokaʻi. South end of Pāpōhaku Beach fronting a concrete tunnel in the backshore, the only remnant of a former sand-mining operation that was terminated in 1975.

 moʻolelo

We rode **Tunnels** first during the summertime as it breaks on some of those northeast trade wind swells. It got its name from those long tube rides you can get there. And it was one of those places where you always had a long swim. Remember, we had those old-style boards, those old-style skegs, and, of course, no leashes. So every wipeout was a guaranteed swim in and over the reef, which seemed to have a lot more *wana* in those days. Anyways, to my recollection, it was always called Tunnels out in the surf before I ever saw anyone diving in the area very much. Like many of the places on the north shore of Kauaʻi, I was diving *those areas before venturing out to surf them, so I knew pretty much what the bottom was like, and there weren't any tunnels. This used to be a favorite spot to cruise through and pick up some lobster, kumu, and 'aweoweo (big ones which I hardly ever see anymore)—and always some big uhu. And then outside where Dumptrucks is, those canyons would always house ulua.*

Nick Beck, January 1, 1999

T

Turkey Bay. Surf site, Sunset Beach, Oʻahu. Nearshore surf site on the west side of Rocky Point between the point and Gas Chambers. Novice surfers, or "turkeys," are often found here.

Turtle. 1. Bay, Kahuku, Oʻahu. Turtles commonly feed in the bay, so former area residents named it Turtle Bay. The name predates the completion of the hotel in May 1972. A ban on catching all sea turtles has been in effect in Hawaiʻi since July 1978, when the green sea turtle was placed on the list of threatened species under provisions of the Endangered Species Act. As a result of the ban, many turtles are found in the bay and elsewhere on the North Shore. 2. Beach, Mākaha, Oʻahu. West of Mauna Lahilahi. Also known as Keawaiki, Papaoneone. 3. Island, Kāneʻohe, Oʻahu. Off the north end of Mōkapu Peninsula near Pyramid Rock. The outline of the island resembles a turtle shell. Also known as Kekepa, Turtleback Island.

Turtle Arches. Dive site, Mākena, Maui. Off the Maui Prince Hotel.

Turtleback. Island, surf site, Kāneʻohe, Oʻahu. The outline of the island resembles the shell or "back" of a turtle. Also known as Kekepa Island, Turtle Island. The surf site is near the island.

Turtle Bay. 1. Dive site, Kīholo, Hawaiʻi. Kīholo Bay is a special fisheries management area, designed to protect the turtles that feed and rest here. It is one of the major habitats on the island for green sea turtles and hawksbill turtles, so divers also know it as Turtle Bay. 2. Gathering site, Hāmākua Poko, Maui. Rocky shore between Hoʻokipa Beach Park and Māliko Bay. Also known as Kaheʻa. 3. Surf site, Kahuku, Oʻahu. On the west side of Kalaeokaunu Point, the point on which the Turtle Bay Hilton Hotel is sited. Turtle Bay was a popular name for the bay to the west of the hotel that was legitimized on August 1, 1983, when the Hilton Hotels in Hawaiʻi took over management of the hotel and changed its name from the Kuilima Resort to the Hilton Turtle Bay Golf and Tennis Resort.

Turtle Bluffs. Dive site, Kalāheo, Kauaʻi. Southwest of Makaokahaʻi Point at approximately 50 feet. Also known as Turtle Hill.

Turtle Canyon. 1. Dive site, Hawaiʻi Kai, Oʻahu. Popular dive charter site, with lava ridges and sand canyons at 30–40 feet,

T

many fish and turtles, and one state underwater mooring buoy. 2. Dive site, Waikīkī, Oʻahu. Same as Canyons Reef, Turtles, Waikīkī Turtles.

Turtle Caves. Dive site, Kahakuloa, Maui. Six pinnacles with caves that rise from 70 feet to 10 feet below the surface. Turtles frequent the caves and the canyons between the pinnacles.

Turtle Haven. Dive site, northeast coast, Lānaʻi. One of the most popular dive sites on the island. At approximately 30 feet.

Turtle Heaven. Dive site, Haleʻiwa, Oʻahu. Pinnacle near the Haleʻiwa Trench that rises from 100 feet to 35 feet below the surface. Turtles are commonly found resting on the pinnacle.

Turtle Hill. Dive site, Kalāheo, Kauaʻi. Same as Turtle Bluffs.

Turtle Hole. Dive site, Hanalei, Kauaʻi. A 30-foot hole in the reef off Puʻu Pōā Beach that is frequented by sea turtles.

Turtle House. Dive site, Kawailoa, Oʻahu. Sea turtles frequent the site.

Turtle Pinnacle. Dive site, Honokōhau, Hawaiʻi. Several pinnacles are at approximately 35 feet off Kaloko-Honokōhau National Historical Park. Sea turtles frequent the site.

Turtle Reef. 1. Dive site, Halepalaoa, Lānaʻi. Off Club Lānaʻi. Sea turtles frequent the site. 2. Dive site, Ala Moana, Oʻahu. Off Magic Island at 40 feet. Turtles commonly rest here in pockets on the side of the reef.

Turtles. 1. Surf site, dive site, Hawaiʻi Kai, Oʻahu. Both the dive and surf sites are on a reef off the Hawaiʻi Kai Boat Ramp. 2. Surf site, Kahe, Oʻahu. Off the east end of Kahe Point Beach Park. 3. Dive site, Waikīkī, Oʻahu. Off the Hilton Hawaiian Village. Also known as Turtle Canyon. All sites are named for the abundance of green sea turtles.

Turtle Street. Dive site, Haleʻiwa, Oʻahu. Reef off the west end of Kaiaka Bay at 30 feet with arches, tunnels, and caves. Turtles are often found here.

Turtle Town. Dive site, Mākena, Maui. Many green sea turtles frequent this area. Also known as Five Caves, Five Graves, Nahuna Point.

Twelve Coconuts. Beach, Waikīkī, Oʻahu. Section of Waikīkī Beach in Kapiʻolani Regional Park that is marked by a cluster of twelve coconut trees in the backshore.

Twenty Minutes. Fishing site, Hawaiʻi Volcanoes National Park, Hawaiʻi. Twenty minutes is the time it takes to reach the site following the coastal trail from the Chain of Craters Road toward ʻĀpua Point. According to the Hawaiʻi Volcanoes National Park rules, fishing on the shore of the park in the Puna District, which includes Twenty Minutes, is limited to residents of Kalapana and their guests. Anyone fishing at Twenty Minutes must be a Kalapana resident or have one with them.

Twin. Islands, Kailua, Oʻahu. Two, or "twin," prominent islands off the east end of Lanikai Beach in Kailua. Also known as the Mokulua Islands.

Twin Sands. Beach, Kahoʻolawe. Calcareous sand beach that is divided into two, or "twin," sections of beach by a rock formation in the center of the beach. Also known as Kaukauka-papa Beach.

Two Humps. Island, Kailua, Oʻahu. Larger of the two Mokulua Islands. From a distance, the outline of the island's summit resembles the back of a two-humped camel. Also known as Moku Nui.

Two Mountains. Fishing site, cinder cones, Kahuku, Hawaiʻi. Named for two prominent cinder cones near the bottom of Road to the Sea that are used as landmarks by boaters offshore. Also known as Nā Puʻu a Pele.

Twos. Surf site, Waikīkī, Oʻahu. Same as Number Twos.

'Ualapu'e. Fishpond, Kamalō, Moloka'i. *Lit.*, hilled sweet potatoes.

Uaoa. Bay, fishing site, landing, Kaupakalua, Maui. Noted site for surround-netting *akule.* A former canoe landing was in a cove on the shore of the bay. Also known as Keone. *Lit.*, light rain, mist.

U Buoy. Fish aggregating device, Kāne'ohe, O'ahu. Buoy anchored at approximately 960 fathoms. Landmarks: Mokoli'i Island, Mōkapu Point.

'Uko'a. 'Fishpond, Hale'iwa, O'ahu.

Ukumehame. Beach park, Maui. The beach park lies within the coastal boundaries of the land division of Ukumehame. A narrow detrital sand beach fronts the park. Also known as Pako'a. *Lit.*, [to] pay for [in] *mehame* wood. *Mehame* was a prized native hardwood.

 mo'olelo

I was born and raised in Ukumehame Canyon. There used to be a beautiful reef from the *pali* down to **Ukumehame,** but it was destroyed by the military in World War II. The little park with the small parking lot was called Pako'a. The beach before Olowalu with the rocks on the shore was Ka'ili'ili, and Kapaiki was the village and the Teen Challenge area where I live now. Awalua was the *'ili'ili* and black sand on the Lahaina side of Olowalu. Launiupoko was a shark-breeding ground, and we had to watch the season when we laid our nets or the big sharks would get caught and break our nets.

 *John Kaaiea, February 11, 1978*

'Ula'ino. Beach, Hāna, Maui. Small pebble beach on an otherwise rocky shore. Site of Pi'ilani Heiau, the largest shrine in the Hawaiian Islands. *Lit.*, stormy red.

Ule Point. Dive site, fishing site, point, rock, east coast, Kaho'olawe. Phallic rock on a point north of Kanapou Bay. The dive site is north of the point and is also known as Ulua Ridge. A bottom fishing site is off the point. *Lit.,* penis.

Ulehawa. 1. Beach park (57.7 acres), Wai'anae, O'ahu. The park fronts almost all of Nānākuli from Nānāikapono Elementary School to Mā'ili Point. The eastern section of the park is known as Depots. 2. Surf site, Nānākuli, O'ahu. Also known as Channels at the mouth of Ulehawa Channel. *Lit.,* filthy penis. Probably the name of a chief who lived here.

Ulua Beach. Beach, dive site, snorkeling site, surf site, Wailea, Maui. One of five calcareous sand beaches fronting the Wailea resort complex. The surf site is a shorebreak that forms on the sandbar fronting the beach. The dive and snorkeling sites are off the beach. In 1971, Maui historian Inez Ashdown identified this beach as Ke One Ulua (literally, "the adult crevalle fish sand") in her book *Ke Alaloa o Maui.* When Wailea was developed, the name was shortened to Ulua. Fronting the Elua Village condominiums. *Lit.,* adult crevalle fish.

Ulua Cave. 1. Dive site, Kohala, Hawai'i. Large cave in Waiaka'īlio Bay that descends from 35 to 80 feet and that sometimes has *ulua,* or adult cravalle fish, in it. Also known as Kohala Estates. 2. Dive site, Mākaha, O'ahu. Large cave below a ledge west of Lahilahi Point at 80 feet that sometimes has *ulua* in it. Also known as Big Mouth Cave.

Ulua Ridge. Dive site, northeast coast, Kaho'olawe. Underwater lava ridge north of Ule Point with abrupt dropoffs at 60 to 120 feet. *Ulua* fish sometimes frequent the ridge.

Ulukou. Beach, Waikīkī, O'ahu. Section of Waikīkī Beach where the Moana Hotel was built. *Lit., kou* tree grove.

Ulupa'u. Crater, headland, Mōkapu, O'ahu. Volcanic tuff cone like Mānana (Rabbit) Island that is saucer shaped from the violent explosions that occurred when hot lava rose through the sea floor and interacted with the ocean. Mokumanu, the large island offshore, is an eroded remnant of Ulupa'u Head. *Lit.,* increasing soot.

Ulupikuli'ili'i. Point, Mākena, Maui. Rocky point at the south end of Ulupikunui. *Lit.,* small fig tree.

Ulupikunui. Beach, Mākena, Maui. Small pocket of calcareous sand in the rocky point south of Po'olenalena Beach. *Lit.,* large fig tree. A large fig tree once grew on the cliffs above the cove.

Underwater Range. Naval site, Mānā, Kaua'i. The range consists of listening devices on the ocean floor off the Pacific Missile Range Facility that can pinpoint a vessel's location within an area of 1,000 square miles. One of the facility's missions is to detect aircraft or vessels in the Pacific.

United States Navy Underwater Demolition Team No. 14. Memorial, Kīhei, Maui. Erected in 1997 in Kama'ole Beach

Park I in memory of the men who served on the teams. The park was the World War II training site for the navy's underwater demolition teams.

'Upolu. 1. Airport, point, North Kohala, Hawai'i. Northernmost point on the island. The airport is a short landing strip that was built by the army in the early 1930s and named Suiter Field. It was eventually acquired by the civilian community and is used infrequently by small aircraft. 2. Point loran station, Honoipu, Hawai'i. Coast Guard Long-Range Aid to Navigation (Loran) station with a navigational light. One of three transmitting stations in the Pacific that enable ships or aircraft to determine their positions at sea or in the air. The station is near Honoipu, several miles south of 'Upolu Point. Possibly named for the island 'Upolu in Western Sāmoa.

Upper Kanahā. Windsurf site, Kanahā, Maui. Same as Uppers.

Uppers. 1. Surf site, Hale'iwa, O'ahu. Originally known as Upper Marijuanas because it is up the coast from Marijuanas when heading toward Waimea Bay from Hale'iwa. 2. Windsurf site, Kanahā, Maui. The site is upwind from Kanahā Beach Park. Also known as Upper Kanahā.

U.S. Army Museum. Waikīkī, O'ahu. On the shore of Fort DeRussy. The museum is housed in Battery Randolph, a coastal artillery defense gun emplacement that was completed in 1911. It contains artifacts, photographs, and reference books that detail the history of the U.S. Army in Hawai'i, the military history of Hawai'i, and the contributions made by Hawai'i and Hawaiians to the nation's defense. The museum opened on December 7, 1976, and is operated by the U.S. Army Support Command, Hawai'i and supported by the Hawai'i Army Museum Society. Also known as the Army Museum.

USS _Arizona_. Memorial, Pearl Harbor, O'ahu. Park and memorial dedicated in 1962 and operated by the National Park Service that commemorates the battleship USS _Arizona._ The memorial straddles the _Arizona,_ where she was bombed and sunk in a surprise attack by aircraft from the Imperial Japanese Navy on Sunday, December 7, 1941, killing 1,177 sailors. The attack engaged the United States in World War II. The _Arizona_ Memorial Vistors Center was completed in 1980 at a cost of $4.9 million.

USS _Bowfin_ Submarine Museum and Park. Memorial, Pearl Harbor, O'ahu. The _Bowfin_ is one of only fifteen U.S. World War II submarines still in existence. In 1972, World War II submariner and Pearl Harbor survivor Admiral Bernard A. "Chick" Clarey and Rear Admiral Paul Lacy approached the Secretary of the Navy about acquiring the _Bowfin_ as a memorial to the U.S. Submarine Force at Pearl Harbor. With the assistance of Senator Daniel Inouye, the acquisition was approved. In 1978, the Pacific Fleet Submarine Memorial Association was chartered and in 1979 acquired the *Bowfin* from the navy. The sub arrived in Hawai'i in 1979, underwent a restoration project at Pier 39 in Honolulu Harbor, and was moved to Pearl Harbor next to the *Arizona* Memorial Visitor Center in December 1980. The museum and park are operated by the Pacific Fleet Submarine Memorial Association.

USS *Missouri*. Memorial, Pearl Harbor, O'ahu. Same as the Battleship *Missouri* Memorial.

UU Buoy. Fish aggregating device, 'Au'au Point, Hawai'i. Buoy anchored at approximately 760 fathoms. Landmarks: Kealakekua Bay Light, Miloli'i.

Val's Reef. Surf site, Sunset Beach, O'ahu. Pioneer surfing photographer Val Valentine lived directly inshore of Sunset, the world-famous surf site. Val's Reef is the shallow reef that forms the inside lineup of the break.

Vancouver Monument. Memorial, Kīhei, Maui. Stone monument designed and erected by J. Gordon Gibson, the original owner of the Maui Lu Hotel, to commemorate Captain George Vancouver's visit here in March 1792. Vancouver went ashore to look for water and to briefly explore the area.

Vanishing Sands. Beach, North Kona, Hawai'i. Same as Magic Sands.

Van Winkles. Surf site, Kalaeloa, O'ahu. Big-wave, second-reef site off the seaward end of the east runway. Also known as Grim Reapers.

V Buoy. Fish aggregating device, Mākua, O'ahu. Buoy anchored at approximately 309 fathoms. Landmarks: Ka'ena Point Light, Lahilahi Point.

Velzyland. Surf site, Kaunalā, O'ahu. In 1958, Bruce Brown was a twenty-year-old lifeguard in San Clemente, California, who also worked for surfboard manufacturer Dale Velzy. Velzy wanted to make a promotional movie about surfing, so he put up $5,000 and hired Brown to produce it. Brown found five other California surfers (Del Cannon, Henry Ford, Freddy Pfhaler, Kemp Aaberg, and Dick Thomas) and flew them to Hawai'i. During the winter of 1958, the six of them "discovered" Velzyland while exploring the North Shore for new surf sites. The name was inspired by Velzy, the man who had sponsored them, and Disneyland, California's world-famous theme park, which had opened three years earlier in 1955. Brown, however, did not tell the Velzyland story in his first surfing movie, *Slippery When Wet* (1958), but included it in his second surfing movie, *Surf Crazy* (1959). *Surf Crazy* featured Joey Cabell and Donald Takayama surfing at Velzyland. The name **369**

was reinforced locally when Velzy opened the first foam surf-board shop in Hawai'i in August 1960 and hired Terry Woodall to manage it. The introduction of inexpensive, light-weight, and mass-produced foam surfboards by California entrepreneurs like Velzy revolutionized surfing in California and Hawai'i—and eventually in the rest of the world. Also known as Kaunalā, V-land.

Veterans Park. Kīhei, Maui. Also known as Kīhei Memorial Park, Mai Poina 'Oe Ia'u Beach Park.

V-land. Surf site, Kaunalā, O'ahu. Same as Velzyland.

Voyager. Reef, Ala Moana, O'ahu. Artificial reef at 110 feet and approximately a mile off Ala Moana Beach Park, built by Voyager Submarines Hawai'i as a viewing attraction for their submarine tours. The reef consists of a 200-foot vessel, the *Sea Tiger*, that was sunk on June 24, 1999. Also known as the Sea Tiger Artificial Reef.

VV Buoy. Fish aggregating device, Kahalu'u, Hawai'i. Buoy anchored at approximately 600 fathoms. Landmarks: Kailua Bay Light, Keauhou Bay Light.

Wa'aiki. Bay, beach, northwest shore, Kaho'olawe. The bay lies within the *'ili*, or land division, of Wa'aiki. A detrital sand beach lines the shore of the bay. *Lit.*, small canoe.

Wahiawa. Anchorage, bay, beach, snorkeling site, Kalāheo, Kaua'i. Calcareous sand beach at the head of a large sand-bottomed bay. The bay is deeply indented and used as an anchorage during normal trade wind conditions. The snorkeling site is in the bay. *Lit.*, place [of the] milkfish. Wahiawa was named for a large stone basin where *awa*, or milkfish, were placed temporarily to keep them alive after they were caught. This stone and other important historical stones are in Kukuiolono Park in Kalāheo.

Wahieli'ili'i. Reef, Waiehu, Maui. Reef between the seventh and eighth holes of the Waiehu Golf Course. *Lit.*, small wood.

Wahikuli. State wayside park, Lahaina, Maui. Between Lahaina and Kā'anapali. *Lit.*, noisy place.

Wahinemakanui. Island (.18 acres, 40 feet high), Puna, Hawai'i. *Lit.*, big-eyed woman.

Wahiopua. Fishing site, reef, Hau'ula, O'ahu. Large, semicircular reef fronting Hau'ula Beach Park. *Lit.*, place of juvenile fish.

Wai'aha. Bay, surf site, Kailua, Hawai'i. Along Ali'i Drive in Kailua. *Lit.*, gathering water.

Waiāhole. Beach park (14.9 acres), Waiāhole, O'ahu. On the shore of Kāne'ohe Bay in the land division of Waiāhole. *Lit.*, adult flagtail fish water.

Wai'ahukini. Beach, surf site, Kahuku, Hawai'i. Calcareous sand beach at the base of Pali o Kūlani, the 500-foot-high sea cliff west of Ka Lae, or South Point. The surf site is off the beach. The beach and surf site are named for Wai'ahukini, a former fishing village. In 1954, archaeologists from the Bishop Museum began surveying the area and discovered that the cave shelters here showed occupation from the earliest settlement of Hawai'i to modern times. Fishhooks were among the artifacts discovered in the successive layers, and they provided an unbroken record of Wai'ahukini's inhabitants. The earliest fish-hooks showed Marquesan cultural traits, validating Hawaiian legends that at least one segment of the precontact Hawaiian population came from the Marquesas. *Lit.,* water of 'Ahukini [a supernatural woman].

Waiaka'aiea. Spring, Ka'ena, O'ahu. Same as Kawaiaka'aiea. *Lit.,* water of the *'aiea* tree.

Waiaka'īlio. Bay, dive site, Kohala, Hawai'i. Bay approximately 3 miles north of Kawaihae Harbor. The bay is also known as Big Sandy Bay. The dive site in the bay is also known as Kohala Estates and Ulua Cave. *Lit.,* water [used] by the dog.

Waiakalua Iki. Beach, Waiakalua, Kaua'i. Large pocket of calcareous sand at the mouth of a small valley. A stream crosses the west end of the beach. *Lit.,* small water [used] by the pit.

Waiakalua Nui. Beach, Waiakalua, Kaua'i. Large pocket of calcareous sand at the mouth of a small valley. Sand extends inland more than 100 yards. A low, rocky shelf fronts the beach. *Lit.,* large water [used] by the pit.

Waiakanaloa. Cave, Hā'ena, Kaua'i. Lava tube cave with water in it in Hā'ena State Park. Also known as the Waikanaloa, Wet Cave. *Lit.,* water [made, used] by [the god] Kanaloa.

Waiākea. 1. Light, Waiākea, Hawai'i. Established in 1904 to mark the southeast side of Hilo Bay. 2. Peninsula, Hilo, Hawai'i. Low-lying peninsula on the southeast coast of Hilo Bay. *Lit.,* broad waters.

Waiakuhi. Pond, Ka'ūpūlehu, Hawai'i. Largest of several brackish-water ponds in the backshore at the south end of Ka'ūpūlehu Beach.

Wai'alae. Beach park (4.4 acres), Honolulu, O'ahu. The park is on the shore of the Wai'alae land division. The park is also located within the community of Kāhala and is commonly called Kāhala Beach Park. *Lit.,* mudhen water. From the name of a spring near the shore that was reserved for Hawaiian royalty.

Waiale'e. 1. Beach, surf site, Waiale'e, O'ahu. Calcareous sand beach between Kaunalā and Waiale'e Beach Park. The surf site is outside a wide, shallow reef at the end of the road through the University of Hawai'i's livestock research farm and is also known as Revelations. 2. Beach park (25.7 acres), Waiale'e, O'ahu.

Wai'ale'ia. Beach, valley, Kalaupapa, Moloka'i. Steep boulder beach on Kalaupapa Peninsula fronting one of the six coastal valleys on Moloka'i's north shore. *Lit.,* gulped water.

Waialua. 1. Bay, Hale'iwa, O'ahu. The bay fronting Hale'iwa Beach Park. Named after the Waialua District. 2. Bay light, Hale'iwa, O'ahu. Navigational light marking Waialua Bay.

3. District, O'ahu. On the shore, the district extends from Waimea Bay to Ka'ena Point. 4. Beach, surf site, Waialua, Moloka'i. Narrow calcareous sand beach with a surf site offshore in the district of Waialua. Perhaps lit., two waters.

Waialua-Kahuku World War II Memorial. Monument, Hale'iwa, O'ahu. Same as Waialua Lions Memorial Monument.

Waialua Lions Memorial Monument. Monument, Hale'iwa, O'ahu. White concrete obelisk on the shore of Hale'iwa Beach Park. The Waialua Lions Club was chartered in February 1947, and the monument was the first community service project for its members. Shotaro Tanabe suggested the obelisk design, with the base to represent the four corners of the world and the pillar to represent the brotherhood of mankind. The top of the pillar was lighted with an electric light that served as a navigational light for incoming boats. The monument was called the Waialua-Kahuku World War II Memorial and included a plaque set into its base listing the names of the men from Waialua and Kahuku who died during War II. The Waialua Lions Club dedicated it on July 4, 1947. In the years that followed, additional plaques were added with the names of other North Shore men who lost their lives in subsequent wars, and the club members changed the monument's name to the Waialua Lions Memorial Monument.

Waialua Ridge. Dive site, Hale'iwa, O'ahu. Same as Waialua Wall.

Waialua Wall. Dive site, Hale'iwa, O'ahu. Long vertical wall, or drop-off, from 10 to 80 feet that is east of Devil's Rock. Also known as Waialua Ridge.

Wai'anae. 1. Artificial reef, Wai'anae, O'ahu. One mile south of Pōka'ī Bay at depths of 85–120 feet. Established in 1963. 2. District park (22.9 acres), Wai'anae, O'ahu. On the shore near the small boat harbor. 3. Small boat harbor, Wai'anae, O'ahu. Facilities include 146 berths, 7 ramps, and a vessel washdown area. 4. Memorial. At the south end of the small boat harbor. Unofficial memorial site with headstones and plaques that primarily commemorate individuals whose ashes were scattered at sea in Wai'anae. Many turtles come here to feed on a favorite seaweed. *Lit.*, mullet water. Perhaps from mullet in the *muliwai,* or brackish-water pools, that were once common in the backshore on many Wai'anae beaches.

Wai'anae Kai Military Reservation. Recreation site, Wai'anae, O'ahu. A 20-acre recreation center on Pōka'ī Bay that the army acquired in 1918. Also known as Army Beach, Wai'anae Rest Camp.

Wai'anae Rest Camp. Recreation site, Wai'anae, O'ahu. Same as Wai'anae Kai Military Reservation.

Wai'ānapanapa. State park (122.1 acres), Hāna, Maui. The park includes many historical sites, cabins, picnic facilities, a coastal hiking trail, and Pa'iloa Beach. Wai'ānapanapa is the name of a large water-filled cave on the park grounds. *Lit.,* glistening water.

Waiawa Unit. Wildlife refuge, Pearl Harbor, O'ahu. One of three satellite sections, or "units," of the Pearl Harbor National Wildlife Refuge. The unit is at the mouth of Waiawa Stream. The other units are Honouliuli and Kalaeloa. *Lit.,* milkfish water.

Waiehu. Beach, beach park, gathering site, Waiehu, Maui. Narrow calcareous sand beach fronting the beach park and the Waiehu Municipal Golf Course. The beach is a popular gathering site for seaweed that washes ashore from the shallow reef offshore. *Lit.,* water spray. Waiehu is one of four famous streams on the east side of the West Maui Mountains that are collectively known as Nā Wai 'Ehā. James Kahale recognized Waiehu in his traditional song, "Inikimalie."

Waihānau. Valley, Kalaupapa, Moloka'i. One of the six coastal valleys on Moloka'i's north shore. *Lit.,* birth water.

Waihe'e. 1. Beach park, gathering site, Waihe'e, Maui. Small park near the driving range at Waiehu Municipal Golf Course with a narrow calcareous sand beach. The beach is a popular gathering site for seaweed that washes ashore from the shallow reef offshore. 2. Reef, Waihe'e, Maui. One of the longest and widest reefs on Maui. Waihe'e Reef begins at Waihe'e Point, where it is 1,000 feet wide, and ends at Paukūkalo, where it is 500 feet wide. *Lit.,* slipping water. Waihe'e is one of four famous streams on the east side of the West Maui Mountains that are collectively known as Nā Wai 'Ehā. James Kahale recognized Waihe'e in his traditional song, "Inikimalie."

Waihī. Falls, Waimea, O'ahu. Waterfall that is the "falls" in Waimea Falls Park on the North Shore. *Lit.,* trickling water.

Waihilahila. Fishpond, Hālawa, Moloka'i. *Lit.,* bashful water.

Waika'ea. Canal, ramp, Kapa'a, Kaua'i. Drainage canal with a small jetty at the south end of Kapa'a Beach. One of several canals in Waipouli and Kapa'a that were built to drain the inland marshes to make the land suitable for agriculture, Waika'ea Canal is large enough to accommodate small boats. The size of the boats is limited by a low pedestrian bridge over the canal seaward of the ramp. Facilities include a two-lane ramp, a loading dock, and a vessel washdown area. The canal is a restricted fishing area.

Waikahalulu. Bay, south shore, Kaho'olawe. One of two large bays with high sea cliffs on the south shore of Kaho'olawe. *Lit.,* water [of] the roaring.

Waikalae. Beach, Kahuku, Oʻahu. Calcareous sand beach below the cabanas on the west side of the Turtle Bay Hilton Hotel. *Lit.*, water [of] the point.

Waikalua. Fishpond, Kāneʻohe, Oʻahu. *Lit.*, water [of] the *lua* fighter or water [of] the pit.

Waikanaloa. Cave, Hāʻena, Kauaʻi. Same as Waiakanaloa.

Waikapuna. Fishing site, Nāʻālehu, Kaʻū, Hawaiʻi. Low, wide rocky terrace at the southern end of the high sea cliffs that begin at Honuʻapo and end below Nāʻālehu. Many tide pools and several springs are found on the terrace. *Lit.*, water [of] the spring.

Waikīkī. 1. Aquarium, Waikīkī, Oʻahu. The Honolulu Rapid Transit Company (HRT) built the Aquarium in 1904 at the east end of Waikīkī. HRT owners hoped the facility would stimulate public ridership to the end of its trolley line. Charles M. Cooke paid for its construction and James B. Castle provided the land. Both were directors of the HRT. The original structure was replaced by the present one in 1955. A research laboratory established as part of the aquarium in 1912 became part of the University of Hawaiʻi in 1919. 2. Beach, Waikīkī, Oʻahu. One of the most famous beaches in the world, Waikīkī Beach is a 2-mile long calcareous sand beach between the Elks Club to the east and the Ala Wai Small Boat Harbor to the west. Formerly a barrier beach between the ocean and an extensive wetland, it is now almost entirely artificial, having been altered with imported sand to enhance the beach and seawalls to reduce erosion. 3. Beach waters, Waikīkī, Oʻahu. Undesignated moorings immediately off the beach from Diamond Head to Fort DeRussy. 4. Historic Trail, Waikīkī, Oʻahu. A 2-mile trail that begins at Kūhiō Beach Park, follows Waikīkī Beach west to the Hilton Hawaiian Village, and ends inland at the King Kalākaua Statue at the intersection of Kalākaua and Kūhiō Avenues. It includes nineteen bronze surfboard-shaped markers, each identifying an important historic, natural, or cultural site. 5. Marine life conservation district (76 acres), Waikīkī, Oʻahu. Established in 1988. The Waikīkī MLCD extends from the Kapahulu Groin (The Wall) to the Waikīkī War Memorial Natatorium and includes the offshore reef. 6. Surf sites, Waikīkī, Oʻahu. There is no single surf site known as Waikīkī. "Surfing at Waikīkī" usually means surfing at either Queen's or Canoes, the two famous surf sites in the center of Waikīkī Beach. 7. War memorial natatorium. Waikīkī, Oʻahu. A 100-meter saltwater swimming pool on the shore of Kapiʻolani Regional Park that was opened in 1927 as a memorial to honor the men from Hawaiʻi who died in World War I. 8. Wreck, Waikīkī, Oʻahu. Same as the Atlantis Wreck. 9. Yacht club. Private recreation facility in the Ala Wai Small Boat Harbor that includes 143 slips and visitor moorings. *Lit.*, spouting water. Perhaps named for springs that were in the now landfilled wetlands behind the beach. Waikīkī was also the name of a chiefess.

Waikīkī-Diamond Head shore Fisheries Management Area. Restricted fishing area, Diamond Head, Oʻahu. The fisheries management area lies between the west wall of the Waikīkī War Memorial Natatorium and Diamond Head Lighthouse. Pole fishing, throw net fishing, and daylight spearfishing are permitted during even-numbered years, and no fishing is permitted during odd-numbered years.

Waikīkī Ocean Waters. Restricted areas, Waikīkī, Oʻahu. Areas in Waikīkī where motorized boats are not permitted, such as at Queen's and Canoes, the famous surf sites in the center of Waikīkī Beach.

Waikīkī Turtles. Dive site, Waikīkī, Oʻahu. Also known as Turtle Canyons.

Waikoko. Beach, reef, surf site, Hanalei, Kauaʻi. Northernmost section of Hanalei Bay's 2 miles of calcareous sand beach. The beach is fronted by Waikoko Reef, and the surf site is seaward of the reef. *Lit.*, blood water. During heavy rains, water washing down from the hills above Makahoa Point colors the ocean red. Perhaps this is the origin of the name.

Waikoloa. 1. Beach, surf site, Hāna, Maui. Pebble beach on the north side of Hāna Bay at the mouth of Waikoloa Stream. The surf site is offshore. 2. Beach, ʻAnaehoʻomalu, Hawaiʻi. The beach was named after the Outrigger Waikoloa Beach Resort, the hotel inland of the beach that opened in 1981. Also known as ʻAnaehoʻomalu Beach. *Lit.*, *koloa* duck water.

Waikoloa Anchialine Pond Preservation Area. ʻAnaehoʻomalu, Hawaiʻi. Undeveloped area with anchialine ponds on the shore between the Outrigger Waikoloa Beach Resort and the Hilton Waikoloa Village. Anchialine ponds are brackish-water pools formed by depressions, crevices, or lava tubes that extend into the water table. The name is from the Greek word *anchialos*, meaning "near the sea." Although the ponds are landlocked and some distance from the ocean, they exhibit tidal fluctuation because of subterranean connections with the ocean through the highly porous lava. Tiny red shrimp, collectively called *ʻopaeʻula* (literally, red shrimp), are a unique feature of the anchialine ponds and are found only in Hawaiʻi. The shrimp are omnivorous and can live for long periods of time in the interstitial groundwater without appearing in the pools. The smaller and more numerous shrimp *(Halocaridina rubra)* is preyed upon by the larger shrimp *(Metabetaeus lohena)*. Some Hawaiians use these *ʻopaeʻula* as fish bait. The clear, larger, and more easily seen glass shrimp *(Palemon debilis)*, or *ʻopaehuna*, is also found in the ponds. It is indigenous to Hawaiʻi and commonly found in estuaries. Two common estuarine snails in Hawaiʻi, *Melania* and *Assiminea*, are also found in the pools. The golden orange algal mats in the pools are common to anchialine ponds. The preservation area was created by the developer and federal agencies and is managed for research and education by the University of Hawaiʻi under an endowment from the Waikoloa Land Company.

Waikolu. Beach, Kalaupapa, Molokaʻi. Steep boulder beach fronting one of the six coastal valleys on Molokaʻi's north shore. The valley was the original source of fresh water for the settlement at Kalaupapa, and a heavy-gauge pipeline once ran from the valley over the boulder beach to the Kalaupapa Peninsula. In 1960, a 5.5-mile water tunnel was built into the western side of the valley to supply water for other areas of the island. The water is stored in a large reservoir at Kualapuʻu. *Lit.,* three waters.

 moʻolelo

I was sent to Kalaupapa on January 13, 1924, and I stayed in the old Baldwin Home. That year there was a severe landslide between Waiʻaleʻia and **Waikolu** that we heard from the home. Our water line ran across the boulders at the bottom of the sea cliffs between Waikolu and Kalaupapa, and the landslide destroyed a section of it. We had to help with the repairs, and it took about twenty-one of us boys to carry one 900-pound section of pipe. Over the years this happened a lot, and I helped make many repairs to the line. Mōkapu Island outside Waikolu had a lobster cave, and one of the Hawaiians had a big canoe that he kept at Waiʻaleʻia near the home. All the boys would go down to help carry it across the rocks, and we'd all go out to the lobster cave. About all that's left of the home now are the rock walls that were part of the kitchen.

 John Cambra, February 15, 1978

Waikomo. Beach, surf site, ʻŌhikilolo, Oʻahu. Center section of ʻŌhikilolo Beach. Also known as Neill's, Ranch. *Lit.,* entering water.

Waikulu. Point, Mōkapu, Oʻahu. Outermost point of Ulupaʻu Crater. *Lit.,* trickling water.

Wailau. 1. Beach, surf site, Wailau, Molokaʻi. Boulder and black detrital sand beach on the shore of the largest of the six coastal valleys on Molokaʻi's north shore. Formerly the site of a fishing and commercial farming community that was abandoned by 1920. The tsunami of April 1, 1946, destroyed what remained of the taro patches and the abandoned village. The surf site is off the east point of the bay. 2. Point, He'eia, O'ahu. Small point in Kāne'ohe Bay that is the site of Laenani Neighborhood Park. *Lit.,* many waters.

Wailaumakai. Fishing site, Punalu'u. Between Punalu'u and Nīnole on the shore of Wailau, a land division. *Lit.,* seaward Wailau.

W

Wailea. 1. Dive site, snorkeling site, state park, marine life conservation district (35 acres), Hāpuna, Hawai'i. Calcareous sand beach fronting a small community of beachfront homes between Puakō and Hāpuna. The waters offshore were established as a marine life conservation district in 1985 and offer opportunities for snorkeling and scuba diving. Several surf sites are on the offshore reefs. Also known as Beach 69. 2. Beach, dive site, reef, surf site, Wailea, Maui. One of five calcareous sand beaches fronting the Wailea resort complex and the namesake of the complex. The surf site is a shorebreak that forms on the sandbar fronting the beach. The dive site is off Wailea Point. The beach is also known as Kahamanini. 3. Fishing shrine, point, Kailua, O'ahu. The point that separates the land divisions of Kailua and Waimānalo. The point takes its name from the fishing shrine, a natural stone formation on the ridge above the point. Alāla, a companion fishing shrine, is located at the north end of Lanikai. *Lit.,* water [of] Lea (the goddess of canoe makers).

Wailea Point. Dive site, Wailea, Maui. Off the point.

Wailele. Gathering site, Waipi'o, Maui. Section of Waipi'o Bay where Waipi'o Stream meets the ocean. *'Opihi* gathering site. *Lit.,* waterfall.

Wailoa. 1. River, Hilo, Hawai'i. One of two major rivers, with the Wailuku River, that empty into Hilo Bay. 2. Sampan basin and small boat harbor, Hilo, Hawai'i. Facilities include forty-nine moorings, two ramps, and a vessel washdown area. *Lit.,* long water.

Wailoa River. State recreation area (131.9 acres), Hilo, Hawai'i. Following the tsunami that devastated downtown Hilo in 1960, approximately 150 acres of demolished buildings were cleared and set aside as a park and a tsunami buffer zone. Called Project Kaiko'o ("rough seas"), the park was completed in 1965 and named the Wailoa River State Recreation Area. The park includes a spring-fed estuary and the Shinmachi Tsunami Memorial.

Wailua. 1. Beach, surf site, Wailua, Kaua'i. Long, wide calcareous sand beach across Kūhiō Highway from the Coco Palms Resort. Wailua River at the south end of the beach is normally barred by beach sand. The surf site is a shorebreak on the shallow sandbar off the beach and is also known as Coco Palms. 2. Monument, Kīpahulu, Maui. The wooden cross in the center of this remote coastal valley was erected on March 12, 1906, to honor Helio Koaeloa, who was called the Apostle of Maui. A devout Catholic, Koaeloa converted many Hawaiians to Catholicism before his death in 1848. He was buried in Wailua, the valley of his birth. 3. Bay, beach, surf site, Wailua, Maui. Bay fronted by a boulder beach with a deep-water surf site offshore. Wailua is one of the most famous taro-producing areas on Maui. 4. Pond, Kahana, Oʻahu. Small pond at the north end of Kahana Beach that was once a *muliwai*—a pond separated from the ocean by the beach. *Lit.,* two waters.

Wailua River. Marina, state park, Wailua, Kauaʻi. Wailua River is one of the few navigable rivers in the state. Daily boat tours take visitors from the Wailua River Marina to the Fern Grotto, one of the island's most famous visitor attractions. Smaller boats launch from a ramp across the river from the marina. The river is also popular for waterskiing, kayaking, and outrigger canoe paddling.

Wailuku. River, Hilo, Hawaiʻi. One of two major rivers, with the Wailoa River, that empty into Hilo Bay. *Lit.,* water [of] destruction.

Wailupe. 1. Beach park (1.2 acres), Honolulu, Oʻahu. On Kalanianaʻole Highway on the west side of Wailupe Peninsula. 2. Boat ramp, Wailupe Peninsula, Oʻahu. A private boat ramp on the west side of the peninsula for Wailupe residents. 3. Channel, ʻĀina Haina, Oʻahu. Man-made channel dredged out of the reef in 1947 by Hawaiian Dredging during the construction of Wailupe Peninsula. 4. Peninsula, ʻĀina Haina, Oʻahu. A man-made peninsula that was a former fishpond. In 1947, a boat channel and anchorage were dredged out of the reef surrounding the fishpond and the dredged material was pumped into the fishpond to create a subdivision. 5. Surf site, ʻĀina Haina, Oʻahu. Off Wailupe Peninsula. Also known as Wailupe Lefts. *Lit.,* kite water (kites were only flown in prescribed places; this was one of them).

 moʻolelo

It was back around 1958 when my brother and his friends first started surfing outside the **Wailupe** area. Pretty much, back then, no one ventured beyond Wailupe Lefts. The next spot over from that toward Diamond Head is a left and right break with emphasis on the left. This spot would break way outside on big south days and the right would usually close out all the way to Wailupe Lefts channel. The left would hold and move inside to a shallow reef ledge and then close out. My brother Fritz and his friend Brian Mulkern from 'Āina Haina named this spot Goofy's. Today Goofy's is also called Kim's. The next spot to the left of Goofy's is Groucho's, also named by my brother and his friend. Groucho's is a left and a right that closes out with Goofy's on big days. My brother can't recall why they named it Groucho's, but it doesn't have anything to do with Groucho Marx. The next spot to the left of Groucho's is a natural channel in the reef. This spot is called Rockies because of the abundance of coral heads in and around the channel. This spot is where I learned to surf in 1962. I can tell you that no one surfed this place but us, and no one surfs it today because it's a kiddie break—and there ain't no kids living along the beach today! The next spot down reef from Rockies is named Incons. Mike DuBois and I named this spot around 1970 because it breaks very inconsistently. It is both a left and a right with the emphasis on the right and peaks out at about 4 feet. From this point Diamond Head, there are no other ridable spots until you reach the right at the channel straight out from the Kāhala Mandarin Oriental Hotel. That was our little surfing world, Wailupe to Incons, during the sixties and seventies.

 Howard Hoddick, December 11, 1998

Wailupe Lefts. Surf site, 'Āina Haina, O'ahu. Also known as Wailupe.

Waimāha'iha'i. Beach, Kīhei, Maui. Calcareous sand beach between Kalama Beach Park and Welakahao Street. *Lit.*, broken water.

Waimānalo. 1. Bay, Waimānalo, O'ahu. Bay between Makapu'u Point to the east and Wailea Point to the west. 2. Beach, Waimānalo, O'ahu. Long calcareous sand beach from Wailea Point to Kaupō Beach Park. 3. Beach park (74.8 acres), Waimānalo, O'ahu. One of several beach parks on Waimānalo Beach, Waimānalo Beach Park was established in 1921. 4. Boat ramp, Waimānalo, O'ahu. Community ramp for small boats built in 1999 at Kaiona Beach Park. Also known as Kaiona Boat Ramp. 5. Landing, Waimānalo, O'ahu. Waimānalo Beach Park was the site of the Waimānalo Landing, a former landing for interisland steamers. The 700-foot pier, built in the 1870s by the Waimānalo Sugar Company, was dismantled in the early 1950s, the plantation having closed in 1947. Ruins of the landing lie on the ocean floor off the park. *Lit.*, potable water.

Waimānalo Bay. Beach park (74.8 acres), Waimānalo, O'ahu. One of several beach parks on Waimānalo Beach. Also known as Sherwood Forest, Sherwoods.

Waimanu. 1. Beach, surf site, valley, Hāmākua, Hawai'i. Waimanu Valley is one of seven isolated coastal valleys on the north side of Kohala Mountain. A black sand beach fronts the west end of the valley and a boulder beach comprises the remainder of the shore. A shallow sandbar lies off the beach. The surf site is a shorebreak on the sandbar. The black sand is detrital material eroded and transported to the shore by Waimanu Stream. 2. Campground, Hāmākua, Hawai'i. The campground is managed by the Division of Forestry and Wildlife, State Department of Land and Natural Resources. Campsites are in the vegetated backshore. The valley is accessible by a foot trail from Waipi'o. 3. National estuarine reserve, Hāmākua, Hawai'i. The estuarine reserve is a large marsh covered primarily by California grass and bulrushes that makes up the lower half of the valley floor. *Lit.,* bird water.

 mo'olelo

People were living in **Waimanu** raising pigs—*hapa's*—pigs that were part wild and part domestic, until the 1946 tidal wave. The pens and rock walls were located on the Waipi'o side of the stream near the end of the trail. We came in on horses and mules. If we killed a pig in the valley and it was too big to carry out, we half-cooked the meat in brine, Hawaiian salt, and fresh water in a *pākini* [tin tub]. Then we dried it for one night and packed it out in slabs. We caught plenty of fish, too—*pāpio, moi,* and *'ō'io.* The fish were so thick, we only took the big ones.

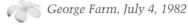 *George Farm, July 4, 1982*

Waima'u. Spring, Nāpo'opo'o, Hawai'i. Freshwater spring on the shore near Nāpo'opo'o Landing. *Lit.,* pleasing water.

Waimea. 1. Fishing site, state recreation pier, Waimea, Kaua'i. Former interisland steamer landing at the end of Moana Road. Primarily a fishing site used by residents of West Kaua'i. 2. Bay, Waimea, O'ahu. One of the North Shore's most popular swimming beaches during the summer and surfing beaches during the winter. 3. Tower, Waimea, O'ahu. The tower on the north side of Waimea Bay, one of the North Shore's most famous landmarks, was originally a storage bin with four vertical chutes to store rocks quarried by the Waimea Quarry Company. In 1929, Carl Winstedt was awarded the contract to build Kamehameha Highway from Waimea to Kahuku. He ran a quarry operation at Waimea from 1930 to 1932 to support the highway's construction but abandoned the site when the job was completed. In 1953, the Catholic mission converted the storage bins and machine sheds into the Saints Paul and Peter Mission. *Lit.,* red water (as from erosion of red soil).

 *mo'olelo*

In 1929 my father was awarded the contract to build roads from **Waimea** to Kahuku, so he set up temporary quarry operations at Waimea from 1930 to 1932. We built a tower that contained four vertical chutes to store rock and used an elevator to bring the rocks down an angular chute attached to the tower. I lived at Waimea for three years and ran the quarry for my dad. The old Hawaiians told me that prior to the flood, the river was always open and that canoes entered and left freely. But the flood deposited thousands of tons of silt at the river mouth and sand began blocking it off. Huge schools of fish came into the bay. It wasn't unusual to see fishermen from Waialua surround several tons of *kala* or 10-pound *pāpio*. No one surfed then, and we only swam from June until the end of September. My dad wanted to make the quarry a permanent operation and ship the materials out of the bay, but I talked him out of it when I saw the surf conditions during the winter months. We closed the quarry in 1932.

Charles Winstedt, January 2, 1974

Waimea Bay. 1. Beach, beach park (22.2 acres), Waimea, O'ahu. Wide calcareous sand beach at the head of the bay. The beach park is one of the most popular parks on the North Shore. 2. Dive site, Waimea, O'ahu. Off the point. 3. Surf site, Waimea, O'ahu. Big-wave surf site where some of the biggest waves in the world are surfed. Waimea Bay is the home of the Quiksilver in Memory of Eddie Aikau Big Wave Invitational surf meet ("The Eddie"), an Association of Surfing Professionals specialty event. Waves for the contest must be consistently 20 feet or higher throughout the event, so it has been completed only four times since it was first held in 1986. Winners were Clyde Aikau (1986), Keone Downing (1990), Noah Johnson (1999), and Ross Clarke-Jones (2001). Clarke-Jones, an Australian, was the first winner not from Hawai'i. The meet was named in honor of former big-wave rider and City and County of Honolulu lifeguard, Eddie Aikau. In 1978, Aikau was a crewmember on the Hawaiian sailing canoe Hokule'a when it overturned in the Moloka'i Channel. He was lost at sea after volunteering to go for help on a 10-foot surfboard. Also known as The Bay. *Lit.*, reddish water.

Waimea Rivermouth. 1. Surf site, Waimea, Kaua'i. Off the mouth of the Waimea River. 2. Surf site, Waimea, O'ahu. A unique surf site that occurs only after heavy rains when the river cuts through the beach and floods into the bay. As the fresh water pours into the ocean, it forms an endlessly breaking wave that can be surfed. After the freshwater runoff subsides and the beach again bars the river, another short-lived surf site is created on the sandbar that forms in front of the rivermouth.

Waimea Shorebreak. Surf site, Waimea, Oʻahu. Spectacular, often-photographed high surf at the edge of the beach in Waimea Bay.

Wainaku. Beach, Hilo, Hawaiʻi. Small pocket of black sand below the site of the former Wainaku Mill. The mill closed on December 30, 1971, and was eventually dismantled. *Lit.,* pushing water.

Wainānāliʻi. Pond (5 acres), Kīholo, Hawaiʻi. Large pond at the north end of Kīholo Bay and at the edge of the 1859 lava flow from Mauna Loa that created Hou Point, the north point of the bay. The flat-bottomed pond is lined with several dozen coconut trees, averages 10–12 feet deep, and opens into Kīholo Bay at its southern end. It is an important habitat for the sea turtles that frequent the bay. The aqua-colored pond is visible from the Kīholo Bay Lookout on Queen Kaʻahumanu Highway. *Lit.,* chief-protected water.

Wainiha. Bay, beach, landing, surf site, Wainiha, Kauaʻi. Long, wide calcareous sand beach at the head of the bay. Wainiha River crosses the south end of the beach. The former inter-island steamer landing was destroyed by the tsunami of April 1, 1946. The surf site is at the point on the east side of the bay. *Lit.,* unfriendly water.

Wainiha Kūʻau. Reef, Wainiha, Kauaʻi. Long reef between Wainiha and Camp Naue. *Lit.,* wading Wainiha. At low tide, fishermen can reach all parts of this reef by wading.

Waiʻohai. Beach, surf site, Poʻipū, Kauaʻi. Calcareous sand beach fronting the Waiʻohai Beach Resort in Poʻipū. The surf site is off the beach. *Lit.,* ʻōhai tree water.

Waiokāne. Spring, Kaʻūpūlehu, Hawaiʻi. Spring on Kaʻūpūlehu Beach fronting the Kona Village Resort's Shipwreck Bar. *Lit.,* water of [the god] Kāne.

Waiolena. Beach, Keaukaha, Hawaiʻi. Eastern shore of Leleiwi Beach Park.

Waiʻoli. 1. Beach park, Hanalei, Kauaʻi. One of three beach parks on Hanalei Bay's 2-mile calcareous sand beach. Also known as Pine Trees. 2. Channel, Hanalei, Kauaʻi. A channel cut through Waiʻoli Reef by the freshwater discharge of Waiʻoli Stream into Hanalei Bay. 3. Surf site, Hanalei, Kauaʻi. Also known as Middles, Middle of the Bay. *Lit.,* joyful water.

Waiono. Fishing site, stream, Punaluʻu, Oʻahu. The name of Punaluʻu Stream where it intersects the shore. Formerly an excellent fishing site for ʻoʻopu, or goby fish, especially the kāni-ʻoniʻo, nākea, ʻōkuhekuhe, and nāpili varieties. *Lit.,* tasty water. In former times the stream was deeper and cleaner. **383**

Wai'ōpae. Fishpond, Keōmuku, Lāna'i. One of two precontact fishponds on the shore of the former Keōmuku village. *Lit.*, shrimp water.

Waipā. Reef, Hanalei, Kaua'i. Isolated offshore reef seaward of the land division of Waipā. *Lit.*, touched water.

Waipā Peak. Surf site, tow-in surf site, Hanalei, Kaua'i. Big-wave, second-reef site that breaks on Waipā Reef.

W

Waipi'o. 1. Beach, surf site, valley, Hāmākua, Hawai'i. Waipi'o Valley is one of seven isolated coastal valleys on the north side of Kohala Mountain. A black sand beach three-quarters of a mile long fronts the valley, the longest beach on the Big Island. A shallow sandbar lies off the beach. The surf site is a shorebreak on the sandbar near the river mouth. High vegetated dunes occupy the backshore. The primary dune vegetation is ironwood trees. The black sand is detrital material eroded and transported to the shore by Waipi'o Stream. The paved road into the valley is only for vehicles with four-wheel drive. The valley floor was once the largest wetland taro cultivation site on the Big Island and one of the largest in the state, but only a small portion of the land is still in production today. 2. Bay, fishing site, Waipi'o, Maui. Large bay near Huelo bordered by high sea cliffs, the highest of which is Palikū. Fishing site for *'āhole, 'āweoweo,* and *'ū'ū. Lit.,* curved water.

 mo'olelo

I was born on November 12, 1899, in **Waipi'o,** a short distance from my present home. Waipi'o means "arching water." My great-grandfather was from Tahiti, so my maiden name Tau'a is Tahitian. There used to be a road down the *pali* to Manawai on the bay below us. Manawai means "two waters" and that's where we spent most of our time *makai.* We usually spent the weekend there. The women would catch *'ōpae* for bait, and the men would night fish for *'āhole, 'āweoweo,* and *'ū'ū.* We would make big bonfires to cook the fish. We kept a canoe in a large cave, but it was lost in the '46 tidal wave, and the cave is now filled with rocks. In 1964 an earthquake caused a landslide and the road to Manawai disappeared. Manawai is where Waipi'o begins and Wailele is where it ends. Palikū in the center is very steep, and no one ever went down there.

 Katheryn Kekapa Tau'a Watson, January 16, 1978

Waipouli. Beach, Kapa'a, Kaua'i. Narrow calcareous sand beach fronted by a rocky shelf that begins at the Coconut Plantation Resort and ends at Waika'ea Canal. Ironwood trees line the backshore. A pedestrian path winds through the trees along the shore. *Lit.*, dark water.

Waipuhi. Fishpond, Mauna Lani, Hawaiʻi. One of four fishponds at Mauna Lani.

Waipunahoe. Fishing site, Kukuihaele, Hawaiʻi. Small rocky point at the mouth of Waipunahoe Gulch. *Lit.*, canoe paddle spring water.

Waiʻulaʻula. Beach, South Kohala, Hawaiʻi. Small pocket of calcareous sand at the head of a narrow gulch north of the Mauna Kea Beach Hotel. *Lit.*, red water.

Waiuli. Spring, Keaukaha, Hawaiʻi. Spring on the point fronting Leleiwi Beach Park. Perhaps lit., blue-green water.

Waiulua. Bay, beach, ʻAnaehoʻomalu, Hawaiʻi. Calcareous sand and coral rubble beach on the shore of Waiulua Bay. *Lit.*, crevalle fish water.

Waiwelawela. Spring, Pohoiki, Hawaiʻi. Pool of volcanically warmed fresh water in a lava sink on the shore of Pohoiki Bay. Also known as Warm Springs. *Lit.*, warm water.

Wakiu. Beach, pool, Kahuku, Oʻahu. Between the Turtle Bay Hilton Hotel and Kawela Bay. *Lit.*, northwest wind sound.

Walker. Bay, Keauhou, Hawaiʻi. Named for the Reverend Shannon Walker of the Kona Union Church in Kealakekua. During the early 1930s he erected a youth camp with four cabins, a meeting hall/cafeteria, and several auxiliary buildings at Heʻeia Bay. A brackish-water spring near the *ʻiliʻili* (pebble) beach was used for bathing, and a catchment system provided drinking water. Also known as Heʻeia Bay.

Wall, The. 1. Sea cliffs, Hawaiʻi Kai, Oʻahu. On the seaward side of Koko Head between Portlock Point and Hanauma Bay. Kayak paddlers from Hawaiʻi Kai and Waimānalo who train here regularly call this section of sea cliffs The Wall. 2. Surf site, Hawaiʻi Kai, Oʻahu. Same as Walls. 3. Bodyboarding site, Waikīkī, Oʻahu. Named for the Kapahulu Groin, a seawall at the intersection of Kalākaua and Kapahulu Avenues. Waves at The Wall break on either side of the groin and are off limits to surfboards. Also known as Walls.

Walls. 1. Surf site, Haleʻiwa, Oʻahu. Waves here have long sections, or "walls." 2. Surf site, Hawaiʻi Kai, Oʻahu. Waves at Kawaihoa, or Portlock Point, break along a low sea cliff as they wrap around the point. The sea cliff is the "wall." Also known as the Point, The Wall. 3. Bodyboarding site, Waikīkī, Oʻahu. The "wall" is the Kapahulu Groin. Also known as The Wall.

Wānanapaoa. Islands, Waimea, Oʻahu. Cluster of small rock islands off the west point of Waimea Bay.

War Memorial Natatorium. Swimming pool, Waikīkī, Oʻahu. A 100-meter saltwater swimming pool adjacent to Kaimana Beach dedicated on August 24, 1927, as a memorial to the men from Hawaiʻi who lost their lives in World War I. The pool

W

was a popular shore recreation facility until it was closed for safety reasons in 1979. The first phase of the Natatorium's restoration, a complete renovation of its bleachers, exterior façade and artwork, was completed under the administration of Mayor Jeremy Harris and dedicated on May 28, 2000. The project included the construction of two restrooms in the east end of the building. Also known as Natatorium.

Warm Springs. Spring, Pohoiki, Hawai'i. Volcanically heated pool of springwater on the shore of Pohoiki Bay. Also known as Waiwelawela.

Wash Rock. 1. Dive site, south shore, Lāna'i. East of Kaunolū. Rock awash that is the top of a 65-foot pinnacle. A ridge nearby has a tunnel through its center. Also known as Lobster Rock. 2. Dive site, Lahaina Pali, Maui. At a rock awash. Also known as Manu'ōhule.

Waste Lands. Dive site, Kahikinui, Maui. Lava formations and ridges at 10–60 feet off the remote, barren lava shore, or "waste lands," of Kahikinui.

Watercress. Bay, Māliko, Maui. Small bay west of the Pa'uwela Light. A man named Taba had a commercial watercress farm here. Also known as 'Ele'ile'i.

Waterhouse. Beach, Po'ipū, Kaua'i. Small pocket of calcareous sand between Hō'ai Bay and Kōloa Landing. The Waterhouse family home borders the beach.

Water Tank. Bay, northwest shore, Kaho'olawe. Two water tanks made of redwood staves were constructed here on the north side of the bay when Kaho'olawe Ranch was operational. Fishermen and hunters using the tanks as landmarks named the bay. Also known as Papaka Nui Bay.

Wawaloli. Beach, dive site, Keāhole, Hawai'i. Narrow calcareous sand beach on a rocky shore. Several shallow tide pools provide swimming sites for small children. Also known as OTEC.

Wāwāmalu. Beach, Hawai'i Kai, O'ahu. Wāwāmalu is an old area name and was the name Alan Davis chose for his ranch. Davis and his family lived at Wāwāmalu Ranch from 1932 until April 1, 1946, when his home and the other ranch buildings were destroyed by a devastating tsunami. Also known as Ka Iwi Coast or Shoreline, Queen's Beach. *Lit.,* shady valley (short for 'Awāwamalu).

Weavers. Channel, surf site, Lanikai, O'ahu. Channel through the east end of Lanikai Reef where Lanikai resident Billy Weaver was killed by a tiger shark in 1959. The surf site adjoins the channel.

Wedge. Surf site, Kawela, O'ahu. Unusual horseshoe or "wedge-shaped" wave that breaks on a shallow reef on the north side of Kawela Bay. Also known as Rainbows.

Weli. Fishpond, Honolulu, O'ahu. *Lit.*, fear.

Weliweli. Surf site, Weliweli, Hawai'i. Between 'Anaeho'o-malu and Keawaiki and off the Von Holt family's beachfront home, Weliweli, with its unique coral and lava walls. *Lit.*, fear.

Weliweli Point. Surf site, Weliweli, Hawai'i. Between 'Anaeho-'omalu and Keawaiki and south of the Von Holt family's beachfront home, Weliweli, with its unique coral and lava wall. *Lit.*, fear point.

West. 1. Beach, Ko 'Olina, O'ahu. During the early 1970s, developer Herbert Horita introduced the name West Beach as the project name for the residential-resort complex that he later renamed Ko 'Olina. 2. Lagoon, Kāne'ohe, O'ahu. One of several man-made lagoons at Coconut Island that were created by Christian Holmes, who owned the island in the 1930s. West Lagoon is the site of the Coconut Island Small Boat Harbor and the primary entry point to the island. West Lagoon is also where large marine animal research is conducted because of its superior water quality and depth. Facilities include floating enclosures for dolphins and false killer whales and several ponds for sharks. 3. Shore, O'ahu. Shore from Kalaeloa Point to Ka'ena Point.

West Kawela. Beach, Kawela, O'ahu. Beach between the west end of Kawela Bay and Waiale'e Beach Park.

West Loch. 1. Bay, Pearl Harbor, O'ahu. One of the three large lochs, or landlocked bays, that make up Pearl Harbor. 2. Shore park (6.36 acres), Honouliuli, O'ahu. On the shore of West Loch Estates, with sixteen recreational fishing piers. No in-water activities are permitted in West Loch.

West Māmala Bay. Shore from the Honolulu International Airport Reef Runway to Kalaeloa Point.

West Maui. Section of Maui defined by the West Maui Mountains.

West Moloka'i. Section of Moloka'i west of an imaginary line approximately from Keonelele at Mo'omomi to Waiakāne on Pālā'au Road. East Moloka'i is east of the line.

 mo'olelo

Forty years ago, I used to fish this stretch of shoreline with the old-timers. I was the "bag boy." In those days vehicle access to the West End was restricted and privy only to the ranch workers. So in order to fish this then remote shoreline, we came by boat from Kaunakakai Wharf and overnighted at Kolo Wharf. Bright and early the next morning, we'd set out around Lā'au Point and head north along the west coast. The names that I learned were the names of the promontories, as they act like "corners" around which you had to go to reach our fishing spots. Four that survive in my mind are "Awa" for Kahaiawa, "Puhi" for Kapuhikani, Koa'e, and Kaiaka.

As soon as you rounded Lā'au, the first point was Awa, which was easily discernable. We seldom stopped between Lā'au and Awa because the water was murky most of the time. But when it was clean, then we would dive a couple of spots and then *pau* because we would have more than enough fish. The next point, Puhi, was another easy marker because it stood way out and was located between Kaupoa and Kaunala Bays. Koa'e and Kaiaka were easy to remember because they are the end points of the long sand beach Pāpōhaku, where we did most of our throw netting for *moi*. Just past Kaiaka was another sand beach called Kepuhi we sometimes visited. This is the beach fronting the Kalua-koi Hotel. I remember coming this far north only two or three times in those days, and only when we didn't catch enough at Pāpō-haku, which was seldom. Between Puhi and Koa'e, we mostly speared. The stretch between Koa'e, Kaiaka, and Kepuhi was used almost exclusively for throw netting at known *moi* holes.

 Bill Puleloa, October 23, 2000

West Peak. Surf site, Sunset Beach, O'ahu. Outside, westernmost section of Sunset.

Wet Cave. Hā'ena, Kaua'i. Lava tube with a freshwater pond that was once a sea cave during a higher stand of the sea. It is called the Wet Cave to differentiate it from another lava tube to the east that has no water in it and is called the Dry Cave. Also known as Waiakanaloa.

Wewehi. Rock formation, Pa'uwela, Maui. Cluster of rocks in the ocean at the west point of Kuiaha Bay. Pa'uwela residents who live inland use the rocks to gauge how rough the ocean is by observing the wave activity on the rocks and the amount of whitewater that the waves generate. Perhaps lit., a deep blue or black spot.

Wharf. Surf site, Kaunakakai, Moloka'i. Generic name for two surf sites, Lefts and Rights, on either side of the wharf.

White Fence. Surf site, Waimānalo, O'ahu. On the east side of Makai Research Pier. This site was partially destroyed when the boat channel to the pier was dredged. The white fence was a former wooden traffic barrier painted white on Kalaniana'ole Highway inshore of the site. A metal traffic barrier replaced it.

White Plains. Beach, surf site, Kalaeloa, O'ahu. Calcareous sand beach on the east shore of Kalaeloa Community Development District. The beach takes its name from White Plains Road, the access road to the beach. When the area was originally developed as Barbers Point Naval Air Station, the majority of the streets were named for battles and ships from World War II. The *White Plains* was an escort aircraft carrier that was built by the Kaiser Shipbuilding Company in 1943 and served as a warship in the Pacific for the duration of the war. She was named after a battle between General George Washington and British forces that occurred in 1776 during the Revolutionary War near White Plains, New York. Today the city of White Plains is the seat of government for Westchester County. Also known as Kualakai.

White Rock. 1. Dive site, island, south coast, Lāna'i. East of Kaunolū. Small island with many small caves. 2. Ridge, Keōmuku, Lāna'i. A wide limestone ridge across Keōmuku Road near the beach homes at Maunalei. Also known as Lae Hi. 3. Historic site, Ka'ena Point State Park, O'ahu. Large limestone rock near Ka'ena Point that was said to be a *leinaaka'uhane*—a place where souls of the dead left the earth. Also known as Leinaaka'uhane.

White Sand Mānele. Beach, Mānele, Lāna'i. Alternate name for Hulopo'e Beach, a calcareous or "white" sand beach that was given to differentiate it from Black Sand Mānele, a detrital or "black" sand beach in Mānele Bay. Also known as Hulopo'e Beach.

White Sands. Beach, surf site, North Kona, Hawai'i. Large pocket of calcareous sand between two rocky points at La'aloa Bay Beach Park. During periods of high surf, waves erode almost the entire beach, exposing the underlying rocks. When the surf subsides, normal surf activity redeposits the sand on shore, covering the rocks. The constant movement of the sand off and onshore keeps it clean and free of debris and, therefore, "white" in appearance. Also known as Disappearing Sands, La'aloa Bay Beach Park, Magic Sands.

White Tip Condos. Dive site, Kainaliu, Hawai'i. One of the Red Hill dive sites. The "condos," or condominiums, are a series of sand-bottomed caves under some ledges in a bay north of Red Hill that almost always have white tip sharks in them.

Whittington. Park, Ka'ū, Hawai'i. Rocky shore that was the site of Honu'apo Landing. The abandoned landing and its port facilities were converted into a beach park by the plantation and several civic groups. In 1948 the park was named for Richard Henry Whittington (1885–1945), a former county road supervisor and longtime resident of Ka'ū. Whittington was born in California and came to Hawai'i as a teenager.

He married a Hawaiian, settled in Ka'ū, built his family home on the hill above the park, and lived there until his death.

 mo'olelo

My father was Richard Henry Whittington, better known as Dick. He was born in California, but he was not sure when. It was about 1885 because he was 60 or 61 when he died in 1945. His father was an old sea captain who came to Hawai'i and eventually settled on Kaua'i at Kalāheo to raise pineapples. My dad followed his father to Hawai'i when he was about sixteen years old. Later my dad moved to Nā'ālehu and worked for the plantation. That's when he met my mom, but they had to wait until my grandfather died before they got married. My grandfather didn't like haoles. We moved all around—O'ahu, Kaua'i, and back to Hawai'i—but my dad was always with the plantation. We had a family soda works for years in Wai'ohinu. It was a family operation with all the kids helping with the bottling and labeling. Later, my dad worked for the county as the road supervisor, and he had a gang of Hawaiians under him. He was well liked and got along well with the young folks.

He built the house on the *pali* above Honu'apo in 1941. We still own the land. There used to be a big Hawaiian village in the flat lands below next to the wharf, but in 1868 a tidal wave wiped the area out, and no one moved back. That's where we swam and had *hukilaus*.

 Winifred Bowman, October 13, 1982

Wild Beach. Kahuku, O'ahu. Center section of Turtle Bay between Kawela Bay and the Turtle Bay Hilton Hotel. There are many erratic or "wild" wave patterns in the bay during periods of high surf.

Wilds. Surf site, Kahuku, O'ahu. Off Wild Beach between Kawela Bay and the Turtle Bay Hilton Hotel.

Wiliwilipe'ape'a. Point, southeast shore, Kaho'olawe. *Lit.,* bushy *wiliwili* tree.

Winch. Surf site, Diamond Head, O'ahu. In 1913 the bark *S.C. Allen*, a lumber carrier bound for Honolulu Harbor, went aground here. All of the cargo and most of her timbers were salvaged, but her heavy winch was left to rust on the shallow reef where it is visible above water. The surf site is seaward of the winch.

Winchells. Surf site, Hā'ena, Kaua'i. Named in the mid 1960s by Carlos Andrade for Winchell's Donut Houses in California. Andrade graduated from Kamehameha Schools in 1962 and spent several years in college in California. Surfers there frequented Winchell's Donut Houses when they were not surfing, so when he discovered this site after returning to Kaua'i, he named it Winchells because the waves are as hollow as a donut.

Windmill. 1. Bay, dive site, Kohala, Hawai'i. First small bay south of Waiaka'īlio Bay. Kahuā Ranch formerly shipped cattle on interisland steamers here. Cattle were penned behind the coral rubble beach. A windmill provided them with water. 2. Beach, Punalau, Maui. During the early 1890s, Henry P. Baldwin started Honolua Ranch, a cattle ranch headquartered at Honolua Bay. In the intermittent streambed at the west end of Punalau Beach, the ranch constructed a windmill to supply water to a water trough for its cattle. Although nothing remains of the windmill today, the beach is still known as Windmill Beach. Also known as Pōhakupule Beach, Punalau Beach, Windmills.

Windmills. 1. Surf site, Kāwā, Hawai'i. Off Kāwā Beach. A small windmill in the pasture inland of the beach supplies water to a trough for cattle. 2. Surf site, Punalau, Maui. The surf site is off an intermittent streambed at the west end of Punalau Beach where a former windmill constructed by Honolua Ranch supplied a water trough for cattle.

Windsock. 1. Dive site, Kā'anapali, Maui. Off the location of the windsock at the former Kā'anapali Airport. 2. Channel marker, Waikīkī, O'ahu. Orange windsock on a pole in the reef fronting Sans Souci Beach. The windsock is permitted on the reef because it is used by sailors from the nearby Outrigger Canoe Club to safely navigate the Kaimana Channel.

Witches Brew. Cove, Hanauma, O'ahu. Rocky cove at the end of the terrace on the west side of Hanauma Bay where floating debris collects as it is blown into the bay by the trade winds. It was named for the swirling movements of the currents in the cove, which were compared to the boiling contents in a witches' cauldron.

Wizard Stones. Historic site, Waikīkī, O'ahu. Same as the Healing Stones, Kapaemāhū stones.

WK Buoy. Fish aggregating device, Wailua, Kaua'i. Buoy anchored at approximately 915 fathoms. Landmarks: Kāhala Point Light, Kamilo Point.

Wrap Arounds. Surf site, Kailua, O'ahu. On the north side of Moku Nui, the larger of the two Mokulua Islands. Waves following the contour of the island "wrap around" it and terminate at the beach.

Wright. Beach park, surf site, Waimea, Kaua'i. On the west bank of Waimea River where the river intersects the detrital sand beach. Named for Lucy Kapahu Aukai Wright (1873–1931), the first native Hawaiian schoolteacher at Waimea School. Wright taught there for thrity-five years and was a member of Waimea Hawaiian Church and many civic organizations. The park named for her is also the site where Captain James Cook first came ashore in the Hawaiian Islands in January 1778. The surf site is off the river mouth.

X Buoy. Fish aggregating device, Kahuku, Oʻahu. Buoy anchored at approximately 945 fathoms. Landmarks: Kaʻena Point, Hale-ʻiwa Channel Buoy Light, Lāʻie Point.

XX Buoy. Fish aggregating device, Puakō, Hawaiʻi. Buoy anchored at approximately 345 fathoms. Landmarks: Māhukona Light, Kawaihae Light, Keāhole Point Light.

Yabui Beach. 'Alaeloa, Maui. The Yabui family owned the property bordering the beach before the Kahana Sunset condominium was built on it. Also known as Keonenui Beach.

Yadao Pavilion. North Hilo, Hawai'i. Picnic pavilion in Kolekole Beach Park that was named for former County Supervisor Elias P. (Epy) Yadao. Among his many accomplishments as a member of the County Board of Supervisors from 1959 until his death in 1966, Yadao was instrumental in obtaining funds for the pavilion named posthumously in his honor.

Yamada Point. North shore, Lāna'i. Lae Wahie section of Shipwreck Beach. Named for Yasukichi Yamada, who moved to Lāna'i from O'ahu in 1929 to work in the plantation's butcher shop and began fishing at Lae Wahie about the same time. Traveling to and from Lāna'i City by mule, he sold the fish he caught in the butcher shop. In 1945 Yamada moved to Maui, where he ran the kitchen in the Kahului Hotel, and two years later he opened his own restaurant, the No Ka 'Oi Inn. Also known as Lae Wahie.

Yamashita Bay. Honouli Malo'o, Moloka'i. Henry Yamashita purchased one of two beachfront parcels here in the 1950s and built a small beach house on it. Also known as Honouli Malo'o.

Y.O. Dive site, Waikīkī, O'ahu. Same as Y.O. 257.

Yokes. Surf site, Ka'ena State Park, O'ahu. An abbreviation of Yokohama.

Yokohama. Bay, beach, dive site, surf site, Ka'ena State Park, O'ahu. Calcareous sand beach on Yokohama Bay. Yokohama is the name of a famous port city in Japan, but the name here apparently came from a Japanese switchman named Yokohama who lived nearby in the early 1900s. He worked for the Oahu Railway and Land (OR&L) Company, which ran trains around Ka'ena Point until 1947. The train stop was named for him, and the name was extended to the beach. The dive and surf sites are off the beach. The surf site is also known as First Dip, Yokes.

Y.O. 257. Dive site, Waikīkī, Oʻahu. Popular scuba wreck dive on a sunken vessel, the *Y.O. 257,* a 175-foot navy ship at 100 feet. Also known as the Atlantis Wreck.

Young's Beach. Kamaʻole, Maui. Charles Clinton Young (1905–1974) came to Hawaiʻi in 1932 as a military reporter to cover the famous Massie Case and decided to make his home in the Islands. He and his wife Betty purchased a beachfront lot north of Kamaʻole I Beach Park in 1940 and built their home there in 1950 after World War II. Young became a well-known public figure as a reporter for the *Maui News* and the *Honolulu Star-Bulletin* and for his involvement in many social, civic, and business activities. The section of Kamaʻole Beach below his home is known as Young's Beach or Charlie Young Beach.

Zablan Beach. Nānākuli, Oʻahu. Section of Nānākuli Beach Park. Named for Benjamin Zablan, district magistrate of the Waiʻanae District from 1916 to 1920 and one of the original Hawaiian homesteaders in Nānākuli. He built his home on the beach next to Nānākuli Stream in 1916 and then relocated to a Department of Hawaiian Homelands lot next to the beach in the 1920s. As other homesteaders moved into Nānākuli and their children began swimming at the beach in front of his home, it became known as Zablan Beach.

Z Buoy. Fish aggregating device, Kīpū Kai, Kauaʻi. Buoy anchored at approximately 892 fathoms. Landmarks: Makahūʻena Point, Kawelikoa Point, Ninini Point.

Zeros. 1. Surf site, Kekaha, Kauaʻi. Off Kekaha Beach Park. Zeros is a play on words with the names of three surf sites to the west: First, Second, and Third Ditch. It is called Zeros because it is before First Ditch. 2. Surf site, Waikīkī, Oʻahu. Outermost surf site in Waikīkī, seaward of First Break. Zeros is a play on words with the name First Break, which is normally the "first" break in Waikīkī on big days—but not when Zeros is breaking. Originally known as Zero Break, it is now shortened to Zeros. 3. Surf site, Waikīkī, Oʻahu. Seaward of Tongg's and named after Zeros in Waikīkī. It breaks only during big south swells.

Zippers. Surf site, Mālaekahana, Oʻahu. Off Mālaekahana State Park on the north side of Kalanai Point. Waves here are small but fast. They "zip" along.

Zombies. Surf site, Mōkapu, Oʻahu. Off Nuʻupia Fishpond on Marine Corps Air Station, Kāneʻohe Bay. In 1959, surfers from Kailua rode the waves on this shallow reef for the first time and named it Zombies Rock Garden for fun. Horror movies creating zombie awareness started with *Zombies* on Broadway in 1944 and continued through the 1960s with cult classics like the *Night of the Living Dead,* starring Duane Jones and Judith O'Dea in 1968.

Z

 mo'olelo

We discovered **Zombies** in 1959 and started surfing it regularly in the early 1960s. We named it Zombies Rock Garden for fun for the rocky bottom conditions of the reef. Our gang was the Harris brothers, Steve and Roger, Scot Muirhead, Roy Mesker, Byron Wright, and John Day. Roy lived near the marine base and everyone parked at his house. We started out surfing at Castle Point off the old skeet range, but the waves were hardly ever good, so we paddled into the base to check out the reefs there for surf. That's how we discovered Zombies, and that was the beginning of the war between the surfers and the marines that is still going on today.

Keith McClure, June 11, 1989

I first surfed Zombies in the winter of 1986 when I was twelve. I'd heard all the stories about the MPs arresting surfers out there from my friends at Shorebreak, but after we moved to Kalāheo Hillside, my dad and I decided to go for it. Zombies was just down the road from our house. Our first time there, we caught it on a perfect day with nobody out. The North Shore was big and there was a 3-, maybe 4-foot wrap coming around Moku-manu. It was glassy, no wind, and these long lefts were breaking from the outside all the way to the beach. We couldn't believe we had it to ourselves.

To get to Zombies you have to trespass on the marine base. First, you go around a chain-link fence. It sticks out over the water after it crosses a sharp reef shelf. Swinging around the fence with your board is tricky, especially when the surf's pounding the rocks. You have to time it just right, or you get nailed. Then you have to walk about a quarter mile on a narrow sand trail between the shelf and the sand dunes. If the MPs come when you're on the trail, it's like you're trapped. If you go back, they'll grab you, so you have to run for the opening at the other end of the shelf where everyone goes out or try to run across the shelf and jump in the water. Crossing the shelf is deadly when you're trying to move fast over sharp rocks in your bare feet carrying your board, but that's the way I went the first time some guys behind me yelled, "MPs." I made it okay, but some of my friends haven't been so lucky. I remember one of them in particular who was trying to run across the shelf with an MP chasing him. He reached the edge of the shelf and just as he jumped, the MP grabbed his leash. He got jerked backwards and slammed into the rocks. The MP couldn't hold on, so my friend managed to paddle away, but not without some bad cuts and some major damage to his board.

The dog incident about 1990 was probably the worst one for

me. My dad and I were just going into the water at Zombies when two MPs with dogs popped up from behind the dunes where they were hiding and yelled, "Hey, you! Halt!" We just kept going, and they started to run toward us. Then one of them released his dog, a big German shepherd. It came in the water right for me, but some waves hit it in the face, so it turned around and went back in. After that, we didn't feel like surfing, so we paddled back down to the fence, but they followed us. So we paddled down to the Castle Point right-of-way, but they followed us there, too. We finally ditched them by paddling across the canal, but I thought the incident was pretty bad—releasing an attack dog on a kid.

The whole MP thing never really got to me, though, maybe because I was always careful and I never got arrested. For me it was part of the adrenalin rush and it just added to thrill of going surfing on base. But you really shouldn't have to go through all of that just to go surf.

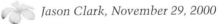 *Jason Clark, November 29, 2000*

Z

REFERENCES

Abbott, Isabella, and Eleanor Williamson. *Limu.* Lawai, Kauai: Pacific Tropical Botanical Garden, 1974.

Adler, Jacob. *Claus Spreckels: The Sugar King in Hawaii.* Honolulu: University of Hawai'i Press, 1966.

AECOS. "Kaua'i Island Coastal Resource Inventory." Prepared for Corps of Engineers, U.S. Army Engineer Division, Pacific Ocean. Kailua, O'ahu, 1982.

———. "Maui Island Coral Reef Inventory." Prepared for Corps of Engineers, U.S. Army Engineer Division, Pacific Ocean. Kailua, O'ahu, 1980.

Aikin, Ross C. *Kilauea Point Lighthouse: The Landfall Beacon on the Orient Run.* Lihue: Kilauea Point Natural History Association, 1988.

Akoi, Rhea. *Kuu Home I Keaukaha.* Hilo: Hui Ho'omau O Keaukaha Panaewa, 1989.

Alford, Johnny. *Mountain Biking the Hawaiian Islands.* Honolulu: 'Ohana, 1997.

Allen, Gwenfread. *Hawaii's War Years.* Honolulu: University of Hawai'i Press, 1950.

Ambrose, Greg. *Surfer's Guide to Hawaii.* Honolulu: Bess Press, 1991.

Apple, Russell. *Trails.* Bishop Museum Special Publication 53. Honolulu: Bishop Museum Press, 1965.

Armitage, George, and Henry Judd. *Ghost Dog and Other Hawaiian Legends.* Honolulu: Advertiser, 1944.

Ashdown, Inez. *Kaho'olawe.* Honolulu: Topgallant, 1979.

———. *Ke Alaloa o Maui.* Wailuku: Ace Printing, 1971.

Balaz, George. *Hawaii's Seabirds, Turtles, and Seals.* Honolulu: World Wide Distributors, 1976.

401

Ball, Stuart, Jr. *The Backpackers Guide to Hawai'i.* Honolulu: University of Hawai'i Press, 1996.

Barrere, Dorothy. *Kamehameha in Kona: Two Documentary Studies.* Pacific Anthropological Records No. 23. Honolulu: Bishop Museum, 1975.

Barrow, Terence. *Captain Cook in Hawaii.* Norfolk Island, Australia: Island Heritage, 1978.

Bartram, Paul, and John Clark. *Reef Study at Nu'alolo Kai, Nā Pali Coast State Park, Kaua'i.* Honolulu: Division of State Parks, Department of Land and Natural Resources, State of Hawaii, 1988.

Becket, Jan, and Joseph Singer. *Pana O'ahu.* Honolulu: University of Hawai'i Press, 1999.

Beckwith, Martha. *Hawaiian Mythology.* Honolulu: University of Hawai'i Press, 1970.

Benedict, Albert. *Ka Iwi: Survival of a Coast.* Woodbridge: Ox Bow Press, 2000.

Bennet, Wendell Clark. *Archaeology of Kauai.* Honolulu: Bishop Museum Press, 1931.

Berry, Paul, and Edgy Lee. *Waikiki: In the Wake of Dreams.* Honolulu: FilmWorks Press, 2000.

Best, Gerald. *Railroads of Hawaii.* San Marino, CA: Golden West Books, 1978.

Bird, Isabella. *Six Months in the Sandwich Islands.* Honolulu: University of Hawai'i Press, 1966.

Blake, Tom. *Hawaiian Surfriders 1935.* Reprint. Redondo, CA: Mountain and Sea, 1983.

Bloomfield, John. *Know-how in the Surf.* Sydney: Angus and Robertson, 1961.

Brennan, Joe. *Duke of Hawaii.* New York: Ballantine Books, 1968.

_____. *The Parker Ranch of Hawaii.* New York: Harper and Row, 1979.

Brundage, Barbara, and Raymond Tabata. *Dive Hawaii.* Sea Grant Publication UNIHI-SEAGRANT-AB-86-01. Honolulu: University of Hawai'i Sea Grant College Program, 1986.

Carlson, Bruce, and Carol Hopper. *Waikiki Aquarium.* Honolulu: Island Heritage, 1999.

Chau, Lisa. *Fishing Practices on the Ala Wai Canal.* Honolulu: Environmental Planning Services, 1997.

City and County of Honolulu. *Index of O'ahu Parks and Facilities.* Honolulu: City and County of Honolulu, 1997.

Clark, John. *Beach and Ocean Recreation Study, Haʻena, Kauaʻi.* Honolulu: Division of State Parks, Department of Land and Natural Resources, 1991.

———. *Beaches of the Big Island.* Honolulu: University of Hawaiʻi Press, 1985.

———. *Beaches of Kauaʻi and Niʻihau.* Honolulu: University of Hawaiʻi Press, 1990.

———. *Hawaiʻi's Best Beaches.* Honolulu: University of Hawaiʻi Press, 1999.

———. *Hawaiʻi's Secret Beaches.* Honolulu: Tongg Publishing, 1989.

———. *The Beaches of Maui County.* Honolulu: University of Hawaiʻi Press, 1980.

———. *The Beaches of Oʻahu.* Honolulu: University of Hawaiʻi Press, 1977

Clark, John, and Wayne Souza. *Statewide Recreation Resources Inventory: Principal Swimming Areas.* Honolulu: Division of State Parks, Department of Land and Natural Resources, State of Hawaii, 1987.

Conde, Jesse, and Gerald Best. *Sugar Trains.* Felton, CA: Big Trees Press and Pacific Bookbinding, Glenwood Publisher, 1973.

Cooke, George P. *Moʻolelo o Molokai.* Honolulu: Honolulu Star-Bulletin, 1949.

Corps of Engineers, U.S. Army Engineer Division, Pacific Ocean. "Hawaii Regional Inventory of the National Shoreline Study." Honolulu: Corps of Engineers, 1971.

Davies, Theophilus H. *Personal Recollections of Hawaii.* Honolulu, 1885.

Davis, Helen Kapililani Sanborn. *Reminiscences of a Life in the Islands.* Honolulu: Barbara Pope Book Design, 2000.

Daws, Gavin. *Shoal of Time.* Honolulu: University of Hawaiʻi Press, 1974.

Dean, Love. *The Lighthouses of Hawaiʻi.* Honolulu: University of Hawaiʻi Press, 1991.

Dondo, Mathurin. *La Perouse in Maui.* Wailuku: Maui Publishing, 1959.

Doyle, David. *Rescue in Paradise: Oʻahu's Beaches and Their Guardians.* Aiea, HI: Island Heritage, 2000.

Doyle, Emma Lyons. *Makua Laiana: The Story of Lorenzo Lyons.* Honolulu: Privately printed, 1945.

Durkin, Pat. *The Kauai Guide to Beaches, Water Activity and Safety.* Lihue: Magic Fishes Press, 1988.

Elbert, Samuel. *Selections from Fornander's Hawaiian Antiquities and Folk-lore.* Honolulu: University of Hawai'i Press, 1959.

Elbert, Samuel, and Noelani Mahoe. *Na Mele o Hawaii Nei.* Honolulu: University of Hawai'i Press, 1970.

Ellis, William. *Journal of William Ellis.* Honolulu: Advertiser, 1963.

Emerson, Nathaniel. *Pele and Hiiaka: A Myth of Hawaii.* Honolulu: Honolulu Star-Bulletin, 1915.

———. *Unwritten Literature of Hawaii.* Rutland, VT: Tuttle, 1965.

Emory, Kenneth. *The Island of Lanai.* Bulletin 12. Honolulu: Bishop Museum Press, 1924.

Emory, Kenneth, and Robert Hommond. *Endangered Hawaiian Archaeological Sites within Maui County.* Report 72-2. Honolulu: Bishop Museum Press, 1972.

Emory, Tiare. "Hawaiian Life in Kalalau, Kauai, According to John Hanohano and His Mother, Wahine-I-Keouli Pa." Manuscript, Bishop Museum Archives, Honolulu, 1949.

Finney, Ben, and James D. Houston. *Surfing: A History of the Ancient Hawaiian Sport.* San Francisco: Pomegranate Artbooks, 1996.

Forbes, David. *Queen Emma and Lawai.* Lihue: Kauai Historical Society, 1970.

Fornander, Abraham. *Hawaiian Antiquities and Folk-lore.* Bishop Museum Memoirs, Vol. 5. Honolulu: Bishop Museum Press, 1918.

Frear, Walter F. *Mark Twain in Hawaii.* Chicago, 1947. Reprint. Golden, CO: Outbooks, 1981.

Freund, Gordon. *Skindiving Guide to Hawaii.* Honolulu: Star-Bulletin Printing, 1958.

Fujii, Jocelyn. *The Book of Bests of Honolulu.* Honolulu: Indigo Publications, 1982.

Gabbard, Andrea. *Girl in the Curl.* Seattle: Seal Press, 2000.

Gault-Williams, Malcolm. *Legendary Surfers.* Internet document, 1996–2000.

Gay, Lawrence. *True Stories of Lanai.* Honolulu: Mission Press, 1965.

Gibbs, James A. *Shipwrecks in Paradise: An Informal Marine History of the Hawaiian Islands.* Seattle: Superior, 1977.

Gilman, G. D. "Journal of a Canoe Voyage Along the Kauai Palis, Made in 1845." Hawaiian Historical Papers No. 14 (1908), pp.3–8.

Grant, Glen, Bennett Hymer. *Hawaii Looking Back: An Illustrated History of the Islands.* Honolulu: Mutual, 2000.

Grigg, Ricky. *Big Surf, Deep Dives and the Islands.* Honolulu: Editions Unlimited, 1998.

Gutmanis, June, Susan Monden, and Theodore Kelsey. *Kahuna La'au Lapa'au.* Honolulu: Island Heritage, 1979.

Handy, E. S. Craighill. *The Hawaiian Planter.* Bulletin 161. Honolulu: Bishop Museum Press, 1940.

Handy, E. S. Craighill, Elizabeth G. Handy, and Mary Kawena Pukui. *Native Planters in Old Hawaii.* Bishop Museum Bulletin 233. Honolulu: Bishop Museum Press, 1972.

Handy, E. S. Craighill, et al. *Ancient Hawaiian Civilization.* Rutland, VT: Tuttle, 1965.

Hancock, Lambreth. *Hawaii Kai: The First 20 Years.* Honolulu: Rotary Club of Hawaii Kai, 1983.

Hansen, Violet, and Marion Kelly. "Cultural and Historical Survey of Kaalualu, District of Ka'u, Island of Hawaii." Department of Anthropology, MS Report 0822972, Bishop Museum, Honolulu, September 1972.

Hapai, Charlotte. *Hilo Legends.* Hilo: Petroglyph Press, 1966.

Haraguchi, Paul. *Weather in Hawaiian Waters.* Honolulu: Hawaii Reprographics, 1979.

Haun, Alan. *An Archaeological Survey of the Naval Air Station, Barbers Point, O'ahu, Hawai'i.* Report including Notes on the History of Honouliuli by Marion Kelly. Honolulu: Applied Research Group, Bishop Museum, 1991.

Hawaiian Mission Children's Society. *Missionary Album.* Sesquicentennial Edition. Honolulu: HMCS, 1969.

Hawaii County. "Inventory of Public Shoreline Access." Report prepared for County of Hawaii Planning Department, Hilo, September 1979.

Hawaii Redevelopment Agency. "Project Kaikoo." Final Report, Hilo, 1971.

Hawaii State. *Hawaii Regional Inventory of the National Shoreline Study.* Prepared by the Corps of Engineers, U.S. Army Engineer Division, Pacific Ocean. Honolulu, 1971.

Hawaii State Department of Land and Natural Resources. *Environmental Assessment of the Statewide System of Day-Use Moorings.* Honolulu: Division of Boating and Ocean Recreation, 1994.

———. *Hawaii Administrative Rules, Part III: Ocean Waters, Navigable Streams and Beaches.* Honolulu: Division of Boating and Ocean Recreation, 1994.

————. *Marine Life Conservation Districts.* Honolulu: Division of Aquatic Resources, 1992.

————. *Na Ala Hele Hawai'i Trail and Access System: Program Plan.* Honolulu: Division of Forestry and Wildlife, 1991.

Hawaii State Department of Land and Natural Resources and Department of Planning and Economic Development. *Na Ala Hele.* Honolulu, 1973.

Hawaii State Department of Planning and Economic Development. *North Kohala Master Plan for Historical Resources.* Honolulu, 1972.

————. *1971 Statewide Surfing Site Survey.* Prepared by Surfing Education Association as part of the 1971 revision of the State Comprehensive Outdoor Recreation Plan. Honolulu, 1971.

Hawaii State Statuary Hall Commission. "The King Kamehameha I and Father Damien Memorial Statues." Senate Document No. 91-54, Washington, D.C., 1970.

Helber, Hastert, and Fee. *Pua'ena Camp: Final Environmental Impact Statement.* Honolulu, 1999.

Hemmings, Fred. *The Soul of Surfing is Hawaiian.* Kailua: Sports Enterprises, 1997.

Hill, S. S. *Travels in the Sandwich and Society Islands.* London: Chapman and Hall, 1856.

Hinds, Norman. *The Geology of Kauai and Niihau.* Honolulu: Bishop Museum Press, 1930. Reprint. New York: Kraus Reprint, 1971.

Hobbs, Jean. *Hawaii: A Pageant of the Soil.* Palo Alto, CA: Stanford University Press, 1935.

Holmes, Tommy. *The Hawaiian Canoe.* Second Edition. Honolulu: Editions Limited, 1993.

Hosaka, Edward. *Sport Fishing in Hawaii.* Honolulu: Watkins Press, 1944.

Hulme, Kathryn. *The Robert Allerton Story.* Kauai: John Gregg Allerton, 1979.

Hungerford, John. *Hawaiian Railroads.* Reseda, CA: Hungerford Press, 1963.

Ii, John Papa. *Fragments of Hawaiian History.* Honolulu: Bishop Museum Press, 1959.

Jarratt, Phil. *Mr. Sunset: The Jeff Hakman Story.* London: Gen X Publishing in association with General Publishing Group, 1997.

Jenkins, Bruce. *North Shore Chronicles.* Berkeley: North Atlantic Books, 1990.

Johnson, Rubellite K. *Kukini 'Aha'ilono.* Honolulu: Topgallant, 1976.

Judd, Gerrit P., IV. *Puleo'o: The Story of Molokai.* Honolulu: Porter Printing, 1936.

Judd, Walter F. *Palaces and Forts of the Hawaiian Kingdom.* Palo Alto, CA: Pacific Book, 1975.

Juvik, Sonia P., and James O. Juvik, eds. *Atlas of Hawai'i.* Third Edition. Honolulu: University of Hawai'i Press, 1998.

Kaaiakamanu, D. M. *Hawaiian Herbs of Medicinal Value.* Rutland, VT: Tuttle, 1972.

Kahele, Mona. "Recollection of Some of the Events of Kapu'a." Unpublished manuscript, author's collection, n.d.

Kalakaua, David. *The Legends and Myths of Hawaii.* Rutland, VT: Tuttle, 1972.

Kamakau, Samuel. *Ka Po'e Kahiko: The People of Old.* Bishop Museum Special Publication 51. Honolulu: Bishop Museum Press, 1964.

———. *Ruling Chiefs of Hawaii.* Honolulu: Kamehameha Schools Press, 1961.

Kasamoto, Hiroshi, Inc., and P. Yoshimura, Inc. *Public Access to the Shoreline: County of Hawaii.* Report prepared for the Planning Department, County of Hawaii. Hilo: 1979.

Kelly, John, Jr. *Folk Songs Hawaii Sings.* Rutland, VT: Tuttle, 1962.

Kelly, Marion. *Kekaha: 'Aina Malo'o.* Bishop Museum, Department of Anthropology Report 71-2. Honolulu, March 1971.

———. *Loko I'a o He'eia Fishpond.* Honolulu: Bishop Museum Press, 1975.

———. *Majestic Ka'u: Mo'olelo of Nine Ahupua'a.* Bishop Museum, Department of Anthropology Report 80-2. Honolulu, May 1980.

Kelly, Marion, Barry Nakamura, and Dorothy Barrère. *Hilo Bay: A Chronological History.* Report prepared for the U.S. Army Engineer District, Honolulu, March 1981.

Kelsey, Theodore. "Kauai Place Names." Unpublished manuscript, Kelsey Collection, Hawaii State Archives, n.d.

———. "Ocean Fish-farming in Ancient Hawaii." Unpublished manuscript, Kelsey Collection, Hawaii State Archives, n.d.

Kinney, Henry W. *The Island of Hawaii.* Hilo: Hilo Board of Trade, 1913.

Kirch, Patrick. *Marine Explorations in Prehistoric Hawaii: Archaeological Inventory at Kalahuipuaa, Hawaii Island.* Bishop Museum, Pacific Anthropological Records No. 29. Honolulu, 1979.

Krauss, Beatrice. "Ethnobotany of Hawaii." Manuscript, University of Hawai'i–Mānoa, Department of Botany. Honolulu, n.d.

Krauss, Bob. *Johnny Wilson.* Honolulu: University of Hawai'i Press, 1994.

———. *Travel Guide to the Hawaiian Islands.* New York: Van Rees Press, 1963.

Kuykendall, Ralph S. *The Hawaiian Kingdom [Vol. I] 1778–1854: Foundation and Transformation.* Reprint. Honolulu: University of Hawai'i Press, 1957.

Lahaina Restoration Foundation. *Story of Lahaina.* Lahaina: Lahaina Restoration Foundation, 1972.

Link, Matthew. *Rainbow Handbook Hawai'i.* Kona: Missing Link Productions, 1999.

Leatherman, Stephen P. *America's Best Beaches.* Miami: Florida International University, 1998.

Lueras, Leonard. *Surfing: The Ultimate Pleasure.* Honolulu: Emphasis International, 1984.

Lyon, Charlie, and Leslie Lyon. *Jaws Maui.* Hong Kong: Everbest Printing, 1997.

Macdonald, Gordon, Agatin Abbott, and Frank Peterson. *Volcanoes in the Sea.* Honolulu: University of Hawai'i Press, 1983.

Macy, William, and Roland Hussey. *The Nantucket Scrap Bucket.* Boston: The Inquirer and Mirror Press, 1916.

Maguire, Eliza D. *Kona Legends.* Hilo: Petroglyph Press, 1966.

Malo, David. *Hawaiian Antiquities.* Bishop Museum Special Publication No. 2. Honolulu: Bishop Museum Press, 1951.

McAllister, J. Gilbert. *The Archaeology of Kahoolawe.* Bulletin 115. Honolulu: Bishop Museum Press, 1933.

———. *Archaeology of Oahu.* Bulletin 104. Honolulu: Bishop Museum Press, 1933.

McBryde, L. R. *Petroglyphs of Hawaii.* Hilo: Petroglyph Press, 1969.

McGaw, Sister Martha M., C.S.J. *Stevenson in Hawaii.* Honolulu: University of Hawai'i Press, 1950.

McGrath, Edward, Kenneth Brewer, and Bob Krauss. *Historic Waianae.* Norfolk Island, Australia: Island Heritage, 1973.

McMahon, Richard. *Camping Hawai'i.* Honolulu: University of Hawai'i Press, 1997.

McPherson, Michael. "Malama." *Hawaii Review* 14, 1981.

———. *Singing with the Owls.* Honolulu: Petronium Press, 1982.

Menzies, Archibald. *Hawaii Nei 128 Years Ago.* Honolulu: New Freedom, 1920.

Mid-Pacific Country Club. *Mid-Pacific Country Club, 1926–2001.* Kailua: Mid-Pacific Country Club, 2001.

Mifflin, Thomas. *Schooner from Windward.* Honolulu: University of Hawai'i Press, 1983.

Mitchell, Donald D. Kilolani. *Hawaiian Games for Today.* Honolulu: Kamehameha Schools Press, 1975.

———. *Resource Units in Hawaiian Culture.* Honolulu: Kamehameha Schools Press, 1982.

Moberly, Ralph, Jr., and Theodore Chamberlain. *Hawaiian Beach Systems.* Report prepared for the Harbors Division, Department of Transportation, State of Hawai'i. May 1964.

Moffatt & Nichols. *Ewa Marina: Evaluation of Project Impacts on Surf Sites: Technical Study.* File 2612-04. Long Beach: Moffatt & Nichols, Engineers, 1990.

Mooney, James L. *Dictionary of American Naval Fighting Ships.* Vol. III. Washington, D.C.: Naval Historical Center, 1981.

Moriarty, Linda Paik. *Ni'ihau Shell Leis.* Honolulu: University of Hawai'i Press, 1986.

Morrison, Boone. *Journal of a Pioneer Builder.* Kilauea, HI: Hawaii Natural History Association, 1977.

National Oceanic and Atmospheric Administration. *United States Coast Pilot 7, Pacific Coast: California, Oregon, Washington and Hawaii.* Washington: National Oceanic and Atmospheric Administration, 1977.

ORCA, Ltd. and D. P. Cheney. *West Hawaii Coral Reef Inventory.* Honolulu: U.S. Army Corps of Engineers, 1981.

Paki, Pilahi. *Legends of Hawaii: Oahu's Yesterday.* Honolulu: Victoria Publishers, 1972.

Patterson, O. B. *Surf-riding: Its Thrills and Techniques.* Tokyo: Tuttle, 1960.

Pratt, H. Douglas, Phillip L. Bruner, and Delwyn G. Berrett. *The Birds of Hawaii and the Tropical Pacific.* Princeton: Princeton University Press, 1987.

Preston, C. *Captain James Cook, R.N., F.R.S., and Whitby.* Whitby, UK: Whitby Literary and Philosophical Society, 1965.

Puakō Historical Society. *Puakō: An Affectionate History*. Vancouver: Creative Connections, 2000.

Pukui, Mary Kawena. *'Olelo Noeau: Hawaiian Proverbs and Poetical Sayings*. Bishop Museum Special Publication No. 71, Honolulu: Bishop Museum Press, 1983.

Pukui, Mary Kawena, and Samuel H. Elbert. *Hawaiian Dictionary*. Honolulu: University of Hawai'i Press, 1971.

Pukui, Mary Kawena, Samuel H. Elbert, and Esther T. Mookini. *Place Names of Hawaii*. Honolulu: University of Hawai'i Press, 1974.

Pukui, Mary Kawena, and Alfons Korn. *The Echo of Our Song*. Honolulu: University of Hawai'i Press, 1973.

Reeve, Roland. *Kaho'olawe Place Names*. Kaho'olawe Island Conveyance Commission Consultant Report No. 16. Honolulu: 1995.

Rice, William Hyde. *Hawaiian Legends*. Bishop Museum Special Publication No. 63. Honolulu: Bishop Museum Press, 1977.

Robinson, Ed. *Ed Robinson's Diving Adventures*. Kihei, HI: Kihei Scuba Services, 1998.

Science Management, Inc. "Mauna Lani Resort: An Interpretive and Management Plan for its Historical Resources at Kalahuipuaa." Honolulu: Science Management, January 1982.

Scott, Edward. *The Saga of the Sandwich Islands*. Lake Tahoe: Sierra-Tahoe, 1968.

Scott, Susan. *Exploring Hanauma Bay*. Honolulu: University of Hawai'i Press, 1993.

Sinoto, Aki. *Archaeological Reconnaissance Survey of Kamoa Point, Holualoa Ahupuaa, Hawaii Island*. Bernice P. Bishop Museum, Department of Anthropology Report 69-5. Honolulu: 1971.

Sinoto, Yosihiko, and Marion Kelly. *Archaeological and Historical Survey of Pakini-Nui and Pakini-Iki Coastal Sites; Waiahukini, Kailikii, and Hawea, Ka'u, Hawaii*. Bernice P. Bishop Museum, Department of Anthropology Report 75-1. Honolulu: 1975.

Souza, Wayne. *Statewide Recreation Resources Inventory: Principal Sand Beaches*. Division of State Parks, Department of Land and Natural Resources, State of Hawaii, 1986.

Stephenson, Larry. *Kohala Keia*. Ka'u, HI: Home Naauao o Ka'u, December 1977.

Sterling, Elspeth. "The Sites of Maui County." Fourteen unpublished volumes. Department of Archaeology, Bishop Museum, Honolulu. Waluku: Hale Ho'ike'ike.

Sterling, Elspeth, and Catherine Summers. *The Sites of Oahu.* Honolulu: Bishop Museum Press, 1962.

Stevenson, Robert L. *Travels in Hawaii.* Honolulu: University of Hawai'i Press, 1973.

Stone, Scott C. S. *Living Treasures of Hawai'i.* Honolulu: Honpa Hongwanji Mission of Hawai'i, 2000.

Stroup, Elaine. *Ports of Hawaii.* Honolulu: Red Dot, 1967.

Summers, Catherine. *Molokai: A Site Survey.* Pacific Anthropological Records No. 14. Honolulu: Bishop Museum Press, 1971.

Surfing Education Association. "1971 Statewide Surfing Site Survey." Honolulu: Surfing Education Association, 1971.

Sutherland, Audrey. *Paddling Hawai'i.* Honolulu: University of Hawai'i Press, 1998.

Tabata, Raymond. *Hawaii's Recreational Dive Industry and Use of Nearshore Dive Sites.* University of Hawai'i Sea Grant College Program and Ocean Resources Branch, Department of Business, Economic Development and Tourism, State of Hawai'i. Honolulu, 1992.

Tabrah, Ruth. *Lanai.* Norfolk Island, Australia: Island Heritage, 1976.

_____. *Ni'ihau: The Last Hawaiian Island.* Kailua: Press Pacifica, 1987.

Taylor, Leighton. *Sharks of Hawai'i: Their Biology and Cultural Significance.* Honolulu: University of Hawai'i Press, 1993.

Thorne, Chuck, and Lou Zitnik. *The Divers' Guide to Hawaii.* Kihei, HI: Hawaii Divers' Guide, 1984.

Thrum, Thomas G. *Hawaiian Folk Tales.* New York: AMS Press, 1907.

Tilling, Robert, et al. *Earthquake and Related Catastrophic Events, Island of Hawaii, November 29, 1975: A Preliminary Report.* Geological Survey Circular 740, U.S. Geological Survey, 1976.

Timmons, Grady. *Waikiki Beachboy.* Honolulu: Editions Limited, 1989.

Tinker, Spencer. *Fishes of Hawaii.* Honolulu: Hawaiian Service, 1982.

_____. *Pacific Sea Shells.* Rutland, VT: Tuttle, 1952.

_____. *Sharks and Rays.* Rutland, VT: Tuttle, 1973.

Titcomb, Margaret. *Native Use of Fish in Hawaii.* Honolulu: University of Hawai'i Press, 1972.

Tuggle, H. David, and P. Bion Griffin. *Lapakahi Hawaii: Archaeological Studies.* Asian and Pacific Archaeological Series No.

411

5, Social Science Research Institute, University of Hawai'i, Honolulu, 1973.

Tuggle, H. David, and M. J. Tomonari-Tuggle. *Synthesis of Cultural Resource Studies of the 'Ewa Plain.* Report prepared for Belt Collins Hawaii by International Archaeological Research Institute, Honolulu, 1997.

U.S. Army Engineer Division, Honolulu. *Hawaii Regional Inventory of the National Shoreline Study.* Honolulu, 1971.

U.S. Department of Commerce, Coast and Geodetic Survey. *Triangulation in Hawaii.* Special Publication No. 156. Washington, D.C.: Government Printing Office, 1930.

Valier, Kathy. *On the Nā Pali Coast.* Honolulu: University of Hawai'i Press, 1988.

Van Dyke, Fred. *30 Years of Riding the World's Biggest Waves.* Kailua: Ocean Sports International, 1988.

Van Steenwyk, Elizabeth. *Let's Go to the Beach: A History of Sun and Fun by the Sea.* New York: Henry Holt and Company, 2001.

Vogelsberger, Paul. *Hawaiian Windsurfing Annual 1988–89.* Paia, HI: Windward Promotions, 1989.

Warren, Mark. *Atlas of Australian Surfing.* Cottage Point, NSW: Dolphin Publications, 1988.

Warshaw, Matt. *Maverick's.* San Francisco: Chronicle Books, 2000.

Westervelt, William. *Hawaiian Historical Legends.* New York: Revell, 1926.

———. *Hawaiian Legends of Volcanoes.* Rutland, VT: Tuttle, 1963.

White, John Wythe. *Short-Timers in Paradise.* Honolulu: Anoai Press, 2000.

Whitney, Henry M. *The Hawaiian Guide Book, 1875.* Reprint. Rutland, VT: Tuttle, 1970.

Wichman, Frederick B. *Kaua'i: Ancient Place-Names and Their Stories.* Honolulu: University of Hawai'i Press, 1998.

Wilkes, Lt. Charles. *Narrative of the United States Exploring Expedition during the Years 1838–1842.* Philadelphia, 1845.

Woods, Amos. *Beachcombing for Japanese Fish Floats.* Portland, OR: Binford and Mort, 1967.

Wright, Bank. *Surfing Hawaii.* Los Angeles: Mountain and Sea, 1972.

Young, Nat. *The History of Surfing.* Revised edition. Angourie, NSW, Australia: Palm Beach Press, 1994.

———. *Surf Rage.* Angourie, NSW, Australia: Nymboida Press, 2000.

ABOUT THE AUTHOR

JOHN R. KUKEAKALANI CLARK is the author of the beaches of Hawai'i series: *The Beaches of O'ahu, The Beaches of Maui County, Beaches of the Big Island, Beaches of Kaua'i and Ni'ihau*, and *Hawai'i's Best Beaches*. A former lifeguard, he is deputy fire chief of the Honolulu Fire Department.